The Military Balance
in the Middle East

Other Books by Anthony H. Cordesman

The Iraq War: Strategy, Tactics, and Military Lessons (Westport, CT: Praeger, 2003)

Saudi Arabia Enters the Twenty-first Century: The Political, Foreign Policy, Economic, and Energy Dimensions (Westport, CT: Praeger, 2003)

Saudi Arabia Enters the Twenty-first Century: The Military and International Security Dimensions (Westport, CT: Praeger, 2003)

The Lessons of Afghanistan: War Fighting, Intelligence, and Force Transformation (Washington, DC: CSIS, 2002)

Iraq's Military Capabilities in 2002: A Dynamic Net Assessment (Washington, DC: CSIS, 2002)

Strategic Threats and National Missile Defenses: Defending the U.S. Homeland (Westport, CT: Praeger, 2002)

A Tragedy of Arms: Military and Security Developments in the Maghreb (Westport, CT: Praeger, 2001)

Peace and War: The Arab-Israeli Military Balance Enters the 21st Century (Westport, CT: Praeger, 2001)

Terrorism, Asymmetric Warfare, and Weapons of Mass Destruction: Defending the U.S. Homeland (Westport, CT: Praeger, 2001)

Cyber-threats, Information Warfare, and Critical Infrastructure Protection: Defending the U.S. Homeland, with Justin G. Cordesman (Westport, CT: Praeger, 2001)

The Lessons and Non-Lessons of the Air and Missile Campaign in Kosovo (Westport, CT: Praeger, 2000)

Iran's Military Forces in Transition: Conventional Threats and Weapons of Mass Destruction (Westport, CT: Praeger, 2000)

Transnational Threats from the Middle East: Crying Wolf or Crying Havoc? (Carlyle, PA: Strategic Studies Institute, 1999)

Iraq and the War of Sanctions: Conventional Threats and Weapons of Mass Destruction (Westport, CT: Praeger, 1999)

U.S. Forces in the Middle East: Resources and Capabilities (Boulder, CO: Westview, 1997)

Perilous Prospects: The Peace Process and Arab-Israeli Military Balance (Boulder, CO: Westview, 1996)

The Lessons of Modern War, Volume IV: The Gulf War, with Abraham R. Wagner (Boulder, CO: Westview, 1995; paperback, 1999)

U.S. Defence Policy: Resources and Capabilities (London: RUSI Whitehall Series, 1993)

After the Storm: The Changing Military Balance in the Middle East (Boulder, CO: Westview, 1993)

Weapons of Mass Destruction in the Middle East (London: Brassey's, 1991)

The Lessons of Modern War, Volume I: The Arab-Israeli Conflicts, with Abraham R. Wagner (Boulder, CO: Westview, 1990)

The Lessons of Modern War, Volume II: The Iran-Iraq Conflict, with Abraham R. Wagner (Boulder, CO: Westview, 1990)

The Lessons of Modern War, Volume III: The Afghan and Falklands Conflicts, with Abraham R. Wagner (Boulder, CO: Westview, 1990)

The Gulf and the West: Strategic Relations and Military Realities (Boulder, CO: Westview, 1988)

The Military Balance in the Middle East

ANTHONY H. CORDESMAN

Published in cooperation with the
Center for Strategic and International Studies,
Washington, D.C.

Westport, Connecticut
London

Library of Congress Cataloging-in-Publication Data

Cordesman, Anthony H.

The military balance in the Middle East / Anthony Cordesman.
p. cm.
"Published in cooperation with the Center for Strategic and International Studies,
Washington, D.C."
Includes bibliographical references and index.
ISBN 0–275–98399–4 (alk. paper)
1. Middle East—Armed Forces. 2. Middle East—Defenses. 3. Middle East—
Military policy. I. Title.
UA832.C6715 2004
355′.033056—dc22   2004053792

British Library Cataloguing in Publication Data is available.

Library of Congress Catalog Card Number: 2004053792
ISBN: 0–275–98399–4

First published in 2004

Praeger Publishers, 88 Post Road West, Westport, CT 06881
An imprint of Greenwood Publishing Group, Inc.
www.praeger.com

Printed in the United States of America

The paper used in this book complies with the
Permanent Paper Standard issued by the National
Information Standards Organization (Z39.48–1984).

10 9 8 7 6 5 4 3 2 1

*With assistance from Patrick B. Baetjer
and G. Ryan Faith*

Contents

Figures

Introduction

This book is intended to be a reference for military analysts, arms control specialists, and experts on the region, and to provide a picture of military developments that few regional governments are willing to make public but that shape security developments in the most heavily armed region in the world. The following chapters provide a detailed picture of the quantitative and qualitative trends in the military balance in the Middle East and North Africa, and of the levels of military forces, the levels of military spending, and the levels of arms imports in each country. They describe national efforts to acquire weapons of mass destruction and provide summary assessments of proliferation and the size and nature of the terrorist and extremist forces in the region.

The analysis in these chapters grew out of a series of annual efforts to introduce analysts and officials to the trends in the regional balance, and how to assess them. As such, it draws largely on unclassified sources provided by the U.S. government, and on the database the International Institute of Strategic Studies compiles with the aid of various governments. It also makes use of the databases developed by Jane's and the Jaffe Center for Strategic Studies, as well as informal inputs from U.S. experts and experts within the region.

The reader should be aware, however, that many of the data are uncertain, and the sources used are often in conflict. In these cases, this document relies largely on U.S. official sources, or on force counts that are seen as accurate by U.S. experts. This choice of sources reflects the fact that the U.S. government has intelligence and analytic resources far beyond those available to most other governments and organizations. It also reflects a deliberate effort to avoid the use of sources designed to prove an ideological point or to choose one side over another in the many conflicts plaguing the region.

There are many cases for which such data are not available, however; and there are many aspects of the balance that cannot be quantified in the form of graphics, charts, and tables; in such cases, judgment is the only valid form of analysis. There are also aspects of the balance that require a far more detailed assessment of country and nonstate military capabilities than is possible in this overview. Similarly, it is not possible to go from assessing force strengths and broad trends to providing a contingency or scenario analysis, although the forces actually brought to bear in a given conflict normally do far more to determine its outcome than the total forces a country has at the outset of conflict. The material presented can help the reader in making such contingency assessments, but measurements of force strength cannot be predictions of the future of war or of the outcome on possible conflicts.

Moreover, the very nature of the military balance in the Middle East is experiencing massive changes. Some of these changes are the result of conflicts in the region. The U.S.- and British-led invasion of Iraq in 2003 removed the country—one of the region's major military powers—from the balance, creating at least a temporary power vacuum in the Gulf. Like the Gulf War and Afghan conflict before it, the Iraq War also demonstrated the power of new battle management, targeting, intelligence, and surveillance and reconnaissance systems, and the potential value of "netcentric warfare." It also demonstrated the crushing power that precision air and missile power, as well as advanced armor and artillery, can have against a technologically inferior opponent.

At the same time, the Iraq War demonstrated just how different the military capabilities of truly professional armed forces are against the highly politicized, poorly trained, and weakly led forces of most Middle Eastern countries. It also demonstrated the importance of the ability to coordinate different military services, or "jointness," and of realistic training and extensive combat experience. The same is true of readiness: operations and maintenance, the ability to project military power at long distances, and the capability to sustain forces in intense combat. These are all capabilities that the United States and Britain possess but most of the military powers in the Middle East lack or have never properly funded and organized. They too illustrate that force quality is often as important as, if not more so than, force quantity.

Other important changes are taking place in the very nature of the military balance. The attacks Al-Qaeda made on the World Trade Center and the Pentagon on September 11, 2001, illustrated that nonstate actors, and violent Islamic extremism, are creating a new security threat in the region that has transformed "terrorism" into a major military force. Low-intensity conflict is scarcely new to the region. Algeria and Morocco have fought such conflicts for well over a decade. At the same time, the fall of Saddam Hussein's regime has been followed by a "war after the war" in Iraq wherein a combination of former regime loyalists and Islamists have shown they can pose a major challenge to even the most advanced conventional forces, and that conflict termination and nation building are as critical to the military balance as combat capability. It is all too clear that the struggle to win a conventional war may increasingly be only a prelude to asymmetric war and the struggle to win the peace.

Finally, proliferation and weapons of mass destruction are changing the calculation of the military balance as it applies to both regular military forces and the use of terrorism. The United States, Britain, and their coalition allies did not find an imminent threat from weapons of mass destruction in Iraq. They did find evidence that Iraq continued to acquire the technology to produce such weapons, however, as well as long-range missiles. Iran was found during 2003 to have key elements of a nuclear weapons program, had previously shown it was developing new long-range missiles, and had declared it had chemical weapons. Nuclear weapons technology was intercepted on the way to Libya, which then admitted it was developing chemical, biological, radiological, and nuclear weapons and missiles and agreed to abandon its efforts. Israel is a major nuclear power, and Algeria, Egypt, Libya, and Syria are all believed to have programs to develop weapons of mass destruction, or are believed to have acquired and deployed them.

The end result is that the regional military balance is becoming more and more asymmetric, and nations and nonstate actors are increasingly likely to use radically different types of military force in terms of strategy, tactics, and technology. This, in turn, means that the military balance is becoming progressively harder to measure. Force strength, and the sheer size of the military forces a given country possesses, still matter. Mass tells. Numbers, however, increasingly are only part of the story, and a modern assessment of the balance must focus more and more on force quality and the capability for asymmetric warfare.

Chapter 1

Defining the Middle East Military Balance

Defining the Middle Eastern military balance, and even the areas to be included in this balance, is not easy. While definitions differ, the Middle East and North Africa is an area that includes a geographic range from Morocco, at the western end of the Atlantic, to Iran on the edge of Central Asia; and from Yemen to the Red Sea and Indian Ocean. It includes over twenty countries, each of which has taken a different approach to shaping its military forces. There are major regional military powers like Egypt and Israel, and small states that have only token forces, like Bahrain and Tunisia.

Figure 1.1 summarizes the military strength of each of these nations, as well as that of major nearby powers. It provides a rough picture of the complexity of the region and the differences between the forces involved. At the same time, the moment force strengths are presented in this manner, it becomes clear why the entire region will never go to war in any cohesive way. Even a cursory reading of the list of countries shows that their national interests involved are too diverse, their interests too localized, and many nations face threats from outside the Middle East.

Equally important, most states cannot project significant amounts of their total military forces much beyond their own borders, much less throughout the region. Out of all the nations in the region, only Egypt and Israel can project and sustain significant conventional forces for long distances, and even these powers face severe limits on how much of their strength can really be projected in a combat effective form. In some cases, such as Libya, countries cannot even deploy the bulk of their forces within their own

Figure 1.1
The Military Forces of the Greater Middle East

Country	Total Active Manning	Total Active Army Manning	Tanks	OAFVs	Artillery	Combat Aircraft	Armed Helicopters
North Africa							
Algeria	127,500	110,000	1,000	1,892	1,100	175	93
Libya	76,000	45,000	800	2,065	1,921	400	41
Morocco	196,300	175,000	520	1,279	452	95	24
Tunisia	35,000	27,000	84	391	117	29	15
Chad	30,350	25,000	60	203	5	2	2
Mauritania	15,750	15,000	35	75	75	8	0
Arab-Israeli							
Egypt	450,000	320,000	3,655[a]	4,682[d]	1,647[a]	579	121
Israel	167,600	125,000	3,950	8,770	1,542	438	100
Jordan	100,500	85,000	1,018[a]	1,595	475	101	22
Lebanon	72,100	70,000	310	1,463	172	0	0
Palestine[b]	(35,000)	(35,000)	—	—	—	—	—
Syria	319,000[d]	215,000	4,500	4,600	2,540	548	71[d]
Gulf							
Iran[c]	540,000	350,000	1,565	1,735	3,284	306	69
Iraq[e]	389,000	350,000	2,600	3,400	2,300	316	62
Bahrain	11,200	8,500	140	306	48	34	40
Kuwait	15,500	11,000	293	731	95	81	20

2

Oman[c]	41,700	117	371	132	40	0
Qatar	12,400	30	334	44	18	19
Saudi Arabia[c]	199,500	710	4,460	390	294	33
UAE	50,500	441	1,305	343	106	59
Yemen[a]	66,700	790	1,040	695	76	8
Peripheral						
Afghanistan	60–70,000	500	345+	210+	5	5
Djibouti	8,000	0	31	6	0	0
Eritrea	200,000	150	80	155	17	?
Ethiopia	160,000	270+	400	400	50	25
Somalia[b]	(35,900)	—	—	—	—	—
Sudan	100,000	200	604	1,070	27	10
Turkey	402,000	4,205	4,543	2,990	483	0

[a]Egypt has 100 additional M-1A1 Abrams MBT, 179 M-109A2/A3 SP ARTY on order. Jordan is awaiting 114 additional Challenger 1 MBT. Yemen has an additional 5 MiG-29S/UB on order.

[b]No current data available for Palestine and Somalia due to recent combat.

[c]Iranian totals include Revolutionary Guard Corps, Saudi totals include the Saudi National Guard Corps, and Omani totals include the Royal Household Guard.

[d]Egypt has 500 BTR-50/OT-62s in storage. Syria has around 1,200 tanks in static positions and an indeterminate number in storage. It is suspected that many of Syria's helicopters are in storage as well.

[e]These are preconflict numbers.

Notes: Totals count all "active" equipment, much of which is not operational. They do not include stored equipment, but are only approximate estimates of combat-ready equipment holdings. Light tanks, APCs, AIFVs, armored recce vehicles, and misc. AFVs are counted as OAFVs (Other Armored Fighting Vehicles). Artillery counts towed and self-propelled tube weapons of 100-mm+ and multiple rocket launchers, but not mortars. Only armed or combat-capable fixed wing combat aircraft are counted, not other trainers or aircraft.

Source: Adapted by Anthony H. Cordesman, CIA, *World Factbook*, various editions and IISS, *The Military Balance*, various editions.

boundaries. They lack the manpower and support capabilities to use their present pool of weapons with any effectiveness.

THE SUBREGIONALIZATION OF THE MIDDLE EAST MILITARY BALANCE

There are patterns within the regional military balance that do reflect the military dynamics of the region, however, and that simplify the analysis of the balance. In practice, the military forces of the Middle East can be divided into several key sub-balances that do reflect the history of warfare in the region, and provide a more tangible basis for estimating the mix of forces that might be involved in future conflicts:

- *The trends within the individual states of North Africa.* These states include Algeria, Libya, Morocco, and Tunisia, with Egypt having a major impact. These countries differ from those of the rest of the Middle East in that they have sometimes had civil conflicts or border clashes, but have had no major external conflicts with each other since achieving independence.

  Libya has had major regional ambitions in the past and fought a war with Chad on its southern border, but never became a significant military power. Morocco has long fought a war to fully annex the former Spanish Sahara, fighting with local forces called the Polisario. This has been a highly local-ized struggle, although Algeria has provided the Polisario with sanctuary and support. The bloodiest war in the region since independence, however, has been a civil conflict: the Algerian civil war, which has now gone on for well over a decade.

  In broad terms, the military balance in North Africa has not consisted of planning to go to war as much as creating forces that can defend a nation's borders, maintain internal security, and serve the purposes of national pres-tige. While several states have sent token forces to past Arab-Israeli forces, such forces have been a truly "token" and have had no military significance.

- *The trends affecting the Arab-Israeli conflict, dominated by Israel versus Syria.* The "Arab-Israeli" states include Egypt, Israel, Jordan, Lebanon, Syria; and a Palestinian entity or protostate. Their forces have been involved in major Arab-Israeli wars in 1948, 1956, 1967, 1970, 1973, and 1982. These con-ventional conflicts have had some elements of a broader regional conflict, and some Gulf and North African countries have sent forces to these conflicts.

  Egypt and Israel—the two most important military powers in the region—have been at peace since the late 1970s, however; and Jordon reached a peace treaty with Israel on October 26, 1994. Lebanon has never been a significant conventional military power, or threat to Israel. This essentially makes the present "Arab-Israeli balance" a largely Israeli-Syrian balance, although it remains possible that Egypt and/or Jordan could again become hostile to Israel in the future.

  There have also been three significant asymmetric Arab-Israeli conflicts. The first is the "First Intifada" between Israel and the Palestinians of Gaza and the West Bank between 1988 and 1993. The second is a struggle between Israel and an allied Christian-led Lebanese force, on the one hand, and Shiite factions in Southern Lebanon led primarily by Hezbollah with Iranian and Syrian support, on the other. This war grew out of the Israeli occupation of Southern Lebanon in 1982, and lasted until Israel withdrew on May 24, 2000. The third is the Israeli-Palestinian War, which began in September 2000, led to the collapse of the Arab-Israeli peace process and has continued ever since.

• *The Gulf military balance, divided largely into the Southern Gulf states, Iran, Iraq, and Yemen.* The military balance in the Gulf has long been a "four-cornered" balance between Iran, Iraq, Saudi Arabia, and the Southern Gulf states, and the power projection forces of the United Kingdom and the United States. Yemen has only been a limited military power, but has still been a significant factor in regional security because of its history of civil wars, large population, common borders with Oman and Saudi Arabia, and strategic position at the entrance to the Red Sea.

There have been several major tests of the Gulf balance. Egypt attempted to dominate North Yemen by intervening in its civil war during the 1960s, and only left in 1967. South Yemen supported Marxist rebels in Oman in what came to be called the "Dhofar Rebellion." Iraq invaded Iran in 1980, and a bloody war lasted until 1988. This led to U.S. reflagging of Kuwait's tankers in 1987, and a series of U.S. and Iranian clashes between 1987 and 1988 that came to be called the "Tanker War." Iraq first threatened to invade Kuwait when Britain withdrew from its role in protecting the Gulf, and then invaded and conquered Kuwait in 1990—only to be driven out by a U.S.-led coalition in 1991.

The fall of Saddam Hussein as a result of the Iraq War of 2003 and the virtual destruction of Iraq's military capabilities have had a much more decisive impact on the balance. The United States and Britain now lead a coalition that occupies Iraq and that is fighting a low-intensity conflict against former regime loyalists and other groups hostile to the coalition. Tensions between the United States and Saudi Arabia have led the former to withdraw its military forces from the latter, but have not led to a severing of U.S. and Saudi military ties. The United States has created new facilities in Kuwait, Qatar, and the United Arab Emirates (UAE) as well as improved its facilities in Oman.

LOOKING BEYOND THE NUMBERS: THE SCENARIO PROBLEM

Breaking down the military balance into functional subregions, however, is only part of the story. As the next chapter discusses, there are trends within the Middle Eastern and North African military balance that make traditional counts of force strength less and less relevant. There are also aspects of the balance like proliferation, asymmetric warfare, and terrorism that cut across the subregions outlined previously, and link the military balance in the Middle East and North African (MENA) region with that in many other areas, including the United States, Europe, Central Asia, South Asia, and Southeast Asia. Their trends all have one thing in common: there are no simple or reliable ways to quantify them.

This analysis does provide important tools for the scenario analysis of contingencies involving these forces and trends, however. It examines different ways to count conventional forces, and possible ways of relating force numbers to force quality. It examines the quality of manpower and weapons by country and service, and the impact of changes in military technology. It then integrates such analysis with an examination of the kinds of contingencies and scenarios most likely to affect the future and how changes in both force quantity and force quality are likely to affect future wars.

There is one problem that cannot be avoided. Counts of national military forces are scarcely definitive measures of war-fighting capability. The most important questions about the military balance, and the most important answers, are scenario and contingency dependent. Even if countries were foolish enough to publish their war plans, history has shown that wars and crises occur in ways that planners do not anticipate and cannot control. Even when conflicts do roughly fit the conditions planners consider in terms of the forces involved, timing, motive, deployment and sustainability of specific forces engaged and factors like geography, mobilization, and preparation shape the outcome of any clash or conflict.

Moreover, efforts to guess at the classified details of comparative doctrine, war plans, and the details of intentions, escalation management, and conflict termination are critical, but ultimately can only be guesses. No one can predict what portion of a given nation's forces will actually be engaged in future conflicts. The only thing that is certain is that no country can ever commit its entire pool of manpower and equipment, and the war-fighting balance almost always differs significantly from one based on a nation's entire order of battle or total inventory of weapons and equipment.

THE STRENGTHS AND LIMITATIONS OF NUMBERS

Like all analytic tools, numbers have inherent limitations. Aside from the many uncertainties inevitable in trying to quantify what every government in the region does its best to conceal, no one can predict what element of a given nation's forces will be used in a given scenario or conflict. Quantitative balances do not apply to many aspects of the asymmetric wars in the region, or provide a meaningful measurement of the capabilities of extremist, guerrilla, or terrorist groups. Wars are also often dominated by "intangibles" like leadership, training, manpower quality, and tactics. Important as manpower and equipment numbers can be in some respects, unquantifiable factors like innovation, flexibility, effective use of combined arms and jointness, command and control capability, and battle management skills shape the outcome of conflicts. No real-world conflict has ever had an outcome determined by easily quantifiable force ratios or preconflict orders of battle.

The inability to predict the forces that will be engaged in a given scenario, and the many "intangibles" that shape the outcome of war, do not mean, however, that comparisons of force strength are not important. Numbers still tell. Force ratios, manpower, and equipment numbers have an important impact on political perceptions of the balance, and they have value in estimating war-fighting capabilities. Force numbers can be particularly valuable when they show the full range of major combat weapons, and show the different force mixes involved in different countries. Simple counts of total manpower, or a few weapons categories like tanks and combat aircraft, often disguise as much as they reveal.

Deciding What to Count

Much depends on what is counted. It is easy to alter a count of total forces to exaggerate or underestimate a threat. As a result, there is no "right" count of Arab-Israeli forces, or of the Gulf or North African military balance. There are rather many different comparisons representing valid pictures of possible scenarios. These can range from counts of the forces that might be involved in a relatively low-intensity conflict to counts estimating the forces in a theaterwide conflict in a "worst case" scenario. No matter how this is done, there also is no way to avoid the fact that counts of total national forces do not reflect the portion of the total force that a given country can actually deploy and sustain in combat and ignore many aspects of force quality. As a result, some estimates are provided of deployable versus total forces. Such estimates are rough judgments.

For example, "classic" Israeli estimates of the Arab-Israeli military balance used to be based on the total conventional forces the Arab states near Israel could deploy against Israel. This "worst case" method of comparison greatly exaggerated both the probability that such coalitions would occur, and the total forces Arab states could actually deploy and sustain. In practice, however, few Israeli military analysts and planners ever based their force-planning and war-fighting assessments on comparisons of Israel's total forces with the total forces that all Arab states could conceivably deploy against Israel.[1] At the same time, some Arab counts only exaggerate Israel's weapons, understate Arab inventories, and ignore factors like geography and Israel's inherent vulnerability as a small, "thin" state with a narrow, exposed territory. This seeks to provide counts that are as neutral and objective as possible. Forces are counted and assessed largely on a national basis to avoid creating regional conflict scenarios that may never occur, and reflect the fact that many states are at peace or have good relations with their neighbors. At the same time, "regionwide" coalitions cannot be totally ignored. Iraq did play a significant role in the October War.

Problems in Counting Major Combat Units

This analysis does not make detailed assessments of unit strength for several reasons. First, few Middle Eastern and North African states have anything approaching standardized combat units with fixed numbers of men and equipment. Instead, each unit differs sharply, and some "divisions" are little more than brigade or regimental in size, while a "brigade" or "regiment" may actually be little more than a reinforced battalion. The same is true of air and air defense regiments and squadrons. Units also differ sharply in terms of manpower and equipment quality, and in readiness and sustainability.

Conventional order of battle analysis has limited value in assessing the Middle Eastern military balance. It can be useful in understanding the way in which individual powers organize their forces, but only if such data can be tied to a realistic estimate of the manpower and equipment strength of such units, and how they differ by individual unit as well as by unit type. It should also be noted that many of the unclassified sources on Middle Eastern and North African major combat unit and air unit strength are badly outdated or simply wrong, and that much of the data that are available will produce invalid comparisons even if one ignores the differences in unit manning and equipment. In general, the International Institute of Strategic Studies has the most accurate counts for land and air units, and Jane's has the most accurate count for combat ships.

The Strengths and Weaknesses of Manpower Numbers

There are other strengths and weaknesses in the numbers provided. Total manpower numbers provide a rough picture of the level of effort given nations devote to their military forces and of the war-fighting capabilities of armies. At the same time, manpower training and experience are as important as manpower numbers. Conscripts, with short terms of service, have less and less value in an era of high-technology forces and rapid tactical maneuver. The quality of a given force's noncommissioned officer (NCO), technician, and junior officers, and the experience of its enlisted men operating as teams, shape the ability to use modern combat equipment effectively. The value of conscript forces depends heavily on their funding and training. For example, Egypt and Syria grossly underfund conscript training; most of their conscripts have too little experience and training, and never realistically train in complex war-fighting scenarios and exercises.

Active manpower is hard to compare to reserve manpower. Much of the reserve manpower in Arab and Iranian forces has limited value due to a lack of training, modern equipment, sustainability, and adequate C^4I/BM capability. The Israeli reserve system is far more effective than that of any of its Arab neighbors, in part because Israel has such a small population that it has no alternative. Even Israel, however, has found it increasingly difficult to give reserve forces the training they need to maintain a capability for advanced maneuver warfare, and most Arab land force reserve manpower has little training, has second- or third-rate equipment, and has little capability in maneuver and demanding combined arms warfare.

Money is a steadily increasing problem that affects both manpower quantity and quality. Modern military forces are so expensive that Middle Eastern states cannot afford to use much of their total manpower pool, because they cannot fund suitable equipment, training, and sustainability. At the same time, states cannot use much of the manpower in their military forces in missions tailored to large-scale wars with their neighbors. Internal security and low-intensity operations degrade training for war fighting, and this presents a serious manpower quality problem for Israel, Egypt, and Syria. It is a problem both countries face difficulties in addressing because of the need to avoid additional unemployment and the feeling that mass conscription aids in political indoctrination and "nation building."

The Strengths and Weaknesses of Equipment Numbers

Comparisons of equipment numbers have somewhat similar strengths and weaknesses. Past Arab-Israeli conflicts, the Iran-Iraq War, and the Gulf War have all shown that equipment quality is often more important than equipment numbers. For example, most regional ground forces experienced a major buildup that continued from the late 1950s to the early 1990s. Holdings of armored forces and artillery increased significantly in size during this period. However, much of the present total inventory of Arab land weapons is now the result of the fact that states have continued to retain large numbers of older and low-quality systems that have only limited capability. The war-fighting value of much of this equipment is uncertain at best, and so is the ability of Arab forces to effectively man and sustain it.

Force quality can also improve strikingly, even if force numbers drop or remain constant. Israel has cut aircraft numbers to fund major improvements in the quality of its combat aircraft. Reductions have also taken place in the size of Arab forces because of factors like attrition and the rising cost of aircraft. At the same time, the combat aircraft in a number of these Arab states have also improved strikingly in relative quality.

Changes in force mix affect the meaning of equipment numbers as well as any counts of major combat unit strength. For example, counts of fixed wing aircraft do not reflect the fact that many countries now have significantly larger numbers of attack helicopters. Further, such totals usually overstate the strength of regional air forces by counting some aircraft housed in storage or training units.

COMPARISONS OF MILITARY EFFORT AND RESOURCES

Comparisons of defense expenditures and arms sales provide additional insights into the broad trends in regional and national military efforts—and put the analysis of both force numbers and force quality in perspective. Countries differ sharply in the size of their economy, and in the relative military effort they make at any given time. Comparisons of the size of national economies, and the strain that military spending puts on economies, provide a measure of both the willingness and capability of given countries to sustain their current military effort, and their ability to pay for future modernization and to "recapitalize" their forces.

The data on military spending as a percentage of gross national product (GNP) and national budgets are a morass of partial reporting and definitional and comparability problems. Nevertheless, enough data are available from declassified U.S. intelligence sources to make the correlation between the size of total national military spending and the burden it places on the economy and state budget relatively clear. It is also obvious in some cases that countries simply do not come close to spending the amount on their armed services and arms imports needed to keep their forces effective. There are four major sources for directly comparable data on military expenditures and arms sales: the Arms Control and Disarmament Agency (ACDA), which is now part of the U.S. State Department, the Congressional Research Service, the Stockholm International Peace Research Institute (SIPRI), and the International Institute of Strategic Studies (IISS).

Out of these sources, only the U.S. State Department and the Congressional Research Service have access to U.S. intelligence data, and can draw on the major analytic effort that goes on within the U.S. intelligence community. The SIPRI data have to be based largely on the estimates of a small group of private analysts. The IISS data rely on a mix of official sources but only report total military expenditures, and sometimes in ways that vary in definition from year to year and country to country, limiting the value of both trend and intercountry comparisons.

While the State Department and Congressional Research Service data are taken from material provided by the U.S. intelligence community, they too have problems:

- The data do not track with national reporting on military expenditures in budget documents, and the data on military expenditures for Egypt, Jordan, Lebanon, and Syria are rough estimates.
- The data on military expenditures are not fully comparable in definition from country to country. They generally exclude expenditures on weapons of mass destruction, and exclude many imports of long-range missiles.
- The data are not fully comparable in terms of the amount of military imports included or in terms of the extent to which they include new foreign debt and/

or past interest payments on military foreign debt—data excluded from the budget reporting of all of the Arab states listed.

- The data are not fully comparable in terms of the amount of nonmilitary goods and services used by the military, and include very different levels of military infrastructure expenditures.

- There is no way to adjust for the very different costs each country pays for manpower. Israel, for example, pays for high-quality regular manpower, but is primarily a reserve force. Arab states pay almost nothing for conscripts and very low salaries for other ranks and many junior officers.

COMPARISONS OF ARMS SALES AND IMPORTS

Comparing the data available on arms imports presents many of the same problems as comparing military expenditures. In addition to the problems mentioned earlier, the data on arms purchases exclude much expenditure on weapons of mass destruction, and exclude many imports of long-range missiles. They are not comparable in terms of the kind of contractor services and advisory efforts, military construction, and civil/dual-use equipment included.

Comparing data on the dollar value of arms imports presents further problems, because there often is only a limited correlation between the dollar figure and the number of weapons transferred or the importance of technology transferred. Dollar-oriented comparisons can be particularly misleading in examining the balance, because Israel has a major military industry and often imports components that are not included in the figures for arms imports. Egypt is the only Arab state with significant military industrial output, although the sophistication of its output does not approach that of Israel.

Many of the data on arms sales have to be based on educated guesses about the very different prices given nations pay for given weapons. They may or may not be properly adjusted for the fact that some countries get weapons that are provided as surplus equipment or pay far less for given types of weapons than do other countries. These factors need to be kept in mind in comparing the data. The trends in the figures are probably broadly accurate, but they do not portray directly comparable data.

Throughout the Cold War the Arab states that bought weapons from the Soviet bloc paid far less per weapon than states that bought from the West. Since the end of the Cold War, states buying from Russia, the People's Republic of China, and Central Europe have had to pay more than in the past, but have still paid far less per weapon than nations buying similar types of weapons from Western countries. These price differences have been so striking in the case of some arms transfers to the Middle East that there is sometimes an inverse correlation between the trends reflected in cost estimates of the size of the arms transfers to given states and the trends in the number of weapons transferred.

Egypt and Israel present special problems. The data on their total arms imports rarely reflect the data available on the size of the U.S. military assistance provided to Egypt and Israel, and there is no way of relating dollar cost to the value of the weapons technologies being purchased. There is an uncertain correlation to actual expenditures in foreign currencies, and to data on military foreign assistance and borrowing. There is little correlation between the State Department's estimates of arms imports and the flow of U.S. foreign military aid and sales. Israel, for example, receives billions of dollars of annual military assistance from the United States and much goes to imports of parts and munitions for Israel's arms, but this often is not counted as arms imports in State Department estimates of Israel's total annual arms imports.

LOOKING BEYOND THE NUMBERS: THE UNQUANTIFIABLE ASPECTS OF FORCE QUALITY

There are other important limits to numbers that must be kept firmly in mind. Unquantifiable factors like morale and training are as important as force strength, and repeated efforts to create models to quantify force and equipment quality have had uncertain results at best. Historically, force quality has always been as—or more—important than force numbers. As a result, the assessments of the balance in this book look at factors like investment in new weapons, the relative quality of major weapons, and acquisitions of advanced intelligence and command and control systems.

The analysis does take a detailed look at the level of resources available to each country and the flow of arms into the region over a period of decades, other methods of measuring force quality both now and in the future. The resulting comparisons show that various countries have grossly different total military expenditures and access to modern arms, and that the forces of some nations have benefited far more from recent arms transfers than have those of others. Unfortunately, reliable data are often missing on critical factors like munitions types and numbers, stock levels and sustainability, and support equipment. Moreover, almost no data are available on other critical "intangibles" like training or manpower quality in terms of numbers of officers, other ranks, technicians, and experienced manpower.

SCORING SYSTEMS, WAR GAMING, AND SIMULATION

This book does not include any effort to assign scores to given weapons systems or types of combat units. An evaluation of the various scoring systems currently available reveals that these systems only have value in a few cases, where the structure of the forces on both sides is consistent, and there is something approaching a common mix of combined arms, and capability for joint operations. These conditions simply do not apply to the forces of virtually all Middle Eastern and North African countries, and the scoring systems involved ultimately break down in reflecting meaningful differences between equipment types and direct and indirect fire. They may have value for bureaucratic reasons in the organizations and countries that use them, but even a cursory review of the scores by unit or weapon shows that such scoring is either little more than guesswork or grossly exaggerates the value of older weapons types.

For similar reasons, no use has been made of computer gaming and simulation. Such techniques can be very useful in interactive modeling, where the course of the game or simulation is transparent to the modelers and the assumptions made are continuously corrected to reflect human judgment as to what might happen under real-world conditions. The key, however, is that the modelers be directly involved in the game, that no part of the computerized model is treated as a "black box" or as valid without an explicit examination of all of the data and assumptions made, and that the game scenario be as realistic as possible rather than being based on force ratios per se. These conditions cannot be met in an analysis of this kind, and where they cannot be met, the end result of gaming and simulation is simply to create a true "black box," which adds new layers of complexity and random error to all of the problems inherent in static force ratios.

Chapter 2

The Changing Face of the Middle East Military Balance

The problems in quantifying and counting Middle Eastern and North African forces are only part of the story in assessing the Middle East military balance. The very nature of warfare is changing in a region where nations have previously tended to focus on building the largest possible forces and obtaining the most advanced major weapons. The force comparisons and trend analyses in the following chapters should be considered with the understanding that major changes are taking place in the way that military forces are shaped and used at a time when many Middle Eastern powers either cannot afford to make the necessary force improvements, or lack the capacity to do so.

CHANGES IN THE NATURE OF WARFARE

Like all regions in the world, the Middle East is being affected by radical changes in tactics, technology, and training. The most critical of these changes include:

- *The "revolution in military affairs."* Changes in tactics, technology, and training that exploit new intelligence, surveillance, and reconnaissance (IS&R) systems, precision targeting and munitions, long-range strike systems, high mobility, and other assets to fundamentally change the pace and intensity of warfare and to exploit a qualitative "revolution" in military technology.

- *Combined arms and joint warfare.* Methods of warfare that eliminate the traditional organization and tactical barriers between the elements of a given military service ("combined arms") and integrate the operations of different military services (joint warfare).

- *C⁴I/BM/IS&R and "netcentric warfare."* C⁴I (command, control, communications, computers, and intelligence), BM (battle management), and IS&R are all subsets of the "revolution in military affairs," but the advances in each area are so great that each is a driving force behind changes in the regional balance. Moreover, the growing ability to link these advances in a "net" that can provide a comprehensive, near–real time picture of the battle-field is fundamentally changing the nature of warfare.

- *Precision and platform upgrades.* Military investment and modernization have seen a shift in emphasis to more advanced munitions and precision weapons, with less investment in new platforms like tanks, aircraft, and ships. Major investments are being made in military electronics.

- *Professionalism and manpower quality—new human factors and capabilities.* Advances in both tactics and technology have made human factors steadily more important. Modern forces, combined arms, and joint warfare all require a far higher degree of professionalism, training, and experience than in the past. They have created a new premium for giving junior officers and other ranks more initiative, and for developing cadres of effective and well-trained noncommissioned offers (NCOs) and technicians. Conversely, they have made short-service conscripts and reserves with limited training steadily less valuable.

- *Sustainability.* Logistics, maintenance, readiness, and repair and recovery have always been critical aspects of military operations. During the past four decades, however, the value of highly ready forces that can be sustained for prolonged periods of intense warfare has become steadily more apparent, while it has become clear that forces without high levels of sustainability cannot fight at levels of maneuver and intensity that allow them to compete.

- *Asymmetric warfare.* New approaches to warfare are being developed whereby each side uses a radically different mix of strategy, tactics, technology, and methods of warfare to best exploit its opponent's weaknesses while minimizing its own weaknesses and vulnerabilities.

- *Proliferation.* Chemical, biological, radiological, and nuclear (CBRN) weapons, and long-range delivery systems like ballistic missiles, are being acquired and deployed. Algeria, Libya, Egypt, Israel, Syria, Iran, and Iraq have all at least made efforts at developing CBRN weapons, and Saudi Arabia has acquired long-range surface-to-surface missiles.

- *Terrorism.* Terrorism is the systematic use of terror, especially as a means of coercion. It has become part of the way in which both states and nonstate actors conduct warfare. The region has suffered from major terrorist attacks since the early phases of the Arab-Israeli conflict, but secular terrorism became a major aspect of the military balance in the late 1960s; and religious terrorism has been a major aspect of the balance since the mid-1990s.

- *Covert and proxy warfare.* Many powers have not been able to keep up in the race to modernize their military forces or are simply too small to confront the major regional military powers or the power projection forces of outside nations like the United States. Shifting to the use of covert warfare, or proxy forces like terrorist and extremist groups, provides a means of conducting asymmetric warfare whereby states can seek to avoid direct confrontation or combat with larger powers.

- *Superterrorism.* The growth of extremist and terrorist threats is increasing the risk that chemical, biological, radiological, and nuclear weapons will be used against states or other opponents and potentially increasing the risk that precision weapons or other devices will be used to produce catastrophic damage through attacks against critical infrastructure targets like desalination plants, major energy facilities, and the like.

- *External and regional coalitions.* State-to-state and internal civil conflicts are still a major aspect of the Middle East balance. Recent wars have shown, however, that coalitions that involve states from outside the Middle East and North Africa (MENA), and assemblies of "coalitions of the willing" that draw together disparate force elements from throughout the region, can be rapidly developed.

- *Information warfare.* Middle Eastern conflicts have always had a significant political and propagandizing dimension. The political and information aspects of the Arab-Israeli conflict, the Gulf War, the Iraq War, and the U.S. "war on terrorism" have all shown, however, that information warfare per se has become steadily more important over time. This process has been accelerated by developments like satellite television, the emergence of major independent broadcasters, the Internet, cell phones, and fax machines.

- *Economic warfare and sanctions.* Oil-exporting nations first tried to use oil as a weapon in the mid-1960s, but did not succeed until after the October War of 1973. Since that time, the United States, Britain, and the United Nations have made aggressive use of economic sanctions, most notably against Libya, Iran, and Iraq.

THE IMPACT OF THE REVOLUTION IN MILITARY AFFAIRS

Not all of the previously mentioned changes can be covered in detail in this analysis, particularly those dealing with complex advances in military technology and tactics. Chapter 9 does analyze the threat of terrorism in more detail, and Chapter 10 discusses proliferation. There are several broader developments, however, that need to be considered in evaluating both the changes in the nature of regional warfare and how well a given country is coping with these changes:

- Figure 2.1 describes the key features of the revolution in military affairs. Middle Eastern and North African states differ radically in the degree to which they have adapted to these changes, and often individual services and force elements have progressed at very different levels—even within a given country. So far, MENA nations lag badly behind advanced military powers like the United Kingdom and the United States, although Israel and Egypt are limited exceptions.

Figure 2.1
The "Revolution in Military Affairs" (RMA)

- *Decoupling of political and military responsibility:* No war is ever free of command controversy or friction between political and military leadership. However, the Coalition forces fought the Gulf War with effective delegation of responsibility for military decisions to military commanders. RMA forces are likely to enjoy the same advantage in mid-to-high-intensity wars where rival military forces will be more politicized and organized more to suit the regime's internal security needs than to conduct modern joint operations.

- *Unity of command:* The level of unity of command, and "fusion," achieved during the Gulf War was scarcely perfect, but it was far more effective than that possible in most states. Advanced powers have improved its unity of command and ability to conduct joint operations.

- *Jointness, combined operations, combined arms, and the "AirLand Battle":* Advanced powers can use technology to train and integrate in ways that allow far more effective approaches to jointness, combined arms, and combined operations. They have developed tactics that closely integrated air and land operations.

- *Emphasis on maneuver:* The United States had firepower and attrition warfare until the end of the Vietnam War. In the years that followed, it converted its force structure to place an equal emphasis on maneuver and deception. This emphasis has been adopted by Britain, France, and other advanced states.

- *Emphasis on deception and strategic/tactical innovation:* No country has a monopoly on the use of deception and strategic/tactical innovation. High technology powers with advanced battle management and information systems will, however, be able to penetrate the enemy's decision-making system and react so quickly that the opponent cannot compete.

- *"24-hour war"—superior night, all-weather, and beyond-visual-range warfare:* "Visibility" is always relative in combat. There is no such thing as a perfect night vision or all-weather combat system, or way of acquiring perfect information at long-ranges. Advanced technology air and land forces, however, have far better training and technology for such combat than they ever had in the past and are designed to wage warfare continuously at night and in poor weather. Equally important, they are far more capable of taking advantage of the margin of extra range and tactical information provided by superior technology.

- *Near–real time integration of $C^4I/BM/T/BDA$:* New $C^4I/BM/T/BDA$ organization, technology, and software systems make it possible to integrate various aspects of command, control, communications, computers, and intelligence (C^4I); battle management (BM); targeting (T); and battle damage assessment (BDA) to achieve a near–real time integration and decision-making-execution cycle.

- *A new tempo of operations:* Superiority in virtually every aspect of targeting, intelligence gathering and dissemination, integration of combined arms, multiservice forces, and night and all-weather warfare make it possible to achieve both a new tempo of operations and one far superior to that of the enemy.

- *A new tempo of sustainability:* Advanced forces will have maintainability, reliability, reparability, and the speed and overall mobility of logistic, service support, and combat support force activity that broadly match their maneuver and

Figure 2.1 (Continued)

firepower capabilities. The benefits of these new capabilities are already reflected in such critical areas as the extraordinarily high operational availability and sortie rates of Western combat aircraft, and the ability to support the movement of heliborne and armored forces

- *Beyond-visual-range air combat, air defense suppression, air base attacks, and airborne C⁴I/BM:* The Coalition in the Gulf had a decisive advantage in air combat training, beyond-visual-range air combat capability, antiradiation missiles, electronic warfare, air base and shelter and kill capability, stealth and unmanned long-range strike systems, IFF and air control capability, and airborne C⁴I/BM systems like the E-3 and ABCCC. These advantages allowed the Coalition to win early and decisive air supremacy. Advanced forces will steadily improve the individual capability of these systems and their integration into "netcentric" warfare.

- *Focused and effective interdiction bombing:* Advanced forces will organize effectively to use its deep strike capabilities to carry out a rapid and effective pattern of focus strategic bombing where planning is sufficiently well coupled to intelligence and meaningful strategic objectives so that such strikes achieve the major military objectives that the planner sets. At the same time, targeting, force allocation, and precision kill capabilities will advance to the point where interdiction bombing and strikes are far more lethal and strategically useful than in previous conflicts.

- *Expansion of the battlefield—"Deep Strike":* As part of its effort to offset the Warsaw Pact's numerical superiority, U.S. tactics and technology emphasized using AirLand battle capabilities to extend the battlefield far beyond the immediate forward "edge" of the battle area (FEBA). The Coalition exploited the resulting mix of targeting capability, improved air strike capabilities, and land force capabilities in ways during the Gulf War that played an important role in degrading Iraqi ground forces during the air phase of the war, and which helped the Coalition break through Iraqi defenses and exploit the breakthrough. Even in Kosovo, the United States and NATO were only beginning to employ advanced "Deep Strike" targeting technologies and precision strike systems and far more advanced systems are in development.

- *Technological superiority in many critical areas of weaponry:* The West and GCC scarcely had a monopoly on effective weapons during the Gulf War, but they had a critical "edge" in key weapons like tanks, other armored fighting vehicles, artillery systems, long-range strike systems, attack aircraft, air defense aircraft, surface-to-air missiles, space, attack helicopters, naval systems, sensors, battle management, and a host of other areas. This superiority went far beyond the technical "edge" revealed by "weapon on weapon" comparisons. Coalition forces exploited technology in "systems" that integrated mixes of different weapons into other aspects of force capability and into the overall force structure.

- *Integration of precision-guided weapons into tactics and force structures:* Advanced forces will exploit a technical "edge" in the ability to use precision-guided weapons with far more realistic training in using such weapons and the ability to link their employment to far superior reconnaissance and targeting capability.

continued

Figure 2.1 (Continued)

- *Realistic combat training and use of technology and simulation:* During the Gulf War, the United States and Britain used training methods based on realistic combined arms and AirLand training, large-scale training, and adversary training. These efforts proved far superior to previous methods and were coupled to a far more realistic and demanding system for ensuring the readiness of the forces involved. They show the value of kinds of training that allow forces to rapidly adapt to the special and changing conditions of war.

- *Emphasis on forward leadership and delegation:* Technology, tactics, and training all support aggressive and innovative leadership.

- *Heavy reliance on NCOs and highly skilled enlisted personnel:* Advanced forces will not rely on conscripts or reserves, but will place heavy reliance on the technical skills, leadership quality, and initiative of NCOs and experienced enlisted personnel.

- *High degree of overall readiness:* Military readiness is a difficult term to define since it involves so many aspects of force capability. RMA forces, however, will have more realistic standards for measuring readiness, ensuring proper reporting, and adequate funding over a sustained period of time.

- Figure 2.2 describes the challenges that poorer and less developed MENA powers face in coping with the revolution in military affairs. Many of the points in this figure help explain the scale and speed of the coalition victories against Iraq in 1991 and 2003, and Israel's military "edge" in comparison with the capabilities most of its neighbors.

- Figure 2.3, however, makes it clear that advanced military powers have vulnerabilities as well, and helps to explain why poorer and less developed MENA powers have turned to asymmetric warfare, proliferation, covert warfare, and terrorism as possible counters to the revolution in military affairs.

Several key points emerge from Figures 2.1–2.3. First, the ability to exploit the revolution in military affairs gives those few countries with the capability to do so a tremendous advantage as long as warfare remains relatively conventional in terms of the forces engaged. Second, few nations will passively cede this advantage to more powerful neighbors or outside powers, and this is even more true of nonstate actors like extremist or terrorist organizations. Finally, there are alternative tactics and "countervailing strategies" that militarily weak nations and powers can use to try to offset the revolution in military affairs, tactics that are now being employed in the Afghan war, the Israeli-Palestinian conflict, and Iraq.

What may be less obvious is the importance of human factors and of having the well-educated, well-trained, and experienced forces capable of adapting to new forms of warfare. Manpower quality is an "intangible"

Figure 2.2
Technology Vulnerabilities of Less Advanced Powers

- *Authoritarianism and overcentralization of the effective command structure:* The high command of many countries is dependent on compartmentalized, over-centralized C⁴I/BM systems that do not support high tempo warfare, combined arms, or combined operations and lack tactical and technical sophistication. Many forces or force elements report through a separate chain of command. C⁴I/BM systems often are structured to separate the activity of regular forces from elite, regime security, and ideological forces. Systems often ensure major sectors and corps commanders report to the political leadership, and separations occur within the branches of a given service. Intelligence is compartmentalized and poorly disseminated. Air force command systems are small, unit-oriented, and unsuited for large-scale force management. Coordination of land-based air defense and strike systems is poorly integrated, vulnerable, and/or limited in volume handing capability. Combined operations and combined arms coordination are poor, and command interference at the political level is common.

- *Lack of strategic assessment capability:* Many nations lack sufficient understanding of Western war fighting capabilities to understand the impact of the revolution in military affairs, the role of high technology systems, and the impact of the new tempo of war. Other countries have important gaps in their assessment capabilities reflecting national traditions or prejudices.

- *Major weaknesses in battle management, command, control, communications, intelligence, targeting, and battle damage assessment:* No Middle Eastern country has meaningful access to space-based systems or advanced theater reconnaissance and intelligence systems. Most lack sophisticated reconnaissance, intelligence, and targeting assets. Beyond-visual-range imagery and targeting is restricted to largely vulnerable and easily detectable reconnaissance aircraft or low performance UAVs. Many rely on photo data for imagery and have cumbersome download and analysis cycles in interpreting intelligence. Many have exploitable vulnerabilities to information warfare. Most are limited in the sophistication of their electronic warfare, SIGINT, and COMINT systems. Their communications security is little better than commercial communications security. They have severe communications interconnectivity, volume handling, and dissemination problems. Additionally, they cannot provide the software and connectivity necessary to fully exploit even commercial or ordinary military systems. They lack the C⁴I/BM capability to manage complex deep strikes, complex large-scale armor and artillery operations, effective electronic intelligence, and rapid cycles of reaction in decision making.

- *Lack of cohesive force quality:* Most countries' forces have major land combat units and squadrons with very different levels of proficiency. Political, historical, and equipment-supply factors often mean that most units have much lower levels of real-world combat effectiveness than the best units. Further, imbalances in combat support, service support, and logistic support create significant additional imbalances in sustainability and operational effectiveness. Many states add to these problems, as well as lack of force cohesion, by creating politicized or ideological divisions within their forces.

continued

Figure 2.2 (Continued)

- *Shallow offensive battlefields:* Most states face severe limits in extending the depth of the battlefield because they lack the survivable platforms and sensors, communications, and data processing to do so. These problems are particularly severe in wars of maneuver, in wars involving the extensive use of strike aircraft, and in battles where a growing strain is placed on force cohesion.
- *Manpower quality:* Many states rely on the mass use of poorly trained conscripts. They fail to provide adequate status, pay, training, and career management for NCOs and technicians. Many forces fail to provide professional career development for officers and joint and combined arms training. Promotion often occurs for political reasons or out of nepotism and favoritism.
- *Slow tempo of operations:* Most military forces have not fought a high-intensity air or armored battle. They are at best capable of medium tempo operations, and their pace of operations is often dependent on the survival of some critical mix of facilities or capabilities.
- *Lack of sustainability, recovery, and repair:* These initial problems in the tempo of operations are often exacerbated by a failure to provide for sustained air operations and high sortie rates, long-range sustained maneuver, and battlefield/ combat unit recovery and repair. Most forces are heavily dependent on resupply to deal with combat attrition whereas Western forces can use field recovery, maintenance, and repair.
- *Inability to prevent air superiority:* Many states have far greater air defense capability on paper than they do in practice. Most have not fought in any kind of meaningful air action in the last decade, and many have never fought any significant air action in their history. C⁴I/BM problems are critical in this near–real time environment. Most countries lack sophisticated air combat and land-based air defense simulation and training systems and do not conduct effective aggressor and large-scale operations training. Efforts to transfer technology, organization, and training methods from other nations on a patchwork basis often leaves critical gaps in national capability, even where other capabilities are effective.
- *Problems in air-to-air combat:* Air combat training levels are low and unrealistic. Pilot and other crew training standards are insufficient, or initial training is not followed up with sustained training. There is little effective aggressor training. AWACS and ABCCC capabilities are lacking. EW capabilities are modified commercial grade capabilities. Most aircraft lack effective air battle management systems and have limited beyond-visual-range and look down shoot down capability. Most Soviet/Communist-supplied air forces depend heavily on obsolete ground-controlled vectoring for intercepts. Key radar and control centers are static and vulnerable to corridor blasting.
- *Problems in land-based air defense:* Many states must borrow or adapt air defense battle management capabilities from supplier states, and have limited independent capability for systems integration—particularly at the software level. They lack the mix of heavy surface-to-air missile systems to cover broad areas, or must rely on obsolete systems that can be killed, countered by EW, and/or bypassed. Most Middle Eastern short-range air defense systems do not protect against attacks with stand-off precision weapons or using stealth.

Figure 2.2 (Continued)

- *Lack of effective survivable long-range strike systems:* Many nations have the capability to launch long-range air and missile strikes, but also have severe operational problems. Refueling capabilities do not exist or are in such small numbers as to be highly vulnerable. Long-range targeting and battle damage assessment capabilities are lacking. Training is limited and unrealistic in terms of penetrating effective air defenses. Platforms are export systems without the full range of supplier avionics or missile warheads. Assets are not survivable, or lose much of their effective strike capability once dispersed.

- *Combined (joint) operations, combined arms, and the AirLand battle:* Many states fail to emphasize the key advances in the integration of warfighting capabilities from the last decade. When they do emphasize combined arms and joint operations, they usually leave serious gaps in some aspects of national warfighting capability.

- *Rough/special terrain warfare:* Although many forces have armed helicopters and large numbers of tracked vehicles and can create effective rough terrain defenses if given time, they have problems in conducting high tempo operations. Many tend to be road-bound for critical support and combined arms functions and lack training for long-range, high-intensity engagements in rough terrain. Many are not properly trained to exploit the potential advantages of their own region. They are either garrison forces, or forces that rely on relatively static operations in predetermined field positions. These problems are often compounded by a lack of combat engineering and barrier crossing equipment.

- *Night and all-weather warfare:* Most forces lack adequate equipment for night and poor weather warfare, and particularly for long-range direct and indirect fire engagement and cohesive, sustainable, large-scale maneuver.

- *Armored operations:* Most countries have sharply different levels of armored warfare proficiency within their armored and mechanized forces. Few units have advanced training and simulation facilities. Most land forces have interoperability and standardization problems within their force structure—particularly in the case of other armored fighting vehicles where they often deploy a very wide range of types. Many are very tank heavy, without the mix of other capabilities necessary to deploy infantry, supporting artillery, and antitank capabilities at the same speed and maneuver proficiency as tank units. Most forces have poor training in conducting rapid, large-scale armored and combined operations at night and in poor weather. Effective battle management declines sharply at the forcewide level—as distinguished from the major combat unit level—and sometimes even in coordinating brigade or division-sized operations.

- *Artillery operations:* Many states have large numbers of artillery weapons but serious problems in training and tactics. They lack long-range targeting capability and the ability to rapidly shift and effectively allocate fire. Many rely on towed weapons with limited mobility, or lack off-road support vehicles. Combined arms capabilities are limited. Many units are only effective in using mass fire against enemies that maneuver more slowly than they do.

continued

Figure 2.2 (Continued)

- *Combat training:* Training generally has serious problems and gaps, which vary by country. Units or force elements differ sharply in training quality. Training problems are complicated by conversion and expansion, conscript turnover, and a lack of advanced technical support for realistic armored, artillery, air-to-air, surface-to-air, and offensive air training. Mass sometimes compensates, but major weaknesses remain.

- *Inability to use weapons of mass destruction effectively:* Any state can use weapons of mass destruction to threaten or intimidate another or to attack population centers and fixed area targets. At the same time, this is not the same as having an effective capability and doctrine to obtain maximum use of such weapons, or to manage attacks in ways that result in effective tactical outcomes and conflict termination. Many states are acquiring long-range missiles and weapons of mass destruction with very limited exercise and test and evaluation capabilities. This does not deny them the ability to target large populated areas, economic centers, and fixed military targets, potentially inflicting massive damage. At the same time, it does present problems in more sophisticated military operations. Many will have to improvise deployments, doctrine, and war fighting capabilities. In many cases, weaknesses and vulnerabilities will persist and they will only be able to exploit a limited amount of the potential lethality of such systems.

that is not easily quantifiable, but that is even more critical to success in dealing with these changes than are investments in equipment and technology. All of the forces shown in Figures 2.1–2.3 are exacerbating long-standing problems in the quality of regional military manpower. The value of conscripts is increasingly uncertain when military forces have to execute complex tactics and operate advanced military equipment. Experience in realistic exercise training, in operating as combat teams, and in joint and combined arms training has become far more important. So has the ability to create and retain technical cadres, NCOs, and "hands-on" officers capable of a high degree of initiative and leadership by example.

THE PROBLEM OF RESOURCES

As the following chapters make clear, these shifts in the nature of war fighting and the MENA military balance interact with major shifts in military resources. In general, the cost of modern forces has gone steadily up while the resources available to fund them have either dropped in real terms or remained constant. Currently, no Middle Eastern state is spending the resources necessary to fully sustain the present size of its force structure, modernizing it in ways that allow competitiveness with the West, or bringing it to the proper level of readiness and sustainment.

Figure 2.3
Asymmetric Warfare and the Vulnerabilities of Advanced Technology Powers

- *Sudden or surprise attack:* Power projection is dependent on strategic warning, timely decision making, and effective mobilization and redeployment for much of its military effectiveness.

- *Saturation:* There is no precise way to determine the point at which mass, or force quantity, overcomes superior effectiveness, or force quality—historically, efforts to emphasize mass have been far less successful than military experts predicted at the time. Even the best force, however, reaches the point where it cannot maintain its "edge" in C⁴I/battle management, air combat, or maneuver warfare in the face of superior numbers or multiple threats. Further, saturation may produce a sudden catalytic collapse of effectiveness, rather than a gradual degeneration from which the Israeli Defense Force could recover. This affects forward deployment, reliance on mobilization, and reliance on defensive land tactics versus preemption and "offensive defense."

- *Taking casualties:* Warfighting is not measured simply in terms of whether a given side can win a battle or conflict, but how well it can absorb the damage inflicted upon it. Many powers are highly sensitive to casualties and losses. This sensitivity may limit its operational flexibility in taking risks, and in sustaining some kinds of combat if casualties become serious relative to the apparent value of the immediate objective.

- *Inflicting casualties:* Dependence on world opinion and outside support means some nations increasingly must plan to fight at least low- and mid-intensity conflicts in ways that limit enemy casualties and collateral damage to its opponents and show that Israel is actively attempting to fight a "humanitarian" style of combat.

- *Low-intensity combat:* Low-intensity conflict makes it much harder to utilize most technical advantages in combat—because low-intensity wars are largely fought against people, not things. Low-intensity wars are also highly political. The battle for public opinion is as much a condition of victory as killing the enemy. The outcome of such a battle will be highly dependent on the specific political conditions under which it is fought, rather than RMA-like capabilities.

- *Hostage taking and terrorism:* Like low-intensity warfare, hostage taking and terrorism present the problem that advanced technology powers cannot exploit their conventional strengths and must fight a low-level battle primarily on the basis of infantry combat. HUMINT is more important than conventional military intelligence, and much of the fight against terrorism may take place in urban or heavily populated areas.

- *Urban and built-up area warfare:* Advanced military powers are still challenged the problem of urban warfare. They did not perform particularly well in urban warfare. Most western forces are not trained or equipped to deal with sustained urban warfare in populated areas during regional combat—particularly when the fighting may affect large civilian populations on friendly soil.

continued

Figure 2.3 (Continued)

- *Extended conflict and occupation warfare:* Not all wars can be quickly termi-nated, and many forms of warfare—particularly those involving peacekeeping and peace-enforcement—require prolonged military occupations.

- *Weapons of mass destruction:* The threat or actual use of such weapons can com-pensate for conventional weakness in some cases and deter military action in others.

Many nations are facing a crisis in terms of recapitalizing their forces. They cannot afford modernization at anything like the rate required to maintain their current equipment numbers and force strengths. In some cases, this underfunding has been chronic for more than a decade. These problems have been particularly serious in countries that once relied on Soviet-bloc aid, low-cost arms, and/or low-cost loans. They have also af-fected countries under sanctions or to which the United States and other Western powers have made efforts to limit arms exports. Only a few coun-tries have funded the same rate of new arms purchases as in the past, or increased them, and none of these countries is a serious regional military power. Even Egypt and Israel—countries receiving massive U.S. military aid—are experiencing serious recapitalization problems.

These problems are compounded by a lack of investment in manpower quality and readiness that is far harder to quantify, but obvious to anyone who studies the region. Far too many Middle Eastern nations still attempt to create the largest possible forces, or invest in the latest and most modern weapons, rather than create balanced mixes of capability. Many govern-ments also distrust their military and emphasize loyalty and security rather than military effectiveness. When they are forced to compromise for finan-cial reasons, they continue to fund force size at the expense of readiness and sustainability. The end result is often impressive force numbers but lim-ited real-world military capability.

Barring a massive change in military spending, these problems will gen-erally get worse for at least the next half decade. The major cutbacks in military investment and modernization that began in the late 1980s and early 1990s could be absorbed for a while, because many countries had large pools of relatively modern equipment to draw from. Most countries sharply cut their new weapons orders in the late 1990s and early 2000s as well. Even if they were to place major orders today, it would take half a decade to obtain delivery and convert to the new weapons systems, and there is little evidence that such orders will be placed.

Proliferation and internal security expenditures put further pressure on Middle Eastern and North African resource problems. Most countries face serious budget constraints, but some are funding major programs to acquire long-range surface-to-surface missiles and CBRN weapons, and most have had to make major increases in their internal security efforts. These programs cannot be funded by cutting civil expenditures, because massive population growth requires more and more civil spending and any cutback in civil programs creates added civil unrest and increases the threat from Islamic extremists. In short, Middle Eastern and North African countries are less and less able to pay for the necessary changes in their military forces at a time when such changes are becoming more and more necessary.

KEY ANALYTIC ISSUES AFFECTING THE MIDDLE EAST MILITARY BALANCE

There are other military and analytic issues that must be considered in assessing force trends and comparisons:

- *Arms control and the Arab-Israeli peace process are, and will remain, an extension of war by other means.* Arms control and peace are both valid ends in themselves, but they are also security struggles and extensions of war by other means. Their impact on regional scenarios, military planning, and war-fighting capability is as meaningful as that of manpower increases or equipment modernization.

- *Military resource problems do not bring stability.* The recapitalization problem does create an incentive for some forms of force reduction, but reductions eliminating older and lower-quality forces will have little impact on war-fighting capability. Recapitalization is also an incentive to proliferate. Moreover, most countries have historically spent twice their present percentages of gross national product (GNP) on military forces. Middle East states have tremendous "surge" capability to make major, unpredictable new equipment purchases.

- *Proliferation is far more complex than nuclear proliferation or the acquisition of long-range missiles.* Proliferation cannot be seen in terms of one type of weapon—specifically, nuclear weapons. In fact, the inability to acquire nuclear weapons creates an incentive to acquire biological and chemical weapons. Delivery systems for proliferation are not driven by ballistic missiles: they may involve terrorism and unconventional and proxy systems as well as cruise missiles and aircraft.

- *Major weapons platforms are increasingly less important than associated equipment.* Command, control, communications, computers, and intelligence; battle management; strategic reconnaissance-targeting; and battle damage assessment can now greatly enhance the capabilities of conventional forces, and smart munitions and highly lethal warheads can compensate for force numbers. The resulting changes in warfare require new methods of reporting on modernization, and assessing its impact, that existing unclassified reporting does not support. Reporting still focuses on major weapons platforms by basic type. Existing sources do not report accurately or in depth on platform upgrades, developments in netcentric warfare, or the acquisition of precision weapons and the systems necessary to use them.

- *New measures of manpower and training quality are needed.* Total active and reserve manpower are uncertain measures of military capability at best. Estimates of the balance need to consider ratios of officers and NCOs to enlisted men, numbers of technicians, training cycles, dependence on conscripts, retention rates, numbers of personnel with combat experience, and other critical factors relating to manpower quality. Such data are rarely, if ever, available in unclassified form.

- *New measures of readiness and sustainability are needed.* Support and sustainability are critical in determining war fighting, and have high-technology, infrastructural, and training dimensions. Existing sources do not report meaningful on support equipment, supply and stock levels, combat engineering capability, repair and recovery capability, logistic structures and capability, deadline line rates or operational availability, or any of the other measures of this aspect of war-fighting capability.

- *Paramilitary, counterterrorism, and asymmetric warfare capabilities need separate reporting and assessment.* Limited data are available on paramilitary and special forces, largely in the form of manpower totals or reporting on special forces and other light units with special value in asymmetric warfare. Such data do little to describe the real-world capabilities of the forces involved, however; and they are grossly inadequate as a means of assessing capabilities for counterterrorism and asymmetric warfare.

It is valid to argue that none of these issues is new. There have long been similar problems in assessing the military balance in the Middle East and North Africa, as in other regions. This past decade has seen a steady rise in the importance of such factors, however; and conflicts like the Gulf War of 1991 have been followed by the Kosovo conflict, Israeli-Palestinian War, Afghan War, and Iraq War, which have all demonstrated the importance of both the revolution in military affairs and asymmetric warfare. Unfortunately, many of these developments simply cannot be assessed without far better data on the qualitative aspects of the military balance than are currently available.

Chapter 3

"The Most Militarized Area in the World":
Regional Military Expenditures, Arms Transfers, and Manpower Resources

The Middle East has long been the most militarized region in the world in terms of raw defense effort. As Figure 3.1 shows, the Middle East spends by far the most on military forces as a percentage of gross national product (GNP), as a percentage of central government expenditures, and in terms of arms as a percentage of total imports. North Africa ranks second, although it scarcely reaches the levels of military effort expended in the Gulf and Arab-Israeli states.

One key issue shaping the future military balance throughout the region is how well such spending levels can be sustained, and their impact on the ability of Middle Eastern and North Africa (MENA) states to fund their civil programs and economic development and create the conditions for internal stability. In many cases, even the current levels of military spending are probably too high for nations to sustain, and the pressures to reduce conventional military expenditures are growing.

THE GROWING RESOURCE CHALLENGE

Important as military security may be, it is economics and demographics that may well prove to present the most serious future challenge to the region's stability. Economic development has been poor since the end of the oil boom in the late 1970s. The Middle East averaged only 1.5 percent annual economic growth from 1990 to 2000, just half of its average annual population growth. This situation has improved since 1990, but growth

Figure 3.1
"The Most Militarized Area in the World"

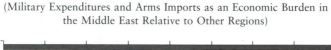

(Military Expenditures and Arms Imports as an Economic Burden in
the Middle East Relative to Other Regions)

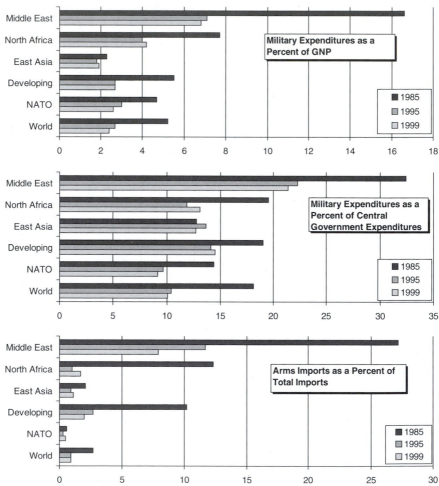

Note: Middle East does not include North African states other than Egypt.
Source: Adapted by Anthony H. Cordesman from U.S. State Department, Bureau of Verification
and Compliance, *World Military Expenditures and Arms Transfers*, 1989–1999.

averaged less than 3 percent before the economic collapse in Asia and the similar collapse in world oil prices in late 1997. Population growth slightly outpaced real economic growth throughout the 1990s.

The World Bank's *Global Economic Development* report for 2003 shows a sharp decline in economic growth in gross domestic product (GDP) in constant prices from 6.5 percent during 1971–1980 to 2.5 percent during 1981–1990. While growth rose to 3.2 percent during 1991–2000, it barely kept pace with population growth. This is reflected in the fact that growth in per capita income in constant prices dropped from 3.6 percent during 1971–1980 to –0.6 percent during 1981–1990, and was only 1 percent during 1991–2000—reflecting static income over nearly twenty years in a region with extremely poor equity of income distribution.

While interregional comparisons may be somewhat unfair, the economic growth in East Asia and the Pacific was 6.6 percent during 1971–1980, 7.3 percent during 1981–1990, and 7.7 percent during 1991–2000. The growth in real per capita income was the economic growth in East Asia and the Pacific: 3 percent during 1971–1980, 4.8 percent during 1981–1990, and 5.4 percent during 1991–2000.

Some states, like Kuwait, Qatar, and the United Arab Emirates (UAE), have so much oil and gas wealth per capita that they may still be able to buy their way out of their mistakes indefinitely. Most Middle Eastern states, however, suffer severely from economic mismanagement and excessive state control of the economy. Structural economic reform has begun in Algeria, Morocco, Tunisia, Egypt, Jordan, Saudi Arabia, Lebanon, and Bahrain. This reform, however, remains highly uncertain and no country as yet has a serious prospect of success.

The other Middle Eastern states have uncertain near to midterm economic prospects, and this is true of most oil exporters as well. The Israeli and Palestinian economies have been crippled by war; Egypt, Jordan, Lebanon, and Syria are all experiencing serious economic and demographic problems; and the Iraqi economy is weak and may soon face the shock of a new war. The Iranian economy is in a serious crisis, compounded by deep ideological conflicts over how to deal with the issue.

Algeria's efforts at economic reform have been partially blocked by corruption and civil war. Qadhafi's mismanagement, and UN and U.S. sanctions, have blocked much of Libya's development. Bahrain no longer has significant oil reserves. Saudi Arabia has experienced over a decade of budget deficits and has only about 40 percent of the real per capita income it had at the peak of the oil boom. Oman is also experiencing serious development problems. While sources differ, work by the World Bank shows that economic growth in many Middle Eastern has lagged behind population growth, and that development in the Middle East has fallen badly behind growth in East Asia and China.

POPULATION GROWTH, DEMOGRAPHIC PRESSURES, AND A "YOUTH EXPLOSION"

These economic pressures are compounded by major demographic problems. The total population of the Middle East and North Africa grew from 78.6 million in 1950 to 101.2 million in 1960, 133.0 million in 1970, 177.9 million in 1980, 244.8 million in 1990, and 307.1 million in 2000. Conservative projections put it at 376.2 million in 2010, 449.3 million in 2020, 522.3 million in 2030, 592.1 million in 2040, and 656.3 million in 2050. This growth will exhaust natural water supplies, force permanent dependence on food imports, and raise the size of the working population aged fifteen to thirty from 20.5 million in 1950, to 87.8 million in 2000, to 145.2 million in 2050.

The end result is that a combination of fluctuating oil revenues, high population growth rates, and a failure to modernize and diversify the overall economy threatens to turn the past oil wealth of the oil-exporting states into oil poverty. The Southern Gulf states have only about 40 percent of the real per capita income they had at the peak of the oil boom in the early 1980s, and little prospect for anything other than a slow decline. Kuwait, Qatar, and the UAE maintain high per capita incomes, but Saudi Arabia's "oil wealth" is becoming increasingly marginal, as its population is growing far more quickly than its economy.

The resulting social turbulence is compounded by the region's extremely young population, overstretched and outdated educational systems, and the failure of the labor market to create productive jobs, or any jobs at all for many of the young men entering the labor force. The fact that over 40 percent of the population of the region is now age fourteen or younger creates an immense bow wave of future strain on the social, educational, political, and economic system. Emigration creates another source of social turbulence, while religious and cultural barriers to the effective employment of women compound other problems in productivity and competitiveness with other developed regions.

Political structures remain fragile, and largely authoritarian, regardless of the formal structure of government. Traditional monarchies often interfere less in human rights and normal social conduct than do supposed democracies. In broad terms, however, no state in the region has yet managed to create a secular political culture that provides effective pluralism, and most competing secular ideologies have failed: pan-Arabism, socialism, capitalism, Marxism, statism, and paternalism have all failed to provide adequate development and meet social needs, and all governments are to some extent repressive. The fact that so many in the region have turned back to more traditional social structures and religion is scarcely surprising, but it is far from clear that they offer any meaningful solution to the problems involved.

DECLINES IN MILITARY EXPENDITURES AND ARMS TRANSFERS

These economic and demographic pressures may explain why the overall trends in Middle Eastern and North African military and arms spending have generally dropped in real terms since the late 1980s and early 1990s. In the most recent year reported by official U.S. sources, the Middle East only spent about half the percentage of GNP that it did during the late 1980s and early 1990s, the time of the Gulf War. The economic burden created by military expenditures has generally dropped significantly, as has the burden on central government expenditures. Arms imports are also down, both as a percentage of total imports and in absolute terms, and new arms orders have generally dropped far more quickly than deliveries—indicating that this aspect of the military burden will drop even more quickly in the future than in the past.

Drops have also occurred in terms of military manpower as a percentage of total population, although this is not a particularly valid measure of military effort. Virtually all Middle Eastern and North African powers have rapidly increasing populations, and manpower quality has become steadily more important relative to manpower quantity. Few nations have needed massive increases in manpower. Instead, they have needed more career professionals, better-trained and better-educated forces, and forces with better and more sophisticated combat and support equipment. The cost per effective soldier has risen sharply over time, not only in capital terms (the amount of military equipment and supplies needed), but in also terms of the salaries, support, and overhead needed to attract and retain qualified personnel.

There are also several reasons to be careful about giving the trends in military expenditures and arms sales too much importance. Such trends are cyclical. Wars lead to major increases and then decreases. Major acquisitions often lead to short-term increases in arms orders followed by cuts as nations pay for previous orders, and are then followed by new waves of military expenditures and arms purchases as new crises or wars arise.

THE STRENGTHS AND WEAKNESSES IN CURRENT SOURCES

As is the case with all of the data on the Middle Eastern military balance, there are problems with the data on military expenditures, demographics, and arms transfers. Some are generic. There is usually no way to estimate what MENA nations are spending on weapons of mass destruction, or even long-range missiles. As a result, the figures available undercount the military effort in most proliferating states. The problem of terrorism and asymmetric warfare has also created a situation wherein many nations have steadily increased internal security expenditures, sometimes making trade-offs that reduce military spending in order to fund stronger national security. This leads to an undercounting of national security expenditures, although not necessarily military expenditures as they have been defined in the past.

Other problems are more country specific. Some governments do not report meaningful data on military expenditures, and most countries do not use comparable definitions. The estimates of military expenditures and arms sales made by most research institutes are little more than sophisticated guesstimates, and the member countries of the United Nations often either do not report to the UN or report highly politicized figures. Many other sources of international statistics, like the Central Intelligence Agency's *World Factbook,* either do not report or report very erratically.

There are, however, three sources that have a reasonable degree of reliability. The U.S. State Department issues a report called *World Military Expenditures and Arms Transfers* that draws on declassified U.S. intelligence estimates based on a serious and comprehensive effort to create directly comparable trend estimates. Another report, by Richard F. Grimmett of the Congressional Research Service, called *Conventional Arms Transfer to Developing Nations,* provides more current data on arms deliveries and orders. Finally, the International Institute of Strategic Studies receives data from a variety of sources, including governments with major intelligence resources, and its reporting has significantly higher credibility than that of most independent research organizations.

DETAILED TRENDS IN MILITARY EFFORT AND EXPENDITURES

If one looks at the trends in military effort in detail, they reveal several trends in the balance:

- Figure 3.1 provides an overview of how the military efforts of the Middle East and North Africa compare with those of other regions in the world. It shows that even though the annual level of military expenditure as a percentage of GNP dropped by nearly 50 percent from 1985 to 1995, it was still nearly twice as high as the level in other regions in 1999—the last year for which there are declassified estimates. It also shows that Middle Eastern military expenditures remain a major burden on central government expenditures at a time when sharply rising populations and poor economic development have created a rising need for civil expenditures. The data for North African countries reflect a smaller percentage burden, but they do not fully reflect the burden of civil war in Algeria or the expenditures Morocco has made in its conflict against the Polisario.

    The data on Middle Eastern arms imports as a percentage of total imports in Figure 3.1 show that the percentage in 1999 was only about one-third of the 1985 rate, but that it was still far higher than the rate for any other region. This was partly a result of the failure of Middle Eastern economies to diversify and grow at the rate of the economies in several other developing regions.

- Figure 3.2 shows these data by country for each of the MENA countries in 1999, and compares the impact of such expenditures on each state. Such statistical "snapshots" can be misleading—because they do not shows averages or trends—but it is clear that burdens vary sharply by country, and often in unexpected ways. This illustrates the dangers of talking in regional terms without examining nations as separate cases.

- Figure 3.3 shows the trend in both military expenditures and arms transfers since the Arab-Israeli conflict of 1967—a conflict that transformed the Middle East and helped trigger a regional arms race that has continued ever since. It should also be stressed that such measures of military effort increasingly interact with demographic pressures on state budgets that force states to spend more on services and leave them less and less discretionary money for investment in infrastructure and economic development.

  The data on military expenditures show just how quickly a war or crisis can lead to radical shifts in military effort, and reflect the fact that expenditures have not dropped as much in absolute terms as they have as a percentage of GNP, largely because of economic growth, The impact of the Iran-Iraq War (1980–1988) and the Gulf War (1990–1991) is particularly apparent.

  The various cycles in arms imports are different for several reasons. A sharp rise took place during the Iran-Iraq War because sufficient time existed for both nations to place major orders and take delivery, with constantly rising levels of sustainment. The Gulf War led to major arms orders, but for major deliveries, too little time elapsed between Iraq's invasion of Kuwait and its liberation, and most regional expenditures went to paying for the deployment of U.S., British, French, Egyptian, and Syrian forces.

  Interestingly enough, if the data were to cover the Iraqi War of 2003, there would be little change in either military expenditures or arms imports, as the United States and Britain essentially self-financed their operations. Similarly, the Israeli-Palestinian War, which began in September 2000, has had a major impact on those two nations but is not large enough to impact heavily on the regional total. Much of the "war on terrorism" is also not reflected in military expenditures or arms imports because these data are classified as internal security expenditures.

- Figure 3.4 shows the cumulative burden that military expenditures and arms transfers, and military manpower, has placed on the nations in the region since 1984. The dramatic cuts after 1991 are a product of the cumulative impact of the end of the Iran-Iraq War, the end of the Gulf War, and sanctions on Iraq after 1980. They are also the result of the fact that Syria ceased trying to compete with Israel in military spending and arms imports after it lost access to low-cost Russian loans, and the fact that Israel and Jordan signed a peace treaty.

- Figure 3.5 shows that this enabled both regions' total GNP and civil expenditures to grow relative to military spending and arms imports.

Figure 3.2
The Burden of Military Expenditures and Arms Transfers on the Economies of Individual Middle Eastern Countries in 1999

(Military spending as a percent of Central Government Expenditures [CGE] and Gross National Product [GNP], and Arms Imports as a Percent of Total)

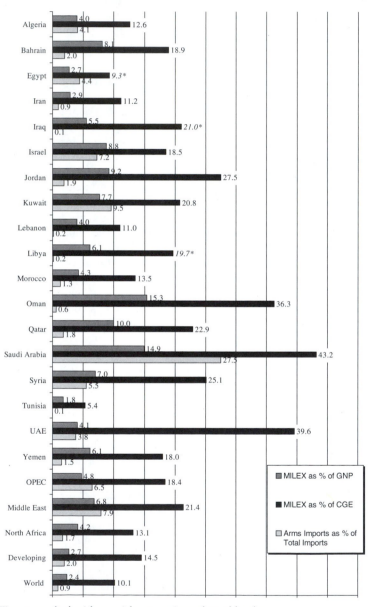

Note: Figures marked with asterisks are estimated or older data.

Source: Adapted by Anthony H. Cordesman from U.S. State Department, Bureau of Verification and Compliance, *World Military Expenditures and Arms Transfers*, various editions.

Figure 3.3
The Trend in Middle Eastern Military Expenditures and Arms Transfers since the "Six Day War" of 1967

(1967–1999 in $Current Billions)

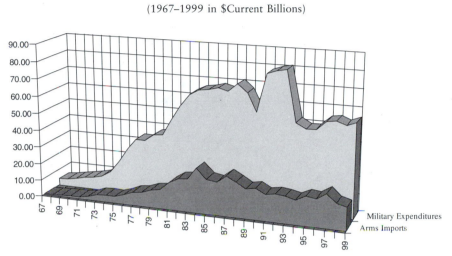

Note: Middle East does not include North African states other than Egypt.
Source: Adapted by Anthony H. Cordesman from U.S. State Department, Bureau of Arms
  Control, *World Military Expenditures and Arms Transfers*, various editions.

- Figure 3.6 highlights the major cuts in military spending after 1991 by Iran
  and Iraq, and the trends in Libya and Syria. These nations have often been
  the source of wars and instability in the region.

BROAD PATTERNS IN MIDDLE EAST ARMS TRANSFERS

There has been a substantial "deradicalization" of Middle East arms
transfers since the early 1990s. This shift in the flow of arms to the more
aggressive countries has been shaped by the following trends:

- The Arab-Israeli peace process, the end of the Iran-Iraq War, the end of the
  Cold War, and the Gulf War have reduced the threat far more than orders of
  battle would indicate.
- Mismanagement of the economy, lower oil prices, and regional recession have
  reduced the purchase of arms.
- New arms order agreements are down to a token share of past levels.
- Iran, Iraq, Libya, and Syria have had to sharply cut their purchases. Moderate states have signed 93 percent of all recent new arms import agreements,
  versus 67 percent before the Gulf War.

Figure 3.4
Middle Eastern Military Efforts Dropped Sharply as a Percentage of GNP,
Government Expenditures, Total Population, and Arms Imports: 1984–1999

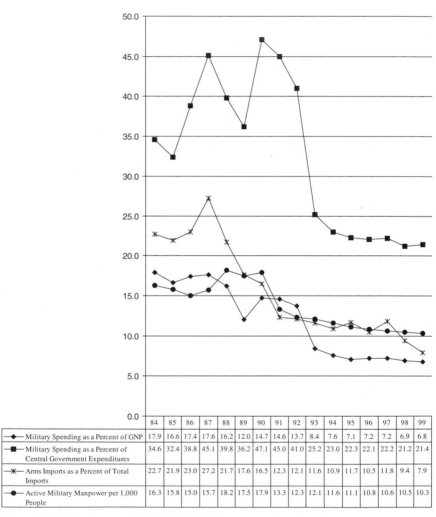

	84	85	86	87	88	89	90	91	92	93	94	95	96	97	98	99
◆ Military Spending as a Percent of GNP	17.9	16.6	17.4	17.6	16.2	12.0	14.7	14.6	13.7	8.4	7.6	7.1	7.2	7.2	6.9	6.8
■ Military Spending as a Percent of Central Government Expenditures	34.6	32.4	38.8	45.1	39.8	36.2	47.1	45.0	41.0	25.2	23.0	22.3	22.1	22.2	21.2	21.4
✳ Arms Imports as a Percent of Total Imports	22.7	21.9	23.0	27.2	21.7	17.6	16.5	12.3	12.1	11.6	10.9	11.7	10.5	11.8	9.4	7.9
● Active Military Manpower per 1,000 People	16.3	15.8	15.0	15.7	18.2	17.5	17.9	13.3	12.3	12.1	11.6	11.1	10.8	10.6	10.5	10.3

Note: Middle East does not include North African states other than Egypt.
Source: Adapted by Anthony H. Cordesman from U.S. State Department, *World Military Expenditures and Arms Transfers*, various editions.

Figure 3.5
Middle Eastern Military Expenditures and Arms Imports Dropped Sharply
Relative to Economic Growth and Government Spending during 1989–1999

(1989=100, and all following years are percentages of 1989 as base year.
All expenditure totals are measured in constant 1989 U.S. dollars.)

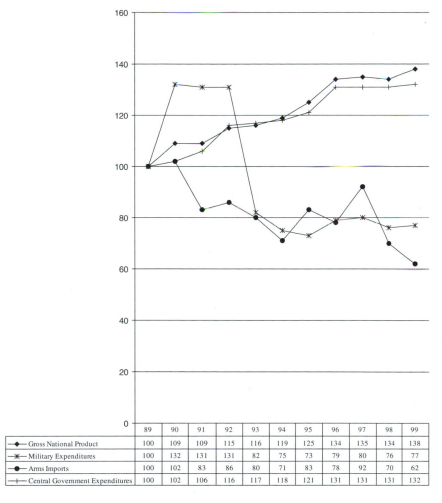

	89	90	91	92	93	94	95	96	97	98	99
◆ Gross National Product	100	109	109	115	116	119	125	134	135	134	138
✳ Military Expenditures	100	132	131	131	82	75	73	79	80	76	77
● Arms Imports	100	102	83	86	80	71	83	78	92	70	62
+ Central Government Expenditures	100	102	106	116	117	118	121	131	131	131	132

Note: Middle East does not include North African states other than Egypt.
Source: Adapted by Anthony H. Cordesman form U.S. State Department, Bureau of Verification and Compliance, *World Military Expenditures and Arms Transfers 1999–2000*.

Figure 3.6
The Cumulative Decline in Military Spending by Selected Major Buyers in
Constant Dollars: 1984–1999

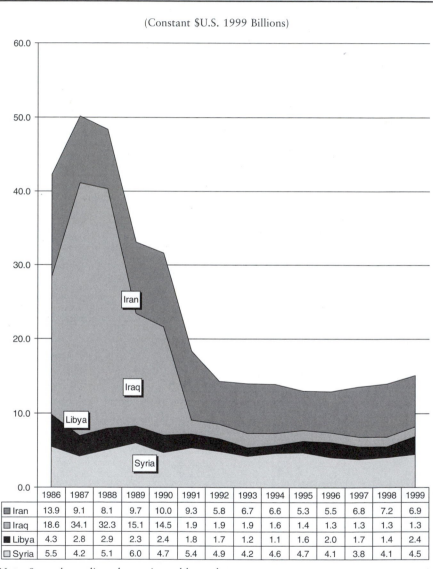

(Constant $U.S. 1999 Billions)

	1986	1987	1988	1989	1990	1991	1992	1993	1994	1995	1996	1997	1998	1999
▨ Iran	13.9	9.1	8.1	9.7	10.0	9.3	5.8	6.7	6.6	5.3	5.5	6.8	7.2	6.9
▨ Iraq	18.6	34.1	32.3	15.1	14.5	1.9	1.9	1.9	1.6	1.4	1.3	1.3	1.3	1.3
■ Libya	4.3	2.8	2.9	2.3	2.4	1.8	1.7	1.2	1.1	1.6	2.0	1.7	1.4	2.4
□ Syria	5.5	4.2	5.1	6.0	4.7	5.4	4.9	4.2	4.6	4.7	4.1	3.8	4.1	4.5

Note: Some data adjusted or estimated by author.
Source: Adapted by Anthony H. Cordesman from U.S. Arms Control and Disarmament
  Agency, *World Military Expenditures and Arms Transfers*, various editions.

- Southern Gulf states have signed over 90 percent of all new arms import agreements—excluding grant aid to Egypt and Israel—versus 53 percent before the Gulf War.
- The most aggressive country—Iraq—had only token imports after 1990.
- Iran did not choose to renew the arms race after its defeat in 1988 and made major further cuts in 1992, after coalition forces weakened Iraq.
- Syria lost all sources of free arms and low-cost credit.
- Libya faced economic problems and UN sanctions.

At the same time, the trends in the dollar value of new arms agreements and past deliveries do not always tell the whole story:

- The previous data do not include many aspects of proliferation and the acquisition of chemical, biological, radiological, and nuclear (CBRN) weapons.
- The end of Cold War has meant more rapid transfer of first-line weapons and technologies to the world market.
- Arms imports are only part of the story. Nations with major defense industries do not have to import as many arms, and "dual-use" technologies aid in proliferation and the C⁴I/BM/IS&R side of the revolution in military affairs.
- Such trends are scarcely stable: past flows of arms are highly cyclical in terms of rises and falls, and Russia may rebuild its former volume of sales.
- There is a relatively free transfer of technology and equipment for new types of wars and battles: information and economic warfare.
- The capability to fight many forms of asymmetric warfare is not affected.
- Modifying platforms is increasingly as important as obtaining new platforms.
- Transfers of "smart" weapons are very difficult to categorize, monitor, and control: "beyond-visual-range"/advanced air-to-air missiles, smart precision and area munitions, black boxes, sensors and secure communications, and the like.
- Controlling or limiting conventional arms can push nations toward proliferation and asymmetric warfare.

The following figures show the broad patterns in regional arms sales far more clearly. They reinforce the fact there has been a major drop in the cost of both new agreements and actual deliveries. At the same time, massive amounts of weapons and equipment are still involved.

- Figure 3.7 shows the cumulative downward trend in arms deliveries in constant dollars. It also shows how Middle Eastern arms deliveries compare with those in other regions. The Middle East clearly remains the dominant world market for arms.

Figure 3.7
The Cumulative Impact of the Arab-Israeli Peace Accords, Sanctioning of Libya,
End of the Iran-Iraq War, Cold War, Gulf War, and Economic Recession:
1985–1999

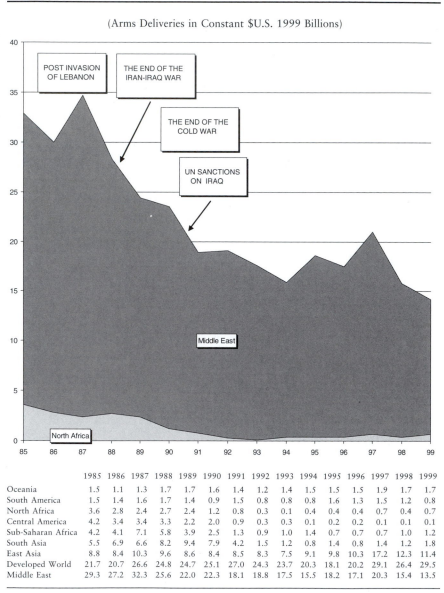

(Arms Deliveries in Constant $U.S. 1999 Billions)

	1985	1986	1987	1988	1989	1990	1991	1992	1993	1994	1995	1996	1997	1998	1999
Oceania	1.5	1.1	1.3	1.7	1.7	1.6	1.4	1.2	1.4	1.5	1.5	1.5	1.9	1.7	1.7
South America	1.5	1.4	1.6	1.7	1.4	0.9	1.5	0.8	0.8	0.8	1.6	1.3	1.5	1.2	0.8
North Africa	3.6	2.8	2.4	2.7	2.4	1.2	0.8	0.3	0.1	0.4	0.4	0.4	0.7	0.4	0.7
Central America	4.2	3.4	3.4	3.3	2.2	2.0	0.9	0.3	0.3	0.1	0.2	0.2	0.1	0.1	0.1
Sub-Saharan Africa	4.2	4.1	7.1	5.8	3.9	2.5	1.3	0.9	1.0	1.4	0.7	0.7	0.7	1.0	1.2
South Asia	5.5	6.9	6.6	8.2	9.4	7.9	4.2	1.5	1.2	0.8	1.4	0.8	1.4	1.2	1.8
East Asia	8.8	8.4	10.3	9.6	8.6	8.4	8.5	8.3	7.5	9.1	9.8	10.3	17.2	12.3	11.4
Developed World	21.7	20.7	26.6	24.8	24.7	25.1	27.0	24.3	23.7	20.3	18.1	20.2	29.1	26.4	29.5
Middle East	29.3	27.2	32.3	25.6	22.0	22.3	18.1	18.8	17.5	15.5	18.2	17.1	20.3	15.4	13.5

Note: Middle East does not include North African states other than Egypt.
Source: Adapted by Anthony H. Cordesman from U.S. State Department, Bureau of Verification
and Compliance, *World Military Expenditures and Arms Transfers*, various editions.

Figure 3.8
Rate of Arms Technology Transfers to MENA Is Declining but Is Still an Issue

(Arms Deliveries in Constant $U.S. 1999 Billions)

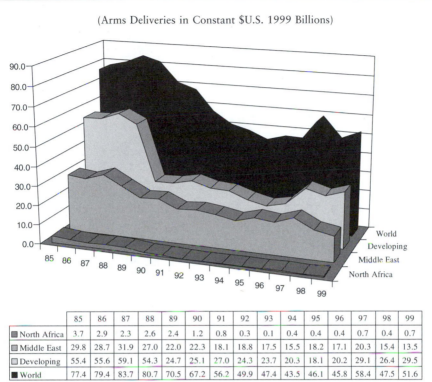

	85	86	87	88	89	90	91	92	93	94	95	96	97	98	99
■ North Africa	3.7	2.9	2.3	2.6	2.4	1.2	0.8	0.3	0.1	0.4	0.4	0.4	0.7	0.4	0.7
■ Middle East	29.8	28.7	31.9	27.0	22.0	22.3	18.1	18.8	17.5	15.5	18.2	17.1	20.3	15.4	13.5
□ Developing	55.4	55.6	59.1	54.3	24.7	25.1	27.0	24.3	23.7	20.3	18.1	20.2	29.1	26.4	29.5
■ World	77.4	79.4	83.7	80.7	70.5	67.2	56.2	49.9	47.4	43.5	46.1	45.8	58.4	47.5	51.6

Note: Middle East does not include North African states other than Egypt.
Source: Adapted by Anthony H. Cordesman from Bureau of Arms Control in the U.S. State Department (formerly U.S. State Department, Bureau of Arms Control), *World Military Expenditures and Arms Transfers*, various editions.

- Figure 3.8 compares the Middle East and North Africa to the total world and total developing world in terms of deliveries. It is clear that deliveries in the MENA area have dropped in relation.
- Figure 3.9 shows that military expenditures have shrunk faster than military expenditures. This is the result of a major recapitalization problem in the military modernization efforts of a number of regional powers, discussed in detail in the following chapters.
- Figure 3.10 shows more recent data on both new arms orders and deliveries. It shows that new orders have continued to drop in recent years, although the backlog in deliveries has led to a much lower drop in this category.
- Figures 3.11 and 3.12 provide a warning, however, that major deliveries of weapons still flow into the area.

Figure 3.9
The Trend in Middle Eastern Military Expenditures and Arms Transfers in Constant Dollars since 1989

(1989–1999 in $U.S. 1999 Constant Billions)

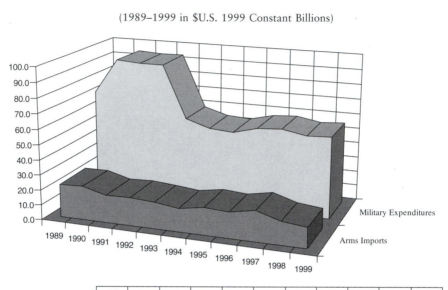

	1989	1990	1991	1992	1993	1994	1995	1996	1997	1998	1999
■ Arms Imports	22.0	22.3	18.1	18.8	17.5	15.5	18.2	17.1	20.3	15.4	13.5
□ Military Expenditures	71	94	93	93	58	53	52	56	57	54	55

Note: Middle East does not include North African states other than Egypt.
Source: Adapted by Anthony H. Cordesman from U.S. State Department, Bureau of Verification and Compliance, *World Military Expenditures and Arms Transfers 1999–2000*.

THE DYNAMICS OF MIDDLE EASTERN MANPOWER AND DEMOGRAPHICS

When most of the Middle Eastern states emerged as independent nations in the 1940s and 1950s, they had relatively small populations, and a lack of military-age manpower was a serious problem. Figure 3.13, however, shows that these days are long gone. Rapid population increases, and a lack of economic reform and diversification, have created a military manpower pool that most MENA states have no way to train and equip, and unemployment is so high that the resulting impact on internal stability has become a major security problem.

- Figure 3.14 dramatizes these problems by showing the projected growth in both the number of youths entering the labor market and the burden placed on regional civil budgets by the growth of pension-age men and women.

Figure 3.10
New Arms Agreements Are Dropping Faster Than Deliveries

(Arms Agreements and Deliveries to the Developing World vs. Total Sales to the Middle East in $U.S. Current Millions)

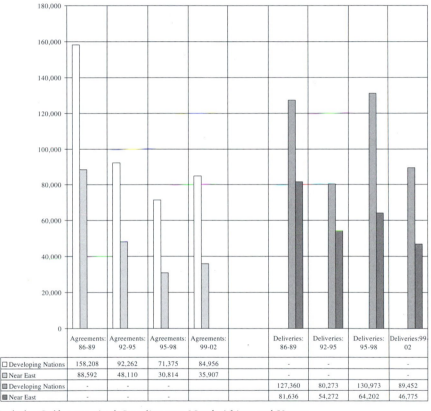

	Agreements: 86-89	Agreements: 92-95	Agreements: 95-98	Agreements: 99-02		Deliveries: 86-89	Deliveries: 92-95	Deliveries: 95-98	Deliveries:99-02
☐ Developing Nations	158,208	92,262	71,375	84,956		-	-		-
☐ Near East	88,592	48,110	30,814	35,907		-	-		-
▨ Developing Nations	-	-	-			127,360	80,273	130,973	89,452
■ Near East	-	-	-			81,636	54,272	64,202	46,775

Includes Gulf states, Arab-Israeli states, North Africa, and Yemen.
0 = less than $50 million or nil, and all data rounded to the nearest $100 million.
Source: Richard F. Grimmett, *Conventional Arms Transfers to the Developing Nations*, Congressional Research Service, various editions.

Figure 3.11
Total Middle Eastern Arms Deliveries by Major Weapon: 1985–1999

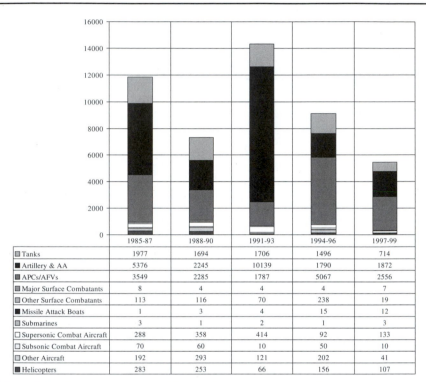

	1985-87	1988-90	1991-93	1994-96	1997-99
▢ Tanks	1977	1694	1706	1496	714
■ Artillery & AA	5376	2245	10139	1790	1872
■ APCs/AFVs	3549	2285	1787	5067	2556
▢ Major Surface Combatants	8	4	4	4	7
▢ Other Surface Combatants	113	116	70	238	19
■ Missile Attack Boats	1	3	4	15	12
▢ Submarines	3	1	2	1	3
▢ Supersonic Combat Aircraft	288	358	414	92	133
▢ Subsonic Combat Aircraft	70	60	10	50	10
▢ Other Aircraft	192	293	121	202	41
■ Helicopters	283	253	66	156	107

Note: Middle East does not include North African states other than Egypt.
Source: Adapted by Anthony H. Cordesman from Bureau of Arms Control in the U.S. State
  Department (formerly ACDA), *World Military Expenditures and Arms Transfers*, various
  editions.

- Figure 3.15 shows that this population increase has taken place in spite of projections of a major drop in the population growth rate. So far, such projections of a decline in the growth rate seem optimistic. Urbanization and the education of women are not producing the rate of decline that has occurred in the West and Asia.

- Figures 3.16 and 3.17 show the projected increases in population by large and small country through 2050, and that sheer population momentum will ensure high growth for decades.

- Figure 3.18 shows the comparative military demographics of the region by country. The growth in military-age males in virtually every country—with the exceptions of Qatar and the UAE—has limited the ability of regional states to fund anything like the manpower pool now available.

Figure 3.12
Transfers of New Weapons Are Still Substantial

(Numbers of New Weapons Delivered by Major Suppliers to Near East During 1998–2001)

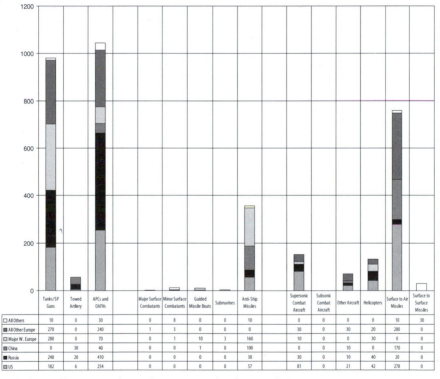

	Tanks/SP Guns	Towed Artlery	APCs and OAFVs	Major Surface Combatants	Minor Surface Combatants	Guided Missile Boats	Submarines	Anti-Ship Missiles	Supersonic Combat Aircraft	Subsonic Combat Aircraft	Other Aircraft	Helicopters	Surface to Air Missiles	Surface to Surface Missiles
☐ All Others	10	0	30	0	8	0	0	10	0	0	0	0	10	30
▣ All Other Europe	270	0	240	1	3	0	0	0	30	0	30	20	280	0
☐ Major W. Europe	280	0	70	0	1	10	3	160	10	0	0	30	0	0
▣ China	0	30	40	0	0	1	0	100	0	0	10	0	170	0
▪ Russia	240	20	410	0	0	0	0	30	30	0	10	40	20	0
▣ US	182	6	254	0	0	0	0	57	81	0	21	42	278	0

Includes Gulf states, Arab-Israeli states, North Africa, and Yemen.

Source: Richard F. Grimmett, *Conventional Arms Transfers to the Developing Nations, 1994–2001*, Congressional Research Service.

Figure 3.13
Living in a Crowded Desert: Massive Ongoing Population Growth in the Total Middle East and North Africa

(UN Estimate—Population in Millions)

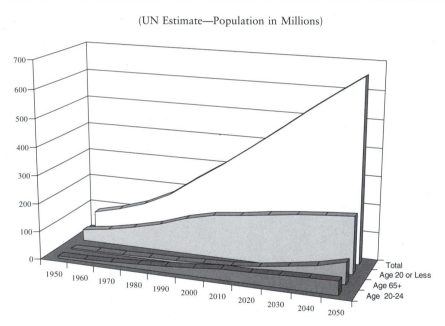

	1950	1960	1970	1980	1990	2000	2010	2020	2030	2040	2050
■ Age 20-24	6.8	8.4	10.9	16.2	21.9	28.7	37.9	38.6	42.7	46.4	48.3
■ Age 65+	3.1	3.6	5.1	6.4	8.2	11.3	15.5	24.6	38	53.9	77.9
■ Age 20 or Less	39.9	53.6	73.1	96.2	128.4	151	161.7	175.7	187.6	196.5	203.6
□ Total	78.7	101.2	133	177.9	244.8	307.7	376.2	449.3	522.4	592.1	656.3

Source: Adapted by Anthony H. Cordesman from data provided by the U.S. Census Bureau.

Figure 3.14
MENA Youth Explosion and the Pensioner Burden

(UN Estimate—Population in Millions)

Roughly 51% of older youths polled expressed a desire to emigrate to other countries. 46% wanted to go to Europe; 36% to the US and Canada.*

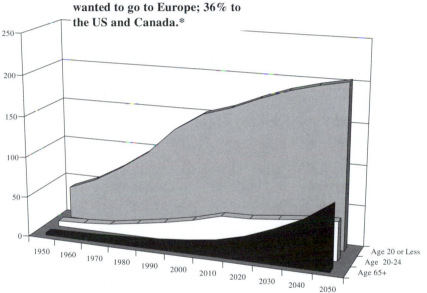

	1950	1960	1970	1980	1990	2000	2010	2020	2030	2040	2050
■ Age 65+	3.1	3.6	5.1	6.4	8.2	11.3	15.5	24.6	38	53.9	77.9
□ Age 20-24	6.8	8.4	10.9	16.2	21.9	28.7	37.9	38.6	42.7	46.4	48.3
▨ Age 20 or Less	39.9	53.6	73.1	96.2	128.4	151	161.7	175.7	187.6	196.5	203.6

*From *Arab Human Development Report, 2202*, p. 30.
Source: Adapted by Anthony H. Cordesman from data provided by the U.S. Census Bureau.

Figure 3.15
Population Growth Rates Are Projected to Decline

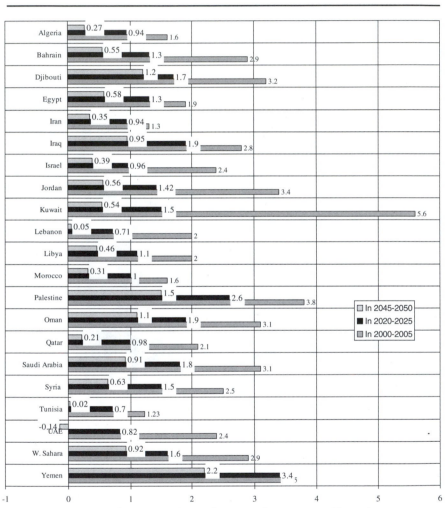

Source: Adapted by Anthony H. Cordesman from United Nations, *World Population Prospects,*
The 2002 Revision, New York: United Nations, ESA/WP 180 February 26, 2003.

Figure 3.16
Population Momentum Continues: Total Population by Larger MENA Countries in 2003

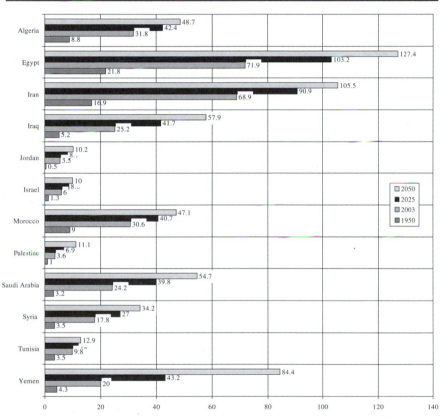

Source: Adapted by Anthony H. Cordesman from United Nations, *World Population Prospects, The 2002 Revision*, New York: United Nations, ESA/WP 180 February 26, 2003.

Figure 3.17
Total Population by Smaller MENA Countries in 2003

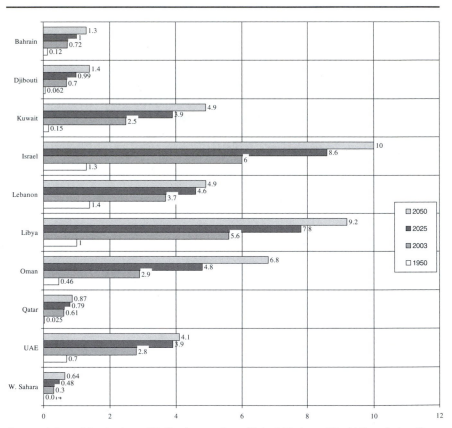

Source: Adapted by Anthony H. Cordesman from United Nations, *World Population Prospects, The 2002 Revision*, New York: United Nations, ESA/WP 180 February 26, 2003.

Figure 3.18
The Military Demographics of the Greater Middle East

Country	Total Population	Males Reaching Military Age Each Year	Males Between the Ages of			Males Between 15 and 49	
			13 and 17	18 and 22	23 and 32	Total	Medically Fit
Egypt	70,993,000	743,305	3,707,000	3,313,000	5,150,000	19,030,030	12,867,160
Gaza	1,274,868*	—	—	—	—	—	—
Israel	6,296,000	51,080	284,000	272,000	535,000	1,542,835	1,279,277
Jordan	5,215,000	58,840	280,000	247,000	454,000	1,517,751	1,113,787
Lebanon	3,532,000	—	216,000	194,000	397,000	1,003,174	630,657
Palestinian	3,510,000*	—	163,000	140,000	233,000	—	—
Syria	16,986,000	210,941	1,076,000	883,000	1,274,000	4,550,496	2,629,148
West Bank	2,237,194*	—	—	—	—	—	—
Iran	72,499,000	870,711	4,735,000	3,960,000	5,959,000	18,868,571	12,094,551
Iraq	24,027,000	292,930	1,472,000	1,270,000	1,899,000	6,135,847	3,541,467
Bahrain	721,000	6,126	35,000	26,000	40,000	222,572	121,739
Kuwait	2,082,000	18,885	124,000	107,000	148,000	812,059	508,399
Oman	2,719,000	29,485	163,000	140,000	233,000	780,292	428,326
Qatar	610,000	7,192	26,000	22,000	38,000	316,885	168,416
Saudi Arabia	21,397,000	253,685	1,391,000	1,177,000	1,725,000	6,007,635	3,431,281

continued

Figure 3.18 (Continued)

Country	Total Population	Males Reaching Military Age Each Year	Males Between the Ages of			Males Between 15 and 49	
			13 and 17	18 and 22	23 and 32	Total	Medically Fit
UAE	2,852,000	26,636	87,000	87,000	143,000	773,938	416,963
Yemen	19,909,000	249,292	1,008,000	803,000	1,328,000	4,272,156	2,493,612
Algeria	32,242,000	412,545	1,986,000	1,834,000	2,962,000	9,016,048	5,646,418
Libya	5,398,000	61,511	387,000	320,000	492,000	1,503,647	914,649
Morocco	30,846,000	351,671	1,780,000	1,612,000	2,726,000	8,393,772	5,411,846
Tunisia	9,697,000	106,513	529,000	505,000	869,000	2,806,881	1,629,241
Chad	8,375,000	86,953	408,000	332,000	518,000	1,881,769	1,015,982
Mauritania	2,774,000	—	149,000	121,000	194,000	644,294	322,288
Western Sahara	261,794*	—	—	—	—	—	—
Afghanistan	22,336,000	275,223	1,499,000	1,194,000	2,053,000	6,896,623	3,837,646
Djibouti	632,000	—	42,000	35,000	57,000	110,221	63,459
Eritrea	3,837,000	—	252,000	210,000	320,000	—	—
Ethiopia	64,734,000	714,165	3,977,000	3,172,000	4,780,000	14,925,883	8,040,381
Somalia	9,234,000	—	626,000	511,000	726,000	1,881,634	1,072,689
Sudan	32,304,000	429,334	1,990,000	1,693,000	2,542,000	8,739,982	5,558,462
Turkey	68,652,000	679,882	3,264,000	3,251,000	6,242,000	19,219,177	11,801,267

*Totals for Palestinians are IISS; totals for Gaza, the West Bank, and the Western Sahara are CIA.

Note: Totals include non-nationals, Total Population, Males Reaching Military Age, and Males Between 15 and 49 are generally CIA data; and the rest are IISS data.

Source: Adapted by Anthony H. Cordesman, CIA, *World Factbook*, 2002, 2004; IISS, *The Military Balance*, various editions.

Chapter 4

North Africa and the Maghreb

THE MILITARY BALANCE IN THE MAGHREB

There is no military balance in North Africa in the classic sense of the term. While there are still rivalries and tensions among Algeria, Libya, Morocco, and Tunisia, no state in the Maghreb now actively prepares for war with its neighbors, and the prospects of such conflict are limited at best. Several countries have had border clashes in the past, but none has approached the point of serious conflicts with another since achieving independence. The Maghreb states project only token forces outside their borders.

While several states have sent token forces to past Arab-Israeli forces, such forces were deployed only at levels approaching "token" contributions, and had no real military significance. This does not mean, however, that the region has been peaceful. Libya has had major regional ambitions in the past and fought a war with Chad on its southern border, but its military adventures largely failed. Libya made mass arms purchases in the 1970s and 1980s, but never developed the manpower and support base to use them effectively and has been unable to sustain its arms buys because of economic problems and sanctions.

Morocco has had minor border clashes with Algeria in the past, but none had major military significance. It has long fought a war to annex the former Spanish Sahara, fighting with local forces called the Polisario. This has been a low-intensity conflict, although Algeria has provided the Polisario with sanctuary and support.

The bloodiest war in the region since independence has been a civil conflict: the Algerian civil war has now gone on for well over a decade. This war has pitted a corrupt military junta, which has ruled behind the façade of an elected government, against Islamists who effectively won a popular election in the early 1990s and were then deprived of power. When civil war broke out, violent extremist elements among these Islamists quickly came to dominate the fighting, while the military increasingly relied on equally violent repression. This civil war consumed so many resources that it led to major cuts in Algerian military modernization, although arms purchases have risen as the military has been able to sharply reduce the Islamist threat.

Today, the military balance in North Africa consists largely of efforts to create military forces that can defend a nation's borders, maintain internal security, and serve the purposes of national prestige. The states of North Africa have also had to adapt to the threats posed by terrorism, asymmetric warfare, and proliferation. These are not new challenges. Libya has supported terrorist and extremist movements in the past, and has been guilty of state terrorism. It has largely ended such efforts in recent years, however; and it is currently making a major effort to be seen as a moderate and pragmatic regime that is primarily interested in economic development and better relations with the West. It is struggling with its own Islamic extremists. Morocco and Tunisia have never supported terrorism or extremism, and Algeria's ruling military junta has had to fight Islamic extremists and terrorists for more than a decade.

Proliferation has been a problem. Algeria made contingency plans to acquire nuclear weapons in the late 1980s, and has examined options for acquiring long-range missiles. There is no current evidence, however, that Algeria has implemented major programs to actually acquire such capabilities or to deploy such forces. Libya has sought chemical and nuclear weapons and long-range missiles, and has some 80 Scud B missile launchers and up to 350–500 missiles. It may have examined options for acquiring biological weapons. It stated in 2003, however, that it would crease all such efforts and opened up its nuclear facilities to inspection by the United States and the International Atomic Energy Agency (IAEA).

RESOURCES AND FORCE TRENDS

The patterns in the North African military balance have been erratic at best. The newly independent Maghreb states followed the same pattern of rapid military buildup that characterized virtually all of the newly independent states in the Near East and Southwest Asia. They embarked on a wasteful military buildup and increased their military forces sharply after the Arab-Israeli conflict in 1973. This eventually led them to spend more than their national incomes could sustain. In the mid-1980s, military spending began to moderately decline, followed by a sharper decline after the collapse of the Soviet Union. Spending rose again in the late 1990s, but has not approached the levels of real spending that occurred in the 1970s.

- Figure 4.1 provides a summary comparison of the present strength of Algerian, Libyan, Moroccan, and Tunisian military forces.

- Figure 4.2 shows the trends in military expenditures and arms imports in constant dollars. The massive decline in spending after the mid-1980s is clearly apparent, as is the fact that arms imports dropped far more quickly than military expenditures. The rise in military expenditures in the late 1990s was driven largely by the Algerian civil war and low-intensity conflict between Morocco and the Polisario. This helps explain why arms imports remained comparatively low, and it is clear that military modernization has been badly undercapitalized for more than a decade.

- Figure 4.3 shows the same trends in terms of military effort as a percentage of gross national product (GNP), central government expenditures, and arms imports as a percentage of total imports. While North African states failed to properly capitalize their military forces, they did significantly reduce the impact of military spending on their economies, national budgets, and imports.

- Figure 4.4 shows the more recent trends in military expenditures in current U.S. dollars, drawn from a different source. Algeria clearly dominates regional military spending, driven partly by civil war and partly by the ambitions and bureaucratic momentum of its ruling military junta, and fueled by its oil and gas exports. Morocco has maintained high spending levels, largely because of the continuing cost of its war with the Polisario. Libyan military spending has continued to decline because of the impact of its economic problems and U.S. and UN sanctions. Tunisia has never attempted to build up major military forces.

- Figure 4.5 shows how the regional trends in North African arms imports compared with those in other regions between 1985 and 1999. It is clear that North Africa was never a significant part of the world arms trade in spite of the ambitions of several regional states.

- Figure 4.6 highlights the sharp decline in arms imports as a percentage of total imports. On the one hand, this reveals a significant drop in the impact of arms imports on local economies. On the other hand, it illustrates just how sharply North African states—none of which has significant domestic military industries—have undercapitalized the modernization of their military forces.

- Figure 4.7 provides more current data on new arms orders and deliveries. They show that recent Algerian new orders have not declined consistently and that significant arms deliveries took place between 1995 and 2002. Libya exhibits a consistent, precipitous decline in arms orders and deliveries. Morocco shows a less steep decline, and Tunisia shows an increase in deliveries during 1995–1998, although the amounts involved are so small that they scarcely constitute a military buildup.

- Figure 4.8 shows recent arms imports by supplier country. Morocco and Tunisia are the only countries to have received U.S. arms, and there have been no recent orders. Morocco has depended largely on Europe for its arms, although, again, new orders dropped sharply between 1987 and 2002. Libya has only placed limited orders, and has not placed significant orders with any country capable of supplying it with the most advanced weapons. It did step up its new orders during 1999–2002, however, reflecting an easing of UN

Figure 4.1
Algerian, Libyan, Moroccan, and Tunisian Forces in 2004

Category/Weapon	Algeria	Libya	Morocco	Tunisia
Manpower				
Total Active	127,500	76,000	196,300	35,000
(Conscript)	75,000	38,000	100,000	23,400
Total Regular	—	76,000	196,300	35,000
Royal/Special Guard and Other	0	?	1,500	—
Total Reserve	150,000	40,000	150,000	—
Total Active and Reserve	277,500	116,000	346,300	35,000
Paramilitary	181,200	?	50,000	12,000
Land Forces				
Active Manpower	110,000	45,000	175,000	27,000
(Conscripts)	75,000	25,000	100,000	22,000
Reserve Manpower	150,000	—	150,000	—
Total Active and Reserve Manpower	260,000	45,000	325,000	27,000
Main Battle Tanks	1,000	800 (1,040)	520 (224)	84
AIFVs/Armored Cars/Lt. Tanks	989	1,000	215	54
APCs/Recce/Scouts/Half-Tracks	903	1,065	1,064	327
ATGM Launchers	—	3,000	720	600
SP Artillery	185	444	227	—
Towed Artillery	406	647	185	117
MRLs	144	830	40	—
Mortars	330+	500	1,470	191
SSM Launchers	—	120	0	0
AA Guns	899	600	425	115
Lt. SAM Launchers	1,000+	2,500+*	107	74

Air & Air Defense Forces

	10,000	23,000	13,500	3,500
Active Manpower	10,000	23,000	13,500	3,500
(Air Defense Only)	NA	?	—	—
Reserve Manpower	—	—	—	—
(Air Defense Only)	NA	?	—	—
Aircraft				
Total Fighter/FGA/Recce	175	400	95	29
Bomber	0	6	0	0
Fighter	83	209	15	0
FGA/Fighter	66	172	54	12
Other Combat Unit (OCU)	—	—	—	5
Recce	12	11	6	0
Airborne Early Warning (AEW/EW)	0	0	4	0
Maritime Reconnaissance (MR)	15	0	0	0
Combat Capable Trainer	10	23	24	—
Tanker	0	0	3	0
Transport	27	83	33	16
Helicopters				
Attack/Armed/ASW	93	41	24	15
Other	50	90	88	43
Total	143	131	112	58
SAM Forces				
Batteries	9	39	—	—
Heavy Launchers	43	236	—	—
Medium Launchers	—	—	—	—
AA guns	—	4+	—	—

continued

Figure 4.1 (Continued)

Category/Weapon	Algeria	Libya	Morocco	Tunisia
Naval Forces				
Active Manpower	7,500	8,000	7,800	4,500
Regular Navy	7,500	8,000	6,300	4,500
Naval Guards	—	—	—	—
Marines	—	—	1,500	—
Reserve Manpower	—	—	—	—
Total Active & Reserve Manpower	7,500	8,000	7,800	4,500
Submarines	2	1(4)	0	0
Destroyers/Frigates/Corvettes	9	2	2	0
Missile	6	2	2	0
Other	3	0	0	0
Missile Patrol	9(2)	8(22)	4	6
Coastal/Inshore Patrol	10	—	23	13
Mine	0	2	0	0
Amphibious Ships	3	3(2)	4	0
Landing Craft/Light Support	3	12	4	2
MPA/ASW/Combat Helicopter	0	7	2	0

*Extensive but unknown amounts inoperable or in storage.

Note: Figures in parenthesis are additional equipment in storage. Total equipment holdings for the Iranian land forces include 470 tanks, 620 other armored vehicles, 360 artillery weapons, 40 rocket launchers, and 140 anti-aircraft weapons with the land units of the Revolutionary Guards. Iranian and Iraqi attack helicopters are in the army. Only about 60% of the U.S. supplied fixed wing combat aircraft in Iran are operational and 80% of the Chinese supplied aircraft.

Source: Adapted by Anthony H. Cordesman from data provided by U.S. experts; IISS, *The Military Balance, 2003–2004.*

Figure 4.2
**North African Military Expenditures and Arms Transfers in Constant Dollars
Have Dropped to Low Levels by Global Standards**

(Algerian, Libyan, Moroccan, and Tunisian spending in Constant $U.S. 1999 Billions)

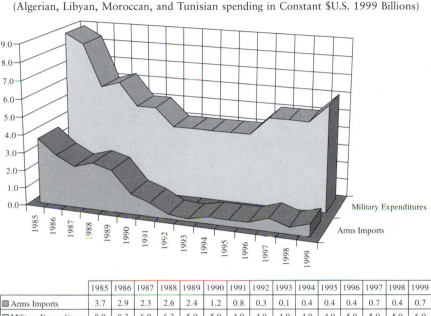

	1985	1986	1987	1988	1989	1990	1991	1992	1993	1994	1995	1996	1997	1998	1999
■ Arms Imports	3.7	2.9	2.3	2.6	2.4	1.2	0.8	0.3	0.1	0.4	0.4	0.4	0.7	0.4	0.7
□ Military Expenditures	8.9	8.3	6.0	6.3	5.0	5.0	4.0	4.0	4.0	4.0	4.0	5.0	5.0	5.0	6.0

Source: Adapted by Anthony H. Cordesman from Bureau of Arms Control in the U.S. State
Department (formerly U.S. State Department, Bureau of Arms Control), *World Military
Expenditures and Arms Transfers*, various editions.

sanctions and the ability to import arms from developing countries that are
less careful about UN sanctions. Algeria has relied largely on Russia and
Eastern Europe, and placed significant new orders during 1995–1998.

- Figure 4.9 highlights just how serious the decline in Libyan military efforts
was between the mid-1980s and 2000, revealing a sharp imbalance between
continued military spending and inadequate arms imports during most of the
1990s.

- Figures 4.10 and 4.11 reveal other imbalances in North African military efforts. Most countries maintained larger manpower and equipment pools than
they could afford to sustain. All of the Maghreb states except Tunisia bought
more military equipment during the 1970s and 1980s than they can now adequately support. Like many less developed countries, the Maghreb states
confused weapons numbers and the "glitter factor" of buying advanced
weapons technology with military effectiveness. Algeria, Libya, and Morocco

Figure 4.3
North African Military Efforts Declined Sharply as a Percentage of GNP,
Government Expenditures, Imports, and Total Population: 1985–1999

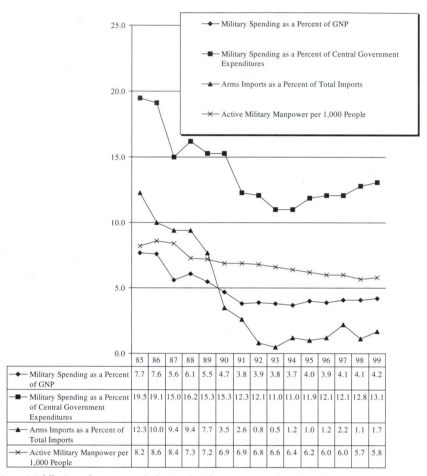

	85	86	87	88	89	90	91	92	93	94	95	96	97	98	99
◆ Military Spending as a Percent of GNP	7.7	7.6	5.6	6.1	5.5	4.7	3.8	3.9	3.8	3.7	4.0	3.9	4.1	4.1	4.2
■ Military Spending as a Percent of Central Government Expenditures	19.5	19.1	15.0	16.2	15.3	15.3	12.3	12.1	11.0	11.0	11.9	12.1	12.1	12.8	13.1
▲ Arms Imports as a Percent of Total Imports	12.3	10.0	9.4	9.4	7.7	3.5	2.6	0.8	0.5	1.2	1.0	1.2	2.2	1.1	1.7
✕ Active Military Manpower per 1,000 People	8.2	8.6	8.4	7.3	7.2	6.9	6.9	6.8	6.6	6.4	6.2	6.0	6.0	5.7	5.8

Note: Middle East does not include North African states other than Egypt.
Source: Adapted by Anthony H. Cordesman from U.S. State Department, *World Military Expenditures and Arms Transfers*, Washington, DC: GPO, various editions.

saturated their military forces with weaponry between 1972 and 1985 without buying proper support, sustainability, and command, control, communications, computers, and intelligence (C⁴I) equipment. They created teeth-to-tail ratios about two to three times the proper ratio for military effectiveness.

- Figure 4.12 shows the most recent data on how North Africa military manpower by service. It should be noted that the training and equipment levels

Figure 4.4
North African Military Expenditures by Country: 1997–2002

(In $U.S. Current Millions)

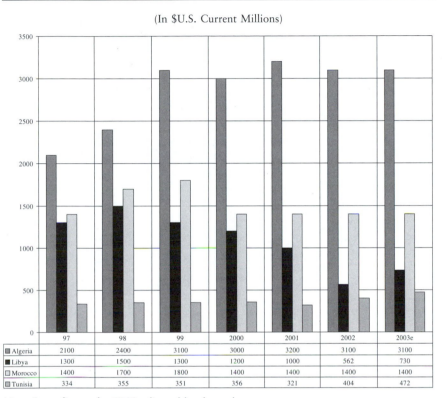

	97	98	99	2000	2001	2002	2003e
Algeria	2100	2400	3100	3000	3200	3100	3100
Libya	1300	1500	1300	1200	1000	562	730
Morocco	1400	1700	1800	1400	1400	1400	1400
Tunisia	334	355	351	356	321	404	472

Note: Some figures for 2003 adjusted by the author.
Source: International Institute of Strategic Studies, *The Military Balance*, various editions.

for almost all reserve forces in Maghreb countries are so low that manpower numbers have little real military value. Algeria's force structure reflects a heavy emphasis on the paramilitary forces needed to fight its civil war. Morocco's large army reflects the need to maintain large forces to protect the south from Polisario attack. As later figures show, Libya has very low manning levels for its total equipment holdings. Tunisia's distribution of military manpower is what might be expected of a small and defensive military power.

The cumulative message of these figures is that the force structures of Algeria, Libya, and Morocco grew to the point where their economies no longer could provide the funding for the equipment, manpower, training, logistics, infrastructure, and sustainability necessary to make these force structures effective. This overexpansion of the total force structure was

Figure 4.5
North African Arms Deliveries Are Declining and Are a Minor Portion of the
World Market: 1985–1999

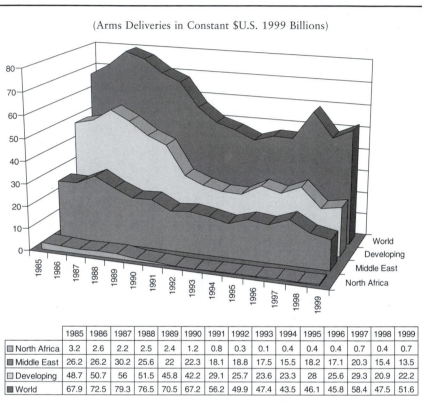

(Arms Deliveries in Constant $U.S. 1999 Billions)

	1985	1986	1987	1988	1989	1990	1991	1992	1993	1994	1995	1996	1997	1998	1999
▢ North Africa	3.2	2.6	2.2	2.5	2.4	1.2	0.8	0.3	0.1	0.4	0.4	0.4	0.7	0.4	0.7
■ Middle East	26.2	26.2	30.2	25.6	22	22.3	18.1	18.8	17.5	15.5	18.2	17.1	20.3	15.4	13.5
▢ Developing	48.7	50.7	56	51.5	45.8	42.2	29.1	25.7	23.6	23.3	28	25.6	29.3	20.9	22.2
■ World	67.9	72.5	79.3	76.5	70.5	67.2	56.2	49.9	47.4	43.5	46.1	45.8	58.4	47.5	51.6

Note: Middle East does not include North African states other than Egypt.
Source: Adapted by Anthony H. Cordesman from Bureau of Arms Control in the U.S. State
Department, *World Military Expenditures and Arms Transfers*, various editions.

particularly severe in the case of Libya, which sized its forces based on its
peak oil revenues in 1981 and 1982, when it spent over 12 percent of its
GNP on its military forces. Libya has never been able to find the resources
or manpower to use more than half of the equipment it bought, and cut
military spending to around 5–6 percent of its GNP after 1993.[1] This resulted in substantial waste, and many purchases were rendered nearly useless by the lack of proper support. As arms spending decreases, nations often
let portions of their older equipment become inoperable or obsolete. Algeria and Libya are only spending a small fraction of their military budget
on the modernization that is necessary to recapitalize their forces.

Figure 4.6
North African Arms Imports as a Percentage of Total Imports: 1985–1999

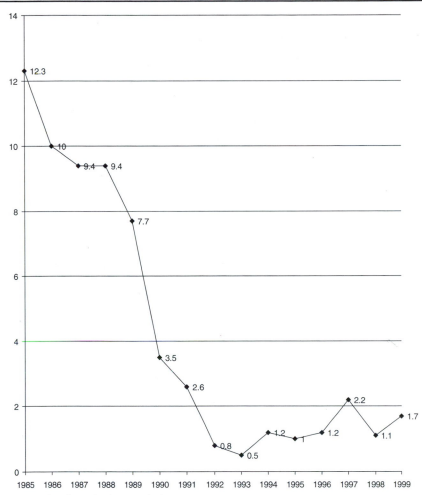

Note: North Africa does not include Egypt.
Source: Adapted by Anthony H. Cordesman from Bureau of Arms Control in the U.S. State
Department, *World Military Expenditures and Arms Transfers*, various editions.

The Maghreb states have seen conscription, and the expansion of military manpower, as a useful means of providing employment and ensuring the loyalty of their youth. These efforts at nation building have complemented a similar expansion of national civil service and employment in the state sector of the economy. This approach to nation building lead to overexpansion of their forces during the early 1980s and the creation of large

Figure 4.7
North African New Arms Agreements and Deliveries by Country: 1987–2002

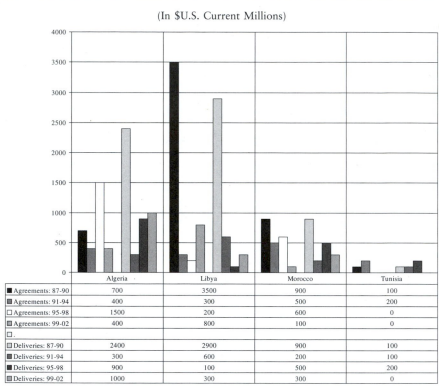

(In $U.S. Current Millions)

	Algeria	Libya	Morocco	Tunisia
■ Agreements: 87-90	700	3500	900	100
▨ Agreements: 91-94	400	300	500	200
☐ Agreements: 95-98	1500	200	600	0
▨ Agreements: 99-02	400	800	100	0
☐.				
☐ Deliveries: 87-90	2400	2900	900	100
■ Deliveries: 91-94	300	600	200	100
■ Deliveries: 95-98	900	100	500	200
☐ Deliveries: 99-02	1000	300	300	0

0 = Data less than $50 million or nil. All data rounded to the nearest $100 million.
Source: Richard F. Grimmett, *Conventional Arms Transfers to the Developing Nations*, Congressional Research Service, various editions.

armies filled with poorly trained men. The cost of maintaining large pools of military manpower helped to diminish economic growth during the early and mid-1980s, and this situation has continued ever since in spite of cuts in total manning after that date.

The military value of such an approach to manpower is dubious for other reasons. Conscript service is often touted as a form of education and nation building. In practice, it has helped disguise unemployment, but the training that conscripts actually receive has little value in training and educating young men. Conscript service has also proven to do little to win the loyalty of young men, aid in internal stability, and serve the cause of nation building. It has often been either a source of added alienation or a schooling in propaganda and repression.

Figure 4.8
New North African Arms Orders by Supplier Country: 1987–2002

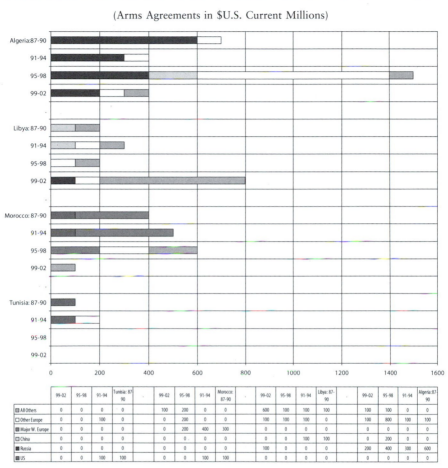

(Arms Agreements in $U.S. Current Millions)

	99-02	95-98	91-94	Tunisia:87-90	.	99-02	95-98	91-94	Morocco:87-90	.	99-02	95-98	91-94	Libya:87-90	.	99-02	95-98	91-94	Algeria:87-90
▨ All Others	0	0	0	0		100	200	0	0		600	100	100	100		100	100	0	0
☐ Other Europe	0	0	100	0		0	200	0	0		100	100	100	0		100	800	100	100
▥ Major W. Europe	0	0	0	0		0	200	400	300		0	0	0	0		0	0	0	0
☐ China	0	0	0	0		0	0	0	0		0	0	100	100		0	200	0	0
▪ Russia	0	0	0	0		0	0	0	0		100	0	0	0		200	400	300	600
▨ US	0	0	100	100		0	0	100	100		0	0	0	0		0	0	0	0

0 = less than $50 million or nil. All data rounded to the nearest $100 million.
Source: Adapted by Anthony H. Cordesman, CSIS, from Richard F. Grimmett, *Conventional Arms Transfers to the Developing Nations*, Congressional Research Service, various editions.

Like most developing countries, the Maghreb states have long under-funded advanced training and the other aspects of manpower quality for their full-time and career forces. None of the Maghreb states has maintained average military expenditures per man in uniform high enough to maintain effective manpower quality and retain technically trained manpower. Morocco and Tunisia have done better than the others. All the Maghreb states have had serious problems in adapting their military organization and discipline to take into account the need for far more skilled junior officers

Figure 4.9
The Decline in Libyan Spending and Arms Imports: 1986–1999

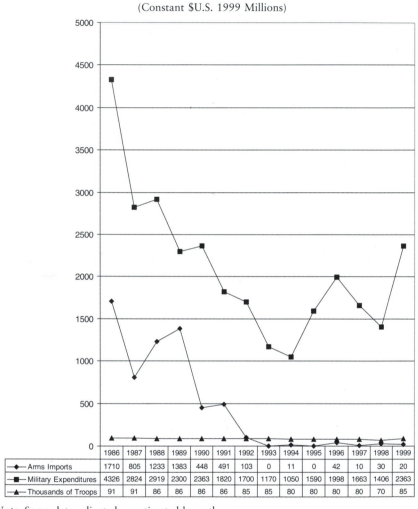

(Constant $U.S. 1999 Millions)

	1986	1987	1988	1989	1990	1991	1992	1993	1994	1995	1996	1997	1998	1999
◆ Arms Imports	1710	805	1233	1383	448	491	103	0	11	0	42	10	30	20
■ Military Expenditures	4326	2824	2919	2300	2363	1820	1700	1170	1050	1590	1998	1663	1406	2363
▲ Thousands of Troops	91	91	86	86	86	86	85	85	80	80	80	80	70	85

Note: Some data adjusted or estimated by author.
Source: Adapted by Anthony H. Cordesman from U.S. State Department, *World Military Expenditures and Arms Transfers*, Washington, DC: GPO, various editions.

and noncommissioned officers (NCOs). The Maghreb states have also demonstrated poor management of military personnel and career structures.

Several detailed national trends that helped shape the trends in the previous figures are worth noting:

Figure 4.10
Trends in North African Military Manpower

(Algerian, Libyan, Moroccan, and Tunisian Military Manpower in Thousands)

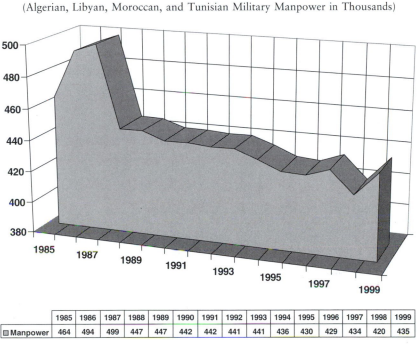

	1985	1986	1987	1988	1989	1990	1991	1992	1993	1994	1995	1996	1997	1998	1999
▢ Manpower	464	494	499	447	447	442	442	441	441	436	430	429	434	420	435

Note: Middle East does not include North African states other than Egypt.
Source: Adapted by Anthony H. Cordesman from U.S. State Department, *World Military Expenditures and Arms Transfers*, Washington, DC: GPO, various editions.

- Algeria has a force structure of over six active division equivalents with a total army manpower of only 124,000 men, 75,000 of whom are poorly trained conscripts. In addition, it has six military regions that require military manpower. This force structure has sharply overstretched its army and made effective force planning impossible. Things have been made worse by rampant corruption at the highest levels of the Algerian officer corps.

- Algeria did a relatively good job of buying armor before its civil war begin in the late 1980s, but it spent too much on artillery quantity and too little on artillery and infantry mobility and quality. It bought a poor mix of relatively low-quality antitank weapons and air defense systems. Since that time, it has increased its paramilitary forces to over 180,000 men to deal with its civil war—compounding all of its military planning, force structure, and force modernization problems.

- The Algerian air force has only bought a limited number of modern air defense fighters for a force with a total of 214 combat aircraft and 65 armed

Figure 4.11
Total Manpower in North African Military Forces in 2003–2004

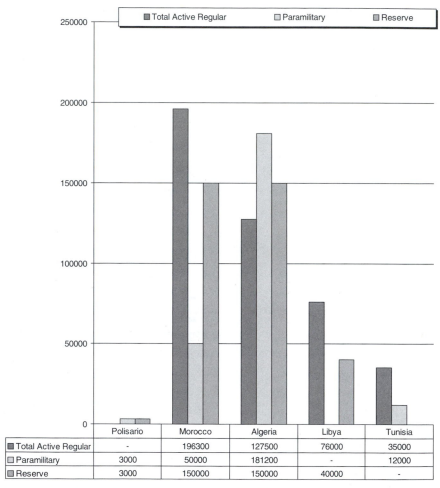

	Polisario	Morocco	Algeria	Libya	Tunisia
Total Active Regular	-	196300	127500	76000	35000
Paramilitary	3000	50000	181200	-	12000
Reserve	3000	150000	150000	40000	-

Source: Adapted by Anthony H. Cordesman from IISS, *The Military Balance*, various editions.

helicopters, and has bought only 10 modern Su-24 attack aircraft. It has long sought to buy aircraft like the MiG-29 and Su-24, but has not had the money. Its surface-to-air missile defenses are of early to late 1970s technology and are now vulnerable to commercially available electronic warfare capabilities and any force with modern antiradiation missiles.

- Until the late 1980s, Algeria gave its more advanced units with heavy armor and advanced aircraft adequate funding, but sharply underfunded its overall

Figure 4.12
Total Regular Military Manpower in North African Forces by Service in 2003–2004

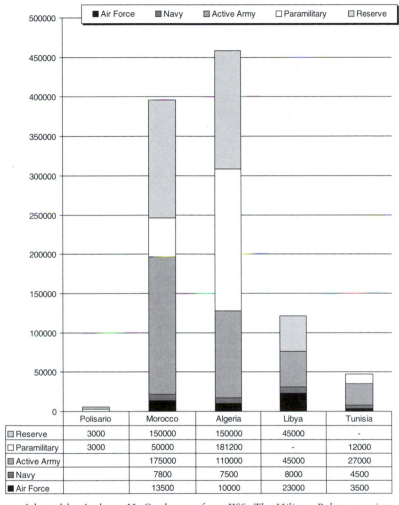

	Polisario	Morocco	Algeria	Libya	Tunisia
Reserve	3000	150000	150000	45000	-
Paramilitary	3000	50000	181200	-	12000
Active Army		175000	110000	45000	27000
Navy		7800	7500	8000	4500
Air Force		13500	10000	23000	3500

Source: Adapted by Anthony H. Cordesman from IISS, *The Military Balance*, various editions; and JCSS, *The Military Balance in the Middle East*, various editions.

manpower and support structure. Since the late 1980s it has had to concentrate its resources on fighting a steadily intensifying civil war, and this means it has had to sharply underfund its equipment modernization.

- Tunisia has provided reasonable wages for its career officers, but has done little to turn its many twelve-month conscripts into effective soldiers.

- Libya has invested in equipment and facilities rather than a sound manpower, infrastructure, and support base. Its poorly trained conscripts, and "volunteers" suffered a decisive defeat in Chad at the hands of lightly armed forces. Its forces have since declined in quality.

- Libya's military equipment purchases have been chaotic. During the Cold War and the period before Libya was placed under UN sanctions, its arms buys involved incredible waste and overexpenditure on equipment. They were made without regard to providing adequate manpower and support forces, and they did not reflect a clear concept of force development or combined arms.

- Libya's adventures in trying to influence events in other states, and its disastrous military intervention in Chad, involved comparatively little actual use of Libya's total forces. Libya did, however, have a powerful catalytic effect on the military buildup of other states in the region. As poor as Libya's military forces were, no neighbor could ignore the buildup of a vast pool of military equipment and Libya's large numbers of Soviet-bloc advisers.

- Libya has to keep many of its aircraft and over 1,000 of its tanks in storage. Its other equipment purchases require far more manpower than its small active army and low-quality reserves can provide. Its overall ratio of weapons to manpower is militarily absurd, and Libya has compounded its problems by buying a wide diversity of equipment types that make it impossible to create an effective training and support base.

- Morocco's continuing low-level tensions with Algeria and Mauritania, and its nearly two-decade-long war with the Polisario over control of the Western Sahara, are the key factors shaping its force trends. It is interesting to note, however, that Morocco's arms purchases were not particularly well suited to dealing with a low-level guerrilla threat until 1982–1983. As late as 1992, Morocco's combat engineering efforts reflected a sounder pattern of purchases for dealing with the Polisario than did its weapons buys. These problems were partly the result of the fact that the Moroccan army was still focusing on a possible confrontation with Algeria, rather than on the conflict with the Polisario.

- Morocco then spent much of its money on maintaining a force of 100,000–150,000 men in the Spanish Sahara. This force became relatively effective by the early 1990s, and has effectively defeated its opposition. Morocco still is unable to fund adequate force modernization, however; and it has bought so many different types of major land weapons over the years that that it finds it difficult to keep its support costs at reasonable levels, to provide proper training, and to maintain suitable C^{4}I battle management capability.

- Morocco has maintained a higher real average of spending per man in its career forces than the other Maghreb states, but it still underfunds and undertrains its conscripts and enlisted men.

- Morocco's air force has a better balance of equipment type than its armed forces or naval forces. Nevertheless, Morocco still relies on obsolescent F-5s and Mirages F-1s, and its purchase of both French and U.S. types of combat aircraft has increased its training and support problems. Morocco also has no meaningful surface-to-air missile defenses.

- Tunisia began to acquire modern armor and fighter aircraft in 1985, but still has bought only limited numbers of weapons. It has done a reasonably good job of expanding its army and air force, but its force size and equipment holdings are inadequate for combat with either of its larger neighbors. Its military forces also include too many types of equipment to allow for effective organization and support.

- Money still severely limits the size and modernization of the Tunisian force structure. In early 2001, it had only 35,000 actives, of whom 23,400 were conscripts. Its only modern armored craft consisted of 54 M-60A3 and 30 older M-60A1 tanks and its 140 M-113 armored personnel carriers. It had no self-propelled artillery, and its most modern aircraft consisted of 15 aging F-E/Fs. It had no modern attack helicopters and no major surface-to-air missiles.

NATIONAL MILITARY FORCES

Each of the nations of North Africa has taken a different approach to developing its military forces.

Morocco

Morocco's only major external threat is Algeria, which no longer presents a significant risk. Its military spending is driven largely by its war with the Polisario for control of the Western Sahara and by factors like bureaucratic momentum, regional rivalries with Algeria and Spain, and the search for status and prestige. This spending consumes some 4–5 percent of Morocco's GNP and 13–14 percent of its national budget. This is not high by regional standards, but Morocco has a sharply rising population, has massive unemployment, and desperately needs resources for economic development. Military spending and the war in the Western Sahara are a major burden on the country.

The trends in Moroccan military forces are shown in Figure 4.13. Morocco's military forces and budget have increased steadily since 1975, with a large jump in expenditures between 1985 and 1990, during its war with the Polisario. Morocco's total manpower and land forces shot up during that period as well. Total manpower increased from 149,000 in 1985 to 192,500 in 1990. Its land forces rose from 130,000 to 175,000 men in that period. Since 1990, there have been only limited changes in total force size.

In 2004, Morocco had a total of 196,300 actives, with 150,000 army reserves. Its land forces had an inventory of 744 main battle tanks, 559 armored infantry fighting vehicles (AIFVs), 785 armored personnel carriers (APCs), 255 self-propelled (SP) artillery, 190 towed artillery, and 39 multiple rocket launchers (MRLs). Its air forces had a total of 89 combat aircraft and 24 attack helicopters. Its navy possessed 1 major surface ship, 4 missile patrol craft, 23 other patrol craft, and 4 amphibious ships.

Figure 4.13
Moroccan Force Developments: 1980–2004

Category/Weapon	1980	1985	1990	1995	2000	2002	2004
Defense Budget (In 96–97, $Current Billions)	0.676	0.504	1.36	1.23	1.8	—	—
Mobilization Base							
Men Ages 13–17	—	—	1,437,000	1,599,600	1,690,000	1,780,000	1,780,000
Men Ages 18–22	—	—	1,343,000	1,439,000	1,526,000	1,612,000	1,612,000
Manpower							
Total Active	116,500	149,000	192,500	195,500	196,300	198,500	196,300
(Conscript)	—	—	—	100,000	100,000	100,000	100,000
Total Reserve	—	—	100,000	150,000	—	150,000	150,000
Total	—	—	292,500	249,500	—	348,500	346,300
Paramilitary	30,000	33,000	40,000	42,000	42,000	48,000	50,000
Land Forces							
Active Manpower	105,000	130,000	175,000	175,000	175,000	175,000	175,000
(Conscripts)	—	—	—	100,000	100,000	100,000	100,000
Reserve Manpower	—	—	—	150,000	—	150,000	150,000
Total Manpower	—	—	—	325,000	—	325,000	325,000
Main Battle Tanks	170	190	284	524	524	744	520
AIFVs/Armored Cars/Lt. Tanks	740	612	474	559	559	539	215

APCs/Recce/Scouts/Half-Tracks	644	806	879	785	785	1,109	1,064
ATGM Launchers	—	—	850	720	720	720	720
SP Artillery/SP Antitank guns	217	174?	230	175	167	227	227
Towed Artillery	132	174	144	164	190	185	185
MRLs	36	20	40	39	39	26	40
Mortars	—	1,290	680+	1,700	1,700	1,470	1,470
SSM Launchers	—	—	—	—	0	0	0
AA Guns	—	140	427	—	425	425	425
Lt. SAM Launchers	—	—	—	107	107	107	107
Air & Air Defense Forces							
Active Manpower	7,000	13,000	13,500	13,500	13,500	13,500	13,500
Reserve Manpower	—	—	—	—	—	—	—
Aircraft							
Total Fighter/FGA/Recce	90	105	93	99	89	74	95
Bomber	0	0	0	0	0	0	0
Fighter	0	0	15	15	15	15	15
FGA/Fighter	68	77	0	0	0	0	0
FGA	0	0	31	34	47	53	54
Recce	0	0	6	2	6	6	6
COIN/OCU	22	28	46	50	0	0	0
Airborne Early Warning (AEW)	0	0	0	0	0	0	0
Electronic Warfare (EW)	0	0	3	3	3	3	4
Maritime Reconnaissance (MR)	0	0	0	0	0	0	0
Combat Capable Trainer	35	52	—	12	23	23	24
Tanker	0	0	4	3	3	3	3
Transport	29	33	33	35	36	33	33

continued

Figure 4.13 (Continued)

Category/Weapon	1980	1985	1990	1995	2000	2002	2004
Helicopters							
Attack/Armed/ASW	0	18	50	24	24	24	24
Other	117	90	24	89	88	89	88
Total	117	108	74	113	112	113	112
SAM Forces							
Batteries	0	0	0	0	0	0	0
Heavy Launchers	0	0	0	0	0	0	0
Naval Forces							
Active Manpower	4,500	6,000	7,000	7,000	7,800	10,000	7,800
Reserve Manpower	—	—	—	—	—	—	—
Total Manpower	—	—	—	—	—	10,000	7,800
Submarines	0	0	0	0	0	0	0
Destroyers/Frigates/Corvettes	0	1	1	3	1	1	2
Missile	0	1	1	3	1	1	2
Other	0	0	0	0	0	0	0
Missile Patrol	2	6	4	4	4	4	4
Coastal/Inshore Patrol	15	17	21	23	23	23	23
Mine	0	0	0	0	0	0	0
Amphibious Ships	4	4	3	4	4	4	4
Landing Craft/Light Support	—	—	—	—	4	4	4
ASW/Combat Helicopter	0	—	—	—	0	0	2

Source: Adapted by Anthony H. Cordesman from data provided by U.S. experts; and IISS, *The Military Balance, 2001–2002, 2003–2004.*

Land Forces

The 175,000-man Moroccan army is the only force in the Maghreb that has recently had to train and organize for serious combat, although this combat has consisted largely of guerrilla warfare. The army is organized into two major commands: Northern Zone (Rabat) and Southern Zone (Agadir). The Northern Zone deals largely with defense of the Algerian border and internal security. The Southern Zone is organized to fight the Polisario. The order of battle alters to deploy the forces necessary to deal with the threat in the Western Sahara at any given time.

The army has 3 mechanized infantry brigade headquarters, 1 light security brigade, 2 paratroop brigades, and 8 mechanized/motorized infantry regiments (2–3 battalions each). It also has an exceptionally large number of small independent units. These include 11 armored battalions, 39 infantry battalions, 3 motorized (camel corps) battalions, 1 mountain battalion, 2 cavalry battalions, 9–12 artillery battalions, 1 air defense group, 7 engineering battalions, 4–7 commando units, and 2 airborne battalions.

The Moroccan army has a significant number of conscripts, but also has a strong cadre of experienced regulars. Morocco's large population and low per capita income have led many poorer Moroccans to make the army a career. The pay and benefits are adequate, and living conditions are acceptable, even in the camps and strong points in the south. Training, however, is still erratic and much of it is conducted at the unit level. This leads to very different levels of effectiveness, depending upon the particular unit involved.

A 50,000-man reserve exists on paper, but—as is the case with virtually all reserve forces in the Middle East—most of this manpower serves little real purpose. There is little reserve training, and there are few combat-ready officers, other ranks, and specialists with the kind of current fighting skills the army would need in war. The only combat-effective reserves would be men called back to units they had recently left. The paramilitary Force Auxillaire is probably more effective. It is a 30,000-man force designed to reinforce the army in a campaign against Algeria, and would provide service support and rear area security. It also includes a 5,000-man Mobile Intervention Force that is fully equipped with light armored vehicles and Land Rovers, and with automatic and crew-served weapons. The Force Auxillaire has also been used successfully in rear area security operations against the Polisario.

The Gendarmerie Royal is a 15,000–20,000-man support force that includes a wide range of state security functions. It is headquartered in Rabat and has heavy elements that can deal with major internal security threats. Its order of battle includes a Special Brigade, Mobile Group South, Mobile Group North, Air Squadron, and Coast Guard Support elements.

The army is deployed to concentrate Morocco's armored forces in the north and a large antiguerrilla force in the south. This reflects its long-standing emphasis on deterring Algeria, while fighting the Polisario. There is one Royal Guard battalion, a mountain battalion, an armored squadron, a mechanized squadron, a cavalry squadron, and an artillery group in the Northwest Atlas. The border is defended by 2 mechanized infantry regiments, 3 infantry battalions, a camel corps battalion, 2 armored squadrons, and 1 artillery group.

There normally are 3 mechanized infantry brigades, 9 mechanized infantry regiments, 25 infantry battalions, 2 paratroop battalions, 2 camel corps battalions, 4 armored squadrons (with UR-416 APCs), and 7 artillery groups in the south. Morocco also plays a significant peacekeeping role. One additional Moroccan battalion with 360 men is deployed in Equatorial Guinea, Moroccan troops are deployed with the UN force in Angola, and Morocco deployed 5,000 men in the UAE during the Gulf War, including a 700-man paratroop unit. In addition, Morocco has deployed 800 soldiers in a motorized infantry brigade to aid the UN peacekeeping efforts in Bosnia.

Morocco's purchases of 224 M-48A5, 300 M-60A1, 120 M-60A3, and 100 T-72 main battle tanks have given the army adequate heavy armor. However, most of the M-48A5s remain in storage. Morocco also had an additional 100 SK-105 Kuerassier light tanks, but these are obsolescent. Overall levels of tank training are limited to adequate, and Morocco only conducts limited maneuver and large-unit training.

Reports differ as to the strength and types of other fighting vehicles in the Moroccan forces, but its armored reconnaissance strength seems to include 16 EBR-75, 80 AMX-10RCs, 190 AML-90s, 38 AML-60-7s, and 20 M-113s. It also had 30 Ratel 20, 30 Ratel 90, 45 VAB-VCIs, and 10 AMX-10P employed as AIFVs. Its APC include 420 M-113s and 320 VAB-VTTs. It may also have 45 OT-62 and OT-64 APCs. This diverse mix of armored fighting vehicles and APCs is often of mediocre quality and readiness, and lacks effective standardization. Morocco's emphasis on armored infantry fighting vehicles and armored personnel carriers does, however, reflect a response to the special needs imposed by its terrain and to its experience in fighting the Polisario. While Algeria poses a somewhat theoretical threat of armored warfare, Morocco has had to fight the Polisario largely using mechanized and light infantry.

Morocco is well equipped with artillery. In early 2004, it had 190 towed weapons. These included 30–35 L-118, 20 M-101, and 36 M-1950 105-mm weapons, 18 M-46 130-mm weapons, and 35 FH-70, 20 M-114, and 26 M-198 155-mm weapons. It had 222 self-propelled weapons: 5 Mk 61 105-mm howitzers, 98 AMX-F3, 20 M-44, 44 M-109/109A1 155-mm howitzers, and 60 203-mm M-110 howitzers. It also had 26 BM-21 and 14 M-1979 122-mm multiple rocket launchers, and some 1,500 81-mm and 120-mm mortars. Roughly 600 of the mortars were 120-mm weapons, 20 of which were mounted on VAB armored vehicles. This artillery strength does not match Algeria's, but it includes a large number of modern self-propelled weapons. Morocco seems to be able to operate most of its artillery weapons effectively as individual units but has problems with combined arms, artillery maneuver, and BVR targeting.

Morocco's holdings of antitank weapons include 440 M-47 Dragon, 80 Milan, 150 BGM-71A TOW, and 50 AT-3 antitank guided missile launchers. Roughly 80 of the TOWs were mounted on M-901 armored vehicles. Its other antitank weapons include 150 3.5-inch M-20. The army also has some 350 M-40A1 106-mm recoilless rifles. Morocco has some 425 anti-aircraft guns, including 200 ZPU-2 and 20 ZPU-4 14.5-mm guns, 40 M-167 and 60 M-163 Vulcan SP 20-mm guns, 90 ZU-23-2s 23-mm guns, and 15 KS-19 towed 100-mm guns. It also has 37 M-54 Chaparral self-propelled surface-to-air missile launchers, and 70 SA-7s.

The army's war-fighting effectiveness is mixed. It is most experienced in dealing with light infantry and guerrilla forces like the Polisario, and is best trained and organized for defense against this kind of warfare. While Morocco has some outstanding battalion-sized elements, most of its heavy armor lacks proper support equipment, technical manpower, and spares. Morocco does not conduct serious large-unit armored maneuver training, and lacks the service support and sustaining capability it needs to fight a prolonged conflict with Algeria. Its artillery is effective against infantry and slow-moving forces, but lacks proficiency in combined arms and armored maneuver speed. Logistic support, however, is adequate; and Morocco has shown that it can maintain an adequate supply line over considerable distances.

Naval Forces

The 7,800-man Moroccan navy is a relatively large force by local standards, although it scarcely makes Morocco a major Mediterranean or Atlantic naval power. It has 2 frigates, 4 missile fast attack craft, 17 large coastal patrol craft, 6 inshore patrol craft, 4 amphibious landing craft, 4 support ships, and 40 customs and coast guard vessels. Fifteen hundred men are organized in a marine naval infantry battalion. The navy is based in Casablanca, Agadir, Al-Hoceima, Dakhla, and Tangier. Casablanca is its headquarters and the key port. Dakhla and Agadier are the main secondary bases on the Atlantic, and Al-Hociema is the key secondary base on the Mediterranean. The Ministry of Fisheries also operates 11 Pilatus Britten-Norman Defender Maritime Surveillance Aircraft.[2]

The navy has two new French-made Mohammed V-class frigates (French Floreal–class): the Mohammed V and Hassan II, commissioned in 2002 and 2003. Each had four Exocet ship-to-ship missiles, two Matra Simbad surface-to-air missile launchers, a 76-mm gun, 2×3 Mk 46 torpedoes, and two 375-mm antiship marine mortars. They also have electronic support measures, and have chaff and IR flare launchers. They have modern Thompson air/surface search radars and can carry one Panther helicopter. Their ASW sonar capabilities are unclear.

The navy also has a 1,480-ton modified Descubierta-class guided missile frigate, named the *Lt. Colonel Errhamani*, commissioned in 1983 and refitted in Spain in 1996. The ship has four MM-38 Exocet launchers (sea-skimming missiles with semiactive radar guidance, a range of 42 kilometers, and a 165-kilogram warhead), an octuple Aspide launcher (semiactive radar homing to 13 kilometers at Mach 2.5), one 76-mm gun, six 324-mm torpedo tubes, and antisubmarine mortars. The navy rarely loaded Exocets, or exercised missile firings, on its guided missile frigate, and its air search radar was removed in 1998. The ability to fight the ship effectively in combat against a force equipped with modern sensors and countermeasures was uncertain, as was its ability to operate effectively with other ships in fleet operations.

The navy has four Lazaga-class 425-ton fast attack craft—all of which are equipped with four M-38 Exocets and one 76-mm gun. The missile ships were generally considerably better-manned and better-equipped than Morocco's other vessels. Individual officer training for these ships ranged from adequate to good, and crew training ranged from mediocre to adequate. The navy has six 425-ton Lazaga-class missile patrol craft with four MM 38 Exocet missiles each, one 76-mm gun, 20- and 40-mm antiaircraft guns, and fire control and surface search radars. These ships date back to the early 1980s. One had its 76-mm gun removed in 1998. It had six 425-ton Cormoran-class large patrol craft with 40-mm and 20-mm guns. The navy also had five 580-ton Rais Bargach-class patrol craft commissioned in the middle to late 1990s. These were French-made craft with 20-mm and 40-mm guns and surface search radars. It had four 475-ton Osprey Mark II-class large patrol craft with one 40-mm and two 20-mm guns each. These were equipped with surface search radars, and were commissioned in the late 1980s and 1990. Some were assigned to the Customs Service.

It had two Okba-class 445-ton large patrol craft with one 76-mm gun each, and with surface search radars. These French-supplied patrol craft dated back to the mid-1980s. It had four El Hahiq (Osprey II) class, 475-ton large patrol craft with 40-mm and 20-mm guns. The navy also had six 89-ton El Wacil-class coastal/inshore patrol craft with 20-mm guns and surface search radars. The training and crew proficiency of these ships were suitable largely for commercial patrol purposes.

The navy had one Newport-class landing ship tank (LST), displacing 8,450 tons fully loaded, and with the capacity to carry 400 troops 500 tons of vehicles, 3 LCVPs, and 1 LCPL. The ship has experienced repeated maintenance and operating problems. It carried three Batral-class 1,409-ton LSTs, and had the capacity to carry 140 troops or 12 vehicles, one 670-

ton LCT, and up to 26 LCMs. Support craft included two small 1,500-ton transports and one Ro-Ro Ferry converted to be a troop transport ship. The navy also had three 1,409-ton Batral-class landing ship (tank) or LSTs, which could carry 140 troops and 12 vehicles or 300 tons of cargo, and 1 Edic-class 670-ton landing craft (tank), which could carry up to 11 vehicles.

The Customs Service and coast guard have 4 P-32 coastal patrol craft, 18 Arcor-class coastal patrol craft, 3 Sar craft, and 15 Arcor 53-class inshore patrol craft.

The Moroccan navy has shown that it can operate these fast attack craft, patrol craft, and transport and amphibious ships reasonably well. It is capable of patrolling local waters, but has limited ability to operate in the Atlantic, and training is said to be mediocre. Its capabilities for antiair and antiship missile warfare are limited. It would not be capable of successfully engaging Spanish naval forces, and would experience serious problems in any engagement with Algeria.

Morocco has limited repair and at-sea replenishment capability, although it does have two logistic support ships, and most of its ships have limited endurance. Morocco is scarcely the possessor of a "blue water" navy that can play a role in the Atlantic or in controlling the entrance to the Mediterranean. The Moroccan navy is adequate for coastal defense and most practical mission requirements, and probably represents the largest and most effective naval force that Morocco can support given its limited defense budget and the need to concentrate on the defense of the western border and south.

Air Forces

In 2004, the 13,500-man Moroccan air force had 95 combat aircraft and 24 armed helicopters. There were major air bases in Kenitra, Marrakesh-Menara, Meknes-Mezergues, Rabat-Sale, and Sidi Slimane, as well as three to four operating bases in the south.

Morocco's forces included fighter ground attack squadron consisting of 8 F-5As, 3 F-5Bs, 24 F-5Es, 4 F-5Fs, and 14 Mirage F-1Ehs; plus one air defense squadron with 15 Mirage F-1CHs. It also had a reconnaissance squadron with 4 OV-10s and 2 CH-130s with side-looking radar; and 2 C-130 and 2 Falcon 20 electronic intelligence and warfare planes. It had 51 training aircraft, including 23 Alphajets with dual capability in light attack missions.

Morocco had relatively modern air munitions, including some AIM-9B/D/Js, R-530s, R-550 Magics, and 125 AGM-65B Mavericks for F-5Es. All of its combat aircraft are aging, however; and Morocco needs to fund more modern fighters during the next decade.

Its transport forces were relatively large and included 12 C-130H, 7 CN-235, 2 Do-28, and 2 Falcon 20, plus 1 Falcon 50, 2 Gulfstream, 4 King Air 100, and 3 King Air 200. Morocco is one of the few air forces with tanker and midair refueling assets; it has 1 B-707 and 2 KC-130H transport/

tanker aircraft. Morocco makes extensive use of air transport and supply in its operations against the Polisario.

Morocco had 24 SA-342 armed helicopters, 12 with high-subsonic optically teleguided (HOT) antiguided missiles and 12 with cannon. These armed helicopters do not have advanced sensors and avionics, but are adequate for day combat. It has 7 CH-47 heavy transport helicopters, 58 medium transport helicopters, and 23 light helicopters. Helicopter mobility and readiness are good by regional standards.

The Moroccan air force is one of the few regional air forces without a major land-based air defense component. Morocco has no medium and heavy surface-to-air missile units and does not have the radars and battlement management systems to support them.

The Moroccan air force experienced considerable political instability in the early 1970s, and then had problems in the war with the Polisario. It lost a considerable number of aircraft to Polisario SA-6s and SA-7s in the early and middle 1980s, and often aborted missions or dropped bombs where they had limited effect. Since that time, however, it has gradually corrected many of its past training, maintenance, and leadership problems. It has achieved a reasonable level of proficiency in using its Mirage F-1s, F-5E/Fs, and Alphajets in basic attack and support missions.

The air force is also effective in using its attack and reconnaissance aircraft, and its CH-130s with SLAR have proven to be of considerable value in monitoring the defensive wall in the Western Sahara and locating and targeting Polisario movements with vehicles. It seems able to make effective use of its 2 C-130 and 2 Falcon 20 ELINT aircraft, and is one of the few regional air forces with such an electronic intelligence capability. It acquired a Westinghouse air defense system in the early 1980s, and has moderately effective warning and combat air control capability.

The air force cannot, however, properly operate all of its Mirage F-1 fighters, which constitute 29 aircraft out of a total combat strength of 95 aircraft. There are 14 Mirage F-1EHs in the attack role and 15 Mirage F-1CHs assigned to the air defense role. It is unclear whether Morocco's problems in operating the Mirage F-1 stem from problems in maintaining the aircraft or from a failure or inability to fund the spare parts and equipment it needs. Its 13 F-5A/Bs and 29 F-5E/Fs are adequate for missions against the Polisario, but are aging aircraft that lack modern avionics. They are not adequate to engage modern fighters with BVR radars and air-to-air missiles, and lack the avionics and sensors to use modern air-to-surface guided weapons at long ranges.

Morocco does not have a significant land-based air defense system. It has upgraded its Northrop Grumman tactical radar system (TPS-63) with new solid-state transmitters and digital signal processors (AN/TPS-63). This upgrade increases detection range by 250 percent and improves reliability, maintainability, and supportability. It has reasonably good warning and air control capability, but no airborne air control and warning assets and only limited surveillance and electronic warfare capabilities.

The air force's other limitations include its lack of advanced or airborne sensors and AC&W capability, its lack of advanced combat training capability, continuing maintenance problems and dependence on foreign technicians, and its limited C⁴I battle management capability in the event of a major Algerian attack. Some of these problems may be solved over the next few years as a result of a 1991 contract that Morocco signed with Westinghouse to modernize its communications, entire air defense system, and air traffic system.

Paramilitary and Security Forces

The military, paramilitary, and security forces of Morocco, like those of all Maghreb states, play a major role in internal security and in safeguarding the power of the regime. Morocco's paramilitary forces total roughly 42,000 men, most of whom can act as land forces. These include 12,000 men in the Gendarmerie Royale, which is organized into 1 brigade, 4 mobile groups, 1 air squadron, 1 paratroop squadron, and a coast guard unit. The gendarmerie has 18 patrol boats, two light aircraft, and 22 helicopters.

The Border Police, the National Security Police, and the Judicial Police are all departments of the Ministry of Interior, while the Royal Gendarmerie reports directly to the presidential palace. Its activities are focused primarily on Islamic extremists, student and labor unrest, and the Sahrawis in the Western Sahara.

Until recently, the Moroccan security apparatus had been repressive, and the security services had often acted a power in their own right, as well as a key source of support for the monarchy. This rule by the security forces, or "makhzen," has been controlled by the minister of interior, which commands several overlapping police and paramilitary organizations. The ministry of interior has also exerted power through the fact that it determined eligibility for some aspects of welfare and free medical care, and supervises the state and public committees dealing with investment and businesses in Morocco's sixteen provinces.

The Ministry of Interior has been responsible for the conduct of elections, cooperation with the United Nations in the referendum on the Western Sahara, the appointment and training of many local officials, the allocation of local and regional budgets, the oversight of university campuses, and the licensing of associations and political parties. The ministry has also exerted substantial influence over the judicial system.

Algeria

Algeria has been long been dominated by a corrupt and inefficient military junta, sometimes called the "Power," which has ruled the country behind the façade of an elected government. Since the early 1990s, Algeria has been involved in a violent civil war with Islamic extremists, after more moderate Islamic political factions were denied power following their victory in an election. This civil war has been vicious on both sides, often involving large-scale atrocities. The armed forces have largely won, but the fight continues.

Algeria has changed its force posture over time to reflect the state of its improving relations with Morocco, the decline in any threat from Libya, its economic problems, and its need to focus on its civil war. The trends in Algerian military forces are shown in Figure 4.14. Algerian regular military manpower peaked at around 170,000 in the mid-1980s, but declined to around 150,000 in 1990. It dropped to less than 122,000 in 1995, but has since increased slowly. Algeria had 127,000–128,000 actives in 2004, including 75,000–85,000 conscripts. It had a paper reserve strength of some 150,000, with little or no real-world readiness or warfighting capability.

Algeria's civil war has led it, however, to increase its paramilitary forces, which rose from around 30,000 men in 1986 to some 181,200 in 2004, with 60,000 in the army-controlled gendarmerie, 20,000 in the Directorate of National Security Forces, 1,200 in the Republican Guard, and around 100,000 in the "Legitimate Defense Groups." To put these figures in perspective, they compare with a peak threat of only about 2,000–3,000 full-time regulars in the Group Islamique Armée (GIA), operating in small groups of 50–100. The Armed Front for Islamic Jihad (FIDA) and Islamic League for the Call and Jihad (LIDD) probably have peaked at less than 1,000 actives each.

Algeria has a large pool of major weapons systems. Its forces have 1,000 main battle tanks, 124–173 armored reconnaissance vehicles, 989 AIFVs, 730 APCs, 185 self-propelled artillery, 406 towed artillery, and 144 multiple rocket launchers. In 2004, its air force consisted of 175 combat aircraft and 93 attack helicopters. Its naval forces included 2 submarines, 8 major surface ships, 12 patrol craft, and 3 amphibious ships.

Land Forces

Algeria's military forces are called the National Popular Army (ANP). The Algerian army is by far the largest element of the ANP and is currently organized into six military regions. Like Morocco and Libya, Algeria has gradually built up a network of roads and facilities in its border areas that are designed to allow its forces to deploy and fight against either Morocco or Libya. Many of its units are not deployed in the border area, however; and the Algerian army is scarcely on a wartime footing. The army has major bases at Algeris, Annaba, Batna, Becher, Biskra, Blida, Constantine, Djanet, Ghardaia, El Golea, Oran, Ouargla, Reggane, In Salah, Skikda, Tamanrasset, Tarat, Timimoun, Tindouf, and Touggourt.

Figure 4.14
Algerian Force Trends: 1975–2004

Category/Weapon	1980	1985	1990	1995	2000	2002	2004
Defense Budget							
(In 96–97, $Current Billions)	0.705	0.938	1.01	1.36	1.9	—	—
Mobilization Base							
Men Ages 13–17	—	—	1,535,000	1,796,000	1,891,000	1,986,000	1,986,000
Men Ages 18–2	—	—	1,328,000	1,551,800	1,693,000	1,934,000	1,834,000
Manpower							
Total Active	101,000	170,000	125,000	121,700	122,000	124,000	127,500
(Conscript)	—	100,000	70,000	90,000	75,000	75,000	75,000
Total Reserve	100,000	150,000	150,000	150,000	150,000	150,000	150,000
Total	201,000	320,000	275,000	271,700	272,000	274,000	277,500
Paramilitary	10,000	30,550	23,000	105,000	146,200	181,200	181,200
Land Forces							
Active Manpower	90,000	150,000	107,000	105,000	105,000	107,000	110,000
(Conscripts)	—	100,000	70,000	90,000	75,000	75,000	75,000
Reserve Manpower	—	—	150,000	150,000	—	150,000	150,000
Total Manpower	—	—	257,000	255,000	—	257,000	260,000
Main Battle Tanks	600	700	900	960	951	1,089	1,000
AIFVs/Armored Cars/Lt. Tanks	250	800	1,055	1,035	1,000	1,174	989
APCs/Recce/Scouts/Half-Tracks	830	550	860	460	680+	945	903
ATGM Launchers	—	—	—	—	—	—	—

continued

Figure 4.14 (Continued)

Category/Weapon	1980	1985	1990	1995	2000	2002	2004
SP Artillery	140	100	120	185	185	185	185
Towed Artillery	340	550	390	405	416	418	406
MRLs	85	170	78	126	126	96	144
Mortars	180	180	—	330	330	330+	330+
SSM Launchers	50	—	—	—	—	—	—
AA Guns	540	280+	855	895	895	980	899
Lt. SAM Launchers	—	—	—	—	1,000+	1,000+	1,000+
Air & Air Defense Forces							
Active Manpower	7,000	12,000	12,000	10,000	10,000	10,000	10,000
Reserve Manpower	—	—	—	—	—	—	—
Aircraft							
Total Fighter/FGA/Recce	278	332	257	170	181	166	175
Bomber	24	0	0	0	0	0	0
Fighter	90	110	146	100	110	114	83
FGA/Fighter	0	0	0	0	0	0	0
FGA	110	150	47	50	50	48	66
COIN/OCU	44	0	18	0	0	0	0
Recce	10	6	3	9	10	10	12
Airborne Early Warning (AEW)	0	0	0	0	0	0	0
Electronic Warfare (EW)	0	0	0	0	0	0	0
Maritime Reconnaissance (MR)	0	8	2	2	15	15	15
Combat Capable Trainer	18	39	60	11	8	10	10
Tanker	0	0	0	0	0	0	0
Transport	20	29	26	26	27	27	27

Helicopters							
Attack/Armed/ASW	20	35	38	60	65	63	93
Other	37	72	91	53	63	50	50
Total	57	107	129	113	138	138	143
SAM Forces							
Batteries	1	5	9	9	9	9	9
Heavy Launchers	18	44	51	51	43	43	43
Naval Forces							
Active Manpower	4,000	8,000	6,500	6,700	7,000	7,000	7,500
Reserve Manpower	—	—	—	—	—	—	—
Total Manpower	—	—	—	—	—	—	—
Submarines	0	2	4	2	2	2	2
Destroyers/Frigates/Corvettes	0	7	6	6	6	8	9
Missile	0	4	3	3	3	5	6
Other	0	3	3	3	3	3	3
Missile Patrol	17	8	11	11	11	9 (2)	9 (2)
Coastal/Inshore Patrol	12	—	11	8	5	3	10
Mine	2	1	1	1	1	0	0
Amphibious Ships	1	3	3	3	3	3	3
Landing Craft/Light Support	—	—	—	—	3	3	3
ASW/Combat Helicopter	—	—	—	—	0	0	0

Source: Adapted by Anthony H. Cordesman from data provided by U.S. experts; and IISS, *The Military Balance, 2001–2002.*

87

At the top of the chain of command is the Higher Council of State to the General Staff, followed by the Army Commander, Navy Commander, and Air Force and Air Defense Commander. The organization of the armed forces has been streamlined since 1996 but still has a highly bureaucratic, grossly overmanned and overranked headquarters, support structure. It would probably be more efficient with one-third less manpower. The army is under the command of the Chief of the General Staff, who has a separate Inspector General and exercises a direct line of command to the major combat units.

In the mid-1980s, the army reorganized its divisions into something approaching a modern regimental structure, added armored forces, and attempted to modernize its command structure. The army is now organized into two armored divisions, each consisting of three tank regiments (95 T-62s or T-72s and 30 BMP-1s or BMP-2s each). Each also has one mechanized regiment (30 T-62s or T-72s, 30 BMP-1s or BMP-2s, and 60 BTR-60s each), an artillery group with 120 guns, a reconnaissance battalion, an air defense battalion, and engineer and logistic elements.

The army has two mechanized divisions, each consisting of three mechanized regiments and an artillery group with 120 guns, a reconnaissance battalion, an air defense battalion, and engineer and logistic elements. The army also has one airborne division with five airborne regiments, plus one independent armored brigade, one tank regiment, four or five independent motorized/mechanized infantry brigades, and one antitank battalion. Depending on the source, it has two to seven artillery battalions and five–seven air defense battalions—one a surface-to-air missile unit. Most of these latter battalions support a given division and are effectively part of its force structure.

Algeria also has large paramilitary forces, which have carried out most of the fighting in the civil war. The Ministry of the Interior has a 16,000–20,000-man National Security Force, used as an antiterrorist and security force in desert and mountain areas. The Republican Guard Brigade is a 1,200-man force with armored reconnaissance vehicles that aids in border surveillance and antiterrorist operations in desert areas. There is a 50,000-man police force and 50,000–60,000-man gendarmerie used for security and antiterrorist as well as police functions. These latter forces are controlled by the Ministry of the Interior.

In 2004, the regular army had about 110,000 full-time actives, about 75,000–85,000 of whom were conscripts. Conscripts serve for eighteen months and generally receive inadequate basic training, in both unit training and field training. Algeria also has a large army reserve on paper, but it has little real structure and only limited and highly selective call-up training. It would take weeks to retrain most reserves to serve basic military functions, and months to create effective reserve units.

The Algerian army had roughly 1,000 tanks, including 320 T-54/55s, 330 T-62s and 350 T-72s—55 of which were delivered during 1999–2000. It had 124 BDRM-2 reconnaissance vehicles (64 with AT-3 Sagger), and possibly 49 Saladins. It had 989 armored infantry fighting vehicles, including 700 BMP-1s and 289 BMP-2s. Continuing deliveries of BMP-2s took place during 1999 and 2000. It had some 730 armored personnel carriers, including 100 Fahds, 30 BTR-50/OT-62s, 400 BTR-60/OT-64s, and 200 BTR-80s. The overall readiness of Algerian armor was limited by significant obsolescence and maintenance problems, little large-unit training, and poor to mediocre training in rapid maneuver, night warfare, support and logistics, and aggressive offensive combat.

The army had 406 major towed artillery weapons, including 28 D-74, 100 M-1931/37, 60 M-30 and 198 D-30 122-mm weapons, 10 M-46 130-mm weapons, and 10 M-1937 152-mm weapons. It also had 185 self-propelled artillery weapons, including 150 122-mm 2S1s and 35 2S3 152-mm weapons. Its multiple rocket launcher strength included 48 122-mm BM-21s, 48 140-mm BM-14 and BM-16s, 30 BM-24 240-mm weapons, and 18 new long-range Smerch 9A52s. It had 120 120-mm, 150 82-mm and 60 160-mm mortars. This artillery strength included far more self-propelled weapons than Algeria had in the mid-1980s, and the army has moderate capabilities for mass fire against static or area targets. However, it has little training in artillery maneuver and poor capabilities for combined arms, counterbattery fire, switching fire, and beyond-visual-range targeting.

The Algerian army had 156 towed 57-mm and 85 antitank guns, plus 3 T-12 and 50 Su-100 100-mm self-propelled weapons in storage. Other antitank weapons included AT-2 Swatter and AT-3 Sagger antitank guided weapons (ATGWs). An unknown number of modern AT-4 Spigot and AT-5 Spandrel ATGWs have been delivered and further deliveries are planned. The army had 178 recoilless rifles. Some of the Saggers are mounted on BRDM-2s. About 156 of the towed antitank guns are obsolete 57-mm weapons, and 80 more are obsolescent 85-mm D-44 with limited antiarmor capability against modern tanks. Few crews have realistic combat training in killing tanks or other armored vehicles.

The army had some 770 air defense guns, including 219 self-propelled, radar-guided ZSU-23-4s. It also had large numbers of manportable SA-7s, SA-14s, and SA-16s and had 20 SA-8 and 20 SA-9 light surface-to-air missile launchers. While most of its air defense weapons have limited lethality, and most crews have limited training, Algeria has enough modern weapons and sheer weapons strength to provide a considerable "curtain fire" capability against low-flying aircraft.

These weapons holdings show that Algeria is relatively well equipped in terms of equipment numbers for a 110,000-man army. However, much of

Algeria's equipment is ten to twenty years old, and some is no longer fully operational. This includes many BTR combat vehicles and a few of Algeria's towed artillery weapons. Algeria needs more self-propelled artillery weapons and more modern short-range air defenses. It needs far more third- and fourth-generation antitank guided missiles. It also needs modern artillery counterbattery radars and fire control equipment and improved command, control, and communications systems. It would have to be extensively re-equipped for effective night combat and BVR range targeting.

The Algerian army has had no meaningful combat experience against a regular army since its border clashes with Morocco in 1963. The army is heavily politicized; it is corrupt and nepotistic, and this affects promotion at the higher levels of command. It spends far more time on internal security problems than on developing its war-fighting capability.

Training tends to be overrigid and repetitive, and combined arms, combined operations, and maneuver training are poor. Leadership is weak at every level, there is considerable corruption and favoritism in promotion and command assignments, and the army has serious organizational, training, logistic, and combat and service support problems. Technical training and maintenance standards are weak. The army often buys new equipment more quickly than it can effectively absorb it. It then fails to follow up with effective training, maintenance, and logistic subsystems.

The military "culture" of the army is also an awkward mix of Algerian ideology and long-outdated and relatively slow-moving Soviet tactics and doctrine. The army relies on mass and attrition, not maneuver and technology. Its leadership has never fully converted from an ideological focus on the army as a popular or revolutionary force to one that is fully capable of modern armored and maneuver combat. Many units lack adequate manning and readiness, and large-scale exercise training is poor. Algeria's internal security problems, and the high degree of politicization and bureaucratization of its forces, may well make it impossible to change this situation during the next decade. High level positions are highly political and so is promotion; there is massive internal corruption among the top leadership.

It is striking that it is the paramilitary forces and militias that have done so much of the actual fighting in the Algerian civil war, and not the regular army—which has drained so many resources out of the nation for so long a period. The National Security Force, Republican Guard Brigade, police force, and gendarmerie have performed most security antiterrorist functions. Much of the responsibility for security has also been turned over to the extensive regional militia forces and the roughly 100,000 men in what are called the "Legitimate Defense Groups." Where Morocco painfully learned how to fight a guerrilla war, the Algerian army largely stood aside and let proxies do much of the fighting.

The relatively small size of the organized military forces of the Islamic opposition is also striking. The GIA is estimated to have small groups of 50–100 men, with a total of less than 3,000 actives. FIDA is estimated to have small groups of 50–100 men, and now an estimate of total active strength is available. The same is true of the Islamic League for the Call and Jihad.[3]

Naval Forces

The 7,500-man Algerian navy is based at Mers-el-Kebir (2nd Region), Algiers (1st Region), Annaba (GG headquarters), and Jijel (5th Region). It is under the command of a general-major and headquartered at Algiers. In addition to the navy, Algeria has 600 naval infantry and 500 men in its coast guard. The navy has a strength of 2 submarines, 3 frigates, 6 corvettes, 9 missile fast attack craft, 10 fast attack craft, and 3 amphibious ships. The navy has 1 survey ship, 1 major auxiliary ship, and several tug and support vessels. It has 2 Kebir-class fast attack craft in construction. The coastal defense force has 4 truck-mounted batteries of SS-C-3 Styx coastal antiship defense missiles that are based at Algiers, Mers-el-Kebir, and Jijel and linked by coastal surveillance radars.[4]

The Algerian navy's two 2,325-ton Kilo-class (type 877E) submarines are equipped with six 533-mm torpedo tubes, long-range torpedoes with active/passive homing, and pattern active/passive homing torpedoes and mines. These submarines were refitted in 1995 and 1996. They are active, but still seem to have little operational training. Algeria used to have two additional Romeo-class submarines, but these left the fleet in 1989 and are now restricted to training. As a result, Algeria has sought to acquire up to two more Kilos. The purpose and mission of Algeria's submarine force is unclear. Its operating standards are as low as those of most Third World navies. Algeria could not use these submarines effectively against a modern Western navy, and it is unclear how they would be used against Libya or Morocco.

The Algerian navy's major surface ships are more capable. The navy has 3 Mourad Rais–class, 1,900-ton ASW frigates (ex-Soviet Koni-class), armed with four 76-mm and four 30-mm guns, twin launcher SA-N-4 Gecko surface-to-air missiles (with a maximum range of 15 kilometers or 8 nautical miles and a speed of Mach 0.9). There are also ASW rocket launchers, mine rails, and depth charges. The ships date back to the early and mid-1980s. The ships have relatively modern air-to-surface radars and fire control systems, but they only have decoys and chaff launchers as countermeasures and do not have torpedo tubes. They are all active, but one ship is used for training purposes. One ship was refitted in Russia during 1997–2000, and has returned to service. A second ship is to be refitted, but no date has been announced.

There are three 660-ton Burya-class missile corvettes (ex-Soviet Nanuchka-class) armed with SS-N-2Cs (active radar or IR homing to 46 kilometers or 25 nautical miles), twin launcher SA-N-4 surface-to-air missiles, and two 57-mm guns. There were delivered as new ships during 1980–1982. One completed a refit in 1998–2000, and a second is scheduled to be refitted, but no date has been announced.

There are two 540-ton Chinese-designed Type 802 or Djebel Chinoise-class coastal patrol corvettes each armed with one 76-mm gun, two twin 40-mm guns, and twin 23-mm guns. They lack effective fire control systems but do have a surface search radar. The ships were delivered in 1985 and 1990, and the second ship ran into financing problems and is not fitted with a main gun. Neither seems fully combat operational.

The navy also has 9 Osa I and II 210–245-ton missile fast attack craft, plus 2 nonoperational 210-ton Osa-I class attack craft. They are each armed with four SS-N-2A antiship missiles with infrared and radar homing, and four 30-mm guns. The SS-N-2A is an aging system vulnerable to countermeasures, but has a maximum speed of Mach 0.9 and range of 46 kilometers (25 nautical miles) with semi-active radar or IR homing. These ships are rarely seen at sea, and it is unclear whether more than 6 Osa II-class craft and their weapons systems are fully operational. They were delivered in the late 1970s and early 1980s and need refitting and reengining.

Algeria has at least 12 active 200-ton Kebir-Class (Brooke Marine) patrol boats with one 76-mm gun each, plus two twin 25-mm guns and two twin 14.5-mm guns, and the navy has ordered 15—although financing problems have delayed construction and delivery of the additional ships. Six have been transferred to the Coast Guard. These boats have surface search radars, but do not have modern countermeasures or serious aid defense capabilities.

The navy's amphibious strength is large enough to give Algeria a potential capability to conduct landings against Morocco or Libya. It includes two British-made 2,450-ton LSLs (capacity 240 troops, 7 tanks, 1 helicopter) and one 834-ton Polnochny B-class LSM (capacity 180 troops, 6 tanks).

The navy also operates 1 survey ship, 2 support ships, 11 oceangoing minesweepers, a number of tugs, 12 fishery protection craft, SSC-3 coastal defense missiles, and 2 Beechcraft Super Knight 200T aircraft with weather radars. These aircraft are only capable of visual reconnaissance. The 500-man coast guard is under navy command. It has 29 small ships and 2 more are under construction. In addition to the Kebir-class ships, it has 7 El Mouderrib-class 388-ton patrol craft with twin 14.5-mm guns; 5 Baglietto-class 44-ton patrol craft with 20-mm guns; and 4 El Mounkid-class patrol craft used for search and rescue missions.

The Algerian navy has reasonable ship strength and a number of modern combat surface ships that have considerable antiship missile capability by regional standards and may have or be acquiring SS-N-25 missiles. Its air defenses and countermeasure capabilities are more limited, however; and a number of its ships are obsolescent and poorly equipped in terms of their sensors and weaponry. It has poor operational performance, overall readiness, training, and equipment quality. It could not defend itself adequately against Western strike aircraft or antiship missile attacks, but would probably be able to defeat either the Moroccan or Libyan navies.

Air Forces

Algeria's air force had roughly 10,000 actives in 2004. It emerged as a modern force as the result of an expansion that took place in the mid-1970s after the clashes between Algerian and Morocco. It had 175 combat aircraft and 93 armed helicopters. The air force was organized along Soviet lines, although Pakistan provided advisers and pilots and Egypt provided air training. Its main missions are the defense of Algerian cities and conducting air defense and attack operations in the event of a conflict with Morocco or Libya. It has bases in central Algeria at Ain Oussera, Blida, Boufarik, and Bou Sfer; near the Moroccan border at Bechar/Oukda, Mecheira, Oran, and Tindouf; and near the Libyan border at Biskra. There are also dispersal bases at Ozukar and Sidid bei Abbas.

The combat strength of the Algerian air force is organized into regiments. In 2004 it had three fighter ground attack regiments, one with 28 Su-24s and two with 28 MiG-23BNs. Algeria is reported to have ordered 22 Su-24s from Russia in October 2000. Deliveries were to start in November 2000 and all were to be delivered and in service by late 2001. The Su-24s were to be the same SU-24M (Fencer D) model already in service in Algeria and were to be taken from Russia's operational inventory, with some upgrading and reconditioning.

The air force had five fighter regiments, one with 20+ MiG-29C/UB, one with 10 MiG-25s, one with 30 MiG-23B/Es, and two with 30 MiG-21MFs. The air force had two reconnaissance squadrons, one with 6 MiG-25Rs and one with 6 Su-24Es. Some reports indicate Algeria also had four Su-24 MR (Fencer E) reconnaissance aircraft.[5]

With the exception of Algeria's 48 Su-24s and MiG-29s, whose designs date back to the 1980s, Algeria's 175 combat aircraft are now badly dated. The Su-24s and MiG-29s are the only aircraft with modern avionics; the capability to fight effectively in night, all-weather, and BVR air-to-air combat; or the ability to use air-to-ground ordnance with high effectiveness. Algeria's attack aircraft lack the avionics, sensors, all-weather navigation aids and computers to take advantage of modern precision-guided weapons.

There were two maritime reconnaissance squadrons in 2004, with 15 Super King Air B-200Ts, but it is unclear that all these aircraft are operational. Algeria had a large numbers of training aircraft, some of which are part of its combat strength. They included three MiG-21Us, five MiG-23Us, and three MiG-25Us.

Unless it receives additional modern aircraft, Algeria faces serious long-term modernization problems. Many U.S. and French experts also seriously question the merit of past Algerian attempts to try to reconfigure its aging Soviet systems to use Western technology. These experts feel that re-engineering Soviet fighters and trying to upgrade Soviet electronics and avionics would raise the life-cycle cost of such equipment above the cost of new Russian or Western equipment.

There were a total of 65 attack helicopters, organized into a regiment. They included 30 Mi-17Js, 33 Mi-24s, and 30 aging Mi-8s and Mi-17s. Russia delivered six Mi-171 upgraded helicopters employing the Geofizika night vision technology, with 36 more to follow.[6] The air force had 63 heavy transport helicopters, including 2 Mi-4s, 5 Mi-6s, 46 Mi-8/17s, and 10 AS 355s. Algeria had an extensive supply of fixed wing transport and VIP aircraft, including 10 C-130Hs, 6 C-130H-30s, 9 IL-76s, 2 Falcon 900s, 3 Gulfstream IIIs, and 2 F-27s.

Algeria's surface-to-air missile forces are organized into three surface-to-air missile regiments. In 2004, there were two major regiments with a total of 30–35 SA-3 and 50–60 SA-6 launchers and one with a total of 30–35 SA-8 launchers. It had three brigades of air defense artillery units with unguided 85-mm, 100-mm, and 130-mm weapons. The Algerian air defense C^{4}I, air defense and warning system, and radar sensor net are now obsolescent and lack modern battle management and electronic warfare capability.

The Algerian air force has no real combat experience, and training is outdated and poorly organized for large-scale attack or air defense operations. Reconnaissance, electronic warfare, and countermeasure capabilities range from poor to mediocre. Maintenance standards are poor and some aircraft are virtually in storage because of a lack of trained manpower and support capability.

The Algerian air force also suffers from limited and obsolescent C^{4}I/BM capability as well as serious problems in the quality and modernization of its air control and warning capability. Its SA-3, SA-6, and SA-8 units and air defense brigades have low readiness and operational capability and poor aircraft and munitions operability and technology. Algeria seems to have poor to mediocre electronic warfare and countermeasure capability and does not seem to have received the level of technical support and upgrading that the USSR provided to Libya.

Paramilitary and Security Forces

Part of Algeria's military weakness is explained by the fact that it faces far more serious internal threats than foreign ones. Beginning in 1992, Algeria has had to actively fight a bitter civil war with horrible abuses and atrocities on both sides. At present, the main function of its military and paramilitary forces is to fight this civil war and maintain the power of the regime. No quarter is given on either side, and much of the government's internal security forces, including virtually all of the 100,000-man Legitimate Self-Defense Force, is little more than an armed rabble. The Legitimate Self-Defense Force is a force of poorly trained and organized local militias that have sometimes carried out massacres and bloody reprisals of their own.

The government's formal paramilitary forces and security apparatus are composed of the army, air force, navy, and the national gendarmerie (the national police). The less formal elements include the communal guards (a local police) and local self-defense forces. The U.S. State Department reports that all of these elements are involved in counterinsurgency (COIN) and counterterrorism operations and are under the control of the government. All have been responsible for numerous and serious human rights abuses.

The best-organized paramilitary forces include the 1,200-man Republican Guard, which is a small elite security force with AML-60s and M-3s. They also include the gendarmerie, which is a force of 25,000 men. This force is assigned to the Ministry of Defense and has 44 AML-60 and M-3 armored vehicles, 200 Fahd armored personnel carriers, and 28 Mi-2 helicopters. It is reasonably well trained, is organized along military lines, and has played a major role in the government's efforts to assert control over the FIS and in its armed clashes with Islamic fundamentalists. The 20,000-man National Security Forces have mediocre training and are equipped largely with small arms.

Libya

Libya has sought to shed its image as an extremist state and supporter of terrorism in recent years. It seems to have reached a settlement over its terrorist attacks on UTA and Pan Am passenger aircraft and to have halted most support for terrorist groups. It agreed in late 2003 to give up its efforts to acquire and deploy weapons of mass destruction and allow inspection by the International Atomic Energy Agency. Libya did so partly because of years of frustration and failure in various political and military adventures, and partly because of the impact of UN and U.S. sanctions, growing economic problems, and the need to deal with a low-level Islamic extremist insurgent threat.

The Libyan armed forces have, however, been sharply affected by Qadhafi's eccentricities and his past efforts to eliminate military ranks and create a people's army. They are divided into an army, navy, and air force, but there are large numbers of both men and women who have at least a paper assignment to paramilitary forces like the People's Militia, Revolutionary Guards Corps, and People's Cavalry Force. The army operates Libya's surface-to-surface missile forces, the National Air Defense Command is part of the air force, and the navy controls the coast guard.

The trends in Libyan military forces are shown in Figure 4.15. On paper, Libya still retains large military assets. Libya's land forces comprise a total of 2,020 tanks 1,130 AIFVs, 990 APCs, 444 SP artillery, 647 towed artillery, and 830 MRLs. Its air forces consist of 400 combat aircraft and 41 attack helicopters. Its naval forces comprise 1 submarine, 2 major surface ships, 8 missile patrol craft, 2 mine warfare ships, and 3 amphibious ships. These totals are impressive for a relatively small country, but much of this force is in storage or nonoperational, combat readiness is exceptionally low, and modernization rates are very poor.

The true result of Libya's military buildup during the 1970s and 1980s is a vast weapons inventory that has turned Libya into the world's largest military parking lot, and Libya's military capabilities are unlikely to evolve much beyond this stage in the foreseeable future. Libya does not have modern military forces; it has a modern military farce. Poor as Libya's forces are, however, Libya's neighbors cannot count on the permanence of the parking lot syndrome and ignore the sheer mass of Libya's arms holdings. Libya can engage in costly and prolonged confrontations and clashes in the border area with its other neighbors.

Land Forces

The Libyan army has a total active strength of only 45,000 men, including 25,000 badly trained conscripts. While the Libyan army is sometimes reported to have some 40,000 men in its People's Militia, this force is more a symbol of Qadhafi's ever changing ideology than a military force. The Revolutionary Guards Corps is at most a brigade-sized force with about 3,000 men and is equipped with tanks, armored personnel carriers, antitank guided weapons, air defense weapons, and helicopters. The People's Cavalry Force is a largely token force. The Libyan army seems to lack anything approaching an effective and well-trained reserve system.

Reports differ sharply over the organization of Libya forces. The IISS seems to be the most credible source and reports that the forces are organized into eleven Border Defense and four Security Zones and have 1 elite regime security brigade, 10 tank battalions, 10 mechanized infantry battalions, 18 infantry battalions, 6 paratroop/commando battalions, 4 surface-to-surface missile brigades, 22 artillery battalions, and 7 air defense artillery battalions. Another source indicates that the Libyan army is organized into 2–3 tank divisions, 2–4 mechanized infantry divisions, 2 independent tank brigades, and 2 independent mechanized brigades. It also has 3 independent tank battalions, 8 mechanized infantry battalions, a Republican Guard brigade, 12–13 paracommando battalions, 7 surface-to-surface missile brigades, 3 surface-to-air missile brigades, 41 artillery battalions, and 2 AA gun battalions.

Regardless of the exact totals, Libya only has about 25–33 percent of the manpower needed to man its strength of combat units and total

Figure 4.15
Libyan Force Trends: 1980–2004

Category/Weapon	1980	1985	1990	1995	2000	2002	2004
Defense Budget ($Current Billions)	0.448	0.709	1.39	0.967	1.3	—	—
Mobilization Base							
Men Ages 13–17	—	—	262,000	312,400	350,000	387,000	387,000
Men Ages 18–22	—	—	216,000	262,200	291,000	320,000	320,000
Manpower							
Total Active	53,000	73,000	85,000	80,000	65,000	76,000	76,000
(Conscript)	—	—	—	—	—	40,000	38,000
Total Reserve	—	—	40,000	40,000	40,000	40,000	40,000
Total	—	—	125,000	120,000	105,000	116,000	116,000
Paramilitary	—	7,000	5,500	—	—	—	—
Land Forces							
Active Manpower	45,000	58,000	55,000	50,000	35,000	45,000	45,000
(Conscripts)	—	—	—	25,000	25,000	25,000	25,000
Reserve Manpower	—	—	—	—	—	—	—
Total Manpower	—	—	—	—	—	—	—
Main Battle Tanks	2,400	2,800	2,300	2,210	2,025	985(1,040)	800(1,040)
AIFVs/Armored Cars/Lt. Tanks	990	1,200	1,635	1,640	1,630	1,438	1,000
APCs/Recce/Scouts/Half-Tracks	900	1,160	950	900	990	1,381	1,065
ATGM Launchers	3,000	3,000	3,000	3,000	3,000	3,000	3,000

continued

Figure 4.15 (Continued)

Category/Weapon	1980	1985	1990	1995	2000	2002	2004
SP Artillery	18	218	370	450	450	265	444
Towed Artillery	590	930	720	720	720	647	647
MRLs	250	600	650	700	700	564	830
Mortars	450	450	—	—	—	—	500
SSM Launchers	2	48	120	120	120	120	120
AA Guns	450	350+	600+	600	600	600	600
Lt. SAM Launchers	—	—	—	—	1,000+	1,000+	2,500+
Air & Air Defense Forces							
Active Manpower	4,000	8,500	22,000	22,000	22,000	23,000	23,000
Reserve Manpower	—	—	—	—	—	—	—
Aircraft							
Total Fighter/FGA/Recce	287	535	513	417	420	360	400
Bomber	17	7	4	6	6	6	6
Fighter	105	285	284	209	212	177	209
FGA/Fighter	0	0	0	0	0	0	0
FGA	140	204	206	164	194	172	172
Recce	25	7	13	12	11	11	11
COIN/CU	0	30	30	30	0	0	0
Airborne Early Warning (AEW)	0	0	0	0	0	0	0
Electronic Warfare (EW)	0	0	0	0	0	0	0
Maritime Reconnaissance (MR)	0	0	0	0	0	0	0
Combat Capable Trainer	25	14	—	—	21	—	23

Tanker	0	0	0	0	0	0	0
Transport	47	62	82	78	75	81	83
Helicopters							
Attack/Armed/ASW	26	42	35	52	52	41	41
Other	62	55	89	98	98	112	90
Total	88	97	124	150	150	153	131
SAM Forces							
Batteries	12	12	33	39	39	39	39
Heavy Launchers	300	76?	150?	236	236	236	236
Naval Forces							
Active Manpower	4,000	6,500	8,000	8,000	8,000	8,000	8,000
Reserve Manpower	—	—	—	—	—	—	—
Total Manpower	4,000	6,500	8,000	8,000	8,000	8,000	8,000
Submarines	3	6	6	4	2	2	1 (4)
Destroyers/Frigates/Corvettes	2	10	10	6	7	5	2
Missile	1	10	10	6	7	3	2
Other	1	0	0	0	0	2	0
Missile Patrol	14	25	24	24	21	13 (8)	8 (22)
Coastal/Inshore Patrol	11	5	23	8	8	—	—
Mine	0	7	8	8	8	6	2
Amphibious Ships	5	3	5	5	5	4 (1)	3 (2)
Landing Craft/Light Support	1	—	4+	10	10	12	12
ASW/Combat Helicopter	0	—	31	30	32	7	7

Source: Adapted by Anthony H. Cordesman from data provided by U.S. experts; and IISS, *The Military Balance, 2001–2002, 2003–2004.*

equipment pool—a factor that explains why so much of its major combat equipment is in storage. Even its best combat units are under strength and have severe training and leadership problems. These manpower problems are compounded by tight political control, promotion based on political favoritism, and training that is often limited to small units and erratic. As has been noted earlier, Qadhafi also rotates officers arbitrarily to prevent coup attempts, and restricts some forms of training because he regards them as a threat to his security.

In 2004 the Libyan army had some 2,020 main battle tanks. Its operational holdings, however, only included some 800 tanks: 145–200 T-72s, 100 T-62s, and 500 T- T-55s. The other 1,225 tanks were in storage, including some 1,040 T-55s, 70 T-62s, and 115 T-72s. Many of both the operational and stored tanks had significant maintenance problems, and Libya was actively negotiating with Russia and the Ukraine in 2000 for modernization and overhaul contracts for these tanks, as well as for its other armor and much of its artillery.

The army had some 130 armored reconnaissance vehicles, including 50 BDRMs and 70 EE-9 Cascavals—a small portion of the number Libya had originally purchased. There were 1,000 aging BMP-1 armored infantry fighting vehicles and about 990 APCs, including 750 BTR-50s and BTR-60s, 100 OT-62s and OT-64s, 40 M-113s, and 100 EE-11 Urutus. These holdings represented far too many types of APCs to allow for effective support and maintenance. Their armament and armor were dated and often of low quality and in disrepair. Like Libya's tanks, many of its other armored vehicles were in storage or had serious maintenance problems. Only a few battalion-sized elements of Libyan armor had even moderate effectiveness in offensive and maneuver operations.

Libya's artillery strength included some 647 major towed artillery weapons, 444 self-propelled artillery weapons, and 830 multiple rocket launchers—many not operational. The towed weapons included 42 105-mm M-101s, 190 D-30 and 60 D-74 122-mm weapons, 330 130-mm M-46 weapons, and 25 M-1937 152-mm weapons. The self-propelled artillery included 130 2S1 122-mm weapons, 160 Palmaria and 14 M-109 155-mm weapons, and 60 2S3 and 80 DANA 152-mm weapons. Libya's multiple rocket launchers included 300 Type 63 107-mm weapons, and 200 BM-11, 230 BM-21, and 100 RM-70 122-mm weapons. Libya also had over 500 82-mm and 120-mm mortars, and some M-160 160-mm mortars. Libya also had some 40 FROG-7 and 80 Scud B surface-to-surface missile fire units. (Some reports indicate an additional 450–500 North Korean No dong missiles but have not been confirmed.)

This artillery strength was numerically impressive, but once again, much of it was in storage or not operational. Libya had poor standardization in terms of weapon and ammunition types. It also lacked the training, organization, and sensors and C[4]I equipment to conduct combined arms operations, maneuver effectively, switch fires rapidly, target beyond visual range, and conduct efficient counterbattery operations.

Libya's antitank weapons included roughly 3,000 ATGW launchers, with Milans, AT-3 Saggers (some mounted on BDRMs), AT-4 Spigots, and AT-5 Spandrels. These antitank guided weapons are effective against any tank other than the M-1A and possibly T-80, but Libya does not normally provide effective live-fire training under realistic conditions. The army also had at least 220 M-40A1 106-mm recoilless rifles, and large numbers of antitank rocket launchers.

Nothing approaching an accurate count of Libya's operational light air defense weapons is available. Some estimates indicate that the army had an inventory of about 600 air defense guns, including large numbers of radar-guided ZSU-23-4 SP and ZU-23 23-mm weapons, M-53 and M-59 30-mm weapons, L/70 40-mm weapons, and 92 S-60 57-mm weapons. Libya also had large numbers of SA-7, SA-9, SA-13, and Crotale light surface-to-air missiles. Many of these weapons are also stored or have limited operational readiness. The overall air defense training of Libyan army forces is poor. The army had O1-E liaison aircraft and the Libyan air force could support it with 34 transport and liaison helicopters. These included 18 CH-47s and 34 Mi8/Mi-17 transport helicopters, 5 AB-206s, and 11 SA-316s.

Libya's combat support, service support, and logistics units and system are capable of little more than sustaining peacetime garrison operations and occasional set-piece exercises. They would break down quickly in the event of war. The army seems to have no real training using support and logistics capabilities at even the major combat unit level.

In summary, Libya's army and paramilitary forces have little military effectiveness. While a few regular army brigades and some independent elements may have moderate effectiveness, Libya can do comparatively little to make use of its massive inventory of land weapons. Training and readiness are very poor. Libya's erratic equipment purchases make logistics, support, and maintenance a military nightmare. Some purchases seem to be made with no regard to whether the equipment will have any military utility or can be absorbed into Libya's force structure. Nearly half the army's equipment is in storage or has limited operational availability, and overall leadership and organization are poor. Even Libya's better units would have difficulty fighting anything other than static defensive battles.

Naval Forces

The Libyan navy and coast guard have a nominal strength of 8,000 men, but may only have 4,000–4,100 actives. The navy has significant combat ship strength, but little real-world war-fighting capability for anything more than surprise or hit-and-run missions. Maintenance and manpower readiness are poor. The navy has little ability to operate outside of coastal waters, and its sea training and patrol activity are far below the level needed for high military proficiency. It cannot count on significant air support in an encounter with a Western navy, and has negligible offensive capability beyond launching a few missiles.[7]

Jane's reports that the navy has its headquarters at Surt, naval bases at Al-Khums and Tobruq, a submarine base at Ras Hilal, a naval air station at Al-Girdabiyah, a naval infantry battalion at Sidi Bilal, and working ports at Tripoli, Derna, and Benghazi. The IISS reports main naval bases at Tripoli, Benghazi, Derna, Tobruk, Sidi Bilal, and Al-Khums.

The Libyan navy's main combat forces consist of 2 aging Foxtrot-class fleet submarines (6 were delivered, but 5 are nonoperational), 3 missile corvettes, 2 guided missile frigates, 2 guided missile corvettes, 14 missile patrol craft (a number in semi-nonoperational reserve), and 5 ocean minesweepers. Libya also had 5 landing ships (2 in reserve), 3 LCTs, 1 training ship, 1 support ship, 1 diving ship, 10 transport ships, 1 salvage ship, 2 floating docks, and 7 coastal tugs. According to the IISS, Libya's operational strength included 2 submarines, 2 frigates, 3 corvettes, 13 missile patrol boats, 6 mine countermeasure vessels, 4 amphibious vessels, and 9 support ships.

Libya has done a poor job of creating operational naval forces. Libya once had six 1,950-ton ex-Soviet Foxtrot-class submarines that were delivered between 1976 and 1982. These were export versions of the submarine from a reactivated production line and were obsolescent when delivered. They were armed with ten 533-mm torpedo tubes and had Soviet Type 53 active/passive and SEAT-60 passive homing torpedoes (15-kilometer range) homing torpedoes. They were only fully operational as long as the crews were trained and supported by the former Soviet Union (FSU), and the ships were maintained by the FSU. This does not seem to have been the case since 1984, and there have been no regular undersea patrols since that time. One submarine sank in 1993. It was raised but was not returned to service. Libya was seeking to overhaul and modernize its remaining submarines when UN sanctions were imposed, but its remaining ships are now so obsolete that there is little point in such modernization. Only two of its submarines are now operational, and only one—the Al-Khybedr—makes occasional surface patrols.

Libya retains two missile frigates, 1,900-ton ex-Soviet Koni-class vessels, delivered in 1986 and 1987. They each were armed with four SS-N-2C Styx missiles (83-kilometer range), four 76-mm guns, four twin 30-mm guns, SA-N-4 Gecko surface-to-air missile launchers, and four 406-mm torpedo tubes. They could fire Soviet Type 40 active/passive antisubmarine torpedoes. These two frigates lack some of the sensors and electronics of Soviet ships but are relatively modern. Both ships are active, but have not had any significant modernization since they were delivered in the late 1980s. Libya's capability to fully operate these two ships in combat is uncertain.

Libya has two 660-ton Soviet Nanuchka II–class corvettes with four SS-N-2C missiles (83-kilometer range), SA-N-4 Gecko surface-to-air missile launchers, and two twin 57-mm guns. It originally had four. One was sunk by the U.S. Navy on March 24, 1986. Another, the *Tariq Ibn Ziyad* (formerly the *Ean Mara*), was severely damaged by the U.S. Navy on March 25, 1986, but was repaired in the FSU and returned to service. It and *Ean Zara* seem to be quasioperational. Another, the *Ean al-Gzala,* has not been at sea for four years and may have been stripped for parts.

Libya has eight 311-ton Combattante IIG-class missile patrol boats, delivered in 1982–1983. Each has with four Otomat Mark I/II launchers (60–80 kilometers) and 12 76-mm guns. Only some of these ships are crewed and operational. Libya's missile patrol craft also include six 245-ton OSA-II class boats, delivered during 1976–1980, each with four SS-N-2C Styx antiship missile launchers (83 kilometers) and two twin 30-mm guns. It is uncertain that their antiship missiles are fully operational.

Libya still has other patrol craft in its navy, including one 100-ton Poluchat-class torpedo recovery vessel, four Garian-class large patrol craft, and three Benina-class large patrol craft. It is not clear that any of these craft are now truly operational.

The navy still has five 804-ton Soviet Natya-class oceangoing mine sweepers in inventory. These represent a moderate threat because they can lay mines with little warning, though Libya has already used commercial cargo ships to lay mines in the Red Sea, and this kind of asymmetric warfare does not require combat ships. At least five are operational, and possibly six. They are used for coastal patrols and training, and have never been observed in minesweeping exercises.

The Libyan navy has five amphibious ships and three LCTs in inventory. These ships include two 2,800-ton PS-700 class landing ship-tanks (240 troops and eleven tanks each). Both have not been modernized since the late 1970s but are operational. One, however, may have been transferred to commercial service. There are three Turkish-made 600-ton landing craft-tanks (100 troops and 5 tanks each), but their operational status is doubtful. Libya has a number of training and support ships. They include one 500-ton training ship, one support ship, a salvage ship, a diving tender, seven tugs, and ten 2,412-ton transport ships. These latter transport ships are now in commercial service and can be used to either move heavy equipment and troops or lay mines.

The navy has the support of two air force squadrons with a total of 32 armed helicopters, including 25 Mi-14 Haze ASW helicopters and 7 SA-321 Frelon and SA-341 Super Frelon ASW and SAR helicopters. They are worn and obsolete and most are not operational. They can carry AM-39 Exocets but do not seem to do so. The operational status of the Hazes is unclear. There were five SA-316B support helicopters assigned to support the police and customs, but none now seems to be operational. The air force also provides support in the naval reconnaissance and surface support roles. In addition, the navy had several shore batteries, including some with Otomat, SSC-3, and SS-N-2d missiles (95 kilometers). Libya also has some kind of coastal radar and surveillance system, and may be using part of its popular militia in a coast watch mission.[8]

The Libyan navy's overall training and readiness levels were never high and declined sharply after the mid-1980s, possibly because of decreased funding and a resulting drop in support from the FSU. The navy suffered badly from UN sanctions, but acquired some Ukrainian technical support in 1995 and received more parts deliveries and repairs after 1998. Some individual ship crews have moderate capability but overall training, readiness, and command standards are low, and weapons systems and combat electronics are rarely exercised. Libya cannot operate as an effective fleet. Maintenance seems to be as badly organized as most aspects of Libyan military activity.

Air Forces

In early 2004, Libya's air force and air defense command had a nominal strength of 23,000 men, although some estimates put the total below 18,000. It had approximately 400 combat aircraft and 41 armed helicopters. It had at least 10 large air bases with shelters and land-based antiaircraft defenses. It had major air bases at Umm Aitqah, Banghazi-Banina, El Adem (General Abdel Nasser), Tripoli (Okba Ibn Nafa), Bengazi, and Zawiyat-El Bayda. Libya's forces were concentrated at bases in Tripoli and Benghazi. There are dispersal bases at Ghat, Sebha, and Tobruk.

Libya's air force includes some advanced aircraft types, but much of it is obsolete or ineffective. It still has one bomber regiment with 6 Tu-22 Blinders. The USSR transferred 12 long-range Tu-22 bombers in April 1979, and 5–6 may still be marginally operational.[9] These aircraft are obsolete medium-altitude bombers that are very vulnerable to both air-to-air and surface-to-air missile defenses.

Libya's air force has 7 fighter ground attack squadrons (down from a peak of 13), 9 fighter squadrons, 2 reconnaissance squadrons, an attack helicopter squadron, and numerous fixed and rotary wing helicopter units. Its squadrons are organized into regiments, some of which have both defense and attack missions but are normally either strike/attack or air defense regiments.

The only Libyan air force unit with advanced combat aircraft was a single Su-24 strike/attack squadron with only six aircraft. Soviet transfers of six to ten Su-24Ds 1989 gave Libya a more serious long-range strike fighter, which was then one of the most advanced aircraft in Soviet inventory. The Su-24 is a twin-seat swing wing aircraft that is roughly equivalent in terms of weight to the F-111, although it has nearly twice the thrust loading, and about one-third more wing loading. It is deployed in five variants. Although it is not clear which variant Libya has received, it seems likely that it is the expert version of the Su-24D.

Although its avionics are now a decade old, the SU-24D has a sophisticated radar warning receiver, an improved electronic warfare suite, an improved terrain avoidance radar, a bean, satellite communications, and an aerial refueling probe and can deliver electro-optical-, laser-, and radar-guided bombs and missiles. The Su-24 can carry payloads of nearly 25,000 pounds and can operate missions with a 1,300-kilometer radius when carrying 6,600 pounds of fuel. With a more typical 8,818-pound (4,000-kilogram) combat load, it has a mission radius of about 790 kilometers in the LO-LO-LO profile and 1,600 kilometers in the LO-HI-LO profile. With extended-range fuel tanks and airborne refueling, the Su-24 can reach Italy, Egypt, Chad, and even Israel, although the latter mission would be demanding, would have to be flown out of an eastern base like Benghazi, and would allow only a limited time over the target.[10] The Su-24 can carry up to three AS-7 Kerry radio command–guided missiles (5-kilometer range), one AS-9 These can include a mix of Kyle antiradiation missiles with passive radar guidance and an active radar fuse (90-kilometer range), three AS-10 Karen passive laser-guided missiles with an active laser fuse (10-kilometer range), and three AS-11 Kilter antiradiation missiles with passive radar guidance and an active radar fuse (50-kilometers range). It also can carry up to three AS-12 Kegler antiradiation missiles with passive radar guidance and an active radar fuse (35-kilometer range), three AS-13 Kingposts, and three AS-14 Kedge semiactive laser-guided missiles with a active laser fuse (12-kilometers range). The Su-24 also can carry demolition bombs, retarded bombs, cluster bombs, fuel air bombs, and chemical bombs.

Libya has acquired a limited long-range refueling capability in order to ease many of the problems that it would face in conducting such strikes. While Libya did not get the modified IL-76 that it had originally sought from the USSR for refueling its Su-24s, it did get the technology that it needed to convert one of its C-130s into a tanker for airborne refueling from West German firms. Libya has experimentally refueled its Mirage F-1s and is seeking a modifiable cargo jet so that it will be able to refuel at higher speeds and without the maneuver problems inherent in trying to refuel a jet fighter from a propeller aircraft.

Libya's six additional fighter ground attack units had a total of 40 MiG-23BNs, 15 MiG-23Us, 30 Mirage 5D/DEs, 14 Mirage 5DDs, 14 Mirage F-1ADs, and 53 Su20/-22s. Some sources indicate there also was still a COIN squadron with 30 J-1 Jastrebs. Libyan attack aircraft performed poorly in close air support and interdiction missions in Chad, and there are no reports that Libya has since developed effective training systems and facilities or has practiced meaningful exercises in low-altitude combat, air defense evasion, countermeasure penetration, or combined arms with the

Libyan army. Libya did, however, have relatively modern AS-7, AS-9, and AS-11 Soviet air-to-surface missiles and some antiradiation missiles. It had large stocks of unguided bombs, including napalm, and seems to have had some laser-guided bombs.

The Libyan air force had nine fighter squadrons, equipped with a total of 15 Mirage F-1ED/BDs, 45 MiG-21s, 70 MiG-23 Flogger Es, 70 MiG-25s, and 3 MiG-25Us. These air defense fighters had aging avionics with limited capability, but advanced air-to-air missiles like the AA-6 Acrid, AA-7 Apex, AA-8 Aphid, R-530, and R-550 Magic. Only the Mirage F-1s and some MiG-25s had more than very limited long-range intercept and look-down shoot-down capabilities, and Libya had major pilot training problems and had lost a number of aircraft to accidents.

Libyan air-to-air training levels and air combat tactics have remained far inferior to those of U.S. pilots and well-trained Middle Eastern pilots like those of Egypt and Saudi Arabia. Libya seems to have had a serious shortage of even mediocre combat pilots and may be dependent on Soviet and other foreign officers and technicians for effective ground-controlled intercepts. It still does not seem to be able to conduct effective electronic warfare.

Libya had two reconnaissance squadrons with four Mirage-5DRs and seven MiG-25Rs. If the MiG-25R is similar to Soviet versions, it has infrared, side-looking radar, and ESM capabilities. Libya also has some remotely piloted vehicles. This gives Libya a reasonable mix of basic reconnaissance capabilities, but it seems doubtful that it has organized to use them effectively. It may well rely on the slow daylight photography system of most Third World nations.[11]

Libya had an attack helicopter squadron with 29 Mi-25s and 12 Mi-35s. Some of these helicopter forces seemed to had moderate training, but the helicopters were equipped obsolescent avionics and with AT-2 Swatter air-to-ground missiles. Readiness was poor and some aircraft had been lost to accidents.

Other air units included seven transport squadrons, transport helicopters, and training aircraft. The transport squadrons had 23 An-26, 7 CH-130s, 2 L-100-20s, three L-100-30s, 6 G-222s, 25 IL-76s, and 15 L-410s. There was a heavy transport helicopter squadron with 17 CH-47Cs, a medium transport squadron with 34 Mi-8s and Mis-17s, and a light unit with 11 SA-316s and 5 AB-206s. The transport forces seemed to be the most effective element of the Libyan air force.

These holdings are impressive in terms of sheer numbers, but the air force still has severe shortages of competent pilots and training levels and quality were poor. The overall readiness of Libyan aircraft is poor, and most Libyan aircraft are now dated or obsolescent in terms of avionics and upgrades. The operational sustainability of even Libya's most combat-ready aircraft is limited, and most bases can evidently only support limited numbers of types of aircraft. The air force seems to be dependent on foreign technicians for training, maintenance, and sometimes even combat missions. Overhaul and combat repair capability is limited, and combat sustainability is poor. Maintenance is mediocre, and an overcentralized and politicized command structure limits air defense proficiency and makes it difficult to effectively plan coherent air attacks and sustain significant numbers of sorties. In 2004, up to half of Libya's aircraft were in storage or of negligible operational value, and the air force still seemed to rely heavily on Syrian, FSU, North Korean, and Pakistani "instructors" to fly actual missions.

Land-Based Air Defenses

Libya's land-based air defenses are badly dated and are largely obsolete or obsolescent. They are, however, among the largest such defenses in the Middle East. In 2004, Libya's air defense forces included four SA-5 brigades, each with two battalions of six launchers (48 total), four air defense gun batteries, and a radar company. According to some reports, these SA-5 units were partly manned by some Russian personnel.

There were five regional surface-to-air missile commands, each with five to six brigades with 18 SA-2 launchers each (160–180 launchers total); two to three brigades with 12 SA-3 launchers each (100 to 110 launchers total); and three brigades with 20–24 SA-6s (130–150 launchers) and some SA-8s each. These missile units were loosely integrated by Libya's Senezh air defense and command system. Both the SAM units and command system of the Air Defense Command were heavily dependent on expatriate support personnel, who sometimes seem to act as operators. Overall capability is low, except for those forces with direct foreign "supervision."

Libya's major surface-to-air missile forces were first placed under an Air Defense Command, which was formed in 1973, the year of the October War. This command was merged and reorganized in the late 1980s after the U.S. air strikes on Libya. The Air Defense Command seemed to be somewhat more effective than the air force. In 2000, it was reasonably well-deployed and provided overlapping coverage by a range of different missiles along the coastal areas. The network of radars was badly dated, however; as were its electronic warfare and command and control assets.

If British reports are correct, Libya still uses a modification of the same kind of Central Command Center and regional Sector Operations Centers that the former Soviet Union set up in Algeria, Syria, Iraq, and many other countries dependent on FSU arms and aid. The Libyan system, however, was upgraded more than Algeria's before the breakup of the Soviet Union. Soviet high capacity communications systems have been installed, and extensive use is made of buried land lines to reduce the electronic and physical vulnerability of the system. The Air Defense Command also seems to have been upgraded with relatively modern early warning radars and electronic warfare equipment.

These problems led Libya to make the acquisition of new surface-to-air missiles a key priority once sanctions were suspended in April 1999. Libya sought a new air defense system from Russia based on the S-300PMU1 and S-300PMU2 air defense missiles and their supporting radars and C⁴I systems. Price was still a major issue during the Russian-Libyan negotiations in 2000, however; and Libya evidently looked at Belarus and Ukrainian versions of the same system.[12]

The obsolescence of Libya's aging Soviet-supplied surface-to-air missiles is scarcely its only problem. Operator training and proficiency remains low. The system is overcentralized and has relatively a slow data process and limited automated analysis capability. Ergonomics and data interfaces are poor and the system is vulnerable to electronic warfare and antiradiation missiles. Overall alert rates are poor to mediocre, and Libyan operators have not fully adapted to the use of Soviet automated systems. It is also unlikely that Libya's electronic warfare assets give it much protection against the level of jamming and countermeasure technology that the United States deployed in Operations Desert Storm and Desert Fox.

Paramilitary and Security Forces

Like most North African states, Libya is better at internal repression than at dealing with foreign threats. Libya has a number of paramilitary forces and security services. They act as a means of controlling the power of the regular military and providing Qadhafi with security.

The data on such forces are uncertain and sources report very different details. There seems to be a 3,000-man Revolutionary Guard Corps (Liwa Haris Al-Jamahirya) to guard Qadhafi, with T-54/55/62 tanks, armored cars, APCs, multiple rocket launchers, and ZSU-23-4s and SA-8s, which are taken from the army inventory. There also seem to be up to 2,500 men in the Islamic Pan African Legion, which may have one armored, one infantry, and one paracommando brigade, although its total manpower strength could only man less than one brigade slice. The Islamic Pan African Legion has at least 75 T-54s and T-55s and some EE-9 MICVs. Roughly 700–1,000 men from the Islamic Pan African Legion were believed to be in the Sudan in 1988, but current deployments are unknown. There is also a People's Cavalry Force, which acts largely as a parade unit, and a people's militia with a nominal strength of about 40,000 men.

As is the case with other North African states, there are comparatively little reliable data on the operations of the government's security forces. The best unclassified reporting comes from the U.S. State Department, and much of this reporting provides reliable insights into the operations of the security forces. The U.S. State Department reports that Libya maintains an extensive security apparatus, consisting of several elite military units, including Qadhafi's personal bodyguards, local Revolutionary Committees, and People's Committees, as well as the "Purification" Committees, which were formed in 1996. The result is a multilayered, pervasive surveillance system that monitors and controls the activities of individuals.

Tunisia

Tunisia has always been a defensive military power. Until recently, its major threat has been Libya. At this point, it faces no serious external threat. Its armed forces are designed largely for border defense, internal security, and protection of key economic facilities. Tunisia lacks the active force and equipment strength necessary to deploy significant strength on either border in peacetime and keeps most of its units near urban centers. It does, however, have special units in the Sahara brigade that cover the border and provide a light screen of security forces.

The armed forces have a conventional organization and command structure, with a minister of defense and an army chief of staff, and an army, national guard, navy, and air force. The trends in Tunisian military forces are shown in Figure 4.16. Tunisia had total force with only some 35,000 men in 2004, including 23,400 conscripts. Its land forces comprised a total of 84 tanks, 149 AIFVs, 268 APCs, and 117 pieces of towed artillery. Its air force possessed 29 combat aircraft and 7 attack helicopters. Its naval forces had 6 missile craft and 13 patrol boats. These small equipment holdings make Tunisia an exception to the "militarism" of most North African states. Its force levels are far closer in size its real strategic needs than the force levels of any of its neighbors are to their needs, but vulnerability is the price of moderation.

Land Forces

The Tunisian army has a total of 27,000 men, of whom some 22,000 are conscripts with limited experience and training. Officer and career other ranks training and proficiency are good by Third World standards. Conscripts are selected to ensure they have a good basic education, but they serve for only twelve months. Overall training standards are physically rigorous, but conscripts gain little proficiency in combined arms and maneuver warfare. The total strength of Tunisia's organized reserves is currently unknown. There is little indication that they are well trained or organized or would be combat effective without months of reorganization and training.

The army was reorganized in the early 1990s to create three mechanized brigades (each with one armored regiment, two mechanized infantry regiments, one artillery regiment, and one air defense regiment), and the chain of command now flows down from the Army Chief of Staff to the First, Second, and Third Mechanized Brigades, the Saharan Brigade, and the Special Forces Brigade. The major Tunisian army base is in Tunis. One report indicates that a typical mechanized brigades is supposed to have a tank battalion with 42 main battle tanks, a mechanized battalion with 45

Figure 4.16
Tunisian Force Trends: 1980–2004

Category/Weapon	1980	1985	1990	1995	2000	2002	2004
Defense Budget							
($Current Billions)	0.114	0.437	0.388	0.262	0.340	—	—
Mobilization Base							
Men Ages 13–17	—	—	459,000	499,000	514,000	529,000	529,000
Men Ages 18–22	—	—	430,000	450,400	478,000	505,000	505,000
Manpower							
Total Active	28,600	35,100	38,000	35,500	35,000	35,000	35,000
(Conscript)	—	27,000	26,400	26,400	23,400	23,400	23,400
Total Reserve	—	—	—	—	—	—	—
Total	28,600	35,100	38,000	35,500	35,000	35,000	35,000
Paramilitary	2,500	9,500	13,500	23,000	12,000	12,000	12,000
Land Forces							
Active Manpower	24,000	30,000	30,000	27,000	27,000	27,000	27,000
(Conscripts)	—	26,000	25,000	25,000	23,400	22,000	22,000
Reserve Manpower	—	—	—	—	—	—	—
Total Manpower	—	—	—	—	—	—	—
Main Battle Tanks	0	68	98	84	84	84	84
AIFVs/Armored Cars/Lt. Tanks	85	110	139	114	114	123	54
APCs/Recce/Scouts/Half-Tracks	80	68	208	268	268	337	327

110

ATGM Launchers	—	—	—	565	565	600	600
SP Artillery	45	54	28	0	0	0	0
Towed Artillery	50	83	123	117	117	117	117
MRLs	0	0	0	0	0	0	0
Mortars	—	—	—	135	161	155	191
SSM Launchers	—	—	0	0	0	0	0
AA Guns	45	—	—	115	115	115	115
Lt. SAM Launchers	—	—	—	73+	73+	73+	74
Air & Air Defense Forces							
Active Manpower	2,000	2,500	3,500	3,500	3,500	3,500	3,500
Reserve Manpower	—	—	—	—	—	—	—
Aircraft							
Total Fighter/FGA/Recce	14	20	50	32	44	51	29
Bomber	0	0	0	0	0	0	0
Fighter	0	0	0	0	0	0	0
FGA/Fighter	0	0	0	0	0	0	0
FGA	0	12	19	15	15	15	12
Recce	0	0	0	0	0	0	0
COIN/OCU	14	8	11	5	5	5	5
Airborne Early Warning (AEW)	0	0	0	0	0	0	0
Electronic Warfare (EW)	0	0	0	0	0	0	0
Maritime Reconnaissance (MR)	0	0	0	0	0	0	0
Combat Capable Trainer	12	7	—	23	25	24	0
Tanker	0	0	0	0	0	0	0
Transport	4	6	4	7	11	13	16

continued

Figure 4.16 (Continued)

Category/Weapon	1980	1985	1990	1995	2000	2002	2004
Helicopters							
Attack/Armed/ASW	1	1	0	7	7	7	15
Other	31	49	0	35	37	38	43
Total	32	50	41	42	44	45	58
SAM Forces							
Batteries	0	0	0	0	0	0	0
Heavy Launchers	0	0	0	0	0	0	0
Naval Forces							
Active Manpower	2,600	2,600	4,500	5,000	4,500	4,500	4,500
Reserve Manpower	—	—	—	—	—	—	—
Total Manpower	—	—	—	—	—	—	—
Submarines	0	0	0	0	0	0	0
Destroyers/Frigates/Corvettes	1	1	1	0	0	0	0
Missile	0	0	0	0	0	0	0
Other	1	1	1	0	0	0	0
Missile Patrol	2	2	6	6	6	6	6
Coastal/Inshore Patrol	18	17	14	17	14	13	13
Mine	2	—	0	0	0	0	0
Amphibious Ships	0	—	0	0	0	0	0
Landing Craft/Light Support	—	—	—	—	3	2	2
ASW/Combat Helicopter	—	—	0	0	0	0	0

Source: Adapted by Anthony H. Cordesman from data provided by U.S. experts; and IISS, *The Military Balance,* 2001–2002, 2003–2004.

armored personnel carriers, a motorized rifle battalion with 34 light armored vehicles, an artillery battalions with 18 guns, an antitank-guided weapons battery with 12 fire units, an antiaircraft battalion, an engineer battalion, a reconnaissance company, and logistic, transport, and supply elements. The army also has one reinforced Sahara brigade, one special forces brigade, and one engineer regiment. These formations are generally relatively small. A Tunisian brigade generally has only about 5,000 men, and a regiment of only 1,000 to 1,500 men.

The army has slowly acquired 84 main battle tanks (30 M-60A1s and 54 M-60A3s). It has 54 obsolescent Steyr SK-105 Kuerassier light tanks, and 69 relatively low-grade armored reconnaissance vehicles, including 24 Saladins and 45 AML-90s. It has about 268 APCs, including 140 M-113 A-1/2s, 18 EE-11 Urutus, and 110 Fiat F-6614s.

Tunisia is learning how to use modern armor but is, at best, capable of largely static defense in the event of a major attack by Libya or Algeria. Its armor is poorly standardized, and many items are aging or obsolete. Overall, Tunisian armored forces have continuing maintenance and standardization problems. They are trained well enough for light defensive operations but have limited maneuver and offensive capability.

The army has made improvements in its artillery strength in recent years, and most Tunisian artillery battalions now seem to have a full complement of weapons. Total strength has risen from 80 artillery pieces in 1988, to about 117 weapons in 1998, and 123 weapons but this strength is all in towed weapons that cannot maneuver with armor. Tunisia has 48 M-101A1/A2 105-mm towed weapons, 12 M-114A1 155-mm towed weapons, and 57 M-198 155-mm towed weapons. It also has 95 81-mm mortars and 66 4.2-inch and 107-mm mortars. It has been able to employ these weapons defensively in small batteries but has limited maneuver, command and control, counterbattery, and BVR targeting capability.

The antitank weapons strength of the Tunisian army is limited, although it includes some modern types like the Milan and TOW. In 1998, Tunisia had a mix of 500 Milan and 100 MGM-71A TOW antitank guided missile launchers, including 35 TOW antitank guided missile launchers mounted on M-901 armored vehicles. It had 140 57-mm M-18 recoilless rifles and 70 M-40A1 106-mm recoilless rifles. It also had 300 M-20 3.5-inch and 300 LRAC-89 89-mm antitank rocket launchers. Few antitank crews have high readiness or realistic training against mobile armor.

The air defense weapons of the Tunisian army include 48 aging RBS-70 and 25 M-48 Chaparral surface-to-air missile fire units. Tunisia also has 100 M-55 20-mm and 15 M-1939/Type 55/-65 37-mm AA guns. These weapons are capable of providing limited low-altitude point defense. Tunisia has no heavy surface-to-air missile systems in either the army or the air force.

Tunisia is only beginning to acquire the elements of modern armored warfare training and faces massive problems in rationalizing its diverse inventory, which now consists of far too many erratic small buys of incompatible or hard-to-support equipment. The Tunisian army badly needs to improve its manpower management, increase emphasis on professionalism and career incentives, and improve support and logistic capabilities. At present, most units cannot operate effectively for any length of time unless they are near their peacetime depots and casernes, and even then, the logistic and service support system is not particularly effective.

Naval Forces

The 4,500-man Tunisian navy is based at Bizerte, Sfax, LaGoulette, and Keliba. It has nearly 700 conscripts, but ship crews tend to be relatively professional. In early 2001, its holdings included 3 missile fast attack craft, 3 missile patrol craft, 2 regular fast attack craft, 5 large patrol craft, 21 coastal patrol craft, 14 small patrol craft, and 5 training/survey ships. Two more regular fast attack craft were on order, and a number of its patrol craft were not truly operational or were laid up.

The navy had three Combattante III–class 425-ton missile guided fast attack craft, each with two quad MM-40 Exocet antiship missile launchers. The Exocet missiles have active radar homing and a maximum range of 70 kilometers (40 miles). They also have one 76-mm gun, and two twin 40-mm Breda guns. There is an air-to-surface search radar, but there are no surface-to-air missile launchers. These ships were all delivered in the mid-1980s and need modernization and refits. Tunisia also had three Bizerte-class 250-ton missile patrol craft with eight Aerospatiale SS12M and four 37-mm guns. The SS-12M is a very short-range missile (5.5 kilometers or 3 nautical miles) with a small warhead. These Bizerte-class ships are all operational but are badly in need of refits.

Other combat ships included three 120-ton Haizhui-class ex-PRC fast attack craft, each with four 25-mm guns. These ships were delivered in the mid-1990s, and are all operational. They included three 250-ton Bizerte-class large patrol craft with 20-mm guns that date back to the late 1970s, but have had their guns updated and are operational. The navy had ten coastal patrol craft. These included four Istiklal-class 80-ton coastal patrol craft with twin 20-mm guns and surface search radars; and six 38-ton coastal patrol craft with 20-mm guns. The remaining vessels include five Kondor-class 377-ton patrol craft with twin 25-mm guns, and five Bremse-class 42-ton patrol craft with twin 14.5-mm guns, operated by the coast guard, plus eleven 32-ton coastal patrol craft operated by customs, four Gabes-class 18-ton patrol boats, and six training/survey ships.

While Tunisia is capable of operating most of its individual ships, it does not seem to be organized for any kind of fleet or combined arms operations. The Tunisian navy is adequate for patrol missions in local waters, but is not capable of engaging the navies of any of Tunisia's neighbors. It is not strong enough to survive an attack by the Libyan or Algerian navies.

Overall logistic and maintenance capabilities seem to be limited. At the same time, Tunisia can probably count on European, U.S., and/or Egyptian naval support in the event of any offensive attack by its neighbors—none of whom can risk confronting these naval powers.

Air Forces

The 3,500-man Tunisian air force (TAF) has some 700 conscripts. It has slowly developed relatively effective manpower policies and is gradually developing the capability to train and retain competent pilots and air crews. It is expanding steadily and had 29 combat aircraft and 15 attack helicopters in early 2004. Its main bases are in Bizerte-Sidi Ahmed, Bizerte-La Karouba, and Sfax-El Maou. Its forces are organized largely along squadron lines with air defense, COIN, and attack training.

The TAF has done a good job of absorbing and operating its 12 F-5E/Fs in the fighter ground attack role and has gradually developed a limited capability for daytime air-to-air combat. It is unclear whether Tunisia still suffers from a shortage of trained F-5 pilots. It also had five MB-326s in the COIN role. Some its 5 MB-326B and 12 L-59 training aircraft seem to have limited combat capability.

These aircraft are reasonably effective in attack missions against troops that are not equipped with modern manportable or short-range guided missiles—a limitation that may present serious problems if the Tunisian air force must deal with regular Libyan or Syrian forces. None of its combat aircraft has advanced air defense or attack capabilities, however; and Tunisia needs 12–24 more modern combat aircraft during the next 5–8 years. Given potential threats, it needs a modern all-weather air defense fighter with beyond-visual-range air-to-air intercept capabilities.

The air force has 2 S-208M liaison aircraft and a training wing with 18 combat-capable SF-260s, 5 MB-326s, and 12 L-59s. It also has a wing with 43 helicopters, including 6 SA-313s, 3 SA-316s, 15 AB-205s, 12 UH-1s, 6 AS-350Bs, and 1 AS-365F. These helicopters give Tunisia's armed forces considerable tactical air mobility for a force of their size.

In broad terms, Tunisia has a primitive air control and warning system and limited sensor coverage of Tunisian air space. It is not organized to fight at the air force level, as distinguished from the formation or squadron level. It has the same problems in terms of retaining and training good personnel as does the army and is heavily reliant upon foreign contractors for logistics and maintenance. Some effort has been made to give the Tunisian air force a combined operations capability based on U.S. doctrine and training concepts, but success is evidently still very limited.

Paramilitary and Security Forces

Tunisia's paramilitary forces consist of a National Guard with 10,000–12,000 men. It has a naval element with some 13 patrol craft and an aerial element with 5 P-6B aircraft and 8 SA-318 and SA-319 helicopters. The National Guard shares responsibility for internal security with the police. The police operate in the capital and a few other cities. In outlying areas, their duties are shared with, or ceded to, the National Guard. Both forces are under the control of the minister of interior and the president.

As is the case with other North African states, there is comparatively little reliable detailed data on the operations of the government's security forces. The best unclassified reporting comes from the U.S. State Department, and much of this reporting provides reliable insights into the operations of the security forces.

FUTURE PATTERNS IN MILITARY DEVELOPMENT

The irony behind the region's problems in military effectiveness is that it is not clear that they really matter all that much to the nations concerned. The Maghreb states have no real foreign enemies, and the future patterns of security in the Maghreb depend more on internal stability and the health of each economy than on strategic goals, military doctrine, and force plans. This helps explain several at the most probable trends in the military developments in both the region and each country within it:

- The Maghreb states are likely to expand their internal security forces and modernize some of their major weapons, in spite of diminished military requirements. This expansion will largely be the result of continuing internal and external political tension, bureaucratic momentum, and demographic pressure. Once the expansion of military forces takes place in a less developed country, it has a powerful "ratchet effect" that has nothing to do with local threats or military requirements. The lack of alternative employment and career paths, coupled with the role of the military in the nation's power structure and the sheer momentum of global military expansion and technological change, leads to military expansion almost regardless of local political conditions.

- Morocco's forces should be able to limit the Polisario threat to militarily, politically, and economically acceptable levels. Morocco should also be able to maintain adequate relations with Algeria so that both states can avoid an arms race. There is no guarantee that this will happen, however; and it is impossible to rule out a long-term return to some form of arms race, or conflict, between Algeria and Morocco.

- Libya will continue its failure to properly man and modernize its military forces, in spite of the suspension of UN sanctions in 1999. As the analysis later in this book shows, it will continue to seek weapons of mass destruction. These Libyan efforts will pressure the other states in the region to maintain higher levels of military spending than they desire.

- Libya and Algeria will experience steadily growing problems with obsolescence. Much of their equipment is worn, aging, improperly maintained, and hard to support. The end result will be a steady decline in the operational readiness of older types of equipment and growing problems in supporting the overall force mix in combat. Given Algeria's and Libya's limited revenues, both states are likely to drop in net military effectiveness, even though they may acquire enough equipment to have an apparent increase in force strength.

- The internal tensions within each country's military forces will make military politics more important than military effectiveness. In Algeria, the army does not serve the country—it owns it. The army suspended elections in 1992 in order to deny Islamic fundamentalists political control of the country. Since that time, Algeria has been engaged in a confusing, bloody internal conflict between the military government and Islamic extremists. Morocco's war with the Polisario now ties down its military and has led to significant economic strains. A civil regime has taken over power from Bourguiba in Tunisia, but the incompetence and profiteering of the civil authorities may lay the groundwork for an eventual military or radical Islamic takeover. Qadhafi has reportedly purged the Libyan military, but it is virtually the only body that could replace him. Qadhafi has endured numerous coup attempts.

- The end of the Cold War has effectively ended the threat of communism and Soviet penetration into the region's military forces. Islamic fundamentalism now represents the greatest threat of instability and is the rival of the secular and regular military forces in Algeria, Tunisia, and Egypt.

- Creeping proliferation is likely to remain a problem. Algeria and Libya have taken some steps to acquire weapons of mass destruction, and Libya has chemical weapons. This proliferation, however, is now severely limited by funding problems and access to technology.

MAJOR TRENDS IN MAGHREB MILITARY FORCES

The trends in the strength of Maghreb military forces become clearer when they are examined by major category of military strength. The data on manpower have already been discussed.

- Figures 4.17 and 4.18 display the trends in armor, tanks, and artillery in the Maghreb. As Figure 4.17 shows, Libya possesses over 4,600 armored vehicles (although some 1,040 tanks are in storage and useless), Algeria has over 2,600, Morocco has over 1,800, and Tunisia has over 400. These inventory figures provide a rough indication of the amount of armor any given force can bring to bear, although Libya can operate only a comparatively small portion of the armor it holds, other nations hold an unknown amount of this armor in storage, and North African armies are not organized to deploy and support massed armored forces.

- Figures 4.18 through 4.20 show the number and type of tanks in each country. Algeria and Libya have the largest holdings, but the disparities in operational tanks are not as great as the total inventory data might indicate. Algeria and Libya have rough parity in operational tanks. Morocco has about half as many tanks, and Tunisia less than 100. Egypt has about four times more operational tanks than the largest North African power, and these include

Figure 4.17
Total North African Armor in 2003–2004

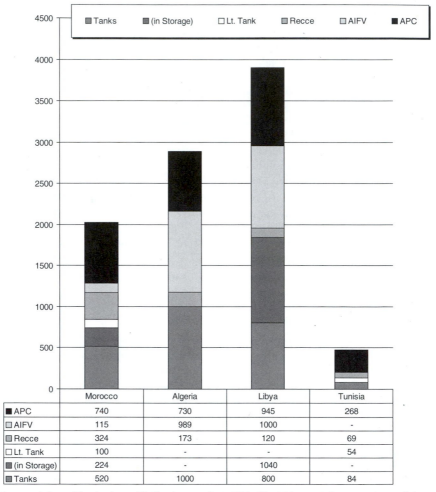

	Tanks	(in Storage)	Lt. Tank	Recce	AIFV	APC

	Morocco	Algeria	Libya	Tunisia
■ APC	740	730	945	268
☐ AIFV	115	989	1000	-
▦ Recce	324	173	120	69
☐ Lt. Tank	100	-	-	54
▨ (in Storage)	224	-	1040	-
▦ Tanks	520	1000	800	84

Source: Adapted by Anthony H. Cordesman from IISS, *The Military Balance*, various editions; and JCSS, *The Military Balance in the Middle East*, various editions.

1,300 M-60A3 and 555 M-1A1 tanks. Morocco has a comparatively large percentage of relatively modern M-60A3s, but a total of only 240. The 350 T-72s in Algerian forces, and 145 in Libyan forces, are roughly comparable to the M-60A3 in quality. However, the export version proved to be far more vulnerable in the Gulf War than many experts had previously estimated and suffered from a lack of modern fire control systems.

Figure 4.18
Total North African Main Battle Tanks in 2003–2004

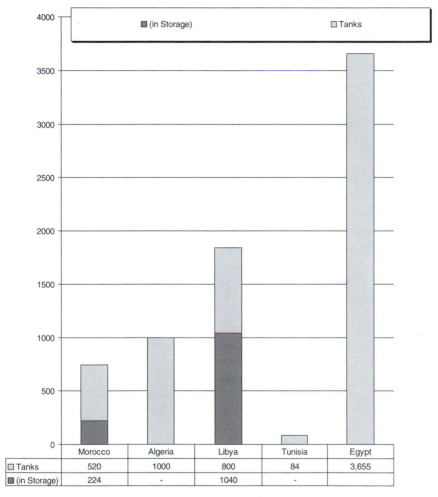

	Morocco	Algeria	Libya	Tunisia	Egypt
☐ Tanks	520	1000	800	84	3,655
◼ (in Storage)	224	-	1040	-	

Source: Adapted by Anthony H. Cordesman from IISS, *The Military Balance*, various editions.

- Figure 4.21 compares the number of armored fighting vehicles. Morocco has large holdings but also has large numbers of different types that are difficult to support. Algeria and Libya also have large holdings and reflect better standardization of equipment types, but they also have large holdings of BMP-1s. The BMP-1 has also proved to be more vulnerable than was initially estimated and to have poor war-fighting ergonomics.

Figure 4.19
Total North African Medium Active Main Battle Tanks by Type in 2003–2004

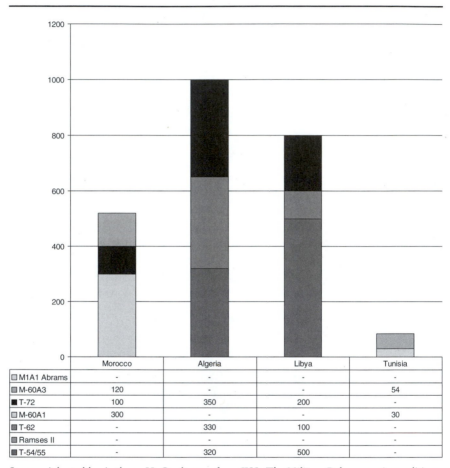

	Morocco	Algeria	Libya	Tunisia
☐ M1A1 Abrams	-	-	-	-
☐ M-60A3	120	-	-	54
■ T-72	100	350	200	-
☐ M-60A1	300	-	-	30
■ T-62	-	330	100	-
■ Ramses II	-	-	-	-
■ T-54/55	-	320	500	-

Source: Adapted by Anthony H. Cordesman from IISS, *The Military Balance*, various editions.

- Figures 4.22 and 4.23 indicate that Libya owns over 1,800 pieces of artillery, Algeria has over 700, Morocco has just under 400, and Tunisia has over 100. Egypt's totals reflect considerably less emphasis on artillery than on armor. The totals for self-propelled weapons provide a rough indication of the capability to carry out combined arms maneuver and to rapidly deploy artillery to a new sector of a front. Algeria and Morocco have moderate to good self-propelled artillery strength relative to their armor. The figures for Libya reflect total inventories. Once again, many of these holdings are in storage and Libya only has the manpower and support capabilities to fight a fraction of its total holdings.

Figure 4.20
Total North African Medium-Quality and Modern Active Main Battle Tanks in 2003–2004

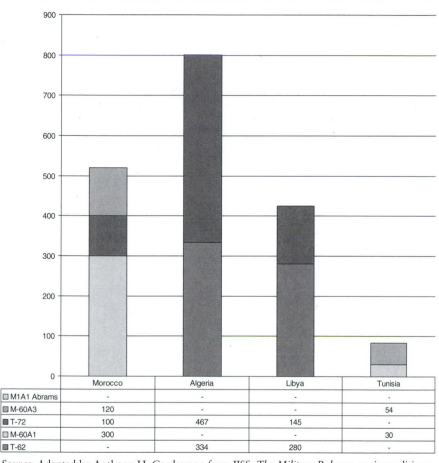

	Morocco	Algeria	Libya	Tunisia
☐ M1A1 Abrams	-	-	-	-
☐ M-60A3	120	-	-	54
■ T-72	100	467	145	-
☐ M-60A1	300	-	-	30
■ T-62	-	334	280	-

Source: Adapted by Anthony H. Cordesman from IISS, *The Military Balance*, various editions.

• Figures 4.24 through 4.27 display data on combat aircraft, armed helicopters, and electronic warfare aircraft. Libya has 420 fixed wing aircraft and 52 armed helicopters. Algeria has 181 fixed wing aircraft and 65 armed helicopters, Morocco 89 and 24, and Tunisia 44 and 7. As Figure 4.20 shows, however, the Maghreb countries have limited numbers of modern combat aircraft and relatively few reconnaissance, air control and warning, and electronic warfare aircraft. Algeria is the only nation now actively modernizing this portion of its military forces.

Figure 4.21
Total North African Medium Quality and Modern Other Armored Fighting Vehicles in 2003–2004 (Less APCs)

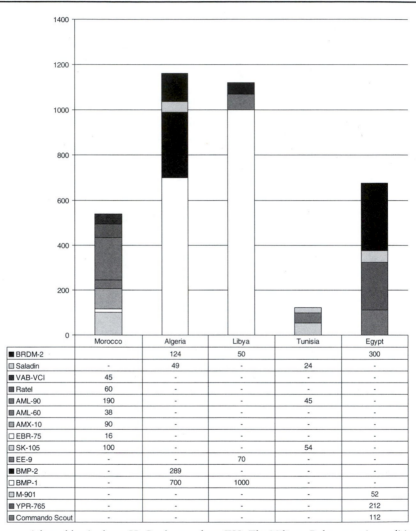

	Morocco	Algeria	Libya	Tunisia	Egypt
■ BRDM-2		124	50		300
☐ Saladin	-	49	-	24	-
■ VAB-VCI	45	-	-	-	-
■ Ratel	60	-	-	-	-
■ AML-90	190	-	-	45	-
■ AML-60	38	-	-	-	-
■ AMX-10	90	-	-	-	-
☐ EBR-75	16	-	-	-	-
☐ SK-105	100	-	-	54	-
■ EE-9	-	-	70	-	-
■ BMP-2	-	289	-	-	-
☐ BMP-1	-	700	1000	-	-
☐ M-901	-	-	-	-	52
■ YPR-765	-	-	-	-	212
■ Commando Scout	-	-	-	-	112

Source: Adapted by Anthony H. Cordesman from IISS, *The Military Balance*, various editions.

- Morocco and Tunisia have no true high-performance combat aircraft. Libya has a token force of 6 Su-24s, but the rest of its holdings are aging 1970s and 1980s designs, and many are inactive or in storage. Egypt, in contrast, has a force of 143 modern F-16CDs, plus 35 F-16A/Bs and 18 Mirage 2000s. It is the only power neighboring the region with airborne battle management as-

Figure 4.22
Total North African Artillery in 2003–2004

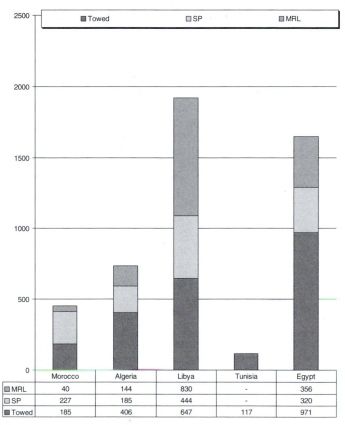

	Morocco	Algeria	Libya	Tunisia	Egypt
▨ MRL	40	144	830	-	356
▫ SP	227	185	444	-	320
▪ Towed	185	406	647	117	971

Source: Adapted by Anthony H. Cordesman from IISS, *The Military Balance*, various editions.

sets and anything approaching modern electronic air warfare capabilities. The large air orders of battle of Algeria and Libya conceal what is becoming a technological museum.

- Figure 4.28 shows the strength of land-based air defense forces. Libya has a large quantity of major and light SAM launchers and 600 AA guns. Algeria has SA-6 and SA-3 major SAMs and 895 AA guns. Morocco and Tunisia have significantly smaller amounts of SAMs and AA guns. Almost all of these weapons systems are obsolescent or obsolete, however; and no North African state has a modern system of sensors, battle management systems, airborne early warning, and integrated air/land-based command and control systems to operate and support its surface-to-air missile systems.

Figure 4.23
North African Self-Propelled Artillery in 2003–2004

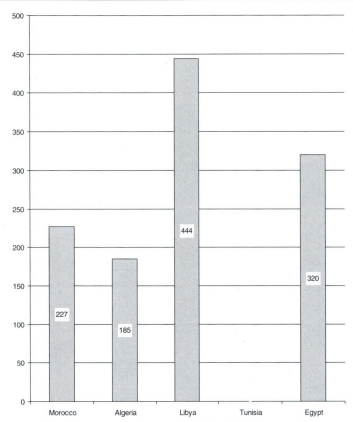

Source: Adapted by Anthony H. Cordesman from IISS, *The Military Balance*, various editions.

- Figures 4.29 and 4.30 display the total naval ship strength in North African forces. The number of ships in inventory, however, provides only a limited picture of comparative ship quality and war-fighting capability. The country-by-country analyses that follow show that many ships are poorly modernization and weaponized and have uncertain operational status or are inactive. Libya, in particular, has many ships that are in reserve to the point where it is questionable whether they will ever be active again or are actually little more than hulks. Most North African combat ships have had little modernization, their air defense capabilities are weak, and their antiship missile defenses are very poor. No North African navies can operate as coherent fleets or task forces or in effective joint operations.

Figure 4.24
North African Total Fixed Combat Aircraft and Armed Helicopters in 2004

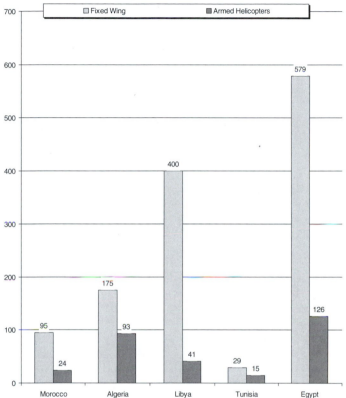

(Totals include all combat-capable, fixed-wing aircraft)

Source: Adapted by Anthony H. Cordesman from IISS, *The Military Balance*, various editions.

- Figure 4.31 shows the strength of the Polisario forces challenging Morocco in the Western Sahara. These forces are small compared to the totals for Morocco. At the same time, Morocco cannot attack them systematically in their relative sanctuary in southern Algeria and must defend a vast territory. This presents a military challenge in spite of an extensive barrier defense system and Morocco's massive advantage in force numbers.

Taken together, these figures provide a good picture of the overall military balance in the region, to the extent that such a balance exists. The figures dealing with equipment types also show the massive obsolescence of much

Figure 4.25
North African Active Bomber, Fighter, FGA, and Strike Combat Aircraft by Type in 2004

(Does not include stored, unarmed electronic warfare or combat-capable recce and trainer aircraft)

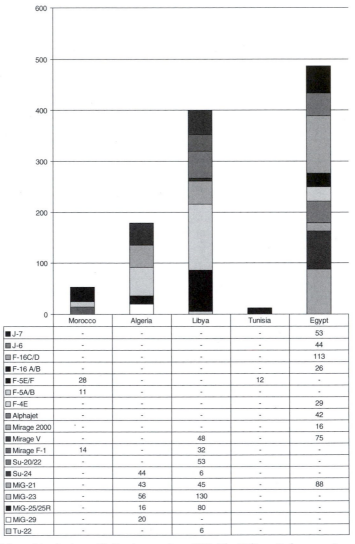

	Morocco	Algeria	Libya	Tunisia	Egypt
■ J-7	-	-	-	-	53
▨ J-6	-	-	-	-	44
▨ F-16C/D	-	-	-	-	113
■ F-16 A/B	-	-	-	-	26
■ F-5E/F	28	-	-	12	-
▢ F-5A/B	11	-	-	-	-
▢ F-4E	-	-	-	-	29
▨ Alphajet	-	-	-	-	42
▨ Mirage 2000	` -	-	-	-	16
■ Mirage V	-	-	48	-	75
■ Mirage F-1	14	-	32	-	-
▨ Su-20/22	-	-	53	-	-
■ Su-24	-	44	6	-	-
▢ MiG-21	-	43	45	-	88
▢ MiG-23	-	56	130	-	-
■ MiG-25/25R	-	16	80	-	-
▢ MiG-29	-	20	-	-	-
▢ Tu-22	-	-	6	-	-

Source: Adapted by Anthony H. Cordesman from IISS, *The Military Balance*, various editions.

126

Figure 4.26
North African Medium- and High-Quality Combat Aircraft by Type in 2003–
2004

(Does not include stored, unarmed electronic warfare or combat-capable recce
and trainer aircraft)

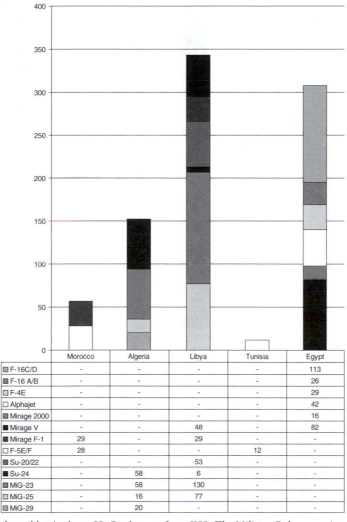

	Morocco	Algeria	Libya	Tunisia	Egypt
▨ F-16C/D	-	-	-	-	113
▤ F-16 A/B	-	-	-	-	26
▢ F-4E	-	-	-	-	29
▢ Alphajet	-	-	-	-	42
▨ Mirage 2000	-	-	-	-	16
▪ Mirage V	-	-	48	-	82
▪ Mirage F-1	29	-	29	-	-
▢ F-5E/F	28	-	-	12	-
▨ Su-20/22	-	-	53	-	-
▪ Su-24	-	58	6	-	-
▨ MiG-23	-	58	130	-	-
▢ MiG-25	-	16	77	-	-
▨ MiG-29	-	20	-	-	-

Source: Adapted by Anthony H. Cordesman from IISS, *The Military Balance*, various editions.

Figure 4.27
North African Active AEW, ELINT, and Electronic Warfare Aircraft by Type in 2003–2004

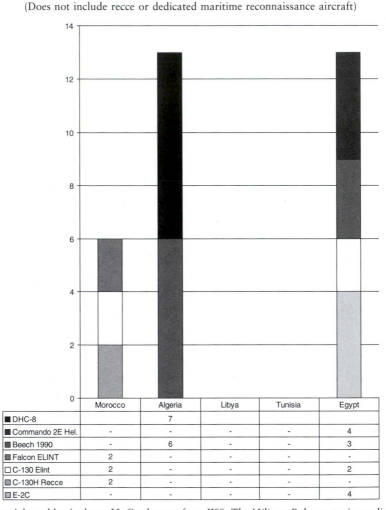

(Does not include recce or dedicated maritime reconnaissance aircraft)

	Morocco	Algeria	Libya	Tunisia	Egypt
■ DHC-8		7			
■ Commando 2E Hel.	-	-	-	-	4
■ Beech 1990	-	6	-	-	3
■ Falcon ELINT	2	-	-	-	-
☐ C-130 Elint	2	-	-	-	2
▨ C-130H Recce	2	-	-	-	-
▨ E-2C	-	-	-	-	4

Source: Adapted by Anthony H. Cordesman from IISS, *The Military Balance*, various editions.

of the Maghreb's military forces. As is discussed in detail in the chapters that follow, these figures also show the end result of a failed military buildup in Algeria and Libya and of decades of war in Morocco. As the country analyses in each chapter reveal, only Tunisia has been relatively immune to the region's tragedy of arms.

Figure 4.28
North African Land-Based Air Defenses in 2004

Country	Major SAM	Light SAM	AA Guns
Morocco	None	37 M-54 Chaparral 70 SA-7	200 ZPU-2 14.5mm 20 ZPU-4 14.5mm 40 M-167 Vulcan 20mm 60 M-163 Vulcan SP 90 ZU-23-2 15 KS-19 100mm
Algeria	1/24 SA-6 1/18 SA-3 SA-2	SA-7 SA-8 SA-8 1 SA-8 SA-9 SA-14 SA-16	895 guns 80 ZPU-2/4 14.5mm 100 20mm 105 ZU-23 219 ZSU-23-4 SP 150 M-1939 37mm 75 S-60 57mm 20 KS-12 85mm 150 KS-19 100mm 10 KS-30 130mm 725 guns 1 85mm regt. 1 100mm regt. 1 130mm regt.

continued

Figure 4.28 (Continued)

Country	Major SAM	Light SAM	AA Guns
Libya	Senez air defense command and control system 4/8/48 SA-5A 5/90-108 SA-2 3/24-36 Twin SA-3 2/48 SA-6	SA-7 SA-9 SA-13 24 Quad Crotale 1/20-24 SA-8	600 guns ZU-23, ZSU-23-4, M-53/59 30mm, S-60 57mm
Tunisia	None	48 RBS-70 25 M-48 Chaparral	100 M-55 20mm 15 T-55/56 37mm
Egypt	664 launchers 40/282 SA-2 53/212 SA-3 14/56 SA-6 12/78 I Hawk (4 Div./100 Btn.)	2,000 SA-7 Ayn as Saqr 20 SA-9 50 M-54 Chaparral SP 14/24 Crotale 72 Amoun Skyguard/ RIM-7F 36 quad SAM Ayn as Saqr 57mm, 85mm, 100mm	200 ZPU-2/4 14.5 mm 280 ZU-23-2 23mm 230- ZSU-23-4 SP 23mm 36 Sinai SP 23mm 200 M-1939 37mm 600 S-60 57mm 40 ZSU-57-2 SP 57mm 14/- Chaparral 2000 20mm, 23mm, 37mm, 36 twin radar guided 35mm guns Sinai radar-guided 23mm guns

Source: Adapted by Anthony H. Cordesman from IISS, *The Military Balance*, various editions; and *Jane's Sentinel*, various editions.

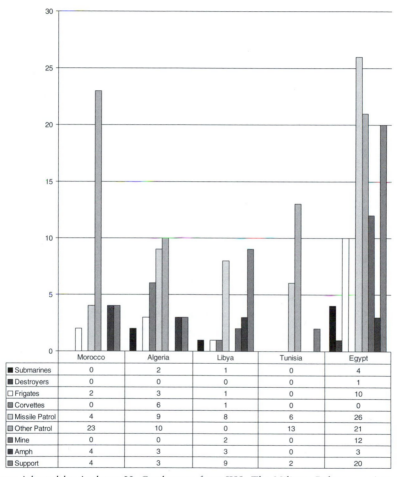

	Morocco	Algeria	Libya	Tunisia	Egypt
■ Submarines	0	2	1	0	4
■ Destroyers	0	0	0	0	1
□ Frigates	2	3	1	0	10
▨ Corvettes	0	6	1	0	0
▧ Missile Patrol	4	9	8	6	26
▨ Other Patrol	23	10	0	13	21
■ Mine	0	0	2	0	12
■ Amph	4	3	3	0	3
▨ Support	4	3	9	2	20

Source: Adapted by Anthony H. Cordesman from IISS, *The Military Balance*, various editions; and *Jane's Fighting Ships*, various editions.

131

Figure 4.30
North African Major Active Combat Ships in 2003–2004

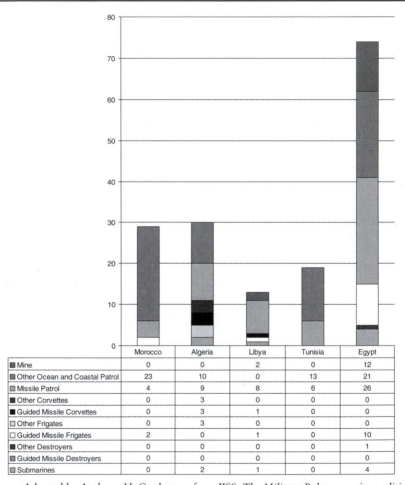

	Morocco	Algeria	Libya	Tunisia	Egypt
■ Mine	0	0	2	0	12
▨ Other Ocean and Coastal Patrol	23	10	0	13	21
▨ Missile Patrol	4	9	8	6	26
■ Other Corvettes	0	3	0	0	0
■ Guided Missile Corvettes	0	3	1	0	0
☐ Other Frigates	0	3	0	0	0
☐ Guided Missile Frigates	2	0	1	0	10
■ Other Destroyers	0	0	0	0	1
▨ Guided Missile Destroyers	0	0	0	0	0
▨ Submarines	0	2	1	0	4

Source: Adapted by Anthony H. Cordesman from IISS, *The Military Balance*, various editions;
and *Jane's Fighting Ships*, various editions.

Figure 4.31
Polisario Forces in 2004

(Sahrawi People's Liberation Army)

Manpower

Weapons

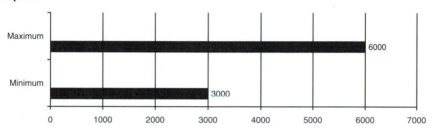

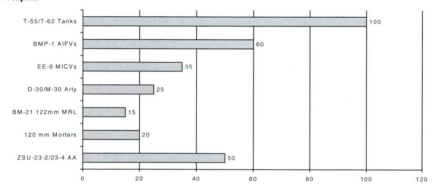

Other Equipment: Numbers Unknown

- Steyr SK-105 light tanks
- Panhard APCs
- Ratel 20 AFVs
- Eland armored reconnaissance vehicles
- AML-90
- AT-3 Sagger antitank guided missiles
- SA-6, SA-7, SA-8, SA-9 surface-to-air missiles

Source: Adapted by Anthony H. Cordesman from data provided by U.S. experts; IISS, *The Military Balance*; and *Jane's Sentinel*.

Chapter 5

The Arab-Israeli States

THE ARAB-ISRAELI MILITARY BALANCE

The "Arab-Israeli" states include Egypt, Israel, Jordan, Lebanon, Syria, and a Palestinian entity or protostate. Their forces have shaped by six Arab-Israeli wars, which took place during in 1948, 1956, 1967, 1970, 1973, and 1982. These conventional conflicts have had some elements of a broader regional conflict, and some Gulf countries have sent forces to such conflict in addition to the North African states mentioned earlier.

The Arab-Israeli wars of the past, however, have been followed by peace agreements between Israel and two of its neighbors and by major changes in the potential role of Arab states outside the immediate Arab-Israeli "confrontation" or "ring" states. Egypt and Israel—the two most important military powers in the region—have been at peace since the late 1970s, and Jordan reached a peace treaty with Israel on October 26, 1994. Lebanon has never been a significant conventional military power, or threat to Israel, although various Lebanese and Palestinian groups have launched attacks from Southern Lebanon, and Israel perceives groups like Hezbollah as a serious unconventional threat.

Iraq is the only nation outside the Arab-Israeli subregion that ever sent significant military forces into an Arab-Israeli conflict, and it only sent significant forces during the 1973 war. Iraq was also the only outside Middle Eastern military power to conduct long-range air or missile strikes against Israel. It fired Scud missiles at Israel during the Gulf War in 1991. (Israel used its long-range strike fighters to destroy Iraq's Osirak reactor a decade earlier.) The fall of Saddam Hussein's regime in 2003 has eliminated Iraq as both a conventional and a missile threat to Israel or any other power. At the same time, the peace proposal advanced by Crown Prince Abdullah of Saudi Arabia in 2002 received support from virtually every outside Arab power, and even former radical opponents of Israel like Libya seem to have abandoned any interest in serious military options.

These developments have made the "Arab-Israeli balance" a largely Israeli-Syrian balance in terms of conventional war fighting, although it remains possible that Egypt and/or Jordan could again become hostile to Israel in the future. One of the underlying realities that shapes the Arab-Israeli balance is that the peace between Egypt and Israel has never led either state to cease making a future war with the other a major unstated aspect of its military planning. Neither Egypt or Israel deploys its forces for such a war, but each state competes with the other in upgrading its conventional forces and prepares for the contingency that the other might attack it. The risk of such a conflict is also a major reason for Egypt's concern over Israel's monopoly of nuclear weapons. Ironically, the resulting arms race has been further fueled by massive U.S. military aid and transfers of advanced weapons and technology to both sates—aid and transfers that originated out of efforts to give both states an incentive to ensure they kept their peace agreement.

The situation is different in terms of asymmetric warfare. As has been touched upon earlier, there have been three significant asymmetric Arab-Israeli conflicts in recent years. The first was the "First Intifada" between Israel and the Palestinians of Gaza and the West Bank between 1988 and 1993. The second was a struggle between Israel and an allied Christian-led Lebanese force, and Shiite factions in Southern Lebanon led primarily by Hezbollah with Iranian and Syrian support. This war grew out of the Israeli occupation of Southern Lebanon in 1982, and lasted until Israel withdrew from Southern Lebanon in 2000. The third is the Israeli-Palestinian War, which began in September 2000, led to the collapse of the Arab-Israeli peace process, and has continued ever since.

The Israeli-Palestinian War is one of the most bitter and polarizing sources of tension in the Middle East. It has led to a brutal struggle in which Israel has exploited its vast superiority in conventional forces to attack Palestinian insurgents and terrorists in ways that have often produced significant civilian casualties and collateral damage. The Arab media is filled with the images of such Israeli military activity, and the Arab world has grown steadily more angry and hostile toward Israel. This same hostility has spilled over toward the United States, as Israel's only major ally and main weapons supplier. At the same time, the Palestinian side has used terrorist attacks against Israeli civilians and "soft" targets as its principle form of military action and has shown little ability to control its extremist and terrorist movements. Neither Israel nor the Palestinians have leadership that seems capable of moving toward peace unless it is forced to do so through sheer military exhaustion, and both peoples have become steadily more distrustful of the other side and less able to understand its motives and needs.

The Israeli-Palestinian War has not involved any direct intervention by outside powers, but Syria and Iran have provided extensive support to Hezbollah, and some support to Hamas, Palestinian Islamic Jihad (PIJ), and other anti-Israeli forces in all of these conflicts. Whether one labels such movements as terrorists, freedom fighters, or nonstate combatants is a matter of perspective. What is clear is that nonstate actors are beginning to play a steadily more significant role in the balance, and that states use them as proxies. Moreover, Israel has already struck at Syrian targets in retaliation for Syrian support of Hezbollah (and tacitly for Syrian support of Hamas and the PIJ). A serious conflict between Israel and Syria seems unlikely, but an escalation to a Syrian proxy war coupled with repeated Israeli retaliation is all too possible.

It is also unclear that nations like Egypt and Jordan can continue to ignore the steady escalation of fighting, and the anger their own people have toward Israel and the United States. The war is particularly destabilizing for Jordan, which has a Palestinian majority. At the same time, it unifies virtually every faction in Egypt. War between Israel and Egypt or Jordan still seems unlikely, but it is increasingly possible. It would also become much more likely if Israel should take any action that were to lead to massive Palestinian civil casualties or a massive expulsion or flight of Palestinians from the West Bank.

Proliferation is a serious problem as well. As is described in depth in Chapter Ten, Israel is a major nuclear power and may have chemical and biological weapons. Israel has the air and missile power to use such weapons to strike at targets anywhere in the great Middle East. Syria has extensive chemical weapons and missiles with chemical warheads and may have biological weapons. Egypt ceased its nuclear weapons research program in the 1970s, but has continued with chemical and biological weapons research and may have small, aging stockpiles of chemical weapons. Moreover, states outside the subregion are coming to play another kind of role in the balance. Iran is acquiring long-range missiles, as well as weapons of mass destruction, though it pledged in 2003 to fully comply with the Nuclear Non-Proliferation Treaty (NNPT) and to allow challenge inspections by the International Atomic Energy Agency.

As is the case with North Africa, many states have far larger force postures than they can properly modernize and support. This is particularly true of Syria, whose concessional arms sales and loans from the former Soviet Union (FSU) and Warsaw Pact ceased when the FSU and the pact collapsed, after years of trying to rival Israel in military power. Much of Syria's conventional force posture is now obsolescent or obsolete, and its failure to properly modernize and "recapitalize" its forces has reached the crisis level.

Egypt and Israel have benefited from massive U.S. military assistance. Egypt, however, is still attempting to maintain a far larger inventory of its aging Soviet-bloc and non-U.S. equipment than it can afford to maintain, modernize, and sustain. Roughly one-third of its force posture is an obsolete and largely hollow shell that wastes resources that would be better spent on force quality than on force quantity.

Israel's forces are better modernized, but even Israel is forced to maintain a "high-low" force mix with substantial numbers of obsolete systems. It also is still heavily reliant on conscript and reserve manpower to free resources for arms imports and its heavily subsidized military industries, and it is unclear that this gives it the manpower quality and readiness it needs to take maximum advantage of its high-technology systems.

Jordan has made a series of painful trade-offs between force quantity and force quality, reducing numbers to pay for modernization, readiness, and training. Even so, Jordan simply has not been able to compete with Egypt and Israel in developing high-technology forces.

Lebanon has never had particularly effective military forces, and is still recovering from the impact of years of civil war. Syrian occupation forces still occupy the country, and independent forces like Hezbollah have arisen to replace the old militias that were largely disbanded at the end of the civil war. The Lebanese forces are badly undercapitalized and are likely to remain more oriented toward internal security than sustained conventional warfare.

The following figures illustrate the economic forces shaping the Arab-Israeli balance:

- Figure 5.1 provides a summary comparison of the current strength of Israeli, Egyptian, Jordanian, Lebanese, and Syrian forces.
- Figure 5.2 shows the trends in military expenditures and arms imports in constant dollars. Israel has a clear lead in military spending over any of its neighbors, but several factors need to be kept in mind. Israel must still plan for a larger Arab-Israeli conflict in spite of its peace treaties with Egypt and Jordan. Israel has substantially higher manpower and maintenance costs because of high salaries and costs, and Israel has been fighting a prolonged series of asymmetric wars while its Arab neighbors have not.

  Syria has had to maintain a high level of military spending in spite of the drop in arms imports shown in the following figures. It is still trying to compete with Israel at levels it cannot afford. The data show that Egypt obtained a substantial "peace dividend" in terms of military spending during the middle to late 1980s and reduced military domestic spending, but it is important to note that the figures do not seem to include U.S. grant aid to Egypt—which would sharply raise the total for Egyptian spending.

- Figure 5.3 shows more recent trends in military expenditures in current U.S. dollars from a different source, and provides a more realistic estimate of Egyptian spending. Israel's edge in military resources remains clear, although it has

Figure 5.1
The Arab-Israeli Balance: Forces in the Arab-Israeli "Ring" States in 2001—Part One

Category/Weapon	Israel	Syria	Jordan	Egypt	Lebanon
Defense Budget					
(In 2000, $Current Billions)	$7.0	$1.8	$0.488	$2.5	$0.846
Arms Imports: 1996–1999 ($M)					
New Orders	4,500	500	800	6,800	100
Deliveries	4,500	300	300	3,800	100
Mobilization Base					
Men Ages 13–17	281,000	1,042,000	274,000	3,634,000	213,000
Men Ages 18–22	270,000	853,000	245,000	3,437,000	195,000
Manpower					
Total Active	172,500	316,000	103,880	448,500	63,750
(Conscript)	107,500	—	—	322,000+	22,600
Total Reserve	425,000	396,000	35,000	254,000	—
Total	597,500	7120,000	139,000	702,000	60,670
Paramilitary	8,050	108,000	10,000	230,000	13,000
Land Forces					
Active Manpower	130,000	215,000	90,000	320,000	60,670
(Conscripts)	85,000	—	250,000+	22,600	—
Reserve Manpower	400,000	300,000	30,000	150,000	—
Total Active & Reserve Manpower	530,000	515,000	120,000	470,000	60,670

Figure 5.1 (Continued)

Category/Weapon	Israel	Syria	Jordan	Egypt	Lebanon
Main Battle Tanks	3,900	3,650 (1200)	1,246 (300)	3,960	327
AIFVs/Armored Cars/Lt. Tanks	408	3,305	241	740 (220)	125
APCs/Recce/Scouts	5,900	1,500	1,450	2,990 (1,075)	1,338
WWII Half-Tracks	500 (3,500)	0	0	0	0
ATGM Launchers	1,300	3,390+	610	2,660	250
SP Artillery	855	450	412	251	0
Towed Artillery	520	1,600	132	971	151
MRLs	198	480	0	156	23
Mortars	6,440	4,500+	800	2,400	377
SSM Launchers	48	72	0	18–24	0
AA Guns	850	2,060	416	834	220
Lt. SAM Launchers	1,298	4,055	1,184	1,146	—
Air & Air Defense Forces					
Active Air Force Manpower	36,000	40,000	13,400	30,000	1,700
Active Air Defense Command	0	60,000	0	80,000	0
Air Force Reserve Manpower	20,000	92,000	—	90,000	—
Air Defense Command Reserve Manpower	0	—	0	70,000	0
Aircraft					
Total Fighter/FGA/Recce	446 (250)	589	106	583	(16)
Fighter	0	310	41	363	0
FGA/Fighter	405	0	0	0	0
FGA	25	154	65	133	0

140

Recce	10	14	0	20	0
Airborne Early Warning (AEW)	6	0	0	5	0
Electronic Warfare (EW)	37	10	0	10	0
Fixed-Wing	37	0	0	6	—
Helicopter	0	10	0	4	—
Maritime Reconnaissance (MR)	3	0	0	2	0
Combat Capable Trainer	26	111	2	64	3
Tanker	6	0	0	0	0
Transport	37	27	12	32	2
Helicopters					
Attack/Armed	133	87	16	129	0
SAR/ASW	6	—	—	—	—
Transport & Other	160	110	52	158	30
Total	299	197	68	287	30
SAM Forces					
Batteries	28	150	14	38+	0
Heavy Launchers	79	848	80	628	0
Medium Launchers	0	60	0	36–54	0
AA Guns	0	4,000	—	72+	—
Naval Forces					
Active Manpower	6,500	6,000	480	18,500	1,200
Reserve Manpower	5,000	4,000	—	14,000	0
Total Manpower	11,500	10,000	480	34,000	1,200
Naval Commandos/Marines	300	0	0	0	0
Submarines	2	0	0	4	0

continued

Figure 5.1 (Continued)

Category/Weapon	Israel	Syria	Jordan	Egypt	Lebanon
Destroyers/Frigates/Corvettes	3	2	0	11	0
Missile	3	2	0	10	0
Other	0	0	0	1	0
Missile Patrol	12	10	0	25	0
Coastal/Inshore Patrol	32	8	6	15	7
Mine	0	5	0	13	0
Amphibious Ships	1	3	0	3	0
Landing Craft/Light Support	4	5	(3)	9	2
Fixed-Wing Combat Aircraft	0	0	0	0	0
MR/MPA	0	0	0	0	0
ASW/Combat Helicopter	0	24	0	24	0
Other Helicopters	—	—	—	—	—

Note: Figures in parenthesis show additional equipment known to be in long-term storage. Some Syrian tanks shown in parenthesis are used as fire points in fixed positions.
Source: Adapted by Anthony H. Cordesman from data provided by U.S. experts; and IISS, *The Military Balance.*

Figure 5.2
National Trends in Arab-Israeli Military Spending in Constant Dollars: The Decline in Arab Forces as a Share of Total Spending: 1985–1999

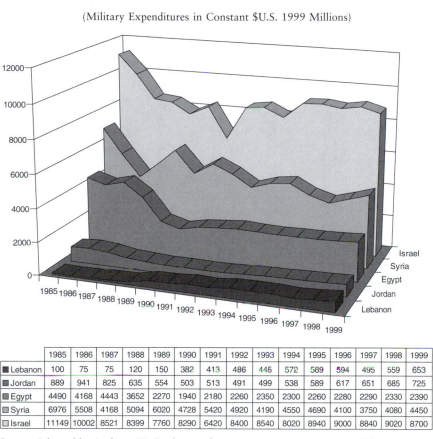

(Military Expenditures in Constant $U.S. 1999 Millions)

	1985	1986	1987	1988	1989	1990	1991	1992	1993	1994	1995	1996	1997	1998	1999
■ Lebanon	100	75	75	120	150	382	413	486	445	572	589	594	495	559	653
■ Jordan	889	941	825	635	554	503	513	491	499	538	589	617	651	685	725
■ Egypt	4490	4168	4443	3652	2270	1940	2180	2260	2350	2300	2260	2280	2290	2330	2390
■ Syria	6976	5508	4168	5094	6020	4728	5420	4920	4190	4550	4690	4100	3750	4080	4450
□ Israel	11149	10002	8521	8399	7760	8290	6420	8400	8540	8020	8940	9000	8840	9020	8700

Source: Adapted by Anthony H. Cordesman from U.S. State Department, *World Military Expenditures and Arms Transfers*, various editions.

had to spend more and more on the Israeli-Palestinian War since 2000, and these figures sharply understate the costs of civil programs like roads and settlements that Israel funds for security reasons. Egypt and Jordan have benefited from both peace and U.S. aid, although it is clear that Jordan faces serious resource limitations and Egypt is only funding its forces at about 30 percent of the level of Israel. Syria's military expenditures continue to decline and are less than one-third of the level needed to pay for the mix of manpower quality, readiness, and modernization it would need to compete with Israel in overall conventional force quality.

Figure 5.3
Arab-Israeli Military Expenditures by Country: 1997–2002

(In \$U.S. Current Millions)

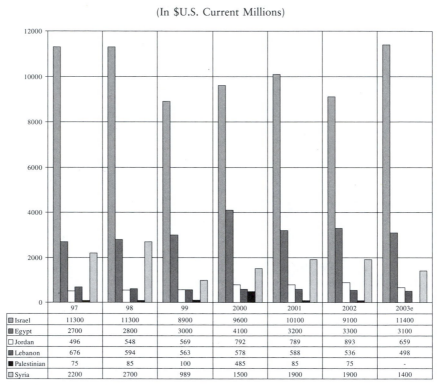

	97	98	99	2000	2001	2002	2003e
Israel	11300	11300	8900	9600	10100	9100	11400
Egypt	2700	2800	3000	4100	3200	3300	3100
Jordan	496	548	569	792	789	893	659
Lebanon	676	594	563	578	588	536	498
Palestinian	75	85	100	485	85	75	-
Syria	2200	2700	989	1500	1900	1900	1400

Note: Palestinian total is rough estimate based on FMA.
Source: International Institute of Strategic Studies, *The Military Balance*, various editions.

- Figure 5.4 shows the trend in military effort as a percentage of gross national product (GNP), and other measures of the military burden on the civil economy. The regional burden has been cut sharply since the mid-1980s, but is still one of the highest of any region in the world. The data also show that Israel still faces the heaviest burden, while Syria has effectively given up trying to compete with Israel in military terms.

- Figure 5.5 shows how the national trends in Arab-Israeli arms imports compare in constant dollars. Such estimates differ sharply by source, and these are drawn from declassified U.S. intelligence data in a U.S. State Department report. It is interesting that these figures show that Egypt and Israel both have received similar average levels of arms imports during the period shown. While technically true, such figures ignore the fact that Israel is the only state in the region with a relative efficient defense industry capable of producing modern military weapons and equipment and that it imports large amounts of U.S.

Figure 5.4
Trend in Percentage of GNP Spent on Military Forces: 1983–1999: Half the
Burden of the Early 1980s

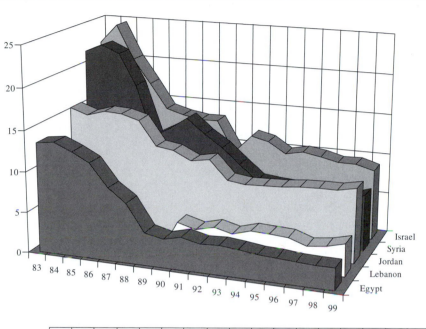

	83	84	85	86	87	88	89	90	91	92	93	94	95	96	97	98	99
■ Egypt	13.4	13.7	12.8	11.7	8.9	7.3	4	3.5	4	3.5	3.6	3.4	3.1	3	2.8	2.7	2.7
☐ Lebanon	-	-	-	-	-	-	-	4.1	3.5	4	3.5	4.1	4	3.9	3.1	3.4	4
☐ Jordan	15.6	14.9	15.5	15.4	14.8	12	11.5	10.4	10.8	8.5	8.2	8.3	8.4	8.6	8.7	8.7	9.2
■ Syria	21.8	22.7	21.8	18	11.7	12.9	14.4	12.6	11.1	9.2	7.4	7.2	7	6.2	6.1	6.3	7
☐ Israel	22.2	24.5	20.3	17.3	14.2	13.6	13.2	13.2	9.4	11.7	11.2	9.8	10.3	9.9	9.4	9.4	8.8

IISS Estimate of Military Spending and Manpower Trends: 1985–2000
Trend: 1985 versus 2000* ($U.S. are in Constant 1999 prices)

Country	Military Expenditures in $U.S. Millions			Military Spending Per Capita ($U.S.)			Military Spending as a % of GDP			Military Manpower (1000s)			
	85	99	00	85	99	00	85	99	00	Active 85	Reserve 00	00	Para 00
Israel	7,486	8,846	9,373	1,768	1,465	1,512	21.2	8.9	8.9	142	172.5	400	8.0
Egypt	3,827	2,988	2,821	79	45	45	7.2	3.4	3.2	445	448.5	254	230
Jordan	891	588	510	255	95	76	15.9	7.7	6.9	70.3	103.9	35	45
Lebanon	296	563	553	111	164	468	9.0	3.4	3.5	17.4	63.6	n.a.	13
Syria	5,161	989	760	491	63	47	16.4	5.6	5.6	402.5	316	396	108.8

Source: Adapted by Anthony H. Cordesman from U.S. State Department, Bureau of Arms
Control, "World Military Expenditures and Arms Transfers," Table I, Washington, DC:
GPO, various editions; and IISS, *The Military Balance*, various editions.

Figure 5.5
National Trends in Arab-Israeli Arms Deliveries in Constant Dollars

(Arms Deliveries in Constant $U.S. 1999 Millions)

	1985	1986	1987	1988	1989	1990	1991	1992	1993	1994	1995	1996	1997	1998	1999
■ Lebanon	74	15	13	13	6	0	6	0	11	11	53	42	41	10	10
■ Jordan	915	889	704	636	428	182	93	46	45	55	85	126	134	122	70
■ Syria	2194	1565	2683	1687	1383	1150	934	445	312	55	117	52	41	142	210
▣ Israel	1609	1565	2951	2336	1761	1695	1869	1825	1782	1200	827	969	1130	2233	2400
☐ Egypt	2486	2134	2683	1427	1258	1573	1869	1825	2227	1854	2242	1780	1644	1015	700

Source: Adapted by Anthony H. Cordesman from U.S. State Department, *World Military Expenditures and Arms Transfers*, various editions.

technology and equipment that it includes in its weapons systems but that are not classified as arms imports under the present definition of the term. This estimate shows a precipitous drop in Jordanian and Syrian arms imports that has had a crippling impact on both countries since the early 1990s. Lebanon has not had significant arms imports.

• Figure 5.6 provides more current data on both new arms orders and arms deliveries, using a different source. It reflects the same general patterns for Israel, and Egypt, and shows that new arms orders have risen sharply in recent years. Jordan also increased its arms orders in 1999–2002, largely as a result of increased U.S. aid resulting from its peace treaty with Israel and cooperation in dealing with Iraq. Syria shows no recovery in either new arms orders

Figure 5.6
Arab-Israeli New Arms Agreements and Deliveries by Country: 1987–2002

(In $U.S. Current Millions)

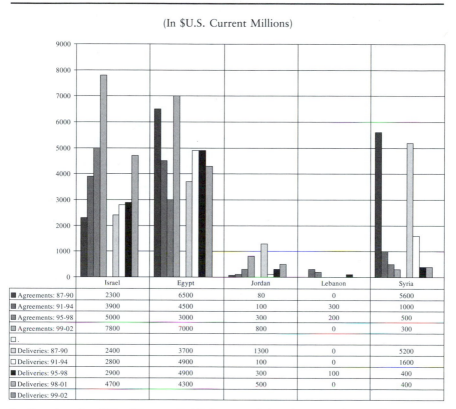

	Israel	Egypt	Jordan	Lebanon	Syria
■ Agreements: 87-90	2300	6500	80	0	5600
■ Agreements: 91-94	3900	4500	100	300	1000
■ Agreements: 95-98	5000	3000	300	200	500
□ Agreements: 99-02	7800	7000	800	0	300
□ .					
□ Deliveries: 87-90	2400	3700	1300	0	5200
□ Deliveries: 91-94	2800	4900	100	0	1600
■ Deliveries: 95-98	2900	4900	300	100	400
■ Deliveries: 98-01	4700	4300	500	0	400
■ Deliveries: 99-02					

0 = Data less than $50 million or nil. All data rounded to the nearest $100 million.
Source: Richard F. Grimmett, *Conventional Arms Transfers to the Developing Nations*, Congressional Research Service, various editions.

or deliveries from 1998 to 2002, in spite of some reports of major agreements with Russia. Lebanon remained a minor player.

• Figure 5.7 shows the source of Arab-Israeli arms imports. It shows that Israel clearly has had large-scale access to U.S. arms imports, including the most modern equipment, and these totals ignore massive imports of parts and subassemblies that are not classified as arms imports. Egypt has also had access to U.S. arms and technology, but has spent significant amounts on Russian, Chinese, and European arms to try to supplement what it can obtain with U.S. grant aid and to keep the Soviet-supplied portion of its forces operational. Jordan has been heavily dependent on the United States since 1990, although it has obtained some European arms. Syria has lost Russia as a major supplier without finding any replacement—particularly one capable of selling advanced arms and technology. Lebanon's arms imports have been too small to be significant.

Figure 5.7
Arab-Israeli Arms Orders by Supplier Country: 1987–2002

(Arms Agreements in $U.S. Current Millions)

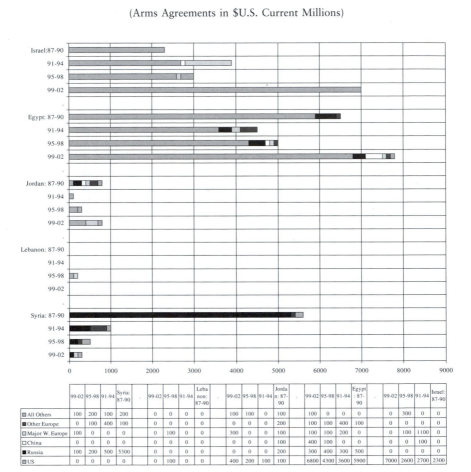

	99-02	95-98	91-94	Syria: 87-90	.	99-02	95-98	91-94	Leba non: 87-90	.	99-02	95-98	91-94	Jorda n: 87-90	.	99-02	95-98	91-94	Egypt : 87-90	.	99-02	95-98	91-94	Israel: 87-90
▨ All Others	100	200	100	200		0	0	0	0		100	100	0	100		100	0	0	0		0	300	0	0
■ Other Europe	0	100	400	100		0	0	0	0		0	0	0	200		100	100	400	100		0	0	0	0
▨ Major W. Europe	100	0	0	0		0	100	0	0		300	0	0	100		100	100	200	0		0	100	1100	0
▢ China	0	0	0	0		0	0	0	0		0	0	0	100		400	100	0	0		0	0	100	0
■ Russia	100	200	500	5300		0	0	0	0		0	0	0	200		300	400	300	500		0	0	0	0
▢ US	0	0	0	0		0	100	0	0		400	200	100	100		6800	4300	3600	5900		7000	2600	2700	2300

0 = less than $50 million or nil. All data rounded to the nearest $100 million.
Source: Adapted by Anthony H. Cordesman, CSIS, from Richard F. Grimmett, *Conventional Arms Transfers to the Developing Nations*, Congressional Research Service, various editions.

- Figure 5.8 puts the previous comparisons of Israeli and Arab arms imports in perspective. It shows that Israel has received far larger amounts of grant military assistance than Egypt and has been able to import far more equipment. These differ from the previous totals in that they include total funding for modernization, including the ability to import goods for military industry, while the other totals only count deliveries classified as "arms."

Figure 5.8
The Comparative Size of U.S. Military Assistance and Commercial Arms Sales to the Arab-Israeli Ring States: 1987–2001

	1987	1988	1989	1990	1991	1992	1993	1994	1995	1996	1997	1998	1999	2000	2001
Israel															
Foreign Military Financing Program	1,800	1,800	1,800	1,800	1,800	1,800	1,800	1,800	1,800	1,800	1,800	1,800	1,860	2,820	1,976
Payment Waived	1,800	1,800	1,800	1,800	1,800	1,800	1,800	1,800	1,800	1,800	1,800	1,800	1,860	2,820	1,976
FMS Agreements	100.5	130.9	327.7	376.7	361.4	96.5	161.0	2,142.9	631.3	828.7	506.4	654.6	2,430.7	782.6	2,882.1
Commercial Exports	1,024.8	474.8	997.2	387.3	169.1	27.9	41.8	34.0	34.7	13.1	12.8	11.5	4.2	26.3	4.0
FMS Construction Agreements	—	—	—	—	—	—	—	—	—	—	—	—	—	0.3	9.9
FMS Deliveries	1,229.6	754.1	230.3	146.3	239.0	718.7	773.9	409.2	327.0	385.8	497.2	1,202.7	1,224.4	570.8	759.8
MAP Program	—	—	—	74.0	43.0	47.0	491.0	165.9	80.0	22.0	—	—	—	—	—
MAP Deliveries	—	—	—	—	114.7	0.6	44.7	—	0.0	—	—	—	—	—	—
IMET Program/ Deliveries	1.9 (0)	1.7 (0)	1.9 (0)	2.1 (0)	1.1 (0.2)	0.6 (0)	0.5 (0)	0.8 (0)	0.8 (0)	—	—	—	—	—	—
Egypt															
Foreign Military Financing Program	1,300	1,300	1,300	1,300	1,300	1,300	1,300	1,300	1,300	1,300	1,300.0.	1,300	1,300	1,300	1,297
Payment Waived	1,300	1,300	1,300	1,300	1,300	1,300	1,300	1,300	1,300	1,300	1,300	1,300	1,300	1,300	1,297
FMS Agreements	330.9	1,306.1	2,646.3	969.5	1,631.7	587.0	435.2	409.5	1,014.8	1,269.1	961.0	978.5	2,058.7	1,612.2	1,720.5
Commercial Exports	55.4	73.1	252.5	206.0	75.6	31.0	18.7	9.6	10.3	3.5	5.0	2.4	0.6	3.8	0.9
FMS Construction Agreements	112.4	118.8	65.1	48.2	269.7	66.9	124.0	139.2	83.0	57.0	45.6	27.3	61.9	93.3	48.9
FMS Deliveries	955.1	473.0	296.8	368.1	482.3	1,026.7	1,236.0	889.0	1,478.7	1,083.2	896.8	570.7	450.4	805.3	881.9
MAP Program	—	—	—	—	—	—	—	13.5	—	—	—	—	—	—	—
MAP Deliveries	—	—	—	—	—	—	—	1.4	1.6	—	—	—	—	—	—

continued

Figure 5.8 (Continued)

	1987	1988	1989	1990	1991	1992	1993	1994	1995	1996	1997	1998	1999	2000	2001
IMET Program/ Deliveries	1.7	1.5	1.5	1.5	1.8	1.5	1.7	0.8	1.0	1.0.	1.0	1.0	1.0	1.0	1.1
Jordan															
Foreign Military Financing Program	—	—	10.0	67.8	20.0	20.0	9.0	9.0	7.3	100.3	30.0	50.0	95.9	124.9	74.8
Payment Waived	—	—	10.0	67.8	20.0	20.0	9.0	9.0	7.3	100.3	30.0	50.0	95.9	124.9	74.8
DoD Guaranty	81.3	—	—	—	—	—	—	—	—	—	—	—	—	—	—
FMS Agreements	33.9	28.7	9.4	26.7	0.4	6.8	14.5	38.7	13.0	199.5	17.5	17.9	14.7	120.5	122.3
Commercial Exports	73.4	18.3	23.5	12.1	0.9	27.9	41.8	34.0	34.7	13.1	12.8	11.5	4.2	26.3	4.0
FMS Deliveries	49.7	55.4	59.5	42.1	22.9	19.5	24.9	31.5	47.0	15.7	41.7	47.0	48.7	52.7	80.4
MAP Deliveries	1.1	0.8	—	—	0.4	—	0.1	—	—	10.7	16.3	50.2	7.5.	8.2	11.5
IMET Program/ Deliveries	1.9	1.7	1.9	2.1	1.1	0.6	0.5	0.8	1.0	1.2	1.7	1.6	1.7	1.7	1.7
Lebanon															
FMS Agreements	4.9	0.5	—	—	—	—	2.4	29.3	64.4	15.8	16.7	12.3	1.6	6.9	5.5
Commercial Exports	0.1	0.0	0.2	0.1	0.5	0.4	1.0	0.8	0.5	0.3	0.8	0.8	0.1	0.1	0.1
FMS Deliveries	12.1	11.9	3.9	2.0	0.3	1.3	4.9	3.6	40.9	31.7	33.0	8.0	7.0	4.9	6.1
IMET Program/ Deliveries	—	0.3	0.3	0.1	—	—	0.6	0.3	0.4	0.5	0.5	0.6	0.6	0.6	0.5

Note: Syria received no U.S. aid or sales during the period shown.
Source: Adapted from U.S. Defense Security Assistance Agency (DSAA), *Foreign Military Sales, Foreign Military Construction Sales and Military Assistance Facts,* Washington, DC: Department of Defense, various editions.

NATIONAL MILITARY FORCES

Each of the Arab-Israeli states has taken a different approach to shaping its military forces.

Israel

For more than a decade, the conventional Arab-Israeli balance has shaped Israel's struggle to maintain a decisive qualitative edge over its Arab neighbors. This balance, however, has changed significantly over time. Before the start of Operation Iraqi Freedom in March 2003, the combined force of Syria, Jordan and Iraq had always outnumbered the Israeli Defense Forces (IDF). During the 1990s, an Israeli estimate of the strength of a coalition of these three Arab armies suggested they could have deployed 39 ground divisions against Israel's 16, including three times as many artillery pieces and twice as many tanks as the IDF. These three countries also had a collective air strength that outnumbered those of Israel—960 to 624 in planes and 865 to 300 in helicopters.[1] This contrast, however, only takes into account potential threats on Israel's eastern front, excluding other countries such as Egypt, Libya, and Iran.

To compensate for this disparity, Israel has long maintained qualitative military superiority in the region. The IDF has consistently demonstrated a significant advantage over Arab militaries in leadership, training, equipment capabilities, and maintenance and in adapting to both tactical and technological developments spurred on by the revolution in military affairs. Furthermore, even taking into consideration recent budget cuts, Israel's defense spending remains higher than the total defense budgets of Egypt, Jordan, Syria, and Lebanon combined.[2]

The United States–led invasion and occupation of Iraq has further strengthened Israel's position in the regional military balance. During the conventional stage of the conflict, the Iraqi military suffered heavy losses in both men and material, and thereafter coalition forces destroyed or disbanded the remaining conventional forces that had existed under Saddam Hussein. The removal of Saddam's Baathist regime and the ongoing coalition occupation have nullified Iraqi armed forces as an immediate conventional threat to Israel despite the ongoing insurgency and Iraq's uncertain long-term political future.

Without Iraq, a statistical balance of the eastern front Arab militaries versus the IDF reveals that the collective armed forces of Syria and Jordan include 16 army divisions—the same number as Israel. In terms of equipment strength, Syria and Jordan have 3,355 artillery pieces (compared to Israel's 1,950), 4,570 tanks (to Israel's 3,895), 5,555 APC/AFVs (to Israel's 8,040), 610 combat aircraft (to Israel's 624), and 365 helicopters (to Israel's 300).[3] The Iraq War has enabled Israel to achieve relative parity on its eastern front while still maintaining its qualitative dominance.

For these reasons, Israel has largely won the struggle for overall force supremacy vis-à-vis its Arab neighbors, although Egypt has made impressive progress in conventional military modernization, and Israel's efforts have been undermined since 2002 by the steadily rising costs of the Israeli-Palestinian War and the need to devote much of Israel's forces to low intensity combat missions. As has been touched upon earlier, the asymmetric military balance is becoming as important as the conventional balance, and proliferation is a growing problem.

Israel is now in its fourth year of asymmetric warfare with the Palestinians. This war has forced it to devote many of its military resources to low-intensity conflict, raids and reoccupations of Palestinian territory, and internal security missions. There is no way to precisely quantify the resulting effort, but it seems to consume nearly half of Israel's military resources in terms of self-financed security expenditures, and some 25 percent of its active and mobilized reserve manpower. The end result has been a steady expansion of the training and equipment IDF units have for low-intensity conflict and internal security missions, although few of the details are public. For example, Israel signed two separate security agreements, one with Russia and one with Turkey, promising to share information about terrorist groups.[4] Israel hopes that the added intelligence will boost the IDF's effectiveness in the low-intensity conflict.

Israel has begun to consider and, in some cases, utilize unorthodox strategies both domestically and internationally in an effort to enhance security. Domestically, Israel has implemented a targeted assassination policy to try and destroy terrorist organizations by decapitating their leadership ranks. This policy has produced critics both abroad and at home. Many Arab nations, and obviously the Palestinians, oppose the policy, seeing it as counterproductive to the peace process while pointing out the strikes frequently incur bystander casualties.

Within Israel, many reservists refuse to serve in either Gaza or the West Bank, and twenty-seven Israeli air force pilots, including the most decorated pilot in Israel's history, refused to carry out further strikes. Four former heads of the Shin Bet security service declared that Israel's activities in the territories actually eroded national security instead of bolstering it.[5] A former deputy chief of staff of the IDF stated that Israel lacked a grand strategy and that the West Bank security fence that Israel is constructing at a cost of $450 million a year precludes the creation of a Palestinian state.[6]

Yet the Israeli government asserts that the strategies are working. The IDF indicates that gunfire attacks on Israelis in the West Bank decreased by 1,016 incidents in almost one year. Israelis and the IDF were bombed 578 times in 2002, compared to around 220 times in 2003. Israel touts these statistics as proof that the controversial strategies are successful. However, the number of *attempts* to kill Israelis, especially by suicide bombers, has risen dramatically.[7]

Israel has entered Syrian airspace on several occasions in a campaign aimed at encouraging Syria to end its support of the Islamic Jihad terror group. In September 2003, Israeli jets intentionally flew over a palace owned by Syrian president Bashar Assad's family. More forcefully, Israel bombed a suspected Islamic Jihad training camp outside of Damascus in October 2003. Israel has reportedly ruled out full air strikes or an invasion to remove the Islamic Jihad, but Israel remains committed to degrading Assad's influence. However, it is unclear as to whether such a campaign would diminish Assad's power or whether it might produce a rally-around-the-leader sentiment in the Syrian populace. Syria refuses to eliminate the Islamic Jihad, claiming that the group is not really a terrorist organization, has broken no Syrian laws, and does not hurt Syria.[8] Overall, it is uncertain whether these unconventional strategies will produce the desired results.

At the same time, Israel continues to emphasize many of its classic conventional military strengths: demanding exercise training, promoting on the basis of competence, maintaining a relatively young and aggressive officer corps, and insisting on forward leadership. It uses training that develops battlefield initiative, and it allows flexibility in executing orders. In contrast, Arab forces often require highly detailed written orders and systems of accountability in order to ensure that orders are obeyed, and commanders are taught not to deviate from orders when presented with new battlefield opportunities or unanticipated problems. Most exercises have predetermined outcomes that sharply limit the initiative of the officers involved, and make it impossible to determine the relative effectiveness of the forces involved.

The IDF has been forced to adopt a new, radical training regimen for its soldiers. In the past, it assumed that soldiers needed to be trained for months prior to deployment. Largely as a result of the Israeli-Palestinian War, however, Israel has instituted a different, three-pronged approach. Training consists of a brief yet difficult month-long training program followed by immediate deployment to either the occupied territories or the border with Lebanon. The training regimen, 40 percent of which has been altered, stresses the challenges soldiers will face during low-intensity conflict in an urban setting. Forgoing the traditional seventeen-week course enables soldiers to acquire "on-the-job training," an experience that, at least an IDF official states, cannot be replicated. The fluidity and rapidly changing tactics of the Israeli-Palestinian War render many forms of lengthy training anachronistic by the time soldiers complete the various courses. Three field schools supplement the regimented and on-the-job training for IDF soldiers. Every month, each soldier spends four to five days in a field school being trained in the latest techniques tailored to their specific functions in the context of the most recent developments. After six months of deployment, soldiers train for yet another month and attend the field schools once more.

Israel makes good use of advanced military technology, and of its access to arms transfers from the United States, and Israel has done more than procure high-technology equipment. While most Arab states focus on the "glitter factor" inherent in buying the most advanced weapons systems, Israel has given the proper weight to battle management, sustainability, and systems integration. Israel integrates technology into its force structure in ways that emphasize tactics, training, and all aspects of technology rather than relying on force strengths and weapons performance.

The recent trends in Israeli forces are shown in Figure 5.9. One key factor behind Israeli military efforts is a continuing emphasis on force quality over force quantity in order to maintain a decisive conventional and nuclear superiority, or "edge," over any likely combination of hostile Arab military forces. The end result is that Israel organizes its forces and military manpower in ways different from those of its Arab neighbors, and comparisons of either total active manpower or total active and reserve manpower have only limited meaning in measuring military effectiveness.

In spite of the Israeli-Palestinian War, Israel has cut its total active manpower in recent years from around 175,000 men and women in its peacetime force structure to 167,600. This total includes some 107,500 conscripts. Israeli male conscripts serve a total of thirty-six months (twenty-one months for women, forty-eight months for officers), and a significant number are still in training or gathering combat experience at any given time.

Israel's military effectiveness depends heavily on the ability to call up the key elements of a reserve manpower pool that has also been cut in recent years from 430,000 to 358,000. A significant number of the personnel now fighting in the Israeli-Palestinian War are reservists. As a result, Israel has far more real-world manpower strength than its total active military manpower would indicate. At the same time, Israel's use of reserves makes it dependent on timely mobilization for its war-fighting capability, and Israel requires thirty-six to forty-eight hours of strategic warning and reaction time to fully prepare its defenses in the Golan—its most vulnerable front. Only about one-third of Israel's total manpower consists of full-time actives, and much of this manpower consists of conscripts. Some of Israel's best troops consist of its younger reserves.

Israel's response to recent budgetary shortfalls and changes in its strategic environment (particularly the elimination of the threat of a conventional eastern front) is reflected in "Kela 2008" (Catapult 2008), the IDF's latest five-year work plan. The "Kela 2008" plan calls for the IDF to reduce its ground forces by nearly 20% over the next five years. Armored units will be cut by more than 25%. By 2008 the IDF Ground Forces Command expects to almost exclusively employ Mekava MK 2, 3, and 4 main battle tanks, with only a few brigades of M-60 Magach 7s remaining in regular service. The rest, along with remaining Merkava Mk1s, will be converted to heavy APCs. The military will outsource maintenance and administration functions in an effort to cut costs further. Other Kela initiatives that will surely raise concerns among soldiers and veterans include plans to

Figure 5.9
Force Trends in Israel

Category/Weapon	1975	1980	1985	1990	1995	2000	2004
Manpower							
Total Active	156,000	169,600	142,000	141,000	172,000	175,000	167,600
(Conscript)	(125,000)	(125,300)	—	(110,000)	(138,500)	(138,500)	(107,500)
Total Reserve	275,000	—	370,000	504,000	430,000	430,000	358,00
Total Actives & Reserves	400,000	400,000	512,000	645,000	602,000	605,000	525,60
Paramilitary	9,000	9,500	4,500	6,000	6,050	6,050	8,050
Land Forces							
Active Manpower	135,000	135,000	104,000	104,000	134,000	134,000	125,000
(Conscripts)	(120,000)	(120,000)	(88,000)	(88,000)	(114,700)	(114,700)	(85,000)
Reserve Manpower	240,000	—	310,000	494,000	365,000	365,000	330,000
Total Reserve & Active Manpower	375,000	375,000	414,000	598,000	499,000	499,000	455,000
Main Battle Tanks	2,700	3,050	3,600	4,288	4,095	4,300	3,950
(Static & in Storage)	—	—	—	—	—	—	—
AIFVs/Armored Cars/Lt. Tanks	365	80+	300	400	408	408	408
APCs/Recce/Scouts	3,000*	4,000*	4,000	5,980	5,980	5,980	7,990
WWII Half-Tracks	*	*	4,000	4,400	3,500	500 (4,000)	500
ATGM Launchers	—	—	—	—	1,005	1,005	1,225
SP Artillery	660**	228	488	816	1,150	1,150	960
Towed Artillery	**	950	570	579	400	400	370
MRLs	**	—	180	175	160	160	212

continued

Figure 5.9 (Continued)

Category/Weapon	1975	1980	1985	1990	1995	2000	2004
Mortars	—	900+	900+	—	2,740	2,740	1,890
SSM Launchers	—	—	—	112	100+	48–96	100
AA Guns	—	900+	900+	850+	850	850+	850+
Lt. SAM Launchers	—	—	—	—	945+	945+	1,298
Air & Air Defense Forces							
Active Air Force Manpower	16,000	38,000	28,000	28,000	32,000	37,000	35,000
Active Air Defense	—	—	—	—	—	—	—
Reserve Manpower	4,000	9,000	9,000	9,000	20,000	20,000	24,500
Air Defense Command Reserve	—	—	—	—	—	—	—
Aircraft							
Total Fighter/FGA/Recce	481	535	684 (90)	553	449	459 (250)	438 (250)
Fighter	0	0	0	0	0	0	0
FGA/Fighter	275	265	402	393 (+83)	373 (+120)	405	340
FGA	200	200	130	121 (+14)	50 (+150)	25	39
Recce	6	14	15	14	22	10	13
Airborne Early Warning (AEW)	—	4	4	4	4	6	6
Electronic Warfare (EW)	—	—	10	26	36	37	39
Fixed-Wing	—	—	—	—	—	37	39
Helicopter	—	—	—	—	—	0	39
Maritime Reconnaissance (MR)	—	0	0	5	3	3	3
Combat Capable Trainer	25	74	123	48	14–24	19	26
Tanker	2	2	2	7	8	8	5
Transport	54–98	58–70	45	58	47	36	22

Helicopters						
Attack/Armed/	—	6	58	74	116	133	100
ASW/SAR	—	—	37	2	2	6	6
Transport & Other	97	145	92	143	145	160	186
Total	97	151	187	219	263	299	292
SAM Forces							
Batteries	15	15	15	17	17	28	25
Heavy Launchers	90	60	60	68	68	79	79
Medium Launchers	—	—	—	—	—	—	—
Naval Forces							
Active Manpower	5,000	6,600	10,000	9,000	6,000–7,000	6,500	7,600
Reserve Manpower	1,000	3,400	10,000	1,000	10,000	5,000	3,500
Total Manpower	6,000	10,000	20,000	10,000	16,000–17,000	11,500	11,100
Submarines	2	3	3	3	2	4	3
Destroyers/Frigates/Corvettes	0	0	6	0	3	3	3
Missile	0	0	6	0	3	3	3
Other	0	0	0	0	0	0	0
Missile Patrol	18	22	24	26	23	14	11
Coastal/Inshore Patrol	36	38	45	37	40	36	39
Mine	0	0	0	0	0	0	0
Amphibious Ships	0	3	3	0	1	1	1
Landing Craft/Light Support	10	6	9	9	4	4	4
Fixed-Wing Combat Aircraft	0	0	0	0	0	0	0
MR/MPA	0	3	0	0	0	0	0
ASW/Combat Helicopter	0	0	0	0	0	0	0
Other Helicopters	—	—	—	—	—	—	—

*Includes all types of other armed vehicles except tanks and self-propelled artillery.

**Includes all medium and heavy self-propelled and towed weapons.

Source: Adapted by Anthony H. Cordesman from data provided by U.S. experts; and IISS, *The Military Balance.*

reduce the amount of training per annum for both regular soldiers and reservists, cut total funding for wages up to 20%, overhaul and drastically
reduce promotion, retention, welfare and pension programs for officers, and
increase the minimum retirement age for most professional military service
paths. Overall, the implementation of Kela will also lead the army to cut
10% of its regular forces and minimize the use of unskilled reservists who
typically incur larger operating expenses.[9]

The effect these cuts will have on the IDF's ability to confront the Palestinian militants is also unclear. Some reports indicate that the IDF believes
that Kela 2008 will streamline their forces, make them more effective, and
cut unnecessary costs. However, some of the measures, such as the pay cuts
and elimination of jobs, are likely to be highly unpopular and run the risk
of fomenting discontent within the military. At a time when Israel is leaning increasingly heavily on the IDF despite reduced threats from Iraq and
Syria, cuts in benefits are likely to discourage Israelis from pursuing long-
term military careers.

In addition, a panel of industrialists, former generals, and security experts recommended further reductions on top of the Kela plan. The panel-
ists want to decrease the number of combat helicopters by 20 percent, the
number of tanks by an additional 10 percent, the older fighter planes by 5
percent, and the patrol boats by 15 percent. Reportedly, the resulting force
numbers would be sufficient to face Israel's threats.[10]

Other reports indicate that Israeli concerns over funding and the threat
of budget reduction has led the navy, army, and air force to fight fiercely
over U.S. Foreign Military Financing allocations. The navy was once
thought to have been assured a lion's share, but the other services have
raised questions as to whether Israel would be best served by using those
funds to purchase additional Arrow missile batteries, Apache AH-64Ds, or
Stryker armored vehicles. It seemed likely that the navy would have used
those funds to purchase additional missile corvettes, ostensibly to counter
threats from Libya. However, Libya is perceived as somewhat less threatening and there has been a second successful test of the Arrow system,
making it unclear which service will secure the funds.[11]

Land Forces

Israel has an active army strength of 125,000 and has a well-trained and
active reserve force of 330,000. It is organized into three territorial and one
home front command, and into a combat structure of four corps. Its active forces have a nominal strength of four armored divisions, five infantry
divisions, and five air-mobile brigades. Its reserves have a nominal strength
of five armored divisions, with a total of fourteen armored brigades, three
infantry brigades, and five artillery regiments. There are four infantry divisions with a total of seventeen infantry brigades and one artillery regiment, and five mobile brigades. In practice, however, Israel adjusts its force

mix to the mission at hand and each of these units has reserve elements. Another six of Israel's eleven armored "divisions" are reserve forces, as is one airmobile mechanized division. These reserve units have a total of ten armored brigades, four infantry brigades, and four artillery regiments.

The IDF's major combat equipment includes 3,950 main battle tanks. It has an inventory of some 7,700 APCs: 670 AIFVs, 4,300 obsolete half-tracks, 960 self-propelled artillery weapons, 370 towed weapons, 212 multiple rocket launchers, some 1,360 mortars, over 1,200 modern anti-tank guided weapons launchers, some 350 recoilless rifles, and over 1,300 light surface-to-air missiles (many obsolete). The land forces are reported to operate Israel's nuclear-armed Jericho missiles, which are described in more detail in Chapter 10.

The cost and forcewide impacts of the Israeli-Palestinian War have had a major impact on Israel's military development. Israel does not face recapitalization problems that approach those of Jordan or Syria, but it does have problems. It cannot afford to convert its armor to a coherent force of first-line systems that has the mix the IDF would like of both the most advanced tanks and the most advanced infantry fighting vehicles.

Israel's 1,790 Merkavas are, however, designed for the specific tactical conditions Israel faces. They are more advanced than any tank in Arab hands, except for Egypt's 550 M1A1s, and can defeat most antitank weapons in Arab forces. This is particularly true of the Merkava IV, Merkava III Baz, and Merkava III, which have excellent protection and some of the best fire control and sighting systems available. The Merkava IV is just becoming operational and is much more powerful that the previous versions without an increase in weight. It also has much better day and night vision systems, and a new and improved version of ballistic protection. The Ministry of Defense recently decided to forgo the development of the Merkava V, citing the success and cost effectiveness of the Merkava IV.[12]

The cost of the existing Merkavas has raised questions about the viability of continuing the thirty-four-year-old program. It has been reported that some elements within the Israeli Ministry of Defense are suggesting that the Merkava line be abandoned in favor of the U.S. M1A2 main battle tank. Viewed as widely successful, the M1A2 would also be paid for by U.S. Foreign Military Financing aid, making it an even more attractive option. Others suggest that Israel should ask for inclusion in the U.S. Future Combat Systems (FCS) program, which aims to develop a future armored force that is far lighter, that is easier to transport, and that integrates manned and unmanned vehicles while maintaining survivability and lethality. Critics argue, however, that while they would be willing to participate in aspects of the program, the FCS program's stress on weight and transportability does little to solve Israel's needs. They maintain that the Merkava line is sufficient and call for an increase in the program's budget.[13] A recent proposal to sell the Merkava tank production line, either to a private Israeli defense firm or to another owned by the government, has further clouded the tank's future. Proponents believe that the sale would increase efficiency and drastically cut the line's costs.[14]

Israel's 600 M-60A3s are not up to the standard of the Merkava, but have an "edge" in fire control and sights, and a marginal advantage in protection, over Syria's 1,500 export versions of the T-72s and T-72Ms—the only relatively modern tanks in Syrian forces, Israel's 300 M-60/M-60A1s, have been upgraded to the point where they may well have a similar advantage. They may not have such an advantage over Egypt's nearly 1,000 M-60A3s and 400 M-60A-1s, or Jordan's 288 M-60A1/A3 or 288 Al-Hussein (Challenger 1)—which also have improved armor and other upgrades. Egypt also has some 1,000 M-60s, which have significant capabilities relative to Israel's first line tanks. Israel has already upgraded at least 180–190 of its M-48s and M-60s to the MAGACH 6 and 7 modifications, with improved passive and reactive armor, power, guns, and fire control. It may upgrade the rest to a further improved version in the MAGACH series, and it has also develop an Sabra upgrade of the M-60, with improvements in fire control, protection, and mobility.

Israel's other tanks are much less advanced than its Merkavas and M-60s. They include 300 Centurions, 560 M-48A5s, 114 Ti-67s (somewhat improved T-54/T-55), and 100 T-62s. This means that 975 of Israel's tanks are of low to medium quality, although many of these tanks have been upgraded and are considerably better than the original U.S.-, British-, and Soviet-supplied versions.

Israel has had to choose between funding improved tanks and funding improvements of other armored fighting vehicles. As a result, it has a relatively limited number of modern AIFVs to supplement its tanks. These include some 400 light wheeled RAMTAs and RBYs, BRDM-2 amphibious scout cars, and 8 Fuchs. Israel's APCs include converted Centurions called Nagmaschons (400?), heavy Achzarit APC conversions of the T-55 designed to accompany the Merkava (270?), Puma combat engineer APCs, and Nakpadons. In addition, large numbers of its 7,700 M-113 Zeldas have been upgraded from APCs to something approaching AIFVs. It is still dependent on a stockpile of some 4,300 half-tracks for support vehicles and reserves—although most are not in storage or will be place in storage shortly.

Israel is seeking to supplement this force, and possibly replace the M113s, by either buying 500 Stryker LAV-IIIs or an undetermined number of Dingo 2 APVs. Reports in early 2004 suggest that the IDF is leaning toward purchasing the Stryker. However, it has been reported that Israel has built a prototype LAV featuring tank treads that rivals the abilities of the Stryker.[15] What affect this prototype will have on the acquisition of the Stryker remains unclear. The IDF hopes that these vehicles will provide the protection and mobility needed in urban areas, where a large majority of its operations take place.[16]

Israel has a wide range of advanced antitank guided weapons. Its holding include 300 TOW 2A/Bs, many mounted on armored vehicles, 90 Dragon man portable weapons, AT-3 Saggers, and an unknown number of Israel-developed weapons including Mapats, Gill, Spike, and Dandy. The Dandy can be fired from either a helicopter or a ground-based vehicle.[17] The Spike, available in medium-range, long-range, and ER, has received a significant upgrade. Named Spike C41, the upgrade includes a GPS receiver, computer, and data link as well as a handheld laser rangefinder, and a laptop command unit and radio system. The C41 decreases the chance of friendly fire incidents while providing a network capability to Spike units in the field.[18] It has large numbers of rocket launchers and some 250 106-mm recoilless rifles.

Israel has built up a modern artillery force of some 960 self-propelled weapons and more than 212 multiple rocket launchers—including 48 U.S. MLRs. Its self-propelled weapons include 148 L-33 and 704 M-109A1/A2 weapons, 72 M-107 175-mm weapons, and 36 M-110 203-mm weapons. It has upgraded its 175-mm M-107 weapons into a version called the Romach, and has upgraded many of its 155-mm M-109 weapons into a version called the Doher, which has improved mobility, NBC protection, and fire control and accuracy. The L-33 Soltam is an aging Israeli system placed on a Sherman M4A3e8 tank chassis. Its operational status is unclear. Some sources indicate that 200 were built and the system is now in reserve. Israel also has 370 towed weapons, including 70 105-mm, 5 122-mm, 15 130-mm, and 280 155-mm weapons.

Israel's multiple rocket launcher strength includes 58 BM-21 122-mm, 50 LAR 160 160-mm, 48 MRLS 227-mm, 36 BM-24 240-mm, and 20 LAR-90 290–350-mm weapons. These weapons often have substantial modifications and upgrades, and the LAR has both three 160-mm and one 290–350-mm versions. The 160-mm version has a range of 12–45 kilometers, and the 350-mm version has a range of 30–100 kilometers. Israel also has some 1,300 81-mm, 400 120-mm, and 130 160-mm mortars, many mounted on armored vehicles.

Additionally, the IDF has absorbed 33 AFB-142F-1 and seven AGM-142 Have Nap Popeye Standoff Attack Missiles.[19] Israeli weapons manufacturers developed a deep-strike, precision-guided missile dubbed LORA, or Long Range Artillery. The LORA, with a range of approximately 120 kilometers, is similar to the SS-21s employed by the Russians or the ATACMS utilized by the Americans. The operational status of the missile remains uncertain, however, as the developers accidentally broadcasted a failed LORA missile test in 2003.[20] Israel has over 100 active variants of the Jericho long-range ballistic missile (IRBM), plus 7 Lance surface-to-surface missile fire units in storage.

Israel is steadily upgrading its battle management and targeting systems, self-propelled artillery force, and is enhancing its long-range strike capabilities with advanced multiple rocket launchers; but it would still would like to acquire much larger stocks of advanced and specialized ammunition, upgrade to weapons like an upgunned version of the M-109 and Soltam Slammer self-propelled 155mm howitzers, and increase its number of MLRS and other advanced multiple rocket launchers. For instance, an infantry modernization program that is already underway is the Ministry of Defense's procurement order for 15,000 of the Israeli Military Industry's 5.56mm Tar-21 Tavor assault rifle to replace the U.S.-made M-16 series rifles that the IDF currently uses.[21]

Due to lack of funding Israel may, however, have to concentrate on upgrading its targeting sensors like radars and UAVs and battlefield management systems. The Ministry of Defense ordered additional special surveillance coverage to be provided by Searcher UAVs that have been in service since 1992.[22] It is not clear that the Searcher will satisfy the IDF's needs. The Israeli Army would like to acquire a number of Skylark mini-UAVs for special operations purposes, but it has yet to place a specific order.[23] Israel also plans to develop a fleet of aircraft that would mimic the abilities of U.S. aircraft equipped with the Joint Surveillance Target Attack Radar System, or JSTARS. This would greatly enhance long-range battle management.[24] The Israel Air Force will have acquired three signals intelligence collection aircraft (SIGINT) by 2006.[25]

In the realm of battlefield management, the IDF acquired the PNR-500 personal radio network system that allows units to communicate in a manner similar to a conference call, enhancing coordination and information relay.[26] By 2008, Israel hopes to complete the "Digital Ground Forces" project, dubbed "Tsayad" ("Hunter"), which calls for the installation of communal broadband communications capabilities first in all command levels and then every ground platform. Although "Tsayad" has been approved in principle, due to its high budget it may only receive partial funding and have to be stretched out over a longer period of time.[27]

Some reports indicate that Israel's Project Anog will seek to apply existing technologies to create an integrated battlesuit system in an effort to boost each individual soldier's effectiveness. It has been reported that the system will sport interconnected weaponry, headgear, and body systems, providing soldiers with GPS receivers, laser rangefinders, wireless communicators, and a combined reflex sight and laser-aiming light. Field trials could begin as early as 2006, with full prototypes available by 2010 at a reported cost of less than $10 million.[28]

The IDF increasingly emphasizes joint operations in its training and doctrine, and seems likely to develop fully mobile and air mobile infantry units that match or exceed the maneuver capability of its armored forces. It is still a twelve-division force, of which some nine divisions are manned by reserves. However, it seems to be moving toward a more flexible task force concept in which the independently controlled infantry brigades could be placed under the overall control of the armored divisions in order to enhance armored combat under fire-saturated battlefield scenarios. The resulting units could operate independently in a number of scenarios.

Israel also is one of the few armies in the Middle East with anything approaching the advanced training facilities that the U.S. Army has at Fort Irwin or that the U.S. Marine Corps has at Twenty-Nine Palms. Egypt and Jordan are the only two Arab powers acquiring somewhat similar capabilities. The Israeli army has a computer corps called Mamram. It has a training center at Mabat in the Negev desert, which uses a modern computerized training range, an advanced command and control simulator, an area-weapons effect system, and over 1,000 MILES II instrumented player outfits for infantry, antitank weapons, and armored vehicles. There are other MILES systems for infantry and special forces training, and some form of equipment is used to simulated helicopter and fixed-wing aircraft in joint training. The facility is scarcely as advanced as its U.S. counterparts, but has well over $50 million worth of equipment.

The IDF has had to concentrate many of its recent efforts on internal security and counterinsurgency/counterterrorism missions, but it has also sought to restructure its support and logistic elements to allow more rapid support of maneuver operations at the brigade or task force level. Such forces would be reequipped with a mix of specialized armored and tracked support vehicles like the Achsarit, Puma, and Nakpadon to provide both better mobility and some degree of NBC protection. Recently, the IDF has been deploying its "Solid Mirror" integrated system along the expanding security fence and on the border of the Gaza Strip. Solid Mirror detects and identifies threats, tracks their progress, and has the ability to warn or set off an alarm. The system utilizes a variety of sensors and automated constructs to perform its mission. It has been deployed along the 120-kilometer border with Lebanon since 1999.[29]

The IDF is examining different ways to man "high-alert" forces. Some include larger numbers of career actives and fewer reserves. Others seem to involve more use of attack helicopters, air support, and long-range firepower systems like rockets with advanced conventional warheads. It has placed an increasing emphasis on improving combined arms and joint operations at every tactical level.

Naval Forces

Israel's naval forces have 7,600 actives and 3,500 reserves. Conscripts serve three years. The Israeli navy has 3 submarines, 3 Sa'ar 5-class corvettes, 11 missile patrol craft, 39 inshore patrol craft, and 1 amphibious ship. It has a small commando force of 300 men, and has 4 AS 565SA Sea Panther antisubmarine warfare helicopters. Its forces are based at Haifa, Ashdod, and Eilat. The Israeli navy is trying to purchase two or three Multi-Mission Combat Ships, dubbed the Sa'ar 5 plus program, by 2005.[30] The vessels would extend the navy's sensor capability and possibly could serve as the platform for a sea-based missile defense system.[31] At this point in time, Israel has little or no capability in the Red Sea—reflecting its peace with Egypt and Jordan.

Israel has replaced its three Gal-class submarines with three modern Dolphin-class submarines (commissioned in 1999 and 2000). Israeli navy plans originally called for the country to maintain all six submarines, but it is unclear that such a force is affordable. The Dolphins give Israel considerably greater strategic depth in operating in Mediterranean waters. They can be operated at ranges of up to 8,000 miles and have an endurance of up to 30 days. They have modern sonar, wire-guided torpedoes, and facilities for the launch of Harpoon antiship missiles. The Dolphins are the most advanced submarines in the Middle East. They weigh 1,700 tons and are twice the size of the Gal-class subs. In addition, Israel is to receive German Seahake heavyweight torpedoes. The navy is considering the acquisition of two more Dolphins, and some opposition seems to have developed to its plans to buy two additional missile corvettes. There is some concern that the corvettes would be vulnerable to terror attacks either in the Suez Canal or in the Straits of Gibraltar. Some within the navy have also stressed the importance of submarines over the corvettes in order to preserve a nuclear second-strike capability in the event of an attack.[32] There are reports that Israel can use its submarines to provide a secure and relatively invulnerable launch platform for nuclear-armed missiles. These initially would be a nuclear-armed version of a system like the Harpoon, with a nominal range of 70 miles, or 130 kilometers. They may be followed by new long-range cruise missiles.

Israel has three new Sa'ar 5 (Eliat or Sa'ar V)–class missile corvettes, with a fourth due to be commissioned in 2004–2005. These are 1,227-ton ships, each of which has two quad launchers for Harpoon missiles with a range of up to 130 kilometers, one 76-mm gun, a Dauphin SA-366G helicopter, a Phalanx close-in defense systems, and six torpedo launchers. They may be equipped with eight IAI MBT Gabriel 5 antiship missiles with radar and optical homing and ranges of up to 36 kilometers, but there are top weight problems. Other upgrades may include giving each ship two 32-cell launchers for Barak air defense missiles The Sa'ar 5s also have modern electronic support and countermeasure systems, and advanced software for target tracking and identification. These facilities include a sophisticated command information center (CIC) sheltered deep within the ship that can act as task group command centers, as well as fight the individual ship. The sea and air tracking and battle management system is also advanced for a ship of this class.[33]

The ships also have extensive countermeasure and some stealth features, and are to be upgraded to use the Barak missile when suitable funds become available. The ships give Israel additional "blue water capability," and are superior to any similar missile ships in service with Israel's Arab neighbors. Israel has sought funds for up to five more ships through U.S. aid, but it is unclear it will have sufficient funds. Nevertheless, the Ministry of Defense continues to pursue funds for and development of sea-based vessels capable of interdicting air-, surface-, and submarine-fired missiles.[34]

Israel has 18 additional missile craft—including 7 Sa'ar 4.5 (Hetz)–class ships with 8 Harpoons and 6 Gabriels each. It has 2 Sa'ar 4.5 (Aliya)–class ships with 4 Harpoons and 4 Gabriels. It retains 2 Sa'ar 4 (Reshef)–class missile patrol boats for spaces. The Sa'ar 4.5s have been extensively modernized under the Nirit (4.5)-class upgrade program, which incorporates a "modernization by cannibalization" approach, scrapping much of the material from the Sa'ar 4s while outfitting the vessels with new hulls, low-radar-signature masts, new fire-control detectors, updated sensors, and four 8-cell launchers for Barak point-defense missiles. All Sa'ar 2s and 3s have been retired.[35]

Israel also has 13 Dvora- and Super Dorva–class fast attack craft with 20-mm guns and short-range Hellfire missiles, and 5 Super Dorvas are in construction that may replace older Dorva-class ships. Two are based at Eliat on the Red Sea. It has 15 land-transportable Dabur-class coastal patrol boats (two are based at Eliat on the Red Sea.) There are 3 small Bobcat (coast guard)-class patrol boats.

The Israeli navy has 1 Ashdod-class LCT (400 tons, 730 tons fully loaded). It may lease a Newport-class LST from the United States. Its 6 Phalcons can provide maritime surveillance, as well as airborne early warning, and it has 19 Bell 212 helicopters for coastal surveillance tasks. It has 2 Sea Panther helicopters for its Sa'ar 5s, and Sea Scan UAVs for maritime surveillance and targeting.

Israel is the only navy in the Middle East supported by an industrial base that has advanced electronic warfare design and modification capabilities, with the ability to manufacture and design its own sensors and antiship missiles. These developments should allow Israel to maintain a decisive edge over Syria in the Mediterranean and more limited advantage in tactics, training, and technology over the Egyptian navy—although the Egyptian navy is now receiving significant modernization.

Sea power is not likely to be a significant issue in any near-term Arab-Israeli conflict—particularly one between Israel and Syria. Israel has massive naval superiority over Syria and Lebanon. It also can probably use joint naval-air operations to win superiority over Egypt except in Egyptian waters.[36] It should be noted, however, that Israel has effectively ended its naval presence in the Red Sea, and has had to make trade-offs that have reduced its naval capabilities. It has had to cut its procurement of new Sa'ar corvettes from eight to three and may have problems in funding all three Dolphin-class submarines. It also had to cut back substantially on its Barak ship defense missiles—although these are armed with Harpoon and Gabriel ship-to-ship missiles. The practical issue is whether this matters given the strategic partnership between the United States and Israel and U.S. dominance of the sea. It simply is not clear that any of Israel's naval trade-offs erode its edge in any probable contingency.

Air Forces

The Israeli air force (IAF) has a nominal strength of 35,000. This includes 20,000 conscripts, largely assigned to land-based air defense forces. It has some 438 active combat aircraft, plus 250 in storage, and some 100 armed helicopters. It has 13 fighter and fighter attack squadrons with a total of 340–360 aircraft authorized. These include 50 F-4E2000, 20 F-4E, 34 F-15A/B, 28 F-15 C/D, 25 F-15I, 102 F-16A/B, 101 F-16C/D, and 102 F-16I now in delivery and conversion. It also has one attack squadron of 39 A4Ns, a reconnaissance unit with 13 RF-4Es, 6 Phalcon AEW aircraft, 27 EW and ELINT aircraft, 95 attack helicopters (16 AH-1E, 39 AH-1S, and 40 AH-64A), and 6 ASW helicopters. It has 5 KC130H tankers, 22 major transport aircraft, and some 186 scout and transport helicopters. It also has a wide range of unmanned aerial vehicles, and a large inventory of advanced air-to-air and precision guided air-to-surface weapons— including both Israeli- and U.S.-made weapons.

The IAF plans to install a new self-protection system, designed to fend off man-portable infrared missiles, on most of its attack and troop-transport helicopters and all new F-16I jet fighters during the next several years. In 2000 the Israeli company Elisra Electronic Systems won an IAF contract to develop and produce the Passive Approach Warning System (PAWS), which uses infrared imagery and signal processing to detect and track the hot smoke plume of an incoming missile. Operational testing of PAWS is expected to last through Summer 2004. After testing is complete, the system is expected to receive certification for deployment.[37]

According to some reports, the IAF is also pursuing the development of multispectral sensor systems to be fitted on UAVs, planes, and helicopters. Replacing forward-looking infrared systems with synthetic aperture radar or millimeter wave radio systems would drastically reduce the effects of poor weather conditions on reconnaissance and targeting. However, development and deployment may be ten to twenty years away by some estimates.[38]

Israel is the only Middle Eastern air force that combines all of the elements of modern air power into an efficient and integrated whole. Israel has advanced combat, electronic warfare, intelligence and targeting, and battle management aircraft. These are supported by a host of advanced and special purpose weapons systems, combat electronics, unmanned airborne vehicles, night and all weather combat systems, and command and control facilities. Israel is one of the few countries capable of creating advanced chaff, electronic warfare, and electronic supporting measures and its own guided air weapons.

Israel has long stressed joint warfare, and combines its skills in land maneuver warfare with one of the most effective air forces in the world. The Israeli air force is one of the most modern air forces in the world. It has systematically improved its conventional attack—or "soft strike"— capability. It now has many of the advantages that U.S. airpower enjoyed during the Gulf War, plus a wide range of subsystems and weapons tailored to deal with threats like Syria and the special conditions in its theater of operations. The IAF has recently absorbed 20–24 F-15Is, 50 surplus USAF F-16s, additional AH-64s, 10 Black Hawk helicopters, advanced new UAVs, and ongoing Israeli upgrades to existing aircraft like the F-15, F-16, and Phantom 2000. The Israelis are considering the purchase of 6 more AH-64D Apache Longbow attack helicopters, bringing their fleet to 18.[39] Additionally, the IAF is buying 102 F-16I fighters. The older F-15Is will be fitted with Mk84 joint direct attack munitions (JDAMs) by late 2005.[40] Israel purchased 4 G550s, with an option for 2 more, to provide an airborne early warning capability.[41] However, they will not be fully operational until 2007.

Israel has the technical resources to steadily modernize and improve the capability of its electronic warfare and reconnaissance aircraft. At the same time, Israel has the C⁴I/BM, training, night warfare, electronic warfare, support, sustainability, and other specialized qualitative capabilities necessary to exploit the revolution in military affairs. Its superior technology is fully supported by superior tactics and training, and this gives it all of the qualitative advantages over Syria that were discussed earlier.

Israeli pilot and aircrew selection and training standards are the highest in the Middle East and some of the highest in the world. In addition, Israel has developed a reserve system that requires exceptional performance from its air force reservists. There are no reserve squadrons in the IAF, and all squadrons can operate without mobilization. However, about one-third of the aircrew in each squadron is reservists. Reserve aircrews train fifty-five to sixty days a year, and fly operational missions with the squadron to which they are assigned. In the event of a call-up, the reserve aircrews and operations support personnel report first, and then support personnel for sustained operations. About 60 percent of the IAF reserves are in air and ground defense units.

In contrast, other Middle Eastern forces are weakened by their failure to enforce rigorous selection procedures for assignments other than combat pilot, and by their failure to create a highly professional class of noncommissioned officers who are paid, trained, and given the status necessary to maintain fully effective combat operations. In most cases, these problems are compounded by poor overall manpower policies and promotion for political and personal loyalty. Other Middle Eastern air forces also tend to be weakened by a failure to see command and control, intelligence and targeting, high-intensity combat operations, and sustainability as being equal in importance to weapons numbers and quality. While Egypt, and Saudi Arabia have moved toward the idea of forcewide excellence in supporting an overall concept of operations, they still have a long way to go before approaching Israel's level of capability.

While the Israeli air defense system is scarcely leak proof—a fact it demonstrated some years ago when a defecting Syrian pilot flew undetected deep into Israeli airspace—a fully alert Israeli air defense is capable of coordinating its sensors, fighters, and land-based defenses with a level of effectiveness that no other Middle Eastern air force can approach.[42] Israel has a better overall mix of systems, better-trained personnel, and a far better ability to integrate all its assets with its own technology and software than any other Middle Eastern air force.

The IAF has an unequaled record in air-to-air combat. It destroyed many of its opponent's aircraft on the ground in the 1967 war and then scored 72 air-to-air kills over the rest. It destroyed 113 Egyptian and Syrian aircraft in air-to-air combat during the war of attrition, and killed 452 Egyptian, Syrian, Iraqi, and Jordanian aircraft during the October War in 1973. It killed at least 23 Syrian aircraft between 1973 and 1982, and killed 71 fixed-wing aircraft during the fighting in 1982. It shot down 3 Syrian fighters between 1982 and 1992. While it has lost 247 aircraft in combat since the beginning of the 1948 war, only 18 have been lost in air-to-air combat. In contrast, Arab forces have lost at least 1,428 fixed-wing and rotary wing aircraft in combat, and 817 have been lost in air-to-air combat.

Israel's advantages in strategic and long-range offensive operations are even greater. The IAF is the only air force in the Middle East that is seriously organized for strategic attacks on its neighbors. Other Middle Eastern air forces may have long-range strike aircraft, effective munitions, and even a limited refueling capacity. They are, however, essentially amateurs in using their assets to inflict strategic damage on an enemy nation or in conducting effective long-range strategic strikes.

Israel has shown it has the ability to strike deep into the Arab world, and has greatly improved its long-range strike capability since its attacks on Osirak in 1981 and on Tunisia in 1985. It has the F-15I and greatly improved refueling capability, targeting capability, standoff precision munitions, and electronic warfare capability. Israel could probably surgically strike a limited number of key targets in virtually any Arab country within 1,500 nautical miles of Israel, and could sustain operations against western Iraq. It would, however, probably be forced to use nuclear weapons to achieve significant strategic impact on more than a few Iraqi facilities, or if it has to simultaneously engage Syrian and Iraqi forces.

Nevertheless, several Arab forces now have combat elements with moderate to high capabilities. Two Arab air forces—Egypt and Saudi Arabia—have relatively good training standards, modern combat aircraft, and advanced battle management systems like the E-3A and E-2C. The IAF faces growing problems over the cost of advanced new aircraft, munitions, sensors, and battle management systems. Modernization will continue to present financial challenges. The IAF would like to buy up to 42 more AH-64 Apache or AH-64D Longbow attack helicopters, including at least 1 more squadron equipped with Longbow long-range, all-weather, fire-and-forget, antiarmor missiles.

More generally, the IAF faces two evolving challenges that could erode its present almost decisive superiority. One is the risk that a nation like Syria will acquire large numbers of truly modern surface-to-air missiles like the S-300 or S-400, and the necessary command and control system and sensors. The other is proliferation. Long-range missiles and weapons of mass destruction pose a risk to all of Israel's conventional forces, but they pose a particular challenge to Israel's air forces because they (a) provide the ability to strike directly at Israel's densely packed main operating bases, and (b) bypass its air combat capabilities. Israel's very strengths drive its opponents toward asymmetric warfare, and to use proliferation as a way to exploit its remaining areas of vulnerability.

Land-Based Air Defenses

The IAF operates Israel's land-based air defense units. These are organized into six brigades covering five geographic regions (central, northwestern, southeastern, southwestern, and northeastern), plus a training unit. Weapons are deployed into battalions organized by weapons type. This includes Israel's Patriot/I Hawk battalions (136, 138, and 139 Battalions) that have one Patriot battery and three I-Hawk batteries each. Israel now has 17 batteries of MIM-23 Improved Hawk surface-to-air missiles, and 3 batteries of upgraded Patriot missiles with improved antitactical ballistic missile capabilities, and has deployed 2 Arrow batteries at Palmahim and Ein Shemer.[43] The Patriot batteries have 3 multiple launcher fire units each. In mid-May 2004 the IAF successfully conducted an experimental launch of Patriot and Hawk missiles at a base in central Israel to test unspecified "technological improvements" in these air defense components.[44]

Israel is the only state that has the resources, technology, organizational skills, war planning capability, and leadership to provide such a comprehensive approach to combining land-based air defense and air warfare. Jordan has the technical understanding, but lacks the equipment and resources. Egypt combines some modern capabilities with large obsolete forces, and has a lack of overall systems integration and military coherence. Syria relies on aging Soviet systems, the most modern of which dates back to the early 1980s. Its air defense deployments and battle management systems are poorly executed in detail, and lack effective systems integration, electronic warfare capability, and modern C^4I/BM capabilities.

The Israeli system is believed to make use of the Hughes technology developed for the U.S. Air Force, including many elements of the USAF

407L tactical command and control system and Hughes 4118 digital computers. The system has main control centers in the Negev and near Tel Aviv. It has a mix of different radars, including at least 2 AN/TPS-43 three-dimensional radars with 3 AN/MPQ-53 radar sets and 3 AN/MSQ-104 engagement control stations bought in 1998. This system is tailored to Israel's local threats and has sufficient technology to meet these threats in combat. Israel also has the ability to coordinate its air defenses from the air, has superior electronic warfare and systems integration capability, and has a clear strategy for suppressing enemy land-based air defenses and the ability to execute it.

The Israeli army also has 8 short-range Chaparral missile fire units and units with large numbers of Stinger, Grail, and Redeye man portable missiles and Vulcan antiaircraft (AA) guns. It has over 250 Stingers, 1,000 obsolescent Redeye man portable surface-to air missiles, and 45 Chaparral crew-served missile launchers. It also has some 850 20-mm AA guns—including TCM-20s and M-167 Vulcans. It has 35 M-163 Vulcan/M-48 Chaparral gun-missile systems, 100 ZU-23 23-mm and 60 ZSU-23-4 23-mm AA guns, and some M-39 37-mm and L-70 40-mm AA guns. The IAF has eight Stinger batteries and eight Chaparral batteries. These assets give Israel fewer land-based air defense forces and mobility than some of its neighbors, but Israel relies primarily upon its air force for such defense.

Two Israeli defense firms have jointly produced a new surface-to-air missile platform dubbed the "SPYDER." The all-weather day/night system is truck-mounted along with a surveillance radar and a command and control unit. The SPYDER is designed to target precision-guided munitions, helicopters, UAVs, and aircraft up to 15 kilometers away and up to 9,000 meters in the air.[45] The IDF has not, however, announced any plans to acquire SPYDER units.

The IDF, in conjunction with the U.S. Army, is developing a mobile tactical high-energy laser (MTHEL) that will target UAVs, some types of cruise missiles, artillery shells, and short-range rockets. A similar system, albeit much larger and in prototype form only, has already been produced in the United States. The Ministry of Defense envisions deploying it by 2007.[46]

Continuing Strategic Challenges

In spite of Israel's conventional military superiority, and its nuclear forces—which are described in Chapter 10—Israel does face continuing strategic challenges:

- The IDF must make hard trade-offs between technology and force size, mass intakes of conscripts for "nation building" and real war-fighting needs, and high-quality, long-call-up reserves and large reserve forces.
- Israel must deal with an ongoing asymmetric war with the Palestinians and the constant threat of extremist and terrorist attacks. These partly offset its

advantages in conventional force strength, force it to constantly devote major resources to offensive missions, and are a major threat to any new peace process.

- Israel must choose between defense at its borders and invasion or counterattack into Arab territory, and decide how to use its new deep-strike air and missile capabilities, and air mobile/air assault forces to defeat Arab enemies or force them to peace. This may lead to more emphasis on airpower, missiles, and long-range artillery to attrite attacking land forces before IDF armor begins a counterattack or to complex joint operations. It also may force the IDF to adapt its tactics and joint force mix under enemy attack, rather than impose it by preempting.

- Israel's need to maintain control over the Jordan River Valley in order to prevent and deter a conventional attack from the east has become less critical because the removal of Saddam's regime in Iraq significantly reduced the short-term likelihood of a conventional Arab-Israeli conflict on the Eastern Front. Nevertheless, the Israeli government still views the Valley as essential to Israel's security because it serves as a buffer zone between Palestinians in the West Bank and Jordan, both protecting Jordan's Hashemite regime from potential Palestinian destabilization efforts and preventing the import of arms and military reinforcements through this avenue. Hence, control over the Jordan Valley is another contentious issue precluding an Israeli-Palestinian final status agreement.

- Israel must plan for continued warfare with the Palestinians even as it seeks a peace. A sovereign Palestinian state or entity would also change the strategic geography of Israel at virtually every level and a failed peace could mean massive problems in terms of terrorism and urban, asymmetric, and occupation warfare.

- Israel must simultaneously plan to deter Syria, to fight Syria, and to make peace with Syria, with or without peace with Lebanon. It must also prepare for low-level war, large-scale conventional combat, and warfare involving chemical and biological weapons. Under worst cases, this could involve outside Arab and/or Iranian intervention.

- The IDF must plan for the risk of an extended low-intensity war on its border with Lebanon.

- Israel cannot count on coalition warfare, but it must decide how to strengthen alliances and secure it peace with Egypt, Jordan, and other powers in the region. So far, this has meant closer strategic cooperation with the United States and Turkey, but the IDF must also be prepared to rethink the way in which it would assist Jordan in the event of Syrian pressure or attack, and the possibility of extending missile defense over Jordan and Palestinian territory.

- The IDF must look beyond defense against its neighbors, most of whom now have peace treaties with Israel, to a broader range of threats like Iran, which is in the process of acquiring very-long-range strike capabilities and which can support proxies in asymmetric warfare.

- Nuclear and retaliatory survivability is becoming a growing problem, as is reliance on an undeclared nuclear deterrent. Israel continued to use its limited resources to build more nuclear warheads, but its shelters are not hardened silos and do not protect its existing warheads and Jericho medium-range missiles from a preemptive surprise nuclear attack.

- Any move to place a number of Israel's nuclear missiles in submarines is likely to be challenged by other Middle Eastern countries, that may respond by acquiring attack subs, helicopters, and planes with antisubmarine warfare capabilities and more sensitive detection devices. Iran has acquired three older submarines, and while they may not be able to challenge the Israeli subs, it may signify a new proliferation arena. Saudi Arabia has expressed interest in purchasing submarines and is seeking ten NH-90 helicopters with antisubmarine warfare capabilities for their Arriyad-class frigates.

- Counterproliferation involves both offense and defense. In 1981 the IAF was able to destroy an Iraqi nuclear reactor before it could start to produce material or waste that could be used for atomic weapons. Now Iran has been successful in using Chinese and Russian support to develop a nuclear program that is spread out and not susceptible to long-range attack. This requires a shift to missile defense, but it also requires a broader counterproliferation strategy and possibly a new approach to deterrence and retaliation—making nuclear deterrence more overt and mixing it with credible long-range precision conventional strikes.

Egypt

Egypt has been at peace with Israel since 1979, and has scrupulously honored the terms of this peace. Nevertheless, it has never been able to plan on a secure peace because of ongoing conflicts between Israel and the Palestinians and the risks illustrated by Israel's past conflicts with Lebanon. Egypt has also planned for the risk of a military confrontation with the Sudan over the control of the Nile, to provide security for the transit of shipping through the Suez Canal and Red Sea, and for potential conflicts with Libya—although the risk of these latter conflicts has diminished steadily in recent years.

These risks, the political and bureaucratic momentum behind maintaining a large force posture for status purposes, and the fact that Egypt's armed forces play a major role in its government have led Egypt to spend far more on military forces than it can really afford. It has also used U.S. grant assistance for military purposes that would be far better spent on economic development and reform. Such spending also limits Egypt's ability to deal with a serious Islamic extremist and terrorist threat, caused in part by deteriorating economic conditions and living standards for much of the population.

The end result is that Egypt has formidable military forces by regional standards. Egypt retains much of the force levels it had during the October War in 1973, and has an active strength of 450,000 men, although

322,000 are conscripts serving 12–36 months, who often lack adequate training. The recent trends in Egyptian forces are shown in Figure 5.10, and indicate that Egypt's greatest strength lies in its pool of advanced modern equipment. Egypt has also benefited from well over a decade of large amounts of U.S. grant aid, and is the only Arab state bordering Israel that has been able to compete in arms imports during the 1990s. Egypt has had massive supplies of U.S. and other Western arms and it has a substantial backlog of new orders. At the same time, Egypt is extremely dependent on U.S. aid. This dependence will present problems if U.S. aid declines in the future, or if Egypt should ever back away from the peace process. Egypt would face an immediate cutoff of U.S. aid and resupply if it should come under extremist Islamist rule, and this would present major near-term problems in Egypt's effort to support U.S.-supplied systems and likely lead to an immediate internal economic crisis.

Egypt has also generally emphasized force strength over force quality, often limiting its ability to make effective use of its modern weapons. Its active forces have serious manpower quality, readiness, and sustainability problems. Egypt also maintains massive 410,000-man reserve forces (300,000 army, 20,000 air force, 70,000 air defenses, 14,000 navy). These have been allowed to collapse into near decay since the 1973 war. Reserves still have nominal assignments to fill in badly undermanned regular units, but most reservists receive little or no training. Those reserves who do train usually do not receive meaningful training above the company to battalion level, and many train using obsolete equipment that is different from the equipment in the active units to which they are assigned.

Land Forces

The Egyptian army has strength of 320,000 actives, including 250,000 conscripts, plus a reserve pool of up to 300,000 men. Egypt's command structure is organized into five military zones: the Central Zone (Cairo), the Eastern Zone (Ismailiya), the Western Zone (Meksa Matrun), the Southern Zone (Alexandria), and the Northern Zone (Aswan). In spite of the fact that Egypt has strictly adhered to the terms of its peace with Israel, the Eastern Zone and defense of Suez and the Sinai is still its major military priority. Its two field armies (the 2nd Field Army and 3rd Field Army) are placed under the Eastern Zone Command.

Egypt's combat strength emphasizes heavy forces. It has four armored divisions, each with a nominal organization of two armored, one mechanized, and one artillery brigades. It has eight mechanized infantry divisions, each with a nominal strength of one armored, two mechanized, and one artillery brigades. It also has one Republican Guard armored brigade, four independent armored brigades, one air mobile brigade, four independent mechanized brigades, two independent infantry brigades, one special forces

Figure 5.10
Force Trends in Egypt

Category/Weapon	1975	1980	1985	1990	1995	2001	2004
Manpower							
Total Active	322,500	367,000	445,000	450,000	450,000	448,500	450,000
(Conscript)	—	—	(250,000)	(252,000)	(320,000)	(322,000)	322,000
Total Reserve	—	—	380,000	623,000	254,000	254,000	410,000
Total	—	—	825,000	1,073,000	704,000	703,500	860,000
Paramilitary	120,000	49,000	139,000	374,000	230,000	230,000	330,000
Land Forces							
Active Manpower	275,000	245,000	320,000	320,000	320,000	320,000	320,000
(Conscripts)	—	—	(250,000)	(180,000)	(250,000+)	(250,000+)	250,000+
Reserve Manpower	500,000	350,000	323,000	500,000	150,000	150,000	300,000
Total Reserve & Active Manpower	775,000	595,000	643,000	820,000	470,000	470,000	620,000
Main Battle Tanks (Fixed & in Storage)	1,945	1,600	2,159	3,190	3,500	3,960	3,655
AIFVs/Armored Cars/Lt. Tanks	130	580	747	770	1,080	740 (220)	470 (220)
APCs/Recce/Scouts/	2,500	2,550	2,550	2,745	3,834	3,990 (1,075)	3,800 (500)
WWII Half-Tracks	0	0	0	0	0	0	0
ATGM Launchers	—	1,000	—	3,340	2,785	2,660	4,600
SP Artillery	200	200	200	185	200	251	320
Towed Artillery	1,300	1,500	1,500	1,120	971	971	971
MRLs	420	300	300	300	296	156	354
Mortars	—	—	—	—	—	2,400	2,370
SSM Launchers	18+	54	—	13	21	18–24	21

AA Guns (Army + ADC)	2,500	2,500+	2,500+	1,070+	1,677+	834	2,674+
Lt. SAM Launchers	—	—	—	1,226+	2,046	1,146	2,096+
Air & Air Defense Forces							
Active Air Force Manpower	30,000	27,000	25,000	80,000	30,000	30,000	30,000
Air Defense Command	(75,000)*	75,000	80,000	30,000	80,000	80,000	80,000
Total Reserve Manpower	20,000	—	42,000	109,000	90,000	90,000	90,000
Aircraft							
Total Fighter/FGA/Recce	608**	363 (305)	427	475	564	583	579
Bomber	30	23	13	0	0	0	0
Fighter	—	45	164	272	339	363	335
FGA/Fighter	200	92	103	0	0	0	0
FGA	205–253	201	73	139	135	133	131
Recce	—	—	34	20	20	20	20
Airborne Early Warning (AEW)	0	0	0	5	5	5	4
Electronic Warfare (EW)	0	2	2	10	10	10	7
Maritime Reconnaissance (MR)	0	0	0	2	2	2	2
Combat Capable Trainer/OCU	153	50	38	48	70	64	64
Tanker	0	0	0	0	0	0	0
Transport	70	65	37	25	32	32	41
Helicopters							
Attack/Armed	0	0	48	74	103	129	101
ASW/SAR	0	0	5	0	14	0	10
Transport & Other	138	168	108	118	115	158	158
Total	138	168	161	192	232	287	259
SAM Forces							
Batteries	—	—	—	—	—	38+	38+
Heavy Launchers	635	635	727	808	702	628	628
Medium Launchers	—	20	16	50	36	36–54	36–54

continued

Figure 5.10 (Continued)

Category/Weapon	1975	1980	1985	1990	1995	2001	2004
Naval Forces							
Active Manpower	17,500	20,000	20,000	20,000	16,000	18,500	20,000
Reserve Manpower	15,000	—	15,000	14,000	14,000	14,000	20,000
Total Manpower	32,500	—	35,000	34,000	30,000	34,000	40,000
Submarines	12	10 (1)	14	10	4	4	4
Destroyers/Frigates/Corvettes	8	8	10	5	7	11	11
Missile	—	5	7	4	6	10	10
Other	—	3	3	1	1	1	1
Missile Patrol	13	22	30	21	25	25	26
Coastal/Inshore Patrol	42	38	32	18	18	15	21
Mine	12	14	15	9	7	13	12
Amphibious Ships	—	3	3	3	3	3	3
Landing Craft/Light Support	14	17	13	—	11	9	20
Fixed-Wing Combat Aircraft	0	0	0	0	0	0	0
MR/MPA	0	0	0	0	0	0	0
ASW/Combat Helicopter	6	(5)	(17)	(14)	24	24	—
Other Helicopters	—	—	—	—	—	—	—

*Included in the army total.

**Includes 108 fighters in the Air Defense Command

Source: Adapted by Anthony H. Cordesman from data provided by U.S. experts; and IISS, *The Military Balance.*

group, one air mobile brigade, and five to six commando groups. Like Syria, a substantial part of this order of battle is composed of relatively low-grade and poorly equipped units, many of which would require substantial fill-in with reservists—almost all of whom would require several months of training to be effective. Major combat support forces include fifteen independent artillery brigades, one FROG surface-to-surface rocket brigade, and one Scud-B surface-to-surface missile brigade.

Each military zone has a nominal strength of one armored division with two armored and one mechanized brigades, except for the Central Zone. The mechanized divisions are concentrated in the Eastern Zone, but some are in the other zones. Each mechanized division has two mechanized and one armored brigade. The Republican Guard is under the command of the Central Zone, but takes its orders directly from the president. The air mobile and paratroop units also seem to be under presidential command. The army's main bases are in Cairo, Alexandria, El Arish, Ismailiya, Luxor, Matruh, Port Said, Sharm el-Sheik, Taba, and Suez.

The Egyptian army has large holdings of modern equipment and continues to modernize. In 2004, Egypt had 550 M-1A1 tanks, plus 400 M-60A1s and 1,000 M-60A3s: 1,950 relatively modern tanks out of a total of 3,855, or 58 percent. These forces compare with 2,880 modern tank for Israel, out of overall holdings of 3,950 tanks (53 percent). A decade earlier, Egypt only had 785 M-60A3s out of a total of 2,425 tanks. Egypt lagged in modern armored fighting vehicles, but had 2,320 M-113s. Egypt is scheduled to produce additional M-1A1s to bring Egypt's total M1A1 fleet to 880 by June 2008.[47] Egypt is seeking to buy 21 M88A2 Hercules heavy recovery vehicle kits from the United States.[48]

Egypt has, however, weakened its ability to use its modern weapons effectively by overextending its force structure. It tries to support far too large a land force structure at the cost of relying on low-quality conscripts, poor training for most of its forces, and increasingly underpaid officers and other ranks. In spite of a decade of ongoing modernization, about 35–40 percent of Egypt's total inventory of major land combat weapons still consists of obsolete and badly worn Soviet-bloc systems supplied in the late 1960s, and none of its Soviet-bloc inventory was supplied after 1974. For example, the rest of its tanks consisted of obsolete to obsolescent Soviet-bloc models, with some conversions and upgrades of dubious value. These included 1,155 T-54/T-55s, only 260 of which had had any real upgrading into the Ramses version, and 550 T-62s. The most Egypt could do to modernize the rest of these tanks was to obtain British aid in upgrading their ammunition.

The IISS estimates that only 225 YPR-765s of Egypt's holdings of 690 AIFVs were relatively advanced types, although *Jane's* reports that some 611 were delivered, including 304 with 25-mm cannon, six command post vehicles with 25-mm cannon, 210 PRAT-TOW vehicles with a twin TOW ATGM launcher, 79 other command post vehicles with 12.7-mm machine gun, and 12 other communications and command post variants. Egypt has some 220 BMP-1s in storage, and its other holdings consisted of 250 Spanish lightly armored, wheeled BMR-600Ps.

Egypt had 300 worn and aging BRDM-2, and 112 more modern Commando Scout light wheeled armored reconnaissance vehicles. Its 4,300 APCs included some 2,400 relatively low-quality systems: 650 Walids, 1,000 Fahds, 500 worn and aging BTR-50/OT-62s (most in storage), and 250 aging BRT-60s. Egypt may upgrade around 350 BTR-50s with the help of Belarus.[49] They also, however, included and some 1,900 variants of the M-113A3. Some of Egypt's M-113s have been upgunned and may have add-on armor. The Egyptian armed forces are trying to procure 100 up-armored armament carrier 4×4 high mobility multipurpose wheeled vehicles.[50]

Egypt had 3,200 numbers of advanced U.S.-made TOW antitank guided weapons (including the TOW-2A, which has a significant capability against reactive armor), 50 mounted on M-901 armored vehicles and 210 on YPR-765s. Egypt was seeking TOW-2B missiles. Egypt also had 200 relatively effective Milan manportable weapons. However, Egypt also had 1,200 aging, second-generation AT-3 Saggers and 200 Swingfires.

Egypt had significant artillery strength. It had 320 self-propelled weapons: 196 modern self-propelled M-109A2 155-mm howitzers, and 169 M-109A2/A3s in delivery, plus 124 122-mm self-propelled systems using a mix of Soviet-supplied and U.S.-supplied chassis. Egypt had some 1,000 towed tube artillery weapons, including 551 FSU-supplied 122-mm and 420 FSU-supplied 130-mm weapons. Its roughly 356 multiple rocket launchers included 96 BM-11 60 BM-21 and, 200 Saqr 10/18/36 122-mm weapons. It had some 26/227-mm MLRS weapons, and 2,850 rockets, entering service and in delivery.

Unlike some Arab states, Egypt has made a major effort to improve and modernize its artillery targeting and fire control systems, and has had AN/TPQ-37 counterbattery radars, UAVs, and RASIT artillery support vehicles to support its artillery in maneuver warfare. However, the rest of its artillery consisted of 76 aging FSU-supplied 122-mm self-propelled weapons, 971 towed weapons, and 156 operational multiple rocket launchers, only a limited number of which had been modernized. Egypt has never fully trained and organized the forces using its older weapons into a modern war-fighting force and most of its artillery forces still lack modern support vehicles, C⁴I, battle management and fire control, and target acquisition and counterbattery radars and sensors. Many of its forces are not trained or equipped for effective BVR targeting, counterbattery fire, and rapid shifts of mass fire.

Egypt has large numbers of short-range air defense weapons, which included over 1,000 antiaircraft guns. Most were obsolete weapons suitable only for suppressive fire, but as many as 118 were radar-guided ZSU-23.4 radar-guided, self-propelled systems. Egypt had over 2,000 manportable surface-to-air missiles, largely versions of the SA-7 but including some Stingers. It had 20 SA-9s, 26 M-54 Chaparrals, and 50 Avengers.

In spite of its obvious successes in many aspects of force modernization, these figures show that the Egyptian army is still heavily dependent on aging and obsolescent Soviet-supplied systems, many of which are inoperable or incapable of sustained combat. Ironically, the Egyptian army could probably be much more effective if it concentrated its manpower and training resources on a much smaller and better-equipped force. It could also use the resulting savings in military spending to either improve its readiness and sustainment or for economic development.

It is also important to note that Egypt has honored its peace treaty. It has never taken the steps necessary to deploy for war with Israel. In spite of ongoing improvements, it has never modernized its infrastructure, support, and sustainment capabilities near the Suez Canal in ways that would allow it to efficiently mobilize and assemble a massive armored force that could rapidly thrust across the Sinai and then sustain itself in intense combat. It has emphasized acquisition and modernization over overall readiness and sustainment, and it is much better postured to defend in depth than to attack in a massive war of offensive maneuver.

Naval Forces

Egypt has a 16,000–20,000-man navy, including a 2,000-man coast guard. Much of this force consists of conscripts with limited experience and training. Its headquarters is in Alexandria, and its forces are based primarily at Port Said, Mersa Matruh, Safaqa, Port Tewfiq, and Hurghada. In the past, the navy has tended to emphasize force quantity over force quality and to try to retain its past strength levels even at the cost of obsolescence and limited readiness.

Egypt's forces are numerically much larger than those of Israel—four submarines and eleven principle surface combatants versus three submarines and five principle surface combatants for Israel.[51] While the Egyptian navy has impressive combat strength, however, this strength comes at the cost of holding on to aging and low-capability ships and limited overall effectiveness—although the navy is improving as it continues to modernize.

Egypt's major combat ships include four ex-Chinese, Romeo-class submarines. These are badly aging designs, but they have been modernized to use Western periscopes, trailing GPS, passive sonars and fire control systems; fire modern wire-guided torpedoes and Harpoon missiles (130-kilometer maximum range); and use modern torpedoes. One of the submarines has not, however, been seen as operational since 1986. Egypt has examined replacing them with two former Royal Dutch-Navy Zwaardvis-class submarines, which could be specially refitted for Egypt. Egypt hopes to use its U.S. FMF grants to purchase these subs and to buy to two new-build RDM-designed Moray 1400 submarines or German Type-209s. These deliveries would significantly increase the capabilities of the Egyptian navy, but there is little evidence as yet that the United States will agree to the use of funds for foreign ships or that the Egyptian navy will get the funding priority it needs to use U.S. aid. Egypt will receive an additional 62 Harpoon missiles by mid-2005.[52]

Egypt has two low-quality 1,425-ton Jianghu 1–class Chinese frigates dating back to the early 1980s, which have never been upgraded and refitted as the Egyptian navy once planned. Each is equipped with four HY-2 antiship missiles (with a maximum range of 80 kilometers) and four 57-mm guns. These ships are both active in the Red Sea, where no other regional navy except Saudi Arabia deploys more modern major combat vessels.

Egypt does, however, have two El Suez (Spanish Descubierta-class) frigates. The ships date back to the early 1970s, but each was modernized in the early 1980s. These are 1,479-ton ships equipped with eight Harpoon antiship missiles (maximum range 70 nautical miles, 130 kilometers) in two quadruple launchers, an octuple Albatros anti–air missile launcher, a 76-mm gun, two triple torpedo tubes, and antisubmarine mortars. Their combat data systems, air search, and fire control radars were updated in 1995–1996. They can be modified to carry up to eight Otomats.

Egypt also has two 3,011-ton Damyat (ex-U.S. FF-1051 Knox)-class guided missile frigates. While they date back to the 1970s, they were recommissioned in 1995. Each has eight Harpoon missiles, ASROC antisubmarine rocket launchers, Phalanx close-in air/missile defenses, and a 127-mm gun. They have two twin torpedo tubes, and relatively modern combat data systems, electronic countermeasures, search and surface radars, and fire control systems. Each can carry one Kaman Seasprite SH-2G helicopter. They have had boiler problems, their ASROC system is now dated, and they lack long-range air defenses. The navy will receive an additional four Phalanx systems by mid-2005.[53]

In 1996 the Egyptian navy began to acquire four Oliver Hazard Perry-class frigates in a $600 million deal with the United States. These frigates are 2,750-ton vessels. They are now in service as the Mubarak-class, and are armed with four Harpoon antiship missiles, 76-mm guns, Standard SM-1 surface-to-air missiles, Vulcan, and six torpedo tubes with Mk 46 antisubmarine torpedoes. All of these ships date back to the early 1980s, but they have been upgrade and have relatively modern radars, sonars, fire control, combat data management, and electronic warfare capability. Each can carry two Kaman Seasprite SH-2G helicopters.

Egypt has twenty-four missile patrol craft, twelve of which are relatively capable ships armed with the Harpoon and Otomat antiship missile. These include six 307-ton Ramadan-class ships, each with four Otomat I antiship missiles and 76-mm guns. They also include five 82-ton October-class craft with two Otomat I missiles and 30-mm guns, and five 234-ton Tiger-class ships armed with Exocet missiles and one 76-mm gun.

Egypt has four aging 68-ton Hegu-class (the Chinese version of the FSU Komar-class) vessels with SY-1 missiles. They were refitted with improved electronic support measures in 1996, but one seems to be laid up on what may be a permanent basis. Egypt still has four obsolete Osa I–class with four SS-N-2A Styx missiles; and has 2 Komar-class vessels with SS-N-2A missiles laid up in reserve. Several of the Hegu-, Osa-, and Komar-class ships have had serious combat damage or been taken out of service, but two Hegus- and four Osa-class boats are still operational.

Egypt has 18–27 other patrol ships (4 Shanghai-class, 6 Shershen-class, 8 Hainan-class, and 5 Type 148 Tiger-class). Some are armed with 122-mm multiple rocket launchers, torpedoes, or 57-mm guns. They can also be used to lay mines. These have some value in the patrol mission and fire support mission in secure waters. Egypt has 15 operational mine vessels, including 5 relatively modern Swiftsure coastal mine hunters and route survey vessels. The rest of its mine vessels can lay mines, but its 4 ex-Soviet Yurka and 6 T-43-class mine vessels have little modern mine detection and minesweeping capability. Plans to modernize their capabilities have never been implemented.

The Egyptian navy has three Polnochny-class amphibious vessels (100 troops and 10 tanks capacity each) and nine Vydra-class landing ships (200 troops capacity each). It has some twenty support ships, including diving and support ships. There are six specialized Seafox ships for deliveries of underwater demolition teams.

The army operates three land-based, truck-mounted batteries of Otomat antiship missiles with Plessey targeting radars, and two brigades of 100-mm, 130-mm, and 152-mm SM-4-1 coastal defense guns. These defenses are located near major ports and the approaches to the Suez Canal and are under Egyptian navy command.

In addition, the Egyptian air force (EAF) is equipping a limited number of F-16s to carry Harpoon antiship missiles, and Egypt wants to acquire 10 antisubmarine warfare helicopters. It currently has 9 operational SA-342L antiship missile-equipped helicopters (out of a total of 12) armed with AS-12 guided missiles, and 10 SH-2(G)E Seasprite helicopters equipped for antisubmarine warfare, which carry sonars and two torpedoes or depth charges. It also has five Mark 47 Sea Kings equipped for both the antiship and antisubmarine warfare roles. The EAF has five E-2C Hawkeyes with search and warning radars and both electronic support and counter measures, and two Beech 1900C surveillance aircraft with surveillance radars and electronic support measures that it can use in the maritime patrol role.

The Egyptian navy has many capable vessels, and a steadily increasing capability to defend Egypt's coast, the approaches to the Suez Canal, and Egypt's interests in the Red Sea. However, its naval modernization is still limited and its training and sustainability have had comparatively limited funding. The Egyptian navy is improving, but it has not yet received the funding necessary to fully modernize its ships, or to carry out the levels of advanced joint warfare training it needs. It has difficulties in maintaining ships from so many different countries, and many of its ships and boats are worn and obsolete and have little operational effectiveness.

Egypt cannot defeat Israel at sea, but has the capability to pose a limited to moderate threat to Israel, although it would face major problems. It does not have the training, electronic warfare, or navy–air force joint operations capabilities to challenge Israel's best Sa'ar-class vessels in joint operations, except in Egyptian waters, where Egyptian ships might have air cover and protection from its submarines. Most importantly, Egypt's navy would not have the air cover and air defense capability necessary to protect itself from the Israeli air force.

The Egyptian navy is, however, the dominant regional naval power in the Red Sea. It has moderate capability to defend the approaches to the Suez Canal. Egypt can play an important role in dealing with the less sophisticated naval and air forces of potentially hostile Red Sea countries and in securing the Egyptian coastline and approaches to the Suez Canal. The better-crewed and funded Egyptian ships have drawn considerable praise from their U.S. counterparts during joint exercises.

Air Forces

Egypt has the only air force in the Arab "ring states" with large numbers of modern fighters capable of advanced strike/attack missions and BVR/look-down shoot-down air-to-air combat. The air force had 30,000 actives in 2004, including 10 conscripts and a reserve pool of 20,000 men. Egypt had 38 F-16A/Bs, 119 F-16C/Ds, and 9 Mirage 2000B/Cs in 2004. This was 163 advanced aircraft out of a total of 579 combat aircraft (29 percent). Egypt's holdings compared with 62 F-15A-Ds, 25 F-15Is, and 203 F-16A-Ds for Israel. Israel had 290 advanced combat aircraft out of a total of 438, or 66 percent.

Egypt's total forces included 131 attack fighters, 335 fighter-attack aircraft, and 20 reconnaissance fighters. Its forces have 7 attack squadrons, equipped with 2/42 Alphajets, 2/44 obsolete PRC-made J-6s, 29 aging F-4Es, and 16 aging Mirage 5E2s. Its fighter attack units included 2/26 F-16A, 7/113 F-16C, 1/16 Mirage 2000C, 2/53 aging Mirage 5D/E, 6/74 obsolete MiG-21, and 3/53 obsolescent J-7s. It had two reconnaissance squadrons, equipped with 6 aging Mirage 5SDR and 14 obsolete MiG 21-R. It also had 12 F-16B, 6 F-16D, 3 Mirage 2000B, 15 MiG-21U, 16 JJ-6, and 35 L-59E armed aircraft in its training units.

Egypt has 121 armed helicopters. It is deploying 36 AH-64 Apache attack helicopters, and has 6/65 SA-342Ks (44 with High-Subsonic Optically Teleguided [HOT] weapons and 25 with 20-mm guns). It also has 5 SA-342L, 5 Sea King 47, and 10 SH-2G ASW helicopters, many serving with the navy.

Egypt is the only Arab air force with AEW aircraft and some modern electronic warfare, intelligence, and reconnaissance aircraft—including 4 E-2Cs, 2 C-130H ELINT, 1–4 Beech 1900 ELINT, and 4 Commando 2E ECM helicopters. It has 2 Beech 1900C surveillance aircraft. Egypt also makes growing use of UAVs, including 20 R-E-50 Skyeyes and 29 Teledyne-Ryan 324 Scarabs. The EAF absorbed the first of a planned 6 E-2C Hawkeye 2000 aircraft. The fleet will eventually replace Egypt's older E-2Cs.[54]

Egypt has significant force improvements under way. It is currently scheduled to receive a total of 220 F-16s and to upgrade its AH-64s to Longbow. Egypt has large numbers of modern air-to-surface, antiradiation, and air-to-air precision-guided weapons. It is taking delivery on the AMRAAM and has the technology to make fuel-air-explosive (FAE) weapons, although it is not clear it has done so. Egypt is seeking an additional 414 AIM-9M-1/2 Sidewinder missiles and 459 Hellfire II missiles.[55] The air force will upgrade 35 of the AH64As with the Modular Mission Support System, or MMSS, that will enable Egypt to integrate its jets with its Apaches.[56] The air force will be equipping several of its F-16s with reconnaissance pods as part of its ongoing Theater Airborne Reconnaissance Systems program. To be completed by 2007, the program will include the construction of two ground stations as well as extensive training and repair programs.[57]

The EAF has large transport assets. It has some 60 fixed-wing transport aircraft, including 22 C-130Hs. It has 141 transport helicopters, including 19 CH-47C/D heavy transports; 62 Mi-8, 25 Command, and 2 S-70 medium helicopters; and 10 Mi-6, 17 UH-12E, 2 UH-60A, 2 UH-60L, and 2 AS-61 light helicopters. The readiness and operational status of its older helicopters is, however, uncertain.

The Egyptian air force is still developing effective joint warfare capabilities, but can already do a far better job of supporting its land and naval forces than most Arab air forces, and some Egyptian squadrons have excellent readiness and proficiency. However, Egyptian air force wastes its resources on ineffective systems like its J-6s, J-7s, and MiG-21s. The EAF has not done well in keeping its Mirage 5s at a high degree of combat readiness. Egypt still has aging Alpha Jets, and well-worn F-4Es. The operational readiness of many of its 65 SA-342K armed helicopters is limited.

More generally, the Egyptian air force cannot compete with the Israeli air force in overall battle management, the exploitation of modern sensors and targeting systems, electronic warfare, beyond-visual-range warfare, and in using precision strike and attack munitions. It also focuses more on numbers than sustainability, and has limited ability to sustain high sortie rates.

Land-Based Air Defenses

As a result of the Canal War of 1970, Egypt has developed one of the largest dedicated air defense forces in the Middle East. It has a separate Air Defense Command with nearly 80,000 personnel. Its forces are organized into four divisions with regional brigades and a countrywide total of 100 air defense battalions. These forces include large numbers of worn, obsolete Soviet-bloc systems that have had only limited upgrading. These assets include 40 SA-2 battalions with 282 launchers, 53 SA-3 battalions with 212 launchers, and 14 SA-6 battalions with 56 launchers. These Egyptian forces have low readiness and operational sustainability, and only limited capability to resist modern jamming and other air defense suppression techniques. They are vulnerable to modern antiradiation missiles.

Egypt does have substantial holdings of more modern and more effective Western-supplied systems. They include 12 batteries of Improved Hawks with 78 launchers. Egypt is also developing an integrated command and control system, with U.S. assistance, as part of Program 776. This system is not highly advanced by U.S. standards, but it will allow Egypt to (a) integrate airborne and land-based air defenses into a common air defense system, (b) create a single C⁴I/BM network, and (c) manage a defense against air attacks that bring a moderate number of sorties together at the same time and near the same area.

Egypt has long been trying to upgrade its older air defense systems and will improve its surface-to-air missile capabilities in the near future. Egypt first considered trying to update some of its systems with modern Russian-made S-300 or S-400 surface-to-air missiles. In 1997, Egypt is reported to have submitted a proposal to Russia whereby it would purchase the S-300 in a package containing 224 missiles and nearly 100 mobile launchers and radar systems at a cost of at least $700 per missile. The S-300 is not only an effective surface-to-air missiles, but also a competent antitactical ballistic missile system and defense against cruise missiles. Egypt lacked the funds to complete this contract, however; and it could not use U.S. aid funds for such a purpose. It limited its buys from Russia to a $125 million contract to upgrade 50 Egypt's SA-3a missile launchers and their associated units by 2003.

As a result, Egypt turned to the United States. In March 1999, the United States agreed to sell Egypt $3.2 billion worth of new weapons, including 24 F-16C/D Block 40 fighter jets, 200 M-1A1 tanks, and 32 Patriot missiles. The sale gave Egypt is first battery of Patriot-3 missiles at a cost of $1.3 billion. The battery consisted of eight firing units, each containing four missiles. At the same time, the United States announced that it would provide Egypt with the same warning data on the launch of any hostile ballistic missile that it provided to Israel. Egypt will almost certainly acquire several more batteries over time, acquiring far better air, cruise, and tactical ballistic missile defenses than it has today.

Egypt is also upgrading its AN/TPS50(V)2 air defense radars to the (V)3 standard. This will provide new software and hardware, including new signal processing centers. It will also give Egypt considerably more ballistic missile attack warning and tracking capability, and advanced long-range, three-dimensional air-surveillance capabilities. The radars are linked to 12 operations centers in Egypt, which will be able to pass intercept data to both airborne and ground-based are defenses and antiballistic missile warning data to Egypt's I-Hawks and Patriots.

The Egyptian ground forces have large numbers of AA weapons. The army's surface-to-air missile assets include some 2,000 obsolete SA-7s and slightly better performing Egyptian-made variants of the SA-7 called the Ayn-as-Saqr. The army also has 12 batteries of short-range Chaparrals with 26 M-54 self-propelled Chaparral fire units, 14 batteries of short-range Crotales with 36 launchers, and at least 20 SA-9 fire units. The Egyptian army's holdings of air defense guns include 200 14.5-mm ZPU-2/4, 280 23-mm ZU-23-2/4, 200 37-mm M-1939, and 200 57-mm S-60 towed-unguided guns. They also include 118 ZSU-23-4 and 36 Sinai radar-guided self-propelled guns. The SA-9s, Chaparrals, ZSU-23-4s, and Sinais provide the Egyptian army with maneuverable air defenses that can accompany Egyptian armored forces.

In addition, Egypt's Air Defense Command has some 2,000 Soviet-bloc-supplied unguided towed AA guns ranging from 20-mm to 100-mm, and a number of light air defense systems. These include 72 Amoun (Skyguard/RIM-7F Sparrow) system with 36 twin guns and 36 quad launchers, a number of ZSU-23-4s, and Sinai-23 systems that are composed of Dassault 6SD-20S radars, 23-mm guns, and short-range Ayn-as-Saqr missiles. These weapons provide low-altitude defense of military installations and critical facilities, and can often be surprisingly effective in degrading attack sorties or destroying attack aircraft that attempt to fly through a "curtain" of massed antiaircraft fire.

Egypt cannot project large mobile land-based surface-to-air missile forces into the Sinai without having to operate individual fire units outside the full sensor and C^{4}I/BM capabilities of its central air defense command and control system. It would have to support its advancing land forces with individual surface-to-air missile units, which would become progressively more vulnerable to the IAF as they moved across the Sinai. Unless Egypt had months to build up its forces near Israel's border, the forces would become progressively more vulnerable to air attack in terms of Israel's ability both to rapidly suppress Egyptian air defenses and target and attack Egyptian land units.

Paramilitary Forces

Egypt has a wide range of paramilitary forces, including the National Guard, Central Security Force, Border Guard, Internal Security Force, General Intelligence Service, and Department for Combating Religious Activity. The National Guard, Central Security Force, and Border Guard are all under the command of the Ministry of Interior. Egyptian military intelligence has a separate, and large, internal security force to preserve the loyalty of the armed forces.

The National Guard had some 60,000 personnel in 2004. Its training and effectiveness have improved steadily in recent years, and it has become a key element of Egypt's efforts to suppress violent Islamic extremists. It is dispersed throughout the country and has automatic weapons, armored cars, and some 250 Walid armored personnel carriers. The Central Security Force is also under the Ministry of Interior and plays a major role in fighting Islamic extremists. It has some 325,000 men, and it was this force that mutinied near the pyramids in 1986. It remains relatively poorly trained, paid, and equipped and is given lower-grade conscripts while the army gets the better-educated intake. The Border Guard includes some 12,000 men in 18 regiments.

Internal Security Force and General Intelligence Service play a major role in dealing with Islamic extremists, other militant opposition groups, and foreign agents. Both services report to both ministers and the president. The Department for Combating Religious Activity is under the command of an army general, and has focused on the most extreme religious groups. These include the Islamic Jihad, Gamaat Islamiya (Islamic Group), and Vanguards of Conquest. The Muslim Brotherhood is the subject of considerable government concern but is more a political party than an extremist movement.

Jordan

Jordan has spent much of its modern history caught up in the pressures of various Arab-Israeli conflicts. Its peace agreement with Israel in 1994 has greatly eased the most serious pressure on its security and military development, and the end of Saddam Hussein's regime in Iraq in 2003 removed the threat to its Eastern border. At this point, the two major threats it faces are securing its border with Israel in the face of the Israeli-Palestinian War and a low-level risk of some crisis with Syria, and the internal instability growing out of its largely Palestinian population and the resulting internal security problems and tensions with Israel. Jordan does, however, face a limited internal security problem in dealing with Islamic extremist groups and domestic opponents of the regime.

The recent trends in Jordanian forces are shown in Figure 5.11. Jordan has long maintained some of the best trained and most professional military forces in the Middle East, and maintains a force structure of 100,500 actives and some 35,000 reserves. At the same time, Jordan has faced massive problems in financing its military modernization. This recapitalization crisis is shown in the steady decline in the value of Jordan arms imports reflected in Figure 5.12.

Jordan has dealt with this situation as effectively as its resources permit. It has focused on buying the key weapons systems that do the most to improve its capabilities, and has developed a steadily improving domestic capability to modify and upgrade its weapons. It has also developed steadily

Table 5.11
Force Trends in Jordan

Category/Weapon	1975	1980	1985	1990	1995	2001	2004
Manpower							
Total Active	80,200	67,200	70,300	82,250	98,800	103,880	100,500
(Conscript)	–	–	–	–	–	–	–
Total Reserve	–	–	35,000	35,000	35,000	35,000	35,000
Total Actives & Reserve	–	–	105,300	117,250	133,800	139,000	135,500
Paramilitary	10,000	10,000	11,000	17,000	10,000	10,000	8,050
Land Forces							
Active Manpower	75,000	60,000	62,750	74,000	90,000	90,000	85,000
(Conscripts)	–	–	–	–	–	–	–
Reserve Manpower	–	–	30,000	30,000	30,000	30,000	30,000
Total Reserve & Active	–	–	92,750	104,000	120,000	120,000	115,000
Main Battle Tanks	440	609	795	1,131	1,141	1,246	1,018
(Fixed & in Storage)	–	(260)	(270)	(300)	(78)	–	–
AIFVs/Armored Cars/Lt. Tanks	240	140	32	188	204	241	226
APCs/Recce/Scouts	440	962	850	1,244	1,100	1,100	1,350
WWII Half-Tracks	0	0	0	0	0	0	0
ATGM Launchers	–	162	610	640	640	610	640
SP Artillery	55	173	144	237	370	412	399
Towed Artillery	160	90	91	89	115	132	76
MRLs	0	0	0	0	0	0	0

continued

Table 5.11 (Continued)

Category/Weapon	1975	1980	1985	1990	1995	2001	2004
Mortars	—	400	500	600	450+	800	740
SSM Launchers	0	0	0	0	0	0	0
AA Guns	200	200	366	408	360	416	395
Lt. SAM Launchers	—	—	—	—	890	1,184	992
Air & Air Defense Forces							
Active Air Force Manpower	5,000	7,000	7,200	10,000	8,000	13,400	15,000
Active Air Defense	—	—	—	—	(2,000)	(3,400)	(3,400)
Air Force Reserve Manpower	—	—	—	5,000	5,000	—	—
Air Defense Reserve Manpower	0	0	0	0	0	0	0
Aircraft							
Total Fighter/FGA/Recce	42	58	121	104	82	106	101
Fighter	18	24	35	32	30	41	31
FGA/Fighter	0	0	0	0	0	0	0
FGA	24	24	68	72	50	65	70
Recce	0	0	0	0	0	0	0
Airborne Early Warning (AEW)	0	0	0	0	0	0	0
Electronic Warfare (EW)	0	0	0	0	0	0	0
(Fixed-Wing)	—	—	—	—	—	—	—
(Helicopter)	—	—	—	—	—	—	—
Maritime Reconnaissance (MR)	0	0	0	0	0	0	0
Combat Capable Trainer/OCU	7	10	18	0	2	2	2
Tanker	0	0	0	0	0	0	0
Transport	11	9	10	13	20	12	12

Helicopters							
Attack/Armed	22	16	24	24	0	0	0
ASW/SAR	0	0	0	0	0	0	0
Transport & Other	37	52	20	32	38	17	13
Total	59	68	44	56	38	17	13
SAM Forces (operated by Army)							
Batteries	14	14	14	14	14	14	0
Heavy Launchers	80	80	80	126	—	—	0
Medium Launchers	—	—	—	40	20	—	0
AA Guns	—	—	—	—	—	—	—
Naval Forces							
Active Manpower	500	480	600	250	350	200	250
Reserve Manpower	—	—	—	—	—	—	—
Total Manpower	500	480	600	250	350	200	250
Submarines	0	0	0	0	0	0	0
Destroyers/Frigates/Corvettes							
Missile	0	0	0	0	0	0	0
Other	0	0	0	0	0	0	0
Missile Patrol	0	0	0	0	0	0	0
Coastal/Inshore Patrol	3	6	5	1	9	9	12
Mine	0	0	0	0	0	0	0
Amphibious Ships	0	0	0	0	0	0	0
Landing Craft/Light Support	17	(3)	3	0	0	0	0
Fixed-Wing Combat Aircraft	0	0	0	0	0	0	0
MR/MPA	0	0	0	0	0	0	0
ASW/Combat Helicopter	0	0	0	0	0	0	0
Other Helicopters	0	0	0	0	0	0	0

Source: Adapted by Anthony H. Cordesman from data provided by U.S. and regional experts; and IISS, *The Military Balance.*

Figure 5.12
The Jordanian Recapitalization Crisis: Arms Deliveries during 1985–1999

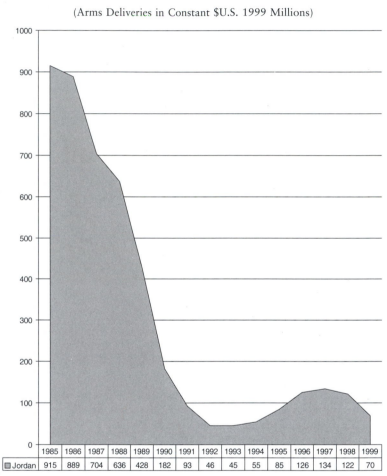

(Arms Deliveries in Constant $U.S. 1999 Millions)

	1985	1986	1987	1988	1989	1990	1991	1992	1993	1994	1995	1996	1997	1998	1999
Jordan	915	889	704	636	428	182	93	46	45	55	85	126	134	122	70

Source: Adapted by Anthony H. Cordesman from U.S. Arms Control and Disarmament Agency, *World Military Expenditures and Arms Transfers*, various editions.

better light forces, include some of the best-trained and most combat effective special forces in the region. These steps, however, have not enabled Jordan to be able to begin to keep up with the rate of military modernization in Israel and Egypt.

Land Forces

The Jordanian army has a total of some 85,000 actives and 30,000 reserves. It is organized into four commands, with a strategic reserve and

Special Operations Command. The North Command has two mechanized, one infantry, one artillery, and one aid defense brigade and defends its border with Syria. The Central Command has one mechanized, one light infantry, one artillery, and one air defense brigade. The Southern Command has one armored and one infantry command. The Eastern Command, which will be reorganized as a result of the fall of Saddam Hussein's regime, has two mechanized, one artillery, and one air defense brigade. The Strategic Reserve is a heavy, highly mobile force composed of the Royal Armored Division, and has three armored, one artillery, and one air defense brigade. The Special Operations Command has two special forces brigades, a ranger unit, and a counterterrorism battalion.

This command structure reflects Jordan's conversion to a lighter force structure emphasizing smaller combat formations and fewer tank battalions. It has become more professional, cheaper, more mobile, and better able to deal with internal security problems and the defense of Jordan's borders against threats like smuggling and infiltration across the Jordanian border. As part of this conversion, Jordan has put more emphasis on special forces, and on equipment like the AB3 Black Iris light utility vehicle and remotely piloted helicopters for border surveillance.

Jordan's Special Operations Command is one of the most effective in the MENA area. It was under the command of King Abdullah II before he became king, and has received strong support from the Jordanian government. It has been extensively reorganized since 1992 and has extensive special equipment, including advanced intelligence, communications, and night vision devices, and special purpose vehicles. It conducts joint training with the British 5th Airborne Brigade and Parachute Regiment. The Special Operations Command also includes the royal guard brigade, elements of the police, and an air wing with AH-1F attack helicopters and UH-1H utility helicopters. The Special Operations Command played a critical role in securing the Iraqi border in the years before the Iraq War, where almost nightly clashes take place with Iraqi smugglers, and in blocking infiltration across the Syrian border.

Jordan also has 10,000 men in its Public Security Directorate, which is under the command of the Ministry of Interior and includes the police and Desert Patrol. The Desert Patrol has about 2,500 men and 25 EE-11 and 30 aging Saracen armored infantry and scout vehicles. The People's Army is a broad pool of reserves with some military training and would assume part of the internal security mission in time of war. It has a large pool of mobilizable manpower, but little equipment and recent training. Its current strength is unclear.

Jordan has reorganized its land force deployments to improve coverage of the Iraqi and Syrian borders, and provide a lighter border force to cover its border with Israel to emphasize border security over defense against Israel. This new border force is highly mobile, has improved surveillance technology, and may be supported by an electrified border fence and systems of thermal TV cameras. These efforts are mainly to provide protection from infiltration and smuggling from Iraq and Syria as well as to counter terrorist threats. Talks are underway between Israel and Jordan on cooperative border surveillance.

Jordan cannot significantly increase its combat unit numbers with reserves. It has had to cut back on reserve training to the point where its reserves now have limited effectiveness, and has recently frozen its intake of conscripts for its active forces to reduce the cost of its forces. This freeze effectively ensures that Jordan's active and reserve forces will not grow with its population, and Jordan may have to make additional cuts in both its active and reserve strength.

Given its resource limitations, the Jordanian army has one of the most effective equipment mixes in the Middle East, and it has been able to retain significant defensive and war-fighting capabilities in spite of its economic problems. Jordan is one of the few countries that can—and has—upgraded and modified much of its land force combat equipment. At the same time, Jordan has been forced to reduce its main battle tank strength from over 1,200 to 1,018. Its first line tanks now consist of 288 Challenger I (Al Hussein) and 288 upgraded M-60A1/A3 conversions, supported by 274 much less capable Khalid (Chieftain) tanks. Jordan has 78 additional M-47/M-48s and 90 Centurions (Tariq).

Some of these older tanks have been heavily modernized but many are not operational or effectively are in storage. Jordan's Al-Hussein capabilities are to be extended by the addition of a 120-mm mechanical load assist system that will give the tanks a 120-mm smoothbore capability.[58] In addition, Jordan is studying a "Hybrid Turret" upgrade to the Al-Hussein that would give the tank a greater degree of system commonality with Jordan's other tanks.[59] 100 of Jordan's M60s will be upgraded with the Integrated Fire-Control System (IFCS), which will boost the tanks' target acquisition and surveillance abilities during mobile conflicts, improve long-range fire, and enable them to engage multiple targets more rapidly.[60] The Jordanian military recently placed an order for 100 Turkish tracked FNSS ACVs to be delivered over the next three years.[61]

Jordan's 245 armored infantry fighting vehicles consist of 19 aging Scorpions, 26 BMP-2s, and 200 Ratel 20s. Jordan has converted some of its roughly 1,200 M-113s from APCs to AIFVs, but some of the rest of its M-113s are not fully operable. Jordan also has 100 Spartan and 50 BTR-94 APCs, for a total of 1,394. Jordan has also developed its own prototype of an AIFV called the Temsah (Crocodile), which would convert a Tariq tank chassis in ways somewhat similar to Israeli conversions of main battle tanks. It would give Jordan one of the few AIFVs with the passive armor and other protection necessary to accompany its tanks into maneuver warfare and deal with well-armed infantry and insurgent threats.

The Jordanian Public Security Directorate ordered 60 AB2 Al-Jawad armored troop carriers in 2002, though it is unclear as to whether these vehicles have been delivered.[62]

Jordan is well armed with antitank guided weapons: 330 TOW and TOW-2As, 20 on M-901 AFVs, with 310 Dragons, and 30 Javelin. It has large numbers of light antitank weapons, including RPG-26s, 2,500 LAW-80, and 2,300 APILAS.

Jordan has relatively large amounts of self-propelled artillery for a force its size, including 35 M-52 105-mm, 29 M-44 155-mm, 253 M-109A1/A2 conversions, and 82 M-110A2 203-mm weapons. It has 76 towed artillery weapons—36 M-107 105-mm, 18 M-114 155-mm, and 18 M-59/M-1 155-mm—and 4 M-115 203-mm guns. Jordan cannot support much of its artillery with advanced target acquisition, fire and battle management, and counterbattery capabilities. The air force intends to replace its existing M102 105-mm field pieces with 18 truck-mounted MOBAT (MOB ArTillery) 105-mm howitzers sometime in 2004.[63] These guns will be fitted with the newly ordered Laser Inertial Automatic Pointing System (LINAPS), which will allow operators to aim them faster and more accurately.[64] Jordan has 450 81-mm mortars (130 on AFVs), 60 107-mm mortars, and 230 120-mm mortars.

Jordan has some 400 AA guns—including 52 ZSU-23-4 radar-guided guns. It has 60 self-propelled SA-8s, plus 92 SA-13s, 50 SA-7B2, 300 SA-14, 240 SA-16, and 250 obsolete Red Eye manportable surface-to-air missile launchers. These are only capable of protecting ground troops at short ranges and against aircraft flying at low altitudes.

Training and readiness are generally good to very good by regional standards. Jordan carries out maneuver exercises, organizes and trains for effective sustainment, and practices combined arms warfare more realistically than most of its neighbors. Jordan as has an effective defense industry for a nation of its size, with capability of modernizing many of its weapons and repairing combat damage.

Naval Forces

Jordan's small naval forces report to the Director of Operations at the headquarters of the general staff and consist of a 500-man force with several coastal patrol boats: three 24-ton Al-Hussein–class, and four small 8-ton Faysal class. Most patrol boats are based at Aqaba, but some can deploy to the Dead Sea.[65] The three 30-meter, Al-Hussein–class boats were built by Vosper and have twin 30-mm guns, radars, and chaff launchers. The Faysal-class boats only have machine guns. Jordan also has three Rotork-class, 9-ton craft capable of carrying 30 troops each.[66]

Jordan currently sees its navy as a coastal patrol force designed to provide inspection for incoming cargo ships and guard its coasts and ports against infiltration. It is not designed to have a war-fighting capability against Israel or any neighboring state.

Air Forces

Jordan's 15,000-man air force now has 101 fully operational combat aircraft, and 22 armed helicopters. Air force training and readiness are good, and air and air-to-ground combat training is more demanding and realistic compared to most regional powers.

The air force has four fighter attack/reconnaissance squadrons with 3/ 55 F-5E/Fs and 1/15 F-1EJ. It has two fighter squadrons with 1/16 Mirage F-1 CJ/BJ and 1/16 F-16A/B. Jordan's aircraft are comparable to those held by Syria but Israel. Its F-16A/Bs are its only modern fighter, but do not have the performance capability of Israel's F-16C/Ds or F-15s. The RJAF has ordered 17 upgrade kits to boost the service life of its F-16s.[67] Jordan's F-5Es are aging although they may be upgraded as a result of an agreement with Singapore. The Mirage F-1 aircraft cannot hope to engage modern IAF fighters with any success, and Jordan lacks any form of AEW aircraft and its ground-based air battle management capabilities have severe technical limitations.

Jordan has 22 AH-1F attack helicopters with TOW antiarmor missiles. These are effective systems, and Jordanian proficiency in using them is good, but they could not fly evasive attack profiles along most of the border with Israel because they would be highly vulnerable to Israeli air power.

Land-Based Air Defenses

Jordan has modernized some aspects of its ground-based air defense C^{4}I/ BM system with U.S. aid, but has lacked the funds to compete with Israel in systems integration, sensor and sensor integration capability, digital data links, and electronic warfare capabilities. It now has two incompatible air defense systems: its air force and Improved Hawk forces use a U.S. system supplied by Westinghouse, and its land forces use a Russian system.

Jordan has 4 batteries of Improved Hawk launchers, organized into 2 brigades with a total of 24 launchers. Jordan's Improved Hawk forces, however, have important limitations. They are not mobile, they have blind spots in their low-altitude coverage, and Israel can easily target them. The Improved Hawks have been upgraded to Phase 3 Pip (product improvement program) status, but may still be vulnerable to Israeli and Syrian electronic countermeasures. The Jordan military maintains 3 Patriot missile batteries around Amman and Irbid.[68]

Lebanon

Lebanon is recovering from a long period of civil war, from the Israeli and Syrian occupations, which resulted from Israel's invasion of Lebanon in 1982, and from Syria's interventions in the civil and enforcement of a peace settlement in 1990. Israel left South Lebanon in 2000, after years of low-intensity civil conflict with Shiite militias like Hezbollah and Amal. Syria is reducing its military presence. Lebanon now, however, faces the risk that Hezbollah may intervene more actively in the Israel-Palestinian War and the resulting conflict may spread to the Israeli-Lebanese border area and lead to Israeli reprisals that strike deep into Lebanon and/or that could involve Syria and Syrian forces.

The Lebanese command structure reflects the nation's serious religious divisions. The president is the nominal commander, but cannot act without Syrian approval. The commander of the army is Maronite Christian, the deputy commander is a Muslim (Shiite), and the Army Council has Druze and Sunni members. Lebanon's military forces total some 72,100 actives, including some 22,600 conscripts. It is unclear, however, that all this strength is actually present, and Lebanese forces are lightly armed, poorly trained and organized for maneuver warfare, and lack both a meaningful air force and modern land-based air defense assets.

The recent trends in Lebanese forces are shown in Figure 5.13. Lebanon is making some progress toward rebuilding its national military forces. Additionally, since the Israeli pullout from Southern Lebanon in May 2000, the Lebanese government has authorized deployment of a small joint force army commandos and military police to join its internal security personnel already in the south. Lebanon, however, shows great caution in attempting to actively control Southern Lebanon and bring Hezbollah under its control. The Lebanese government must evaluate every use of military force in the context of its history of civil war, and the risk of dividing its military forces if they are used for any mission that all major factions do not perceive as being in Lebanon's national interest.

Syria has reduced its force presence in Lebanon, but still has some elements of one mechanized infantry brigade and special forces battalions near Beirut, much of a mechanized division in the Bekaa Valley area, and forces near Metn, Tripoli, Batrum, and Kfar Falous.

Land Forces

The Lebanese army is the only element of Lebanon's military forces that has any serious potential war-fighting capability against a well-organized military force. It has played a steadily more important internal security role since the final battles of the civil war in October 1990. It has deployed south from Beirut and occupies Lebanese territory as far south as Sidon and Tyre, north to Tripoli, and in the Shuf Mountains. Most militias have been contained to their local territory, and most are largely disarmed. Some militias have been integrated into the army, and most have turned over or sold their heavy weapons. Furthermore, the command structure is tightly linked to Syria (to the dismay of many Lebanese) and might deploy in support of Syria if it came under intense pressure to do so.

Figure 5.13
Force Trends in Lebanon

Category/Weapon	1975	1980	1985	1990	1995	2001	2004
Manpower							
Total Active	15,300	23,000	17,400	21,000	44,300	63,750	72,100
(Conscript)	—	—	—	—	—	(22,600)	(22,600)
Total Reserve	—	—	—	—	—	—	—
Total	—	—	17,400	21,000	44,300	63,750	94,700
Paramilitary	5,000	—	13,000	8,000	13,000	13,000	13,000
Land Forces							
Active Manpower	14,000	22,250	16,000	21,000	43,000	60,670	70,000
(Conscripts)	—	—	—	—	—	22,600	—
Reserve Manpower	—	—	—	—	—	—	—
Total Reserve & Active Manpower	14,000	22,250	16,000	21,000	43,000	60,670	70,000
Main Battle Tanks	60	0	50	200	300	327	310
(Fixed & in Storage)	—	—	—	—	—	—	—
AIFVs/Armored Cars/Lt. Tanks	43	17	150	102	175	125	40
APCs/Recce/Scouts	180	80	420	340	740	1,388	1,423
WWII Half-Tracks	0	0	0	0	0	0	0
ATGM Launchers	—	—	—	—	200	250	70
SP Artillery	0	0	0	0	0	0	0
Towed Artillery	50	28	125	111	200	151	147
MRLs	0	0	0	—	30	23	25

Mortars	—	—	200+	120+	280+	377	369
SSM Launchers	0	0	0	0	0	0	0
AA Guns	—	—	—	—	—	220	220
Lt. SAM Launchers	—	—	—	—	—	—	20
Air & Air Defense Forces							
Active Manpower	1,000	500	1,100	800	800	1,700	1,000
Reserve Manpower	—	—	—	—	—	—	—
Aircraft	19	—	—	—	—	—	—
Total Fighter/FGA/Recce	7	7	3	3	(16)	(11)	—
Fighter	6 (5)	(9)	0	0	0	0	0
FGA/Fighter	0	0	0	0	0	0	0
FGA	13	7	7	3	3	0	0
Recce	0	0	0	0	0	0	0
Airborne Early Warning (AEW)	0	0	0	0	0	0	0
Electronic Warfare (EW)	0	0	0	0	0	0	0
Maritime Reconnaissance (MR)	0	0	0	0	0	0	0
Combat Capable Trainer	0	0	0	0	0	3	3
Tanker	0	0	0	0	0	0	0
Transport	3	2	2	2	2	2	2
Helicopters							
Attack/Armed	0	4	4	1	4	0	0
ASW/SAR	0	0	0	0	0	0	0
Transport & Other	16	17	28	15	46	30	38
Total	21	32	16	50	30	38	—

continued

Figure 5.13 (Continued)

Category/Weapon	1975	1980	1985	1990	1995	2001	2004
SAM Forces							
Batteries	0	0	0	0	0	0	0
Heavy Launchers	0	0	0	0	0	0	0
Medium Launchers	0	0	0	0	0	0	0
Naval Forces							
Active Manpower	300	250	300	—	500	1,200	1,100
Reserve Manpower	0	0	0	—	0	0	0
Total Manpower	300	250	300	—	500	1,200	1,100
Submarines	0	0	0	—	0	0	0
Missile	0	0	0	—	0	0	0
Other	0	0	0	—	0	0	0
Missile Patrol	0	0	0	—	0	0	0
Coastal/Inshore Patrol	5	6	4	—	9	7	7
Mine	0	0	0	—	0	0	0
Amphibious Ships	0	0	0	—	0	0	0
Landing Craft/Light Support	1	1	1	—	2	2	2
Fixed-Wing Combat Aircraft	0	0	0	—	0	0	0
MR/MPA	0	0	0	—	0	0	0
ASW/Combat Helicopter	0	0	0	—	0	0	0
Other Helicopters	0	0	0	—	0	0	0

Note: Lebanese combat aircraft shown in parenthesis are in storage or are for sale.
Source: Adapted by Anthony H. Cordesman from data provided by U.S. experts; and IISS, *The Military Balance.*

The army has an authorized strength of about 65,000–70,000 men. Its order of battle has 11 regular infantry brigades, a Presidential Guard brigade, a Ranger regiment, three special forces regiments, an air assault regiment, and two artillery regiments. Its major combat equipment includes 310 tanks—with an estimated 110M-48A1 and M-48A5 tanks and 200–212 T-54 and T-55 tanks. It has phased out its Ferret and Staghound light armored reconnaissance vehicles. It does, however, have 132 other armored fighting vehicles: 40 AMX-13 light tanks, 67 AML-90, and 25 Saladins. It has some 1,338 APCs, including the operational portion of an inventory of 1,164 M-113s, 81 VAB-VCIs, 81 AMX-VCI, and 12 Panhards.

The Lebanese army has 203 towed artillery weapons—of which some 147 are counted as operational: 13 105-mm M-101A1s, 32 M-1938, and 24 D-20 122-mm weapons, 16 1130-mm M-46s, and 15 Model 50, 15 M-114A1, and 32 M-198 155-mm weapons. It also has 23–25 multiple BM-11 and BM-21 rocket launchers, and over 280 81-mm, 82-mm, and 120-mm mortars. It has 24 BGM-71A TOWs 16 Milan and 30 ENTAC antitank guided missiles, plus large numbers of light antitank weapons—including 50 M-40A1 106-mm recoilless rifles. It has 20–60 SA-7A/B fire units, and large numbers of 20-mm and 23-mm AA guns, plus 10 M-42A1 40-mm guns.

Since the end of Lebanon's civil war in 1990, Beirut has benefited from its relationship with the U.S. military. The United States has either donated, or sold at minimal prices, sixteen Huey helicopters, and earmarked another sixteen for future delivery, comprising the entirety of Lebanon's air force. The United States has furnished a large portion Lebanon's ground transportation, including 850 armored personnel carriers, 3,000 trucks and jeeps, and 60 ambulances. The Pentagon has provided much equipment, labeled as "excess defense articles," which has included small weapons, spare parts, grenade launchers, night vision goggles, and communications equipment. Much of the army's inventory is worn or obsolete, however; and it is useful largely for internal security purposes. The Lebanese army is far too lightly equipped, and its equipment is too old or limited in capability to engage either Israeli or Syrian forces.

More broadly, the Lebanese army underwent a massive reorganization in 1997, integrating Muslim and Christian brigades in an attempt to end factional rivalries and bias. Units became subject to rotation to prevent any regional bias from forming and commanders within units are rotated regularly to ensure that religious prejudice does not create informal hierarchies. Although these changes cannot compensate for Lebanon's weaknesses in matériel or its client relationship with Syria, many hope they will insulate the military from the religious tensions that plague the country.

In spite of these improvements, the army is still emerging from the chaos of civil war. Lebanon may have some excellent individual officers and some good combat elements, but there are still ethnic and sectarian divisions within its forces. Its "brigades" and "regiments" are often badly undermanned.

Conscripts train for only one year. Career soldiers still tend to be politicized, are generally low in quality, and receive limited training for anything other than defensive infantry combat. The Lebanese army's seemingly impressive equipment pool is worn, often obsolescent, and much of it is inoperative.

The army is seeking to re-create itself as an independent national force and many Lebanese officers are struggling hard to maintain the army's independence. The fact remains, however, that it still is heavily under Syrian influence, and even the best leaders cannot quickly overcome its heritage of incompetence, corruption, and ethnic divisions. It will be years before the Lebanese army can emerge as an independent fighting force that could engage Israeli or Syrian forces in anything other than well-positioned defensive combat.

Naval Forces

Lebanon has some 1,000–1,150 men assigned to its navy, including 100 marines. Its forces are based in Beirut and Jounieh. It has seven coastal patrol craft, including five British-made, 38-ton, Attacker-class inshore patrol craft with radars and twin 23-mm guns. It also has two British-made, 31-ton Tracker-class inshore patrol craft with radars and twin 23-mm guns. It has two aging 670-ton Sour-class (French Edic-class) landing craft, which can carry about 33 troops each. The navy has other small-armed boats in inventory, including thirteen 6-ton inshore patrol craft and two more Tracker-class boats in the Customs Service. It is not clear how many are operational.[69]

The Lebanese navy has a coastal patrol capability, and some troop lift capability, but no war-fighting capability against Israel or any neighboring state. It can perform a surveillance role, inspect cargo ships, and intercept small infiltrating forces along a limited part of Lebanon's coastline.[70]

Air Forces

Lebanon has no real air force or navy. Its air force has 800–1,000 men on paper, but its real strength is much lower. It only has six worn, obsolete, low-capability Hunter light attack and five Fouiga fixed-wing aircraft, all in storage. It has four SA-342 attack helicopters armed with obsolete short-range AS-11 and AS-12 missiles, of which two seem to be operational. It has no significant surface-to-air missile defenses. The only significant assets of the Lebanese air force are its transport helicopters, which consist of about 24 UH-1Hs, 1 SA-318, 5 Bell-212s, and 3 SA-330s. A substantial number of these helicopters need major overhauls or are only semioperational.

Paramilitary Forces and Hezbollah

Lebanon's paramilitary forces include a large 13,000-man internal security force that is part of the Ministry of Interior, and that includes the regional and Beirut gendarmerie and the Judicial Police. It is armed with automatic weapons and has some Chaimite APCS. There is a small customs force, equipped with light patrol boats.

The most important paramilitary elements in Lebanon, however, is Hezbollah. Estimates differ regarding its force strength, but Figure 5.14 provides a rough estimate of its current military capabilities. Hezbollah has already defeated the South Lebanese Army and driven Israel out of Lebanon. It would have far more difficulty in attacking across the Israeli border or infiltrating into the country, but it does have rockets and other weapons that it can fire into Israel and has shown it can conduct small border raids and shown it could kidnap Israeli soldiers in the Shebaa Farms area. Hezbollah has had significant Iranian and Syrian support in the past, and is helping to train anti-Israeli Palestinian groups.

Figure 5.14
Developments in Hezbollah Military Forces in Lebanon in 2004

- Roughly 2,500–3,500 men, heavily dependent on part-time and irregular forces. Many are now highly experienced, often well-educated forces.

- Composed of a core of around 300 guerrillas. Has deliberately cut its force over the past years to prevent infiltration and leaks.

- Hezbollah fighters are old by comparison to Israeli fighters. Any age up to 35, usually married, often university students or professional men.

- Still seems to have Iranian Revolutionary Guards as advisors. Heavily supplied and financed by Iran, but Syrian personnel seem to be involved in training and in coordinating with Iran. Iranian and Syrian coordination of support for military supply and possibly operations of Hezbollah seems to occur at the general officer, deputy minister level.

- Conflicting intelligence reports estimate Iranian aid to Hezbollah to involve tens of million dollars a year.

- Equipped with APCs, artillery, multiple rocket launchers, mortars, antitank-guided missiles (including AT-3 Sagger, AT-4 Spigot ATGWs, and captured TOWs), recoilless rifles, SA-7s, antiaircraft guns.

- Guerrilla mortar strikes have improved in both accuracy and range, indicating better range-finding systems, low signature weapons, and the use of mortar boosters that enable consistent hits for 2 to 3 miles.

- Supply of rockets is estimated to have risen to 1,000. These include Iranian produced 240mm rockets with a range of 40 km, according to Israeli intelligence reports. Most of the rockets are 120mm and 127mm variants with a maximum range of 22 km. Types include the Katyusha, Fajr 3/5, and Zelzal-2.

- Has great expertise in using improvised explosive devices like the improved radio detonated roadside bombs that proved effective against the Israelis. Some are disguised as large rocks. These rock-like explosives are reportedly produced in Iran.

Palestine

The Palestinian Authority is a protostate that has been effectively at war with Israel since September 2000. The security forces of the Palestinian Authority have taken massive losses during the course of the fighting and independent antipeace groups like Hamas and Palestinian Islamic Jihad have also suffered major losses. It is currently almost impossible to make a detailed assessment of Palestinian military capabilities, most of which now consist of scattered elements of irregular forces plus organizations that make extensive use of covert and terrorist attacks. A nominal estimate of Palestinian forces is shown in Figure 5.15, and a more detailed estimate of the Palestinian and Lebanese forces that can pose a threat to Israel is shown in Figure 5.16.

It is not clear at this point how much progress the IDF is making in reducing the Palestinian threat. It has certainly crippled the Palestinian security forces that existed when the war began, which are shown in Figure 5.15. At the same time, the Jaffee Center estimates that the size of the Palestinian security forces increased from 36,000 in 2000 to 45,000 in 2002. It estimates that in 2002, the Palestinian Authority had the following force strength: Public Security or National Security Force, 14,000; Coastal Police, 1,000; Aerial Police, 50(?); Civil Police, 10,000; Preventive Security Force, 5,000;

Figure 5.15
Military and Paramilitary Strength of Key Palestinian Factions and Hezbollah at the Start of the Israel-Palestine War

---

Palestinian Authority
- 29,000 Security and paramilitary pro-PLO forces enforcing security in Gaza and Jericho, including:
  - Public Security (14,000)—6,000 in Gaza and 8,000 in West Bank,
  - Civil police (10,000)—4,000 in Gaza and 6,000 in West Bank,
  - Preventive Security (3,000)—1,200 in Gaza and 1,800 in West Bank,
  - General Intelligence (1,000),
  - Presidential Security (500),
  - Military Intelligence (500), and
  - Additional forces in Coastal Police, Air Force, Customs and Excise Police Force, University Security Service, and Civil Defense.
- Equipment includes 45 APCs, 1 Lockheed Jetstar, 2 Mi-8s, 2 Mi-17s, and roughly 40,000 small arms. These include automatic weapons and light machine guns. Israeli claims they include heavy automatic weapons, rocket launchers, antitank rocket launchers and guided weapons, and manportable antiair missiles.
- The PA wants 12,000 more security forces after further withdrawals. Israel has proposed some 2,000.

continued

Figure 5.15 (Continued)

Pro-PLO

- Palestinian National Liberation Army (PNLA)/Al Fatah—5,000–8,000 active and semiactive reserves that make up main pro-Arafat force, based in Algeria, Egypt, Iraq, Lebanon, Libya, Jordan, Sudan, Syria, and Yemen under the tight control of the host government.
- Palestine Liberation Front (PLF)—Abu Abbas Faction—200 men led by Al-Abbas, based in Syria.
- Arab Liberation Front (ALF)—500 men led by Abdel al Rahim Ahmad, based in Lebanon and Iraq.
- Democratic Front for the Liberation of Palestine (DFLP)—400–600 men led by Naif Hawatmeh, which claims eight battalions, and is based in Syria, Lebanon, and elsewhere.
- Popular Front for the Liberation of Palestine (PFLP)—800–1000 men led by Ahmed Sadaat, based in Syria, Lebanon, West Bank, and Gaza.
- Palestine Popular Struggle Front (PSF)—200 men led by Samir Ghawsha and Bahjat Abu Gharbiyah, based in Syria.

Anti-PLO

- Palestinian Islamic Jihad (PIJ)—500 men in various factions, led by Assad Bayud al-Tamimi, Fathi Shakaki, Ibrahim Odeh, Ahmad Muhana, and others, based in the West Bank and Gaza.
- Hamas—military wing of about 300 men, based in the West Bank and Gaza.
- As-Saiqa—600–1,000 men in pro-Syrian force under Issam al-Qadi, based in Syria.
- Fatah Revolutionary Council (FRC)/Abu Nidal Organization (ANO)—300 men led by Abu Nidal (Sabri al-Bana), based in Lebanon, Syria, and Iraq.
- Popular Front for the Liberation of Palestine—General Command (PFLP-GC)—500 men led by Ahmad Jibril, based in Syria, Lebanon, elsewhere.
- Popular Front for the Liberation of Palestine—Special Command (PFLP-SC)—50–100 men led by Abu Muhammad (Salim Abu Salem) based in Lebanon, Syria and Iraq.
- Palestine Liberation Army (PLA)—2,000 men, based in Syria.
- Fatah Intifada—400–1,000 men led by Said Musa Muragha (Abu Musa), based in Syria and Lebanon.

Hezbollah (Party of God)

- About 300–500 actives with 2,000 men in support, Shi'ite fundamentalist, APCs, artillery, MRLs (107 and 122 mm), rocket launchers, recoilless launchers, AA guns, SA-7 SAMs, antitank missiles (AT-3 Saggers, AT-4 Spigots).

Source: Adapted from U.S. Department of State, *Patterns of Global Terrorism*, various editions; IISS, *The Military Balance*, various editions.

Figure 5.16
Current Palestinian and Lebanese Forces

Origin	Organization and Aims (Remarks)	Established	Estimated Strength	Status	Operates
Lebanon	**Asbat al-Ansar** Advocates Salafism, opposed to any peace with Israel	1990s	300	Active	Lebanon
Lebanon	**Hizbullah** (Party of God) **Islamic Jihad-Revolutionary Justice Organization** **Organization of the Oppressed on Earth*** Iran-style Islamic republic in Lebanon; all non-Islamic influences removed from area (Shi'ite; formed to resist Israeli occupation of south Lebanon with political representation in Lebanon Assembly).	1982	2,000+	Active	Bekaa Valley, Beirut, south Lebanon, Shebaa Farms
Palestinian Autonomous Areas of Gaza and Jericho	**Al-Aqsa Martyrs Brigade*** Associated, though not officially backed, by Arafat Military offshoot of Fatah	2000	Not known	Active	Palestinian Autonomous Areas of Gaza and Jericho, Israel
Palestinian Autonomous Areas of Gaza and Jericho	**Al Saika** Military wing of Palestinian faction of Syrian Ba'ath Party (Nominally part of PLO)	1968	300	Active	Palestinian Autonomous Areas of Gaza and Jericho, Israel
Palestinian Autonomous Areas of Gaza and Jericho	**Arab Liberation Front** Achieve national goals of Palestinian Authority (Faction of PLO formed by leadership of Iraq Ba'ath party)	1969	500	Dormant	Palestinian Autonomous Areas of Gaza and Jericho, Israel
Palestinian Autonomous Areas of Gaza and Jericho	**Democratic Front for the Liberation of Palestine** (DFLP) Achieve Palestinian national goals through revolution (Marxist-Leninst; splintered from PFLP)	1969	100+	Active	Palestinian Autonomous Areas of Gaza and Jericho, Israel
Palestinian Autonomous Areas of Gaza and Jericho	**Fatah Tanzim** Armed militia link to Fatah	1995	1000+	Active	Palestinian Autonomous Areas of Gaza and Jericho, Israel
Palestinian Autonomous Areas of Gaza and Jericho	**Harakat al-Muqawama al-Islamiyya (HAMAS) Islamic Resistance Front** Establish an Islamic Palestinian state in place of Israel	1987	Not known	Active	Palestinian Autonomous Areas of Gaza and Jericho, Israel
Palestinian Autonomous Areas of Gaza and Jericho	**Izz al-Din al-Qassam Brigades (IDQ)*** Replace Israel with Islamic state in Palestinian Areas (Armed wing of Harakat al-Muqawama al-Islamiyya (Hamas); separate from overt organization)	1991	500	Active	Palestinian Autonomous Areas of Gaza and Jericho, Israel
Palestinian Autonomous Areas of Gaza and Jericho	**Palestine Islamic Jihad** (PIJ)* Destroy Israel with holy war and establish Islamic state in Palestinian areas (One of the more extreme groups from the Palestinian areas.)	1970s	Estimated 500	Active	Palestinian Autonomous Areas of Gaza and Jericho, Israel
Palestinian Autonomous Areas of Gaza and Jericho	**Palestine Liberation Front** (PLF)* Armed struggle against Israel (Splintered from PFLP)	1977	300-400	Dormant	Palestinian Autonomous Areas of Gaza and Jericho, Israel
Palestinian Autonomous Areas of Gaza and Jericho	**Popular Front for the Liberation of Palestine** (PFLP) Armed struggle against Israel (Marzist-Leninst)	1967	1000	Active	Palestinian Autonomous Areas of Gaza and Jericho, Israel

continued

Figure 5.16 (Continued)

Origin	Organization and Aims (Remarks)	Established	Estimated Strength	Status	Operates
Palestinian Autonomous Areas of Gaza and Jericho	**Popular Front for the Liberation of Palestine—General Command (PFLP-GC)*** Armed struggle against Israel (Marzist-Leninist; Split from PFLP to focus on fighting rather than politics)	1968	500	Dormant	Palestinian Autonomous Areas of Gaza and Jericho, Israel

Notes:
*Group known to carry out suicide attacks
A—active
C—cease-fire
D—dormant (inactive for the past 12 months)

Source: Adapted from IISS, *The Military Balance*, 2003–2004.

General Intelligence, 3,000; and Presidential Security Force, 3,000. There were additional men in the Military Intelligence and Civil Defense forces.

Hard-line extremist groups have also gained in strength, and this includes militias in the Palestinian Authority like the Fatah-based Tanzim. The Palestinian forces also have begun to acquire longer-range weapons like mortars and rockets such as the Oassim-2 and Qassim-3. The Qassim-3 has a range of more than 10 kilometers.

Syria

The trends in Syrian forces are shown in Figure 5.17. They reflect the fact that Syria still treats Israel as an enemy power, but has had to abandon its search for conventional parity. As a result, it has had to minimize the risk of a future military clash with Israel, and make shifts in its strategy and procurement effort, which includes a new focus on "asymmetric warfare." These shifts:

- Emphasize the procurement of long-range ballistic missiles and weapons of mass destruction as a relatively low cost offset to Israel's conventional superiority while giving Syria a limited counterweight to Israel's nuclear strike capability.

- Give priority to elite commando and special forces units that can be used to defend key approaches to Syria and spearhead infiltrations and attacks. Many of these forces are equipped with modern antitank guided weapons and other modern crew and manportable weapons that allow them to disperse without relying on armored weapons and other systems Israel can target more easily. They are supported by attack helicopters.

- Maintain a large tank force both as a deterrent to any Israeli attempt to penetrate Syria and to maintain a constant threat to the Golan, even if Syria has no hope of achieving overall parity.

- Use Hezbollah and Amal as proxies to attack Israel and the SLA in Southern Lebanon, the Golan Heights, and the Shebaa Farms area. Following the

Figure 5.17
Force Trends in Syria

Category/Weapon	1975	1980	1985	1990	2000	2004
Manpower						
Total Active	177,500	247,500	402,500	404,000	320,000	319,000
(Conscript)	—	—	—	—	—	—
Total Reserve	102,500	—	273,500	400,000	500,000	354,000
Total	280,000	—	676,000	804,000	820,000	673,000
Paramilitary	9,500	9,500	6,300	10,800	8,000+	108,000
Land Forces						
Active Regular Manpower	150,000	200,000	270,000	300,000	215,000	215,000
(Conscripts)	—	(140,000)	(135,000)	(130,000)	—	—
Republican Guards	—	—	—	10,000	—	—
Reserve Manpower	100,000	—	270,000	392,000	400,000	280,000
Total Reserve & Active Manpower	250,000	—	540,000	702,000	615,000	495,000
Main Battle Tanks	1,400	2,920	4,200	2,900	3,450	4,500
(Static & in Storage)	—	—	(1,100)	(1,200)	(1,200)	—
AIFVs/Armored Cars/Lt. Tanks	70	700	1,400	2,800	3,010	2,200
APCs/Recce/Scouts	1,100	1,600	1,600	1,500	1,500	2,400
WWII Half-Tracks	0	0	0	0	0	0
ATGM Launchers	—	—	—	1,100	3,390	4,390
SP Artillery	75	800*	—	186	450	430
Towed Artillery	700	*	—	2,000	1,630	1,630
MRLs	57	—	—	250	480	480
Mortars	—	—	—	—	4,500+	710

	1	2	3	4	5	6
SSM Launchers	—	54	54	61	62	82
AA Guns	—	—	1,000	1,700	2,060	2,050
Lt. SAM Launchers	—	—	—	—	4,055	4,335
Air & Air Defense Forces						
Active Air Force Manpower	25,000	45,000	70,000	40,000	40,000	40,000
Air Force Reserve Manpower	—	—	—	—	92,000	70,000
Active Air Defense Command	—	(15,000)	60,000	60,000	60,000	60,000
Air Defense Command Reserve	—	—	—	—	—	—
Aircraft						
Total Fighter/FGA/Recce	400	395	500	558	589	548
Bombers	4	0	0	0	0	0
Fighter	250	225	280	312	310	300
FGA/Fighter	0	60	0	0	0	0
FGA	140	110	193	170	154	130
Recce	0	0	10	6	14	46
Airborne Early Warning (AEW)	0	0	0	0	0	0
Electronic Warfare (EW)	0	0	—	8	10	0
(Fixed-Wing)						
(Helicopter)						
Maritime Reconnaissance (MR)	0	0	0	0	0	0
Combat Capable Trainer	—	20	10–60	76–96	111	111
Tanker	0	0	0	0	0	0
Transport	9	17	23	28	49	23
Helicopters						
Attack/Armed	0	0	100	100	72	36
ASW/SAR	0	35	23	25	0	0
Transport & Other	60	82	160	155	110	120
Total	60	117	283	280	182	156

continued

Figure 5.17 (Continued)

Category/Weapon	1975	1980	1985	1990	2000	2004
SAM Forces						
Batteries	—	75	126	126	130	130
Heavy Launchers	—	—	658	640	728	728
Medium Launchers	—	—	—	60	60	60
AA Guns	—	—	—	—	—	—
Naval Forces						
Active Manpower	2,500	2,500	2,500	6,000	6,000	4,100
Reserve Manpower	2,500	—	2,500	8,000	4,000	4,000
Total Manpower	5,000	—	5,000	14,000	10,000	8,100
Submarines	0	0	0	3	0 (3)	0
Destroyers/Frigates/Corvettes	0	0	0	2	2	2
Missile	0	2	2	2	2	2
Other	0	0	0	0	0	0
Missile Patrol	6	18	22	12	10	10
Coastal/Inshore Patrol	12	9	7	8	8	8
Mine	1	3	4	9	5	5
Amphibious Ships	—	—	2	3	3	3
Landing Craft/Light Support	—	—	—	—	5	4
Fixed-Wing Combat Aircraft	0	0	0	0	0	0
MR/MPA	0	0	0	0	0	0
ASW/Combat Helicopter	—	—	—	17	24	25
Other Helicopters	—	—	—	—	—	—

*Includes all types of towed and self-propelled artillery, but not multiple rocket launchers.
Source: Adapted by Anthony H. Cordesman from data provided by U.S. experts; and IISS, *The Military Balance.*

October 5, 2003, bombing of a suspected Islamic Jihad training camp near Damascus by Israel, it was speculated that the Golan Heights in particular could become a new battleground. However, critics of such a view argue that it would be very difficult for Syria to establish a credible resistance movement among the Syrians in the Golan Heights, mostly the Druze, since they have faced little repression. Some Druze serve in the IDF. They contend that attacks on the Shebaa area by Hezbollah are much more likely.[71]

These shifts cannot compensate for the recapitalization crisis reflected in Figure 5.18, and a lack of modern arms and military technology. Syria has attempted to remedy some of its growing modernization problems by

Figure 5.18
The Syrian Recapitalization Crisis: Arms Deliveries during 1985–1999

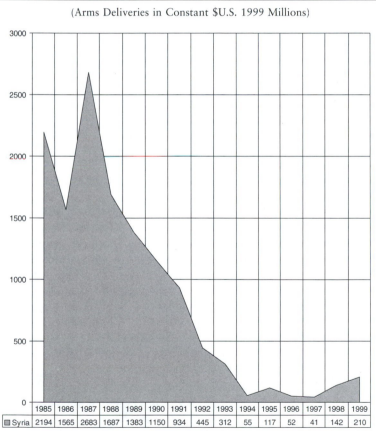

(Arms Deliveries in Constant $U.S. 1999 Millions)

	1985	1986	1987	1988	1989	1990	1991	1992	1993	1994	1995	1996	1997	1998	1999
Syria	2194	1565	2683	1687	1383	1150	934	445	312	55	117	52	41	142	210

Source: Adapted by Anthony H. Cordesman from U.S. State Department, *World Military Expenditures and Arms Transfers*, various editions.

procuring upgrades and technology from Russia and the West, but Syria has not done well in obtaining such help. Its only major conventional force improvements during the middle and late 1990s were some Ukrainian modifications for part of the T-55 tank fleet and AT-14 Kornet antitank guided missiles. Some reports indicate that the Syrian Armed Forces did acquire an additional 1,500 Kornets as well as upgrade packages for up to a brigade of T-72 tanks. The upgrade will boost the T-72's armor while adding an attachment that would enable the tank to fire ATGMs.[72] Yet it is important to note that Syria has tried four previous times to upgrade the T-72s with little success and past attempts to incorporate elements of the current upgrade package met with great difficulty.

Syria, however, has not yet succeeded in negotiating major new arms agreements with Russia and other suppliers. Western firms want solid cash guarantees and are reluctant to sell to Syria. China and North Korea cannot supply the quality of conventional arms Syria needs, and any purchase of equipment that does not come from Russia will create interoperability problems that will compound Syrian weaknesses in sustainability and combined arms.

Bulgaria, for example, could supply Syria with much of the Soviet-era replacement parts that it needs, as an illegal sale by a Bulgarian firm of 50 sets of gear boxes and engines for T-55s in 2001 illustrates, but the country has expressed its desire to join the North Atlantic Treaty Organization (NATO), which clearly does not support the export of arms to Syria, and Bulgaria has launched an investigation into the sale of Soviet APC parts to Syria in 2003, culminating in at least six arrests. Bulgaria hopes to rid itself of the perception that it will sell arms to almost any group interested to support its flagging defense industry and thus is unlikely to continue or strengthen ties with Syria.[73]

Russia is Syria's most logical source of new conventional arms, and there were reports during the early 1990s that indicated that Syria would be able to spend some $1.4 billion on military modernization between 1992 and 1994. Syria found, however, that post-Communist Russia did not make concessionary arms sales that approached the level of gifts, or show the past tolerance for unpaid loans. This was a major stumbling block throughout the 1990s. Syria had plied up a massive debt over the years. It owed Russia roughly $7–11 billion for past arms purchases, and a total of $20 billion for both its military and civil debt. Russia was well aware that there was little prospect that it would ever be paid and this had a chilling impact on Syria's ability to obtain arms.[74]

Russia and Syria have claimed to have resolved the issue on several occasions. Syria signed a new cooperation agreement with Russia in April 1994, for "defensive weapons and spare parts." Syria held extensive new arms purchasing talks with Russia in 1997 and 1998. In February 1999, Syria announced plans to spend as much as $2 billion on a range of Russian armaments, including more antitank systems—which seem to have included deliveries of more AT-14 Kornets.[75] Syria and Russia held talks in May 1999 to discuss expanding military cooperation, and in particular to arrange the sale of Russian advanced weapons systems to Syria.[76] According to some reports, Russia seemed willing to put repayments of its debt on hold.[77] A five-year, $2 billion contract was under discussion.[78] According to one report, Syria apparently requested Su-27 fighters and the S-300 air defense system, but was offered the cheaper MiG-29 fighters and Tor-M1 air defense systems.[79] Syrian president Hafez Assad visited Moscow in July 1999.

Syria and Russia held new highly level talks on military cooperation in September 1999. These talks seem to have again involved a $2–2.5 billion deal over five years, and the possible purchase of the S-300 surface-to-air missile defense system, the Sukhoi Su-27 multi-role fighter, MiG-29SMT fighters, T-80 tanks, and more antitank weapons. Once again, however, the contractual status of such agreements, the weapons involved, and delivery schedules remained unclear.[80]

What is a cause for concern on Syria's part, however, is that Russia may be seeking to develop a closer relationship with Israel. Israeli prime minister Ariel Sharon stated that Russia had decided not to sell the SA-18 Grouse surface-to-air missile systems to Syria over Israeli concerns that the weapons might fall into the hands of Hezbollah.[81] Sharon indicated that Israel and Russia intend on sharing intelligence in their respective fights against "terrorism." If Israel and Russia continue to strengthen their ties, Syria could face additional weapons procurement problems, as Israel is likely to pressure Russia on other arms sales.

It is not clear how Hafez Assad's death, and Bashar's succession, will ultimately affect this situation. Even if reports of major new Russian arms sales in 2002 and 2003 should eventually prove true, any foreseeable new agreements will still leave Syria with far fewer funds than it needs to re-capitalize its current force structure and compete with Israel in modernization. It is hard to see how Syria can finance even half the funds and projected deliveries necessary to replace its older land force equipment and aircraft in the near to middle term. Furthermore, if Syria could order all of the arms it wants, it would still take some three to five years to fully absorb all of the new technology it needs, integrate it into effective combat systems, and retrain its forces—assuming it recognizes the need to do so. Barring massive outside aid, Syrian forces are almost certain to continue to go "hollow" for the foreseeable future, although moderate deliveries of advanced modern aircraft, tanks, and surface-to-air missile systems like the S-300 could still help correct key Syrian weaknesses.

Syria's limitations will be further compounded by its problems in absorbing new equipment. These include the endemic corruption. They also include its politicized and compartmented command structure, inadequate military pay, poor manpower management, poor technical training, and poor overall training—particularly in realistic combat exercises and aggressor training. Syrian forces have inadequate combat and service support, equipment for night and poor weather warfare, long-range sensors and targeting systems, and mobile rapidly maneuverable logistics, recording, and combat repair capability. While individual Syrian officers have shown a keen understanding of many of these problems, Syria has never taken effective action to deal with them.

Land Forces

Syria organizes its ground forces into two corps that report to the Land Forces General Staff and Commander of the Land Force. The chain of command then passes up to the Chief of the General Staff and Deputy Defense Minister, Minister of Defense, Deputy Commander in Chief of the Armed Forces, and Supreme Commander of the Armed Forces. The Syrian 1st Corps is headquartered near Damascus, and commands forces in southeastern Syria, opposing Israel. The 2nd Corps is headquartered near Zabadani, near the Lebanese border, and covers units in Lebanon. The command relationships involving Jordan, Turkey, and Iraq are unclear. The 1st Corps has two armored and three mechanized divisions. The 2nd Corps has three armored and two mechanized divisions.

The Syrian army has a total of 215,000 active men and is organized into five to seven armored divisions, including the 1st, 3rd, 9th, 11th, and 569th. Syrian armored divisions vary in size. They have 2–3 armored brigades, 1–2 mechanized brigades, and 1 artillery regiment. A typical division has around 8,000 men. A typical armored brigade has 93 main battle tanks, and 30 other armored fighting vehicles like the BMP. The Syrian army has 3 mechanized divisions. They normally have about 11,000 men, but vary in structure. They have 1–2 armored brigades, 2–3 mechanized brigades, and 1 artillery regiment. A typical mechanized brigade has 40 main battle tanks, and 90 other armored fighting vehicles like the BMP.

Syria also has 1 Republican Guard division, with 3 armored brigades, 1 mechanized brigade, and 1 artillery regiment that reports directly to the Commander of the Land Forces, plus a special forces division with 3 special forces regiments and 8 independent special forces regiments.

Syria's other independent formations include 3 independent infantry battalions, 2 independent artillery brigades, and 2 independent antitank brigades. Its active smaller formations include 1 border guard brigade, 3 infantry brigades, 1 antitank brigade, 1 independent tank regiment, 8 special forces regiments, 3 surface-to-surface missile brigades with an additional coastal defense brigade, and 2 artillery brigades. According to some reports, it has 1 reserve armored division, and 30 reserve regiments, including infantry and artillery formations.[82]

On paper, Syria has 1 low-grade reserve armored unit with about half the effective strength of its active divisions, plus 30 infantry and 1 artillery reserve regiment. Most of these Syrian reserve units are poorly equipped and trained. Those Syrian reserves that do train, usually do not receive meaningful training above the company to battalion level, and many train using obsolete equipment that is different from the equipment in the active units to which they are assigned. The Syrian call-up system is relatively effective, but the Syrian army is not organized to make use of it. Virtually all of the Syrian reserves called up in the 1982 war had to be sent home because the Syrian army lacked the capability to absorb and support them.

Although Syria now has a total of some 4,650 tanks, at least 1,200 of these are in static positions or in storage. Roughly half are relatively low-grade T-54s and T-55s, and only 1,500 are relatively modern T-72s. Even the T-72s lack the advanced thermal sights, fire control systems, and armor to engage the Israeli Merkavas and M-60s on anything like a one-to-one basis. The T-72 also performed surprisingly poorly in Iraqi hands during the Gulf War. Its armor did not prove to be as effective against modern Western antitank rounds as was previously expected, and its sensors and fire control systems proved inadequate for night and poor visibility combat and could not keep up with Western thermal sights in range and target acquisition capability.[83]

Syria has some 4,600 armored vehicles, of which approximately 2,400 are BMPs. These armored fighting vehicles can supplement and support Syria's tanks in combined arms combat, and increase its potential ability to overwhelm unmobilized Israeli forces with sheer mass. Only about 100 of these BMPs are the more modern BMP-2s, plus a limited number of BMP-3s. Nearly half of Syria's other armor consists of low-grade BRDM-2 and BTR-40, 50, 60, and 152 reconnaissance vehicles and APCs. Even the BMP-2 has relatively light armor, and retains many of the ergonomic problems in fighting from the vehicle and using its guns and antitank guided missile launchers as with the BMP-1. The BMP has only moderate ability to escort tanks in a combat environment where the opponent has modern sensors and antitank guided weapons. U.S. experts believe Syria has made relatively limited progress in improving its combined arms and armored warfighting capabilities since 1982, although it does have more advanced antitank guided weapons like the Milan, AT-10, and AT-14. They believe that Syrian exercise and command post training is weak above the battalion or regimental level, that Syrian tactics are rigid, and that Syrian reaction times are slow.

Syria can mass large numbers of towed artillery weapons and multiple rocket launchers. Syria maintains an inventory of 150 122-mm M-1938, 600 122-mm D-30, 100 122-mm M-1931 (mostly in storage), 600 130-mm M-46, 20 152-mm D-20, 50 152-mm M-1937, and 10 180-mm S23 towed weapons. Additionally, Syria employs 200 107-mm Type-63 and 280 122-mm BM-21 rocket launchers. This could have a major impact in an area like the Golan where ranges are relatively short and where Syria normally deploys much of its artillery. At the same time, massed artillery fire has only limited lethality against well dug in defenses and armor, and Syria lacks the sensors and battle management systems to concentrate its artillery fire with great precision and to rapidly switch fires. Syria will also have problems in maneuvering its artillery. Only about 28 percent of Syria's artillery consists of modern self-propelled weapons. These weapons include 380 122-mm 2S1 and 50 152-mm 2S3s.

Syria does have good physical defenses of its own positions on the Golan. Syria has spent decades in improving its terrain barriers and creating anti-tank barriers and ditches, and many of its units in the area between Damascus and the Golan have considerable readiness and effectiveness. However, Syria has not come close to Israel in developing the kind of capabilities for combined operations that the IDF takes virtually for granted. For example, Syria's only modern third-generation antitank guided missile launchers consist of 200 Milans, 40 AT-5s, and an unknown number of AT-10s and AT-14s, out of total holdings of some 3,390 antitank guided missile launchers.[84] Most of its systems are still relatively low-grade antitank guided missiles systems can hardly be ignored, but they greatly reduce the effectiveness of Syrian antitank forces both in the defensive mode and in providing mechanized infantry support for armored operations.

Naval Forces

Syria has a small 3,000–4,000-man navy, manned largely by conscripts with 18 months; service. It is based in Latakia, Tartus, Baniya, and Minet el-Baida. Junior naval officers receive training at the Jableh Naval Academy. Senior officers receive training as part of the normal program of the general staff's center at Quabon. Petty officer and enlisted training is conducted at Minet el Baida, Lattakia, and on-ship. Training standards are low. Syria has some 2,500–4,000 naval reserves, but they have little training and war fighting capability. The navy has 25 surface ships and 3 nonoperational Romeo-class submarines moored at Tartus.[85]

Syria's only significant surface ships include two obsolete Petya III–class frigates. These ships are equipped with torpedo tubes and rocket launchers, but have no modern air defense capability or antiship missiles. Their seagoing status is unclear and one may no longer be functional. It has two obsolescent Osa I and eight Osa II missile patrol boats dating back to the 1970s. Each is equipped with four SS-N-2 Styx antiship missiles. Some have only limited operational capability while others are on the edge of being laid up or may already lack operational capability. Syria did, however, modernize some of its Osas in the mid-1980s.[86]

Syria has eight light Soviet Zhuk-class patrol boats. These light 39-ton coastal patrol boasts have little firepower and combat capability. It has five operational obsolescent FSU-supplied mine warfare craft, including one Natya-class, one T-43, one Sonya, and three Yevenya-class ships. Only some of these mine craft are operational; the Natya-class vessel has had its minesweeping gear removed and the Sonya may not be operational. They can lay mines, but have little minesweeping capability except for the one Sonya-class vessel. Syria has three Class-class landing ships (LSMs) with a lift capacity of 100 troops and 10 tanks.

There is a small naval aviation branch with 24 armed helicopters. These include 11–20 operational Mi-14P Hazes and 4 Kamov Ka-28 Helixes, and are manned with air force operators. The Mi-14 does have dipping sonar, radar, MAD, and can use sonobouys, and can launch torpedoes, depth bombs, or mines. The Ka-28s are relatively modern and also have dipping sonar, radar, and MAD, can use sonobouys, and can launch torpedoes, depth bombs, or mines.

The coastal defense force was placed under naval command in 1984. It has two infantry brigades for coastal surveillance and defense, two artillery brigades with 18 130-mm M-46 coastal guns and around 6 KS-19 antiaircraft guns. Its main armament consists of 8–12 batteries of aging SSC-1B Sepal and SS-N-2 Styx antiship missiles.[87]

The Syrian navy's primary mission is the defense of Syria's ports at Lattakia and Tartous, coastal surveillance and defense, and peacetime patrol missions. Its major bases are at Banias, Mina el Beida, Lattakia, and Tartous, with small marine detachments at Banias, Lattakia, and Tartous. There are Scuba and UDT units at Mina el Beida. Most surface forces are based at Lattakia and Tartous, and the submarines at Tartous.[88] Overall readiness, training, and funding levels are low. It rarely practices meaningful exercises, has almost no joint warfare training, and it has little warfighting capability against either Israel or Turkey.[89] It is largely a coastal surveillance and patrol force.

Air and Air Defense Forces

The Syrian air force and Air Defense Command have more severe problems than Syrian land forces. Although Syria possesses 548 combat aircraft and a force of 40,000 men, the 20 Su-24s are its only truly modern attack fighters and they lack the avionics and precision all-weather strike capabilities of first-line Israeli attack aircraft. Similarly, Syria's 20 MiG-29s and 8 Su-27s are its only modern fighters with advanced BVR and look-down, shoot-down capabilities, and Syria so far has shown little ability to use such aircraft effectively in training and simulated combat or to generate high sortie rates. Other aircraft include 50 Su-22s, 120 MiG-23 and MiG-23 BNs, 160 MiG-21s, and 30 MiB-25s. Of these, the exact number in service is unclear. The bulk of Syria's air defense fighters have poor look-down, shoot-down capabilities and BVR combat capability, and still operate largely using obsolete and electronically vulnerable ground-controlled intercept (GCI) techniques.

Syria has also been slow to modernize its attack helicopter tactics. While Syria's attack helicopter tactics were successful in the 1982 war, they were successful largely because the IDF did not expect them and was often trying to rush its advances without adequate coordination. The IDF has now greatly improved its counterattack helicopter training and tactics, arms its helicopters to attack other helicopters, and its antiaircraft systems and light air defense weaponry. Syria has some 36 Mi-25s and SA-3421s in service, with up to another 35 in storage.

Syria has no airborne early warning and electronic intelligence and warfare aircraft that approach Israel's capabilities. Syria has vast holdings of land-based air defenses, but these consist largely of obsolescent SA-2, SA-3, SA-5, and SA-6 surface-to-air missile systems and shorter-range systems. Israel was able to defeat all of these systems in 1982, except for the SA-5, which was only deployed late in 1982, after the fighting.

Syria has not modernized its C⁴I/BM system to anything approaching a high-capability automated system, and virtually all of its systems require active radar to operate—which makes them very vulnerable to Israeli antiradiation missiles, target location and identification systems, and electronic warfare capabilities. While such land-based air defenses can scarcely be disregarded, and are certain to force Israel to both conduct a massive air defense suppression campaign and fly attack missions that avoid or minimize exposure to surviving defenses, Syrian air defenses do not have the quality necessary to match their quantity.

Syria has a large separate Air Defense Command with nearly 60,000 personnel. Its forces are organized into 25 regional brigades and a country-wide total of 130 air defense batteries. There are two major air defense commands, a North Zone and a South Zone. The defenses are concentrated to protect the south, but Syria has recently redeployed some forces to strengthen the North Zone and defenses against Turkey and Iraq. Some forces are deployed to cover Lebanon.

These forces include large numbers of worn obsolete Soviet-bloc systems, which have only had limited upgrading. These assets include 11 SA-2 and SA-3 brigades with 60 batteries and some 480 launchers. They include 11 brigades with 27 batteries that are armed with 200 SA-6 launchers and some air defense guns. In addition, there are two regiments that have two battalions with two batteries each, and that are armed with 48 SA-5 and 60 SA-8 surface-to-air missile launchers. The SA-5s seem to be deployed near Dumayr, about 40 kilometers east of Damascus, and at Shansur near Homs.

The SA-2 and SA-3 are effectively obsolete. They are hard to move, large enough to be easy to target, and are vulnerable to Israeli, Jordanian, and

Egyptian countermeasures. The SA-5 is an obsolescent long-range system whose primary value is to force large, fixed-wing aircraft like Israel's E-2Cs to stand off outside their range. The SA-6 is Syria's only moderately effective long-range system. The SA-8 is a mobile medium-range system that is effective, but limited in capability.

Syria badly needs a new type of missile system to develop the range of air defense capabilities it requires. Its SA-2s, SA-3s, SA-6s, SA-5s, and SA-8s are vulnerable to active and passive countermeasures. If Syria is to create the land-based elements of an air defense system capable of dealing with the retaliatory capabilities of the Israeli air force, it needs a modern, heavy surface-to-air missile system that is part of an integrated air defense system. Such a system will not be easy for Syria to obtain. No European or Asian power can currently sell Syria either an advanced ground-based air defense system, or an advanced heavy surface-to-air missile system. The United States and Russia are the only current suppliers of such systems, and the only surface-to-air missiles that can meet Syria's needs are the Patriot, S-300 series, and S-400.

In practice, Russia is the only potential source of the required land-based air defense technology. This explains why Syria has sought to buy the S-300 or S-400 heavy surface-to-air missile/antitactical ballistic missile systems and a next generation warning, command, and control system from Russia.[90] The SA-10 (also named the Fakel 5300PMU or Grumble) has a range of 90 kilometers or 50 nautical miles. It has a highly sophisticated warning radar, tracking radar, terminal guidance system and warhead, and has good electronic warfare capabilities. The SA-10 is a far more advanced and capable system than the SA-2, SA-3, SA-5, or SA-6.[91]

Much depends on Russian willingness to make such sales in the face of Syria's debt and credit problems. Russia has the capability to provide Syria with the SA-300 or S-400 quickly and in large numbers, as well as to support it with a greatly improved early warning sensor system, and an advanced command and control system for both its fighters and its land-based air defenses.

Such a Russian-supplied system would, however, still have important limits. Russia has not fully completed integration of the S-300 or S-400 into its own air defenses. It also has significant limitations on its air defense computer technology, and relies heavily on redundant sensors and different, overlapping surface-to-air missiles to compensate for a lack of overall system efficiency. A combination of advanced Russian missiles and an advanced sensor and battle management system would still be vulnerable to active and passive attack by the United States.

It would take Syria at least three to five years to deploy and integrate such a system fully, once Russia agreed to the sale. Its effectiveness would also depend on Russia's ability to both provide suitable technical training, and to adapt a Russian system to the specific topographical and operating conditions of Syria. A Russian system cannot simply be transferred to Syria as an equipment package. It would take a major effort in terms of software, radar deployment and technology—and considerable adaptation of Russian tactics and sighting concepts—to make such a system fully combat effective. As a result, full-scale modernization of the Syrian land-based air defense system is unlikely to occur before 2005 under the most optimistic conditions, and will probably lag well beyond 2010.[92]

As for Syria's short-range air defenses, Syria is keenly aware that Iraqi short-range air defenses proved relatively ineffective in the Gulf and Iraq Wars, and that Israel is now equipped with standoff air-to-ground missiles, high-speed antiradiation missiles (HARMs), UAVs that can target mobile and concealed systems, and extensive countermeasures.

The Syrian army has roughly 4,000 manportable light surface-to-air missiles, including SA-7s. It has a number of vehicle-mounted, infrared systems that include 20 SA-9s and 35 SA-13s. Syria's 60 radar-guided SA-8 fire units are assigned to its air force as part of its Air Defense Command. Like all similar weapons in Arab forces, these systems have low individual lethality, but help keep attacking aircraft at standoff distances, can degrade the attack profile of aircraft they are fired at, and have some cumulative kill probability.

The Syrian army has over 2,000 antiaircraft guns, including some 400 radar-guided 23-mm ZSU-4-23s, and 10 57-mm unguided ZSU-57-2 self-propelled guns. It also has 650 23-mm ZU-23, 300 M-1939 37-mm, 675 57-mm S-60, and 25 100-mm KS-19 unguided towed guns. These antiaircraft guns have limited lethality even at low altitudes, except for the ZSU-23-4. They can, however, be used effectively in "curtain fire" to force attacking aircraft and helicopters to attack at high altitudes or at standoff ranges.

MAJOR TRENDS IN ARAB-ISRAELI FORCES

The trends in the strength of Arab-Israeli military forces become clearer when they are examined by major category of military strength. The data on manpower have already been discussed.

- Figure 5.19 shows Israel's force strength relative to all of the Arab states combined. This comparison may fit the traditional "worst case," but is extremely unlikely to ever occur. Egypt and Jordan are at peace with Israel and Lebanon has little real-world military capability.

- Figure 5.20 shows the balance between Israel and Syria. This is a far more realistic balance for scenario purposes, although Syria could not sustain anything like its total force numbers in combat. Such numbers also disguised the major qualitative weaknesses in Syrian forces.

- Figure 5.21 emphasizes the difference in force modernization between Israel and Syria. Even so, it sharply understates Israel's qualitative advantage. Israel has excellent access to the most advanced U.S. military technology and has a

Figure 5.19
Israel versus Egypt, Syria, Jordan, and Lebanon in 2004

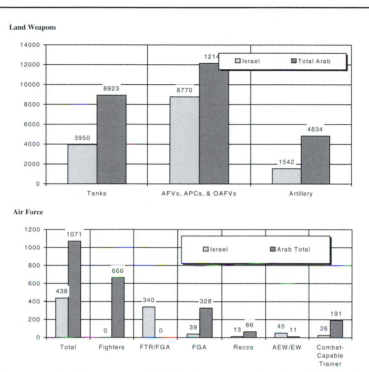

Note: Israel has 3 Gulfstream V ELINT aircraft on order, Egypt has 100 M-1A1 tanks, 179 M-109A2/3 artillery and 1 E-2C AEW aircraft on order, Jordan is awaiting delivery of 47 Challenger 1 tanks. AEW/EW Arab totals include 4 Commando 2E ECM helicopters. Total Artillery includes towed and self-propelled tube artillery and multiple rocket launchers. Total air forces include operational fixed-wing combat and combat-capable aircraft, including fighters, attack, fighter-attack, and combat-capable reconnaissance and training aircraft.
Source: Adapted by Anthony H. Cordesman from data provided by U.S. experts; and IISS, *The Military Balance*, various editions.

large and effective military industry in addition to being able to import far more arms.

- Figure 5.22 serves as a reminder of just how small the area of operations is in an Arab-Israeli conflict, and of Israel's problems in defending its borders.

- Figure 5.23 compares Arab and Israeli military manpower. It is clear that Egypt and Syria have an advantage in terms of active manpower numbers, but such an advantage is of little practical meaning because of their problems in manpower quality, readiness, and sustainability.

- Figure 5.24 shows that much of the Egyptian or Syrian advantage in manpower disappears when the superior quality of Israel's reserve manpower is considered.

Figure 5.20
Israeli versus Syrian Operational Force Strength in 2004

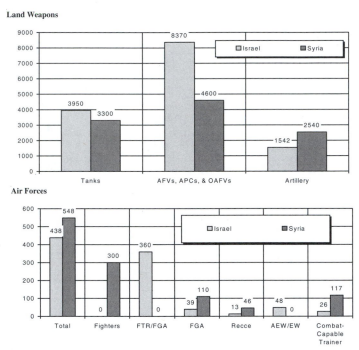

Land Weapons

Air Forces

Note: Israel has 3 Gulfstream V ELINT aircraft on order. Total Artillery includes towed and self-propelled tube artillery and multiple rocket launchers. Total air forces include operational fixed-wing combat and combat-capable aircraft, including fighters, attack, fighter-attack, and combat-capable reconnaissance and training aircraft.
Source: Adapted by Anthony H. Cordesman from data provided by U.S. experts; and IISS, *The Military Balance*, various editions.

- Figures 5.25 through 5.30 display the trends in armor, tanks, and artillery. As Figure 5.25 shows, Israel does not have a significant numerical superiority over Syria or Egypt and would have a severe numerical inferiority if it had to face a broad attack from all of its Arab neighbors.

- Figures 5.26 through 5.27, however, show the number and type of tanks in each country. Israel has a massive qualitative advantage over Syria and a major advantage over Egypt.

- Figure 5.28 shows the number of other armored fighting vehicles in each. Israel has large numbers, and a highly mechanized force, although its total includes large numbers of obsolescent systems. Figure 5.29 shows that Syria is much better equipped in terms of armored infantry fighting vehicles, although they remain highly vulnerable to Israel armor and airpower. Figure 5.30 shows

Figure 5.21
Syrian-Israeli Arms Agreements and Deliveries: 1986–2001

($U.S. Current Millions)

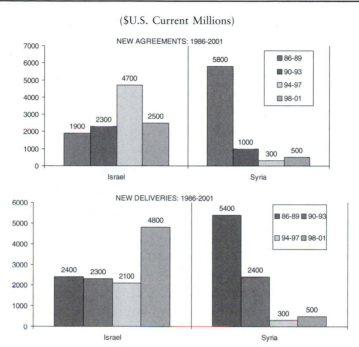

Source: Adapted by Anthony H. Cordesman, CSIS, from Richard F. Grimmett, *Conventional Arms Transfers to Developing Nations*, Washington, DC: Congressional Research Service, various editions.

Israel's advantage in APC—some of which it has armed and uparmored, but that it also retains significant numbers of obsolete half-tracks.

- Figures 5.31 shows that Syria has massive artillery strength, while Egypt's, Israel's, and Jordan's totals reflect considerably less emphasis on artillery than on armor. Most of this artillery is towed, however; and it cannot rapidly or effectively maneuver. Moreover, Syrian lacks the command and control, sensor, and counterbattery radar assets to rapidly shift and concentrate fires, carry out efficient beyond line of sight targeting, and provide efficient counterbattery fire. Israel has all of these capabilities.

- The totals for self-propelled weapons provided in Figures 5.32 and 5.33 show the number of self-propelled weapons, and provide a rough indication of the capability to carry out combined arms maneuver, and rapidly deploy artillery to a new sector of a front.

- Figures 5.33 and 5.34 reflect the major emphasis region power place on multiple rocket launchers, although only Israel has effective BVR targeting capabilities and the technology to use such weapons with relative precision.

Figure 5.22
Arab-Israeli Borders

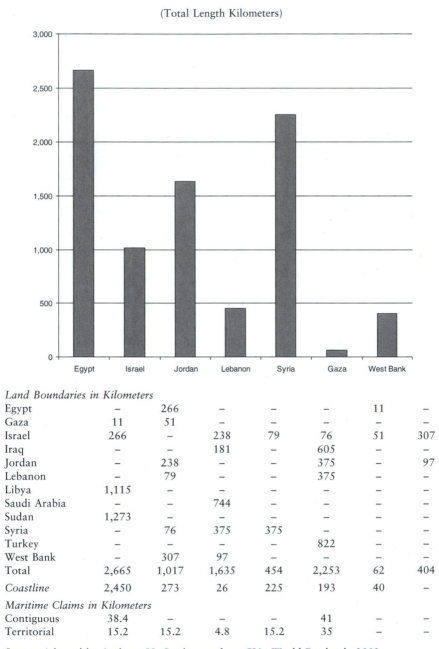

(Total Length Kilometers)

Land Boundaries in Kilometers

	Egypt	Israel	Jordan	Lebanon	Syria	Gaza	West Bank
Egypt	–	266	–	–	–	11	–
Gaza	11	51	–	–	–	–	–
Israel	266	–	238	79	76	51	307
Iraq	–	–	181	–	605	–	–
Jordan	–	238	–	–	375	–	97
Lebanon	–	79	–	–	375	–	–
Libya	1,115	–	–	–	–	–	–
Saudi Arabia	–	–	744	–	–	–	–
Sudan	1,273	–	–	–	–	–	–
Syria	–	76	375	375	–	–	–
Turkey	–	–	–	–	822	–	–
West Bank	–	307	97	–	–	–	–
Total	2,665	1,017	1,635	454	2,253	62	404
Coastline	2,450	273	26	225	193	40	–

Maritime Claims in Kilometers

	Egypt	Israel	Jordan	Lebanon	Syria	Gaza	West Bank
Contiguous	38.4	–	–	–	41	–	–
Territorial	15.2	15.2	4.8	15.2	35	–	–

Source: Adapted by Anthony H. Cordesman from CIA, *World Factbook, 2002.*

Figure 5.23
Total Arab-Israeli Active Military Manpower: 1973–2004

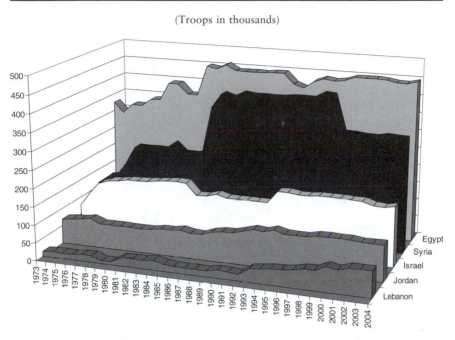

(Troops in thousands)

	'73	'76	'79	'82	'85	'88	'91	'94	'97	'00	'04
Lebanon	14.3	15.3	7.8	23.8	20.3	16.7	20.6	41.3	48.9	67.9	72.1
Jordan	69.3	80.3	67.9	67.5	76.3	80.3	93.3	106.0	98.7	104.0	100.5
Israel	77.0	156.0	164.0	172.0	141.0	141.0	141.0	176.0	175.0	173.5	167.6
Syria	111.8	177.5	227.5	222.5	362.5	407.5	404.0	408.0	421.0	316.0	319.0
Egypt	325.0	322.5	395.0	367.0	460.0	445.0	448.0	430.0	440.0	450.0	450.0

Note: Some data adjusted or estimated by the author.
Source: Adapted by Anthony H. Cordesman from IISS, *The Military Balance*, various editions.

- Figures 5.35 through 5.39 display data on combat aircraft, armed helicopters, and electronic warfare aircraft.
- Figure 5.35 shows that Egypt and Syria now each have numerical superiority over Israel in terms of total combat aircraft.
- Figure 5.36, however, shows that these aircraft differ radically by type and capability.
- Figure 5.37 shows that comparisons of high-quality aircraft give Israel a significant lead over Egypt and a massive lead over Syria. Recent wars have also shown that the quality of air forces is far more important than force numbers.
- Figure 5.38 shows that Israel also has major lead in both the quantity and quality of the air battle management, intelligence, warning, and targeting systems critical to making use of modern airpower and precision weapons, and

Figure 5.24
Arab Active versus Israeli Mobilized Army Manpower: 1973–2004

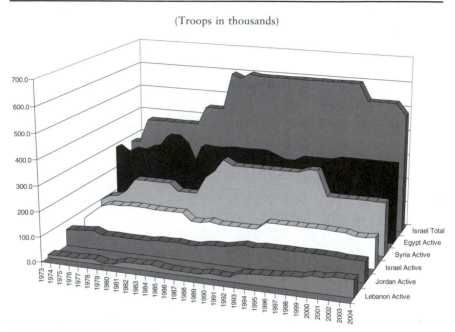

(Troops in thousands)

	'73	'76	'79	'82	'85	'88	'91	'94	'97	'00	'04
Lebanon Active	13.0	14.0	7.0	22.3	19.0	15.0	19.3	40.0	47.5	65.0	70.0
Jordan Active	65.0	75.0	61.0	60.0	68.0	70.0	82.0	90.0	90.0	90.0	85.0
Israel Active	65.0	135.0	138.0	135.0	104.0	104.0	104.0	134.0	134.0	130.0	125.0
Syria Active	100.0	150.0	200.0	170.0	240.0	300.0	300.0	300.0	315.0	215.0	215.0
Egypt Active	285.0	275.0	350.0	235.0	315.0	320.0	305.0	310.0	310.0	320.0	320.0
Israel Total	275.0	375.0	375.0	450.0	600.0	598.0	598.0	598.0	598.0	530.0	483.0

Note: Some data adjusted or estimated by the author.
Source: Adapted by Anthony H. Cordesman from IISS, *The Military Balance*, various editions.

this advantage is greatly enhanced by superior Israeli tactics, overall training, and other technologies. Egypt, along with Saudi Arabia, has acquired some of these capabilities, but cannot truly compete. Syria has little or no meaningful capability.

• Figure 5.39 reflects the growing emphasis regional powers are putting on combat and attack helicopters. Israel again leads in both numbers and quality, although Egypt has substantial modern assets. Syria's helicopter assets are approaching obsolescence, and readiness is dropping.

Figure 5.25
Arab-Israeli Armored Forces in 2004

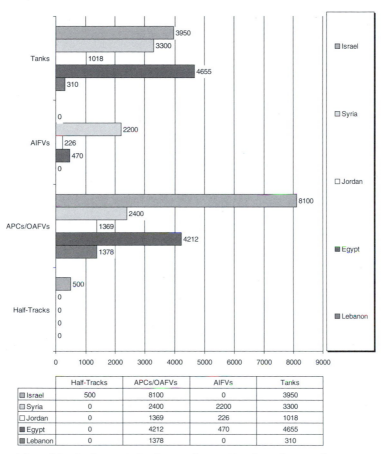

	Half-Tracks	APCs/OAFVs	AIFVs	Tanks
Israel	500	8100	0	3950
Syria	0	2400	2200	3300
Jordan	0	1369	226	1018
Egypt	0	4212	470	4655
Lebanon	0	1378	0	310

Source: Adapted by Anthony H. Cordesman from IISS, *The Military Balance*, various editions. Other data based upon discussions with U.S. experts.

- Figure 5.40 shows the strength of land-based air defense forces. Egypt, Israel, and Syria all have large forces, but only the forces of Egypt and Israel are relatively modern, and Egypt dilutes its force capability by retaining large numbers of obsolete Soviet-bloc systems. It also has a weak command and control system and training and readiness problems. Syria's system is obsolete in weapons, sensors, and command and control capability. Jordan has improved a cost-effective system with reasonable readiness and proficiency but has never had the resources to compete with the larger Arab-Israeli powers.

Figure 5.26
Israel versus Egypt, Syria, Jordan, and Lebanon: Operational Tanks by Type

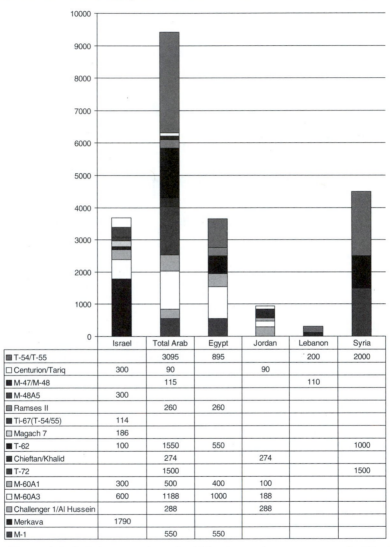

	Israel	Total Arab	Egypt	Jordan	Lebanon	Syria
■ T-54/T-55		3095	895		˙ 200	2000
□ Centurion/Tariq	300	90		90		
■ M-47/M-48		115			110	
■ M-48A5	300					
▨ Ramses II		260	260			
■ Ti-67(T-54/55)	114					
□ Magach 7	186					
■ T-62	100	1550	550			1000
■ Chieftan/Khalid		274		274		
■ T-72		1500				1500
▨ M-60A1	300	500	400	100		
□ M-60A3	600	1188	1000	188		
▨ Challenger 1/Al Hussein		288		288		
■ Merkava	1790					
■ M-1		550	550			

Note: The totals include large numbers of vehicles that are in storage or are fixed in place. In 2000, these included 300 M-47/M-48A5s for Jordan, 1,200 tanks for Syria and an unknown number for Egypt, Israel, and Lebanon. Some data adjusted or estimated by the author. Data differ significantly from estimated by U.S. experts.

Source: Adapted from IISS, *The Military Balance*, various editions.

Figure 5.27
Israel versus Egypt, Syria, Jordan, and Lebanon: High-Quality Tanks by Type

(High Quality Tanks include T-62s, T-72s, M-60s, M-1s, Merkavas, Challenger 1s)

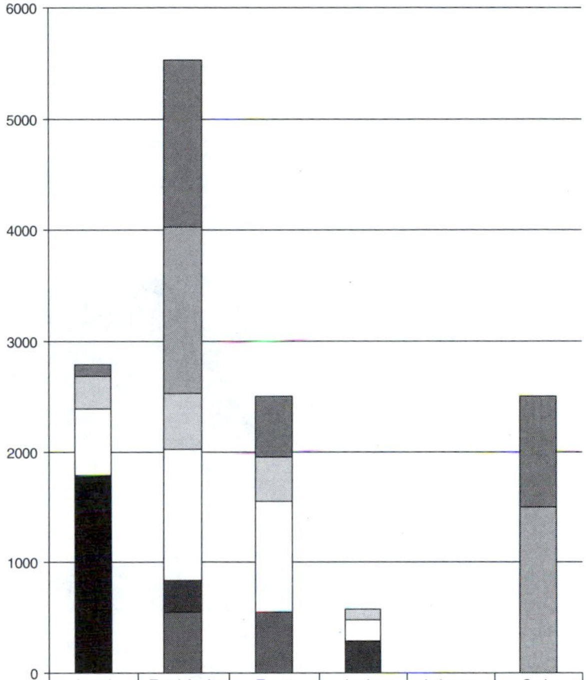

	Israel	Total Arab	Egypt	Jordan	Lebanon	Syria
■ T-62	100	1500	550			1000
▩ T-72		1500				1500
▨ M-60A1	300	500	400	100		
▫ M-60A3	600	1188	1000	188		
■ Challenger 1/Al Hussein		288		288		
■ Merkava	1790					
▥ M-1		550	550			

Note: Some data adjusted or estimated by the author. Data differ significantly from estimated by U.S. experts.
Source: Adapted from IISS, *The Military Balance*, various editions.

- Figure 5.41 compares the combat ship strength in Arab-Israeli forces. The qualitative issues affecting the forces have been described earlier. Israel had relatively modern and effective submarines and surface forces, backed by effective airpower. Egypt is less proficient, and again dilutes force quality but maintaining too many obsolete and ineffective ships, but has effective force elements. Syria's navy is obsolete and ineffective. Jordan and Lebanon have only token navies.

Figure 5.28
Arab-Israeli Other Armored Fighting Vehicles

(Lt. Tanks, AFVs, APCs, Scouts, Recce, OAFVs): 1973–2004

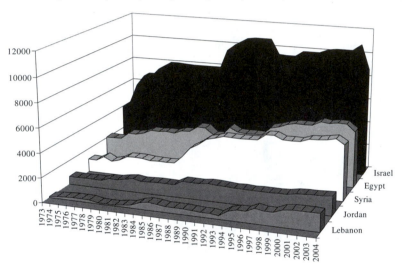

	'73	'75	'77	'79	'81	'83	'85	'87	'89	'91	'93	'95	'97	'99	'01	'04
Lebanon	80	204	239	80	80	245	658	470	470	402	312	915	1232	1085	1463	1463
Jordan	670	670	680	860	1102	1022	1022	1372	1374	1403	1324	1304	1304	1324	1501	1595
Syria	1100	1470	1300	1700	1600	1600	2200	3400	4100	4275	4250	4800	4510	4510	4785	4600
Egypt	2100	2100	2630	3080	3130	3330	3830	3245	4045	3660	3660	4501	4889	4886	5172	4682
Israel	4015	6100	6965	8080	8065	8000	8000	9800	10700	10780	8488	9488	9888	10188	10308	8770

Note: Includes APCs, scout cars, half-tracks, mechanized infantry fighting vehicles, reconnaissance vehicles, and other armored vehicles other than tanks. The totals include large
numbers of vehicles that are in storage or not operational. In 2003, they included 3,000–
3,500 half-tracks for Israel, 220 BMP-1s and 1,075 BTR-60/OT-62s for Egypt, and an unknown number for Lebanon and Syria. Some data adjusted or estimated by the author.
Source: Adapted by Anthony H. Cordesman from IISS, *The Military Balance*, various years.

Figure 5.29
Israel versus Egypt, Syria, Jordan, and Lebanon: "True AFVs"

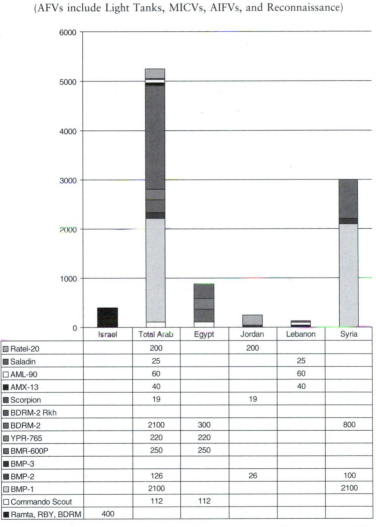

(AFVs include Light Tanks, MICVs, AIFVs, and Reconnaissance)

	Israel	Total Arab	Egypt	Jordan	Lebanon	Syria
▨ Ratel-20		200		200		
■ Saladin		25			25	
☐ AML-90		60			60	
■ AMX-13		40			40	
■ Scorpion		19		19		
■ BDRM-2 Rkh						
■ BDRM-2		2100	300			800
▨ YPR-765		220	220			
■ BMR-600P		250	250			
■ BMP-3						
■ BMP-2		126		26		100
☐ BMP-1		2100				2100
☐ Commando Scout		112	112			
■ Ramta, RBY, BDRM	400					

Note: Some data adjusted or estimated by the author on the basis of comments by U.S. experts.
Source: Adapted by Anthony H. Cordesman from IISS, *The Military Balance*.

Figure 5.30
Operational Arab-Israeli Armored Personnel Carriers in 2004

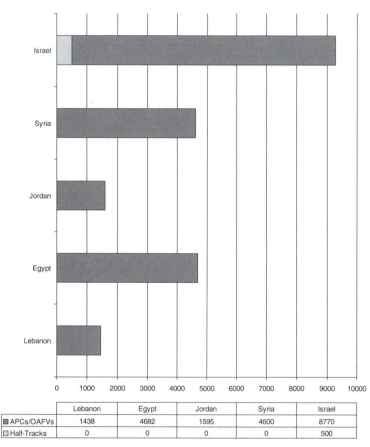

	Lebanon	Egypt	Jordan	Syria	Israel
■ APCs/OAFVs	1438	4682	1595	4600	8770
□ Half-Tracks	0	0	0	0	500

Note: Includes APCs, scouts cars, half-tracks, mechanized infantry fighting vehicles, reconnaissance vehicles, and other armored vehicles other than tanks. The totals do not include large numbers of vehicles that are in storage or not operational. In 2000, they included 3,000–3,500 half-tracks for Israel, 1,075 BTR-60/OT-62s for Egypt, and an unknown number for Lebanon and Syria. Some data adjusted or estimated by the author on the basis of comments by U.S. experts.

Source: Adapted by Anthony H. Cordesman from IISS, *The Military Balance*.

Figure 5.31
Arab-Israeli Artillery Forces by Category of Weapon in 2003

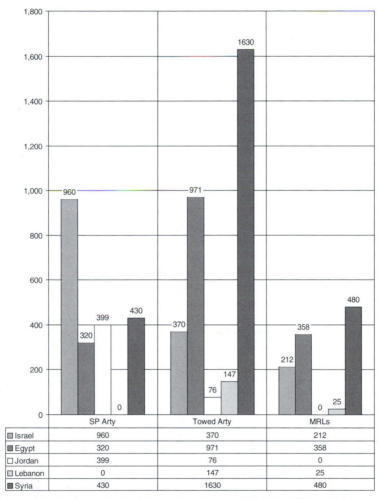

	SP Arty	Towed Arty	MRLs
Israel	960	370	212
Egypt	320	971	358
Jordan	399	76	0
Lebanon	0	147	25
Syria	430	1630	480

Source: Prepared by Anthony H. Cordesman, based upon IISS, *The Military Balance*; and discussions with U.S. experts.

231

Figure 5.32
Israel versus Egypt, Syria, Jordan, and Lebanon: High-Performance Artillery in 2004

Modern Self Propelled Artillery

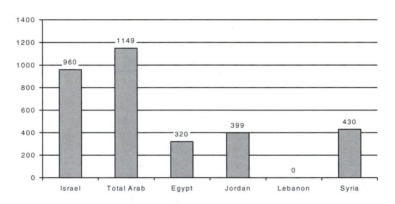

Multiple Rocket Launchers

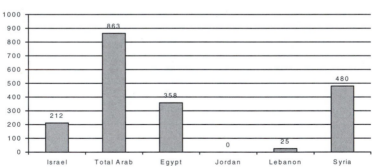

Source: Prepared by Anthony H. Cordesman, based upon IISS, *The Military Balance*; and discussions with U.S. and regional experts.

Figure 5.33
Arab-Israeli Self-Propelled Artillery by Caliber in 2004

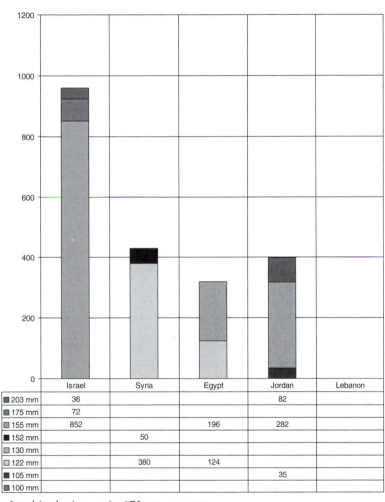

	Israel	Syria	Egypt	Jordan	Lebanon
■ 203 mm	36			82	
■ 175 mm	72				
▢ 155 mm	852		196	282	
■ 152 mm		50			
▢ 130 mm					
▢ 122 mm		380	124		
■ 105 mm				35	
■ 100 mm					

Note: Israel is phasing out its 175-mm weapons.
Source: Prepared by Anthony H. Cordesman, based upon IISS, *The Military Balance*; and
discussions with U.S. and regional experts.

233

Figure 5.34
Arab-Israeli Multiple Rocket Launchers by Caliber in 2004

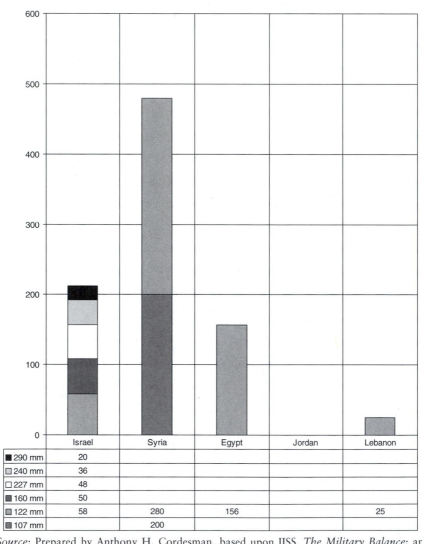

	Israel	Syria	Egypt	Jordan	Lebanon
■ 290 mm	20				
☐ 240 mm	36				
☐ 227 mm	48				
■ 160 mm	50				
▨ 122 mm	58	280	156		25
▩ 107 mm		200			

Source: Prepared by Anthony H. Cordesman, based upon IISS, *The Military Balance*; and discussions with U.S. and regional experts.

234

Figure 5.35
Trends in Total Arab-Israeli Combat Aircraft: 1973–2004

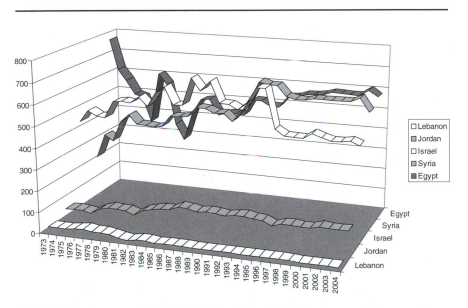

	'73	'75	'77	'79	'81	'83	'85	'87	'89	'91	'93	'95	'97	'99	'01	'04
Lebanon	18	18	27	21	7	8	3	5	4	3	3	3	3	3	0	0
Jordan	50	50	66	76	58	94	103	119	114	104	113	102	97	93	106	101
Israel	432	466	543	543	535	634	555	629	577	553	662	478	449	474	446	438
Syria	210	300	440	392	395	450	503	483	448	558	639	591	579	589	589	548
Egypt	768	568	488	612	363	429	504	443	441	517	492	551	567	585	580	579

Source: Prepared by Anthony H. Cordesman, based upon IISS, *The Military Balance*; and discussions with U.S. and regional experts.

235

Figure 5.36
Total Operational Arab-Israeli Combat Fighter, Attack, Bomber by Type in 2004

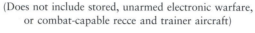

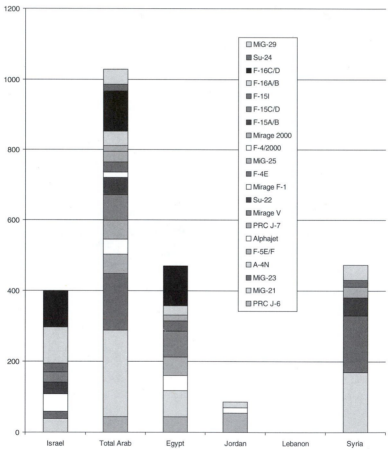

Source: Prepared by Anthony H. Cordesman, based upon IISS, *The Military Balance*; and discussions with U.S. and regional experts.

Figure 5.37
High-Quality Operational Arab-Israeli Combat Aircraft in 2004

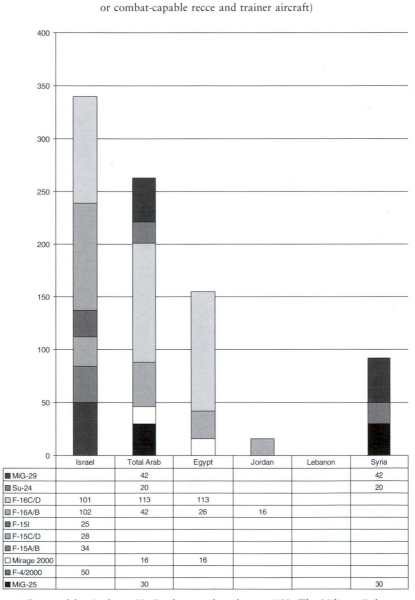

(Does not include stored, unarmed electronic warfare,
or combat-capable recce and trainer aircraft)

	Israel	Total Arab	Egypt	Jordan	Lebanon	Syria
■ MiG-29		42				42
▨ Su-24		20				20
▨ F-16C/D	101	113	113			
▨ F-16A/B	102	42	26	16		
■ F-15I	25					
▨ F-15C/D	28					
■ F-15A/B	34					
□ Mirage 2000		16	16			
■ F-4/2000	50					
■ MiG-25		30				30

Source: Prepared by Anthony H. Cordesman, based upon IISS, *The Military Balance*; and discussions with U.S. and regional experts.

237

Figure 5.38
Unarmed Fixed- and Rotary-Wing Recce, Electronic Warfare, and Intelligence
Aircraft in 2004

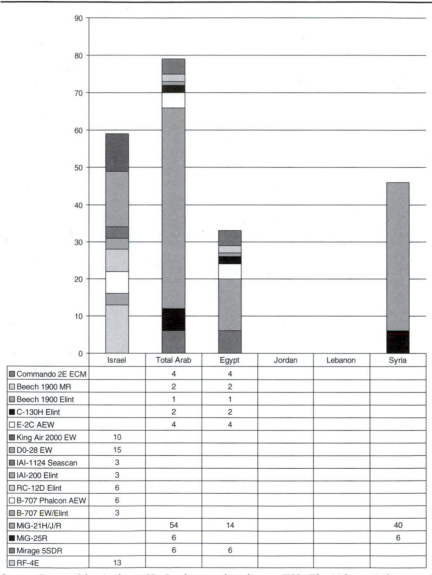

	Israel	Total Arab	Egypt	Jordan	Lebanon	Syria
■ Commando 2E ECM		4	4			
☐ Beech 1900 MR		2	2			
■ Beech 1900 Elint		1	1			
■ C-130H Elint		2	2			
☐ E-2C AEW		4	4			
■ King Air 2000 EW	10					
☐ DO-28 EW	15					
■ IAI-1124 Seascan	3					
■ IAI-200 Elint	3					
☐ RC-12D Elint	6					
☐ B-707 Phalcon AEW	6					
■ B-707 EW/Elint	3					
☐ MiG-21H/J/R		54	14			40
■ MiG-25R		6				6
■ Mirage 5SDR		6	6			
☐ RF-4E	13					

Source: Prepared by Anthony H. Cordesman, based upon IISS, *The Military Balance*; and
discussions with U.S. and regional experts.

Figure 5.39
Operational Arab-Israeli Attack and Armed Helicopters in 2004

(Does not include ASW or antiship helicopters)

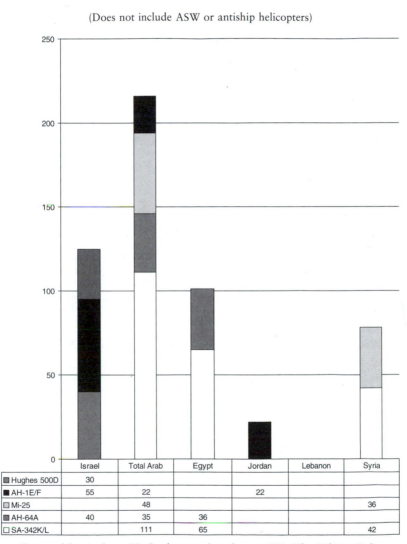

	Israel	Total Arab	Egypt	Jordan	Lebanon	Syria
Hughes 500D	30					
AH-1E/F	55	22		22		
Mi-25		48				36
AH-64A	40	35	36			
SA-342K/L		111	65			42

Source: Prepared by Anthony H. Cordesman, based upon IISS, *The Military Balance*; and discussions with U.S. and regional experts.

Figure 5.40
Arab-Israeli Land-Based Air Defense Systems in 2004

Country	Major SAM	Light SAM	AA Guns
Egypt	664+ launchers *40/~300 SA-2* *53/232 SA-3A* *14/56 SA-6* *12/78 I Hawk*	2000 SA-7 Ayn as Saqr 20 SA-9 50 Avenger Stinger 26 *M-54 Chaparral SP* *14/24 Crotale* *18 Amoun Skyguard/* *RIM-7F* *36 quad SAM* *Ayn as Saqr*	200 ZPU-2/4 14.5 mm 280 ZU-23-2 23mm 118 ZSU-23-4 SP 23mm 36 Sinai SP 23mm 200 M-1939 37mm 200 S-60 57mm 40 ZSU-57-2 SP 57mm *14/- Chaparral* 2000 20mm, 23mm, 37mm, 57mm, 85mm, 100mm 36 twin radar guided 35mm guns *Sinai-23 radar-guided 23mm guns*
Israel	*3/18 Patriot Bty* *17/102 I Hawk Bty* *2 Bty Arrow 2*	250 Stinger 1,000 Redeye *8/48 Chaparral* *8 Stinger Bty*	*850 20 mm: including 20mm,* *Vulcan, TCM-20, M-167* *35 M-163 Vulcan/* *Chaparral* 150 ZU-23 23mm 60 ZSU-23-4 SP M-39 37mm 150 L-70 40mm 8 Chaparral Bty (IAF)

Jordan	2 bde/14 Bbty/80 I Hawk	50 SA-7B2	395 guns
		60 SA-8	139 M-163 SP 20mm
		92 SA-13	40 ZSU-23-4 SP
		300 SA-14	216 M-42 SP 40mm
		240 SA-16	
		250 Redeye	
Lebanon	None	20 SA-7/B	20mm
		SA-14	ZU-23 23mm
			10 M-42A1 40mm
Syria	25 Ad Brigades	35 SA-13	2,050 Guns
	150 SAM Bty	20 SA-9	650 ZU-23-2
	11/60/600 SA-2/3	4,000 SA-7	400 ZSU-23-4 SP
	11/27/200 SA-6	160 SA-8	300 M-1938 37mm
	1/2/48 SA-5	20 SA-11	675 S-60 57mm
		100 SA-14	25 KS-19 100mm
			10 ZSU-5-2 SP
			Some 4,000 AD arty

Note: Syria has S-300 SAMs on order from Russia. Figures in italics are systems operated by the Air Force or Air Defense commands. Some data adjusted or estimated by the author.

Source: Adapted by Anthony H. Cordesman from the IISS, *The Military Balance*.

Figure 5.41
Arab-Israeli Major Combat Ships by Category in 2004

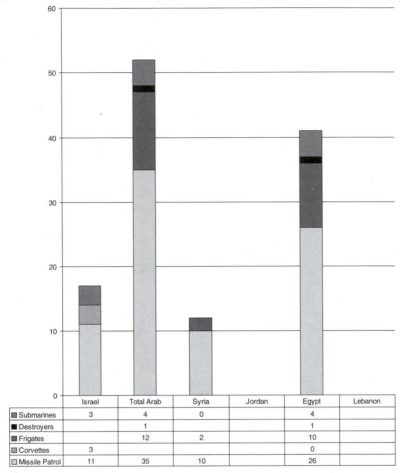

	Israel	Total Arab	Syria	Jordan	Egypt	Lebanon
■ Submarines	3	4	0		4	
■ Destroyers		1			1	
■ Frigates		12	2		10	
▨ Corvettes	3				0	
▢ Missile Patrol	11	35	10		26	

Source: Adapted by Anthony H. Cordesman from IISS, *The Military Balance*, and *Jane's Fighting Ships*, various editions. Other data based upon discussions with U.S. experts.

Taken together, these figures provide a good picture of the overall military balance in the region, to the extent that such a balance exists. The figures dealing with equipment types also show the massive obsolescence of much of the Maghreb's military forces. As is discussed in detail in the chapters that follow, these figures also show the end result of a failed military buildup in Algeria and Libya and of decades of war in Morocco. As the country analyses in each chapter reveal, only Tunisia has been relatively immune to the region's tragedy of arms.

Chapter 6

The Gulf Military Balance and Force Developments in the Northern Gulf

The Gulf military balance has long been a "four-cornered" balancing act among Iran, Iraq, Saudi Arabia, and the Southern Gulf states, and the power projection forces of the United Kingdom and the United States. Yemen has only limited military power, but is still a significant factor in regional security because of its large population, common borders with Oman and Saudi Arabia, and strategic position at the entrance to the Red Sea.

DYNAMICS OF THE GULF MILITARY BALANCE

There have been many tests of this balance. Egypt attempted to dominate North Yemen by intervening in its civil war during the 1960s, and only left in 1967. South Yemen supported Marxists rebels in Oman in what came to be called the "Dhofar Rebellion." Iraq invaded Iran in 1980. The most serious tests, however, have come from two rival Northern Gulf powers—Iran and Iraq—which have dominated both regional conflicts and the regional arms race since the 1960s. This rivalry led to a bloody war between them during 1980–1988, followed by an Iraqi victory.

Iraq's status as the dominant power, however, was very short lived. In 1990 Iraq invaded Kuwait, and triggered a war with a UN coalition that not only destroyed much of its military power, but that led to more than a decade of UN sanctions and confrontation with the United States and its allies. In 2003, a U.S.- and British-led coalition invaded Iraq, removed the regime of Saddam Hussein, and effectively destroyed Iraq's armed forces.

The end result was to create a major power vacuum in the Gulf whose future impact and implications are now far from clear.

The military balance in the Gulf has always been shaped by players from outside the region. First Britain and then the United States have effectively counterbalanced the power of both Iran and Iraq. Britain effectively guaranteed the security of the Southern Gulf states until abandoned its dominant military role in the region between 1966 and 1968. The United States then turned to Iran as a "pillar" of regional security until the fall of the Shah in 1979—which led to the Iranian seizure of U.S. diplomats as hostages and a crisis in U.S.-Iranian relations.

The United States and Europe supported Iraq in the Iran-Iraq War after 1982, when Iranian counteroffensives threatened Iraq's survival. Kuwait pressured the United States into "reflagging" its tankers in 1986, to protect them from Iranian attacks, which led to a brief "tanker war" between the United States and Iran during 1987–1988, crippling part of the Iranian navy. This situation changed radically in the summer of 1990, when Iraq invaded Kuwait. The United States, Britain, Saudi Arabia, and Egypt led a coalition that liberated Kuwait in 1991, and Iraq was placed under sanctions that continued until 2003—when the United States and Britain led another coalition that invaded Iraq and overthrew the regime of Saddam Hussein.

The Southern Gulf states—Bahrain, Kuwait, Oman, Qatar, Saudi Arabia, and the United Arab Emirates (UAE)—have built up their own military forces. This effort has been led by a massive military investment by Saudi Arabia, the only Southern Gulf state large and wealthy enough to play such a role. Unlike Iran and Iraq, however, the military efforts of the Southern Gulf states were carried out with the knowledge that the United States and its allies could provide power projection forces to protect them, and that such protection would almost certainly be forthcoming because of the role the Gulf played in the world's oil exports and the fact it had more than 60 percent of the world proven oil reserves.

As a result, the military buildup in the Southern Gulf has lacked cooperation and cohesion. Although the Southern Gulf states created a Gulf Cooperation Council (GCC) in 1980—largely as a reaction to the perceived threat from a revolutionary Iran—the GCC never resulted in more than token military cooperation. Each of the Southern Gulf states pursued its own path in creating military forces, often emphasized the purchase of modern major weapons systems that were perceived to provide prestige and a "glitter factor" in terms of regional status. Rivalries and past tensions between the Southern Gulf states prevented serious efforts at developing joint capabilities and interoperability. At the same time, a number of states limited their military efforts because of the fear of coups. The end result was that the Southern Gulf states largely preferred de facto dependence on U.S. and British power projection forces over effective regional and national military efforts.

As discussed in Chapter 2, other changes are radically affecting this balance. These include the "revolution in military affairs," but the primary factors have been proliferation, asymmetric warfare, and terrorism—driven by Islamic extremism. As this chapter makes clear, Iraq's defeat and Iran's military weakness have sharply reduced the conventional threat from the Northern Gulf. Iraq is no longer able to proliferate, though a new insurgency since Saddam's fall has shown the ability of asymmetric warfare to challenge even the most effective conventional forces.

Iran has organized its Revolutionary Guards Corps to support asymmetric warfare and has supported violent nonstate groups in the struggle against Israel such as Hezbollah, Hamas, and Palestinian Islamic Jihad. Iran has also had more freedom to acquire weapons of mass destruction, although it has joined the Chemical Weapons Convention and has pledged to destroy its chemical weapons. It also agreed to allow full inspection of its nuclear facilities in 2003, and to permit challenge inspections by the International Atomic Energy Agency (IAEA), after disclosures regarding its covert nuclear programs prompted the threat of UN sanctions.

ANALYSIS OF THE GULF MILITARY BALANCE

There is no simple way to portray all of these trends within a single chapter, particularly when the goal of such analysis is to look beyond the uncertainties of the moment, and show what trends have dominated the balance over time. Accordingly, the analysis of the Gulf balance is divided into three chapters:

- This chapter analyzes the dynamics of the military forces in the North Gulf, and the impact of past wars on that balance.
- Chapter 7 analyzes the very different dynamics of the military forces in the Southern Gulf.
- Chapter 8 describes the overall trends in the conventional forces of both the Northern and Southern Gulf states.

It should be noted that two further chapters also play a major role in this analysis. Chapter 9 describes the emerging threat from Islamic extremism and terrorism. This is currently most active in Saudi Arabia, Iraq, and Yemen, but elements of such groups exist in all of the Gulf countries. Chapter 10 describes the threat of proliferation. While this threat is now less severe as a result of the fall of Saddam Hussein, and Iran's agreement to allow IAEA inspections, it has scarcely gone away. Other regional powers like Israel and Syria continue to make steady improvements in their chemical, biological, radiological, and nuclear (CBRN) capabilities, and Israel has the ability to strike at targets throughout the Gulf. No Gulf power can ignore the fact that India and Pakistan—two major powers on the eastern edge of the Gulf—are both involved in a major nuclear arms race.

DEVELOPMENTS IN THE NORTH GULF

Figure 6.1 sets the stage by showing how Iranian and Iraqi forces compared with those of the Southern Gulf states in 2003, before the Iraq War began. The military buildup in the northern Gulf has long dominated both conflict and perceptions of risk in the Gulf region. This buildup began in the 1960s, and accelerated during the 1970s. It involved an arms race between Iran and Iraq that Iran largely dominated until the fall of the Shah in 1979. Most Western arms shipments halted as a result of both the turmoil that followed and Iran's seizure of U.S. diplomats as hostage. The end result was to deprive Iran of major resupply of its large U.S. and British forces from 1980 to the present—a development that forced Iran to turn to suppliers like Russia, China, North Korea, and Vietnam with limited success.

In 1980, war broke out between Iran and Iraq and continued until 1988—a conflict that proved to be the bloodiest in the history of the Middle East and the first in which extensive use was made of chemical weapons. Iraqi victories in the spring and summer of 1988 destroyed between 40 percent and 60 percent of the inventory. The result was to make Iraq the dominant military power in the Gulf, although Iraq had been largely impoverished by the war. This helped trigger Iraq's invasion of Kuwait in 1990, and the Gulf War that followed. The UN-imposed sanctions on any Iraqi import of arms in 1990, lasting until 2003, and Iraq lost some 30–40 percent of its military inventory in the Gulf War.

Iraq's military development remained crippled from 1990 to 2003, when a U.S.- and British-led coalition invaded Iraq, destroyed much of Iraq's remaining military forces, and caused the collapse of Saddam Hussein's regime. While Iraq did smuggle in some arms during 1992–2003, such efforts were limited, as were its efforts to create the means to deliver weapons of mass destruction.

Iran had a greater ability to import arms after the end of the Gulf War in 1990, but faced major financial problems and could not obtain resupply or new weapons from most Western states. It was able to rebuild some of its conventional capabilities during 1988–2003, and make progress toward acquiring weapons of mass destruction and long-range missiles. In practice, however, its forces had far less war-fighting capability than in 1979, the year the Shah fell from power.

As has been discussed earlier, the virtual destruction of Iraq's military forces and capability to deploy or acquire weapons of mass destruction in 2003 has fundamentally changed the Gulf military balance. Yet the longer-term trends described earlier have also had a major effect. While some Southern Gulf states have faced recent problems in recapitalizing their forces, these problems have been far more severe in the case of Iran and Iraq and have affected their military development far longer.

Figure 6.1
Gulf Military Forces in 2004

	Iran	Iraq*	Bahrain	Kuwait	Oman	Qatar	Saudi Arabia*	UAE	Yemen
Manpower									
Total Active	540,000	424,000	11,200	15,500	41,700	12,400	124,500	50,500	66,700
Regular	350,000	375,000	11,200	15,500	25,000	12,400	124,500	50,000	66,700
National Guard & Other	120,000	0	0	0	6,400	0	75,000	0	0
Reserve	350,000	650,000	0	23,700	0	0	20,000	0	40,000
Paramilitary	40,000	42,000+	10,160	6,600	4,400	0	15,500+	1,100	70,000
Army and Guard									
Manpower	540,000*	375,000	8,500	11,000	31,400	8,500	150,000	50,500	60,000
Regular Army Manpower	350,000	375,000	8,500	11,000	25,000	8,500	75,000	50,500	60,000
Reserve	350,000	650,000	0	0	0	0	20,000	0	40,000
Total Main Battle Tanks***	1,565	2,200	140	385	117	30	1,055	439	790
Active Main Battle Tanks	1,565	1,900	140	293	117	30	710	330	790
Active AIFV/Recce, Lt. Tanks	865	1,300	71	355	167	80	1,270+	780 (40)	330
Total APCs	670	2,400	235	321	204	190	3,190	620	710
Active APCs	670	1,800	205	281	204	172	2,630	570	240
ATGM Launchers	75	100+	15	118	48	148	480+	305	71
Self-Propelled Artillery	310	150	13	68 (18)	24	28	170	181	25
Towed Artillery	2,085	1,900	26	0	108	12	238 (58)	90	310
MRLs	889+	200	9	27	?	4	60	72 (48)	164

continued

Figure 6.1 (Continued)

	Iran	Iraq*	Bahrain	Kuwait	Oman	Qatar	Saudi Arabia*	UAE	Yemen
Mortars	5,000	2,000+	21	78	101	45	400	155	502
SSM Launchers	51	56	0	0	0	0	12	6	28
Light SAM Launchers	?	1,100	78	0	72	0	650	100	800
AA Guns	1,700	6,000	27	0	26	0	10	62	530
Air Force Manpower	52,000	20,000	1,500	2,500	4,100	2,100	18,000	4,000	5,000
Air Defense Manpower	15,000	17,000	0	0	0	0	16,000	0	2,000
Total Combat Aircraft	306	316	34	81	40	18	348	106	76 (40)
Bombers	0	6	0	0	0	0	0	0	0
Fighter/Attack	163+	130	12	40	12	18	172	48	40
Fighter/Interceptor	74+	180	22	14	0	0	108	22	30
Recce/FGA Recce	6	5	0	0	12	0	10	8	0
AEW C4I/BM	1	0	0	0	0	0	5	0	0
MR/MPA**	5	0	0	0	0	0	0	0	—
OCU/COIN/CCT	0	0	0	28	16	0	14	28	0
Other Combat Trainers	35	157	0	0	0	0	50	0	6
Transport Aircraft****	68	12	4	4	16	6	61	21	18
Tanker Aircraft	4	2	0	0	0	0	16	0	0
Total Helicopters	628	375	47	28	30	23	137	115	25
Armed Helicopters***	104	100	40	20	0	19	21	59	8
Other Helicopters****	524	275	7	8	30	4	116	56	17

Major SAM Launchers	250+	400	15	84	40	9	106	39	57
Light SAM Launchers	?	1,100	—	60	28	90	309	134	120
AA Guns	—	6,000	—	60	—	—	340	—	—
Total Naval Manpower	38,000*	2,000	1,200	2,000	4,200	1,800	15,500	2,500	1,700
Regular Navy	15,400	2,000	1,200	2,000	4,200	1,800	12,500	2,500	1,700
Naval Guards	20,000	0	0	0	0	0	0	0	0
Marines	2,600	—	—	—	—	—	3,000	—	—
Major Surface Combatants									
Missile	3	0	3	0	0	0	8	4	0
Other	0	0	0	0	0	0	0	0	0
Patrol Craft									
Missile	10	1	6	10	6	7	9	8	6
(Revolutionary Guards)	10	—	—	—	—	—	—	—	—
Other	42	5	4	0	7	—	17	8	5
Revolutionary Guards (Boats)	40	—	—	—	—	—	—	—	—
Submarines	3	0	0	0	0	0	0	0	0
Mine Vessels	7	3	0	0	0	0	7	0	6
Amphibious Ships	9	0	0	0	1	0	0	0	1
Landing Craft	9	—	4	2	4	0	8	5	5
Support Ships	23	2	5	4	4	—	7	2	2
Naval Air	2,000	—	—	—	—	—	—	—	—
Naval Aircraft									
Fixed-Wing Combat	5	0	0	0	0	0	0	0	0
MR/MPA	10	0	0	0	(7)	0	0	0	0

continued

Figure 6.1 (Continued)

	Iran	Iraq*	Bahrain	Kuwait	Oman	Qatar	Saudi Arabia*	UAE	Yemen
Armed Helicopters	19	0	0	0	0	0	21	7	0
SAR Helicopters	—	0	0	0	0	0	4	4	0
Mine Warfare Helicopters	3	0	0	0	0	0	0	0	0
Other Helicopters	19	—	2	—	—	—	19	—	—

*Iranian total includes roughly 100,000 Revolutionary Guard actives in land forces and 20,000 in naval forces. Iraqi totals are preconflict counts.

**Saudi Totals for reserve include National Guard Tribal Levies. The total for land forces includes active National Guard equipment. These additions total 450 AIFVs, 730 (1,540) APCs, and 70 towed artillery weapons.

***Total tanks include tanks in storage or conversion.

****Includes navy, army, national guard, and royal flights, but not paramilitary.

*****Includes in Air Defense Command

Note: Equipment in storage shown in the higher figure in parenthesis or in range. Air Force totals include all helicopters, including army operated weapons, and all heavy surface-to-air missile launchers.

Source: Adapted by Anthony H. Cordesman from interviews; International Institute for Strategic Studies, *The Military Balance* (London: IISS); *Jane's Sentinel*, *Periscope*; and Jaffee Center for Strategic Studies, *The Military Balance in the Middle East* (Tel Aviv: JCSS).

Figure 6.2
Northern Gulf Military Expenditures by Country: 1985–2002

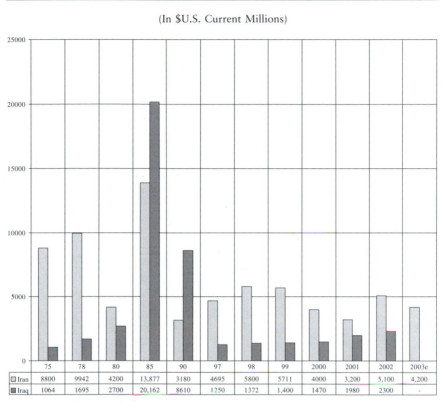

(In $U.S. Current Millions)

	75	78	80	85	90	97	98	99	2000	2001	2002	2003e
□ Iran	8800	9942	4200	13,877	3180	4695	5800	5711	4000	3,200	5,100	4,200
■ Iraq	1064	1695	2700	20,162	8610	1250	1372	1,400	1470	1980	2300	-

Note: Figures for Iraq adjusted by the author.
Source: International Institute of Strategic Studies, *The Military Balance*, various editions.

Three other figures help explain the trends involved:

- Figure 6.2 shows the trends in Iranian and Iraqi military expenditures. While the time scale is altered to highlight key periods, it shows that Iran massively outspent Iraq until the fall of the Shah of Iran in 1979. Iraq was able to dramatically reverse this situation during the Iran-Iraq War, largely as a result of Kuwaiti and Saudi loans and arms sales loans from the former Soviet Union (FSU) and Europe. The Gulf War, however, led to UN sanctions that prevented arms sales to Iraq and created an economic crisis. As a result, Iran sharply outspent Iraq from 1991 onward—although any estimates of Iraqi spending after 1991 are highly uncertain.

- Figure 6.3 shows the long-term trends in Iranian and Iraqi arms orders and deliveries. It shows that Iraq had a massive advantage over Iran in arms orders

Figure 6.3
Agreements and Deliveries to Iran and Iraq: 1994–2002

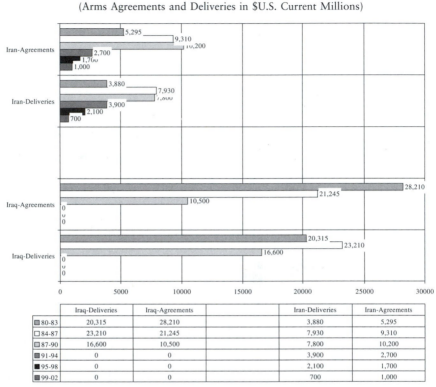

(Arms Agreements and Deliveries in $U.S. Current Millions)

	Iraq-Deliveries	Iraq-Agreements		Iran-Deliveries	Iran-Agreements
80-83	20,315	28,210		3,880	5,295
84-87	23,210	21,245		7,930	9,310
87-90	16,600	10,500		7,800	10,200
91-94	0	0		3,900	2,700
95-98	0	0		2,100	1,700
99-02	0	0		700	1,000

0 = Data less than $50 million or nil. All data rounded to the nearest $100 million.
Source: Richard F. Grimmett, *Conventional Arms Transfers to the Developing Nations*, Congressional Research Service, various editions.

during the Iran-Iraq War and until its arms imports became subject to UN sanctions in 1990. From that point onward, U.S. intelligence estimates Iraq's arms imports at less than $50 million a year. Thereafter, Iraq was free to import arms, but Iraq was not. A careful look at Figure 7.1 shows, however, that Iran never came close to importing the same amount of arms after the end of the Iran-Iraq War that it did before the war in spite of its massive equipment losses in 1988. Moreover, the trend in Iranian arms orders as deliveries has moved steadily downwards in each for year period since 1991.

- Figure 6.4 shows the sources of Iranian and Iraqi imports. Neither received significant deliveries of U.S. arms. Iraq had large deliveries of arms from Europe and the FSU before 1990, but only token deliveries from any source between 1991 and the Iraq War, largely from Eastern Europe between 1999 and 2002—the point at which Iraq's oil exports gave it significant surplus resources for the first time since 1991. Iran depended heavily on Russia before and immediately after the Iran-Iraq War, but placed only limited orders between 1995 and 2002. There are reports of a new $1+ billion dollar order from Russia in 2003, but they have not been confirmed. Its arms came largely from China and East European suppliers.

Figure 6.4
Northern Gulf New Arms Orders by Supplier Country: 1987–2002

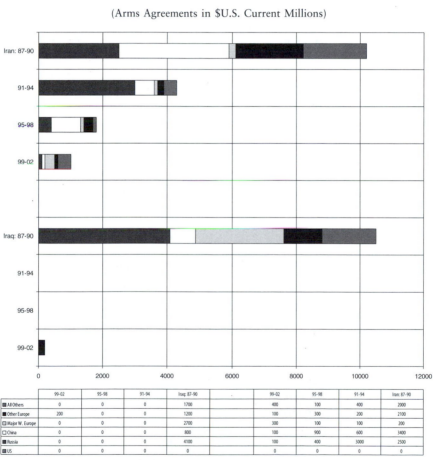

(Arms Agreements in $U.S. Current Millions)

	99-02	95-98	91-94	Iraq: 87-90		99-02	95-98	91-94	Iran: 87-90
All Others	0	0	0	1700		400	100	400	2000
Other Europe	200	0	0	1200		100	300	200	2100
Major W. Europe	0	0	0	2700		300	100	100	200
China	0	0	0	800		100	900	600	3400
Russia	0	0	0	4100		100	400	3000	2500
US	0	0	0	0		0	0	0	0

0 = less than $50 million or nil. All data rounded to the nearest $100 million.
Source: Adapted by Anthony H. Cordesman, CSIS, from Richard F. Grimmett, *Conventional Arms Transfers to the Developing Nations*, Congressional Research Service, various editions.

IRAN'S ERRATIC MILITARY MODERNIZATION

Iran is still a major military power by Gulf terms. It has active forces of some 540,000 men, although some 220,000 of this total are 18-month conscripts who generally receive limited training and have marginal military effectiveness. It also has an army reserve of some 350,000 men, although these reserves receive negligible training and Iran lacks the equipment, supplies, and leadership cadres to make effective use of such reserves without months of reorganization and training.

Iran's problems in military modernization have been compounded by a number of factors. The combat-trained manpower Iran developed during the Iran-Iraq War has virtually all left service. Iran is now a largely conscript force with limited military training and little combat experience. The deep divisions between "moderates" and "hard-liners" in Iran's government have inevitably politicized the armed forces, which remain under the command of the supreme religious leader, the Ayatollah Khamenei. Iran has also divided armed forces, split between the regular forces that existed under the Shah, and the Revolutionary Guards created under the Ayatollah Khomeini. This split is compounded by a highly bureaucratic force, which has made limited progress in joint warfare.

Land Forces

The Iranian army is still large by regional standards. It has some 350,000 men (20,000 conscripts), organized into four corps, with four armored divisions, six infantry divisions, two commando brigades, an airborne brigade, and other smaller independent formations. It has some 1,565 main battle tanks, although only 480–580 can be described as "modern" by Gulf standards, 865 other armored fighting vehicles, 550–670 armored personnel carriers, 2,085 towed artillery weapons, 310 self-propelled artillery weapons, more than 890 multiple rocket launchers, some 1,700 air defense guns, large numbers of light antiaircraft missiles, large numbers of antitank weapons and guided missiles, and some 50 attack helicopters. This is a large inventory of major weapons, although many are worn and obsolete.

In practice, each Iranian division has a somewhat different organization. For example, only one Iranian division (the 92nd) is equipped well enough in practice to be a true armored division and two of the armored divisions are notably larger than the others. Two of the infantry divisions (28th and 84th) are more heavily mechanized than the others.[1] The lighter and smaller formations in the regular army include the 23rd Special Forces Division, which was formed in 1993–1994, and the 55th Paratroop Division. According to one source, the 23rd Special Forces Division has 5,000 full-time regulars, and one of the most professional units in the Iranian army. The airborne and special forces are trained at a facility in Shiraz.[2] The regular army also has a number of independent brigades and groups. These include some small armored units, 1 infantry brigade, 1 airborne and 2–3 special forces brigades, coastal defense units, a growing number of air defense groups, 5 artillery brigades/regiments, 4–6 army aviation units, and a growing number of logistic and supply formations. The land forces have 6 major garrisons and 13 major casernes. There is a military academy at Tehran, and a signal training center in Shiraz.[3]

Iran has steadily rebuilt its armored strength since the Iran-Iraq War. The International Institute of Strategic Studies (IISS) estimates that Iran's inventory of 1,565 main battle tanks now includes some 150 M-47/M-48 and 150–160 M-60A1, 200 Chieftain Mark 3/5s, 75 T-62s, 400 T-72/T-72S, 250 T-54/T-55, 150–250 T-59s, 50 T-62s, and 150–250 T-69II, and 100 Zulfiqars. Other estimates indicate that Iran may have as many as 300 Type 59s. These totals include the remainder of 187 improved FV4030/1 versions of the Mark 5 Chieftain that were delivered to Iran before the fall of the Shah.

Only part of Iran's tank inventory is fully operational, however; and it is uncertain how many Chieftains and M-47/M-48s are operational. Some experts estimate that Iran's sustainable *operational* tank strength may be fewer than 1,000. Further, its Chieftains and M-60s are at least 16–20 years old, and the T-72 is Iran's only tank with advanced fire control systems, sights, and antiarmor ammunition.

Iran's T-72Ss are export versions of the Soviet T-72B. Some have been built under license in Iran, and are armed with a 125-mm 2A46M smoothbore gun. They have a relatively modern IA40–1 fire control system and computer, a laser rangefinder, and a night and day image-intensifying sighting system. The T-72S is powered by an 840-horsepower V-84MS diesel engine, has an upgrade suspension and mine protection, and has a combat weight of 44.5 tons. Russian sources indicate that Iran has ordered a total of 1,000 T-72s from Russia.

As has been touched upon earlier, Iran has developed a main battle tank called the Zulfiqar, with a 125-mm smoothbore gun and welded steel turret of Iranian design. According to one report, the Zulfiqar is powered by a V-46-6-12 V-12 diesel engine with 780 horsepower and uses a SPAT 1200 automatic transmission. This engine is used in the Soviet T-72, but the tank transmission design seems to be closer to that of the U.S. M-60. It seems to have a relatively modern fire control system and Iran may have improved its T-72s with a similar upgrade. The Zulfiqar's combat weight is reported to be 36 tons, and it is reported to have a maximum speed of 65 kilometers per hour and a power to weight ratio of 21.7 horsepower per ton. It has a 7.62-mm coaxial and a 12.7-mm roof mounted machine gun. It uses modern Slovenia Fontana EFCS-3 computerized fire control system to provide a fully stabilized fire on the move capability. It may have a roof-mounted laser warning device and it could use the same reactive armor system discussed earlier. Roughly 100 Zulifqar seem to be in service.

Iran has extended the life of some of its T-54s, T-55s, and T-59s by improving their armor and fire control systems, and by arming them with an Iranian-made M-68 rifled 105-mm gun similar to the one used on the M-60A1. This weapon seems to be made by the Armament Industries Division of the Iranian Defense Industries Organization. The Revolutionary Guard is reported to have a special conversion of the T-54 called the Safir-74. Iran has developed explosive reactive armor add-ons for its tanks, although the effectiveness of such armor and the extent of such uparmoring of any given model of tank is unclear.

Iran's 150 M-47/M-48s include Iran's surviving upgraded M-47Ms. These M-47s were upgraded by the U.S. firm Bowen-McLaughlin York between 1970 and 1972, which also built a vehicle manufacturing plant in Iran. They have many of the components of the M-60A1, including the diesel engine, automatic transmission, suspension, gun control, and fire components. The conversion extended the operating range of the M-47 from 130 to 600 kilometers, and increased space to hold 79 rounds by eliminating the bow mounted machine gun and reducing the crew to four. A total of about 150 conversions seem to have been delivered to Iran.

In spite of its tank deliveries and production since the Iran-Iraq War, Iran's total operational main battle tank holdings are only sufficient to fully equip five to seven of its divisions by Western standards, and Iran could only sustain about half this force for any period of extended maneuver warfare. At present, however, they are dispersed in relatively small lots among all of its regular Army and some of the Iranian Revolutionary Guards Corps (IRGC) combat units—all the IRGC units generally only have small tank force cadres and it is unclear how heavy these forces will really be in the future. The 92nd Armored Division is the only Iranian division that has enough tanks to be a true armored division, even by regional standards.

Iran seems to have about 1,000–1,360 armored infantry fighting vehicles (AFVs) and armored personnel carriers (APCs) in its operational inventory, although counts are contradictory and it is difficult to estimate what parts of Iran's holdings are fully operational and/or sustainable for any length of time in combat. The IISS, for example, estimates 515 light tanks and armored infantry fighting vehicles, and 500 APCs. Virtually all estimates indicate, however, that Iran only has about half of the total holdings it would need to fully mechanize its forces.[4] This total compares with around 3,800 such weapons for Iraq and 3,000–3,600 for Saudi Arabia.

Iran appears to retain 70–80 British-supplied Scorpions out of the 250 it received before the fall of the Shah. These are tracked weapons equipped with 76-mm guns. However, the Scorpion is more than 20 years old, and as few as 30 may be fully operational. These problems may explain why Iran has developed a new light tank called the Tosan ("Wild Horse" or "Fury") with a 90-mm gun, some of which may now be in service.

Iran has some 350 BMP-1 and 400 BMP-2 equivalents in service. The BMPs are Soviet-designed systems, but have serious ergonomic and weapons suite problems. They are hard to fight from, hard to exit, and too slow to keep pace with modern tanks. They lack thermal vision systems and modern long-range fire control systems, and their main weapons are hard to operate in combat even from static positions. Nevertheless, many have smoothbore antitank guns and antitank guided missiles. Iran also has at least 35 EE-9 Cascavel armored reconnaissance vehicles, and one estimate indicates 100. The Cascavel is an acceptable design for Third World combat, although it lacks modern sensors and weapons.

Iranian forces have some 230–240 M-113s and other Western APCs, and a mix of 300–320 BTR-40s, BTR- 50s and BTR-60s. Iran is producing an armored fighting vehicle called the Boragh (Boraq) and a lighter APC called the Cobra or BMT-2, and some 120 may be in service. The Boragh seems to be a copy of a Chinese version of the BMP-1. It is a fully tracked and amphibious and has a combat weight of 13 tons. It can carry 8–12 people, plus 2 crew. Reports differ as to its armament—perhaps reflecting different variants. Initial reports indicated that it has a turret armed with a 73-mm smoothbore gun and antitank guided missile launcher. It may, however, lack the commander's position that exists in the BMP-1, and be armed with a 12.7-mm machine gun. Iran has developed an armor package designed to fit over the hull of the Boragh to provide protection against 30-mm armor-piercing ammunition.[5] Variants with 120-mm mortars, one-man turrets with Iranian-made Toophan ATGMs, and AT-4 ATGMs, and others with 73-mm BMP-2 turrets guns also seem to be deploying.

The Cobra or BMT-2 is a low-profile, wheeled troop carrier, which can hold 7 personnel. Some versions may have twin 23-mm AA guns.

Iran has an unknown number of British Chieftain bridging-tanks and a wide range of specialized armored vehicles, and some heavy equipment transporters. Iran is steadily improving its ability to support armored operations in the field, and to provide recovery and field repair capability. However, its exercises reveal that these capabilities are still limited relative to those of U.S. forces and that a lack of recovery and field repair capability, coupled with poor interoperability, will probably seriously limit the cohesion, speed, and sustainability of Iranian armored operations.

Iran's armored warfare doctrine seems to be borrowed from U.S., British, and Russian sources without achieving any coherent concept of operations. Even so, Iran's armored doctrine is improving more quickly than its organization and exercise performance. Iran's armored forces are very poorly structured, and Iran's equipment pool is dissipated among far too many regular and IRGC units. Iran has only one armored division—the 92nd Armored Division—with enough tanks and other armor to be considered a true armored unit.

Iran has large holdings of antitank guided weapons and has been manufacturing copies of Soviet-systems, while buying missiles from China, Russia, and the Ukraine. It has approximately 50–75 TOW and 20–30 Dragon antitank guided missile launchers that were originally supplied by the United States, although the operational status of such systems is uncertain. It has Soviet and Asian versions of the AT-2, AT-3, and AT-4. Iran seems to have at least 100–200 AT-4 (9K111) launchers, but it is impossible to make an accurate estimate because Iran is producing its own copies of the AT-3. Iran also has some 750 RPG-7V, RPG-11, and 3.5-inch rocket launchers, and roughly 150 M-18 57-mm, 200 M-20 75-mm and B-10 82-mm, and 200 M-40 106-mm and B-11 107-mm recoilless guns.

Iran makes a number of antitank weapons. These include an improved version of the manportable RPG-7 antitank rocket with an 80-mm tandem HEAT warhead instead of the standard 30-mm design, the NAFEZ antitank rocket, and a copy of the Soviet SPG-9 73-mm recoilless antitank gun. Iran also makes a copy of the Russian AT-3 9M14M (Sagger or Ra'ad) antitank guided missile. This system is a crew-operable system with a guidance system that can be linked to a launcher holding up to four missiles. It has a maximum range of 3,000 meters, a minimum range of 500 meters, and a flight speed of 120 meters per second. Iran is also seeking more advanced technology from Russian arms firms. The United States maintains that a firm sold Iran Krasnopol artillery shells, while the company denies any connection with Iran.[6] Prospective sanctions are likely to deter arms manufacturers from filling the many needs of the Iranian military.

The Iranian copy of the AT-3 is made by the Shahid Shah Abaday Industrial Group in Tehran, and seems to be an early version of the missile that lacks the semiautomatic guidance that would allow the operator to simply sight the target, rather than use a joystick to guide the missile to the target by using the light from the missile to track it. The Iranian version also seems to have a maximum armored penetration capability of 500-mm, which is not enough to penetrate the forward armor of the latest Western and Russian main battle tanks. Russia has, however, refitted most of its systems to semiautomatic line of sight guidance and warheads capable of penetrating 800-mm. Iran may have or be acquiring such capability, and it would significantly improve the lethality of its antiarmor forces.

Iran has some 3,000–3,200 operational medium and heavy artillery weapons and multiple rocket launchers. This total is very high by regional standards, and reflects Iran's continuing effort to buildup artillery strength that began during the Iran-Iraq War. Iran used artillery to support its infantry and Islamic Revolutionary Guards Corps in their attacks on Iraqi forces. Iran had to use artillery as a substitute for armor and air power during much of the Iran-Iraq War, and generally used relatively static massed fires.

Some 2,085 of Iran's weapons are towed tube artillery weapons, versus 310 self-propelled tube weapons, and 889 vehicle-mounted or vehicle-towed multiple rocket launchers. The Falaq 1 and 2 series are examples of some of the vehicle mounted unguided rocket systems in the Iranian arsenal. The Falaq 1 fires a 240-mm rocket with 50 kilograms of explosives, and can reach a target up to 10 kilometers away. The Falaq 2 is slightly larger, carries ten more kg of explosives, and flies almost a full kilometer further.[7] Iran's reliance on towed artillery and slow moving multiple rocket launchers limits Iran's combined arms maneuver capabilities, and Iran has failed to develop effective night and BVR targeting capability. Iran's holdings of self-propelled weapons still appear to include a substantial number of U.S.-supplied systems, including 25–30 M-110 203-mm howitzers, 20–30 M-107 175-mm guns, and 130–150 M-109 155-mm howitzers. These U.S.-supplied weapons are worn, have not been modernized in over fifteen years, and lack modern fire control systems and artillery radars. Many lack sustainability, and a number may not be operational.

Iran understands that it has less than a quarter of the self-propelled artillery it needs to properly support its present force structure, and that maneuverable artillery is critical to success in dealing with Iraqi and other maneuver forces. It is attempting to compensate for the resulting lack of modern artillery and artillery mobility by replacing its U.S. self-propelled weapons with other self-propelled systems. Iran has purchased 60–80 Soviet 2S1 122-mm self-propelled howitzers, and has developed an Iranian-made designs called the Raad (Thunder) 1 and Raad (Thunder) 2. The Thunder 1 is a 122-mm weapon similar to Russian designs. The Thunder 2 is a "rapid fire" 155-mm self-propelled weapon. Both systems are now in deployment.

Iran bought large numbers of mortars during the Iran-Iraq War for the same reasons it bought large numbers of towed tube artillery weapons. It has some 5,000 weapons, including 107-mm and 120-mm heavy mortars, and 800–900 81-mm and 82-mm mortars. Iran mounts at least several hundred of its heavy mortars in armored vehicles.

Iran's emphasis on massed, static area fire is also indicated by the fact it has 700–900 multiple rocket launchers. It is difficult to estimate Iran's inventory, but its holdings include roughly 10 M-1989 240-mm multiple rocket launchers, 500–700 Chinese Type 63 and Iranian Haseb and Fadjir-1 107-mm multiple rocket launchers, and 100+ Soviet BM-21 and Soviet BM-11 122-mm launchers. Iran has produced its own multiple rocket launchers. These include some 50 122-mm, 40-round Hadid rocket launcher systems. In addition, Iran is producing variants of Chinese and Russian 122-mm rockets called the Arash and Noor. Iran has produced some 10 large 240-mm artillery rockets with a range of up to 40–43 kilometers called the Fadjr 3. The Iranian state television announced the production of the

DM-3b seeker for the Noor. The DM-3b is an active radar sensor that is used in the final stages of flight to acquire and home on to ship targets. A joint program between Iran's Aerospace Industries Organisation (AID) and the China Aerospace Science and Industry Corp developed Noor.[8] Iran's land forces operate a number of long-range unguided rockets, including the Shahin 1 and 2, Oghab, and Nazeat. The key longer-range systems seem to include:[9]

- The Shahin 1 (sometimes called the Fadjr 4) is a trailer-launched 333-mm caliber unguided artillery rocket. Two rockets are normally mounted on each trailer, and they have with a solid propelled rocket motor, a maximum range of 75 kilometers, and a 175-kilogram conventional or chemical warhead. The Shahin evidently can be equipped with three types of warheads: a 180-kilogram high-explosive warhead, a warhead using high-explosive submunitions, and a warhead that uses chemical weapons. There is a truck-mounted version, called the Fadjr 5, with a rack of four rockets. A larger Shahin 2, with a range of 20 kilometers, is also deployed.

- The Fadjr-3 is a truck-mounted system with a 12-round launcher for 240-mm rockets. It has a maximum range of 43 kilometers, and a 45-kilogram payload in its warhead.

- The Fadjr 5 is a truck-mounted 333-mm caliber unguided artillery rocket with a solid propelled rocket motor, a maximum range of 75 kilometers, and a 175-kilogram conventional or chemical warhead. It carries four rockets, and they can evidently be equipped with three types of warheads: a kilogram high-explosive warhead, a warhead using high-explosive submunitions, and a warhead that uses chemical weapons.

- The Oghab is a 320-mm caliber unguided artillery rocket that is spin-stabilized in flight, has a maximum range of 34 kilometers, and a 70-kilogram HE fragmentation warhead—although chemical warheads may be available. While it may have a chemical warhead, it has an operational CEP that has proved to be in excess of 500 meters at maximum range. Further, Iran has no way to target accurately the Oghab or any other long-range missile against mobile or point targets at long ranges, other than a limited ability to use RPVs.

- The Nazeat is a TEL launched system with conventional and possibly chemical and biological warheads. The full details of this system remain unclear, but it seems to be based on Chinese technology and uses a solid fuel rocket, with a simple inertial guidance system. Nazeat units are equipped with communications vans, meteorological vans, and a global positioning system for surveying the launch site. Some reports indicate there are two variants of the Nazeat solid fuel rocket system—a 355.6-mm caliber rocket with 105 kilometers range and a 150-kilogram warhead, and a 450-mm caliber rocket with a reported range of 130–150 kilometers and a 250-kilogram warhead. Both systems have maximum closing velocities of Mach 4–5, but both also appear to suffer from poor reliability and accuracy. Other reports indicate all Nazeats are 335.6-mm and there are four versions of progressively larger size, with ranges from 80 to 120 kilometers. It is claimed to have a CEP within 5 percent of its range.

- The Zelzal 2 is a 610-mm long-range rocket, with a warhead with a 600-kilogram payload and a maximum range of 210 kilometers. A single rocket is mounted on a launcher on a truck. It is unguided, but is spin-stabilized, and is claimed to have a CEP within 5 percent of its range.

- The Fateh A-110 is a developmental system believed to by similar to the Chinese CSS-8, which is a surface-to-surface system derived from the Russian SA-2 surface-to-air missile.

Iran has only limited artillery fire control and battle management systems, counterbattery radar capability, and long-range target acquisition capability (although it does have some RPVs) to support its self-propelled weapons. Iran has actively sought more modern fire control and targeting systems since the mid-1980s. It has had some success in deploying and testing RPVs as targeting systems, and has obtained some additional counterbattery radars, but it is unclear how many it obtained or put in service.

Iranian land forces have a total of some 1,700 antiaircraft guns, including 14.5-mm ZPU-2/4s, 23-mm ZSU-23-4s and ZU-23s, 35-mm M-1939s, 37-mm Type 55s, and 57-mm ZSU-57-2s. Iran also has 100–180 Bofors L/70 40-mm guns, and moderate numbers of Skyguard 35-mm twin antiaircraft guns (many of which may not be operational). Its largest holdings consist of unguided ZU-23-2s (which it can manufacture) and M-1939s. It is unclear how many of these systems are really operational as air defense weapons and most would have to be used to provide very short-range "curtain fire" defense of small point targets. They would not be lethal against a modern aircraft using an air-to-ground missile or laser-guided weapon. The only notable exception is the ZSU-23-4 radar-guided antiaircraft gun. Iran has 50–100 fully operational ZSU-23-4s. The weapon is short-range, and vulnerable to electronic countermeasures (ECMs), but is far more lethal than Iran's unguided guns.

Iran has large numbers of SA-7 (Strela 2M) and SA-14 (Strela) manportable surface-to-air missiles. Iran also has some RBS-70 low-level surface-to-air missiles and large numbers of HN-5 manportable surface-to-air missiles. It has some U.S.-made Stinger manportable surface-to-air missiles it bought from Afghan rebels. Iran seems to be producing some version of the SA-7, perhaps with Chinese assistance. It is not clear whether Iran can do this in any numbers. Iran's land-based air defense forces are also acquiring growing numbers of Chinese FM-80s, a Chinese variant of the French-designed Crotale.

In June 2003, development of the Shahab-3 was completed. It is understood to have a range of 1,300 kilometers—enough to hit Israel—and to be capable of carrying a 1,000-kilogram warhead. The Shahab-3 underwent nine tests, and only four of them could be considered successful. A Central Intelligence Agency (CIA) report to Congress on November 10, 2003, indicated that upgrading the Shahab-3 was underway. It reported that the Islamic Republic was developing a "Shahab-4" ballistic missile with a range of 2,000 kilometers. The Iranian government has repeatedly denied that it is upgrading the Shahab-3. Iran claimed that the program that the West refers to as "Shahab-4" is a program aiming to develop a booster rocket for launching satellites into space. On January 2004, Iran's defense minister claimed that the government would launch a domestically built satellite within eighteen months.[10]

Iran pioneered the use of army aviation and attack helicopters during the time of the Shah, but built up its holdings of helicopters far more quickly than it expanded its training and maintenance capability. As a result, it had a hollow force at the time the Shah fell, and its inability to obtain adequate spare parts and help in modernizing the aircraft means Iranian operational helicopter holdings have become uncertain. The Iranian army seems to retain 50 AH-1J Sea Cobra attack helicopters, and 20 CH-47C, 110–130 Bell-214A, 30–35 AB-214C, 35–40 AB-205A, 10 AB-206, and 25 Mi-8/Mi-27 transport and utility helicopters. Iran's Western-supplied transport and support helicopters have low operational readiness, and they have little sustained sortie capability. Iran is also seeking to create a significant RPV force that borrows in many ways from Israeli technical developments and doctrine. It has produced some such RPVs and several exercise reports refer to their use. However, insufficient data are available to assess this aspect of Iranian capabilities.

Iranian army communications have improved, as have Iranian battle management and communications exercises. They are now capable of better coordination between branches, the density of communications equipment has improved, and the functional lines of communication and command now place more emphasis on maneuver, quick reaction, and combined arms. However, Iranian battle management and communications capabilities seem to remain relatively limited. Iran's holdings still consist largely of aging VHF radio with some HF and UHF capability. This equipment cannot handle high traffic densities and secure communications are poor. Iran still relies heavily on analogue data handling and manually switched telephone systems. It is, however, acquiring a steadily growing number of Chinese and Western encryption systems and some digital voice, fax, and telex encryption capability.

Iran's army has improved its organization, doctrine, training, and equipment for land force operations. Iran still, however, is a slow-moving force with limited armored maneuver capability and artillery forces better suited to static defense and the use of mass fires than the efficient use of rapidly switched and well-targeted fire. Sustainability is limited, as is field recovery and repair capability. Overall manpower quality is mediocre because of a lack of adequate realistic training and a heavy reliance on conscripts.

Islamic Revolutionary Guards Corps (Pasdaran)

The Iranian Revolutionary Guards Corps (IRGC) add some 120,000 additional men to Iran's forces. Roughly 100,000 are ground forces, including many conscripts. Some 20,000 are in the naval branch, and there is a small air force. Estimates of its fighting strength are highly uncertain. The IISS estimates that it has some 470 tanks, 620 APCs, 360 artillery weapons, 40 multiple rocket launchers, and 150 air defense guns. The naval branch has at least 40 light patrol boats, 10 Houdong guided missile patrol boats armed with C-802 antiship missiles, and a battery of HY-2 Seersucker land-based antiship missiles. The air branch is believed to operate Iran's three Shahab-3 IRBM units, and may have had custody of its chemical and any biological weapons. Iran's supreme leader, Ayatollah Ali Khamenei, announced that Shahab-3 missiles had been delivered to the Islamic Revolutionary Guards Corps. In addition, six Shahab-3s were displayed in Tehran during a military parade in September 2003.[11] According to the IISS, the IRGC now has command of Iran's Marine Brigade of some 5,000 men. Other sources show this force subordinated to the navy.

Sources differ sharply on the organization of the IRGC, and its combat formations seem to be much smaller than the title implies, and to differ sharply from unit to unit. The IISS reports a strength of 2 armored, 5 mechanized, 10 infantry, and 1 special forces division, plus 15–20 independent brigades, including some armed and paratroop units. In practice, its manning would support 3–5 real divisions, and many of its divisions have an active strength equivalent to large brigades.

The IRGC has a complex structure that is both political and military. It has separate organizational elements for its land, naval, and air units, which include both military and paramilitary units. The Basij and the tribal units of the Pasdaran are subordinated to its land unit command, although the commander of the Basij often seems to report directly to the commander in chief and Minister of the Pasdaran and through him to the Leader of the Islamic Revolution. The IRGC has close ties to the foreign operations branch of the Iranian Ministry of Intelligence and Security (MOIS), particularly through the IRGC's Quds force. The MOIS was established in 1983, and has an extensive network of offices in Iranian embassies. It is often difficult to separate the activities of the IRGC, VEVAK, and the Foreign Ministry and many seem to be integrated operations managed by a ministerial committee called the "Special Operations Council," which includes the Leader of the Islamic Revolution, the President, the Minister of Intelligence and Security, and other members of the Supreme Council for National Defense.[12]

The IRGC's growing involvement in Iran's military industries, and its lead role in Iran's efforts to acquire surface-to-surface missiles and weapons of mass destruction, gives it growing experience with advanced military technology. As a result, the IRGC is believed to be the branch of Iran's forces that plays the largest role in Iran's military industries.[13] It also operates all of Iran's Scuds, controls most its chemical and biological weapons, and provides the military leadership for missile production and the production of all weapons of mass destruction.

The IRGC plays a major role in internal security. Nevertheless, it seems best to treat the IRGC primarily as a military land force that parallels the Iranian regular army, and that would operate with it in most contingencies. As has been discussed earlier, the IRGC has been placed under an integrated command with Iran's regular armed forces at the general staff level. It retains an independent command chain below this level, however; and it generally continues to exercise as an independent force. It rarely exercises with the regular Iranian army—and then usually in large, set-piece exercises that do not require close cooperation.[14]

It is difficult to estimate the proficiency of IRGC units. It seems likely, however, that they vary sharply by unit and that only a portion of the IRGC land forces are intended to participate in joint operations with the regular army in regular combat. These forces seem to have improved steadily in their training, organization, and discipline since the early 1990s, and have also expanded their joint training with the regular army, navy, and air force.

Quds (Qods) Forces

The IRGC has a large component for intelligence operations and unconventional warfare. Roughly 5,000 of the men in the IRGC are assigned to the unconventional warfare mission. The IRGC has the equivalent of one special forces "division," plus additional smaller formations, and these forces are given special priority in terms of training and equipment. In addition, the IRGC has a special Quds force that plays a major role in giving Iran the ability to conduct unconventional warfare overseas using various foreign movements as proxies. This force is under the command of General Ahmad Vahidi (Wahidi), who used to head the information department in the IRGC General Command and had the mission of exporting the revolution.[15]

The budget for this part of the force is a classified budget directly controlled by Khamenei, and is not reflected in the Iranian general budget. It operates primarily outside Iran's borders, although it has bases inside and outside of Iran. The Quds troops are divided into specific groups or "corps" for each country or area in which they operate. There are directorates for Iraq; Lebanon, Palestine, and Jordan; Afghanistan, Pakistan, and India; Turkey and the Arabian Peninsula; and the Asiatic republics of the FSU, Western Nations (Europe and North America), and North Africa (Egypt, Tunisia, Algeria, Sudan, and Morocco).

The Quds has offices or "sections" in many Iranian embassies, which operate as closed sections. It is not clear whether these are integrated with Iranian intelligence operations, or that the ambassador in such embassies has control of, or detailed knowledge of, operations by the Quds staff. However, there are indications that most operations are coordinated between the IRGC and offices within the Iranian Foreign Ministry and Ministry of Intelligence and Security. There are separate operational organizations in Lebanon, Turkey, Pakistan, and several North African countries. There also indications that such elements may have participated in the bombings of the Israeli Embassy in Argentina in 1992, and the Jewish Community Center in Buenos Aires in 1994—although Iran has strongly denied this.[16]

The Quds force seems to control many of Iran's training camps for unconventional warfare, extremists, and terrorists in Iran and countries like the Sudan and Lebanon. It has at least four major training facilities in Iran. The Quds forces has a main training center at Imam Ali University that is based in the Sa'dabad Palace in northern Tehran. Troops are trained to carry out military and terrorist operations, and are indoctrinated in ideology. There are other training camps in the Qom, Tabriz, and Mashhad governates, and in Lebanon and the Sudan. These include the Al-Nasr camp for training Iraqi Shiites and Iraqi and Turkish Kurds in northwest Iran, and a camp near Mashhad for training Afghan and Tajik revolutionaries. The Quds seems to help operate the Manzariyah training center near Qom, which recruits from foreign students in the religious seminary and which seems to have trained some Bahraini extremists. Some foreigners are reported to have received training in demolition and sabotage at an IRGC facility near Isfahan, in airport infiltration at a facilities near Mashad and Shiraz, and in underwater warfare at an IRGC facility at Bandar Abbas.[17]

The Basij and Other Paramilitary Forces

The rest of Iran's paramilitary and internal security forces seem to have relatively little war-fighting capability. The Basij (Mobilization of the Oppressed) is a popular reserve force of about 90,000 men with an active and reserve strength of up to 300,000 and a mobilization capacity of nearly 1 million men. It is controlled by the Islamic Revolutionary Guards Corps, and consists largely of youths, men who have completed military service, and the elderly. It has up to 740 regional battalions with about 300–350 men each, which are composed of three companies or four platoons plus support. These include the former tribal levies, and are largely regional in character. Many have little or no real military training or active full-time active manning, however; Iran has used the Basij to provide local security ever since the popular riots of 1994. It called up over 100,000 men in 19 regions in September 1994, and began far more extensive training for riot control and internal security missions. It also introduced a formal rank structure and a more conventional system of command and discipline, and created specialized Ashura battalions for internal security missions. Some reports indicate that 36 of these battalions were established in 1994. The primary mission of the Basij now seems to be internal security, monitoring the activities of Iranian citizens, acting as replacements for the military services, and serving as a static militia force tied to local defense missions.

Iran also has 45,000–60,000 men in the Ministry of Interior serving as police and border guards, with light utility vehicles, light patrol aircraft (Cessna 185/310 and AB-205 and AB-206s), 90 coastal patrol craft, and 40 harbor patrol craft.

Naval Forces

The Iranian navy has some 18,000 men, and is based at Bandar-e Abbas, Bushehr, Kharg Island, Bander-e Anzelli, Chah Bahar, Bander-e Mahshahar, and Bander-e Khomeini. It has 3 submarines, 3 frigates, 2 corvettes, 10 missile patrol craft, 7 mine warfare ships, 44 coastal and inshore patrol craft, and 9 amphibious ships. Its naval aviation branch is one of the few air elements in any Gulf navy, and has 5 maritime patrol aircraft, and 19 armed helicopters. It has a two brigade marine force of some 2,600 men and a 2,000-man naval aviation force. In addition, the IRGC has some 20,000 men in its naval branch, trained in asymmetric warfare, including a 5,000-man marine branch. It is equipped with 10 Hudong missile patrol boats with C-802 antiship missiles, 40 Boghammer patrol boats, and numerous patrol craft. It has bases on islands and coastal areas in the Gulf like Al-Farisyah, Sirrir, Abu Musa, Khorramshahr, Larak, and Bandar-e Abbas, and on Halul (an offshore oil platform). It also controls Iran's coastal defense forces, including naval guns and an HY-3 Seersucker land-based antiship missile unit deployed in 5–7 sites along the Gulf coast.

Iran has given the modernization of its naval forces high priority. Since the end of the Iran-Iraq War, Iran has obtained new antiship missiles and missile patrol craft from China, midget submarines from North Korea, submarines from Russia, and modern mines. Iran has expanded the capabilities of the naval branch of the IRGC, acquired additional mine warfare capability, and upgraded some of its older surface ships. Iran's exercises have included a growing number of joint and combined arms exercises with the land forces and air force. Iran has also improved its ports and strengthened its air defenses, while obtaining some logistic and technical support from nations like India and Pakistan. In August 2000, the Islamic Republic announced that it had launched its first domestically produced light submarine, which is called the Al-Sabiha 15. It can be used for reconnaissance and laying mines.[18]

Iran's ability to compensate for the weaknesses of its surface missiles depends heavily on its ability to use antiship missiles to make up for its lack of airpower. Iran's Western-supplied missiles are now all beyond their shelf life and their operational status is uncertain. Iranian forces are now operating four systems that Iran has obtained from China:

- *The Seersucker* is a long-range, mobile antiship missile, which is designated the HY-2 or Sea Eagle-2 by the People's Republic of China. It is a large missile with a 0.76-meter diameter and a weight of 3,000 kilograms. It has an 80–90-kilometer range and a 450-kilogram warhead. There are two variants. One uses radar active homing at ranges from the target of 8 kilometers (4.5 nautical miles). The other is set to use passive IR homing and a radar altimeter to keep it at a constant height over the water.

- *The CS-801* antiship missile, also called the Yinji (Hawk) missile, is a solid fueled missile. It can be launched from land and ships. It has a range of approximately 74 kilometers in the surface-to-surface mode, and uses J-Band active radar guidance. It has a 512-kilogram warhead and cruises at an altitude of 20–30 meters.

- *The CS-802* is an upgraded CS-801. It uses a turbojet propulsion system with a rocket booster instead of the solid fueled booster in the CS-801. It has a range of 70–75 miles, has a warhead of up to 363 pounds, and can be targeted by a radar deployed on a smaller ship or aircraft operating over the radar horizon of the launching vessel.[19]

- *The CS-801K* is a Chinese-supplied, air-launched antiship missile and variant of the CS-801. It too is a sea-skimming, high-subsonic cruise missile and has a range in excess of 20 nautical miles. It has been test fired by Iran's F-4Es, but Iran may be able to use other launch aircraft. This air delivery capability gives Iran what some analysts have called a "360 degree" attack capability, since aircraft can rapidly maneuver to far less predictable launch points than Iranian combat ships.[20]

Iran has sought to buy advanced antiship missiles from Russia, North Korea, and China, and sought to buy antiship missile production facilities and possibly even Chinese-made missile armed frigates. Some sources have claimed that Iran has bought eight Soviet-made SS-N-22 "Sunburn" or "Sunburst" antiship missile launch units from Ukraine, and has deployed them near the Straits of Hormuz. However, U.S. experts have seen no evidence of such a purchase and doubt that Iran has any operational holdings of such systems. The "SS-N-22" is a title that actually applies to two different modern long-range supersonic sea skimming systems—the P-270 Moskit (also called the Kh-15 or 3M80) and the P80 or P-100 Zubi/Onika.

Iran's main launch platforms for antiship missiles include three British-supplied Vosper Mark 5 Sa'am-class frigates—called the *Alvand, Alborz,* and *Sabalan*—each is a 1,100-ton frigate with a crew of 125–146 and maximum speed of 39 knots. Each was originally armed with one 5-missile Sea Killer Mark II surface-to-surface missile launcher and one Mark 8 4.5-inch gun mount. They have since had their Sea Killer's replaced with

C-802 antiship missiles and new fire control radars. The Sea Killer has a relatively effective beam-riding missile with radio command or optical guidance, a maximum range of 25 kilometers. All are active, but the *Sabalan* took serious damage from the U.S. Navy during the tanker war of 1997–1998. The ASW capabilities of these ships seem to be limited. Iran has two U.S. PF-103 (Bayandor-class) corvettes called the *Bayandor* and the *Naghdi.* These ships are 900-ton vessels, with crews of 140, two 76-mm guns, and a maximum speed of 18 knots. They were laid down in 1962, and delivered in 1964. The *Bayandor* and the *Naghdi* are probably the most active large surface ships in the Iranian navy. However, neither is equipped with antiship and antiair missiles, sophisticated weapons systems, sonars, or advanced electronic warfare equipment and sensors.

The rest of Iran's major surface vessels consist of missile patrol boats. These include ten 68-ton Chinese Hudong (Hudong)-class fast attack craft or missile patrol boats. The Hudong (Hudong)-class fast attack craft are equipped with I-band search and navigation radars, but do not have a major antiair missile system. Iran ordered these ships for the naval branch of its Iranian Revolutionary Guards Corps in 1992, and all ten were delivered to Iran by March 1996. The vessels have a crew of 28. They carry four antiship missiles, and are armed with the CS-801 and CS-802 missile. Iran now has at least 100 CS-801s and CS-802s. Iran's missile patrol boats also include ten 275-ton French-made Combattante II (Kaman-class) fast attack boats, out of an original total of twelve. These boats are armed with antiship missiles and one 76-mm gun, and have a maximum speed of 37.5 knots. They were originally armed with four U.S. Harpoon missiles, but their Harpoons may no longer be operational. At least five had been successfully converted with launchers that can carry two to four CS-801/CS-802s.

Iran has a number of large patrol craft and fast attack craft. The operational ships of this type include: three North Korean-supplied 82-ton Zafar-class (Chaho-class) fast attack craft with I-band search radars and armed with 23-mm guns and a BM-21 multiple rocket launcher; two Kavian-class (U.S. Cape-class) 148-ton patrol craft armed with 40-mm and 23-mm guns; and three Improved PGM-71 Parvin-class 98-ton patrol craft supplied in the late 1960s and armed with 40-mm and 20-mm guns. There are some 35 other small patrol boats plus large numbers of small boats operated by the IRGC. Most of these craft are operational and can be effective in patrol missions. They lack, however, sophisticated weapons systems or air defenses, other than machine guns and SA-7s and SA-14s. Iran has 5–6 BH-7 and 7–8 SRN-6 Hovercraft, believed to be operated by the IRGC. About half of these Hovercraft may be operational. They are capable of speeds of up to 60–70 knots. They are lightly armed and vulnerable, but their high speed makes them useful for many reconnaissance and unconventional warfare missions, and they can rapidly land troops on suitable beaches.

Mine warfare, amphibious warfare, antiship missiles, and unconventional warfare offer Iran other ways of compensating for the weakness of its conventional air and naval forces. Iran's mine warfare vessels include two to three Shahrock-class MSC-292/268 coastal minesweepers (one used for training in the Caspian Sea). Two of these three ships, the *Shahrock* and *Karkas,* are known to be operational. They are 378-ton sweepers that can be used to lay mines as well as sweep, but their radars and sonars date back to the late 1950s and are obsolete in sweeping and countermeasure activity against modern mines. Iran has one to two Cape-class (Riazzi-class) 239-ton inshore minesweepers; and seems to have converted two of its Iran Ajar-class LSTs for mine warfare purposes. Many of its small boats and craft can also lay mines. Both the Iranian navy and the naval branch of the IRGC are expanding their capability for mine warfare. While Iran has only a limited number of specialized mine vessels, it can also use small craft, LSTs, Boghammers, helicopters, and submarines to lay mines. As a result, it is impossible to determine how many ships Iran would employ to plant or lay mines in a given contingency, and some of its mines might be air dropped or laid by commercial vessels, including dhows.

Iran has a range of Soviet-, Western-, and Iranian-made moored and drifting contact mines, and U.S. experts estimate that Iran has at least 2,000 mines. Iran has significant stocks of antiship mines, and has bought Chinese-made and North Korean–made versions of the Soviet mines. It has claimed to be making its own nonmagnetic, acoustic, free-floating and remote-controlled mines, and has had Chinese assistance in developing the production facilities for such mines. It may have acquired significant stocks of nonmagnetic mines, influence mines, and mines with sophisticated timing devices from other countries.[21] There also are reports that Iran has negotiated with China to buy the EM-52 or MN-52 rocket-propelled mine. The EM-52 is a mine that rests on the bottom until it senses a ship passing over it, and then uses a rocket to hit the target. The maximum depth of the Straits of Hormuz is 80 meters (264 feet), although currents are strong enough to displace all but firmly moored mines.[22] Combined with modern submarine laid mines and antiship missile systems like the CS-801/802, and SS-N-22, the EM-52 would give Iran considerable capability to harass Gulf shipping and even the potential capability to close the Gulf until U.S. naval and air power could clear the mines and destroy the missile launchers and submarines. Even obsolete moored mines have proven difficult to detect and sweep when intelligence does not detect the original laying and size of the minefield, and free-floating mines can be used to present a constant hazard to shipping. Bottom-influence mines can use acoustic, magnetic, or pressure sensors to detect ships passing overhead. They can use multiple types of sensor/actuators to make it hard to deceive the mines and force them to release, can be set to release only after a given number of ships pass, and some can be set to attack only ships of a given size or noise profile.

Such mines are extremely difficult to detect and sweep, particularly when they are spaced at wide intervals in shipping lanes.

Iran has significant amphibious assets by Gulf standards, and the regular navy and naval branch of the IRGC have independent marine forces. These assets are large enough to move a battalion-sized force relatively rapidly and include: four Hengam-class (Larak-class) LST amphibious support ships (displacement of 2,940 tons loaded) that can carry up to six tanks, 600 tons of cargo, and 227 troops; and three Iran Hormuz-class (South Korean) LSTs (2,014 tons loaded) that can carry up 9 tanks and berth 140 troops. They also include three Hormuz 21–class 180-ton LSTs and three Fouque-class 176-ton LSLs. Iran's amphibious ships give it the theoretical capability to deploy about 1,000 troops, and theoretically about 30–40 tanks in an amphibious assault—but Iran has never demonstrated that it has an effective over-the-shore capability. Iran might use commercial ferries and roll-on, roll-off ships if it felt they could survive. Iran has also built up its capability to hide or shelter small ships in facilities on its islands and coastline along the Gulf, and the ability to provide them with defensive cover from antiair and antiship missiles. However, all of Iran's training to date has focused on amphibious raiding and not on operations using heavy weapons or larger operations. Iran lacks the air and surface power to move its amphibious forces across the Gulf in the face of significant air/sea defenses, or to support a landing in a defended area.

Iran has support ships, but these are generally insufficient to sustain "blue water" operations and support an amphibious task force. It has one Kharg-class 33,014-ton replenishment ship, two Bandar Abbas-class 4,673-ton fleet supply ships and oilers, one 14,410-ton repair ship, two 12,000-ton water tankers, seven 1,300-ton Delva-class support ships, five to six Hendijan-class support vessels, two floating dry-docks, and twenty tugs, tenders, and utility craft to help support a large naval or amphibious operation.

The Iranian navy's air capability consists of two to three operational P-3F Orion maritime patrol aircraft out of an original inventory of five. According to reports from the Gulf, none of the surviving P-3Fs have fully operational radars and their crews often use binoculars. It also has up to 12 Sikorsky SH-3D ASW helicopters, two RH-53D mine laying helicopters, and seven Agusta-Bell AB-212 helicopters. It uses air force AH-1J attack helicopters, equipped with French AS-12 missiles, in naval missions, and has adapted Hercules C-130 and Fokker Friendship aircraft for mine laying and patrol missions. The most significant recent development in Iran's capabilities to use airpower to attack naval targets has been the acquisition of the CS-801K for its regular air force.

Iran has attempted to offset the weakness of its major surface forces by obtaining three Type 877 EKM Kilo-class submarines. The Kilo is a relatively modern and quiet submarine that first became operational in 1980.

The Iranian Kilos are Type 877 EKM export versions that are about 10 meters longer than the original Kilos and are equipped with advanced command and control systems. Each Type 877 EKM has a teardrop hull coated with anechoic tiles to reduce noise. It displaces approximately 3,076 tons when submerged and 2,325 tons when surfaced. It is 72.6 meters long, 9.9 meters in beam, has a draught of 6.6 meters, and is powered by three 1,895 HP generator sets, one 5,900 SHP electric motor, and one six-bladed propeller. It has a complement of 52 men and an endurance of 45 days. Its maximum submerged speed is 17 knots and its maximum surface speed is 10 knots.

Each Kilo has six 530-mm torpedo tubes, including two wire-guided torpedo tubes. Only one torpedo can be wire-guided at a time. The Kilo can carry a mix of 18 homing and wire-guided torpedoes or 24 mines. Russian torpedoes are available with ranges of 15–19 kilometers, speeds of 29–40 knots, and warheads with 100-, 205-, and 305-kilogram weights. Their guidance systems include active sonar homing, passive homing, wire guidance, and active homing. Some reports indicate that Iran bought over 1,000 modern Soviet mines with the Kilos, and that the mines were equipped with modern magnetic, acoustic, and pressure sensors. The Kilo has a remote antiaircraft launcher with one preloaded missile in the sail and Soviet versions have six SA-N-5 (Igla/SA-16) surface-to-air missiles stored inside. However, Russia only supplied Iran with the SA-14 (Strela). The Kilo has a maximum surface speed of 10 knots, a maximum submerged speed of about 17 knots, a minimum submerged operating depth of about 30 meters, an operational diving depth of 240 meters, and a maximum diving depth of 300 meters. The submarine also has a surface cruise range of 3,000–6,000 nautical miles and a submerged cruise range of 400 nautical miles—depending on speed and combat conditions.[23]

Iran's ability to use its submarines to deliver mines and fire long-range wake-homing torpedoes gives it a potential capability to strike in ways that make it difficult to detect or attack the submarine. Mines can be laid covertly in critical areas before a conflict, and the mines can be set to activate and deactivate at predetermined intervals in ways that make mining difficult to detect and sweep. Long-range homing torpedoes can be used against tanker-sized targets at ranges in excess of 10 kilometers, and to attack slow-moving combat ships that are not on alert and/or that lack sonars and countermeasures. At the same time, many Third World countries have found submarines to be difficult to operate. For example, Russia delivered the first two Kilos with two 120-cell batteries designed for rapid power surges, rather than power over long periods. They proved to last only 1–2 years in warm waters versus 5–7 years for similar batteries from India and the UK. Iran had to turn to India for help in developing batteries that are reliable in the warm waters of the Gulf. Iran has also had problems with the air conditioning in the ships, and their serviceability has been erratic.

There are serious questions about crew capability and readiness, and all three submarines already need significant refits.

Iran faces significant operational problems in using its submarines in local waters. Many areas of the Gulf do not favor submarine operations. The Gulf is about 241,000 square kilometers in area, and stretches 990 kilometers from the Shatt al-Arab to the Straits of Hormuz. It is about 340 kilometers wide at is maximum width, and about 225 kilometers wide for most of its length. While heat patterns disturb surface sonars, they also disturb submarine sonars, and the advantage seems to be slightly in favor of sophisticated surface ships and maritime patrol aircraft. The deeper parts of the Gulf are noisy enough to make ASW operations difficult, but large parts of the Gulf—including much of the Southern Gulf on a line from Al-Jubail across the tip of Qatar to about halfway up the UAE—are less than 20 meters deep. The water is deeper on the Iranian side, but the maximum depth of the Gulf—located about 30 kilometers south of Qeys Island—is still only 88 meters. This means that no point in the Gulf is deeper than the length of an SN-688 nuclear submarine. The keel to tower height of such a submarine alone is 16 meters. Even smaller coastal submarines have maneuver and bottom suction problems, and cannot hide in thermoclines or take advantage of diving for concealment or self-protection.

The Straits of Hormuz are about 180 kilometers long but have a minimum width of 39 kilometers, and only the two deep water channels are suitable for major surface ship or submarine operations. Each of these channels is only about 2 kilometers wide. Further, a limited flow of fresh water and high evaporation makes the Gulf extremely saline. This creates complex underwater currents in the main channels at the Straits of Hormuz and complicates both submarine operations and submarine detection. There are some areas with considerable noise, but not of a type that masks submarine noise from sophisticated ASW detection systems of the kind operated by the United States and United Kingdom. Further, the minimum operating depth of the Kilo is 45 meters, and the limited depth of the area around the Straits can make submarine operations difficult. Submarines are easier to operate in the Gulf of Oman, which is noisy enough to make ASW operations difficult, but such deployments would expose the Kilos to operations by U.S. and British nuclear attack submarines. It is unlikely that Iran's Kilos could survive for any length of time if hunted by a U.S. or British navy air-surface-SSN hunter-killer team.[24]

In any case, the effectiveness of the Iran's submarines is likely to depend heavily on the degree of Western involvement in any ASW operation. If the Kilos did not face the U.S. or British ASW forces, the Iranian Kilos could operate in or near the Gulf with considerable impunity. If they did face U.S. and British forces, they might be able to attack a few tankers or conduct some mining efforts, but are unlikely to survive extended combat. This makes the Kilos a weapon that may be more effective in threatening Gulf shipping, or as a remote minelayer, than in naval combat. Certainly, Iran's purchase of the Kilos has already received close attention from the Southern Gulf states and convinced them that they must take Iran more seriously.

Finally, Iran's unconventional warfare capabilities include the naval branch of the Islamic Revolutionary Guards Corps, which operates Iran's land-based antiship missiles and coastal defense artillery. In addition to its land- and sea-based antiship missile forces, the naval guards can use large numbers of small patrol boats equipped with heavy machine guns, grenade launchers, antitank guided weapons, manportable surface-to-air missies, and 106-mm recoilless rifles. The IRGC also uses small launches and at least 30 Zodiak rubber dinghies to practice rocket, small arms, and recoilless rifle attacks. Its other small craft were armed with a mix of machine guns, recoilless rifles, and man- and crew-portable antitank guided missiles. These vessels are difficult to detect by radar in anything but the calmest sea state. Iran bases them at a number of offshore islands and oil platforms, and they can strike quickly and with limited warning. The naval branch of the IRGC also has naval artillery, divers, and mine laying units. It had extensive stocks of Scuba equipment, and an underwater combat center at Bandar-e Abbas.[25] Iran is also improving the defenses and port capabilities of its islands in the Gulf, adding covered moorings, more advanced sensors, and better air defenses.

Iran can use IRGC forces to conduct the kind of low-intensity/guerrilla warfare that can only be defeated by direct engagement with land forces, and filter substantial reinforcements into a coastal area on foot or with light vehicles, making such reinforcement difficult to attack. Iran can use virtually any surviving small craft to lay mines, and to place unmoored mines in shipping lanes. Its IRGC forces can use small craft to attack offshore facilities and raid coastal targets. Finally, the United States did not successfully destroy a single land-based Iraqi antiship missile launcher during the Gulf War, and the IRGC now has many dispersal launch sites and storage areas over a much longer coast. It also has a growing number of caves, shelters, and small, hardened facilities. Such targets are sometimes difficult to detect until they are used, and present added problems because they usually are too small and too numerous to attack with high-cost ordnance until it is clear they have valuable enough contents to merit such attack.

The main forces of the Iranian navy are concentrated in the Gulf. Iran gives more importance to the security of its territorial sea in the Gulf area since in this direction it has highly complicated relations with various Arab nations, United States, and Israel. After the collapse of the Soviet Union, however, Iran's policy toward the Caspian has changed. According to the contracts between the Soviet Union and Iran, Tehran was not allowed to hold its navy in the Caspian Sea. After the disintegration of the USSR, however, the 4th Naval Region forces started representing the Iranian navy in the Caspian.[26]

The Islamic Republic has almost 3,000 personnel in the Caspian. The forces include up to 50 fighting ships and support vessels, the marine corps, coastal guard forces, and the sea aircraft. There are also training vessels in the fleet, including one Shahrokh MSC minesweeper, two Hamzeh ships, and others. Currently, Iran has the second largest fleet in Caspian after Russia. The fleet, however, is outdated. This is why Tehran has been trying to strengthen its naval forces in the Caspian through various programs. It is reported that the government has numerous plans to modernize its fleet. According to these projects, the future fleet will include several divisions and sperate battalions of ships and submarines.[27]

In summary, Iran's efforts have steadily improved its capabilities to threaten Gulf shipping and offshore oil facilities, its capability to support unconventional warfare, and its ability to defend its offshore facilities, islands, and coastline. They have not, however, done much to help Iran to act as an effective "blue water" navy. Iranian naval forces still have many limitations, but the military capability of Iranian naval forces should not be measured in terms of the ability to win a battle for sea control against U.S. and British naval forces, or any combination of Southern Gulf states supported by U.S. and British forces. For the foreseeable future, Iran's forces are likely to lose any such battle in a matter of days. As a result, it is Iran's ability to conduct limited or unconventional warfare, or to threaten traffic through the Gulf, that gives Iran the potential ability to threaten or intimidate its neighbors.

Air Forces

The Iranian air force has some 15,000 men and over 300 combat aircraft in its inventory (the IISS estimates 306). Many of these aircraft, however, are either not operational or cannot be sustained in air combat. This includes 50–60 percent of Iran's U.S.- and French-supplied aircraft and some 30–40 percent of its Russian- and Chinese-supplied aircraft. It has nine fighter ground attack squadrons with 162–186 aircraft; seven fighter squadrons, with 70–74 aircraft; a reconnaissance unit with 4–8 aircraft; and a number of transport aircraft, helicopters, and special purpose aircraft. It operates most of Iraq's land-based air defenses, including some 150 I-Hawks, 45 HQ-21s, 10 SA-5sm 30 Rapiers, and additional forces equipped with light surface-to-air missiles.

The Iranian air force is headquartered in Teheran with training, administration, and logistics branches, and a major central Air Defense Operations Center. It has a political directorate and a small naval coordination staff. It has three major regional headquarters: Northern Zone (Badl Sar), Central Zone (Hamaden), and Southern Zone (Bushehr). Each regional zone seems to control a major air defense sector with subordinate air bases and facilities. The key air defense subzones and related bases in the Northern

Zone are at Badl Sar, Mashhad, and Shahabad Kord, the subzones and bases in the Central Zone are at Hamadan and Dezful, and the subzones and bases in the Southern Zone are at Bushehr, Bandar Abbas, and Jask. Iran has large combat air bases at Mehrabad, Tabriz, Hamadan, Dezful, Bushehr, Shiraz, Isfahan, and Bandar-e Abbas. It has smaller bases at least eleven other locations. Shiraz provides interceptor training and is the main base for transport aircraft.

As is the case with most aspects of Iranian military forces, estimates differ by source. The IISS estimates the air force has 18 main combat squadrons. These include 9 fighter ground attack squadrons, with 4/55–65 U.S.-supplied F-4D/E and 4/55–65 F-5E/FII, and 1/27–30 Soviet-supplied Su-24. Iran had 7 Su-25K and 24 Mirage F-1 Iraqi aircraft it seized during the Gulf War, and some may be operational. Iran had 7 air defense squadrons, with 2/20-25, -60 U.S.-supplied F-14, 2/25-30 Russian/Iraqi-supplied MiG-29, and 1/25-35 Chinese-supplied F-7M.[28] The Iranian air force had a small reconnaissance squadron with 3–8 RF-4E. It 5 C-130H MP maritime reconnaissance aircraft, 1 RC-130 and other intelligence/reconnaissance aircraft, together with large numbers of transports and helicopters. Most Iranian squadrons could perform both air defense and attack missions, regardless of their principal mission—although this was not true of Iran's F-14 (air defense) and Su-24s (strike/attack) units. Iran's F-14s have not been able to use their Phoenix air-to-air missiles since the early 1980s. Iran has claimed that it is modernizing its F-14s by equipping them with I-Hawk missiles adapted to the air-to-air role, but it is far from clear that this is the case or that such adaptations can have more than limited effectiveness.[29]

Russian firms and the Iranian government tried to reach an agreement over license-production of the MiG-29, but repeated attempts have failed. Likely due to the difficulty the regime has had in procuring new aircraft, Iran has been developing three new attack aircraft. The indigenous design and specifics of one of the fighters in development, the Shafagh, were unveiled at the Iran Airshow in 2002. Engineers hope to have a prototype by 2008, though it is unclear what the production numbers will be and what the timetable for deployment may be. Little is known about the other two fighters in development, the Saeghe and the Azarakhsh, other than they have been reportedly derived from the F-5.[30]

Iran has moderate airlift capabilities for a regional power. The Iranian air force's air transport assets included 3 B-707 and 1 B-747 tanker transports, and 5 transport squadrons with 4 B-747Fs, 1 B-727, 18C-130E/Hs, 3 Commander 690s, 10 F-27s, 1 Falcon 20A, and 2 Jetstars. Iran will have 14 Xian Y-7 transports by 2006.[31] Its helicopter strength includes 2 AB-206As, 27–30 Bell 214Cs, and 2 CH-47, 30 Mi-17 and Iranian-made Shabaviz 206-1 and 2-75 transport helicopters.

The IRGC also has some air elements. It is not clear what combat formations exist within the IRGC, but the IRGC may operate Iran's 10 EMB-

312 Tucanos.[32] It seems to operate many of Iran's 45 PC-7 trainers, as well as some Pakistani-made trainers at a training school near Mushhak, but this school may be run by the regular air force. It has also claimed to manufacture gliders for use in unconventional warfare. The IRGC has not recently expanded its combat air capabilities.[33]

Iran seems to have assigned about 12,000–15,000 men in its air force to land-based air defense functions, including at least 8,000 regulars and 4,000 IRGC personnel. It is not possible to distinguish clearly between the major air defense weapons holdings of the regular air force and the IRGC, but the air force appeared to operate most major surface-to-air missile systems. Total holdings seem to include 30 Improved Hawk fire units (12 battalions/150+ launchers), 45–55 SA-2 and HQ-2J/23 (CSA-1) launchers (Chinese-made equivalents of the SA-2), and possibly 25 SA-6 launchers. The air force also had three Soviet-made long-range SA-5 units with a total of 10–15 launchers—enough for six sites. Iran has developed and deployed its own domestically manufactured SAM dubbed the Shahab Thaqeb. The SAM requires a four-wheeled trailer for deployment and closely resembles the R440 SAM.[34]

Iran's holdings of lighter air defense weapons include five Rapier squadrons with 30 Rapier fire units, 5–10 Chinese FM-80 launchers, 10–15 Tigercat fire units, and a few RBS-70s. Iran also hold large numbers of manportable SA-7s, HN-5s, and SA-14s, plus about 2,000 antiaircraft guns—including some Vulcans and 50–60 radar-guided and self-propelled ZSU-23-4 weapons.[35] It is not clear which of these lighter air defense weapons were operated by the army, the IRGC, or the air force. The IRGC clearly had larger numbers of manportable surface-to-air launchers, including some Stingers that it had obtained from Afghanistan. It almost certainly had a number of other light air defense guns as well.

There are no authoritative data on how Iran deploys air defenses, but it seems to have deployed its new SA-5s to cover its major ports, oil facilities, and Tehran. It seems to have concentrated its Improved Hawks and Soviet- and Chinese-made SA-2s around Tehran, Isfahan, Shiraz, Bandar-e Abbas, Kharg Island, Bushehr, Bandar Khomeini, Ahwaz, Dezful, Kermanshah, Hamadan, and Tabriz. Iran's air defense forces are too widely spaced to provide more than limited air defense for key bases and facilities, and many lack the missile launcher strength to be fully effective. This is particularly true of Iran's SA-5 sites, which provide long-range medium- to high-altitude coverage of key coastal installations. Too few launchers are scattered over too wide an area to prevent relatively rapid suppression. Iran also lacks the low altitude radar coverage, overall radar net, command and control assets, sensors, resistance to sophisticated jamming and electronic countermeasures, and systems integration capability necessary to create an effective air defense net. Its land-based air defenses must operate largely in the point defense mode, and Iran lacks the battle management systems and data links are not fast and effective enough to allow it to take maximum advantage of the overlapping coverage of some of its missile systems—a problem further complicated by the problems in trying to net different systems supplied by Britain, China, Russia, and the United States. Iran's missiles and sensors are most effective at high to medium altitudes against aircraft with limited penetrating and jamming capability.

In spite of Iran's efforts, readiness and force quality remain major issues. The Iranian air force still has many qualitative weaknesses, and it is far from clear that its current rate of modernization can offset the aging of its Western-supplied aircraft and the qualitative improvements in U.S. and Southern Gulf forces. The air force also faces serious problems in terms of sustainment, command and control, and training. Iran has a pilot quality problem. Many of its U.S.-trained pilots were purged at some point during the revolution. Its other U.S.-trained pilots and ground-crew technicians are aging to the point where many should soon retire from service, and have not had advanced air-to-air combat and air attack training for more than fifteen years. While Iran practices realistic individual intercept training, it fails to practice effective unit- or forcewide tactics and has shown only limited capability to fly large numbers of sorties with its U.S.-supplied aircraft on even a surge basis. It has limited refueling capabilities—although it has four B-707 tanker/transports and may have converted other transports. The Iranian air force lacks advanced training facilities, and has only limited capability to conduct realistic training for BVR combat and standoff attacks with air-to-surface munitions. Ground crew training and proficiency generally seem mediocre—although the layout of Iranian air bases, aircraft storage and parking, the deployment of equipment for maintenance cycles, and the other physical signs of air unit activity are generally better organized than those of most Middle Eastern air forces.

The Iranian air force must also deal with the fact that its primary challenge now consists of the U.S., British, and Saudi air forces. There are high-technology air forces that operate the AWACS airborne control system, have some of the most advanced electronic warfare and targeting systems in the world, and have full refueling capability. They use sophisticated, computer-aided aggressor training and have all of the range and training facilities for beyond-visual-range combat and standoff attacks with air-to-surface munitions. Iran has no airborne control system, although it may be able to use the radars on its F-14s to support other aircraft from the rear. Its overall C⁴I system is a totally inadequate mix of different sensors, communications, and data processing systems. It has limited electronic warfare capabilities by U.S. standards, although it may be seeking to acquire two Beriev A-50 Mainstay AEW aircraft, and has converted some aircraft to provide a limited ELINT/SIGINT capability.

Iran is slowly improving its capability for joint land-air and air-sea operations. Iranian exercises and statements provide strong indications that

Iran would like to develop an advanced air defense systems, the ability to operate effectively in long-range maritime patrol and attack missions, effective joint warfare capabilities, and strike/attack forces with the ability to penetrate deep into Iraq, the southern Gulf states, and other neighboring powers. Iran's exercises, military literature, and procurement efforts also make it clear that its air planners understand the value of airborne early warning and C^4I systems, the value of airborne intelligence and electronic warfare platforms, the value of RPVs, and the value of airborne refueling. Iran has even sought to create its own satellite program.[36] Further, the air force's efforts at sheltering and dispersal indicate that it understands the vulnerability of modern air facilities and the standoff attack capabilities of advanced air forces like those of the United States.

Detailed Trends in Iranian Forces

The following figures illustrate the factors driving Iranian military developments and modernization in more depth:

- Figure 6.5 provides a general overview of military developments in Iran, now the only remaining Gulf military power with a history of hostility to the United States and its neighbors.

Figure 6.5
Iran—Overview

- Iran is still a much poorer nation in terms of export earnings than it was at the time of the Shah, with only about two-thirds of the real export earning it had in the early 1980s. This limits its ability to import arms.
- Iran's military effort is only a small fraction of the share of GNP that Iran spent during the Iran-Iraq War, and Iran's increasing GDP is steadily reducing the impact of its military effort on its economy.
- Although Iran is often said to be involved in a major military buildup, comparisons of the trends in total central government expenditures, military expenditures, arms imports, and export earnings show that Iran has devoted a steadily dropping percentage of its available resources to military spending and arms imports. The IISS estimates that Iran spent $7.9 billion on military forces in 1985, or 7.7% of its GNP. It spent $3.128 billion in 2001 (3.8% of GNP) and $4.9 billion in 2002 (4.6% of GNP). According to a report released by Forecast International, Iran's defence spending will be about $4.5 billion by 2007. These are not inconsiderable defense expenditures, but they represent roughly half the defense effort Iran made during the Iran-Iraq War and time of the Shah, and to put them in perspective, a minor Gulf military power like Kuwait spent $3.3 billion on military forces in 2002.
- At the same time, the data in the CIA *World Factbook* reveals that Iran's domestic government expenditures have been allowed to rise sharply and that im-

Figure 6.5 (Continued)

ports have been allowed to exceed exports. Iran has clearly emphasized public spending on civil programs at the expense of both military spending and private investment.

- Iran's economy is under acute pressure in terms of per capita income and relative wealth. Iran's population increased from 38.2 million in 1980 to over 68 million in 2002. Real per capita income is now about half what it was at the time of the Iranian revolution—a key indicator of the pressures Iran faces to limit military spending.

- As Figure 7.1 shows, major cuts have taken place in both Iran's arms orders and arms deliveries since 1990, and new orders have dropped faster than deliveries. Iran is spending about 25–35% of what it would need to modernize and recapitalize the force levels in had under the Shah.

  - Iran has received no arms transfer from the United States since 1980, and received only $100 million worth of arms from any major West European power during 1985–2002. It received only $1.2 billion worth of arms from Russia, $400 million from other European powers during this period, and only $400 million worth of arms from either source during 1999–2002. As a result, Iran has had only limited access to any source of modern arms.
  - Iran does have more arms in the pipeline. It ordered $1.7 billion worth of arms during 1995–1998, and $800 million of this total will come from Russia, the major West European powers, and other European states. It ordered $1 billion worth of arms during 1995–1998, and $500 million of this total will come from Russia, the major West European powers, and other European states.
  - Recent Iranian arms sales agreements do not reflect Iran a high dependence on Russia, relative to Europe ($400 million vs. $800 million in 1995–1998 and $100 million vs. $400 million in 1999–2002).

- Iran has made important and potentially destabilizing purchases of arms whose content seems targeted at strengthening its air defenses along its Gulf coast, and improving its antiship and unconventional warfare capabilities to threaten Gulf shipping and attack targets in the Southern Gulf.

- At the same time, Iran has a massive inventory of worn and decaying obsolete or obsolescent Western-supplied equipment and low performance Chinese- and North Korean–supplied systems.

- Iran seems to have placed more emphasis on the acquisition of weapons of mass destruction and new long-range missiles than on obtaining modern conventional weapons and equipment.

- Figure 6.6 shows the long-term trend in arms deliveries to Iran. It is important to note that more recent data from a different source indicate that the downward trend from 1986 to 1999 has been arrested—although arms deliveries only average $175 million a year during 1999–2002.

Figure 6.6
Value of Iranian Arms Deliveries

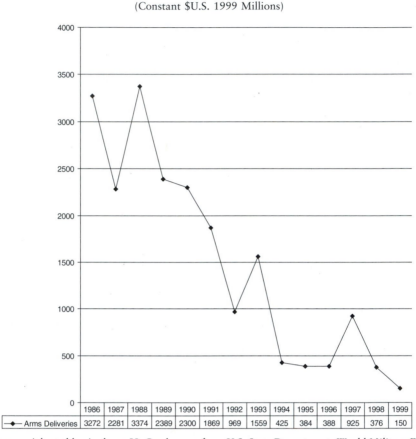

(Constant $U.S. 1999 Millions)

	1986	1987	1988	1989	1990	1991	1992	1993	1994	1995	1996	1997	1998	1999
Arms Deliveries	3272	2281	3374	2389	2300	1869	969	1559	425	384	388	925	376	150

Source: Adapted by Anthony H. Cordesman from U.S. State Department, *World Military Expenditures and Arms Transfers*, various editions.

- Figure 6.7 discusses key Iranian equipment developments since 1990, but many of these developments consist of plans for equipment product and new orders that have not yet materialized. In general, the pace of Iranian land force modernization has been very slow, while it has made little real progress in modernizing its air forces and land-based air defense forces.

- Figure 6.8 shows that Iran remains acutely dependent on worn, aging, and obsolescent Western weapons systems delivered during the time of the Shah.

- Figure 6.9 summarizes the current uncertainties surrounding Iran's ability to substitute for arms imports by producing modern combat equipment. Iran does seem to be making progress in producing armor and artillery, but its progress in aircraft and naval systems is slower.

Figure 6.7
Key Iranian Equipment Developments

Land

- Russian, and Polish T-72 Exports. Reports indicate Iran has procured about 380 T-72Ss from Russia (100 of which are kits for local assembly), and 100 T-72M1s from Poland since 1990. This gives Iran an inventory of about 480 T-72s—now its only truly modern tank and one where it has only taken delivery of 13 such tanks since 1995.

- Claims to be producing the Iranian-made Zolfaqar (Zulfiqar) MBT, an M-48/M-60-like tank, but no more than 100 have been produced.

- Has upgraded to T-54/T-54 called "Safir-74." Claims to have upgraded Iraqi T-54s captured in Iran-Iraq War. Has 400 T-54/55 in inventory. Number of upgrades unknown.

- Purchased Russian BMPs. Inventory of 350 BMP-1s and 400 BMP-2s out a total of 865 armored infantry fighting vehicles and light tanks.

- Russia may be licensing Iranian production of T-72 (100 units) and BMP-2 (200 units).

- Claims domestic production of a Chinese version of the BMP called the Boragh. May have an inventory of 120.

- Claims domestic production of an APC called the BMT-2 or Cobra.

- Possible purchase of 100 M-46 and 300 D-30 artillery weapons from Russia.

- Claims deployment of locally manufactured 122-mm and 155-mm self-propelled guns called Thunder 1 and Thunder 2, respectively. Some seem to be deployed but numbers are not available. Has 60 2S1 122-mm and 180 M-109 155-mm self-propelled weapons and some estimates indicate the Thunder series weapons are with these units.

- May have 15+ Chinese and North Korean 146-mm self-propelled weapons.

- Has 60 Russian 2S1 122-mm self-propelled howitzers in inventory.

- Growing numbers of BM-24 240-mm, BM-21 122-mm and Chinese Type 63 107-mm MRLs.

- Iranian Hadid 122-mm—40 round MRL.

- Manufacturing Iranian Arash and Noor rockets (variants of Chinese and Russian 122-mm rockets).

- Manufacturing Iranian Haseb rockets (variants of Chinese 107-mm rockets).

- Manufacturing Iranian Shahin 1 and 2, Oghab, Nazeat 5 and 10 (may be additional versions), and Fajr battlefield rockets.

- Has shown a modified heavy equipment transporter called the "Babr 400."

- Russian and Asian AT-2, AT-3, AT-4, and AT-5 antitank guided weapons. Reports of 100 Chinese Red Arrows seem incorrect.

- Claims to have developed the Saeque-1 ATGW.

- Possible installation of a Russian T-72S main battle tank crew-training center.

continued

Figure 6.7 (Continued)

- The Shebab-3 MRBM is assessed to enter its early operational status and it is estimated that Iran has some 20 missiles.
- Iran renewed its negotiation with Russia in early 2002 for large weapons deals. None, however, has materialized.

Air/Air Defense

- Keeping up to 115 combat aircraft that Iraq sent to Iran during Gulf War. Seem to include 24 Su-24s and four MiG-29s.
- Has 25 MiG-29s with air-to-air refueling capability in inventory. Reports may be receiving 15–20 more from Russia, but no confirmation.
- Has 30 Su-24s in inventory (Su-24MK). Reports may be receiving 6–9 more from Russia, but no confirmation.
- Has purchased AS-10, AS-11, AS-12, AS-14/16s from Russia.
- Has 7 Su-25Ks (formerly Iraqi), although has not deployed.
- Reports may be trying to purchase more Su-25s, as well as MiG-31s, Su-27s, and Tu-22Ms
- Considering imports of Chinese F-8 fighter and Jian Hong bomber.
- Has 24 Chinese F-7M fighters with PL2A, and PL-7 AAMs.
- Has purchased 15 Brazilian Tucano trainers and 22 Pakistani MiG-17 trainers.
- Has bought 12 Italian AB-212, 20 German BK-117A-3, and 2 Russian Mi-17 support and utility helicopters (30 Mi-17 to be delivered by the end of 2003).
- Claims to have fitted F-14s with I-Hawk missiles adapted to the air-to-air role.
- Claims to produce advanced electronic warfare systems.
- IRGC claims to be ready to mass produce gliders.
- The first Iran-140 transport aircraft assembled under a joint program with Ukrain. Planning to develop two versions of this aircraft for military use.
- The Iranian industry announced that it is planning to move the Azarakhsh combat aircraft and Shabaviz helicopters program into serial production.
- 20 Shahed-5 Helicopter Gunships in production. F-5 Derived Indigenous Attack Aircraft in development.

Land-Based Air Defense

- Most systems now aging or obsolescent in spite of some modifications.
- May be negotiating purchase of S-300 and more SA-14/16s from Russia.
- Has acquired four HQ-23/2B (CSA-1) launchers and 45–48 missiles, plus 25 SA-6 and 10 SA-5 launchers.
- Has acquired Chinese FM-80 launchers and a few RBS-70s.
- More SA-7s and HN-5s man-portable missiles; may have acquired 100-200 Strelas.
- Reports seeking to modernize Rapier and 10-15 Tigercat fire units.
- May be modifying and/or producing ZSU-23-4 radar-guided antiaircraft guns.
- Claims to produce advanced electronic warfare systems.

Figure 6.7 (Continued)

Sea

- Claims will soon start producing 3 corvettes.
- Has taken delivery on three Russian Type 877 EKM Kilo-class submarines, possibly with 1,000 modern magnetic, acoustic, and pressure sensitive mines.
- Reports of North Korean midget submarines have never been confirmed. Has produced small swimmer delivery vehicles called the Al-Sabehat 15 minisub.
- Main surface ships are 3 Alvan (Vosper 5)-class frigates dating back to late 1960s and early 1970s, and two Bayandor-class frigates from early 1980s.
- Obtained 10 Hudong-class Chinese missile patrol boats with CS-802 during early to mid-1990s. Has 10 Kaman-class missile patrol boats from late 1970s, early 1980s.
- U.S. Mark 65 and Russian AND 500, AMAG-1, KRAB antiship mines.
- Reported that Iran is negotiating to buy Chinese EM-52 rocket-propelled mine.
- Claims to be developing nonmagnetic, acoustic, free-floating and remote controlled mines. May have also acquired nonmagnetic mines, influence mines, and mines with sophisticated timing devices.
- Wake-homing and wire-guided Russian torpedoes.
- Seersucker (HY-2) sites with 50–60 missiles—working to extend range to 400 km.
- Has 60–100 Chinese CS-801(Ying Jai-1 SY-2) and CS-802 (YF-6) SSMs.
- Developing FL-10 antiship cruise missile, which is copy of Chinese FL-2 or FL-7.
- Boghammer fast interceptor craft.
- Navy received fast patrol boats and C-701 ship-borne missiles from China.
- Iran received 15 small patrol boats from North Korea.

Missiles

- Obtained up to 300 Scud Bs with 17 launchers.
- Some 175 Chinese CSS-8 surface-to-surface missiles with 25–30 launchers.
- Reports that China is giving Iran technology to produce long-range solid fuel missiles.
- Mushak-90, -120, -160, -200 missiles based on the Chinese CSS-8.
- Has bought North Korean Scud Cs with 5–14 launchers. South Korea reports Iran has bought total of 100 Scud Bs and 100 Scud Cs from North Korea.
- May be developing the Zelzal-3 missile with a range of 900 kilometers with Chinese and North Korean support.
- Has tested the Shahab-3 (which may have a 1,500 km range and is based on the North Korean No-Dong 1) and may have started production.
- May be planning to purchase North Korean No-Dong 1/2s.
- Has shown interest in technology for interested in North Korea's developmental Tapeo Dong 1 or Tapeo Dong 2.

continued

Figure 6.7 (Continued)

- Claims will launch its first experimental satellite by 2000 with Russian aid.
- Reports of tunnels for hardened deployment of Scuds and SAMs.
- Possible deployment of locally produced Nazeat series missiles, based on Russian FROG missiles.

CBW

- Chemical weapons (sulfur mustard gas, hydrogen cyanide, phosgene and/or chlorine; possibly Sarin and Tabun).
- Biological weapons (possibly Anthrax, hoof and mouth disease, and other biotoxins).
- Nuclear weapons development (Russian and Chinese reactors).

Source: Based on interviews; reporting in various defense journals; *Jane's Fighting Ships*; IISS, *The Military Balance*, various editions; and JCSS, *The Middle East Military Balance*.

IRAQ'S MILITARY COLLAPSE

Iraq was still a major regional military power when the U.S.-led coalition invaded in March 2003. Its armed forces had an active strength of around 340,000–380,000 men, with some 650,000 reserves. The bulk of Iraq's actives, however, were also poorly trained conscripts, and its reserves had little training and could only be equipped and sustained for light infantry warfare. The army had some 300,000 men, some 2,600 main battle tanks, 1,600 other armored vehicles, 1,800 armored personnel carriers, 1,900 towed artillery weapons, 200 self-propelled artillery weapons, and 200+ multiple rocket launchers, with 164 helicopters, including armed and attack helicopters.

Iraq's navy had negligible strength: some 2,000 men with 6 aging patrol boats, 3 mine warfare ships, and 2 support ships. Its air force, however, still had some 20,000 men and 307–316 combat aircraft, with 6 bombers, 130 fighter ground attack aircraft, 180 fighters, and 5 reconnaissance aircraft. Its Air Defense Command had some 17,000 men, up to 3,000 air defense guns, and some 850 surface-to-air missile launchers, including several hundred SA-2s, SA-3s, and SA-6s.

Nevertheless, Iraq's military forces put up only limited resistance to a much smaller U.S.- and British-led coalition. Iraq was unable to deal with the high-quality coalition forces that invaded it on March 19, 2003, and all of its conventional forces were destroyed, collapsed, or deserted by May 1. This collapse reflected the impact of many of the changes in the military balance discussed in Chapter 2 as well as the impact of many of the defects common to most Middle Eastern forces.

Figure 6.8
Iranian Dependence on Decaying Western Supplied Major Weapons

Military Service	Weapon Type	Quantity	Comments
Land Forces			
	Chieftain tank	140–200	Worn, under-armored, underarmed, and underpowered. Fire control and sighting system now obsolete. Cooling problems.
	M-47/M-48	150	Worn, under-armored, underarmed, and underpowered. Fire control and sighting system now obsolete.
	M-60A1	150–160	Worn, under-armored, underarmed, and underpowered. Fire control and sighting system now obsolete.
	Scorpion AFV	70–80	Worn, light armor, underarmed, and underpowered.
	M-114s	70–80	Worn, light armor, underarmed, and underpowered.
	M-109 155-mm SP	150–160	Worn, fire control system now obsolete. Growing reliability problems due to lack of updates and parts.
	M-107 175-mm SP	20–30	Worn, fire control system now obsolete. Growing reliability problems due to lack of parts.
	M-110 203-mm SP	25–30	Worn, fire control system now obsolete. Growing reliability problems due to lack of parts.
	AH-1J Attack heli.	50	Worn, avionics and weapons suite now obsolete. Growing reliability problems due to lack of updates and parts.
	CH-47 Trans. heli.	20–25	Worn, avionics now obsolete. Growing reliability problems due to lack of updates and parts.
	Bell, Hughes, Boeing, Augusta, Sikorsky helicopters	145–185	Worn, Growing reliability problems due to lack of updates and parts.

continued

Figure 6.8 (Continued)

Military Service	Weapon Type	Quantity	Comments
Air Force			
	F-4D/E FGA	35–65	Worn, avionics now obsolete. Critical problems due to lack of updates and parts.
	F-5E/F FGA	50–60	Worn, avionics now obsolete. Serious problems due to lack of updates and parts.
	F-5A/B	10–20	Worn, avionics now obsolete. Serious problems due to lack of updates and parts.
	RF-4E	5–6	Worn, avionics now obsolete. Serious problems due to lack of updates and parts.
	RF-5E	0–5	Worn, avionics now obsolete. Serious problems due to lack of updates and parts. (May be in storage)
	F-14 AWX	25	Worn, avionics now obsolete. Critical problems due to lack of updates and parts. Cannot operate some radars at long ranges. Phoenix missile capability cannot be used.
	P-3F MPA	5	Worn, avionics and sensors now obsolete. Many sensors and weapons cannot be used. Critical problems due to lack of updates and parts.

Key PGMs	—	Remaining Mavericks, Aim-7s, Aim-9s, Aim-54s are all long past rated shelf life. Many or most are unreliable or inoperable.
I-Hawk SAM	150	Worn, electronics, software, and some aspects of sensors now obsolete. Critical problems due to lack of updates and parts.
Rapier SAM	30	Worn, electronics, software, and some aspects of sensors now obsolete. Critical problems due to lack of updates and parts.
Tigercat SAM	15	Worn, electronics, software, and some aspects of sensors now obsolete. Critical problems due to lack of updates and parts.
Navy		
Alvand FFG	3	Worn, weapons and electronics suite obsolete, many systems inoperable labor partly dysfunctional due to Critical problems due to lack of updates and parts.
Bayandor FF	2	Obsolete. Critical problems due to lack of updates and parts.
Hengeman LST	4	Worn, needs full-scale refit.

Note: Different equipment estimates are used later in the text. The IISS figures are used throughout this chart to preserve statistical consistency.
Source: Estimate made by Anthony H. Cordesman based on the equipment counts in IISS, *The Military Balance;* and discussions with U.S. experts.

Figure 6.9
Can Iran Mass Produce Major New Weapons Systems?

Land

- Can produce nearly 50 types of munitions, including tank rounds, artillery shells, and rockets. Probably meets between 50% and 75% of Iran's needs in a major regional contingency and their output is steadily building up Iran's reserves.

- Manufacturers most of Iran's assault rifles, mortars up though 120-mm in caliber, and antitank rocket launchers

- Showed prototype of a main battle tank called the Zulfiqar (Zolfaqar) in 1994. Tank has undergone field trials ever since the Velayat military exercises of May 1996. Its drive train and suspension seems to be modeled on the U.S.-designed M-48A5 and M-60A1 series of tanks and to have either a 105-mm or 125mm rifled gun. Reports differ as to the Zulfiqar's production status. One report indicates that Iran announced on July 8, 1997, that President Rafsanjani opened the "first phase" of a plant to produce the tank in Dorud, some 300 kilometers southwest of Tehran. Another report indicates that it is produced at the Shahdid Industrial Complex. Up to 100 may have been produced.

- T-72S (Shilden) tanks being assembled under license.

- Upgrading T-54s, T-55s, T-59s with 105-mm gun made in Iran and new fire control system.

- Claims ready to produce light tank for "unconventional warfare" called the Towan (Wild Horse) with 90-mm gun.

- Developed Iranian-made modification of the Chinese Type WZ 501/503 armored infantry fighting vehicle that Iran calls the Boragh. The WZ 501/503 is itself a Chinese copy of the Russian BMP, and is 30-year-old technology. Up to 120 may be in inventory.

- Displayed APC called the Cobra or BMT-2, which seems to be an indigenous design armed with a 30-mm gun or the ZU-23-2 antiaircraft gun—a light automatic weapons system that Iran has been manufacturing for some years. Like the Zulfiqar, the Cobra has been undergoing field trials in Iranian military exercises since May, 1996.

- Iran now makes a number of antitank weapons. These include an improved version of the man-portable RPG-7 antitank rocket with an 80-mm tandem HEAT warhead instead of the standard 30-mm design, the NAFEZ antitank rocket, and a copy of the Soviet SPG-9 73-mm recoilless antitank gun. Iran also makes a copy of the Russian AT-3 9M14M (Sagger or Ra'ad) antitank guided missile.

- Claimed in May 1996, to have produced a self-propelled version of a Russian 122-mm gun that it called the Thunder-1, with a firing range of 15,200 meters and a road speed of 65 kilometers per hour.[1] It may use the Boragh chassis for this weapon. It also claimed to have tested a "rapid fire" 155-mm self-propelled weapon in September, 1997, called the Thunder 2. some seem to have been deployed.

- Makes military radios and low-technology RPVs like the 22006, Baz, and Shahin.

- Has developed tactical radios ART 2000, VHF frequency-hopping radio with a range of 30-88 MHz, and the PRC-110 HF fixed-frequency manpack radio, which covers the 1.6-29.999 H MHz band in 100Hz steps. (JIDR 6/1998: 22)

Figure 6.9 (Continued)

- Has developed low-drag 155mm high explosive base-bleed projectile. The 155BB HE-TNT incorporates a 16kg TNT and has a range of 35km when fired with an M11 top charge from a 45-caliber gun. Range is 17 km without base bleed. A new low-drag HE projectile for 120-mm smoothbore mortars with a range of 13.2 km. (JIDR 6/1998: 22)

Air/Air Defense

- Necessary technical sophistication to rebuild the jet engines for many of its American fighters and helicopters.
- Produce parts and modifications for some of its radars, missile systems, avionics, ships, and armored personnel carriers.
- Claims to have built its first Iranian-designed helicopter, and to have tested a locally-built fighter plane. Brigadier General Arasteh, a deputy head of the General Staff of the Armed Forces (serving under Major General Ali Shahbazi, the joint chief of staff) stated in April, 1997 that the "production line of this aircraft will begin work in the near future."
- Chinese F-7 assembled in Iran.
- Defense Industries Organization claimed that Iran was soon going to start producing two trainers, a jet-powered Dorna (Lark) and propeller-driven Partsu (Swallow).
- There had been reports in 1996 that Iran had obtained Ukrainian aid in producing the Antonov An-140 at a factory in Isfahan. In September, 1997, Iran indicated that it had signed a contract to buy 10 Antonov An-74 transport jets, and reports surfaced that it might co-produce the An-T74T-200. In November, 1998, it was reported that the first of the 52-seat An-140 will roll off the assembly line next year. (JDW 4 November 1998: 20)
- Iran has upgraded some of its F-4s, F-14s, and C-130s
- Iranian military claimed that Iran has begun mass production of a jet strike aircraft, the Azarakhsh (Lightning), which reportedly resembles the F-4 Phantom. (JDW 4 November 1998: 20)
- Iranian Air Force claims that it is developing two combat aircraft based on the F-5 and a third indigenously designed. (JDW 20 November 2002: 15)
- Armed Forces Air Industries Organization was discussing in November 1998, a deal with Ukraine's Aviant Aviatsiny Zavod, co-producer of the new Tupolev-334, to build the planes in Iran. The deal would be for the production of 100 of the 100-seat aircraft over 15 years. (JDW 4 November 1998: 20; Reuters 12 October 1998)
- Iran has reportedly developed a TV-guided missile for carriage on F-4 Phantoms.
- Iran claims to have deployed an air-to-air adapted variant of the SM1 Standard missile for its fleet of F-4D/E Phantom II fighter bombers. (JDW 29 April 1998: 17)

Land-Based Air Defense

- President Rafsanjani announced on October 11, 1997, that Iran had test-launched a major new surface-to-air missile system with a range of 250 kilometers, although he gave no further details. The description of the missile sounded vaguely

continued

Figure 6.9 (Continued)

like the Russian SA-5, which is deployed in Iran. Reports has acquired four HQ-23/2B (CSA-1) launchers and 45-48 missiles, plus 25 SA-6, and 10-15 SA-5 launchers.
- May be modifying and/or producing ZSU-23-4 radar-guided antiaircraft guns.
- Claims to produce advanced electronic warfare systems.

Sea
- Claims will soon start producing 6 multi-purpose destroyers, with initial production run of three.
- Constructing small submarine?
- Iran claims to be developing non-magnetic, acoustic, free-floating and remote controlled mines. It may have also acquired non-magnetic mines, influence mines and mines with sophisticated timing devices.
- Wake-homing and wire-guided Russian torpedoes.
- Iran is developing FL-10 antiship cruise missile that is copy of Chinese FL-2 or FL-7.
- Reportedly assembled domestic variants the YJ-1 (C-801) solid-propellant antiship missile under the local name of Karus, and the YJ-2 (C-802) turbojet-powered antiship missile under the local name of Tondar. (JDW 9 December 1998)
- Boghammer fast interceptor craft.

Missiles
- Iranian made IRAN 130 rocket with 150+ kilometers range.
- Iranian Oghab (Eagle) rocket with 40+ kilometers range.
- New SSM with 125 mile range may be in production, but could be modified FROG.
- Developing the Zelzal-3 missile with a range of 900 kilometers with Chinese and North Korean support.
- Claims that Russia is helping Iran develop four missiles. These missiles include:
  - Shahab 3—a liquid fueled missile with a range of 810 miles (1,200–1,500 kilometers) and a payload of 1550 pounds, based on North Korean Nodong missile. Israel claims the Shahab might be ready for deployment as early as 1999.
  - Shahab 4, with a range of 1,250 miles (1,995 kilometers) and a payload in excess of one ton, based on the Russian R-12, may be in service in 2001. However, the Ministry of Defense released a statement declaring that Iran had no intention of building the Shahab 4 and would continue to rely on the Shahab 3 and potential future variants.[2]
  - Other two missiles are longer-range systems with a maximum ranges of 4,500 and 10,000 kilometers.
- Iran is reportedly receiving or trying to receive steel from China and Russia for the production of missiles.
- Has tested Iranian made Fajr-4 ballistic missiles and new version of Fajr-3 missile, with a range of 28 miles (45 kilometers).

Figure 6.9 (Continued)

- Has developed solid-propellant surface-to-surface missiles: the Zelzal 2, Nazeat, and Shahin.

- Reports of tunnels for hardened deployment of Scuds and SAMs.

- Experimenting with cruise missile development, although no links as yet to the employment of such missiles with warheads using weapons of mass destruction.

CBW

- Chemical weapons (sulfur mustard gas, hydrogen cyanide, phosgene and/or chlorine; possibly Sarin and Tabun).

- Biological weapons (possibly Anthrax, hoof and mouth disease, and other biotoxins).

- Nuclear weapons development (Russian and Chinese reactors).

---

[1]*Jane's Defense Weekly*, June 5, 1996, p. 15.
[2]Robin Hughes, "Iran Denies Shahab 4 Development," *Jane's Defense Weekly*, November 12, 2003, http://jdw.janes.com. Accessed January 8, 2004. Labeled 46.
**Source*: Based on interviews; reporting in various defense journals; and IISS, *The Military Balance*, various editions.

Iraqi Failures in Leadership and Command and Control

- Saddam Hussein's regime had always given internal security against a coup much higher priority than military effectiveness per se. There were exceptions during the most threatening periods in the Iran-Iraq War. But many of the best officers were retired or shoved aside into positions of limited importance, and some suffered suspicious fatal accidents. Political control not only affected independence and initiative, but extended to limiting or preventing the use of ammunition in live-fire exercises, the scale of maneuver exercises, and forward stockpiling of ammunition and supplies that might be used in a coup.

- Iraq's overlapping structure of forces and security elements were often better at watching one another and at securing the regime than at fighting. There was little coordination except at the local level, and command and control could not direct cohesive action. Iraq also suffered from the fact that it had rebuilt its post–Gulf War forces more around internal security missions, regime stability, and static defense than around the lessons of that war.

- Large parts of the Iraqi force structure were designed to cover the Iranian border, secure the Kurdish security zone, and fight a low-level battle against the Shiites in the south. Others were designed to protect the regime against other elements of the armed forces. The result was a garrison force optimized around the wrong missions that was not trained to fight as a cohesive force and whose command and control structure was focused around the command of disparate force elements in border defense and internal security missions, and had limited capability for actual war fighting. This, in turn, exacerbated the divisions between the different elements of the ground forces and security forces, effectively leaving coordinated to Saddam, his sons, and the elite around him rather than creating a C⁴I structure capable of developing any kind of comprehensive operational picture, coordinating maneuver on a national level, and reacting within the tight time limits forced on Iraq by the speed and intensity of the U.S. drive deep into Iraq.

- Iraqi command and control system was not effective, and Iraq could not establish effective command and control in the face of coalition airpower and the speed of its advance, although it is unclear how much of the Iraqi collapse was the result of attacks on its C⁴I assets, the ability of allied airpower to paralyze its operations, and the slow-moving nature of Iraq's land forces. Iraq had no satellites, minimal UAV assets, no survivable reconnaissance assets, poor artillery radar capability, and no other airborne intelligence assets. It conducted minimal active reconnaissance. If its C⁴I problems deprived it of a functioning brain, its lack of modern IS&R assets effectively left it blind in most aspects of combat beyond visual range.

- The almost universal failures in Saddam Hussein's strategic leadership cannot be explained as the result of ignorance or "shock and awe." The Iraqi regime had already lost one war to a U.S.-led coalition and joint arms. It had seen what the United States and Britain could do in some twelve years of postwar clashes and in the fighting in Afghanistan. The broad details of the coalition buildup were fully revealed in the media during the months of debate within the UN, and so were many of the details of the coalition war plan.

- If there are excuses for the failures of the Iraqi leadership, they could include the following:

  - A belief that the UN debate would paralyze the ability of the coalition to take military action.

  - A belief that Turkey's decision not to base coalition land and air forces would delay or prevent military action (while Iraq's uncertainty regarding Turkey's ultimate intentions led it to leave its forces in the north).

  - A belief that a Popular Army that did not in reality exist could be mobilized.

  - An inability to support and sustain most forces outside their peacetime barracks OK and bases, which forced Iraq to wait to deploy them until the war began.

  - An inability to translate a theoretical knowledge of coalition joint warfare capabilities into practical estimates of the lethality of the coalition's airpower, rates of maneuver, and capability to disrupt Iraqi movement and command and control capability once the war began.

  - An unrealistic faith in unconventional and asymmetric warfare and the impact of delay, deception, and potential casualties on the willingness of the United States and Britain to sustain the war.

  - A worldview that mixed the cult of the leader with an inability to realistically assess the strengths and weaknesses of Iraqi forces.

  - A series of actions to conceal and destroy Iraq's weapons of mass destruction in the face of UNMOVIC that continued virtually until the war began and meant that Iraq could never make effective use of any such weapons that remained.

Lack of Military Modernization and Supply

- Sanctions and the impact of the Gulf War had a major impact on Iraqi war-fighting capabilities. Iraq was not able to fund and/or import any major new conventional warfare technology to react to the lessons of the war or to produce any major equipment; Iraq's inability to recapitalize and modernize its forces meant that much of its large order of battle was obsolescent or obsolete, that its combat readiness was uncertain, and that much of its equipment was difficult to sustain in combat. It also limited the ability of its forces to conduct long-range movements or maneuvers and then sustain coherent operations.

- In addition to lack of funds and spare parts, Iraq lacked the production capabilities to help sustain the quality of its consolidated forces. It had domestic military production facilities, but they were limited to the production of guns and ammunition and had never succeeded in mass-producing more advanced weapons. Many of its modernization efforts showed some technical skill, but others were little more than unintentional technical practical jokes.

Problems in Land Forces

- The Iraqi forces of March 2003 had lost most of the battle-experienced personnel of the Iran-Iraq War and Gulf War. They generally had had only low-level combat experience against the Shiite opposition in southern Iraq, and most forces had limited exercise training and had never mastered combined arms and joint operations by Western standards.

- No cohesive prewar effort was made to create an in-depth defense of Baghdad or to protect the lines of advance up the Euphrates. Although one division was moved south from the area around Mosul to the area around Tikrit, Iraq's Republican Guard did not begin to move to position themselves where they could oppose the U.S. advance from the south until the war began and they were exposed to coalition airpower. The Republican Guard then moved largely in response to the coalition advance and had to fight mainly in scattered engagements rather than as part of a coherent, in-depth defense. In many cases, they intermingled their brigade elements with scattered elements of regular army forces and paramilitary units in ways that made well-organized defensive action difficult or impossible and compounded the impact of coalition strikes on Iraq's weak command and control capabilities.

- There was no real effort to prepare the regular army in the south for defense in depth. The coalition seems to have successfully subverted the Iraqi 51st Mechanized Division in Basra to the point it disrupted the defense of Basra. It largely bypassed the Iraqi regular army corps defending the Iranian border, although elements of that corps did move to challenge the 1st Marine Division's advance on Al-Kut.

- Iraq had no ability to resist U.S. and allied air power. The Iraqi Republican Guards and other ground forces became the major focus of the coalition air attacks and its use of precision weapons. While the numbers the United States and Britain issue do not always agree from briefing to briefing, Lt. General T. Michael Mosley, the commander of coalition air operations during the war, stated that some 1,800 aircraft delivered some 20,000 strikes, and that 15,800 of these were directed against Iraqi ground forces versus 1,800 against the Iraqi government, 1,400 against Iraqi air force and Air Defense Command targets, and 800 against suspected sites, forces, and installations that might have weapons of mass destruction or surface-to-surface missiles. This meant that 80 percent of the coalition air strikes hit Iraqi ground forces.[37] Many Guard and regular units had mass desertions after their initial clashes with U.S. land forces or after they began to take serious equipment losses because of coalition air attacks. The end result was that casualties were probably surprisingly limited, as the forces ceased to be operational when they came under air attack and often could not recover from the resulting desertions.[38]

- Iraq was thrown off balance by the speed of U.S. maneuver as well as by the flanking movement through the western edge of the Euphrates and, then by the drive along the eastern edge of the Tigris. Once the United States approached Baghdad, Iraqi forces could neither maneuver quickly enough to establish a cohesive, in-depth defense, nor cope with U.S. penetrations. The Iraqi decisionmaking cycle fell steadily behind the realities on the ground. By the time the United States entered Baghdad, Iraq had lost force cohesion and committed its best forces—the Republican Guards—in a piecemeal way in meeting engagements that virtually ensured its destruction.

- Iraq effectively wasted most of the Baghdad, Medina, Nebuchadnezzar, and Hammurabi divisions of its Republican Guard by sending them into exposed positions some 100 miles south of the capital. They could then be located by UAVs and aircraft like the E-8C and hit from the air. Some reports indicate that more than half of the air munitions dropped by U.S. forces were directed against the Guard units.

- When Iraqi units did clash with U.S. Army, U.S. Marines, and British land forces, which had advanced sensors, helicopters, tanks, artillery, and antitank guided weapons, the Western forces could generally destroy the forward elements of Iraqi forces before they could close within effective range of the coalition forces.

- Iraq had no modern tanks by U.S. and British standards, although it did have some 700 moderately capable T-72 tanks and 200–300 T-62s. But even the T-72s and T-62s had poor ergonomics. They were limited by lack of thermal vision and modern night warfare systems, and their sights and fire control systems could not approach the engagement range of coalition tanks. The 120-mm gun on the M-1A1, for example, has a nominal maximum engagement range of about 3,000 meters. The T-72 can fire accurately out to about 2,500 meters but has far worse sights, fire control systems, and sensors. The older T-55 is limited to about 2,000 meters but has poor fire control systems and stabilization.[39] The Coalition tanks could normally engage Iraqi tanks at 50 percent to 100 percent longer engagement ranges in open maneuver combat, and the coalition tanks had much better armor and mobility.

- Iraq's doctrine and tactics for using tanks were poor. Iraqi corps and division commanders often set personal standards for training and employing tanks.

- The Iraqi army's other major weapons had similar problems. They included some 400 aging Soviet-bloc and French armored reconnaissance vehicles (AML-60/90s, BDRM-2s, EE-3s, and EE-9s). The army had some 1,200 BMP-1/2 armored infantry fighting vehicles, of which about 900 BMP-series seem to have been active. It had some 1,800 aging, worn, armored personnel carriers made up of 10 major types.

- Iraq's lack of standardization in spare parts, and lack of common weapons and operating features, created major sustainability and cross-training/interoperability problems. Iraq faced a logistic and maintenance nightmare in supporting and providing combat and field repairs for so many types of vehicles with such different firepower, mobility, and endurance. Many were nonfunctional due to a lack of spare parts or otherwise limited operational capability. Furthermore, Iraq was forced to equip its divisions with different mixes of armor, with different maneuver capabilities and often with different training requirements for both the weapons crew and maintenance and support teams. It also had difficulties ensuring that its infantry could keep up with its tanks.

- Iraq's tactical doctrine for using other armored vehicles varied with the major combat unit using a given mix of equipment. Some heavy Republican Guard units and regular army units used other armored vehicles much more effectively in supporting tanks than most of the Iraqi army. Iraq generally overrelied on tanks, however, and had not used its other armored vehicles aggressively in scouting or combat support operations. Its forces were best suited to defensive operations against relatively slow-moving mechanized infantry at short to moderate ranges.

- Iraq had some 200 to 250 active self-propelled artillery weapons—with Soviet 122-mm 2S1s and 152-mm 2S3s—largely in Republican Guard and a few elite regular army heavy divisions. The bulk of Iraqi artillery consisted of some 1,200–1,900 towed weapons, mostly 122-mm, 152-mm, and 155-mm. Iraq had some 200 multiple rocket launchers—largely 122-mm and 127-mm systems but also some longer-range 400-mm Ababil-100 systems. Iraq also had large numbers of 81-mm, 120-mm, 160-mm, and 240-mm mortars.

- Iraqi artillery had relatively long range. Iraq never demonstrated, however, that it could approach U.S. and British capability to rapidly target moving forces and switch fire. It relied heavily on mass fire and area suppression. Its ability to target beyond line of sight was limited, and sensor and command problems severely limited the ability to target maneuver forces at long ranges (although Iraq did have some RASIT artillery surveillance vehicles and French Cymbeline countermortar radars).

- Only a few Iraqi artillery units had the radars, training, and organization to allow them to conduct effective counterbattery fire. Their targeting and observed fire was heavily dependent on forward observers, and it was often slow and unresponsive. Their ability to use UAVs and other techniques to acquire targets beyond visual range was limited, and artillery support of mobile Iraqi armored units had previously been consistently poor—even when the forward armored unit called in targets and requested support.

- Iraq never demonstrated the ability to quickly shift fire and deal with rapidly moving armored forces. Its towed artillery was relatively slow moving and often road bound, unless sufficient time existed to support rear areas. Iraqi artillery units usually needed extensive time to deploy large amounts of ammunition into prepared rear areas in order to maintain high rates of fire, and had to presurvey the battlefield to mass artillery fire effectively. Iraq also relied heavily on the "feed forward" of large amounts of ammunition, without prior request from the user unit, to make up for its slow-moving and unresponsive logistic and support system. Iraqi self-propelled artillery units frequently had problems extracting themselves from prepared positions and moving rapidly under defensive conditions. Field repair and recovery of artillery systems were poor.

- Iraqi land forces had extensive stocks (2,000+) of relatively modern AT-3 (AM14), AT-4 (M136), Milan, and high-subsonic optically teleguided (HOT) antitank guided weapons. Iraq also had significant numbers of obsolescent 85-mm and 100-mm antitank guns and 73-mm, 82-mm, and 107-mm rocket launchers and recoilless rifles. Iraq had rarely employed these weapons well in previous battles. During the Gulf War, it showed little understanding of the range at which modern Western armor could engage; the rate of advance and scale of maneuver of modern well-led armor; the limiting effects of night and poor weather warfare on crew-served weapons without night vision aids; the need to rapidly maneuver crew-served weapons rather than rely on static positions; and the need to continuously conduct actual training firings of such equipment to develop and maintain proficiency. Iraq was also unprepared for the rapidly moving precision of coalition artillery and the ability of helicopters and tanks to bypass prepared defenses using such weapons.

- Iraqi army aviation had roughly 100 attack and 275 utility/transport helicopters, but Iraq's combat helicopter performance was consistently poor to bad before the Iraq War. Training, operational readiness, and sustainability were all believed to be poor, and Iraq never demonstrated the ability to use these assets effectively against coalition forces. Further, Iraq had to operate a fleet with 12 different types of helicopters of very different ages, using different technologies and sources of spare parts. The sensor and weapons mixes on Iraqi attack helicopters were at least 15 years old. Even those helicopters equipped with HOT guided weapons lacked the sensors and fire control systems to effectively use the missiles without closing to ranges that made the helicopter vulnerable.

- The Iraqi army and semimobile elements of Iraq's 17,000-man Air Defense Command were capable of deploying large numbers of manportable surface-to-air missiles like the SA-14 Strela 3, plus SA-7, SA-8, SA-9, and Roland vehicle-mounted surface-to-air missiles. Iraq is believed to have had an inventory of well over 1,000 such missiles, but the types are unclear. These systems had limited effectiveness against high-flying U.S.-UK fighters with standoff weapons but sometimes presented a significant threat at low altitudes.

Problems in Paramilitary and Irregular Forces

- Iraq had a reserve pool of some 650,000 and a large pool of annual conscripts. The U.S. Central Intelligence Agency estimated that some 274,000 males entered military service each year. Iraq also could include more than 100,000 men from the security services and police forces in some military or paramilitary roles, and it had at least lightly armored combat elements in each of its three main civilian security and intelligence services. It also had a popular force called the Fedayeen Saddam (Saddam's Men of Sacrifice) and a youth corps that received some form of military training. Iraq had small arms enough to equip several hundred thousand men for light infantry warfare and to play a limited role in urban warfare. It did not, however, have enough heavy weapons to properly equip such forces, and it rapidly became clear during the war that most Iraqi reserve and popular forces lacked the motivation to show up and fight.

- Iraq badly exaggerated the potential importance of using irregular forces and trying to draw U.S. and British forces into the cities in the south. In practice, these tactics produced clashes and occasional successes. But the United States quickly adjusted its own tactics to bypass most cities, secure key bridges and routes, and give the pacification of cities secondary importance.

- The regime fundamentally misjudged the popular support it could obtain from its own people. It cached massive levels of arms in facilities for an "Al-Quds," or Popular Army, it was never able to call up, arm, and deploy. This may in part have been a function of time and disorganization at the top; but it seems clear that many, if not most, of the Popular Army simply did not support the regime and had no willingness to fight.

- Iraq deployed some of its most loyal irregular forces, like Saddam's Fedayeen, in the south. These units had some successes in ambushes, but could not survive open combat with U.S. or British forces and lacked mobility other than light civilian vehicles. This made them relatively easy to bypass or force out into open combat. One ironic sublesson of the war is that the bypasses and roads that went around many cities in Iraq greatly reduce their importance as potential defenses and barriers, and that one way to win an urban war is to avoid one.

Problems in Air and Air Defense Forces

- The Iraqi air force never even engaged coalition forces, but it is unclear that it would have mattered if they did. The Iraqi air force lacked anything approaching the level of technology of coalition forces and had very weak organization and training. It did little to improve its capability to conduct joint operations with any element of the Iraqi ground forces during the period between the end of the Gulf War in 1991 and the beginning of the Iraq War in 2003. It did equally little to improve its tactics and operations to deal with large-scale air operations. Rather than prepare for war during the months before the war, it executed plans it had been developing and exercises since 1991 to strip the wings from its combat aircraft and disperse them in fields, towns, and shelters. For reasons that are not yet fully apparent, this plan was executed in February 2003, effectively taking the Iraqi air force out of the fight.

- The regime seems to have compounded these problems by largely ignoring the air force in its command and communications activity once the war began. Moreover, coordination among the military services was so poor that the Iraqi air force did not receive the additional weapons it requested to defend its air bases, and many air force units were left with little more than assault rifles to defend their bases.[40]

- Iraq did little or nothing to develop a coordinated defensive strategy between its air force and Air Defense Command. It failed to develop a cohesive strategy for relocating the sensors and fire units of the Air Defense Command, although it did attempt such activity on a largely uncoordinated basis once the war began. It did not take steps to make effective use of the mobile forces of the Air Defense Command to provide cover for Iraqi land maneuver units like the Republican Guards. Moreover, once the war began, the Iraqi Special Republican Guards and security forces interfered with ground-based air defense operations in the Baghdad area, and further complicated the problems the Iraqi Air Defense Command had in the face of coalition air dominance and constant attacks on its command centers, radars, and fire units.

- The Iraqi air force's air-to-air and air-to-ground training was limited and unrealistic. Its command and control was overcentralized, and its mission planning often set impossible goals. The two no-fly zones further limited air training and combat experience. It had no modern airborne sensor, command and control, or intelligence capabilities, other than its small number of UAVs. Its air control and warning was still heavily dependent on outdated ground-based intercept capabilities.

- Iraqi land-based air defenses were too old and too ineffective to counterbalance the coalition's air dominance or even seriously degrade the quality of most coalition attack missions. Iraq's mix of SA-2s, SA-3s, and SA-6s was badly outdated, going back to the 1950s and 1960s. The coalition had shown it could suppress them during the Gulf War in 1991 and had had years of practice in dealing with Iraqi tactics and technology. It had long developed effective countermeasures it could use in most areas to launch strikes that avoided Iraqi defenses or penetrated them and then launched standoff strikes from outside the range of Iraq's shorter-range air defenses, which were more difficult to suppress.

- Iraq also had lost much of its land-based air defense forces to carefully focused U.S. and British strikes on its air defense facilities during the time of the UN debate and particularly from March 1, 2003, to the start of the war. This "enforcement" of the no-fly zones effectively allowed the coalition to begin the suppression of enemy air defense (SEAD) phase of the war long before G-Day on March 19. During the struggle in the no-fly zones, the United States claimed it destroyed some 20 to 33 percent of the launchers and major radars Iraq still had.

- Nevertheless, the sheer density of Iraqi defenses made them dangerous until the last stages of the fighting around Baghdad. Low-altitude penetration missions in close air support remained dangerous and sometimes fatal until the end of the war—particularly for helicopters.

• Iraq never made use of its weapons of mass destruction, if it had them.

Military Forces since the Iraq War

Iraq must now rebuild its military forces from the ground up. Its Republic Guard units were largely destroyed in combat, and its regular army forces suffered badly and largely deserted. Iraq had scattered and buried its aircraft before the war began, but many were destroyed and the vast majority of those that survived were badly damaged when they were buried or dispersed. Its navy is no longer a functioning entity. Mass desertions and repeated looting left few facilities intact, and permanently crippled most of Iraq's order of battle. Many of Iraq's arms depots and stockpiles were destroyed in the war or were scattered throughout the country for the use of popular army forces that largely failed to mobilize and appear. With the exception of some units in its 5th Corps, and some forces along the Iranian border in the North and Center, Iraq's military forces effectively ceased to exist. The U.S.-led coalition formally disbanded Iraq's armed forces during March and April 2003.

The rise of a major insurgent campaign during June 2003, however, forced the coalition to begin rebuilding some of Iraq's capabilities. The coalition had succeeded in rushing the creation of substantial security forces by the end of 2003. There were some 60,000 Iraqi police, 48,000 security guards, 12,200 border and customs officers, and 8,500 troops in the Iraqi civil defense corps—which may come to include at least one 800-man force of the militias now controlled by Iraqi leaders and ethnic groups.

The Border Police and Customs and Immigration Service totaled around 10,000 at the end of 2003: Border Police, 5000; border enforcement officials (immigration, etc.), 3000; and support staff, 2000 The Facilities Protection Service had some 65,000 men (the various ministries hire FPS people to guard installations and facilities that come under their respective jurisdictions). The Iraqi Civil Defense Corps (ICDC) had been formed to work in conjunction with coalition forces, serve as a liaison between the coalition and the local communities, and provide human intelligence. It was recruited from local communities, trained, and then sent back to that community to work with the coalition.

The coalition also sought to recruit and train new units in a New Iraqi Army (NIA). This force was originally planned to reach 7,000 men in 2004, but the rise of a major insurgent threat in Iraq led the United States to expand its plans to call for as many as 15,000 men in combat units, plus a matching number in support. Nevertheless, the New Iraqi Army had only one active battalion (the 1st) at the end of 2003, and some 300 of this unit's 700 men had refused to serve. Some 800 men were in training for the 2nd Battalion, and another 800–1,000 had signed up and were scheduled to begin training in January. The forces in the "pipeline" at the end of 2003, however, added up to little more than a light infantry regiment/brigade.

The coalition stated it would expandi the New Iraqi Army to 35,000 men by the fall of 2004, but did not announce detailed plans for doing so by the end of 2003, or plans for creating the mix of land, air, and naval forces Iraq must have to replace the other types of military forces Iraqi lost in 2003. As a result, Iraq may only have begun to create a meaningful self-defense capability by the time the United States must fully transfer sovereignty between 2005 and 2008. This may be a source of future regional instability given the fact that Iraq has problematic neighbors like Iran, Syria, and Turkey that have massive conventional forces.

Other Factors Shaping Iraq's Military Performance

Given these events, many of the past military developments in Iraq's military forces are now moot. At the same time, there are some details and trends that do provide insight into both the reasons for Iraq's defeat and the problems in dealing with Saddam's military legacy:

- Figure 6.10 summarizes the problems in Iraq's military efforts between 1990 and 2003. Iraq's conventional war-fighting capabilities were costly but were steadily crippled by a lack of modernization and resupply.

Figure 6.10
Iraq's Military Status in the Period before the Iraq War Began

---

- The broad trends in Iraqi central government expenditures, military expenditures, and arms spending reflect the near collapse of Iraq's economy, and a near cut off of military imports between 1991 and 2003, although higher oil exports did lead to increased arms smuggling after 1998.
  - Iraq's military effort had already placed a massive burden on its economy throughout the Iran-Iraq War, and during the period between Iran-Iraq War and its invasion of Kuwait. Its efforts to rebuild its forces after the Gulf War involved such high military expenditures relative to Iraq's GDP that they reached the crisis level and were a critical factor in the decline in living standards in Iraq.
  - The trends in Iraq's military expenditure per capita versus GDP per capita were worse than the trend in gross military expenditures versus total GDP. Iraq clearly had a government which cared little for the welfare of its people, and which emphasized guns over butter—even at the cost of a devastating cut in per capita income.
- A detailed comparison of the trends in the Iraqi economy versus the Iraqi military and arms import effort reveals that Iraq began to encounter critical problems in funding its military efforts as early as 1985. It also reveals that Iraq has chosen guns over butter since the Gulf War at an immense cost in terms of the resulting share of GDP.

Figure 6.10 (Continued)

- As a result, Iraq began to experience a crisis in recapitalizing its military forces as early as 1985, and the Gulf War turned this crisis into a virtual catastrophe. Iraq's military machine may retain a massive order of battle, but Iraq's lack of arms imports means that its military readiness and sustainability is only a fraction of what it was in 1990.
- Iraqi purchases matched Saudi purchases during the mid-1980s, but Iraqi deliveries in current U.S. dollars dropped from $11 billion annually during 1988–1991 to below $200 million annually in 1992–1995.
- Comparisons of Iraqi new agreements and arms deliveries by supplier country reveal a drastic decline in new agreements before the Gulf War that would have seriously compromised Iraq's import-dependent forces even without the Gulf War.
- New agreements with Russia dropped from $11.8 billion in 1983–1986 to $4.1 billion in 1987–1990, before dropping to zero after 1991.
- New agreements with China dropped from $1.7 billion in 1983–1986 to $0.6 billion in 1987–1990, before dropping to zero after 1991.
- New agreements with E. Europe dropped from $4.0 billion in 1983–1986 to $1.0 billion in 1987–1990, before dropping to zero after 1991.
- In contrast, new agreements with the major West European states rose from $1.0 billion in 1983–1986 to $2.7 billion in 1987–1990, before dropping to zero after 1991—reflecting Iraq's growing interest in advanced military technology before the cutoff of arms imports.
- In spite of various claims during 1980–2003, Iraq's domestic military production capability only played a major role in allowing Iraq to sustain its modern weapons and ability to use advanced military technology. Iraq remains an import dependent country.
- Iraq's past pattern of arms imports makes it highly dependent on access to a wide range of suppliers—particularly Western Europe and Russia. Even if one nation should resume supply, Iraq could not rebuild its military machine without broad access to such suppliers and would be forced to convert a substantial amount of its order of battle to whatever supplier(s) were willing to sell.
- No accurate data are available on Iraqi military spending and arms imports since 1991, but estimates of trends in constant dollars, using adjusted U.S. government data, strongly indicate that Iraq would have had to spend sums approaching $20 billion to recapitalize its force structure, and only succeeded in smuggling in an average of less than $50 million of arms a year during 1992–2003.

- Figure 6.11 shows Iraq's military strength at the time of the Gulf War and before the U.S.-led coalition invaded. These totals reflect a severe decline in force strength, but nothing like the decline that occurred as a result of the Iraq War. It should be noted that the figures for post–Iraq War weapons strength are guesstimates based on discussed in Iraq, and assume substantial efforts to recover and recondition most of the weapons listed.
- Figure 6.12 shows Iraq's acute dependence on worn and obsolete weapons before the Iraq War, systems for which it could not obtain more than limited supplies of parts and munitions between 1990 and 2003.

Figure 6.11
Iraq before the Gulf and Iraq Wars and Now

	1990	February 2003	Post-War Guesstimate
Manpower			
Total Active	1,000,000	389,000	400–700
Regular	425,000	375,000	—
National Guard & Other	0	0	—
Reserve	850,000	650,000	—
Paramilitary	40,000	44,000+	—
Army and Guard			
Manpower	955,000	350,000	400–700
Regular Army Manpower	—	375,000	—
Reserve	480,000 (recalled)	650,000	—
Total Main Battle Tanks	5,500–6,700	2,200–2,600	200–500
Active Main Battle Tanks	5,100	1,900–2,200	?
Active AIFV/Recce, Lt. Tanks	2,300	1,300–1,600	?
Total APCs	7,100	2,400	200–300
Active APCs	6,800	1,800	?
ATGM Launchers	1,500	900+	?
Self-Propelled Artillery	500+	150–200	10–50
Towed Artillery	3,000+	1,900	200–300
MRLs	300+	200	20–30
Mortars	5,000	2,000+	?
SSM Launchers	?	56	?

Light SAM Launchers	1,700?	1,100	50–75?
AA Guns	?	6,000	200–300?
Air Force Manpower	40,000	20,000	—
Air Defense Manpower	10,000	17,000	—
Total Combat Aircraft	513	316	?
Bombers	20	6	?
Fighter/Attack	284+	130	?
Fighter/Interceptor	223+	180	?
Recce/FGA Recce	10	5	?
AEW C⁴I/BM	1	0	0
MR/MPA	0	0	0
OCU/COIN/CCT	0	0	0
Other Combat Trainers	157	73	40
Transport Aircraft*	63	12	3–4
Tanker Aircraft	4?	2	0
Total Helicopters	584	375	10–25
Armed Helicopters*	160	100	?
Other Helicopters*	424	275	?
Major SAM Launchers	600+	400	?
Light SAM Launchers	?	450	?
AA Guns	—	3,000	200–300
Total Naval Manpower	5,000	2,000	—
Regular Navy	5,000	2,000	—
Naval Guards	0	0	—
Marines	—	—	—

continued

Figure 6.11 (Continued)

	1990	February 2003	Post-War Guesstimate
Major Surface Combatants			
Missile	4	0	0
Other	1	0	0
Patrol Craft			
Missile	8	1	0
Other	6	5	0
Submarines	0	0	0
Mine Vessels	8	3	0
Amphibious Ships	6	0	0
Landing Craft	9	—	—
Support Ships	3	2	0

*Includes navy, army, national guard, and royal flights, but not paramilitary.
Source: Adapted by Anthony H. Cordesman from interviews, International Institute for Strategic Studies, *The Military Balance* (London: IISS); *Jane's Sentinel*, *Periscope*; and Jaffee Center for Strategic Studies, *The Military Balance in the Middle East* (Tel Aviv: JCSS).

Figure 6.12
Iraqi Dependence on Decaying, Obsolete, or Obsolescent Major Weapons before the Iraq War of 2003

Land Forces

- 600–700 M-48s, M-60s, AMX-30s, Centurions, and Chieftains captured from Iran or which it obtained in small numbers from other countries.
- 1,000 T-54, T-55, T-77 and Chinese T-59 and T-69 tanks.
- 200 T-62s.
- 1,500-2,100 (BTR-50, BTR-60, BTR-152, OT-62, OT-64, etc.
- 1,600 BDRM-2, EE-3, EE-9, AML-60, AML-90.
- 800–1,200 towed artillery weapons (105-mm, 122-mm, 130-mm, and 155-mm).
- Unknown number of AS-11, AS-1, AT-1, crew-portable antitank-guided missiles.
- More than 1,000 heavy, low-quality antiaircraft guns.
- Over 1,500 SA-7 and other low-quality surface-to-air guided missile launchers & fire units.
- 20 PAH-1 (Bo-105); attack helicopters with AS-11 and AS-12, 30 Mi-24s and Mi-25s with AT-2 missiles, SA-342s with AS-12s, Allouettes with AS-11s and AS-12s.
- 100–180 worn or obsolete transport helicopters.

Air Force

- 6–7 HD-6 (BD-6), 1-2 Tu-16, and 6 Tu-22 bombers.
- 100 J-6, MiG-23BN, MiG-27, Su-7 and Su-20.
- 140 J-7, MiG-21, MiG-25 air defense fighters.
- MiG-21 and MiG-25 reconnaissance fighters.
- 15 Hawker Hunters.
- Il-76 Adnan AEW aircraft.
- AA-6, AA-7, Matra 530 air-to-air missiles.
- AS-11, AS-12, AS-6, AS-14; air-to-surface missiles.
- 25 PC-7, 30 PC-9, 40 L-29 trainers.
- An-2, An-12, and Il-76 transport aircraft.

Air Defense

- 20–30 operational SA-2SA-2 batteries with 160 launch units.
- 25–50 SA-3SA-3 batteries with 140 launch units.
- 36–55 SA-6SA-6 batteries with over 100 fire units.
- 6,500 SA-7sSA-7s.
- 400 SA-9sSA-9s.
- 192 SA-13s.

continued

Figure 6.12 (Continued)

Navy

- *Ibn Khaldun.*
- Osa-class missile boat.
- 13 light combat vessels.
- 5-8 landing craft.
- *Agnadeen.*
- 1 Yugoslav Spasilac-class transport.
- Polnocny-class LST.

Source: Estimates made by Anthony H. Cordesman based on discussions with U.S. experts.

Figure 6.13
The Recapitalization Crisis before the Iraq War: Cumulative Arms Import Deficit
Enforced by UN Sanctions

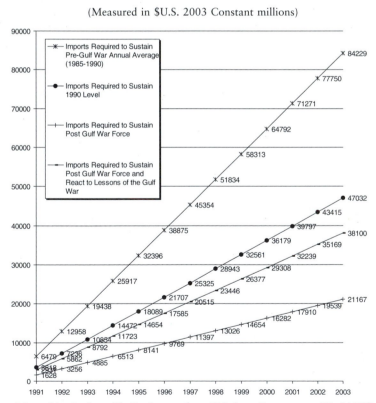

(Measured in $U.S. 2003 Constant millions)

Source: Adapted by Anthony H. Cordesman from U.S. State Department, *World Military Expenditures and Arms Transfers*, various editions.

Figure 6.14
Problems in Iraqi Military Production before the Iraq War

- Iraq developed significant ammunition, small and light arms, and gun barrel production facilities before the Gulf War, and many survive and function. However, Iraq focused most resources on weapons of mass destruction.

- Left even high tech service (e.g. French and Russian aircraft) to foreign technical support teams. Did not attempt to develop major in-house capabilities.

- Pre-1991 production was heavily prototype-oriented and largely prestige-oriented in nature.

- Did import T-72 kits, in theory as transition to production facilities. However, far from clear that Iraq has industrial base for such manufactures.

- Iraqi modifications sometimes succeeded, but many failed and had an "impress the maximum leader character." E.g. T-72 upgrades.

- Historically, assembly of major weapons does not lead to technology transfer or effective reverse engineering capability without extensive foreign support. Net impact is to create over-specialized facilities, waste resources.

- No developing state, including India and China, has yet demonstrated that it can successfully mass manufacture an advanced fighter plane or tank, even on a turn-key basis.

- Few nations have made useful major equipment upgrades for armor and aircraft. Jordan and South Korea, Turkey are among few successes. Egypt, India, Pakistan are more typical.

- Iraq has effectively been cut off from all major imports of parts and specialized equipment since 1990s, although dual use items, civilian electronics and sensors, and computer gear are not effectively controlled.

- Black market imports, substitution, and local manufactures can only provide an erratic and inefficient substitute for large-scale re-sources.

- Some indications that Iraq is giving priority to importing equipment for weapons of mass destruction.

307

Figure 6.15
Major Iraqi Military Production Facilities before the Iraq War

- Tank assembly plant operating under Polish and Czech licenses at Al-Amen.
- Major armor refitting center at Base West World (Samawa).
- Manufacture of proximity fuses for 155-mm and cluster munitions at April 7 (Narawan Fuse) Factory.
- Manufacture of 122-mm howitzers, Ababil rockets, tank optics and mortar sights at Sa'ad 5 (Sa'ad Engineering Complex).
- Manufacture of wheeled APCs under East European license, other armor, and artillery pieces at Al Taji.
- Manufacture and repair of artillery, vehicle parts, and cannon barrels at SEHEE heavy engineering complex (Al Dura).
- Aircraft assembly and manufacturing plant under construction at Sa'ad 38 (Fao).
- Manufacture of aerial bombs, artillery pieces, and tungsten-carbide machine tool bits at Badr (al Yusufiyah).
- Production of explosives, TNT, propellants, and some vehicle production capability at Al Hiteen (Al Iskandariyah).
- Production of cluster bombs and fuel-air explosives at Fao.
- Production of aerial bombs, TNT, and solid rocket propellants at Al Qaqaa.
- Manufacture of small naval boats at Sawary (Basra).
- Production and modification of defense electronics at Mansour (Baghdad).
- Production and modification of defense electronics, radars, and frequency-hopping radios at Sa'ad 13 (Salah al Din—Ad Dawr).
- Digital computer software, assembly of process line controllers for weapons plants, and plastic castings at Diglia (Zaafarniyah).
- Precision machining at Al Rabiyah.
- Manufacture of non-ferrous ammunition cases at Sa'ad 21 (Mosul).
- Liquid nitrogen production at Al Amil.
- Production of ethylene oxide for fuel-air explosives at PCI.
- Production of HMX and RDX explosives at Fallujah chemical plant at Al Muthanna.
- Manufacture of gas masks at Sa'ad 24 (Mosul).

- Figure 6.13 provides a rough estimate of the cumulative rise in the cost of properly modernizing and recapitalizing Iraq's military forces after the Gulf War in 1990. It is clear that this would have been unaffordable regardless of whether the U.S.-led coalition invaded.

- Figure 6.14 summarizes the acute problems in Iraq's military production base. Like most military industrial and production efforts in the Middle East, Iraq's efforts consumed far more resources than their output was worth.

- Figure 6.15 lists Iraq's key military production facilities. Most were looted or destroyed during the Iraq War and now have little value.

Chapter 7

Force Developments in the Southern Gulf

The Southern Gulf states generally have large inventories of military equipment for nations of their size, and a few have comparatively largely military forces for nations their size. In practice, however, all of the Southern Gulf states have limited real-world war-fighting capabilities, readiness and training are poor to mediocre, and there is far more emphasis on buying the most modern military equipment—the "glitter factor" in military procurement—than on creating effective and sustainable forces.

This emphasis on acquiring the shell of military capability, rather than the reality, is partly a result of de facto reliance on the power projection capabilities of the United States and Britain, partly a result of a tendency to treat military forces as royal playgrounds or status symbols, partly a lack of expertise and effective military leadership, and partly a result of the fear that effective military forces might lead to a coup. The end result, however, is that Southern Gulf forces have far less national and collective military capability than their force strengths, and vast investment in arms imports, would otherwise imply.

KEY FACTORS SHAPING SOUTHERN GULF FORCES

Any analysis of the Southern Gulf military balance—and the real-world war-fighting capabilities of Bahrain, Kuwait, Oman, Qatar, Saudi Arabia, and the United Arab Emirates (UAE)—reveals the following major trends:

• Bahrain, Kuwait, Oman, Qatar, Saudi Arabia, and the UAE are all members of the Gulf Cooperation Council (GCC), which has a large military headquarters in Riyadh. The GCC has proposed a wide range of useful projects to improve military interoperability and cooperation since its founding in 1980, but has made only token progress. The GCC is a myth in war-fighting and force development terms:

- The one joint combat force the GCC has created—the GCC rapid deployment force—has always been a hollow, token force, and now has no clear mission with the fall of Saddam Hussein and the end of Iraq as a serious threat.

- Current member country arms orders and inventories preclude standardization and many aspects of standardization for a decade.

- There is little on no focus on developing effective, interoperable forces common missions.

- An air defense integration contract offers some hope for future, but has few of the features needed to actually integrate land-based and fighter aid defense operations in a real-world combat environment.

- Some cooperation has developed in naval exercises, but it would have little real-world effectiveness without U.S. or British support.

- All Southern Gulf states now have closer real-world military cooperation with the United States than with each other:

  - U.S. and Saudi military cooperation was a key to the quick coalition victory in the Gulf War, and U.S. and Saudi cooperation was much closer in the Iraq War than is generally apparent. This cooperation has, however, been sharply curtailed as a result of the events of September 11, 2001, and tensions over the war on terrorism. Active U.S. combat forces left Saudi Arabia in 2003, following the Iraq War.

  - The United States has shifted the focus of its prepositioning, basing, and command and control facilities to Bahrain, Qatar, and Oman, with some presence in the UAE.

- The Southern Gulf states have previously divided into those seeing Iran as a primary threat and those seeing Iraq as a primary threat:

  - The lower Gulf states focused on the naval, air, and subversion threats from Iran.

  - Kuwait and Saudi Arabia focused on Iraq, although Saudi Arabia saw Iran as a serious threat.

  - They now must redefine their strategy and threat perceptions, but so far have shown little practical effort to do so either on a national or on a GCC level.

- The Southern Gulf states have largely resolved their past border and territorial disputes, but some tensions remain:

  - Lingering tensions between Bahrain and Qatar, although these seem to be rapidly diminishing.

  - A fear of Saudi "dominance" that still affects Qatar and Oman.

  - Internal divisions in the UAE and a lingering fear of Omani ambitions to take UAE territory.

- Kuwaiti concern over border issues with Saudi Arabia.
- Saudi Arabia concern over smuggling of arms and explosives across the Yemeni border and the risk Yemen could become a future threat.

KEY ISSUES IN FORCE DEVELOPMENT

It will take the Southern Gulf states several years to adjust their national force plans to take account of the disappearance of Iraq as a major regional threat. In the interim, improving political relations have already led several Southern Gulf states to limit or cut back on their military efforts, and it seems unlikely that Iraq will emerge as a focusing threat that will lead to more effective military cooperation even in the lower Gulf. In order to understand the full range of military dynamics involved, it is necessary to understand that there are new priorities for military spending, as well as for effective force planning and development:

- "Oil wealth" in terms of per capita income is now 25–35 percent of its peak in early 1980s in real terms.
- Internal stability and economic development are generally higher priorities than increased military strength.
- "Statism" is a major problem, compounded by poor overall budgeting and programming and continuing budget deficits.
- Force modernization must be accompanied by creating arms transfer and military assistance programs that support key missions against real threats is "help."
- Effective force planning must take probable Southern Gulf and joint coalitions with Western power projection forces into account and encourage interoperability and standardization.
- Modernization must be based on realistic force mixes, life-cycle costs, attention to human factors, and sustainability.

The military mission has also shifted to the point where the Southern Gulf states need to focus more on dealing with internal divisions and stability, and particularly the threat of Islamic extremism and terrorism, than the creation of more or better military forces. This focus on internal security is already the new driving force behind Saudi security planning. At the same time, the Southern Gulf states also need to make much more effective and collective efforts to improve their conventional forces. They need to:

- Create an effective planning system for collective defense, and truly standardized and/or interoperable forces.
- Integrate C^4I and sensor nets for air and naval combat, including BVR and night warfare.

- Create joint air defense and air attack capabilities.
- Establish effective cross reinforcement and tactical mobility capabilities.
- Set up joint training, support, and infrastructure facilities.
- Create joint air and naval strike forces.
- Deploy joint land defenses of the Kuwaiti/northwestern Saudi borders.
- Prepare for outside or over-the-horizon reinforcement.
- Create common advanced training systems.
- Create of improved urban and area security for unconventional warfare and low-intensity combat.
- Emphasize both effective leadership and delegation.
- Place a steadily higher emphasis on officer initiative and truly competitive career selection. Increase reliance on noncomissioned officers (NCOs) and enlisted personnel.
- Balance forces to achieve proper readiness.
- Establish the ability to limit and manage collateral damage.

The wild card in such planning is proliferation, although the fall of Saddam's regime, and Iran's seeming agreement to fully comply with the Nuclear Non-Proliferation Treaty and allow surprise inspections by the International Atomic Energy Agency (IAEA), may reduce the seriousness of this threat.

TRENDS IN MILITARY EXPENDITURES AND ARMS IMPORTS

The prospects for success in meeting all of these objectives is limited, both in terms of the effective management of military spending and improving the quality and relevance of arms sales. The Southern Gulf states have made truly massive investments in military forces and equipment, although often with equally massive inefficiency and waste:

- Figure 7.1 shows the trends in Gulf military spending in constant dollars during 1984–1999. It clearly reflects the impact of the end of the Iran-Iraq War in 1988, and then the massive impact of the Gulf War of 1991 on military spending in Kuwait and Saudi Arabia. It is clear that Saudi Arabia has overwhelmingly dominated military spending during the period since the Gulf War.
- Figure 7.2 highlights the recent trends in Gulf military expenditures. It shows clearly how much Saudi Arabia has dominated regional military spending, and any comparison with the figures in Chapter 6 shows that Saudi Arabia and the Southern Gulf states have continued to massively outspend Iran.
- Figure 7.3 shows that there is little correlation between country size and the burden military spending places on its economy. It shows that Iraq was forced to make massive cuts in its military spending effort when an embargo was placed on its arms imports in 1990. Iran, however, always kept its military

Figure 7.1
Comparative Military Expenditures of the Gulf Powers: 1984–1999

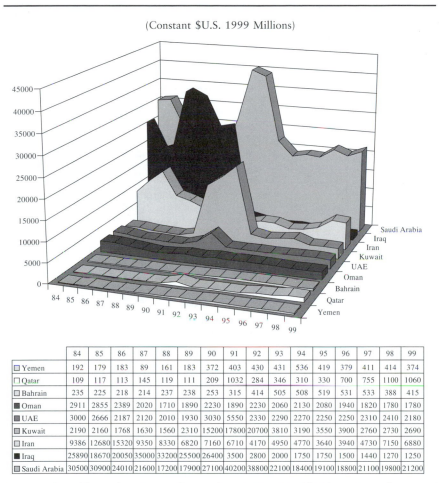

(Constant $U.S. 1999 Millions)

	84	85	86	87	88	89	90	91	92	93	94	95	96	97	98	99
☐ Yemen	192	179	183	89	161	183	372	403	430	431	536	419	379	411	414	374
☐ Qatar	109	117	113	145	119	111	209	1032	284	346	310	330	700	755	1100	1060
☐ Bahrain	235	225	218	214	237	238	253	315	414	505	508	519	531	533	388	415
■ Oman	2911	2855	2389	2020	1710	1890	2230	1890	2230	2060	2130	2080	1940	1820	1780	1780
■ UAE	3000	2666	2187	2120	2010	1930	3030	5550	2330	2290	2270	2250	2250	2310	2410	2180
☐ Kuwait	2190	2160	1768	1630	1560	2310	15200	17800	20700	3810	3190	3550	3900	2760	2730	2690
☐ Iran	9386	12680	15320	9350	8330	6820	7160	6710	4170	4950	4770	3640	3940	4730	7150	6880
■ Iraq	25890	18670	20050	35000	33200	25500	26400	3500	2800	2000	1750	1750	1500	1440	1270	1250
☐ Saudi Arabia	30500	30900	24010	21600	17200	17900	27100	40200	38800	22100	18400	19100	18800	21100	19800	21200

Source: Adapted by Anthony H. Cordesman from ACDA, *World Military Expenditures and Arms Transfers, 1995*, Washington, DC: ACDA/GPO, 1996; and U.S. State Department, *World Military Expenditures and Arms Transfers, 1999–2000*, Washington, DC: Bureau of Arms Control, 2001.

efforts relatively low, clearly choosing not to try to directly compete with the Southern Gulf states after 1988. As might be expected, the Saudi level of effort is consistently high, imposing a major strain on the Saudi economy. The same is true of Bahrain and Oman, which have very high levels of effort. Kuwait's level of effort was so high during the Gulf War that the wartime peaks have been removed from the chart to make the data easier to compare, but it

Figure 7.2
Southern Gulf Military Expenditures by Country: 1997–2002

(In $U.S. Current Millions)

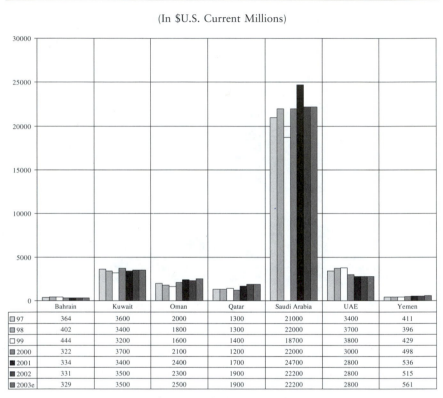

	Bahrain	Kuwait	Oman	Qatar	Saudi Arabia	UAE	Yemen
97	364	3600	2000	1300	21000	3400	411
98	402	3400	1800	1300	22000	3700	396
99	444	3200	1600	1400	18700	3800	429
2000	322	3700	2100	1200	22000	3000	498
2001	334	3400	2400	1700	24700	2800	536
2002	331	3500	2300	1900	22200	2800	515
2003e	329	3500	2500	1900	22200	2800	561

Source: International Institute of Strategic Studies, *The Military Balance*, various editions.

gradually dropped to more comparable levels during 1999–1997. Yemeni levels have remained high in spite of border settlements and the lack of a clear external threat. The UAE has a low level of effort in spite of major arms purchases, largely because of its high oil export revenues and the fact its small native population limits civil expenditures.

- Figure 7.4 shows the trends in the value of arms deliveries to the Gulf in constant dollars during 1984–1999. It clearly reflects the impact of the end of the Iran-Iraq War in 1988, the impact of sanctions on Iraqi arms imports after mid-1990, and then the massive impact of the Gulf War of 1991 on military spending in Kuwait and Saudi Arabia. It is again clear that Saudi Arabia has overwhelmingly dominated military spending during the period since the Gulf War.

- Figure 7.5 the recent trends in Southern Gulf spending of new arms orders and in the value of actual arms deliveries. It also shows a significant decline in spending levels since the Gulf War. The data shown are in current dollars and the decline is much sharper in real terms.

Figure 7.3
Comparative Military Expenditures of the Gulf Powers as a Percentage of GNP: 1989–1999

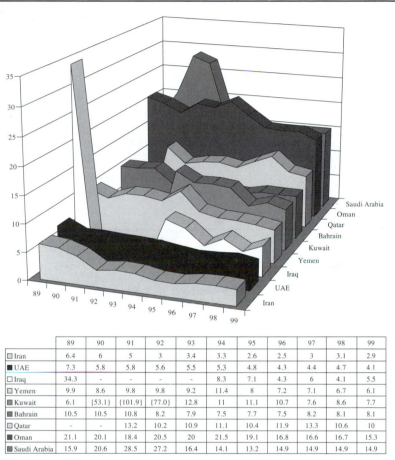

	89	90	91	92	93	94	95	96	97	98	99
Iran	6.4	6	5	3	3.4	3.3	2.6	2.5	3	3.1	2.9
UAE	7.3	5.8	5.8	5.6	5.5	5.3	4.8	4.3	4.4	4.7	4.1
Iraq	34.3	-	-	-	-	8.3	7.1	4.3	6	4.1	5.5
Yemen	9.9	8.6	9.8	9.8	9.2	11.4	8	7.2	7.1	6.7	6.1
Kuwait	6.1	{53.1}	{101.9}	{77.0}	12.8	11	11.1	10.7	7.6	8.6	7.7
Bahrain	10.5	10.5	10.8	8.2	7.9	7.5	7.7	7.5	8.2	8.1	8.1
Qatar	-	-	13.2	10.2	10.9	11.1	10.4	11.9	13.3	10.6	10
Oman	21.1	20.1	18.4	20.5	20	21.5	19.1	16.8	16.6	16.7	15.3
Saudi Arabia	15.9	20.6	28.5	27.2	16.4	14.1	13.2	14.9	14.9	14.9	14.9

Source: Adapted by Anthony H. Cordesman from ACDA, *World Military Expenditures and Arms Transfers, 1995*, Washington, DC: ACDA/GPO, 1996; and U.S. State Department, *World Military Expenditures and Arms Transfers, 1999–2000*, Washington, DC: Bureau of Arms Control, 2001.

• Figure 7.6 shows that the Southern Gulf states have had better and more consistent access to the United States, Western Europe, and other suppliers of the most advanced combat equipment than other Arab states. At the same time, it reflects the lack of standardization and concern for interoperability that has been a continuing problem limiting effective military cooperation within the GCC states.

Figure 7.4
Cumulative Saudi Arms Imports Relative to Those of the Other Gulf States:
1984–1997

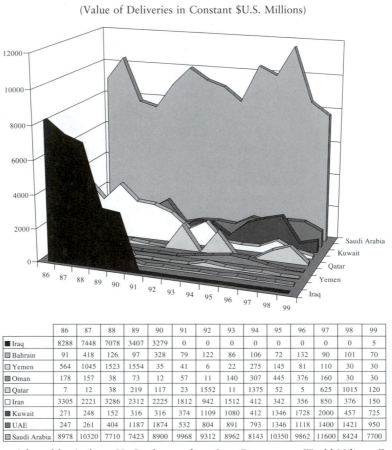

(Value of Deliveries in Constant $U.S. Millions)

	86	87	88	89	90	91	92	93	94	95	96	97	98	99
■ Iraq	8288	7448	7078	3407	3279	0	0	0	0	0	0	0	0	5
□ Bahrain	91	418	126	97	328	79	122	86	106	72	132	90	101	70
□ Yemen	564	1045	1523	1554	35	41	6	22	275	145	81	110	30	30
□ Oman	178	157	38	73	12	57	11	140	307	445	376	160	30	30
□ Qatar	7	12	38	219	117	23	1552	11	1375	52	5	625	1015	120
□ Iran	3305	2221	3286	2312	2225	1812	942	1512	412	342	356	850	376	150
■ Kuwait	271	248	152	316	316	374	1109	1080	412	1346	1728	2000	457	725
■ UAE	247	261	404	1187	1874	532	804	891	793	1346	1118	1400	1421	950
□ Saudi Arabia	8978	10320	7710	7423	8900	9968	9312	8962	8143	10350	9862	11600	8424	7700

Source: Adapted by Anthony H. Cordesman from State Department, *World Military Expenditures and Arms Transfers,* Washington, DC: GPO, various editions.

There are dangers in any generalizations about the way Southern Gulf states
buy major combat equipment and manage military procurement and modernization, and the problems that result. It is also clear that properly managed acquisition of advanced weapons and technology can offer major
advantages.

Actually achieving such advantages, however, requires the Southern Gulf
states to pay far more attention to manpower quality, readiness, and
sustainability and to focus their military expenditures and arms efforts on
the following key procurement priorities:

Figure 7.5
Southern Gulf Arms Agreements and Deliveries by Country: 1987–2002

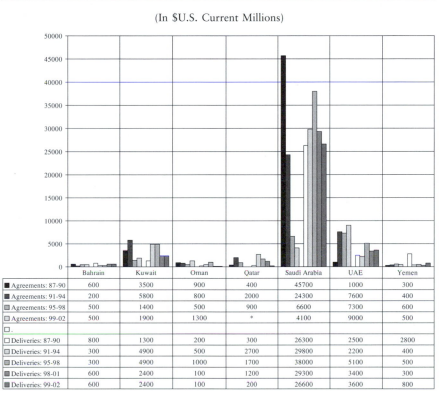

(In $U.S. Current Millions)

	Bahrain	Kuwait	Oman	Qatar	Saudi Arabia	UAE	Yemen
■ Agreements: 87-90	600	3500	900	400	45700	1000	300
■ Agreements: 91-94	200	5800	800	2000	24300	7600	400
▨ Agreements: 95-98	500	1400	500	900	6600	7300	600
▢ Agreements: 99-02	500	1900	1300	*	4100	9000	500
▢ .							
▢ Deliveries: 87-90	800	1300	200	300	26300	2500	2800
▨ Deliveries: 91-94	300	4900	500	2700	29800	2200	400
■ Deliveries: 95-98	300	4900	1000	1700	38000	5100	500
■ Deliveries: 98-01	600	2400	100	1200	29300	3400	300
■ Deliveries: 99-02	600	2400	100	200	26600	3600	800

0 = Data less than $50 million or nil. All data rounded to the nearest $100 million.
Source: Richard F. Grimmett, *Conventional Arms Transfers to the Developing Nations*, Congressional Research Service, various editions.

- Advanced heavy armor, artillery, attack helicopters, and mobile air defense equipment.
- Interoperability and standardization with U.S. and British power projection forces.
- Interoperable offensive air capability with standoff, all-weather precision weapons and antiarmor/antiship capability.
- Interoperable air defense equipment, including heavy surface-to-air missiles, BVR/AWX fighters, AEW and surveillance capability, and ARM and ECM capability (growth in ATBM and cruise missile defense capability).
- Maritime surveillance systems, and equipment for defense against maritime surveillance and unconventional warfare.
- Mine detection and clearing systems.

Figure 7.6
Southern Gulf New Arms Orders by Supplier Country: 1987–2002

(Arms Agreements in $U.S. Current Millions)

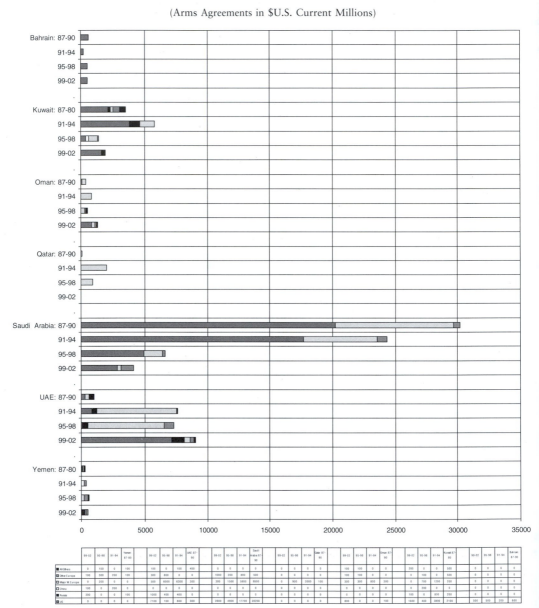

	99-02	95-98	91-94	Yemen 87-80	99-02	95-98	91-94	UAE 87-90	99-02	95-98	91-94	Saudi Arabia 87-90	99-02	95-98	91-94	Qatar 87-90	99-02	95-98	91-94	Oman 87-90	99-02	95-98	91-94	Kuwait 87-80	99-02	95-98	91-94	Bahrain 87-90
All Others	0	100	0	100	100	0	100	400	0	0	0	0	100	100	0	0	200	0	0	500	0	0	0	0	0	0	0	0
Other Europe	100	300	200	100	300	800	0	0	1000	200	800	500	0	0	0	0	100	100	0	0	0	100	0	500	0	0	0	0
Major W Europe	0	200	0	0	500	6000	6300	300	300	1500	5800	9500	0	800	2000	100	300	300	800	300	0	700	1200	200	0	0	0	0
China	100	0	200	0	0	0	0	0	0	0	0	0	0	0	0	0	0	0	0	0	0	200	0	0	0	0	0	0
Russia	300	0	0	100	1000	400	400	0	0	0	0	0	0	0	0	0	0	0	0	0	100	0	650	200	0	0	0	0
US	0	0	0	0	7100	100	800	300	2800	4900	17700	20200	0	0	0	0	800	0	0	100	1600	400	3800	2100	300	500	200	600

0 = less than $50 million or nil. All data rounded to the nearest $100 million.

Source: Adapted by Anthony H. Cordesman, CSIS, from Richard F. Grimmett, *Conventional Arms Transfers to the Developing Nations*, Congressional Research Service, various editions.

- Improved urban, area, and border security equipment for unconventional warfare and low-intensity conflict.
- Advanced training aids.
- Support and sustainment equipment.

The Southern Gulf states have bought much of the equipment and technology they need. Unfortunately, they generally have paid at least as much attention to the wrong procurement priorities as to the right ones. These "nonpriorities" include:

- Attempting every mission or showing no real mission focus.
- Mood swings in one major official, or leader, driving major procurements.
- Buying on the basis of unrealistic threat and net assessment.
- No serious force-planning effort, no long-term program budget; military budget decoupled from national budget.
- Focusing on a few narrow performance parameters and conducting unrealistic trials. Ignoring broader issues of jointness, combined operations, and interoperability.
- Purchasing "glitter factor" weapons and developmental equipment and technology for status purposes. "He who dies with the most advanced new toys wins."
- Focusing on high-visibility major weapons platforms at the expense of funding IS&R and battle management, C⁴I, maintenance, and sustainability. "All teeth and no brain or body."
- Lack of serious interest in regional coalitions; every nation for itself.
- Purchasing unique equipment types and one-of-a-kind modifications status purposes and/or purchasing equipment purely on the basis of national calculations without coordination with other Southern Gulf states or the United States and United Kingdom. Deliberately buying noninteroperable weapons and systems or without concern for interoperability.
- Purchasing equipment for divided or "dual" forces even within a given country, such as divisions within the UAE and between the Saudi regular forces and National Guard.
- Buying new types of equipment, while deliberately failing to fund the required maintenance, sustainability, and training.
- Layering new types of military equipment and technology over old, retaining older equipment to have the largest possible force structure at the expense of waste, and underfunding the effective conversion to new equipment. Retaining too much old equipment, ignoring need for manpower and budget tradeoffs
- Ignoring the need to provide balancing funding of manpower quality. Creating inflated force structures; too many older officers and generals, too few technicians and NCOs. Skilled manpower not properly paid.

- Maximizing the investment in weapons. Ignoring infrastructure, parts, facilities, manpower, and sustainability.
- Making impossible offset demands, and creating domestic "military industries" with little real value or cost-effectiveness.
- Ignoring life-cycle costs; going with a seemingly lower bid.
- Allowing fees and corruption. Something for the buyer on the side.

In fairness to the Southern Gulf states, there are also major problems in the ways seller countries and companies behave, and in the seriousness of their efforts to help Southern Gulf states modernize. The list of seller problems is as long and as impressive as the list of buyer problems:

- A clear lack of Western cohesion in tying arms sales to strategic needs, policy toward buyer countries, and power projection in effective coalitions.
- Neither seller national strategic interests nor corporate profits and survival are altruistic. Seller governments face massive problems in keeping national defense industries viable. Governments may talk strategy and go for bottom-line savings on equipment costs. Governments interfere in market-oriented decisions and often micromanage sales.
- For industry, neo-Darwinism often means survival of the most opportunistic, whether a new U.S. "superfirm," a disunited European firm, or a desperate Russian and Chinese firm.
- Arms sales are Ministry of Defense–driven and compartmentalized from overall policy toward Southern Gulf economic and reform needs. In contests between strategy and money, government policy leans toward more sales.
- No meaningful forum exists for supplier cooperation, and none is likely to come into existence.
- For governments, keeping defense industries alive means ruthless competition, political pressure to sell, and giving the customer what he wants regardless of effectiveness.
- Declining European and Russian power projection capabilities in the region mean these states place steadily less emphasis on effectiveness.
- The customer knows that industry is vulnerable and increasingly exploits the situation politically. Margins are minimal, and exaggerated offset requirements are the rule. Seller states and industries defend themselves through under-costing and avoiding upfront life-cycle and support costs. False terms of sale are often critical to seller survival.

The end result of these buyer and seller actions has been to create a "royal mess" in regional military development and arms sales with the following general characteristics:

- Emphasis on weapons numbers and high-prestige "glitter factor" buys of advanced weapons and technologies.

- Suboptimization based on minor military specifications or advanced technologies for key weapons platforms over balanced and integrated arms buys, and creating a "system of systems."

- National and service rivalries are given emphasis over standardization, integration, and the creation of regional deterrent and war-fighting capabilities.

- Episodic "boom and bust" buys from different suppliers greatly complicate the problems of force expansion and conversion.

- Maneuver capabilities, sustainability and maintenance, recovery and repair, and training are given far too little priority.

- A failure to understand conversion times and the real-world difficulties in absorbing major new weapons and technologies.

- Weapons and other imports from different suppliers are layered over other systems and equipment, creating a steadily growing problem in force integration and support.

- Cost analysis is lacking or based on engineering cost estimates of procurement costs. Realistic life-cycle cost analysis is almost nonexistent.

- A lack of long-term force planning and procurement planning leads to recurring efforts to overexpand force structures and equipment pools at a time when limited oil revenues and growing civil spending burdens make such plans unsustainable.

- A "buy it and they will come" approach to obtaining trained and effective manpower.

- Tendency to mix advanced weapons designed for aggressive joint operations with static tactical concepts divided by service and "stove piped" within individual services.

- Sale-oriented suppliers with little strategic concern for the end result in terms of regional stability and deterrent/war-fighting capability.

NATIONAL MILITARY FORCES

A country-by-country review of national forces provides a clear picture of the strengths and weaknesses of Southern Gulf forces, as well insights into key capabilities and trends. One key insight from such an examination is that it is the quality of Saudi forces that is pivotal to any effective regional defense efforts in the Southern Gulf. This is a matter of both geography and force size. Saudi Arabia is the only Southern Gulf state capable of funding and creating modern forces on any significant scale.

Saudi Arabia

The Saudi armed forces now dominate the Southern Gulf forces. The regular forces now total some 124,500 men, plus some 75,000 actives in the National Guard, and another 15,500 men in various paramilitary forces: some 10,500 in the Frontier force, 4,400 in the Coast Guard, and 500 in a special security forces. These totals do not include massive additional internal security, intelligence, and police forces in the Ministry of Interior.

Saudi forces must now deal with two significant potential threats—Iran and Yemen—and must still deploy forces to cover its border with Jordan and Syria. They must defend a territory roughly the size of the United States east of the Mississippi, and this mix of potential threats means that the Saudi Army cannot normally concentrate its forces to meet a single threat and must disperse its forces over much of the kingdom. Saudi Arabia has, however, reached a full border settlement with Yemen, no longer is threatened by Iraq, and has established good diplomatic relations with Iran. As a result, the primary threat it now faces comes from internal Islamic extremists, which have been a growing problem since the Gulf War, and which became far more violent in 2003.

Saudi Arabia faces a major threat from both Al-Qaeda and independent extremist groups. It also has experienced increasing tension with the United States over the fact that fifteen Saudis were involved in the terrorist attack on the United States on September 11, 2001, because of a U.S. response that often seemed harshly anti-Saudi, and because Saudi Arabia feels the United States has often uncritically backed Israel in the Israeli-Palestinian War. Saudi Arabia cooperated closely with the United States and Britain during the Iraq War, providing extensive basing facilities and other support, but did so as quietly as possible. It also did so with the agreement that the active U.S. Air Force combat forces, and Patriot units, based near Riyadh would leave the country after the war, which they did in the summer of 2003. A major U.S. military assistance mission still operates in Saudi Arabia, and the United States and Britain would certainly support Saudi Arabia in dealing with any threat from Iran or Yemen. Saudi Arabia and the United States also now cooperate far more closely in the war on terrorism. Nevertheless, Saudi Arabia's military relations with the United States are substantially more distant than in the early 1990s.

Like most states in the Middle East and North Africa (MENA), Saudi Arabia faces major problems because of the massive population growth described in Chapter 3, and a failure to diversify its economy. Saudi Arabia now has a population of nearly 23 million. Its real per capita oil income dropped to $2,296 per person in 2002, versus $23,820 in 1980, in constant dollars. Saudi Arabia still has vast oil wealth, and had extremely high oil export earnings in 2003, giving it its first major budget surplus in recent years. It still, however, faces major problems in reforming its economy, already has official levels of unemployment approach 12 percent and disguised levels of unemployment in excess of 20 percent, and faces a "youth explosion" that will double the number of young men and women entering its labor force over the next two decades.

In spite of its recent high oil export earnings, Saudi Arabia has growing problems in funding both its normal civil expenditures, and the longer term investments it must make in infrastructure, energy export capabilities, and economic growth and reform. Military expenditures are a major burden on the Saudi economy, and Saudi Arabia has had to cut back significantly on its new arms orders. It still, however, continues to import significant combat equipment, including new ships, LAVs, helicopters, and munitions. Reportedly, the country is close to signing a massive contract to provide vastly increased border surveillance in an effort to restrict possible infiltration by terrorists.[1] Saudi Arabia has allocated more than $18 billion in its budget to be spent on defense each year until at least 2007.[2]

Land Forces

The Saudi army has about 75,000 actives, an inventory of 1,055 medium tanks on-hand or in delivery, plus over 3,000 other armored vehicles and 500 major artillery weapons. It is headquartered in Riyadh, and has five staff branches: G1 Personnel, G2 Intelligence and Security, GS Operations and Training, G4 Logistics, and G5 Civil and Military Affairs. It also has field commands organized into eight military zones.

The combat strength of the Saudi Army consists of three armored brigades, five mechanized infantry brigades, one airborne brigade, and one Royal Guard regiment. It also had five independent artillery brigades and an aviation command. The Saudi army deployed the 12th Armored Brigade and 6th Mechanized Brigade at King Faisal Military City in the Tabuk area. It deployed the 4th Armored Brigade and 11th Mechanized Brigade at King and Al-Aziz Military City in the Khamis Mushayt area. It deployed the 20th Mechanized Brigade and 8th Mechanized Brigade at King Khalid Military City near Hafr al-Batin. The 10th Mechanized Brigade is deployed at Sharawrah, which is near the border with Yemen and about 150 kilometers from Zamak.

A typical Saudi armored brigade has an armored reconnaissance company, three tank battalions with 42 tanks each, two tank companies with a total of 30 tanks, three tank troops with a total of 12 tanks, a mechanized infantry battalion with 54 AIFVs/APCs, and an artillery battalion with 18 self-propelled guns. It also has an army aviation company, an engineer company, a logistic battalion, a field workshop, and a medical company. A typical Saudi mechanized brigade has an armored reconnaissance company, one tank battalion with 37–42 tanks, three mechanized infantry battalions with 54 AIFVs/APCs each, two infantry companies with a total of 33 APCs, three infantry platoons with a total of 12 APCs, and an artillery battalion with 18 self-propelled guns. It also has an army aviation company, an engineer company, a logistic battalion, a field workshop, and a medical company. It has 24 antitank guided weapons launchers and 4 mortar sections with a total of eight 81-mm mortars.

The Airborne Brigade and Royal Guard Brigade are normally deployed near Riyadh. The Airborne Brigade has two parachute battalions and three special forces companies. The special forces companies report directly to Prince Sultan. The Royal Guard Brigade has three battalions, and is equipped with light armored vehicles. It reports directly to the king and is recruited from loyal tribes in the Najd. The army also has an Aviation Command, which was formed in 1986 and operated Saudi Arabia's Bell 406 armed helicopters and AH-64s. There also were security garrisons at most major Saudi cities, including Dhahran, Jeddah, and Riyadh.

This is an impressive order of battle, but the Saudi army only has around 75,000 full-time actives for a force structure and equipment holdings that require up to twice as many men. This level of manpower is adequate to man about two U.S. division "slices," with minimal manning for combat, combat support, and service support units. In the U.S. Army, it could support a total force with a maximum of around 600 tanks and 1,000 other armored vehicles. In practice, however, the Saudi army's manpower must be divided into force—structure has an order—of battle equivalent to around three heavy divisions, and with an equipment pool at least that size. This requires more manpower than Saudi Arabia has available.

The Saudi army's problems in expansion, planning, manpower, organization, and deployment have been compounded by need to absorb the massive equipment buildup that took place before and after the Gulf War. The army faces the need to operate a complex mix of equipment supplied by many nations, and then be able to operate effectively with the equipment mixes in the forces of regional allies, the United States, and Britain. The diversification of the Saudi army's sources of army equipment has reduced its dependence on the United States, but it has also increased its training and support burden, and has raised its operations and maintenance costs.

Saudi Arabia has also made some purchases of army equipment from its major oil customers that do not serve the army's needs. Saudi Arabia still operates three types of tanks and five different types of major armored fighting vehicles and armored personnel carriers, with an inventory of more than 20 subtypes. It has major artillery holdings from five different countries, antitank weapons from four, and helicopters from two. This equipment is broadly interoperable, but each additional type increases the army's training and sustainability problems.

Saudi Arabia's unique weather, terrain, and desert warfare conditions create special demands in terms of support and sustainability. Much of the equipment the Saudi army has purchased has required modification, or extensive changes to its original technical and logistic support plan, before it could be operated in large numbers. As a result, most new systems present major servicing and support problems, and will continue to do so until new maintenance procedures are adopted and modifications are made to failure-prone components. These problems will increase strikingly the moment the Saudi army is forced to operate away from its bases, conduct sustained maneuvers, and deal with combat damage.

Contractor support is not a substitute for uniformed Saudi combat support and service support capabilities that can deploy and fight in the field, and the Saudi army's standardization and interoperability problems are compounded by the need to support equipment in remote and widely dispersed locations. The Saudi army has tried to reduce such problems by creating an advanced logistic system, but some experts feel this effort has been overly ambitious and has lacked proper advisory management.

Fortunately, Saudi equipment numbers are more than adequate now that Iraq has ceased to be a threat. Saudi Arabia has an inventory of 1,055 main battle tanks and more than 300 tank transporters. In 2004, its tanks included 315 M-1A2s, 450 M-60A3s, and 290 French-made AMX-30s. About half of the AMX-30s were in storage, however, and only about 700–765 of Saudi Arabia's main battle tanks were operational. Saudi Arabia was also experiencing major problems in converting to the M-1A1 tanks and this left it with a core strength of around 380 well-manned M-60A3s, about 100–175 M-1A2s that were combat ready with good crew proficiency, and a residual force of around 160–170 AMX-30s.

Saudi Arabia has a large inventory of other mechanized armored equipment. It has roughly 2,600 armored vehicles in addition to its tanks (300 reconnaissance, 970 armored infantry fighting vehicles, and 1,900 armored personnel carriers), and has a ratio of about 27 actives per other armored vehicle. In contrast, Iran has 1,455 other armored vehicles for 325,000 actives (450,000 if the Revolutionary Guards are included), and Iraq has about 2,700 for 375,000 men. These comparisons are shown in more detail in Figures 4.10 to 4.13. The Saudi army also has large numbers of French- and U.S.-made armored recovery vehicles and armored bridging units, and large numbers of special purpose armored vehicles.

It is not possible to separate all of the Saudi Army's holdings of other armored vehicles from those of the National Guard, Frontier Force, and other paramilitary forces. As of early 2002, however, the Saudi army's holdings of armored infantry fighting and command vehicles seem to have included 400 M-2A2 Bradleys, 150 M-577A1s, and 570 AMX-10Ps. It had 300–330 AML-60, AML-90, and AML-245 reconnaissance vehicles, of which roughly 235 remained in active service.

The Saudi army had 1,750 variants of the M-113, including 950–850 M-113A1s and M-113A2s. Saudi Arabia had 250 to 300 armored mortar carriers, including M-106A1s and M-125s. It also had 30 EE-11 Brazilian Urutus, 110 German UR-416s, 120 Spanish BMR-600s, and 270–290 Panhard M-3/VTT armored personnel carriers in inventory, but only 150 Panhard M-3s, however, remained in active service.

It is obvious from these totals that the Saudi army's holdings of OAFVs include enough U.S.-supplied equipment to provide reasonable levels of standardization for all of the its full-time active manpower, as well as a high degree of interoperability with U.S. forces. At the same time, the Saudi army's total inventory of such weapons still includes far too many types of weapons bought from far too many suppliers over the years. It presents serious problems in operability, standardization, and modernization. Many types are highly specialized and difficult to properly integrate into Saudi forces in small numbers. Some purchases are also the result of political efforts to give foreign suppliers a share of the Saudi market, regardless of military need. The end result is that the Saudi army has so many different types of other armored vehicles that many are no longer in active service— or even useful as spare parts—and even the equipment that is active is still so diverse that it presents training, maintenance, logistic, maneuver, and readiness problems.

The Saudi army has a good mix of small arms, light weaponry, and antitank weapons. These include massive stocks of mobile, crew-portable, and manportable TOW, HOT, and Dragon antitank guided missiles. Saudi Arabia has a total of some 950 TOW launchers with some 200 TOW launchers mounted on VCC-1 armored fighting vehicles, and an additional 300 mounted on M-113A1s or other U.S.-supplied armored vehicles. It had 100 HOT launchers and 90 HOT launchers mounted on AMX-10P armored fighting vehicles. The army also has large numbers of TOW crew-portable and roughly 1,000 Dragon manportable antitank guided weapons systems.

It also has 300 Carl Gustav rocket launchers, 400 M-20 3.5-inch rocket launchers, thousands of M-72 LAWs, and extensive numbers of 75-mm, 84-mm, 90-mm (100), and 106-mm (300) rocket launchers and recoilless rifles. Unlike the older antitank guided weapons in some Gulf armies, the Saudi army's TOW-2A missiles can kill T-72A, T-72M1, T-80, and other modern tanks.

The Saudi army has large numbers of modern artillery weapons. Its inventory includes 60–70 Astros II multiple rocket launchers, and 110–120 M-109A1/A2 and 90 GCT 155-mm self-propelled howitzers.[3] The army had 24 Model 56 and 90–100 M-101/M-102 105-mm towed howitzers, and 40 FH-70 105-mm towed howitzers, in storage. It had 40 M-198 and 50 M-114 155-mm towed howitzers in service and 5–10 M-115 203-mm towed howitzers and some other older towed weapons in storage. Its total mortar strength included over 400 120-mm and 4.2-inch weapons, over 1,000 81-mm weapons, and large numbers of light 60-mm weapons. It had 70 81-mm, and 150 M-30 4.2-inch mortars on M-106 and M-125A1 armored vehicles, and roughly 200 81–120-mm towed mortars.

Many Saudi artillery units, however, lack key targeting, command and control, and battle management capabilities and suffer from manpower quality, mobility, and support problems. Training is poor, and many units only shoot in serious training exercises every one and a half years. The Saudi army needs more and better ballistic computers mobile fire control and ammunition-supply equipment, and desperately needs new target acquisition radars—such as the AN/PPS-15A, MSTAR, or Rasit 3190B. It also needs a modern and fully integrated mix of counterbattery radars and fire control systems to rapidly mass and shift fires.

The Saudi army has limited-to-moderate ability to use artillery in maneuver and combine arms warfare, to target effectively in counterbattery fire or at targets beyond visual range, and to shift and concentrate fires. Unless the kingdom takes combined arms and maneuver warfare far more seriously in the future than it has to date, Saudi artillery units will continue to seriously degrade the overall war-fighting and defense capabilities of Saudi land forces.

Saudi Arabia has relatively large numbers of modern air defense weapons by Gulf standards. It is not easy to separate the Saudi army's air defense assets from those in the Saudi Air Defense Force, and sources disagree over which force operates given systems. However, the Saudi army seems to have had 17 antiaircraft artillery batteries, and is organized and equipped to protect its maneuver forces in combat. Total Saudi holdings of short-range air defenses include 73 Crotale (Shahine) radar-guided missiles on tracked armored vehicles and 19 shelter-mounted firing units, and 36 AMX-30 self-propelled and 10 shelter-mounted Shahine acquisition units. Saudi Arabia also had large holdings of manportable surface-to-air missiles. Its holdings included 700 Mistrals, some 200–500 Stingers (reporting on numbers is unusually uncertain), and 570 obsolescent Redeye man portable surface-to-air missiles. Saudi Arabia may have an unknown number of Kolomna KBM Igla (SA-16 Gimlet) weapons. It bought 50 Stinger launchers and 200 Stinger missiles on an emergency basis in August 1990, and ordered additional Crotales and 700 French Mistral launchers and 1,500 missiles.

It is equally difficult to separate the army's air defense gun holdings from those of the National Guard, but Saudi Arabia's total holdings of light antiaircraft weapons seems to include 10 M-42 40-mm, and 92 Vulcan M-163 20-mm antiaircraft guns. It also seems to have 150 Bofors L-60/L-70 40-mm and 128 Oerlikon 35-mm towed guns, and possibly 15 M-117 90-mm towed antiaircraft guns.

This is a reasonable mix of air defense assets, but training and readiness levels are moderate to low. The separate Saudi Air Defense Force—which controls Saudi Arabia's heavy surface-to-air missiles and fixed air defenses—is also a relatively static force that cannot easily support the army in mobile operations. The army's air defense units also consist largely of independent fire units, rather than an integrated system of netted C^{4}I/BM capabilities, although such capabilities are planned.

The Saudi army's helicopter forces are an important area for future force improvement. Much of the Saudi army is now deployed at least 500 miles from the kingdom's main oil facilities in the Eastern Province, although a brigade is stationed in the new King Fahd military city there, and combat elements of another brigade are deployed to the new Saudi Army base at

King Khalid City, near Hafr al-Batin, in 1984. For the foreseeable future, the Saudi army will be dispersed so that much of its strength will be deployed near Saudi Arabia's borders, with the angles located at Tabuk, Hafr al-Batin, and Sharurah-Khamis Mushayt. Helicopters offer a partial solution to these deployment problems. They can provide rapid concentration of force and allow Saudi Arabia to make up for its lack of experience in large-scale maneuver. These factors first led the Saudi army to seek attack helicopters in the early 1980s.

Saudi Arabia initially experienced political problems in obtaining such helicopters from the United States, and this led the Saudi army to obtain an option to buy 88 Sikorsky-designed S-70 Blackhawk helicopters from Westland in Britain. Roughly 80 of these Westlands were to be attack helicopters equipped with TOW-2. The rest were to be configured for SAR missions. The order was divided into batches of 40 and 48 aircraft. The Gulf War changed this situation and created the political conditions in which Saudi Arabia could buy the AH-64 from the United States. Saudi Arabia ordered 12 AH-64 Apache attack helicopters, 155 Hellfire missiles, 24 spare Hellfire launchers, 6 spare engines, and associated equipment from the United States.

The AH-64s began to enter Saudi service in 1993, and the Saudi army now has a helicopter strength that includes 12 AH-64 attack helicopters, 15 Bell 406CS armed helicopters, 12 S-70A1 Sikorsky Blackhawk transport helicopters, 6 SA-365N medical evacuation helicopters, and 10 UL-60 Blackhawk medical evacuation and 12 UH-60 transport helicopters. The Saudi army has had maintenance problems with its helicopter fleet, although standards seem to be much higher than in Iran and Iraq. It also tends to use helicopters more for service and medical evacuation functions than to achieve tactical mobility. This again presents problems in compensating for the dispersal of the Saudi army and in deploying forward defenses.

The Saudi army has the facilities, infrastructure, and equipment to support its forces in peacetime and some of its ongoing construction of facilities near Yemen may prove to be superfluous because of the improvement in Saudi-Yemeni relations. The army has excellent support facilities, although it has progressively under funded logistic and support vehicles and equipment since the mid-1990s. Nevertheless, the Saudi army has made major purchases of support equipment, along with the purchase of its M-1A2s and M-2A2s. It is improving its field support vehicle strength and ordered 10,000 support vehicles from the United States on September 27, 1990, including 1,200 high-mobility multipurpose wheeled vehicles (HMMWVs). The Saudi army still has extensive foreign support in spite of cutbacks in foreign manpower and support contracts.

The Saudi army has not, however, created the sustainment and support capabilities necessary to support mobile combat operations in the field. While it made progress toward converting to maneuver warfare during the

Gulf War, it then reverted to a largely static and caserne-oriented pattern of peacetime behavior, and it has failed to give sustainability the same priority as firepower and mobility. The lack of standardization within the Saudi army adds to these problems, as does excessive dependence on base facilities and foreign civilian support. So does the lack of progress in these areas in the rest of the Southern Gulf, and the lack of an effective and integrated organization for the defense of Kuwait and the Saudi border with Iraq. There are exceptions like attack helicopters and long-range artillery, but the Saudi army needs the specialized training, organization, and manpower necessary to improve its support structure, and ability to sustain its existing forces in combat, far more than it needs more weapons.

The Saudi army showed during the Gulf War that it could fight well against Iraqi armored forces, and the kind of threats it faces in the Gulf region. Nevertheless, the previous analysis has shown that the Saudi army faces continuing problems in many areas. It does not have the manpower and training necessary to operate all of its new major equipment orders properly. It is also still an army that normally operates near its peacetime casernes, and that will experience serious problems in redeploying its major combat forces unless it has extensive strategic warning.

While Saudi Arabia can move a brigade set of armor relatively rapidly, it would take the Saudi army a minimum of 7–10 days to redeploy a combat sustainable brigade to a new front. The Saudi army does not have a single combat brigade that is now truly combat ready in terms of the ability to rapidly deploy at full strength and then sustain operations at any distance from its peacetime casernes. Every brigade has shortfalls in its active combined arms strength, usually in artillery and mechanized elements, or both. Every brigade is short with some elements of combat and service support capability.

These are issues the Saudi army must now address in the light of the fact Iraq has ceased to be a threat. It should be possible to consolidate Saudi forces around the mission of defending against any incursions by Iran or Yemen, cut major equipment purchases and eliminate older and less capable equipment, and stress training and readiness. The Saudi army also needs to focus on developing more light and heavily mobile forces, and on creating special forces and counterterrorism units.

National Guard

Saudi Arabia divides its land force manpower between the army and the Saudi Arabian National Guard (SANG). The National Guard is the successor of the Ikhwan, or White Army. It is a tribal force forged out of those tribal elements loyal to the Saud family. It was created in 1956, and was originally administered directly by the king until King Faisal appointed Prince Abdullah its commander in 1962. A year later, Abdullah requested a British military mission to help modernize the guard. Since the late 1970s, however, the U.S.–Saudi Arabian National Guard program and U.S. contractors have provided most of the SANG's advisory functions.[4]

The National Guard is sometimes viewed as a counterweight to any threat from the regular military forces, and a counterbalance within the royal family to Sudairi control over the regular armed forces. Over time, however, it has become a steadily more effective internal security force, as well as a force that can provide rear area security for the army and can help defend Riyadh. The five major current missions of the guard are:

- Maintain security and stability within the kingdom.
- Defend vital facilities (religious sites, oil fields).
- Provide security and a screening force for the kingdom's borders.
- Provide a combat ready internal security force for operations throughout the kingdom.
- Provide security for Crown Prince Abdullah and the royal family.

Estimates of the current full-time strength of the National Guard differ sharply. The International Institute of Strategic Studies (IISS) reports it had 75,000 actives and 25,000 tribal levies in 2000. A senior U.S. expert quoted a strength of 105,000 in February 2001. Regardless of the exact numbers, it is clear that the guard is now far larger than it was at the time of the Gulf War, and that it has a full-time active strength approaching that of the Saudi army.

The guard is organized into four mechanized brigades with a fifth forming. These brigades had modern light armored vehicles (LAVs), and each brigade had some 800 men each and some 360 vehicles. There were also five light infantry brigades, equipped primarily with V-150s. These forces were deployed so that there were two mechanized brigades, and another forming, near Riyadh, plus one light infantry brigade. The Western Sector had three light infantry brigades, and the Eastern Sector has one mechanized and one light infantry brigade.

The guard does not have a complex or sophisticated mix of equipment, but has chosen to standardize on some of the best wheeled armored weapons available. The guard's forces operational forces are equipped with about 1,117 LAV light armored vehicles in its mechanized units. According to the IISS, these include 394 LAV-25s, 184 LAV-Cps, 130 LAV-Ags, 111 LAV-AT, 73 LAV-Ms, 47 LAV, plus 190 LAV support vehicles. It also has 290 V-150 Commando armored vehicles in active service in its light infantry forces, plus 810 more V-150s in storage. The guard prefers wheeled vehicles because of their superior speed, endurance, and ease of maintenance. The guard also had a significant number of towed artillery weapons.

The guard is in the midst of a major modernization campaign. Saudi Arabia recently agreed to a contract that could total over $900 million to supply the guard with replacement parts for its LAVs and APCs, as well as additional vehicles, artillery pieces, and training. The goal is for the guard to become a modernized, 75,000-man force.[5]

The major problem with the National Guard is that it must now adapt to more demanding security missions, to counter terrorism, and internal security operations on a far more demanding level in the past. The defeat of Iraq means there is little point in building up the guard as a supplement to the regular army. At the same time, the growth of a serious terrorist threat, the critical importance of Saudi petroleum facilities and civil infrastructure, and the problem of securing the Yemeni border create a clear set of new and more demanding mission priorities for the guard.

Naval Forces

The Saudi navy has slowly improved its readiness and effectiveness, but still has major problems. Only its fleet on the Gulf coast, however, is regarded as making significant progress as a war-fighting force. Its force on the Red Sea is seen more as a symbol than a war-fighting force. Joint warfare capabilities are limited, and the navy is not integrated into either a GGC or Saudi-U.S.-UK concept of operations. It must also restructure is plans and capabilities to focus on Iran, now that Iraq has ceased to be a threat, and on defense of the Red Sea.

The Saudi navy has a nominal strength of 15,500 men, including 3,000 marines. It is headquartered in Riyadh and has major bases in Jeddah, Jizan, Al-Wajh in the Red Sea, and in Jubail, Dammam, Ras al-Mishab, and Ras al-Ghar in the Gulf. Its combat strength includes 4 Madina-class (F-2000) frigates, 3 Arriyad-class (F-3000S) guided missile frigates (*Jane's Defense Weekly,* August 7, 2002, p. 16, labeled 49), 4 Badr-class missile corvettes, and 9 Al-Siddiq-class guided missile ships. It includes 3 Dammam-class (German Jaguar) torpedo boats, 20 Naja 12 inshore fast craft, 17 Halter-type coastal patrol craft (some in the Coast Guard), and 3 Al-Jawf (British Sandown) and 4 Safwa (Addriyah)-class (ex-U.S. MSC-322 Bluebird) mine warfare ships. The Sawari-IIs are to be fitted with Oto Melara stealth 76/62 guns.[6]

It has 4 Afif-class LCU amphibious craft, 4 LCMs, 2 other amphibious craft, 2 10,500-ton Boraida-class (French Durance) support ships, 4 smaller support vessels, 14 tug boats, and large numbers of small patrol boats including 40 Simmoneau Type 51 inshore patrol boats. Auxiliary ships included 3 Radhwa-class oceangoing tugs, 3 Radhwa-class coastal tugs, 2 Buraida-class replenishment oilers (French Durance-class), 1 Al-Riyadh royal yacht, and the Al-Azizah hydrofoil yacht tender. The royal yachts are based at Dammam. Saudi Arabia is considering acquiring up to 4 diesel-electric submarines. Reportedly, the Saudis are looking into the Swedish Kockums Type 471, the German IKL 200, and an undetermined French submarine.[7]

The 3,000-man Saudi marine forces are organized into one regiment with two battalions. It initially was equipped with 140 BTR-60Ps. It is now equipped with 140 Spanish Santa Barbara SBB BMR-600 6×6 amphibious APCs. It seems to have received nearly 100 Al-Fahd 8×8 armored personnel carriers during 2001.

Saudi naval aviation is based at Al-Jubail. Various sources report different holdings for Saudi naval aviation. It seems to have included 15 operational SA-565F Dauphin ASW and antiship missile helicopters with AS-15TT missiles, and 4 SA-565s equipped for the search and rescue mission. The SA-365Fs have only limited ASW capability, and are configured primarily for the surface search and attack roles. Each combat-equipped SA-365F carries 4 missiles and has an Agrion search/attack system. They have Crouzet MAD systems and can carry two Mark 46 torpedoes. The Saudi navy also has 3 Westland Sea King Mark 47 ASW helicopters, and 12–21 land-based AS-332SC(B/F) Super Puma helicopters. Some reports indicate the AS-332s included 12 aircraft with Omera search radars, 9 with Giat 20-mm cannon, and 12 with Exocet or Sea Eagle air-to-ship missiles. Other reports indicate the AS-332s included only 6 transport aircraft, plus another 6 with Exocet air-to-ship missiles. The Saudis are pursuing the sale of 10 NH 90 helicopters with antisubmarine warfare capabilities for the new Arriyad-class frigates.[8]

The Saudi coast guard has up to 4,500 men and has its main base at Azizam. Its equipment includes 2 large Yarmouk-class patrol boats, 2 fast missile attack craft with AS-15TT missiles, 4 large Al-Jouf-class patrol boats, 2 large Al-Jubatel-class patrol boats, 25 Skorpion-class patrol boats, 13 other coastal patrol boats and 4 SRN-6, Model 4 Hovercraft, 16 Slingsby SAH 2200 Hovercraft, large numbers of inshore patrol craft, 3 royal yachts, 3 small tankers, fire-fighting craft, and 3 tugs. Its primary mission is anti-smuggling, but it does have an internal security mission as well.[9]

Air Forces

The Saudi air force is the most advanced air force in the Gulf, but it still has major defects. These defects include:

- An overemphasis on air defense at the expense of offensive air capabilities, and particularly capabilities designed to deal with advancing Iraqi armor or the naval threat from Iran.

- A failure to develop effective joint warfare capabilities and realistic joint warfare training capabilities, and transform joint warfare doctrine into effective war-fighting plans to support the army, national guard, and navy.

- A failure to develop a truly integrated air defense and war-fighting capability with other Southern Gulf states.

- A failure to rapidly modernize the RSAF C⁴I/SR and battle management system and to develop high-capacity secure communications, and to expand the role of sensor, electronic warfare, and intelligence aircraft to support offensive and joint warfare missions.

- A lack of overall readiness, and poor aircrew and maintenance to aircraft ratios, which has forced the near-grounding of its F5s, and has severely reduced the effectiveness of its F-15s and Tornados. Since 1994, the poor leadership of the air force, the mishandling of overall training and readiness, underfunding, and poorly managed Saudization have brought readiness to the point of near-crisis and led to a severe increase in the air force's accident rate.

- A failure to modernize training to support realistic offensive and joint warfare missions.

- A decline in leadership since the Gulf War, and particularly in focusing the modernization of the RSAF on key missions. Slow promotion and turnover, coupled with corruption in the highest ranks, have compounded these problems.

The RSAF has about 18,000 men, not including another 16,000 men in the Air Defense Force. USCENTCOM estimates the air force's strength at a total of 16,500 men. According to one source, the RSAF's combat forces were organized into six wings with a total of 15 combat squadrons and about 259 operational first-line, fixed-wing combat aircraft, and 39 combat capable trainers. The IISS estimated that Saudi Arabia had a total inventory of about 432 combat aircraft with about 294 active combat aircraft. The Saudi army operates an additional force of 12 AH-64 attack helicopters, and the navy has 21 more armed helicopters. These armed naval helicopters include 19 AS-56 helicopters, of which four are equipped for the search and rescue mission and 15 has AS-15TT anti ship missiles, six AS-332B transports, and six AS-332Bs equipped with Exocet antiship missiles.[10]

Saudi Arabia's total inventory of major combat aircraft includes 72 F-15Ss, 67 F-15Cs, 20 F-15Ds, 85 Tornado IDSs (10 Tornado GR.1 recce-attack equipped), 22 Tornado ADVs, and 5 E-3A AWACS. Until recently, the RASF also had 56 F-5Es, 21 F-5Fs, 10 RF-5Es, and 14 F-5Bs. By early 2001, however, most of the F-5s were grounded and in storage. Only 14 F-5B still seem to be operational in a combat-capable training unit.[11]

Combat aircraft strength includes four fighter-attack squadrons, three with 85 Tornado IDS, and one with 14 F-15B/F/RFs. In theory, there were still three squadrons with 53 F-5Es, but virtually all of these aircraft were grounded. The IDS squadrons had dual-capable trainer aircraft, and 10 had a dual-mission in the reconnaissance role. These squadrons were equipped with a wide range of attack munitions, including AS-15, AS-30, AGM-45 Shrike, and AGM-65 Maverick air-to-surface missiles and the Rockeye, Sea Eagle, and Alarm air-to-ground weapons. Saudi Arabia has MQM-74C Chukar II and Banshee remotely piloted vehicles for reconnaissance and target acquisition.

The Tornado squadrons provide much of the offensive strength of the Saudi air force, but are configured more for bombing against fixed targets than joint warfare or operations against armor. The Tornado does, however, have superior low-altitude flight performance in attack missions to the F-15S, and was specifically designed to fly nap-of-the-earth missions, while the F-15S is subject to buffeting because of its large wing area. The Tornado also has superior air-to-surface missile armament. It can deliver the ALARM antiradiation missile and Sea Eagle antiship missile, while the Saudi F-15S is currently limited to the Maverick, which only has a strike range of around 10 miles. Both aircraft can deliver laser-guided bombs and self-illuminate their targets.

The RSAF has nine interceptor squadrons for defensive missions. There were five squadrons with a total of 87 F-15C/Ds (67 F-15C and 20 F-15Ds), and more squadrons with 72 F-15Ss. F-15Ds were deployed to each F-15 squadron to perform both training and operational missions. There was one Tornado ADV squadron with 22 aircraft, which also included dual-capable trainer aircraft. Saudi fighters were equipped with modern air-to-air missiles, including AIM-9L and AIM-9P infrared guided missiles, and AIM-7F Sparrow and Skyflash radar-guided missiles. The RSAF is acquiring the AMRAAM air-to-air missile, which will give it substantial BVR all-weather air combat capability. Saudi F-15 fighter units are capable in the air defense role, but most aircrews now lack adequate advanced fighter combat training. The Tornado ADS has not proved to be an effective fighter except in a standoff missile defense role and is being shifted to other missions.

During the middle and late 1990s, the training of Saudi aircrews became weak to the point where it presented serious safety problems in advanced mission profiles, and led to a number of fatal accidents. Saudi Arabia's remaining active F-5 units present particular problems. They have poor readiness and proficiency levels and their aircraft have little combat capability. This loss of the F-5E led Saudi Arabia to obtain U.S. permission to deploy some of its F-15s to Tabuk in western Saudi Arabia in 2003, although it had previously agreed not to do so because of Israel concerns over security. This deployment has little, if any, practical impact on Israel's security.

Saudi Arabia has been the only Southern Gulf air force with meaningful numbers of reconnaissance aircraft. Until recently, the RSAF had two aging reconnaissance squadrons with a total of 10 RF-5Es. These aircraft have reached obsolescence in terms of their sensors and survivability, however, and most are now deadlined or in storage. The 10 Tornado IDS-Rs in the fighter-ground attack force could probably perform most missions, and Saudi Arabia is acquiring reconnaissance and electronic warfare pods for its F-15s and has deployed some of this equipment.

The RSAF has an airborne early warning squadron with five E-3As. These aircraft now have Saudi crews, but the crews have shown only limited capability to manage complex air battles and the RSAF must rely on the USAF for help in such missions. The Saudi E-3As also lack adequate secure communications and data links, and need an upgrading of their software and improved electronic support measures. The remaining multi-purpose squadron with 14 F-5Bs has both a training and a combat mission, but had little real operational capability. Most aircraft were "parked" and without real operational capability.

The RSAF has 25 armed Hawk Mark 65 jet trainers, and 20 armed Hawk Mark 65A jet trainers. Saudi holdings of 36 BAC-167 turboprop COIN and training aircraft were phased out of service in the late 1990s. The Hawk units were technically capable of performing COIN and light attack functions with machine guns, cannons, and rockets, as well as training missions but the combat mission training of the Hawk aircrews is limited. RSAF does not plan to use them in that role. The RSAF also had 13 Cessna 172s, 1 Jetstream, and 50 PC-9 aircraft in training units that were not armed for combat.

The RSAF is the only Gulf air force with an effective midair refueling capability. Its support units included a tanker squadron with 8 KE-3A tanker/transports, and 8 KC-130H tankers. It had three transport squadrons with 38 C-130 cargo-transports (7 E, 29 H, and 2 H-30), 1 KE-3B (EW), 3 L-100-30HS hospital aircraft, and 4 CN-235s. There were also two helicopter squadrons with 22 AB-205s, 13 AB-206s, 17 AB-212s, 40 AB-41EP (SAR) and 10 AS-5323A2 (SAR). There AS-532A2 Cougar search and rescue helicopters were ordered from France in September 1996, at a cost of $590 million.[12] The Royal Flight provided substantial additional airlift assets, including 2 B-747SP, 1 B-737-200, 4 Bae 125–800, 2 Gulfstream III, 2 Learjet 35, 4 VC-130H, and 5 utility helicopters.

Saudi Arabia has moderate but aging inventories of air munitions and spares—a marked decline from the large inventories of cutting edge munitions and high inventories it had at the time of the Gulf War. The kingdom has not continued to properly maintain and modernize its munitions inventory, however, and has not procured all of the air-to-ground and antiship ordnance it needs for joint warfare.

Up until the mid-1990s, the Saudi air force had excellent foreign support. There have, however, been growing financing and payment problems since the mid 1990s, and they grew worse after the "oil crash" of late 1997. Saudization has not helped, nor has adequate use been made of the offset program. Foreign contractors have often been replaced with Saudis selected more for their contacts than their skills, and training programs for Saudis nave not enforced the proper qualification standards. Saudi air forces facilities remain excellent. No U.S. or NATO base has sheltering or hardening equal to the Saudi bases at Dhahran and Khamis Mushayt, and similar facilities will be built at all of Saudi Arabia's main operating bases.

The Saudi air force's most important challenges are to improve its readiness, training, and capability for joint operations. Fortunately, Iraq's defeat has great reduced the potential threat, as has the slow rate of Iranian air modernization. As a result, Saudi Arabia has no immediate need to replace its F-5Es, or for any other form of major procurements. It can consolidate around its most advanced aircraft, creating a smaller and more effective force.

Land-Based Air Defenses

The Saudi Air Defense Force had a nominal strength of 16,000 men in 2004, and some 33 surface-to-air missile batteries. Some reports indicated its total major surface-to-air missile strength included 16 Improved Hawk batteries with 128 fixed and mobile fire units, 9 Crotale batteries with 48 Crotale fire units (currently being modernized), 16 air defense batteries with 72 Shahine fire units, and 50 AMX-30SA 30-mm self-propelled guns. The IISS reported a strength 16 Improved Hawk batteries with 128 fire units, 17 air defense batteries with 68 Shahine fire units and AMX-30SA 30-mm self-propelled guns, and 73 Crotale and Shahine fire units in static positions. It reported a total inventory of 50 AMX-30 SAs, 141 Shahine launchers, and 40 Crotale launchers. It also reported 92 M-163 20-mm Vulcan antiaircraft guns and 50 AMX-30SA antiaircraft guns, plus 70 L/70 40-mm antiaircraft guns in storage.

Most of Saudi Arabia's Shahine units were deployed in fixed locations for the defense of air bases and key targets. All of the Shahine systems have been upgraded as the result of an agreement with France signed in 1991. These units provide close-in defense capability for virtually all of Saudi Arabia's major cities, ports, oil facilities, and military bases.

Total Saudi army holdings of manportable surface-to-air missiles include 500–700 Mistrals, 350–400 Stingers, and 500–600 Redeyes. The number and type of antiaircraft guns currently operational is uncertain. Some reports state it has 35 35-mm Oerlikon-Contraves twin AA guns with Skyguard fire control systems, 72 40-mm L-70 AA guns, 53 30-mm AMX-30 DCA twin antiaircraft guns, and an unknown number of 20-mm Vulcan M163 guns. Other reports indicate it has 92 M-163 Vulcan 20-mm antiaircraft guns, 30 V-150s with Vulcan 20-mm guns, 30 towed 20-mm Vulcans, 128 35-mm AA guns, and 150 L/70 40-mm guns (most in storage).

Reports differed as to whether Saudi Arabia had two or three major operational Patriot fire units, and there was one report it had a fourth. The United States deployed an additional Patriot battalion near Riyadh in 2001, and some reports indicate equipment was prepositioned for a second. Another source cites only eight active MIM-104 fire units. There seems to be agreement that operational readiness is limited. Live-fire exercises only really began to improve in the fall of 2000, and mobile operations have taken years to develop. The first mobile deployment approaching a combat exercise was a road march from Dhahran to a site near King Khalid Military City in the fall of 2000.

The Saudi Air Defense Force still needs to improve its capability for joint operations with the Saudi air force and army, and the fact that active U.S.

air forces and army forces have left Saudi Arabia means that it must develop far more effective air defense and air force capabilities to use its C4 and IS&R assets effectively. The end of an Iraqi threat greatly eases the potential burden on both the Saudi air force and army, however; and Saudi I-Hawk and Patriot units have improved Saudi Arabia's low- to high-level air defense capability along Gulf coast, while providing some defense against medium-range and theater ballistic missiles.

Bahrain

Bahrain is a small, strategic island in the middle of the Southern Gulf. It has a population of only about 730,000, and cannot support large military forces. Bahrain has long hosted the U.S. naval presence in the Gulf, however, and had close military ties to the United States ever since Britain ceased to act as the military protector of the Southern Gulf states. It now is the site of the headquarters of the U.S. 5th Fleet, and Bahrain provided major basing facilities and support to U.S. forces during the "Tanker War" with Iran in 1987–1998, the Gulf War of 1990–1991, and the Iraq War in 2003.

The United States provides de facto security guarantees to Bahrain against any foreign threat, and Saudi Arabia provides major amounts of economic aid as well as the capability to rapidly reinforce Bahrain's internal security forces. The fall of Saddam Hussein's regime and improvements in relations with Iran have also greatly reduced the level of internal threat. Bahrain's new ruler has also made significant political reforms that have greatly eased the tensions between Bahrain's ruling Sunni elite and its Shiite majority. Nevertheless, these tensions now remain Bahrain's greatest security concern, and Bahrain does have small cadres of Sunni Islamic extremists.

Bahrain is not a wealthy state and has always been careful about its military expenditures. It does, however, selectively modernize its military forces. It bought 8 I-Hawk surface-to-air missile batteries and 30 ATACMs launchers in the 1990s, and ordered 10 F-16C/D with advanced air combat munitions like the AMRAAM in 2000. In the future, further military expenditures will be even more closely monitored by the newly established parliament. The first deputy chairman of the National Assembly indicated that defense spending would be minimal given the amicable relations it has in the region. The defense budget for 2004–2005 was slashed by $10.6 million, though the armed forces are seeking to add additional landing craft, helicopters, and an upgrade to the existing C^4I/SR systems.[13]

Land Forces

Bahrain's small army has 8,500 men and its combat units include one armored brigade, one infantry brigade, one artillery brigade, one special forces battalion, one Amiri Guard battalion, and one air defense battalion with two missile and one AA gun battery. Its major combat equipment includes 140 M-60A3 main battle tanks; 22 AML-90 and 8 Saladin armored reconnaissance vehicles and 16 other obsolescent armored cars; 25 Dutch YPR-765 AIFVs, and 235 APCs: 115 M-113s, 110 Panhard M-3, and 10 AT-105s. It has 15 TOW antitank guided weapons launchers. Its artillery strength now includes 9 MRLS multiple rocket launchers, 13 towed M-110 203-mm self-propelled weapons, 8 light towed 105-mm weapons, 18 M-198 towed 155-mm weapons, and 21 81-mm and 120-mm mortars. Air defense weapons include 8 I-Hawk, 7 Crotale, 60 RBS-70, and 24 Stingers.

This force is roughly the equivalent of one heavy brigade. It is well equipped for its size, but has so many diverse types of equipment that it is difficult to sustain and support. It has moderate levels of combat readiness and training, and is largely suited to service as a local deterrent, with very limited ability to deploy outside Bahrain.

Naval Forces

The Bahraini navy has 1,200 men and it's a relatively large force for such a small country. The navy is not capable of independent operations against a power like Iran, but has reasonable manpower quality, readiness, and sustainability and good training and at sea rates by regional standards. It is based at Mina Salman, and has a combat strength of one frigate, two corvettes, four missile patrol craft, and four inshore patrol craft. It has four LCU landing craft utility. The frigate, the *Sabha*, is an ex–Oliver Hazard Perry class ship with Harpoon ship-to-ship missiles and Standard anti-aircraft missiles. It is equipped with torpedoes, a 76-mm gun, and modern radars and fire control systems. The ship entered Bahraini service in 1997. It is active, but does not have helicopters and cannot adequately perform its ASW mission without them.

The two Al-Manama class corvettes are 632-ton ships with 2 twin MM-40 Exocet launchers, and a 76-mm gun. They have 40-mm AA guns and can carry a helicopter, but are not so equipped. They have moderate radar and combat electronics capabilities and entered service in the late 1980s. The four Ahmad El Fateh class missile patrol boats are 259-ton vessels equipment with 2 twin MM-40 Exocet launchers and a 76-mm gun. Bahrain has four gun-equipped patrol boats: two of 205 tons and two of 33 tons. Its three LCUs have a cargo capacity of 167 tons. It also has one Ajerra-class supply ship. Its small coast guard has 20 light patrol boats, 17 small craft, a support craft, and a landing craft.

Air Forces

The Bahraini air force has 1,500 men, 54 combat aircraft, and 40 armed helicopters, and benefits substantially from U.S. aid and support. It has one fighter attack squadron with 8 F-5E and 4 F-5F, a fighter squadron with 18 F-016C and 4 F-16CD, and 24 AH-1E, 6 TAH-1P, and 10 AB-212 attack and armed helicopters. It has a small transport unit with 4 aircraft, and 7 utility and transport helicopters (often used for royal flights). Bahrain has made a well-planned transition to advanced combat aircraft, and pilot training standards are moderate to good. Readiness is acceptable, and Bahrain has stocks of modern air munitions. Bahrain is dependent on the United States, however, for assistance in battle management, air control and warning, and targeting and battle damage assistance. In spite of various planning efforts, it does not have a fully integrated air defense system with any of its Gulf neighbors, although it does have some data links.

Kuwait

Kuwait's location on the western edge of the Upper Gulf, and at a point where it has common borders with Iraq and Saudi Arabia and is with a few minutes flight of Iran, has made this small country of some 2.1 million people uniquely vulnerable. Iraq has invaded it once, Iran threatened it repeatedly during the Iran-Iraq War, and its wealth and vulnerability continue to make it a potential strategic prize if more aggressive regimes should emerge in Iran and Iraq. At present, however, the fall of Saddam Hussein, and a relatively moderate regime in Iran, has given it as higher level of security than it has enjoyed in many years. In addition, the Kuwaiti deputy prime minister signed a memorandum of understanding with Iran's minister of defense, pledging military cooperation on numerous levels.[14] Kuwait is also making progress toward democracy, and while it has some Islamic extremists, it does not seem to face significant internal security threats.

Kuwait's military readiness and training levels have improved to moderate in recent years, and its training is now effective at the brigade and squadron level. Reports indicate that Kuwaiti defense spending increased by 30 percent by the end of 2003.[15] It has, however, suffered from a past tendency to politicize arms sales, rather than seek the best and most interoperable systems to meet its needs. Recent major purchases include AH-64 attack helicopters and F/A-18E/F fighters. Kuwait was seeking to purchase several C^4I systems, but the parliament blocked the move, claiming that the Ministry of Defense had improperly negotiated a specific C^4I contract. It is unclear if an investigation is under way into the allegations and it is equally uncertain whether Kuwait will continue to pursue the systems in question.[16]

Land Forces

Kuwait has armed forces with some 11,500 actives. It has reserves with some 23,700 men, although few ever receive anything like their theoretical 30 days of training per year. Its army has 11,000 men and is organized into three armored brigades, two mechanized infantry brigades, one mechanized reconnaissance brigade, one artillery brigade, and one engineer brigade. It has a commando battalion and Amiri Guard battalion, and one reserve brigade. In practice, Kuwait barely has enough manpower for two brigades and its "brigades" are actually the equivalent of small regiments or large battalions. Kuwait's paramilitary force include a 6,600-man national guard armed with light armored vehicles (20 VBL, 70 Pandur, and some S-600 APCs) organized into five battalions, including a special force battalion.

Its army is equipped with 218 M-1A2 main battle tanks, plus 150 M-84s (well over half of which are in storage). It has a comparatively large number of AIFVs, including 76 BMP-2s, 120 BMP-3s, and 254 Desert Warriors. It has 230 M-113, 50 M-577, and 11 Tpz-1 Fuch APCs, plus 30–40 Fahds in storage. It has 23 M-109A2 18 F-3 and 27 PLZ 45 155-mm self-propelled artillery weapons, plus 18 GCTs in storage. It also has 27 Russian-made Smerch long-range multiple rocket launchers and 78 mortars, some mounted in armored vehicles. It has comparatively large numbers of TOWs—many mounted on vehicles—and Dragons, plus 200 Carl Gustav unguided antitank recoilless rifles. At least two brigades are now capable of deploying with their full equipment strength, although their maintenance and sustainment needs can only be met while operating in Kuwait and within relatively short range of their bases. Kuwait is seeking to purchase 60 heavy equipment transporters (HETs) to increase the mobility of its M-1A2s. The three vehicles under consideration are the T816-6VWN9T 8×8, the MAN 40.633 6×6 DFAETX, and the Actros 4160AS 8×8.[17]

Naval Forces

The Kuwaiti navy has some 2,000 men, including 500 coast guards. It is based at Ras al-Qalaya. It has 10 surface combatants—all missile patrol boats. They include 8 French-made Ubn Almaradin–class. These are comparatively new 245-ton vessels, armed with 4 Sea Skua missiles and 40-mm gun, and are fitted for launchers for 6 Sadaral air-to-surface missiles. The crews are French trained and Kuwait has sought to develop a strength of 10 crews to allow the boats to be kept at sea. All were delivered during 1998–2000.

It also has one Istiqlal-class (Lurssen FPB-57) missile patrol boat, armed with 2 twin MM-40 Exocet launchers. The ship was extensively refitted in 1995. It has one Al-Sanbouk-class (Lurssen TNC-45) missile patrol boat, armed with 2 twin MM-40 Exocet launchers. This boat escaped to Bahrain in 1990, during Iraq's invasion of Kuwait. It has been laid up since 1997, and is awaiting a major refit or decommissioning. Kuwait also has four Inttisar 150-ton gun patrol boats and three 104-ton Al-Shaheed-class gun patrol boats in its coast guard, and plans to buy nine more Shaheeds. It has 12 Manta-class inshore patrol boats that are inoperable due to design defects, and 23 operational light inshore patrol craft, and plans to buy 3 more. It has 2 LCU 215-ton amphibious ships, and 2 support craft.

These are small naval forces, with limited capability and readiness, but Iraq is no longer a threat. The United States makes extensive use of basing facilities in Kuwait and prepositions a brigade set and air equipment there. Kuwait can count on U.S. military support against any threat from Iran.

The Kuwaitis have committed to significantly upgrading their communication and surveillance capabilities. Kuwait will spend $50 million to acquire the Advanced Tactical Communications System VHF radio.[18] The Kuwaiti Defense Ministry has procured an aerostat, along with the necessary components, that will provide low-altitude airborne surveillance.[19]

Air Forces

The Kuwaiti air force consists of some 2,500 men, 49 combat aircraft, and 16 armed helicopters. Its forces include fighter-ground attack units equipped with 32 F/A-18C and 8 F/A-18D. It is phasing out a fighter unit with 14 Mirage F-1C/K/BK fighters, which are nonoperational. It also has 11 Hawk 64 and 16 Tucanos in a combined light attack and training unit. It has 16 SA-342 attack helicopters with HOT. Purchases of the Ah-64 and F/A-18 E/F should significantly increase its strength in the near future. Kuwait purchased 16 AH-64D Longbow helicopters in 2003, though the dates of delivery and timetable for deployment are unknown.[20] It has a small transport force and 12 utility and other unarmed helicopters. The air force operates 4 I-Hawk batteries with a total of 24 launchers, and Patriot surface-to-air missile forces with 40 launch units. Its lighter air defense forces include 6 Amoun batteries, each with a Skyguard radar, 2 Aspide launchers, and 2 twin Oerlikon 35-mm AA guns. Training and readiness are good by Gulf standards, although Kuwait would have to depend on United States aid for effective AEW, battle management, reconnaissance and intelligence, and targeting support.

Oman

Oman has a strategic location in the lower Gulf. It controls the Mussandam Peninsula and its base at Goat Island is on the edge of the key tanker routes from the Indian Ocean to the Gulf. It has a 1,129 nautical mile coastline, and is the only member of the GCC with meaningful ports on the Indian Ocean. Oman has long had close ties to Britain and the United States, and has granted the United States extensive prepositioning facilities on the Island of Masirah. Iran is the major potential threat to Oman, although relations have improved steadily since the mid-1990s, and there are few signs of current tensions. Yemen too is a potential threat, although both countries have resolved their border issues, and again there have been few signs of recent tension.

Land Forces

Oman has 41,700 actives in its armed forces, plus some 2,000 foreign advisers—largely British. It has maintained relatively large armed forces, with a moderate degree of readiness, ever since the Dhofar Rebellion. It also has exported military manpower to other Southern Gulf states like the UAE. In spite of a comparative large military spending effort, however, it has made comparatively limited equipment purchases and has been relatively slow to modernize its forces.

Oman's army now has 25,000 actives, plus a small contingent of Royal Household troops. Its army is organized into one armored and two infantry brigades, two armored regiments, one armored reconnaissance regiment, eight infantry regiments, one infantry reconnaissance regiment, one airborne regiment, four artillery regiments, an air defense regiment, and a field engineer regiment. These regiments are small and are largely battalion equivalents. It has a number of independent company sized formations, including the Musandam Security Force. The Royal Household has an additional 6,400 troops include two special forces regiments (1,000 men) and a 5,000-man Royal Guard Brigade. There is a small, 150-man Royal Yacht Squadron, and a 250-man Royal Flight.

The army's equipment includes 6 M-60A1, 73 M-60A3, and 38 Challenger 2 main battle tanks. It has 37 aging Scorpion light tanks, 139 VBL armored reconnaissance vehicles, and more than 204 APCs, including 175 variants of the Piranha, 6 Spartans, 13 Sultans, 10 Stormers, and up to 50 WZ 551s.[21] It has 10 TOWs, some on armored vehicles, and at least 30–40 Milan manportable antitank guided weapons, and a mix of RPG-7 and LAW rocket launchers. It has 25 G6 155-mm self-propelled artillery weapons and 108 towed weapons, including 42 ROF 105-mm, 30 D-20 122-mm, 12 M-46 130-mm, and 12 Type 59-1 155-mm plus some FH-70s. It has a mix of roughly 100 81-mm, 107-mm, and 120-mm mortars. Its air defense assets include 14 Javelin, 34 SA-7, and vehicle-mounted Mistral surface-to-air weapons; plus 4 ZSU-23-2 3-mm, 10 GDF-005 35-mm with Skyguard, and 12 Bofors 40-mm AA guns. The Royal Household has an additional 9 VBC-90 armored fighting vehicles, 14 VAB-VCIs, 50 WZ-551s, and 9 VAB-DDA. It has 6 Type 90A multiple rocket launchers, Milan antitank guided weapons, and 14 Javelin light surface-to-air missiles.

Naval Forces

The Omani navy has a critical strategic location because Oman controls the Strait of Hormuz and has a long coast and important ports on the Indian Ocean. It is a 4,200- to 4,500-man force that is headquartered at Seeb, and with bases at Ahwi, Ghanam Island, Mussandam on the Mussandam Peninsula, and Salalah on Oman's south coast. It has thirteen surface vessels. These include two 1,450-ton Qahir-class corvettes, each armed with 8 MM-40 II Exocets, Crotale air-to-surface missiles, and 1 76-mm gun. They have a helicopter platform and can be fitted with ASW gear. The ships are nearly new and were delivered in 1996 and 1997. It has one old 900-ton patrol ship formally used for training, which it has classified as a corvette.

Oman has seven oceangoing patrol boats. These include four Dhofar-class missile patrol boats, armed with twin three or four MM-40 Exocet missiles and one 76-mm gun, which were delivered in the early and middle 1980s. They also include three 475-ton Al-Bushra-class, armed with 76-mm guns and delivered in the mid-1990s. They have no ASW capability. Oman has four Seeb 74-ton coastal patrol craft, plus 15 light inshore patrol boats in its police force. The navy has placed an order for 12 9.5-mm high-speed rigid assault boats, though the date of delivery is unclear.[22]

The Omani Navy has one 2,500-ton Nasr al-Bahr-class LSL (240 troops, 7 tanks) with a helicopter deck. It under went a limited refit in 1997 and is fully operational. It also has four landing craft: three 230-ton LCMs and one 85-ton LCU, as well as a number of support ships and survey craft.

Oman must rely on the United States and Britain for antimine and ASW warfare, and in any major confrontation with Iran. It has shown, however, that it will confront Iran over any infringement of its waters and maintains relatively high readiness by Gulf standards.

Air Forces

The Omani air force has some 4,100 men, with 40 combat aircraft and no armed helicopters. Its aircraft are aging and have limited capability although a number are being upgraded. It has two fighter-attack squadrons with 24 Jaguars that are being upgraded to the GR-3 standard. It has a fighter-reconnaissance unit with 12 Hawk 203s plus a small light attack and training unit with 12 PC-9s and 4 Hawk 103s. It has three fixed-wing transport squadrons, with 3 BAC-11s, 3 C-130H, and 10 Skyvans, and two medium transport helicopter squadrons with 30 aircraft: 19 AB-205, 3 AB-206, 3 AB-2123, and 5 AB-214. The Royal Flight has 2 B-747s, 1 DC-8. Two Gulfstream IV transports and 3 AS-330s, 2 AS-332Cs, and 1 AS-332L.

The Omani air force has sought advanced U.S. combat aircraft for some years and ordered 12 F-16C/D Block 50 fighters from the United States in November 2003. Oman, by mid-2006, will receive the 12 F-16s.[23] Two of these F-16s are to be fitted with F-9120 Advanced Airborne Reconnaissance Systems (AARS).[24] The air force will upgrade seven of its attack aircraft with Precision Attack Navigation and Targeting for Extended-Range Acquisition (PANTERA) pods, enhancing their strike capabilities.[25] Given the importance of Oman's airfields to the United States, it can almost certainly count on effective training and support for these aircraft.

Qatar

Qatar is a small country whose location as a peninsula located in the center of the Southern Gulf places it in a critical strategic location. It shares a massive offshore gas formation with Iran. While Iran is the primary potential threat, there have never been serious recent tensions between the two countries. In contrast, Qatar had several clashes with Saudi Arabia before the two countries finally agreed on a border settlement, and Qatar accused several of its Southern Gulf neighbors of supporting a coup attempt by the present Emir's father, who made an attempt to return to power.

It has limited military forces with a total of only 12,400 men, plus reserves. It makes no pretense to be a major Gulf military power, but maintains just enough forces to provide minimal border defense against Saudi Arabia and some deterrent to Iran. Qatar is now the site of the main U.S. air base and headquarters in the Gulf, however, and of the equipment for one U.S.-prepositioned brigade. It is defended by U.S. power projection forces for all intensive purposes.

Land Forces

Qatar's small 8,500-man army has a force structure with a Royal Guard regiment, a tank battalion, four mechanized infantry battalions, a special forces company, a field artillery regiment, a mortar battalion, and an antitank battalion. These formations are very small, and Qatar's entire army is equivalent to about one brigade slice by the standards of most other armies.

Its equipment includes 30 obsolescent AMX-30 main battle tanks and 40 AMX-10P armored infantry fighting vehicles. It also has armored reconnaissance forces equipped with 16 VBL, 12 AMX-10RC, 8 V-150, 20 EE-9 Cascaval, and 12 obsolete Ferrets. It has 36 Piranha light armored vehicles as well as 160VAB and 30 AMX-VCI APCs. Its artillery strength consists of 28 F-3 155-mm self-propelled artillery weapons, 12 towed GS 155-mm artillery weapons, 4 ASTROS II multiple rocket launchers, 30 L16 81-mm mortars (some on vehicles), and 15 Brant 120-mm mortars. It has 48 HOT (24 on VABs) and 100 Milan antitank guided weapons. Its forces are equipped with rocket launchers and small arms. Land-based air defense weapons are held by the air force.

This is not a bad mix of equipment for a small force, but it includes so many different types that it presents support and sustainment problems even when based near its peacetime casernes. The Qatari army has shown that it can project small forces, and played a small role in the Gulf War. It is, however, not capable of engaging any significant Iranian or other land force.

Naval Forces

Qatar has a small 1,800-man navy, including its marine police force. It is headquartered at Doha and has a base at Halul Island. Its forces include three 396-ton Damsah (Combattante III)-class missile patrol boats. Each is equipped with 8 MM-40 missiles and 1 76-mm gun. They vessels were delivered in the early 1980s, but were refitted in 1997.

It also has 4 376-ton Barzan (British Vita)-class vessels. Each is equipped with 8 Exocet MM-40s, 1 76-mm gun, a six-round Matral Sandral launcher carrying Mistral surface-to-air missiles, and four torpedo tubes. They have modern electronics and radars and were delivered in mid-1996. Qatar is still training its crews and bringing them to full readiness.

The navy recently purchased four DV 15 fast interceptor craft, armed with unknown machine guns, from a French shipbuilder.[26] It has some 20 small craft, which are operated by the Marine police. Its coastal defense forces have four batteries with three quad Exocet MM-40 missile launchers.

Air Forces

Qatar has a small 2,100-man air force with 18 combat aircraft and 19 armed helicopters. These include two fighter-attack squadrons with 6 Alpha Jets 9 Mirage 2000–5 EDA, and 3 Mirage 2000 DDA. Its attack helicopters include 11 SA342L with HOT air-to-surface missiles, and 8 Commando Mark 3 armed with Exocet antiship missiles. Qatar has no heavy surface-to-air missiles, but has 9 Roland 2 fire units, 24 Mistrals, and a mixture of older manportable surface-to-air missiles including Stingers, 30 Sa-7s, and 10 Blowpipe (may not be operational).

Its transport units include 2 B-707, 1 B-727, 2 Falcon 900, and 1 Airbus A340. Its transport and support helicopters include 4 Commandos.

The air force's small air units have low to moderate readiness, with reasonable pilot training for basic missions and foreign support for most ground activities.

The United Arab Emirates

The UAE is a small and extremely wealthy nation. Much of this wealth is due to its position as a major oil exporter and trading nation in the lower Gulf. It is composed of seven emirates, and while its unity has steadily improved over time, questions still exist about its unity and stability once its current leader, Sheik Zayed of Abu Dhabi, dies. Like Bahrain, Qatar, and Oman, the UAE has cooperated closely with the United States and Britain militarily, and it agreed to provide prepositioning facilities for a U.S. brigade before the Iraq War. The UAE also provided facilities and some support for the United States and Britain during the Iraq War, although Sheik Zayed and most of its leaders opposed the conflict.

These links to the United States and Britain give it the same de facto assurance it will receive protection in the event of invasion by other Gulf states. At the same time, that does not mean it will receive any military support in its dispute with Iran over Iran's seizure of full control over three islands in the Gulf that are claimed by the UAE: Abu Musa and the Greater and Lesser Tunbs. Similarly, the other GCC states have backed the UAE politically in this dispute but are not likely to risk military confrontation with Iran. There also is a history of low-level tension between the UAE, Oman, and Qatar, although such tensions seem to have largely faded in recent years. The end result is that the UAE has pursued its own military development, and not without tension among its member emirates, in spite of the formal unification of its forces.

The UAE has a small native population and has encountered political problems in its attempts to retain foreign manpower. It claims to have 50,500 actives, about 30 percent of whom are expatriates. In practice its active manpower is significantly smaller. It has been a major and often overambitious arms importer, possessing far too little manpower to properly use all its equipment, and has little ability to organize its forces into an effective and combat-ready structure, and project and sustain them at any distance. Recent purchases include 390 LeClerc main battle tanks, nearly 150 other armored vehicles, a number of combat ships, 80 F-16C/D Block 60s with advanced air and air to surface munitions, 10 AH-64s and the upgrade of 30 to the Apache-Longbow, and what may come to total over 90 Mirage 2000 fighters.

Land Forces

The army has a claimed strength of 44,000 men, which makes it large by Southern Gulf standards. This total includes 15,000 men in the forces of Dubai, which has two brigades that are not fully integrated into the other forces. The integrated army is dominated by Abu Dhabi and includes a Royal Guard brigade, two armored brigades, three mechanized infantry brigades, and an artillery brigade. Both a number of the UAE's combat units and support units are badly understrength, and army training and readiness quality is low to moderate by regional standards. There is a large total army equipment pool, although of very mixed quality. It includes 45 aging and worn AMX-30s, 36 OF-40 Mark II, and 360 modern LeClerc main battle tanks—which are either being delivered or converted. The UAE would like to acquire 120 HETs to boost the mobility of the LeClercs.[27] The are 76 Scorpion light tanks, 45 AML-90 armored reconnaissance vehicles, 15 AMX-10P and 415 BMP-3 armored infantry fighting vehicles, and 750 APCs and variants: 370 Panhard M-3, 100 EE-11 Urutu, 136 AAPC, 80 VCR, and 64 Tpz-1 Fuchs. The UAE is close to placing an order for armored nuclear, biological, and chemical detecting reconnaissance vehicles. The front-runner is the Transportpanzer 1 Fuchs NBC.[28] This is a very diverse mix of armor, is hard to support, and a number of vehicles are deadlined. The UAE also has 230 Milan, 25 TOW, and 50 HOT antitank guided weapons (a number on armored vehicles), and 250–300 Carl Gustav 84-mm and 12 M-40 120-mm antitank rocket launchers.

Artillery assets include 181 self-propelled 155-mm weapons: 18 F-3, 78 G-6, and 85 M-109A3; and 90 towed weapons: 70 105-mm ROF and 20 130-mm Type 59. The UAE has some 76 operational multiple rocket launchers and an inventory with 18 LAU-97 70-mm, 48 FIROS-25 and Type 90, and 6 Smerch 9A52 300-mm weapons. The UAE has about 155 81-mm and 120-mm mortars. It also has 6 Scud-B surface-to-surface missile launchers. Its antiaircraft weapons include some 20 Blowpipe and 20 Mistral light surface-to-air missiles, 42 20-mm M-3VDA, and 20 30-mm GCF-BMs self-propelled AA guns.

Naval Forces

The UAE navy has approximately 2,500 men and is based at Abu Dhabi with facilities at Dalma, Mina Zayed. There are also facilities at Mina Rashid and Mina Jabal in Dubai, Mina Sakr in Ras al-Khaimah, and Mina Khalid and Khor Fakkan in Sharjah. Its combat strength consists of two frigates, two corvettes, eight missile patrol craft, six coastal patrol craft, five amphibious craft, two support ships, a small naval aviation branch with 4 SA-316 Alouette and 7 AS-585 Panther helicopters.

Its two Kortenaer class frigates are 3,630-ton Dutch vessels recommissioned and refitted in the late 1990s. They have 2×4 Harpoon launchers, and Sea Sparrow antiair missiles. Their radars, fire control, and battle management systems are relatively modern. The crews were trained in the Netherlands and the ships are active and participate in exercises. The two Muray Jib class corvettes are 630-ton ships commissioned in the early 1990s. They have eight MM-40 Exocet ship-to-ship missiles, and a 1×8 Crotale surface-to-air missile launcher, plus a helicopter hanger. They are well-equipped modern ships, although they lack ASW capability. Both are active.

The UAE has two 260-ton Mubarraz-class and six 2350-ton Ban Yas–class missile patrol boats, with 4 MM-40 Exocet missiles each. They were delivered in the early 1980s and are operational. The Ban Yas–class vessels are being modernized. The UAE is acquiring six Bayunah-class missile patrol boasts with Harpoon or MM-40 ship-to-ship missiles and RAM or Sigma surface-to-air missiles. There are 6 175-ton gunned patrol craft, and 20 light 4-ton patrol craft. The UAE has 4 850-ton LCTs, and is considering buying 3 more. It has 3 650-ton LCUs, and is buying 12 Transportbat 43-ton ships. The Abu Dhabi Shipyards are supplying the navy with 12 Ghannatha-class amphibious troop transports. The transports can carry up to 42 personnel or can be used to deliver mines. Additionally, Abu Dhabi will deliver three landing crafts and will upgrade the Ban Yas missile boats with Block 3 Exocet 2 missiles.[29] Support ships include 1 dividing tender and 3 tugs. The coast guard has 37 inshore patrol craft and 35 harbor patrol craft. The navy has placed an order for an additional 30 9.5m high-speed rigid assault boats.[30]

The UAE navy is not capable of fleet operations without British or U.S. support, and has little joint warfare training or readiness. It is slowly improving in training and readiness, however, and has considerable anti–surface ship firepower.

Air Forces

The air force has a claimed strength of 4,000 men, including the police air wing. It has 106 combat aircraft and 59 armed helicopters. There are three fighter ground attack squadrons with a total of 9 Mirage 2000Es, 17 Hawk 102s, 17 Hawk 63 trainers, and a reconnaissance squadron with 8 Mirage 2000 RADs. There is one fighter squadron with 27 Mirage 2000EADs, a light training attack squadron with 8 MB-326 and 5 MB-339A, and a mixed combat unit with 5 Hawk Mk 61, 4 MB-339, and 6 Mirage 2000 DAD trainers. There is a transport squadron with 14 fixed-wing aircraft, including 4 C-130Hs and 4 leased IL-76s.

The UAE recently ordered an additional 33 Mirage 2000–9 and 80 F-16 Block 60s. The first F-16s will arrive in mid-2004 with the rest to follow over a five-year period. The Mirages will be delivered by mid-2005. The UAE may immediately experience problems with the F-16s as the supplying company has demanded a new contract before any upgrades will be made available.[31] To complement this influx of new aircraft, the air force is looking to purchase approximately 12 jet aircraft trainers to replace its older Hawk trainers. The UAE's 30 Pilatus PC-7 turboprop trainers are also earmarked for retirement, with the Swiss PC-21 the likely successor.[32] The air force would like to acquire up to three E-2C Hawkeye 2000s to for electronic warfare and warning purposes, but the UAE is not likely to come to an agreement anytime soon.[33]

Its attack helicopter assets include 5 AS-332F antiship helicopters with Exocet, 10 SA-342K with HOT, 7 SA-316/319 with AS-11 or AS-12s, 7 AS-565 Panther, and 30 AH-64As. The UAE bought approximately 18 CH-47 Chinook helicopters from Libya. The helicopters, which will be utilized by the special forces, they are in dire need of a complete overhaul. They will not be operational for some time.[34] Last, there are 71 utility and transport helicopters.

There are two air defense brigades with a total of six battalions. These include two I-Hawk battalions, and three light air defense battalions with Rapier, Crotale, Mistral, RBS-70, Javelin, and Igla fire units. Reportedly, the UAE air defense commander stated that the UAE, along with the rest of the GCC, had been studying the possible deployment of both a low- and a high-level ballistic missile interception system. The potential provider and other specifics remain unknown. A study, due by the end of 2003, was interrupted by the Iraq war. However, it is believed that the expenses incurred by such a system would be prohibitive despite the GCC's oil revenue.[35]

Pilot training standards are good by regional standards, as are most aspects of readiness. It should improve strikingly in combat strength and capability once its F-16C/D Apaches and additional Mirage 2000s are delivered.

The air force lacks modern AEW and AC&W assets, however, as well as adequate electronic warfare and maritime patrol capabilities. In a positive development for the air force, the UAE will boost the capabilities of

11 air surveillance radar systems at the cost of $23.8 million.[36] However, the lack of a true, integrated air battle management and sensor system, adequate airborne battle management, sensor, and electronic warfare systems now seriously undermines the UAE's ability to use its other air and air defense assets with maximum effectiveness.

This situation may be changing. The recently built Air Warfare Center at the Al-Dhafra Airbase could have a major impact on the military balance in the Middle East. Built by France, the United States, and Britain, the facility could become the center of coalition operations for the Gulf countries, Egypt, and Britain. Such missions would be limited in scope as the three countries that helped build the center would have to take part. In this manner, though a greater integration of Middle Eastern forces is likely, operations will still be dependent on the West.[37]

Yemen

Yemen is the wild card in the Southern Gulf. In strict terms, it is not a southern Gulf power. It has coasts and islands on the Indian Ocean and Red Sea, and occupies a strategic position at the Bab el Mandab—the narrow strait that controls the entrance to the Red Sea and that every ship passing through the Suez Canal must also traverse. It does, however, share borders with Oman. While Yemen has resolved its border disputes with Oman and Saudi Arabia, there has been a long history of tension between Yemen and its neighbors. Yemen sponsored a violent Marxist insurgent movement and provided it with military support and sanctuary during the Oman's Dhofar rebellion. The Saudi-Yemeni border has a long history of clashes, and smuggling from Yemen to Saudi Arabia—including the supply of arms and explosives for Islamic terrorists—is a continuing problem.

Although Yemen is making progress toward democracy and stability, it has a long history of civil war and violence. It also has a large and rapidly growing population of over 20 million, which its economy cannot support. Only remittances from workers oversea and foreign aid allow the nation to function. This economic and demographic instability, coupled with a long history of tolerating the presence of extremist and terrorist movements when they do not directly threaten the regime, makes Yemen a potential threat to both Oman and Saudi Arabia. Yemen's economic problems have also severely limited its military development, although it has continued to import T-72 (35) and T-55 tanks (100) as well as Su-27 (14) and Mig-29 (50+) combat aircraft.

Land Forces

The Yemeni army has a nominal strength of 60,000 men, many of whom are two-year conscripts. It has some 40,000 reserves, with little or no meaningful reserve training. Its force structure includes 11 armored brigades, 16 infantry brigades, 9 mechanized brigades, 2 airborne and commando brigades, 1 special forces brigade, a central guard force, 7 artillery brigades, and 1 air defense brigade with 4 AA gun and 1 surface-to-air missile battalions. It has 1 surface-to surface missile brigade with 12 FROG, 10 SS-21, and 6/33 Scud missiles. The operational status of most of these missiles is uncertain.

The army has a mix of a wide variety of equipment types, many of which are obsolete or worn. It has 790 main battle tanks, including 30 T-34, 450 T-54/55, 200 T-62, 50 M-60A1, and 60 T-72. Its other armored fighting vehicles include 130 reconnaissance (80 AML-90 and 50 BDRM-2), 200 AIFV (200 BMP-1/2), and 210 operational APCs out of a pool of over 700 (60 M-113s plus a mix of BTR 40, 60, and 152). Yemen has 12 TOW, 24 Dragon, and 35 AT-3 antitank guided weapons, large numbers of rocket launchers, and 75-mm, 82-mm, and 107-mm recoil rifles. Armor and antiarmor training is limited, while armored maneuver warfare capability and sustainability are low.

Yemen has only 25 2S1 122-mm self-propelled artillery weapons, plus 30 worn and obsolescent SU100 100-mm assault guns. It has 310 towed artillery weapons, including 25 M-101a1 105-mm; 30 M-1931/1937, 40 M-1938, and 130 D-30 122-mm weapons; 60 M-46 130-mm, 10 D-20 152-mm, and 15 M-114 155-mm weapons. It also has 36 SM-4-1 coastal defense guns. It has roughly 160–170 operational multiple rocket launchers, including 150 BM-21 122-mm and 14 BM-14 140-mm weapons. Yemen is capable of using artillery effectively in static massed fires, but have very limited capability to rapidly shift fires or target effectively beyond visual range. It has little or no modern fire control, counterbattery radar, and fire management capability.

It has some 302 81-mm, 82-mm, 107-mm, 120-mm, and 160-mm mortars. It has several hundred AA guns include 50 M-167 and 20 M-163 20-mm, 100 ZSU-23-2 and 50 ZSU-23-4 23-mm, 150 M-1939 37-mm, 120 S-60 57-mm, and 40 KS-12 85-mm weapons. It has large numbers of SA-7, Sa-9, SA-13, and Sa-14 light surface-to-air missiles. Air defense training and maneuver warfare capability is minimal to limited.

Yemen has sought ballistic missiles since the 1970s. The Soviet Union was the traditional supplier, but with its eventual breakup North Korea became the primary source. It is believed that Yemen has bought missiles and related items from North Korea for the last ten years. Most recently, Spain intercepted a North Korean ship on December 9, 2002, that was loaded with 15 complete Scud missiles (possibly Scud Cs) as well as fuel and additional warheads. The shipment did not break international law, and the vessel was released after officials stated that the missiles would not be transferred to a third party. Though it is unclear exactly how many and what type of ballistic missiles Yemen possesses due to the secretive nature of their procurement and the use of many in the 1994 civil war, it is believed that it maintains a variety of weapons. It is believed that Yemen has up to 12 9k21 FROG 7-TELs, approximately 10 9P129 SS-21 TELs, around 12 9P117 TELs, and up to 75 Scud B/C missiles. Some of these weapons were delivered in the 1970s, and their effectiveness, especially in light of their performance in the 1994 civil war, is uncertain. A Russian firm has inspected many of Yemen's SS-21s, but both the results and Yemen's upgrade plans remain unknown.[38]

Yemen has large internal security forces, indicative of a country with many internal divisions and tensions. The Ministry of Interior has some 50,000 men and there are at least 20,000 tribal levies.

Naval Forces

The Yemeni navy has 1,700 men and is based on the Indian Ocean and Red Sea at Aden and Hodeida, with smaller bases at Al-Mukalla and at the islands of Perim and Socotra. It is a relatively small navy with six missile patrol boats, six minewarfare ships, one amphibious ship (LCM), and five support ships. Yemen has ordered ten additional patrol boats for the purposes of interdicting traffickers and disrupting terrorists.[39] Readiness, training, and war-fighting capabilities are minimal. Yemen is establishing a small coast guard, but it will only be capable of light patrol duties.

Two of the missile patrol boats—Osa II–class vessels are probably not operational at all. A Tarantul 1–class vessel is operational, but without missiles. The Huganfen-class missile patrol boats are equipped with C-801 ship-to-ship missiles, but only one is fully operational with missiles on board. The operational status of one of the mine ships, a Natya-class minesweeper, is uncertain. At least two of the other five Yevgenya-class minehunters are operational, but probably can only be used for mine-laying purposes. The smaller patrol boats—two 39-ton Zhuck-class, and 6 12-ton Baklan-class are operational. The LCM is a new, 1,388-ton ship, delivered in 1999, and is an update of the Polnochny-class. The support ships include two 165-ton LCUs dating back to the 1980s, and three modern Polish-made 221-ton LCUs.

The navy is not capable of independent operations against a regional naval power like Iran, Oman, Saudi Arabia or Egypt, but could mine the Strait of Bab el Mandab or shipping routes in the Red Sea. It could also harass shipping traffic.

Air Forces

The Yemeni air force has a nominal strength of 4,500–5,000 men, including its air defense element. It has suffered badly from a lack of modernization and foreign support in recent years. At least 40 of its aircraft are in storage, and large numbers of the 76 aircraft counted as active combat aircraft have limited or no real operational capability. It will not be able to recover as an effective force unless it receives the MiG-29s and Su-17s said to be on order. Pilot training is limited, and Yemen lacks anything approaching a modern command and control, battle management, or air control and warning system for either its air units or land-based air defenses.

Yemen's air assets include 10 F-5E and 30 Su-20/22 attack fighters, and 20 MiG-21 and 10 MiG-29 fighters. A total of 2 F-5B and 4 Mig-21 training aircraft are said to be combat capable. It has 8 Mi-35 attack helicopters of unknown readiness and sustainability. Its transport assets include 2 AN-123, 6 An-26, 3 C-130H, 4 IL-14, and 3 IL-76, and its utility and transport helicopters include 2 AB-212, 1'4 Mi-8, and 1 AB-47.

Its land based air defense units have a nominal strength of some 1,500–2,000 men. They are equipped with SA-2, SA-3, and Sa-6 heavy surface-to-air missiles, but it is unclear how many are operational or sustainable in combat and few—if any—have been modernized to improve their resistance to jamming and detection. Yemen also has large numbers of AA guns and lighter SA-7, SA-9, SA-13, and SA-14 manportable and vehicle mounted light surface-to-air missiles, but their operational status is unknown.

Chapter 8

Gulf Conventional Military Forces

Chapters 6 and 7 have shown in depth why comparisons of Gulf conventional military forces disguise major problems in military capability. This does not, however, make such comparisons unimportant. The figures in the present chapter describe very real military capabilities that history has shown may become involved in conflicts with little or no warning. At the same time, comparisons of the strength of the conventional forces, and the military buildup of the various Gulf states, provide important insights into the military strengths and weaknesses of each state, and the problems they face in modernizing and restructuring their forces.

- Figure 8.1 shows the radical shifts taking place in Gulf demographics, and that high population growth is greatly reducing the problems the Southern Gulf states have had in manning their forces. At the same time, it shows that Iranian, Iraqi, Saudi, and Yemeni population growth is so high that it is placing a massive strain on their respective economies and ability to fund military forces. In any case, the problem all the Gulf states face is manpower quality and not manpower quantity.

- Figure 8.2 shows the massive level of spending on new arms imports during 1994–2003. It is clear that Saudi Arabia has outspent all of the other Gulf states, and equally clear that Iran and Iraq were virtually forced to drop out of the regional arms race—at least in terms of comparative spending on conventional arms. It is also clear that the United Arab Emirates (UAE) is spending far more than is justified by the effectiveness of the forces it is creating.

- Figure 8.3 provides a count of comparative major equipment strength. The fact Iraq's 2,600 main battle tanks and 316 combat aircraft are no longer part

Figure 8.1
Population Growth in the Gulf

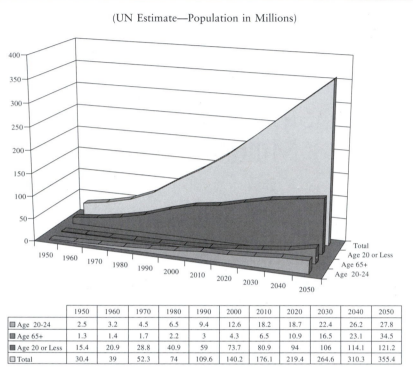

(UN Estimate—Population in Millions)

	1950	1960	1970	1980	1990	2000	2010	2020	2030	2040	2050
▣ Age 20-24	2.5	3.2	4.5	6.5	9.4	12.6	18.2	18.7	22.4	26.2	27.8
▣ Age 65+	1.3	1.4	1.7	2.2	3	4.3	6.5	10.9	16.5	23.1	34.5
▣ Age 20 or Less	15.4	20.9	28.8	40.9	59	73.7	80.9	94	106	114.1	121.2
▢ Total	30.4	39	52.3	74	109.6	140.2	176.1	219.4	264.6	310.3	355.4

Source: Adapted by Anthony H. Cordesman from data provided by the U.S. Census Bureau.

of the count illustrates just how much the regional balance has changed as a result of the Iraq War. At the same time, it is clear that weapons strength is in no way proportionate to the comparative size of arms imports—reflecting the tendency to keep large amounts of obsolescent and low grade equipment in service even if it contributes little to military effectiveness.

- Figure 8.4 shows the historical trend in military manpower. It is clear that Iran and Iraq long had far larger forces than those of the Southern Gulf states. Once again, the elimination of Iraq makes a critical difference. Iran continues to have far more military manpower than Saudi Arabia, but the effectiveness of this manpower is severely limited by the problems in Iran's pool of military equipment.

- Figure 8.5 provides a similar comparison, but with the actual manpower numbers for each country. It is clear that Saudi manpower has increased sharply relative to that of Iran over time, and that the Southern Gulf states have the cumulative manpower to support effective collective defense. In practice, how-

Figure 8.2
Gulf Arms Agreements and Deliveries by Country: 1994–2002

(Arms Agreements and Deliveries to North African nations in $U.S. Current Millions)

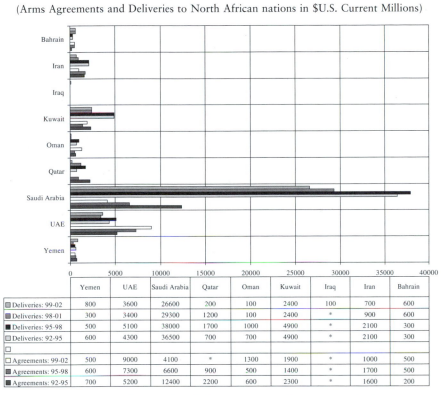

	Yemen	UAE	Saudi Arabia	Qatar	Oman	Kuwait	Iraq	Iran	Bahrain
▨ Deliveries: 99-02	800	3600	26600	200	100	2400	100	700	600
▥ Deliveries: 98-01	300	3400	29300	1200	100	2400	*	900	600
■ Deliveries: 95-98	500	5100	38000	1700	1000	4900	*	2100	300
☐ Deliveries: 92-95	600	4300	36500	700	700	4900	*	2100	300
☐									
☐ Agreements: 99-02	500	9000	4100	*	1300	1900	*	1000	500
■ Agreements: 95-98	600	7300	6600	900	500	1400	*	1700	500
■ Agreements: 92-95	700	5200	12400	2200	600	2300	*	1600	200

0 = Data less than $50 million or nil. All data rounded to the nearest $100 million.
Source: Richard F. Grimmett, *Conventional Arms Transfers to the Developing Nations*, Congressional Research Service, various editions.

ever, coordination and interoperability remains extremely limited, robbing the smaller Gulf states of much of their potential military effectiveness.

- Figure 8.6 shows military manpower by service. It illustrates a relatively heavy emphasis on air force and air defense manpower for most countries, and naval manning too small to support effective navies without extensive foreign civilian support. If the data on land forces are compared to the later figures on land force equipment, it is also clear that the manpower pool of most smaller Southern Gulf countries is too small to properly crew and support the pool of weaponry in their land forces.

- Figures 8.7 through 8.16 display the trends in armor, tanks, and artillery. Figure 8.7 again shows that Iran and Iraq had a far larger pool of equipment

Figure 8.3
Major Measures of Key Combat Equipment Strength in 2004

Total Main Battle Tanks in Inventory

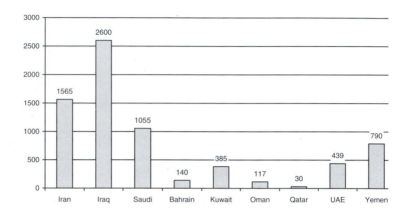

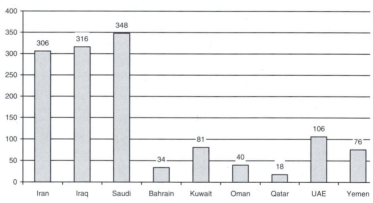
Total Fixed-Wing Combat Aircraft

Source: Adapted by Anthony H. Cordesman from various sources 2003–2004; and IISS, *The Military Balance.*

than their recent arms imports could possibly maintain and modernize. It is also again clear how much the destruction of Iraq's forces have affected the conventional balance.

- Figure 8.8 shows the trends in main battle tanks and the impacts that the Iran-Iraq War and Gulf War had on the respective holding of Iran and Iraq. It also shows the cumulative growth in the holdings of the Southern Gulf states, although Saudi strength has been relatively static since the early 1990s.

Figure 8.4
Comparative Trends in Gulf Total Active Military Manpower: 1979–2004

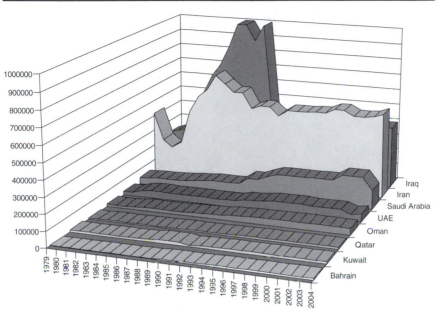

Note: Saudi totals include full-time active National Guard, Omani totals include Royal Guard, Iranian totals include Revolutionary Guards, and Iraqi totals include Republican Guards and Special Republican Guards.
Source: Estimated by Anthony H. Cordesman using data from various editions of IISS *The Military Balance*; *Jane's Sentinel*; and *Military Technology*.

- Figure 8.9 shows that the trends in high quality tanks are radically different from those in the previous figure, and that Saudi numbers have near parity with Iran (whose tanks are generally still sharply inferior to those of Saudi Arabia and most of the smaller Southern Gulf states).

- Figure 8.10 shows that Iran does not have anything like the number of other armored fighting vehicles necessary to support its strength in main battle tanks, and how much the destruction of Iraq's land forces have changed this aspect of the balance. In general, the smaller Southern Gulf states have also developed a good balance of tanks and other armored vehicles.

- Figure 8.11 shows the distribution of current holdings of other armored vehicles by kind. It reflects that lack of armored mobility in Iran's forces. At the same time, it is clear that each Southern Gulf state has developed a different force mix with little regard to interoperability.

- Figure 8.12 provides a breakout of current holdings of other armored vehicles by specific type (although it does not attempt to show the submodels). The

Figure 8.5
Total Active Military Manpower in All Gulf Forces: 1993–2004

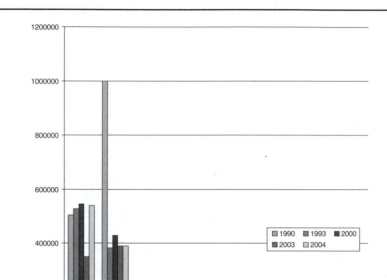

	Iran	Iraq	Saudi Arabia	Bahrain	Kuwait	Oman	Qatar	UAE	Yemen
1990	504000	1000000	102500	6000	20300	29500	7500	44000	38500
1993	528000	382500	157000	6150	11700	35700	7500	54000	38500
2000	545600	429000	162500	11000	15300	43500	11800	64500	66300
2003	350000	389000	199500	10700	15500	41700	12400	41500	66500
2004	540,000	389000	150,000	11,200	15,500	41,700	12,400	50,500	66,700

Note: Saudi totals include full-time active National Guard, Omani totals include Royal Guard, Iranian totals include Revolutionary Guards, and Iraqi totals include Republican Guards and Special Republican Guards.
Source: Estimated by Anthony H. Cordesman using data from various editions of IISS, *The Military Balance*; *Jane's Sentinel*; and *Military Technology*.

lack of standardization is even more apparent. So is the tendency to retain and rely on older and obsolescent types in a number of Gulf armies.

• Figure 8.13 compares total numbers of APCs—a measure of infantry mobility and maneuver capability. The lack of Iranian capability is particularly striking, although Saudi Arabia, Kuwait, and the UAE are the only Southern Gulf states with a proper balance of such mobility.

• Figure 8.14 compares artillery strength. Iran's massive buildup of such weapons during the Iran-Iraq War is still a major factor in the Gulf balance. This

Figure 8.6
Total Gulf Military Manpower by Service in 2004

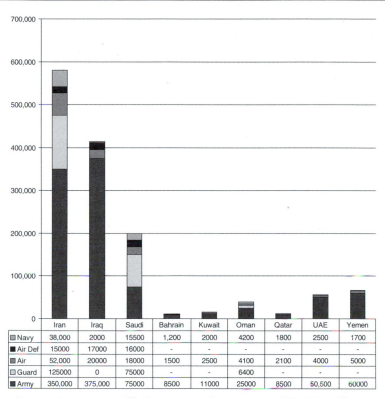

	Iran	Iraq	Saudi	Bahrain	Kuwait	Oman	Qatar	UAE	Yemen
☐ Navy	38,000	2000	15500	1,200	2000	4200	1800	2500	1700
■ Air Def	15000	17000	16000	-	-	-	-	-	-
■ Air	52,000	20000	18000	1500	2500	4100	2100	4000	5000
☐ Guard	125000	0	75000	-	-	6400	-	-	-
■ Army	350,000	375,000	75000	8500	11000	25000	8500	50,500	60000

Source: Estimated by Anthony H. Cordesman using data from IISS, *The Military Balance*, various editions.

is the area where Iran has its greatest lead over the Southern Gulf states. It is also clear, however, that almost all of the Iranian lead is in towed weapons, and its artillery maneuver strength is severely limited.

- Figures 8.15 and 8.16 show the comparative strength of multiple rocket launchers. Once again, Iran has a major lead. Yemen also has comparatively large numbers of such weapons. Multiple rocket launchers provide a partial substitute for air power and can deliver large amounts of area fire, although generally with limited accuracy.

- Figures 8.17 through 8.22 display data on combat aircraft, armed helicopters, and electronic warfare aircraft.

- Figure 8.17 shows total operational combat air strength. Iran has slowly built up much of the strength it lost after the fall of the Shah and in the Iran-Iraq War. The Iraqi air force lost roughly half of its strength during the Gulf War in 1991, and effectively ceased to exist in 2003. Saudi Arabia has good strength

Figure 8.7
Total Gulf Operational Armored Fighting Vehicles in 2004

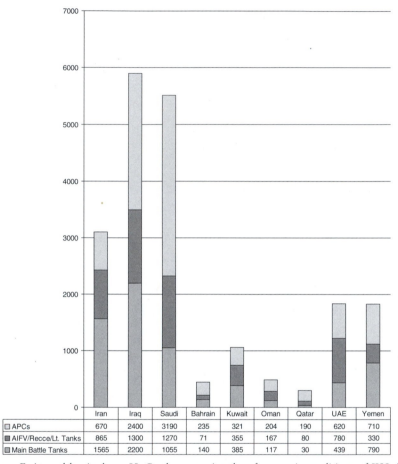

	Iran	Iraq	Saudi	Bahrain	Kuwait	Oman	Qatar	UAE	Yemen
APCs	670	2400	3190	235	321	204	190	620	710
AIFV/Recce/Lt. Tanks	865	1300	1270	71	355	167	80	780	330
Main Battle Tanks	1565	2200	1055	140	385	117	30	439	790

Source: Estimated by Anthony H. Cordesman using data from various editions of IISS, *The Military Balance*; and *Jane's Sentinel*.

figures, but limited training, readiness, and sustainability. The UAE has good numbers for a country its size, but limited real-world effectiveness. The Yemeni air force lost much of its forces because of civil war and funding reasons.

- Figure 8.18 compares total fixed-wing and armed helicopter strength. The growing importance of armed helicopters in the Southern Gulf is apparent. The Iranian holdings are largely worn and obsolescent and the Iraqi armed helicopter forces no longer exist.

Figure 8.8
Total Operational Main Battle Tanks in All Gulf Forces: 1979–2004

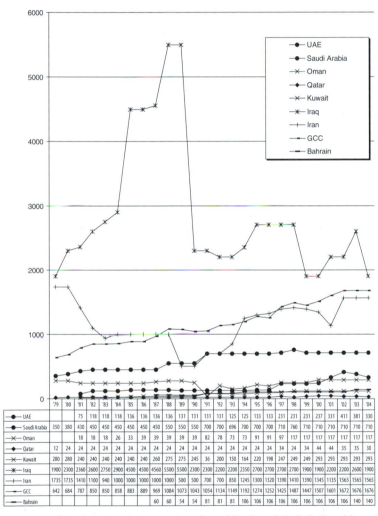

	'79	'80	'81	'82	'83	'84	'85	'86	'87	'88	'89	'90	'91	'92	'93	'94	'95	'96	'97	'98	'99	'00	'01	'02	'03	'04
●— UAE				75	118	118	118	136	136	136	136	131	131	131	131	125	125	133	133	231	231	237	331	411	381	330
●— Saudi Arabia	350	380	430	450	450	450	450	450	450	550	550	550	700	700	696	700	700	700	710	760	710	710	710	710	710	710
—✕— Oman			18	18	18	26	33	39	39	39	39	39	82	78	73	73	91	91	97	117	117	117	117	117	117	117
—◆— Qatar	12	24	24	24	24	24	24	24	24	24	24	24	24	24	24	24	24	24	34	24	34	44	44	35	35	30
—✕— Kuwait	280	280	240	240	240	240	240	240	260	275	275	245	36	200	150	164	220	198	247	249	249	293	293	293	293	293
—✳— Iraq	1900	2300	2360	2600	2750	2900	4500	4500	4560	5500	5500	2300	2300	2200	2200	2350	2700	2700	2700	2700	1900	1900	2200	2200	2600	1900
—+— Iran	1735	1735	1410	1100	940	1000	1000	1000	1000	1000	500	500	700	700	850	1245	1300	1320	1390	1410	1390	1345	1135	1565	1565	1565
—— GCC	642	684	787	850	850	858	883	889	969	1084	1073	1043	1054	1134	1149	1192	1274	1252	1425	1487	1447	1507	1601	1672	1676	1676
—■— Bahrain								60	60	54	54	81	81	81	106	106	106	106	106	106	106	106	106	106	140	140

Note: Iranian totals include Revolutionary Guards, and Iraqi totals include Republican Guards and Special Republican Guards.

Source: Estimated by Anthony H. Cordesman using data from IISS, *The Military Balance*, various editions.

Figure 8.9
Medium- to High-Quality Main Battle Tanks by Type in 2004

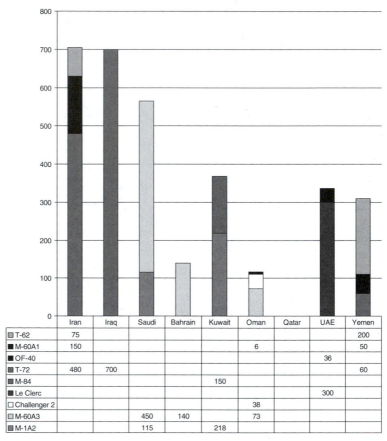

	Iran	Iraq	Saudi	Bahrain	Kuwait	Oman	Qatar	UAE	Yemen
▦ T-62	75								200
■ M-60A1	150					6			50
■ OF-40								36	
▩ T-72	480	700							60
▩ M-84					150				
■ Le Clerc								300	
☐ Challenger 2						38			
☐ M-60A3			450	140		73			
▩ M-1A2			115		218				

Source: Estimated by Anthony H. Cordesman using data from IISS, *The Military Balance*, various editions.

- Figure 8.19 shows Saudi Arabia's advantage over Iran in terms of high-quality aircraft. At the same time, it again shows the lack of standardization and the interoperability problems of the Southern Gulf states.

- Figure 8.20 reflects the limited emphasis on reconnaissance aircraft capability in the Gulf region, and the limitations to situation awareness and targeting. The problems for the Southern Gulf states will, however, be of limited importance if they operate in a coalition with the United States.

- Figure 8.21 shows that Saudi Arabia has a monopoly of airborne warning and control systems, and that its AWACS aircraft give it a major advantage in battle management, some forms of intelligence collect and air force maritime patrol

Figure 8.10
**Total Operational Other Armored Vehicles (Lt. Tanks, LAVs, AIFVs, APCs, Recce)
in Gulf Forces: 1993–2004**

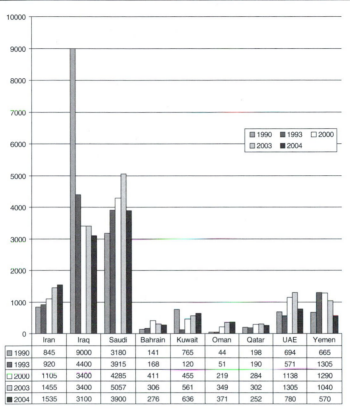

	Iran	Iraq	Saudi	Bahrain	Kuwait	Oman	Qatar	UAE	Yemen
1990	845	9000	3180	141	765	44	198	694	665
1993	920	4400	3915	168	120	51	190	571	1305
2000	1105	3400	4285	411	455	219	284	1138	1290
2003	1455	3400	5057	306	561	349	302	1305	1040
2004	1535	3100	3900	276	636	371	252	780	570

Note: Iranian totals include active forces in the Revolutionary Guards. Saudi totals include
active National Guard. Omani totals include Royal Household Guard.
Source: Adapted by Anthony H. Cordesman from various sources; and IISS, *The Military
Balance*, various editions.

capability—although Iran still operates aging U.S.-supplied maritime patrol
aircraft.

- Figure 8.22 shows the balance of combat helicopters. Saudi Arabia has been
  relative slow to build up its forces, but those of Iran are worn and obsolescent and Iraq's forces have effectively ceased to exist.

- Figure 8.23 shows that Saudi Arabia has the only modern mix of advanced
  land-based defenses in the Gulf, Iran has extensive assets, but many are obsolete or obsolescent, and they are poorly netted and vulnerable to electronic
  warfare. Iraq's assets have effectively ceased to exist. The smaller Southern
  Gulf states have a wide mix of assets, purchased with little attention to

Figure 8.11
Gulf Other Armored Fighting Vehicles (OAFVs) by Category in 2004

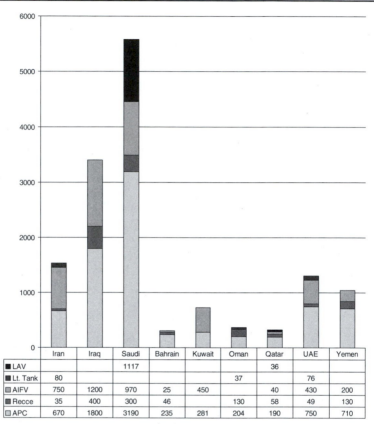

	Iran	Iraq	Saudi	Bahrain	Kuwait	Oman	Qatar	UAE	Yemen
■ LAV			1117				36		
■ Lt. Tank	80					37		76	
▨ AIFV	750	1200	970	25	450		40	430	200
■ Recce	35	400	300	46		130	58	49	130
▨ APC	670	1800	3190	235	281	204	190	750	710

Note: Iranian totals include active forces in the Revolutionary Guards. Saudi totals include active National Guard. Omani totals include Royal Household Guard.
Source: Adapted by Anthony H. Cordesman from various sources; and IISS, *The Military Balance*, various editions.

interoperability, which generally would have limited effectiveness because of a lack of effective long-range sensors, battle management systems training and readiness, and strategic depth.

• Figures 8.24 through 8.28 compares combat ship strength. The qualitative issues affecting the forces have been described earlier. Iran has the only significant Gulf navy. Saudi Arabia has significant total ship strength, and better and more modern ships, but limited readiness and proficiency. The lack of interoperability, specialization, and orientation around key missions leaves most Southern Gulf navies with only limited ability to cooperate. So does a lack of effective airborne surveillance, modern minewarfare ships, and ASW capabilities.

Figure 8.12
Armored Infantry Fighting Vehicles, Reconnaissance Vehicles, LAVs, and Light
Tanks by Type in 2004

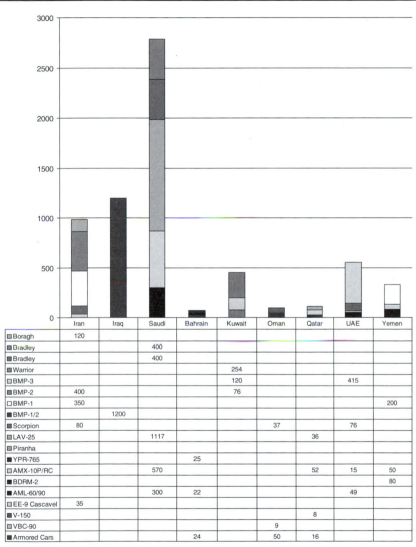

	Iran	Iraq	Saudi	Bahrain	Kuwait	Oman	Qatar	UAE	Yemen
Boragh	120								
Bradley			400						
Bradley			400						
Warrior					254				
BMP-3					120			415	
BMP-2	400				76				
BMP-1	350								200
BMP-1/2		1200							
Scorpion	80					37		76	
LAV-25			1117				36		
Piranha									
YPR-765				25					
AMX-10P/RC			570				52	15	50
BDRM-2									80
AML-60/90			300	22				49	
EE-9 Cascavel	35								
V-150							8		
VBC-90						9			
Armored Cars				24		50	16		

Note: Iranian totals include active forces in the Revolutionary Guards. Saudi totals include
  active National Guard. Omani totals include Royal Household Guard.
Source: Adapted by Anthony H. Cordesman from various sources; and IISS, *The Military
  Balance*, various editions.

Figure 8.13
Armored Personnel Carriers (APCs) in Gulf Armies in 2004

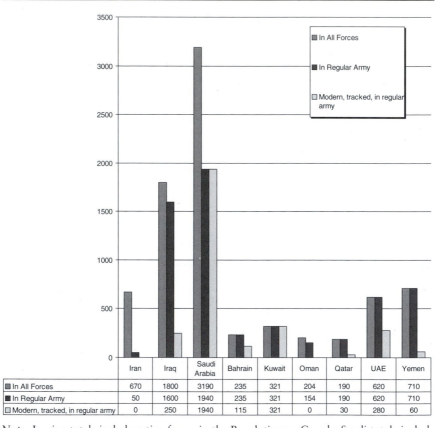

	Iran	Iraq	Saudi Arabia	Bahrain	Kuwait	Oman	Qatar	UAE	Yemen
■ In All Forces	670	1800	3190	235	321	204	190	620	710
■ In Regular Army	50	1600	1940	235	321	154	190	620	710
☐ Modern, tracked, in regular army	0	250	1940	115	321	0	30	280	60

Note: Iranian totals include active forces in the Revolutionary Guards. Saudi totals include active National Guard. Omani totals include Royal Household Guard.

Source: Adapted by Anthony H. Cordesman from various sources; and IISS, *The Military Balance*, various editions.

Figure 8.14
Total Operational Self-Propelled and Towed Tube Artillery and Multiple Rocket
Launchers in Gulf Forces: 1993–2004

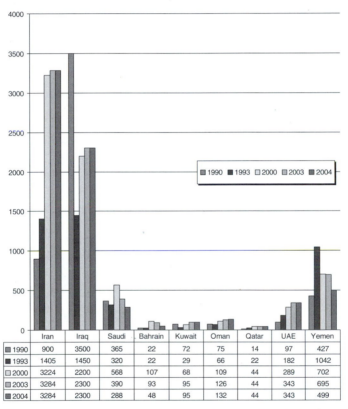

	Iran	Iraq	Saudi	Bahrain	Kuwait	Oman	Qatar	UAE	Yemen
■ 1990	900	3500	365	22	72	75	14	97	427
■ 1993	1405	1450	320	22	29	66	22	182	1042
□ 2000	3224	2200	568	107	68	109	44	289	702
□ 2003	3284	2300	390	93	95	126	44	343	695
■ 2004	3284	2300	288	48	95	132	44	343	499

Note: Iranian totals include active forces in the Revolutionary Guards. Saudi totals include
   active National Guard. Omani totals include Royal Household Guard.
Source: Adapted by Anthony H. Cordesman from various sources; and IISS, *The Military
   Balance*, various editions.

Figure 8.15
Total Operational Gulf Artillery Weapons in 2004

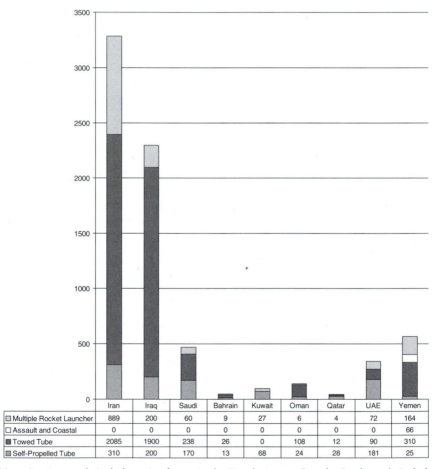

	Iran	Iraq	Saudi	Bahrain	Kuwait	Oman	Qatar	UAE	Yemen
☐ Multiple Rocket Launcher	889	200	60	9	27	6	4	72	164
☐ Assault and Coastal	0	0	0	0	0	0	0	0	66
■ Towed Tube	2085	1900	238	26	0	108	12	90	310
▨ Self-Propelled Tube	310	200	170	13	68	24	28	181	25

Note: Iranian totals include active forces in the Revolutionary Guards. Saudi totals include
active National Guard. Omani totals include Royal Household Guard.
Source: Adapted by Anthony H. Cordesman from various sources; and IISS, *The Military
Balance*, various editions.

Figure 8.16
Gulf Inventory of Multiple Rocket Launchers by Caliber in 2004

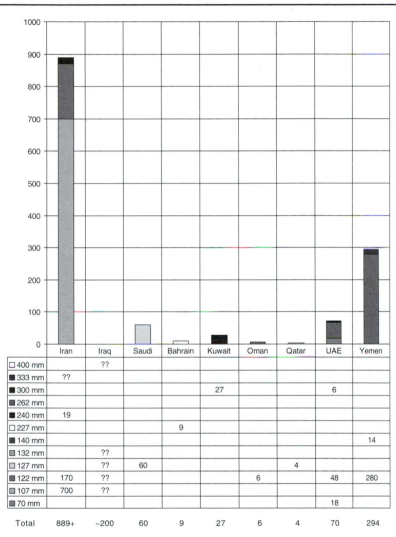

	Iran	Iraq	Saudi	Bahrain	Kuwait	Oman	Qatar	UAE	Yemen
☐ 400 mm		??							
■ 333 mm	??								
■ 300 mm					27			6	
■ 262 mm									
■ 240 mm	19								
☐ 227 mm				9					
■ 140 mm									14
▨ 132 mm		??							
☐ 127 mm		??	60				4		
■ 122 mm	170	??				6		48	280
▨ 107 mm	700	??							
▨ 70 mm								18	
Total	889+	~200	60	9	27	6	4	70	294

Note: Iranian totals include active forces in the Revolutionary Guards. Saudi totals include active National Guard. Omani totals include Royal Household Guard. Iraq has a total of approximately 200 Multiple Rocket Launchers.

Source: Adapted by Anthony H. Cordesman from various sources; and IISS, *The Military Balance*, various editions.

371

Figure 8.17
Total Operational Combat Aircraft in All Gulf Forces: 1993–2003

(Does not include stored or unarmed electronic warfare, recce or trainer aircraft)

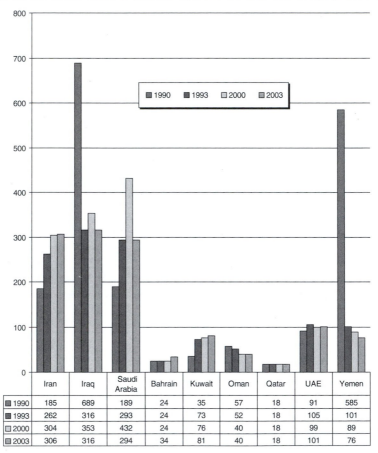

	Iran	Iraq	Saudi Arabia	Bahrain	Kuwait	Oman	Qatar	UAE	Yemen
■ 1990	185	689	189	24	35	57	18	91	585
■ 1993	262	316	293	24	73	52	18	105	101
□ 2000	304	353	432	24	76	40	18	99	89
■ 2003	306	316	294	34	81	40	18	101	76

Source: Adapted by Anthony H. Cordesman from various sources; and IISS, *The Military Balance*, various editions.

372

Figure 8.18
Total Gulf Holdings of Combat Aircraft in 2004

Fixed-Wing Combat Aircraft

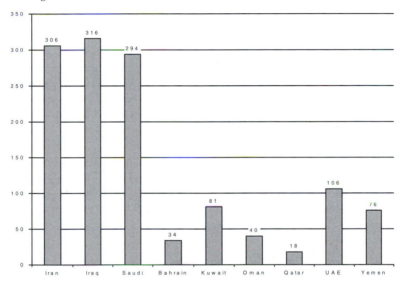

Armed and Attack Helicopters

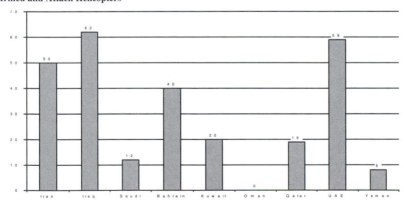

Note: Only armed or combat-capable fixed-wing combat aircraft are counted, not other trainers or aircraft. Yemen has an additional 5 MiG-29S/UB on order.
Source: Adapted by Anthony H. Cordesman from IISS, *The Military Balance*, various editions.

Figure 8.19
Gulf High- and Medium-Quality Fixed-Wing Fighter, Fighter Attack, Attack, Strike, and Multirole Combat Aircraft by Type in 2004

(Totals do not include combat-capable recce but do include OCUs and Hawk combat-capable trainers)

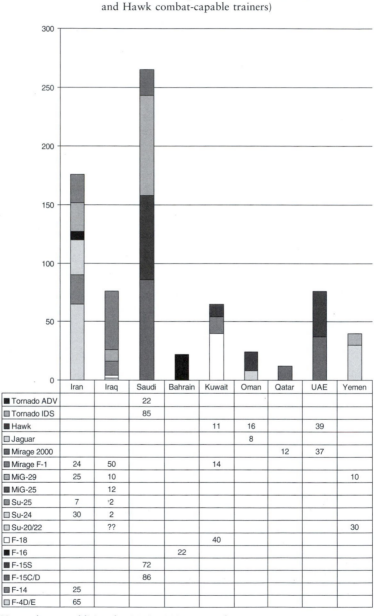

	Iran	Iraq	Saudi	Bahrain	Kuwait	Oman	Qatar	UAE	Yemen
■ Tornado ADV			22						
▢ Tornado IDS			85						
■ Hawk					11	16		39	
▢ Jaguar						8			
■ Mirage 2000								12	37
■ Mirage F-1	24	50			14				
▢ MiG-29	25	10							10
■ MiG-25		12							
▢ Su-25	7	‘2							
▢ Su-24	30	2							
▢ Su-20/22		??							30
▢ F-18					40				
■ F-16				22					
■ F-15S			72						
■ F-15C/D			86						
■ F-14	25								
▢ F-4D/E	65								

Note: Yemen has an additional 5 MiG-29S/UB on order.
Source: Adapted by Anthony H. Cordesman from various sources; and IISS, *The Military Balance*, various editions.

374

Figure 8.20
Gulf Reconnaissance Aircraft in 2004

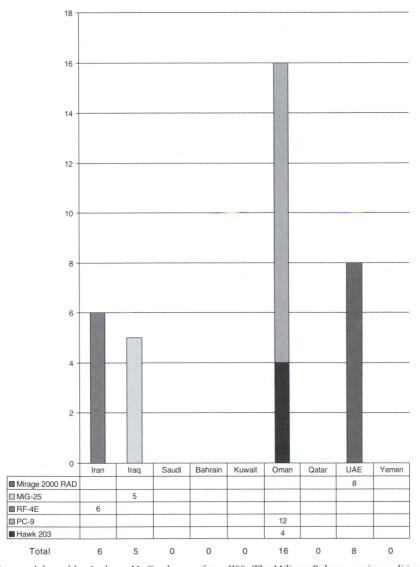

	Iran	Iraq	Saudi	Bahrain	Kuwait	Oman	Qatar	UAE	Yemen
■ Mirage 2000 RAD								8	
□ MiG-25		5							
■ RF-4E	6								
□ PC-9						12			
■ Hawk 203						4			
Total	6	5	0	0	0	16	0	8	0

Source: Adapted by Anthony H. Cordesman from IISS, *The Military Balance*, various editions.

Figure 8.21
Sensor, AWACS, C⁴I, EW, and ELINT Aircraft in 2003

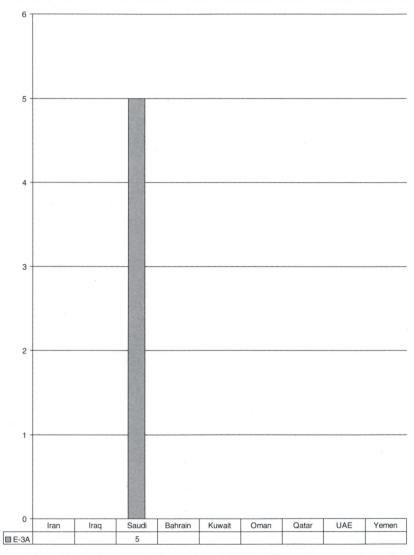

	Iran	Iraq	Saudi	Bahrain	Kuwait	Oman	Qatar	UAE	Yemen
E-3A			5						

Source: Adapted by Anthony H. Cordesman from IISS, *The Military Balance*, various editions.

Figure 8.22
Gulf Attack, Antiship, and ASW Helicopters in 2004

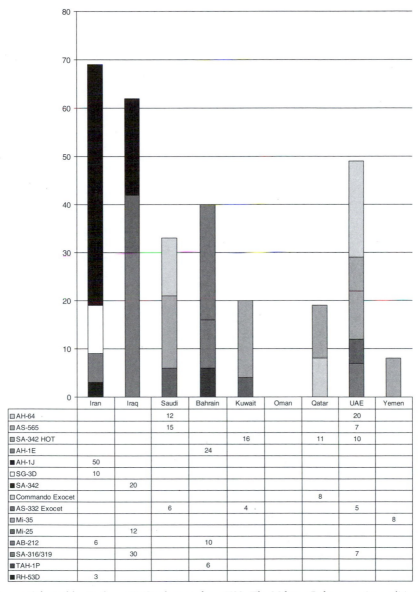

	Iran	Iraq	Saudi	Bahrain	Kuwait	Oman	Qatar	UAE	Yemen
☐ AH-64			12					20	
▨ AS-565			15					7	
▩ SA-342 HOT					16		11	10	
■ AH-1E				24					
■ AH-1J	50								
☐ SG-3D	10								
■ SA-342		20							
☐ Commando Exocet							8		
■ AS-332 Exocet			6		4			5	
▨ Mi-35									8
■ Mi-25		12							
▨ AB-212	6			10					
▨ SA-316/319		30						7	
■ TAH-1P				6					
■ RH-53D	3								

Source: Adapted by Anthony H. Cordesman from IISS, *The Military Balance*, various editions.

Figure 8.23
Gulf Land-Based Air Defense Systems in 2004

Country	Major SAM	Light SAM	AA Guns
Bahrain	8 I Hawk	60 RBS-70 18 Stinger 7 Crotale	15 Oerlikon 35-mm 12 L/70 40-mm
Iran	16/150 I Hawk 3/10 SA-5 45 HQ-2J (SA-2) ? SA-2	SA-7/14/16, HQ-7 HN-5 30 Rapier FM-80 (Ch Crotale) 15 Tigercat SA-7 Stinger (?)	1,700 Guns ZU-23, ZSU-23-4, ZSU-57-2, KS-19 ZPU-2/4, M-1939, Type 55
Iraq	SA-2 SA-3 SA-6	Roland 1,500 SA-7 850 (SA-8, SA-9 SA-13, SA-14, SA-16)	6,000 Guns ZSU-23-4 23-mm, M-1939 37-mm, ZSU-57-2 SP, 57-mm 85-mm, 100-mm, 130-mm
Kuwait	4/24 I Hawk 4-5/40 Patriot	6/12 Aspede 48 Starburst	6/2×35-mm Oerlikon
Oman	None	Blowpipe 2 Mistral SP 34 SA-7 14 *Javelin* 40 Rapier	10 GDF 35-mm/Skyguard 4 ZU-23-2 23-mm 12 L-60 40-mm

378

Qatar	None	10 Blowpipe 12 *Stinger* 9 Roland 20 SA-7, 24 Mistral	?
Saudi Arabia	16/128 I Hawk 4-6/16-24 Patriot 17/68 Shahine Mobile	189 Crotale 400 Stinger 500 Mistral *500 Redeye* 40 Crotale 73-141 Shahine static	50 AMX-30SA 30-mm 92 M-163 Vulcan 20-mm 150 L-70 40-mm (in store)
UAE	5/30 I Hawk Bty.	20+ Blowpipe *Mistral* 12 Rapier 9 Crotale 13 RBS-70 100 Mistral Javelin Igla (SA-16)	42 M-3VDA 20-mm SP 20 GCF-BM2 30-mm
Yemen	SA-2, SA3, SA-6 SA-7, SA-9, SA-13 SA-14	SA-7, SA-9, SA13, SA-14 800 SA-7/9/13/14	52 M-167 20-mm 20 M-163 Vulcan 20-mm 100 ZSU-23-4 23-mm 150 M-1939 23-mm 120 S-60 37-mm KS-12 85-mm

Note: Some data adjusted or estimated by the author.
Source: Adapted by Anthony H. Cordesman from IISS, *The Military Balance; Periscope;* JCSS, *Middle East Military Balance; Jane's Sentinel;* and *Jane's Defense Weekly.*

Figure 8.24
Gulf Naval Ships by Category in 2004

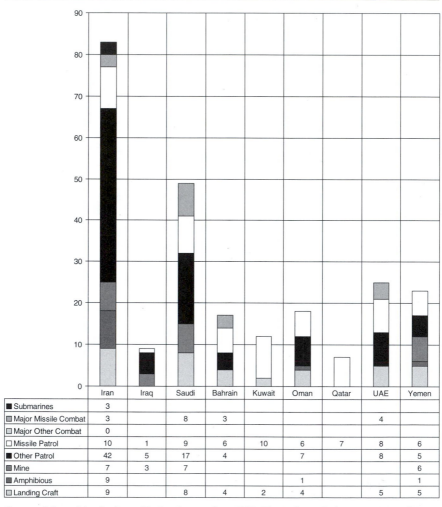

	Iran	Iraq	Saudi	Bahrain	Kuwait	Oman	Qatar	UAE	Yemen
■ Submarines	3								
▨ Major Missile Combat	3		8	3				4	
▢ Major Other Combat	0								
▢ Missile Patrol	10	1	9	6	10	6	7	8	6
■ Other Patrol	42	5	17	4		7		8	5
▨ Mine	7	3	7						6
■ Amphibious	9					1			1
▢ Landing Craft	9		8	4	2	4		5	5

Source: Adapted by Anthony H. Cordesman from IISS, *The Military Balance*, various editions.

Figure 8.25
Gulf Warships with Antiship Missiles in 2004

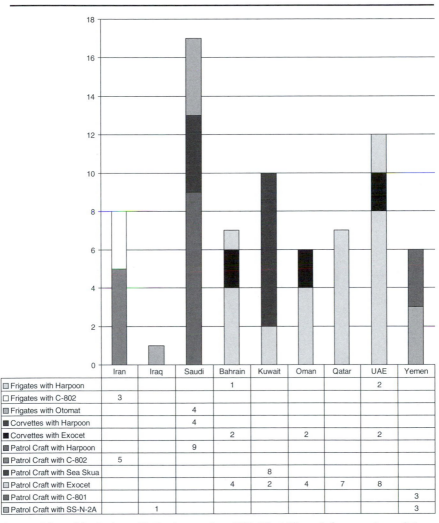

	Iran	Iraq	Saudi	Bahrain	Kuwait	Oman	Qatar	UAE	Yemen
☐ Frigates with Harpoon				1				2	
☐ Frigates with C-802	3								
▨ Frigates with Otomat			4						
■ Corvettes with Harpoon			4						
■ Corvettes with Exocet				2		2		2	
■ Patrol Craft with Harpoon			9						
■ Patrol Craft with C-802	5								
■ Patrol Craft with Sea Skua					8				
☐ Patrol Craft with Exocet				4	2	4	7	8	
■ Patrol Craft with C-801									3
▨ Patrol Craft with SS-N-2A		1							3

Source: Adapted by Anthony H. Cordesman from IISS, *The Military Balance*, various editions;
and material provided by U.S. experts.

Figure 8.26
Gulf Mine Warfare Ships in 2004

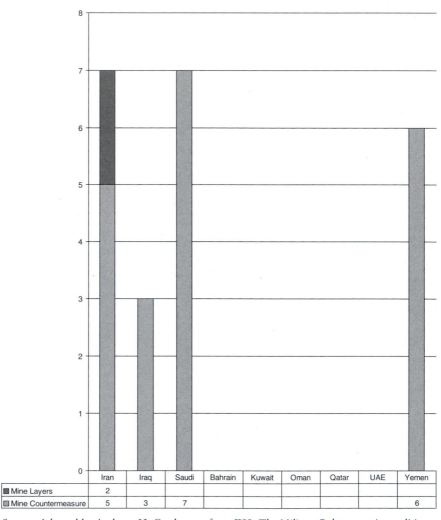

	Iran	Iraq	Saudi	Bahrain	Kuwait	Oman	Qatar	UAE	Yemen
■ Mine Layers	2								
▨ Mine Countermeasure	5	3	7						6

Source: Adapted by Anthony H. Cordesman from IISS, *The Military Balance*, various editions; and material provided by U.S. experts.

382

Figure 8.27
Gulf Amphibious Warfare Ships in 2004

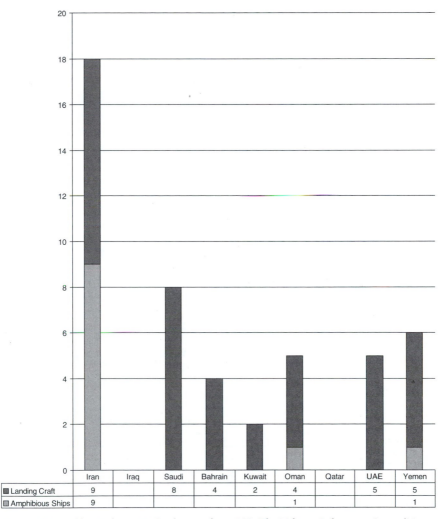

	Iran	Iraq	Saudi	Bahrain	Kuwait	Oman	Qatar	UAE	Yemen
■ Landing Craft	9		8	4	2	4		5	5
▨ Amphibious Ships	9					1			1

Source: Adapted by Anthony H. Cordesman from IISS, *The Military Balance*, various editions;
and material provided by U.S. experts.

Figure 8.28
Gulf Naval Aircraft and Helicopter Aircraft in 2004

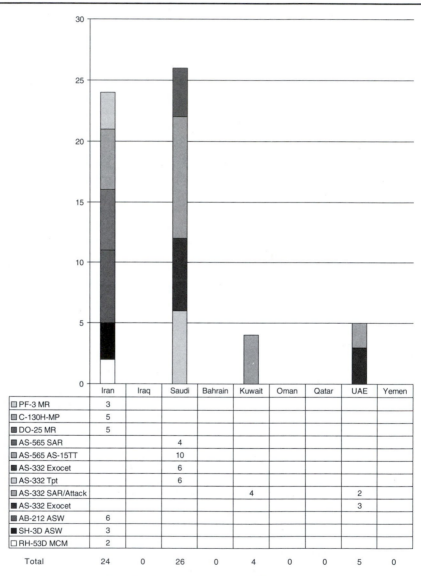

	Iran	Iraq	Saudi	Bahrain	Kuwait	Oman	Qatar	UAE	Yemen
☐ PF-3 MR	3								
☐ C-130H-MP	5								
■ DO-25 MR	5								
■ AS-565 SAR			4						
☐ AS-565 AS-15TT			10						
■ AS-332 Exocet			6						
☐ AS-332 Tpt			6						
☐ AS-332 SAR/Attack					4			2	
■ AS-332 Exocet								3	
■ AB-212 ASW	6								
■ SH-3D ASW	3								
☐ RH-53D MCM	2								
Total	24	0	26	0	4	0	0	5	0

Source: Adapted by Anthony H. Cordesman from IISS, *The Military Balance*.

Taken together, these figures provide a good picture of the overall size of the forces in the region. At the same time, Chapters 6 and 7 have shown that total numbers usually disguise serious problems in actual war-fighting capability, and that the Gulf states are even less able than states of the Middle East and North Africa to make effective use of their total military assets, and provide suitable training, readiness, and sustainability.

Chapter 9

Terrorist and Extremist Movements

Terrorism and asymmetric warfare are scarcely new features of the Middle Eastern military balance, and Islamic extremism is scarcely the only source of extremist violence. There are many serious ethnic and sectarian differences in the Middle East, and these have long led to sporadic violence within given states, and sometimes to major civil conflicts. The civil wars in Yemen and the Dhofar Rebellion in Oman are examples, as are the long history of civil war in Lebanon and Syria's violent suppression of Islamic political groups that opposed the regime of Hafez al-Asad. The rising power of the Palestinian Liberation Organization (PLO) led to a civil war in Jordan in September 1970. The Iranian revolution in 1979 was followed by serious political fighting, and an effort to export a theocratic revolution that helped trigger the Iran-Iraq War. Bahrain and Saudi Arabia have both had civil clashes between their Sunni ruling elites and hostile Shiites and these led to significant violence in the case of Saudi Arabia.

There also, however, has been a long history of violent Islamic extremism in the region, sometimes encouraged by regimes that later became the target of the very Islamists they initially supported. Sadat attempted to use Islamic movements as a counter to his secular opposition in Egypt only to be assassinated by one such movement after his peace agreement with Israel. Israel thought it safe to sponsor Islamic movements after 1967 as a counter to the PLO, only to see the rapid emergence of violently anti-Israeli groups. North and South Yemen were the scene of coups and civil wars since the early 1960s, and it was a civil war in South Yemen that ultimately led to the collapse of its regime and its merger with North Yemen in 1990.

The fall of the Shah led to an Islamist takeover in Iran, and resistance to the Soviet invasion of Afghanistan triggered an Islamist reaction that still influences the Middle East and the entire Islamic world. Saudi Arabia had to deal with an uprising at the Grand Mosque in Mecca in 1979. The religious character of this uprising shared many elements of the movements that arose after the Soviet withdrawal from Afghanistan and the Gulf War in 1991.

Algerian efforts to suppress the victory of Islamic political parties in a democratic election in 1992 were followed by a civil war that has lasted ever since. Egypt fought a long and largely successful battle with its own Islamic extremists in the 1990s, but Egypt has only managed to have suppressed such movements rather than eradicated them. In the rest of the Arab world, the civil wars in Kosovo and Bosnia helped create new Islamic extremist cadres. Saudi Arabia suffered from two major terrorist attacks before 2001. These attacks struck at a National Guard Training center and U.S. Air Force barracks at Al-Khobar, and at least one seems to have been the result of Islamic extremists. Morocco, Libya, Tunisia, Jordan, Bahrain, Qatar, Oman, and Yemen have all seen hard-line Islamist movements become a serious national threat.

While not directly part of the region, the Sudan has fought a fifteen-year civil war that has probably cost over 2 million lives, and this war had been supported by hard-line Islamist elements in the Arab north. Somalia has also been the scene of a civil war since 1991 that has allowed Islamist cells to operate in that country.

THE PROBLEM OF ISLAMIC EXTREMISM AND VIOLENCE

Islamist extremist violence has proved to be exceptionally dangerous and destabilizing. Every nation in the Middle East, no matter how moderate, faces some level of internal and external threat from such movements. Active internal fighting has taken place in Algeria, Libya, Egypt, Lebanon, Syria, Saudi Arabia, and Yemen. Iran is torn between Islamic "hard-liners" and "moderates," and the fall of Saddam Hussein has unleashed new Islamist forces in Iraq. Every other country in the Middle East and North Africa (MENA) has had to establish new security procedures, and cope with its own Islamist extremists. The problem is also an international one that reaches far outside the MENA area. It now involves Central Asia, South Asia, the Islamic countries of Southeast Asia, and movements in Europe and North America.

While militarism and proliferation pose potential threats to the region's development and energy exports, the most active threat of violence now comes from this violent extremism. It does not, however, have one source or represent one cause. Some movements have arisen in response to state terrorism, some movements have arisen in response to regional conflicts like the Israeli-Palestinian War, and other elements have developed more in response to the pressures of social change. The end result is a complex mix of threats including national movements, regional movements, and truly international movements like Al-Qaeda.

The ideology and goals of these movements differs from group to group, but there are often loose alliances of groups with different goals. What most do have in common is that their ideology is based on an extremist version of Shiite, Sufi, Salafi, and Wahhabi Islam and that the religious goals of each movement are mixed with an antisecular political agenda and a rejection of modern economic priorities and reform. So far, they are all small extremist groups that do not represent the views and hopes of the vast majority of the people in the MENA region, but several have already proven to be dangerous both inside and outside the Middle East.

THE REGIONAL AND GLOBAL IMPACT OF ISLAMIC EXTREMIST TERRORISM

Long before September 11, 2001, the attacks on Al-Khobar, the U.S.S. *Cole,* and the World Trade Center showed that terrorism posed a threat to the moderate regimes in the Middle East and a transnational threat to the West. There have been many serious terrorist attacks on Western targets in the Middle East in the past, such as the bombing of the U.S. Marine Corps Barracks in Beirut.[1]

The November 13, 1995, truck bombing of the National Guard Headquarters in Riyadh killed 5 U.S. service men and two Iranians. The June 25, 1996 bombing of the Khobar Towers killed 19 U.S. servicemen. The attacks on the U.S. Embassies in Kenya and Tanzania involved large numbers of innocent casualties—247 dead and over 5,000 wounded in the case of Kenya, and 10 dead and more than 75 wounded in the case of Tanzania. These attacks involved truck bombs with 600–800 pounds of explosives.

Civil tension in the Middle East has made Western businesses and tourists a target as well as embassies and military facilities. For example, the worst terrorist attack in Egypt's history occurred on November 17, 1997. Six gunmen belonging to the Egyptian terrorist group Al-Gama'at al-Islamiyya (Islamic Group [IG]) entered the Hatsheput Temple in Luxor. For nearly half an hour, they methodically shot and knifed tourists trapped inside the Temple's alcoves. Fifty-eight foreign tourists were murdered, along with three Egyptian police officers and one Egyptian tour guide. The gunmen then fled the scene, although Egyptian security forces pursued them and all six were killed. Terrorists launched a grenade attack on a tour bus parked in front of the Egyptian National Antiquities Museum in Cairo on September 18, 1997, killing nine German tourists and an Egyptian bus driver, and wounding eight others.

The West began to respond to these threats long before September 11. The U.S. cruise missile attacks on targets in Afghanistan and the Sudan on August 20, 1998, reflected the fact that U.S. intelligence had reliable information that Osama bin Laden, a leading sponsor and financier of terrorism, was planning large-scale attacks on U.S. targets. The goal of the U.S. preemptive attack on the Shifa Pharmaceutical Plant in Khartoum was to prevent the production and use of VX nerve gas by bin Laden's organization. These attacks, however, show that the wrong use of military power can do more to provoke than deter.

Nevertheless, the attack that truly revealed globalized Middle Eastern terrorism was the series of attack on the World Trade Center and the Pentagon on September 11. There have been many previous attempts at such attacks, and many smaller successful attacks on targets in Europe. It was September 11, however, that showed the United States that its territory and civil population could be as vulnerable as the nations of the Middle East.

While Al-Qaeda has emerged as the most visible current threat, there are many causes of transnational terrorism in the Middle East, and many different targets:

- The United States is a major target because it projects the most power into the region, because of its close ties to Israel, because attacks on the United States produce the most worldwide publicity, and because the United States can often be used as a proxy for less popular attacks on Middle Eastern regimes.

- The breakdown in the Arab-Israeli peace process has triggered a wave of Palestinian "terrorism" in response to steadily escalating Israeli "excessive force." It is a tragedy that could trigger a broader Arab-Israeli conflict and make Americans a target, both out of frustration and in an effort to break up the peace process.

- The failures of Middle Eastern secular governments, state terrorism and authoritarianism, economic hardship, social dislocation, and the alienation of youth, combine to create extremist groups that not only attack their governments, but use Western targets as proxies. Motives can include attempting to drive out the Western military forces that provide Middle Eastern countries with security, cripple the economy to weaken governments, or win public recognition in the region. While some of these groups are secular, most are Islamic in character. Some totally reject both secularism and any ties to the West or what are perceived as Western values.

- The West can be attacked on the basis of its perceived values, and for corrupting Islamic countries and supporting secular regimes. While the United States is the primary target of such attacks, figures like Saudi terrorist financier Osama bin Laden want to drive the West out of the region. Unlike more conventional forms of terrorism, such attacks deliberately seek to create a "clash of civilizations" and to build on other regional problems and tensions to divide the West and Arab worlds.[2]

- European nations can become the battleground for opposition groups to attack the Embassies of Middle Eastern regimes, or by opposition groups attacking each other. Iran has sponsored state terrorist attacks on the People's Mujahideen and Kurdish opposition groups in France, Germany, Switzerland, and Turkey. Israel has killed Palestinians in nations like Norway. France has become the scene of fighting between Algerian factions.

- Western tourists and businessmen can become the focus of much more intense terrorist attacks, as such groups seek to put economic pressure on local regimes, or prove their status and power. For example, an Algerian terrorist group called the GIA (Armed Islamic Group) killed 7 foreigners in Algeria in 1997, bringing the total number of foreigners the GIA has killed in Algeria to 133 (since 1992). Bombs have been used in civilian areas in Bahrain, although Westerners have not been major targets. Four U.S. Union Texas Petroleum employees and their Pakistani driver were shot and killed in Karachi on November 12, 1998, when the vehicle they were riding in was attacked by terrorists that seem to have been affiliated with Middle Eastern extremist groups.

THE CLASH WITHIN A CIVILIZATION, THE ARAB-ISRAELI CONFLICT, AND THE WESTERN COUNTERREACTION

It is still unclear how Islamic extremism and the aftermath of September 11, 2001, will play out in the MENA area, and how they will change the regional military balance. What is clear is that broad historical and social forces are at work, and new patterns of attack continue to emerge. Al-Qaeda launched a new series of bloody attacks in Saudi Arabia in May 2003, major attacks have taken place in Iraq since the fall of Saddam Hussein, and now extremist Islamic cells continue to emerge in virtually every MENA state. Extremism and terrorism are likely to remain a major threat to MENA governments for the next few decades, and the end result is likely to be a continuing clash within an Islamic civilization rather than a clash between Islam and the Arab world, and the West.

The primary goal of most Islamic extremist movements is not to attack the West but to create Islamic regimes based on ill-defined concepts of religious Puritanism, radical socialism or economic change, and conservative social customs. Such extremism is often an attack on secularism per se, and explains why such movements oppose MENA secular governments as well as social and economic modernization without clearly articulating the kind of government, society, and economy that should replace them. Islamic extremists know what they are against. They have only vague and impractical ideas of what they are for.

There are, however, other forms of terrorism and extremist violence. The fact that the Arab-Israeli peace process has given way to an Israeli-Palestinian war has led to a new wave of violence on both sides. The Israeli side has used conventional forces to occupy and attack the Palestinians. The Palestinians have used asymmetric and guerrilla warfare in addition to terrorism—most notably in the form of suicide bombings. The Palestinian terrorist attacks have been overwhelmingly by Islamist groups like Hamas and Palestinian Islamic Jihad, but have increasingly involved support from the hard-line elements of secular Palestinian groups as well.

Unlike most forms of Islamic extremism and terrorism, the Israeli-Palestinian conflict also polarizes the Arab world at a popular level. If the Israeli image is one of Palestinian terrorism, the Arab image is one of excessive Israeli use of force, continued occupation, and continued settlements. This allows extremist and terrorist groups to exploit the conflict to win popular support and to reinforce the image of the United States as Israel's ally and supporter. More generally, it enables them to cast the West as the exploiter of the Arab world.

At the same time, the lines between Islamic extremism and the Arab-Israeli conflict have been further blurred by the role Shiite groups like Hezbollah played in driving Israel out of Lebanon, and the role Iran and Syria have played in supporting Hezbollah. Syria at least tolerates terrorist groups on its soil that oppose Israel. Iran has increasingly funded non-Shiite groups like Hamas and the PIJ, while money has flowed to such groups from the Gulf and other Arab states—partly to support their charities and partly to support the groups in attacking Israel. Yet Sunni and Salafi extremism also targets Shiites and other Islamic threats. As events in Iraq have shown, there is the risk of Sunni versus Shiite terrorism and conflicts.

The West, particularly the United States, has often reacted by confusing the very different of Islamist extremism and terrorism with Islam, the Arab world, and Iran. U.S. officials have tried to avoid such stereotypes and dangerous generalizations, but many analysts and those in the U.S. and Western media have not. One of the ironies of September 11 is that Osama bin Laden and Al-Qaeda have succeeded in part in producing a Western counterreaction that does to some extent reflect a "clash between civilizations." The U.S. and British invasion and occupation of Iraq have increased such tensions, as have the failures to bring effective security and development to Afghanistan, as well as U.S. talk of a broad regime. Ironically, such talk of future "democracies" is as vaguely defined as the future desired by most Islamist extremists.

STATE SUPPORT OF TERRORISM AND THE USE OF TERRORIST PROXIES

The regional security problems created by independent terrorist movements are further compounded by state support of terrorism or state use of terrorist proxies. Several states have actively sponsored external terrorist movements or have conducted acts of terrorism outside their own territory. These states have included Iran, Iraq, Libya, and Syria.

As Chapter 10 discusses in some depth, such states may help extremist movements acquire weapons of mass destruction in the future. The most serious challenge proliferation poses to MENA energy facilities may well prove to be the interaction with terrorism. At present, this is only a possibility, but terrorist attacks using weapons of mass destruction would present a fundamentally different kind of threat. They would represent a vastly more lethal brand of terrorist threat than the region and the West have yet faced.

Under many conditions, a single act of such terrorism could kill thousands of people and or induce levels of panic and political reaction that governments cannot easily deal with. Under some conditions, the use of weapons of mass destruction can pose an existential threat to the existing social and political structure of a small country—particularly one where much of the population and governing elite is concentrated in a single urban area.

IDENTIFYING STATE SPONSORS OF TERRORISM AND REGIONAL TERRORIST ORGANIZATIONS

The threat of terrorism and violent extremism involves a wide range of regional and local actors, including both states and independent organizations. Many scattered incidents have arisen from extremist groups with tenuous or no ties to Al-Qaeda. New linkages may be developing between Sunni and Shiite movements, and that tie extremist groups in the Gulf to groups like Hezbollah, Hamas, and Palestinian Islamic Jihad in the Arab-Israeli countries. There are massive demographic, social, economic, and political shifts going on in the Middle East that are likely to cause turmoil for decades, and some—at least—will be a source of further internal violence.

Complicating matters further, the tensions and divisions within the Middle East make it difficult to characterize all violent nonstate actors as "terrorists." The Arab-Israeli conflict makes one side's "terrorists" the other side's "freedom fighters." In addition, there are violent and oppressive regimes like Algeria whose legal and human rights abuse provoke terrorist and extremist opposition.

There are no easy ways to resolve these issues or measure the strength and effectiveness of terrorist and extremist movements. The International Institute of Strategic Studies (IISS) has, however, developed a survey of the violent extremist movements in the world as part of its annual military balance. Figure 9.1 adapts this IISS summary, and a report by the Congressional Research Service, to focus on the key movements in the Middle East.

Figure 9.1
Key Violent and Extremist Movements in the Middle East and North Africa

Origin	Organization and Aims (Remarks)	Established	Operates	Estimated Strength	Status
Algeria	**Armée Islamique du Salut** (AIS) Socialist republic in Algeria within framework of Islamic principles. Truce 1997. Armed wing of Front Islamique du Salut (FIS)	1992	Algeria	Not known	Cease-fire
Algeria	**Groupe Islamique Armée*** Armed Islamic Group (GIA)* Fundamentalist Islamic state in Algeria (Refused January 2000 peace plan)	1992/93	Algeria	>500	Active Hard-line violence
Algeria	**Groupe Salafiste pour la Prédication et le combat** (GSPC)-al-Safayya Fundamentalist Islamic state in Algeria (Splinter faction of GIA)	1998	Algeria, possibly Western Europe, Middle East, and North Africa	500+	Active Hard-line violence
Egypt	**Al-Jihad• Egyptian Islamic Jihad• Jihad Group• Islamic Jihad• Vanguards of Conquest*** Islamic state in Egypt. Merged with al-Qaeda in June 2001	1973	International	1,000+	Active Hard-line violence
Egypt	**Islamic Group• al-Gama'at al-Islamiyya** Islamic state in Egypt (Largest militant group in Egypt)	1970s	South Egypt	1,000+	Cease-fire
Israel	**Kahane Chai** (Kach) Restore the biblical state of Israel	1990	West Bank, Israel, possibly US	Not known	Active Limited, low-level violence
Iran	**Democratic Party of Iranian Kurdistan** (DPKI) **Kurdish Democratic Party of Iran** (KDPI) Kurdish autonomy in Iran	1995	Iran	1,200-1,800	Dormant
Iran	**Kurdistan Organization of the Communist Party of Iran** (KOMALA) Communist government in Iran (Formed Communist Party of Iran in 1983)	1967	Iran	200	Active
Iran/Iraq	**National Liberation Army** (NLA) 'Democratic, socialist, Islamic republic in Iran' (Largest and most active armed Iranian dissident group of Mujahideen-e Khalq Organization)	1987	Iran, Iraq	6,000-8,000	Disrupted and largely disarmed by Iraq War
Iraq	**Kurdish Democratic Party** Overthrow Iraq government (Ongoing conflict with PUK)	1946	Iraq	15,000	Active Reduced level of recent violence
Iraq	**Patriotic Union of Kurdistan** (PUK) 'Revitalize resistance and rebuild a democratic Kurdish society' (Evolved into a political movement	1975	Iraq	10,000	Active
Iraq	**Ansar al Islam • Jund al-Islam • Army of Islam*** Pro al-Qaeda group, opposed to *Operation Enduring Freedom*. Opposes secular Kurdish parties in Iraq	2001	Iraq	700	Active May be a major source of terrorism in Iraq

Figure 9.1 (Continued)

Origin	Organization and Aims (Remarks)	Established	Operates	Estimated Strength	Status
Iraq	Abu Nidal Organization (ANO) • Fatah Revolutionary Council • Black September • Arab Revolutionary Brigades • Revolutionary Organization of Socialist Muslims* ? Black June Destroy Israel (Operations in Libya and Egypt shut down by governments in 1999)	1974	International	300	Largely dormant
Iraq	**Badr Corps** Opposed Iraq aggression against Iran (Shi'ite; mutual agreement signed with the Patriotic Union of Kurdistan against Iraq) Armed wing of Supreme Council for Islamic Revolution in Iraq (SCIRI)	1982	Baghdad and South Iraq	5,000	Active As elements of militia in Iraq
Iraq	**Mujahedin-e Khalq Organization** (MEK or MKO) Advocate Secular Muslim regime	1960	Iran, Iraq, France	3,000	Now more political, but some cells active in Iran and Iraq
Lebanon	**Asbat al-Ansar** Advocates Salafism, opposed to any peace with Israel, establish an Islamic state in Lebanon	1990s	Lebanon	300	Active
Lebanon	**Hezbollah** (Party of God) • **Islamic Jihad-Revolutionary Justice Organization** • **Organization of the Oppressed on Earth*** Iran-style Islamic republic in Lebanon; all non-Islamic influences removed from area (Shi'ite; formed to resist Israeli occupation of south Lebanon with political representation in Lebanon Assembly).	1982	Bekaa Valley, Beirut, south Lebanon, Shebaa Farms Cells in North America, South America, Europe, Asia, and Africa	2,000+	Active Some incidents of violence in Israeli border area. Build up of long-range rockets. Training violent Palestinian elements
Morocco	**Assirat Al-Moustakim** Claimed Casablanca blast		Morocco	Not known	Active Limited recent violence
Morocco	**Moroccan Islamic Combatant Group** (GICM) Establish an Islamic state in Morocco and support al-Qaeda's jihad against the West	1990s	Western Europe Africa, Morocco	Not known	Active Source of concern to Moroccan security services
Morocco	**Sahrawi People's Liberation Army** Independent Western Sahara (Armed wing is the Frente Popular para la Liberacion de Saguia el-Hamra y del Rio de Oro (Polisario Front)	1973	Morocco	3,000-6,000	Cease-fire with some continuing elements of violence. Moroccans claim has Algerian support.
Morocco	**Salafya Al-Aihadya Jihad** Claimed Casablanca blast		Morocco	Not known	Active Limited recent violence
Palestinian Autonomous Areas of Gaza and Jericho	**Al-Aqsa Martyrs Brigade*** Associated, though not officially backed, by Arafat Military offshoot of Fatah. Aims to expel Israelis from Gaza and West Bank	2000	Palestinian Autonomous Areas of Gaza and Jericho, Israel	Not known	Active Attempted infiltrations and bombings, shootings, kidnappings
Palestinian Autonomous Areas of Gaza and Jericho	**Al Saika** Military wing of Palestinian faction of Syrian Ba'ath Party (Nominally part of PLO)	1968	Palestinian Autonomous Areas of Gaza and Jericho, Israel	300	Active

continued

395

Figure 9.1 (Continued)

Origin	Organization and Aims (Remarks)	Established	Operates	Estimated Strength	Status
Palestinian Autonomous Areas of Gaza and Jericho	**Arab Liberation Front** Achieve national goals of Palestinian Authority (Faction of PLO formed by leadership of Iraq Ba'ath party)	1969	Palestinian Autonomous Areas of Gaza and Jericho, Israel	500	Dormant
Palestinian Autonomous Areas of Gaza and Jericho	**Democratic Front for the Liberation of Palestine** (DFLP) Achieve Palestinian national goals through revolution (Marxist-Leninist; splintered from PFLP)	1969	Palestinian Autonomous Areas of Gaza and Jericho, Israel	100+	Active
Palestinian Autonomous Areas of Gaza and Jericho	**Fatah Tanzim** Armed militia link to Fatah	1995	Palestinian Autonomous Areas of Gaza and Jericho, Israel	1000+	Active Continuing clashes with Israeli forces
Palestinian Autonomous Areas of Gaza and Jericho	**Harakat al-Muqawama al-Islamiyya (HAMAS) Islamic Resistance Front** Establish an Islamic Palestinian state in place of Israel	1987	Palestinian Autonomous Areas of Gaza and Jericho, Israel	Not known	Active Key source of suicide bombings
Palestinian Autonomous Areas of Gaza and Jericho	**Izz al-Din al-Qassam Brigades** (IDQ)* Replace Israel with Islamic state in Palestinian Areas (Armed wing of Harakat al-Muqawama al-Islamiyya (Hamas); separate from overt organization)	1991	Palestinian Autonomous Areas of Gaza and Jericho, Israel	500	Active
Palestinian Autonomous Areas of Gaza and Jericho	**Palestine Islamic Jihad** (PIJ)* Destroy Israel with holy war and establish Islamic state in Palestinian areas (One of the more extreme groups from the Palestinian areas.)	1979	Palestinian Autonomous Areas of Gaza and Jericho, Israel, Damascus, Beirut, Tehran. Possibly Khartoum	Estimated 500	Active Key source of suicide bombings
Palestinian Autonomous Areas of Gaza and Jericho	**Palestine Liberation Front** (PLF)* Armed struggle against Israel (Splintered from PFLP)	1977	Palestinian Autonomous Areas of Gaza and Jericho, Israel, Iraq	300-400	Dormant
Palestinian Autonomous Areas of Gaza and Jericho	**Popular Front for the Liberation of Palestine** (PFLP) Armed struggle against Israel (Marzist-Leninist), end American influence in the region	1967	Palestinian Autonomous Areas of Gaza and Jericho, Israel, Lebanon, Damascus	1000	Active
Palestinian Autonomous Areas of Gaza and Jericho	**Popular Front for the Liberation of Palestine—General Command** (PFLP-GC)* Armed struggle against Israel (Marzist-Leninist; Split from PFLP to focus on fighting rather than politics)	1968	Palestinian Autonomous Areas of Gaza and Jericho, Israel, Lebanon, Syria	500	Dormant
Yemen	**Islamic Army of Aden** (IAA) Overthrow of the Yemeni Government and operations against US and other Western interests in Yemen	1998	South Yemen	Not known	Active Ties to Al Qaeda and other scattered, extremist and terrorist elements unclear

*Group known to carry out suicide attacks

Source: Adapted from IISS, *The Military Balance*, 2003–2004; Audrey Kurth Cronin, *Foreign Terrorist Organizations*, Washington, DC: Congressional Research Service, RL32223, February 6, 2004; with additional comments by author.

While there may be a Western bias in such lists, such movements do exist and often threaten Middle Eastern states far more than the West.

The U.S. State Department provides further lists and descriptions of states and movements that it sees as either supportive of terrorism or terrorist in nature and that already play a role in the Middle Eastern military balance or could do so at any time. While such lists are written from a U.S. perspective, they do provide important insights into the way states that support extremist movements as well as how individual movements could affect the Middle Eastern military balance.

- Figure 9.2 provides a summary description of the State Department list of the movements it designates as terrorist.
- Figure 9.3 provides a summary description of other extremist and terrorist groups in the MENA region that are listed by the State Department.

Figure 9.2
Designated Foreign Terrorist Organizations in the Middle East

---

Abu Nidal Organization (ANO) a.k.a. Fatah—the Revolutionary Council, Arab Revolutionary Brigades, Black September, and Revolutionary Organization of Socialist Muslims

Description:
International terrorist organization founded by Sabri al-Banna (a.k.a. Abu Nidal). Split from PLO in 1974. Made up of various functional committees, including political, military, and financial. In November 2002, Abu Nidal died in Baghdad; the new leadership of the organization is unclear.

Activities:
Has carried out terrorist attacks in 20 countries, killing or injuring almost 900 persons. Targets include the United States, the United Kingdom, France, Israel, moderate Palestinians, the PLO, and various Arab countries. Major attacks included the Rome and Vienna airports in December 1985, a failed attempt to bomb the U.S. embassy in Cairo, the Neve Shalom synagogue in Istanbul and the Pan Am Flight 73 hijacking in Karachi in September 1986, and the City of Poros day-excursion ship attack in Greece in July 1988. Suspected of assassinating PLO deputy chief Abu Iyad and PLO security chief Abu Hul in Tunis in January 1991. ANO assassinated a Jordanian diplomat in Lebanon in January 1994 and has been linked to the killing of the PLO representative there. Has not staged a major attack against Western targets since the late 1980s.

Strength:
Few hundred plus limited overseas support structure.

Location/Area of Operation:
Al-Banna relocated to Iraq in December 1998, where the group maintains a presence. Has an operational presence in Lebanon including in several Palestinian

continued

Figure 9.2 (Continued)

refugee camps. Authorities shut down the ANO's operations in Libya and Egypt in 1999. Has demonstrated ability to operate over wide area, including the Middle East, Asia, and Europe. Financial problems and internal disorganization have reduced the group's activities and capabilities.

External Aid:
Has received considerable support, including safehaven, training, logistic assistance, and financial aid from Iraq, Libya, and Syria (until 1987), in addition to close support for selected operations.

Al-Aqsa Martyrs Brigade (al-Aqsa)

Description:
The al-Aqsa Martyrs Brigade comprises an unknown number of small cells of Fatah-affiliated activists that emerged at the outset of the current intifada to attack Israeli targets. It aims to drive the Israeli military and settlers from the West Bank, Gaza Strip, and Jerusalem and to establish a Palestinian state. It does not claim to seek the destruction of the Israeli state.

Activities:
Al-Aqsa has carried out shootings and suicide operations against Israeli military personnel and civilians and has killed Palestinians who it believed were collaborating with Israel. At least five U.S. citizens, four of them dual Israeli-U.S. citizens, were killed in al-Aqsa's attacks. The group probably did not attack them because of their U.S. citizenship. In January 2002, al-Aqsa claimed responsibility for the first suicide bombing carried out by a female.

Strength:
Unknown.

Location/Area of Operation:
Al-Aqsa operates mainly in the West Bank and has claimed attacks inside Israel and the Gaza Strip. It may have followers in Palestinian refugee camps in southern Lebanon.

External Aid:
Unknown.

Armed Islamic Group (GIA)

Description:
An Islamic extremist group, the GIA aims to overthrow the secular Algerian regime and replace it with an Islamic state. The GIA began its violent activity in 1993 after Algiers voided the victory of the Islamic Salvation Front—the largest Islamic opposition party—in the first round of legislative elections in December 1991. It is composed of radical Islamists and Algerian veterans of the war against the Soviet Union in Afghanistan.

Activities:
Frequent attacks against civilians and government workers. Since 1992, the GIA has conducted a terrorist campaign of civilian massacres, sometimes wiping out entire villages in its area of operation, although the group's dwindling numbers have caused a decrease in the number of attacks. The Algerian military was once thought to have aided the GIA in some of its massacres, but a military crackdown suggests that such

Figure 9.2 (Continued)

cooperation has ceased. Since announcing its campaign against foreigners living in Algeria in 1993, the GIA has killed more than 100 expatriate men and women—mostly Europeans—in the country. The group uses assassinations and bombings, including car bombs, and it is known to favor kidnapping victims and slitting their throats. The GIA hijacked an Air France flight to Algiers in December 1994. In 2002, a French court sentenced two GIA members to life in prison for conducting a series of bombings in France in 1995.

Strength:
Precise numbers unknown, probably fewer than 100.

Location/Area of Operation:
Algeria.

External Aid:
None known.

'Asbat al-Ansar

Description:
'Asbat al-Ansar—the League of the Followers—is a Lebanon-based, Sunni extremist group, composed primarily of Palestinians and associated with Osama Bin Laden. The group follows an extremist interpretation of Islam that justifies violence against civilian targets to achieve political ends. Some of those goals include overthrowing the Lebanese Government and thwarting perceived anti-Islamic and pro-Western influences in the country.

Activities:
'Asbat al-Ansar has carried out multiple terrorist attacks in Lebanon since it first emerged in the early 1990s. The group assassinated Lebanese religious leaders and bombed nightclubs, theaters, and liquor stores in the mid-1990s. The group raised its operational profile in 2000 with two attacks against Lebanese and international targets. It was involved in clashes in northern Lebanon in December 1999 and carried out a rocket-propelled grenade attack on the Russian Embassy in Beirut in January 2000.

In 2002, there was an increase in anti-U.S. attacks, including bombings of U.S.-franchised restaurants and the murder of an American missionary. The perpetrators are believed to be Sunni extremists that may be linked to 'Asbat al-Ansar.

Strength:
The group commands about 300 fighters in Lebanon.

Location/Area of Operation:
The group's primary base of operations is the 'Ayn al-Hilwah Palestinian refugee camp near Sidon in southern Lebanon.

External Aid:
Probably receives money through international Sunni extremist networks and Bin Laden's al-Qaeda network.

Al-Gama'a al-Islamiyya (Islamic Group, IG)

Description:
Egypt's largest militant group, active since the late 1970s; appears to be loosely organized. Has an external wing with supporters in several countries worldwide.

continued

Figure 9.2 (Continued)

The group issued a cease-fire in March 1999, but its spiritual leader, Shaykh Umar Abd al-Rahman, sentenced to life in prison in January 1996 for his involvement in the 1993 World Trade Center bombing and incarcerated in the United States, rescinded his support for the cease-fire in June 2000. The Gama'a has not conducted an attack inside Egypt since August 1998. A senior member signed Osama Bin Laden's fatwa in February 1998 calling for attacks against the United States.

Unofficially it is split in two factions; one that supports the cease-fire led by Mustafa Hamza, and one led by Rifa'i Taha Musa, calling for a return to armed operations. Taha Musa in early 2001 published a book in which he attempted to justify terrorist attacks that would cause mass casualties. Musa disappeared several months thereafter, and there are conflicting reports as to his current whereabouts. In March 2002, members of the group's historic leadership in Egypt declared use of violence misguided and renounced its future use, prompting denunciations by much of the leadership abroad.

For members still dedicated to violent jihad, primary goal is to overthrow the Egyptian Government and replace it with an Islamic state. Disaffected IG members, such as those potentially inspired by Taha Musa or Abd al-Rahman, may be interested in carrying out attacks against U.S. and Israeli interests.

Activities:
Group conducted armed attacks against Egyptian security and other government officials, Coptic Christians, and Egyptian opponents of Islamic extremism before the cease-fire. IG agents were convicted of aiding the group al-Jihad in killing Egyptian President Anwar Sadat in 1981. From 1993 until the cease-fire, al-Gama'a launched attacks on tourists in Egypt, most notably the attack in November 1997 at Luxor that killed 58 foreign tourists. Also claimed responsibility for the attempt in June 1995 to assassinate Egyptian President Hosni Mubarak in Addis Ababa, Ethiopia. The Gama'a never has specifically attacked a U.S. citizen or facility but has threatened U.S. interests.

Strength:
Unknown. At its peak the IG probably commanded several thousand hard-core members and a like number of sympathizers. The 1999 cease-fire and security crackdowns following the attack in Luxor in 1997 and, more recently, security efforts following September 11, probably have resulted in a substantial decrease in the group's numbers.

Location/Area of Operation:
Operates mainly in the Al-Minya, Asyut, Qina, and Sohaj Governorates of southern Egypt. Also appears to have support in Cairo, Alexandria, and other urban locations, particularly among unemployed graduates and students. Has a worldwide presence, including in the United Kingdom, Afghanistan, Yemen, and various locations in Europe.

External Aid:
Unknown. The Egyptian Government believes that Iran, Bin Laden, and Afghan militant groups support the organization. Also may obtain some funding through various Islamic nongovernmental organizations (NGOs).

Figure 9.2 (Continued)

HAMAS (Islamic Resistance Movement)

Description:
Formed in late 1987 as an outgrowth of the Palestinian branch of the Muslim Brotherhood. Various HAMAS elements have used both political and violent means, including terrorism, to pursue the goal of establishing an Islamic Palestinian state in place of Israel. Loosely structured, with some elements working clandestinely and others working openly through mosques and social service institutions to recruit members, raise money, organize activities, and distribute propaganda. Hamas's strength is concentrated in the Gaza Strip and the West Bank. Also has engaged in peaceful political activity, such as running candidates in West Bank Chamber of Commerce elections.

Activities:
HAMAS activists, especially those in the Izz al-Din al-Qassam Brigades, have conducted many attacks—including large-scale suicide bombings—against Israeli civilian and military targets. In the early 1990s, they also targeted suspected Palestinian collaborators and Fatah rivals. HAMAS increased its operational activity during 2001-2002 claiming numerous attacks against Israeli interests. The group has not targeted U.S. interests—although some U.S. citizens have been killed in HAMAS operations—and continues to confine its attacks to Israelis inside Israel and the territories.

Strength:
Unknown number of official members; tens of thousands of supporters and sympathizers.

Location/Area of Operation:
HAMAS currently limits its terrorist operations to Israeli military and civilian targets in the West Bank, Gaza Strip, and Israel. The group's leadership is dispersed throughout the Gaza Strip and West Bank, with a few senior leaders residing in Syria, Lebanon, and the Gulf States.

External Aid:
Receives some funding from Iran but primarily relies on donations from Palestinian expatriates around the world and private benefactors in moderate Arab states. Some fundraising and propaganda activity take place in Western Europe and North America.

Hezbollah (Party of God) a.k.a. Islamic Jihad, Revolutionary Justice Organization, Organization of the Oppressed on Earth, and Islamic Jihad for the Liberation of Palestine.

Description:
Formed in 1982 in response to the Israeli invasion of Lebanon, this Lebanon-based radical Shi'a group takes its ideological inspiration from the Iranian revolution and the teachings of the late Ayatollah Khomeini. The Majlis al-Shura, or Consultative Council, is the group's highest governing body and is led by Secretary General Hassan Nasrallah. Hezbollah is dedicated to liberating Jerusalem, ultimately eliminating Israel, and has formally advocated ultimate establishment of Islamic

continued

Figure 9.2 (Continued)

rule in Lebanon. Nonetheless, Hezbollah has actively participated in Lebanon's political system since 1992. Hezbollah is closely allied with, and often directed by, Iran but may have conducted operations that were not approved by Tehran. While Hezbollah does not share the Syrian regime's secular orientation, the group has been a strong tactical ally in helping Syria advance its political objectives in the region.

Activities:
Known or suspected to have been involved in numerous anti-U.S. and anti-Israeli terrorist attacks, including the suicide truck bombings of the U.S. Embassy and U.S. Marine barracks in Beirut in October 1983 and the U.S. Embassy annex in Beirut in September 1984. Three members of Hezbollah, 'Imad Mughniyah, Hasan Izz-al-Din, and Ali Atwa, are on the FBI's list of 22 Most Wanted Terrorists for the hijacking in 1985 of TWA Flight 847 during which a U.S. Navy diver was murdered. Elements of the group were responsible for the kidnapping and detention of U.S. and other Westerners in Lebanon in the 1980s. Hezbollah also attacked the Israeli Embassy in Argentina in 1992 and the Israeli cultural center in Buenos Aires in 1994. In fall 2000, it captured three Israeli soldiers in the Shebaa Farms and kidnapped an Israeli noncombatant whom it may have lured to Lebanon under false pretenses. In early 2004, Hezbollah released the non-combatant and returned the remains of the three IDF soldiers to Israel in exchange for the release of several Hezbollah members, including two senior officials.

Strength:
Several thousand supporters and a few hundred terrorist operatives.

Location/Area of Operation:
Operates in the southern suburbs of Beirut, the Bekaa Valley, and southern Lebanon. Has established cells in Europe, Africa, South America, North America, and Asia.

External Aid:
Receives financial, training, weapons, explosives, political, diplomatic, and organizational aid from Iran and diplomatic, political, and logistic support from Syria.

Al-Jihad a.k.a. Egyptian Islamic Jihad, Jihad Group, Islamic Jihad, Vanguards of Conquest

Description:
Egyptian Islamic extremist group active since the late 1970s. Merged with Bin Laden's al-Qaeda organization in June 2001, but may retain some capability to conduct independent operations. Primary goals are to overthrow the Egyptian Government and replace it with an Islamic state and to attack U.S. and Israeli interests in Egypt and abroad.

Activities:
Historically specialized in armed attacks against high-level Egyptian Government personnel, including cabinet ministers, and car bombings against official U.S. and Egyptian facilities. The original Jihad was responsible for the assassination in 1981 of Egyptian President Anwar Sadat. Assassinated the People's Assembly Speaker Rifaat el-Mahgoub in October 1990. Claimed responsibility for the attempted

Figure 9.2 (Continued)

assassinations of Interior Minister Hassan al-Alfi in August 1993 and Prime Minister Atef Sedky in November 1993. Has not conducted an attack inside Egypt since 1993 and has never targeted foreign tourists there. Responsible for Egyptian Embassy bombing in Islamabad in 1995; in 1998 an attack against U.S. Embassy in Albania was thwarted. Egyptian President Hosni Mubarak has taken staunch measures to crack down on the group's operational capability since the 1980's.

Strength:
Unknown, but probably has several hundred hard-core members.

Location/Area of Operation:
Historically operated in the Cairo area, but most of its network is outside Egypt, including Yemen, Afghanistan, Pakistan, Lebanon, and the United Kingdom, and its activities have been centered outside Egypt for several years.

External Aid:
Unknown. The Egyptian Government and U.S. intelligence services claim that Iran supports the Jihad. Its merger with al-Qaeda also boosts Bin Laden's support for the group. Also may obtain some funding through various Islamic nongovernmental organizations, cover businesses, and criminal acts.

Kahane Chai (Kach)

Description:
Stated goal is to restore the biblical state of Israel and the implementation of Jewish law. Kach (founded by radical Israeli-American rabbi Meir Kahane) and its offshoot Kahane Chai, which means "Kahane Lives," (founded by Meir Kahane's son Binyamin following his father's assassination in the United States) were declared to be terrorist organizations in March 1994 by the Israeli Cabinet under the 1948 Terrorism Law. This followed the groups' statements in support of Dr. Baruch Goldstein's attack in February 1994 on the al-Ibrahimi Mosque—Goldstein was affiliated with Kach—and their verbal attacks on the Israeli Government. Palestinian gunmen killed Binyamin Kahane and his wife in a drive-by shooting in December 2000 in the West Bank.

Activities:
The group has organized protests against the Israeli Government and has harassed and threatened Palestinians in the West Bank. Kach members have threatened to attack Arabs, Palestinians, and Israeli Government officials. Has vowed revenge for the death of Binyamin Kahane and his wife. Suspected of involvement in a number of low-level attacks since the start of the al-Aqsa intifada. Allegedly plotted to kill a U.S. Representative and to attack Muslim groups and mosques in Los Angeles.

Strength:
Unknown.

Location/Area of Operation:
Israel and West Bank settlements, particularly Qiryat Arba' in Hebron.

External Aid:
Receives support from sympathizers in the United States and Europe.

continued

Figure 9.2 (Continued)

Mujahedin-e Khalq Organization (MEK or MKO)
a.k.a. The National Liberation Army of Iran
(NLA, the militant wing of the MEK),
the People's Mujahedin of Iran (PMOI),
National Council of Resistance (NCR),
the National Council of Resistance of Iran (NCRI),
Muslim Iranian Student's Society
(front organization used to garner financial support)

Description:
The MEK philosophy mixes Marxism and Islam. Formed in the 1960s, the organization was expelled from Iran after the Islamic Revolution in 1979, and its primary support now comes from the Iraqi regime. The MEK's history is studded with anti-Western attacks as well as terrorist attacks on the interests of the clerical regime in Iran and abroad. The MEK now advocates a secular Iranian regime.

Activities:
The worldwide campaign against the Iranian Government stresses propaganda and occasionally uses terrorist violence. During the 1970s, the MEK killed U.S. military personnel and U.S. civilians working on defense projects in Tehran and supported the takeover in 1979 of the U.S. Embassy in Tehran. In 1981, the MEK detonated bombs in the head office of the Islamic Republic Party and the Premier's office, killing some 70 high-ranking Iranian officials, including chief Justice Ayatollah Mohammad Beheshti, President Mohammad-Ali Rajaei, and Premier Mohammad-Javad Bahonar. Near the end of the 1980-88 war with Iran, Baghdad armed the MEK with military equipment and sent it into action against Iranian forces. In 1991, it assisted the Government of Iraq in suppressing the Shia and Kurdish uprisings in southern Iraq and the Kurdish uprisings in the north. Since then, the MEK has continued to perform internal security services for the Government of Iraq. In April 1992, the MEK conducted near-simultaneous attacks on Iranian Embassies and installations in 13 countries, demonstrating the group's ability to mount large-scale operations overseas. In recent years, the MEK has targeted key military officers and assassinated the deputy chief of the Armed Forces General Staff in April 1999. In April 2000, the MEK attempted to assassinate the commander of the Nasr Headquarters—the interagency board responsible for coordinating policies on Iraq. The normal pace of anti-Iranian operations increased during the "Operation Great Bahman" in February 2000, when the group launched a dozen attacks against Iran. In 2000 and 2001, the MEK was involved regularly in mortar attacks and hit-and-run raids on Iranian military and law-enforcement units and government buildings near the Iran-Iraq border, although MEK terrorism in Iran declined throughout the remainder of 2001. Since the end of the Iran-Iraq war, the tactics along the border have garnered almost no military gains and have become commonplace. MEK insurgent activities in Tehran constitute the biggest security concern for the Iranian leadership. In February 2000, for example, the MEK launched a mortar attack against the leadership complex in Tehran that houses the offices of the Supreme Leader and the President. Assassinated the Iranian Chief of Staff. France decided to end its policy of giving the group asylum in 2003, and arrested several top members who had been living there for some time. In 2003, as part of the Iraq War, the U.S. signed a cease-fire with the MEK and has since disarmed them.

404

Figure 9.2 (Continued)

Strength:
Several thousand fighters are scattered throughout Iraq, and most are organized in the MEK's National Liberation Army (NLA). Some NLA units possess tanks, armored vehicles, and heavy artillery. The U.S. has seized much of this equipment. The MEK also has an overseas support structure.

Location/Area of Operation:
In the 1980s, the MEK's leaders were forced by Iranian security forces to flee to France. Since resettling in Iraq in 1987, almost all of its armed units are currently stationed in fortified bases near the border with Iran. In the mid-1980s, the group did not mount terrorist operations in Iran at a level similar to its activities in the 1970s, but by the 1990s the MEK had claimed credit for an increasing number of operations in Iran.

External Aid:
Beyond receiving all of its military assistance, and most of its financial support, from the Iraqi regime, the MEK uses front organizations to solicit contributions from expatriate Iranian communities.

The Palestine Islamic Jihad (PIJ)

Description:
Originated among militant Palestinians in the Gaza Strip during the 1970s. PIJ-Shiqaqi faction, currently led by Ramadan Shallah in Damascus, is most active. Committed to the creation of an Islamic Palestinian state and the destruction of Israel through holy war. Also opposes moderate Arab governments that it believes have been tainted by Western secularism.

Activities:
PIJ activists have conducted many attacks including large-scale suicide bombings against Israeli civilian and military targets. The group increased its operational activity since 2002, claiming numerous attacks against Israeli interests. The group has not yet targeted U.S. interests and continues to confine its attacks to Israelis inside Israel and the territories, although U.S. citizens have died in attacks mounted by the PIJ. The group announced in February 2003 that it would not target American nationals even though the U.S. indicted eight members of the PIJ.

Strength:
Unknown.

Location/Area of Operation:
Primarily Israel, the West Bank, and Gaza Strip, but the group's leaders reside in other parts of the Middle East, including Lebanon and Syria.

External Aid:
Receives financial assistance from Iran and limited logistic support assistance from Syria.

Palestine Liberation Front (PLF)

Description:
Broke away from the PFLP-GC in the late 1970s. Later split again into pro-PLO, pro-Syrian, and pro-Libyan factions. Pro-PLO faction led by Muhammad Abbas (a.k.a. Abu Abbas), currently based in Baghdad.

continued

405

Figure 9.2 (Continued)

Activities:
The Abu Abbas–led faction is known for aerial attacks, including the use of hang gliders and hot air balloons, against Israel. Abbas's group also was responsible for the attack in 1985 on the Italian cruise ship Achille Lauro and the murder of U.S. citizen Leon Klinghoffer. A warrant for Abu Abbas's arrest was outstanding in Italy. He was captured by the U.S. military in Iraq in early 2004 and died of natural causes shortly thereafter. Launched an assault on the Israeli beach area at Nizanim in 1990. Has become more active since the start of the al-Aqsa intifada, and several PLF members have been arrested by Israeli authorities for planning attacks in Israel and the West Bank.

Strength:
Unknown.

Location/Area of Operation:
Based in Iraq since 1990; has a presence in Lebanon and the West Bank.

External Aid:
Receives support mainly from Iraq. Has received support from Libya in the past.

Popular Front for the Liberation of Palestine (PFLP)

Description:
Marxist-Leninist group founded in 1967 by George Habash—as a member of the PLO—when it broke away from the Arab Nationalist Movement. The PFLP views the Palestinian struggle as a legitimate struggle against illegal occupation. The PFLP is opposed to negotiations with Israel.

Activities:
Committed numerous international terrorist attacks during the 1970s. Since 1978 has conducted attacks against Israeli or moderate Arab targets, including killing a settler and her son in December 1996. The PFLP has stepped up its operational activity since the start of the current intifada highlighted by its assassination of the Israeli Tourism Minster in October 2001 to avenge Israel's killing of the PFLP Secretary General earlier that year. The PFLP leader, Ahmed Sadat, was arrested by the Palestinian Authority in 2002. The PA has received threats from PFLP supporters.

Strength:
Unknown.

Location/Area of Operation:
Syria, Lebanon, Israel, West Bank, and Gaza Strip.

External Aid:
Receives safehaven and some logistic assistance from Syria. Iran contributes financially.

Popular Front for the Liberation of Palestine–General Command (PFLP-GC)

Description:
Split from the PFLP in 1968, claiming it wanted to focus more on fighting and less on politics. Opposed to Arafat's PLO. Led by Ahmad Jabril, a former captain in the Syrian Army. Jabril's son, Jihad, was killed by a car bomb in May 2002. Closely tied to both Syria and Iran.

Figure 9.2 (Continued)

Activities:
Carried out dozens of attacks in Europe and the Middle East during 1970s-80s. Known for cross-border terrorist attacks into Israel using unusual means, such as hot-air balloons and motorized hang gliders. Primary focus now on guerrilla operations in southern Lebanon and small-scale attacks in Israel, West Bank, and Gaza Strip. The PFLP-GC killed two IDF soldiers on patrol in the West Bank in November, 2003.

Strength:
Several hundred.

Location/Area of Operation:
Headquartered in Damascus with bases in Lebanon. Operates in Israel and the Palestinian territories.

External Aid:
Receives logistic and military support from Syria and Libya. Libya provided the hang gliders used in several raids.

Al-Qaeda a.k.a. Qa'idat al-Jihad

Description:
Established by Osama Bin Laden in the late 1980s to bring together Arabs who fought in Afghanistan against the Soviet Union. Helped finance, recruit, transport, and train Sunni Islamic extremists for the Afghan resistance. Current goal is to establish a pan-Islamic Caliphate throughout the world by working with allied Islamic extremist groups to overthrow regimes it deems "non-Islamic" and expelling Westerners and non-Muslims from Muslim countries—particularly Saudi Arabia. Issued statement under banner of "the World Islamic Front for Jihad Against the Jews and Crusaders" in February 1998, saying it was the duty of all Muslims to kill U.S. citizens—civilian or military—and their allies everywhere. Merged with Egyptian Islamic Jihad (Al-Jihad) in June 2001.

Activities:
In 2002, carried out bombing on 28 November of hotel in Mombassa, Kenya, killing 15 and injuring 40. Probably supported a nightclub bombing in Bali, Indonesia, on 12 October that killed about 180. Responsible for an attack on U.S. military personnel in Kuwait, on 8 October, that killed one U.S. soldier and injured another. Directed a suicide attack on the MV Limburg off the coast of Yemen, on 6 October that killed one and injured four. Carried out a firebombing of a synagogue in Tunisia on 11 April that killed 19 and injured 22. On 11 September 2001, 19 al-Qaeda suicide attackers hijacked and crashed four U.S. commercial jets, two into the World Trade Center in New York City, one into the Pentagon near Washington, DC, and a fourth into a field in Shanksville, Pennsylvania, leaving about 3,000 individuals dead or missing. Directed the 12 October 2000 attack on the U.S.S *Cole* in the port of Aden, Yemen, killing 17 U.S. Navy members, and injuring another 39. Conducted the bombings in August 1998 of the U.S. Embassies in Nairobi, Kenya, and Dar es Salaam, Tanzania, that killed at least 301 individuals and injured more than 5,000 others. Claims to have shot down U.S. helicopters and killed U.S. servicemen in Somalia in 1993 and to have conducted three bombings that targeted U.S. troops in Aden, Yemen, in

Figure 9.2 (Continued)

December 1992. Taliban and al-Qaeda elements are responsible for continuing attacks on relief workers and Afghans working with the coalition in Afghanistan. An affiliated group has been linked to the bombing of a series of Spanish trains in March 2004. It is suspected that the group or groups affiliated with al-Qaeda have carried out attacks against coalition forces in Iraq.

Al-Qaeda is linked to the following plans that were disrupted or not carried out: to assassinate Pope John Paul II during his visit to Manila in late 1994, to kill President Clinton during a visit to the Philippines in early 1995, to bomb in midair a dozen U.S. trans-Pacific flights in 1995, and to set off a bomb at Los Angeles International Airport in 1999. Also plotted to carry out terrorist operations against U.S. and Israeli tourists visiting Jordan for millennial celebrations in late 1999. (Jordanian authorities thwarted the planned attacks and put 28 suspects on trial.) In December 2001, suspected al-Qaeda associate Richard Colvin Reid attempted to ignite a shoe bomb on a transatlantic flight from Paris to Miami. Attempted to shoot down an Israeli chartered plane with a surface-to-air missile as it departed the Mombassa airport in November 2002.

Strength:
Al-Qaeda probably has several thousand members and associates. The arrests of senior-level al-Qaeda operatives have interrupted some terrorist plots. Also serves as a focal point or umbrella organization for a worldwide network that includes many Sunni Islamic extremist groups, some members of al-Gama'a al-Islamiyya, the Islamic Movement of Uzbekistan, and the Harakat ul-Mujahidin.

Location/Area of Operation:
Al-Qaeda has cells worldwide and is reinforced by its ties to Sunni extremist networks. Was based in Afghanistan until Coalition forces removed the Taliban from power in late 2001. Al-Qaeda has dispersed in small groups across South Asia, Southeast Asia, and the Middle East and probably will attempt to carry out future attacks against U.S. interests. It is suspected that a number of Al-Qaeda operatives remain active in the border regions between Pakistan and Afghanistan.

External Aid:
Al-Qaeda maintains moneymaking front businesses, solicits donations from like-minded supporters, and illicitly siphons funds from donations to Muslim charitable organizations. U.S. efforts to block al-Qaeda funding have hampered the group's ability to obtain money.

The Salafist Group for Call and Combat (GSPC)

Description:
The Salafist Group for Call and Combat (GSPC), an outgrowth of the GIA, appears to have eclipsed the GIA since approximately 1998, and is currently the most effective armed group inside Algeria. In contrast to the GIA, the GSPC has gained popular support through its pledge to avoid civilian attacks inside Algeria. Its adherents abroad appear to have largely co-opted the external networks of the GIA, active particularly throughout Europe, Africa, and the Middle East.

Activities:
The GSPC continues to conduct operations aimed at government and military targets, primarily in rural areas, although civilians are sometimes killed. Such attacks

Figure 9.2 (Continued)

include false roadblocks and attacks against convoys transporting military, police, or other government personnel. According to press reporting, some GSPC members in Europe maintain contacts with other North African extremists sympathetic to al-Qaeda. In late 2002, Algerian authorities announced they had killed a Yemeni al-Qaeda operative who had been meeting with the GSPC inside Algeria. Attacks by the GSPC increased in 2003.

Strength:
Unknown; probably several hundred fighters with an unknown number of support networks inside Algeria.

Location/Area of Operation:
Algeria, possibly Western Europe

External Aid:
Algerian expatriates and GSPC members abroad, many residing in Western Europe, provide financial and logistic support. In addition, the Algerian Government has accused Iran and Sudan of supporting Algerian extremists in years past.

Figure 9.3
Other Terrorist and Extremist Groups

Al-Ittihad al-Islami (AIAI) a.k.a. Islamic Union

Description:
Somalia's largest militant Islamic organization rose to power in the early 1990s following the collapse of the Siad Barre regime. Its aims to establish an Islamic regime in Somalia and force the secession of the Ogaden region of Ethiopia have largely been abandoned. Some elements associated with AIAI maintain ties to al-Qaeda.

Activities:
Conducted terrorist attacks against Ethiopian forces and other Somali factions in the 1990s. The group is believed to be responsible for a series of bomb attacks in public places in Addis Ababa in 1996 and 1997 as well as the kidnapping of several relief workers in 1998. AIAI sponsors Islamic social programs, such as orphanages and schools, and provides pockets of security in Somalia.

Strength:
Estimated at some 2,000 members, plus additional reserve militias. Sustained significant losses at the hands of the Ethiopian military in the late 1990s, and members are now relegated to operating in small cells.

Location/Area of Operation:
Primarily in Somalia, with limited presence in Ethiopia and Kenya.

External Aid:
Receives funds from Middle East financiers and Western diaspora remittances and suspected training in Afghanistan. Past weapons deliveries from Sudan and Eritrea.

continued

Figure 9.3 (Continued)

Ansar al-Islam (AI) a.k.a. Partisans of Islam, Helpers of Islam, Supporters of Islam

Description:
Ansar al-Islam is a radical Islamist group of Iraqi Kurds and Arabs who have vowed to establish an independent Islamic state in northern Iraq. It was formed in September 2001 and is closely allied with al-Qaeda. Its members trained in al-Qaeda camps in Afghanistan and now provide safe haven to al-Qaeda fighters fleeing Afghanistan. (Ansar al-Islam was designated on 20 February 2003, under E.O. 13224. The UNSCR 1267 Committee designated Ansar al-Islam pursuant to UNSCRs 1267, 1390, and 1455 on 27 February 2003.)

Activities:
The group is challenging one of the two main Kurdish political factions, the Patriotic Union of Kurdistan (PUK) and has mounted ambushes and attacks in PUK areas. AI members have been implicated in assassinations and assassination attempts against PUK officials and claim to have produced cyanide-based toxins, ricin, and alfatoxin. AI may be a major source of terrorism in Iraq.

Strength:
Approximately 700 members.

Location/Area of Operation:
Ansar al-Islam is based in northern Iraq near the Iranian border outside Baghdad's control.

External Aid:
The group receives funding, training, equipment, and combat support from al-Qaeda.

Islamic Army of Aden (IAA) a.k.a. Aden-Abyan Islamic Army (AAIA)

Description:
The Islamic Army of Aden (IAA) emerged publicly in mid-1998 when the group released a series of communiques that expressed support for Osama Bin Laden and appealed for the overthrow of the Yemeni Government and operations against U.S. and other Western interests in Yemen. IAA's assets were frozen under E.O. 13224 in September 2001, and it was designated for sanctions under UNSCR 1333 in the same month.

Activities:
Engages in bombings and kidnappings to promote its goals. Kidnapped 16 British, U.S., and Australian tourists in late December 1998 near Mudiyah in southern Yemen. Since the capture and trial of the Mudiyah kidnappers and the execution in October 1999 of the group's leader, Zein al-Abidine al-Mihdar (a.k.a. Abu Hassan), individuals associated with the IAA have remained involved in terrorist activities on a number of occasions. In 2001, the Yemeni Government convicted an IAA member and three associates for their role in the bombing in October 2000 of the British Embassy in Sanaa. The current status of the IAA is unknown. Despite the appearance of several press statements attributed to the IAA and released through intermediaries and the Internet in 2002, Yemeni officials claim that the group is operationally defunct.

410

Figure 9.3 (Continued)

Strength:
Not known.

Location/Area of Operation:
Operates in the southern governorates of Yemen—primarily Aden and Abyan.

External Aid:
Not known.

<h2 style="text-align:center">Libyan Islamic Fighting Group
a.k.a. Al-Jam'a al-Islamiyyah al-Muqatilah, Fighting Islamic Group,
Libyan Fighting Group, Libyan Islamic Group</h2>

Description:
Emerged in 1995 among Libyans who had fought against Soviet forces in Afghanistan. Declared the government of Libyan leader Muammar Qadhafi un-Islamic and pledged to overthrow it. Some members maintain a strictly anti-Qadhafi focus and organize against Libyan Government interests, but others are aligned with Osama Bin Laden's al-Qaeda organization or are active in the international mujahadeen network. The group was designated for asset freeze under E. O. 13224 and UNSCR 1333 in September 2001.

Activities:
Claimed responsibility for a failed assassination attempt against Qadhafi in 1996 and engaged Libyan security forces in armed clashes during the mid-to-late 1990s. Continues to target Libyan interests and may engage in sporadic clashes with Libyan security forces.

Strength:
Not known but probably has several hundred active members or supporters.

Location/Area of Operation:
Probably maintains a clandestine presence in Libya, but since late 1990s, many members have fled to various Middle Eastern and European countries.

External Aid:
Not known. May obtain some funding through private donations, various Islamic nongovernmental organizations, and criminal acts.

<h2 style="text-align:center">Lord's Resistance Army (LRA)</h2>

Description:
Founded in 1989 as the successor to the Holy Spirit Movement, the LRA seeks to overthrow the Ugandan Government and replace it with a regime that will implement the group's brand of Christianity.

Activities:
Since the early 1990's, the LRA has kidnapped and killed local Ugandan civilians in order to discourage foreign investment, precipitate a crisis in Uganda, and replenish their ranks.

Strength:
Estimated 1,000.

continued

Figure 9.3 (Continued)

Location/Area of Operation:
Northern Uganda and southern Sudan.

External Aid:
While the LRA has been supported by the Government of Sudan in the past, the Sudanese are now cooperating with the Government of Uganda in a campaign to eliminate LRA sanctuaries in Sudan.

Moroccan Islamic Combatant Group (GICM)

Description:
The goals of the Moroccan Islamic Combatant Group (GICM) reportedly include establishing an Islamic state in Morocco and supporting al-Qaeda's jihad against the West. The group appears to have emerged in the late 1990s and comprises Moroccan recruits who trained in armed camps in Afghanistan. GICM members interact with other North African extremists, particularly in Europe. On 22 November 2002, the United States designated the GICM for asset freeze under E.O. 13224. This followed the submission of the GICM to the UNSCR 1267 sanctions committee.

Activities:
GICM members, working with other North African extremists, engage in trafficking falsified documents and possibly gunrunning. The group in the past has issued communiques and statements against the Moroccan Government.

Strength:
Unknown.

Location/Area of Operation:
Western Europe, Afghanistan, and possibly Morocco.

External Aid:
Unknown.

The Tunisian Combatant Group (TCG)

Description:
The Tunisian Combatant Group (TCG), also known as the Jama'a Combattante Tunisienne, reportedly is seeking to establish an Islamic regime in Tunisia and targets U.S. and Western interests. Probably founded in 2000 by Tarek Maaroufi and Saifallah Ben Hassine, the loosely organized group has come to be associated with al-Qaeda and other North African extremist networks that have been implicated in terrorist plots during the past two years. The group was designated for sanctions under UNSCR 1333 in December 2000. Belgian authorities continue to hold Maaroufi, whom they arrested in December 2001.

Activities:
Tunisians associated with the TCG are part of the support network of the broader international jihadist movement. According to European press reports, TCG members or affiliates in the past have engaged in trafficking falsified documents and recruiting for terror training camps in Afghanistan. Some TCG associates are suspected of planning an attack against the U.S., Algerian, and Tunisian diplomatic missions in Rome in January 2001. Some members reportedly maintain ties to the Algerian Salafist Group for Preaching and Combat (GSPC).

Figure 9.3 (Continued)

Strength:
Unknown.

Location/Area of Operation:
Western Europe, Afghanistan.

External Aid:
Unknown.

Source: Adapted from IISS, *The Military Balance*, 2003–2004; and CRS, Report on Foreign
  Terrorist Organizations, with additional comments by author.

Chapter 10

Proliferation and Weapons of Mass Destruction

Proliferation is one of the least-understood aspects of the Middle East military balance, but it is also one of the most important. Conventional wars are certainly capable of destroying whole nations, and particularly small ones like Israel, Jordan, and the emerging Palestinian entity. In the real world, however, the probable outcome of conventional warfare in any of the previous contingencies is likely to be limited—at least in the sense that such wars are unlikely to escalate to levels of conflict that threaten the existence of one or more states, or produce massive civilian casualties.

The proliferation of weapons of mass destruction (WMD), however, poses a growing risk of wars that could threaten the major population centers of Israel and its Arab neighbors. Proliferation could destroy the very existence of Israel and change beyond all recognition the leadership and character of Iran and any Arab state that became involved in a large-scale exchange using biological or nuclear weapons.

The destruction of Saddam Hussein's regime in Iraq has removed one of the most dangerous proliferators in the region, but many proliferators remain. These include the nations shown in Figure 10.1. At the same time, this figure shows that the Middle East is only one region where nations are acquiring weapons of mass destruction, and that many other countries have the technology base to become proliferators. This raises the specter of the transfer of such weapons from outside the region or wars involving the forces of outside powers such as Pakistan.

Figure 10.1
Who Has Weapons of Mass Destruction?

Country	Type of Weapon of Mass Destruction		
	Chemical	Biological	Nuclear
East-West			
Britain	Breakout	Breakout	Deployed
France	Breakout	Breakout	Deployed
Germany	Breakout	Breakout	Technology
Sweden	—	—	Technology
Russia	Residual	Residual	Deployed
U.S.	Residual	Breakout	Deployed
Middle East			
Algeria	Technology	Technology	Interest
Egypt	Residual	Breakout	—
Israel	Breakout	Breakout	Deployed
Iran	Deployed?	Breakout	Technology
Iraq	Destroyed	Destroyed	Destroyed
Libya	Deployed?	Research	—
Syria	Deployed	Technology?	—
Yemen	Residual	—	—
Asia and South Asia			
China	Deployed?	Breakout?	Deployed
India	Breakout?	Breakout?	Deployed
Japan	Breakout	Breakout	Technology
Pakistan	Breakout?	Breakout?	Deployed
North Korea	Deployed	Deployed	Deployed (?)
South Korea	Breakout?	Breakout	Technology
Taiwan	Breakout?	Breakout	Technology
Thailand	Residual	—	—
Vietnam	Residual	—	—
Other			
Argentina	—	—	Technology
Brazil	—	—	Technology
South Africa	—	—	Technology

THE NATURE OF THE PROBLEM:
THE WEAPONS AND THEIR EFFECTS

Weapons of mass destruction are divided into four major categories: chemical, biological, radiological, and nuclear (CBRN). In practice, radiological weapons that actually act as weapons of mass destruction, as distinguished from terror weapons that can attack and contaminate a relatively small area, are extremely difficult to manufacture and weaponize and such weapons are probably both beyond the current capabilities of Middle Eastern powers and lack the cost-effectiveness that will lead countries to pursue them.

As Figure 10.2 shows, chemical, biological, and nuclear weapons also differ strikingly in terms of effectiveness, and strengths and weakness. It is important to note that each different type of CBRN weapon differs sharply in its war-fighting characteristics and lethality. Although all are called weapons of mass destruction, biological and nuclear weapons present by far the greatest threat.

Chemical weapons are the least lethal form of weapon of mass destruction, but are also the easiest to manufacture, weaponize, deploy, and use. There is no way to know what weapons given countries are developing or have deployed, but mustard gas, nerve agents, and blood agents seem most likely. Figure 10.3 does, however, show the weapons most likely to be in regional military forces and their general characteristics. Figure 10.4 shows how chemical weapons might be involved in combat, scarcely a theoretical possibility. Iraq prepared massive stockpiles of biological weapons during the end of the Iran-Iraq War and before the Gulf War of 1990.

Figure 10.5 shows the most likely form of biological weapons that may be deployed in the Middle East. This table does not include genetically modified agents, and assumes a moderate level of regional technological capability. If weapons are developed and transferred from more advanced countries, they could be much more lethal, harder to detect, and harder to treat.

Figure 10.6 shows the comparative lethality of chemical, biological, and nuclear weapons using the agents most likely to be used in a missile or line source attack. The differences between the lethality of different types of weapons are clear, although it should be noted that properly weaponized biological weapons are as lethal as fission nuclear weapons. Figure 10.7 extends the comparisons in Figure 10.6 to show the relative area that would be covered by different types of weapons and how increases in the yield of nuclear weapons affect lethality.

The broad characteristics of nuclear weapons are well understood, and a detailed discussion of design issues is beyond the scope of this analysis. Several factors should, however, be kept in mind:

- The physics and design aspects of conventional nuclear weapons are well understood, but actual production of fissile material, and the creation of small, efficient, and reliable weapons, remains at the limits of the state-of-the-art in applied engineering and systems integration in most countries.

- Building small and efficient conventional gun or implosion weapons requires a high level of engineering and design skill and highly enriched material. Large weapons, with unpredictable yields and lower reliability, can use material with much lower levels of enrichment.

Figure 10.2
Strengths and Weaknesses of Weapons of Mass Destruction

Chemical Weapons
Destructive Effects: Poisoning skin, lungs, nervous system, or blood. Contaminating areas, equipment, and protective gear for periods of hours to days. Forcing military units to don highly restrictive protection gear or use incapacitating antidotes. False alarms and panic. Misidentification of the agent, or confusion of chemical with biological agents (which may be mixed) leading to failure of defense measures. Military and popular panic and terror effects. Major medical burdens which may lead to mistreatment. Pressure to deploy high cost air and missile defenses. Paralysis or disruption of civil life and economic activity in threatened or attacked areas.
Typical Military Targets: Infantry concentrations, air bases, ships, ports, staging areas, command centers, munitions depots, cities, key oil and electrical facilities, desalinization plants.
Typical Military Missions: Killing military and civilian populations. Intimidation. Attack of civilian population or targets. Disruption of military operations by requiring protective measures or decontamination. Area or facility denial. Psychological warfare, production of panic, and terror.
Military Limitations: Large amounts of agents are required to achieve high lethality, and military and economic effects are not sufficiently greater than careful target conventional strikes to offer major war-fighting advantages. Most agents degrade quickly, and their effect is highly dependent on temperature and weather conditions, height of dissemination, terrain, and the character of built-up areas. Warning devices far more accurate and sensitive than for biological agents. Protective gear and equipment can greatly reduce effects, and sufficiently high numbers of rounds, sorties, and missiles are needed to ease the task of defense. Leave buildings and equipment reusable by the enemy, although persistent agents may require decontamination. Persistent agents may contaminate the ground the attacker wants to cross or occupy and force use of protective measures or decontamination.

Biological Weapons
Destructive Effects: Infectious disease or biochemical poisoning. Contaminating areas, equipment, and protective gear for periods of hours to weeks. Delayed effects and tailoring to produce incapacitation or killing, treatable or non-treatable agents, and be infectious on contact only or transmittable. Forcing military units to don highly restrictive protection gear or use incapacitating vaccines antidotes. False alarms and panic. High risk of at least initial misidentification of the agent, or confusion of biological with chemical agents (which may be mixed) leading to failure of defense measures. Military and popular panic and terror effects. Major medical burdens, which may lead to mistreatment. Pressure to deploy high cost air and missile defenses. Paralysis or disruption of civil life and economic activity in threatened or attacked areas.
Typical Military Targets: Infantry concentrations, air bases, ships, ports, staging areas, command centers, munitions depots, cities, key oil and electrical facilities, desalinization plants. Potentially fare more effective against military and civil area targets than chemical weapons.

Figure 10.2 (Continued)

Typical Military Missions: Killing and incapacitation of military and civilian populations. Intimidation. Attack of civilian population or targets. Disruption of military operations by requiring protective measures or decontamination. Area or facility denial. Psychological warfare, production of panic, and terror.

Military Limitations: Most wet agents degrade quickly, although spores, dry encapsulated agents, and some toxins are persistent. Effects usually take some time to develop (although not in the case of some toxins). Effects are unpredictable, and are even more dependent than chemical weapons on temperature and weather conditions, height of dissemination, terrain, and the character of built-up areas. Major risk of contaminating the wrong area. Warning devices uncertain and may misidentify the agent. Protective gear and equipment can reduce effects. Leave buildings and equipment reusable by the enemy, although persistent agents may require decontamination. Persistent agents may contaminate the ground the attacker wants to cross or occupy and force use of protective measures or decontamination. More likely than chemical agents to cross the threshold where nuclear retaliation seems justified.

Nuclear Weapons

Destructive Effects: Blast, fire, and radiation. Destruction of large areas and production of fall out and contamination—depending on character of weapon and height of burst. Contaminating areas, equipment, and protective gear for periods of hours to days. Forcing military units to don highly restrictive protection gear and use massive amounts of decontamination gear. Military and popular panic and terror effects. Massive medical burdens. Pressure to deploy high cost air and missile defenses. Paralysis or disruption of civil life and economic activity in threatened or attacked areas. High long-term death rates from radiation. Forced dispersal of military forces and evacuation of civilians. Destruction of military and economic centers, and national political leadership and command authority, potentially altering character of attacked nation and creating major recovery problems.

Typical Military Targets: Hardened targets, enemy facilities and weapons of mass destruction, enemy economy, political leadership, and national command authority. Infantry and armored concentrations, air bases, ships, ports, staging areas, command centers, munitions depots, cities, key oil and electrical facilities, desalinization plants.

Typical Military Missions: Forced dispersal of military forces and evacuation of civilians. Destruction of military and economic centers, and national political leadership and command authority, potentially altering character of attacked nation and creating major recovery problems.

Military Limitations: High cost. Difficulty of acquiring more than a few weapons. Risk of accidents or failures that hit friendly territory. Crosses threshold to level where nuclear retaliation is likely. Destruction or contamination of territory and facilities attacker wants to cross or occupy. High risk of massive collateral damage to civilians if this is important to attacker.

Source: Adapted by the Anthony H. Cordesman from Office of Technology Assessment, *Proliferation of Weapons of Mass Destruction: Assessing the Risks*, Washington, DC: U.S. Congress OTA-ISC-559, 1993, pp. 56–57.

Figure 10.3
Major Chemical Agents

Nerve Agents: Agents that quickly disrupt the nervous system by binding to enzymes critical to nerve functions, causing convulsions and/or paralysis. May be ingested, inhaled, and absorbed through the skin. Very low doses cause a running nose, contraction of the pupil of the eye, and difficulty in visual coordination. Moderate doses constrict the bronchi and cause a feeling of pressure in the chest, and weaken the skeletal muscles and cause filibration. Large doses cause death by respiratory or heart failure. Reaction normally occurs in 1–2 minutes. Death from lethal doses occurs within minutes, but artificial respiration can help and atropine and the oximes act as antidotes. The most toxic nerve agents kill with a dosage of only 10 milligrams per minute per cubic meter, versus 400 for less lethal gases. Recovery is normally quick, if it occurs at all, but permanent brain damage can occur:

> Tabun (GA)
> Sarin (GB)—nearly as volatile as water and delivered by air. A dose of 5 mg/min/m^3 produces casualties, a respiratory dose of 100 mg/min/m^3 is lethal. Lethality lasts 1–2 days.
>
> Soman (GD)
> GF
> VR-55 (Improved Soman) A thick oily substance which persists for some time.
> VK/VX—a persistent agent roughly as heavy as fuel oil. A dose of 0.5 mg/min/m^3 produces casualties, a respiratory dose of 10 mg/min/m3 is lethal. Lethality lasts 1–16 weeks.

Blister Agents: Cell poisons that destroy skin and tissue, cause blindness upon contact with the eyes, and which can result in fatal respiratory damage. Can be colorless or black oily droplets. Can be absorbed through inhalation or skin contact. Serious internal damage if inhaled. Penetrates ordinary clothing. Some have delayed and some have immediate action. Actual blistering normally takes hours to days, but effects on the eyes are much more rapid. Mustard gas is a typical blister agent and exposure of concentrations of a few milligrams per meter over several hours generally at least causes blisters and swollen eyes. When the liquid falls onto the skin or eyes it has the effect of second or third degree burns. It can blind and cause damage to the lungs leading to pneumonia. Severe exposure causes general intoxication similar to radiation sickness. HD and HN persist up to 12 hours. L, HL, and CX persist for 1–2 hours. Short of prevention of exposure, the only treatment is to wash the eyes, decontaminate the skin, and treat the resulting damage like burns:

> Sulfur Mustard (H or HD) A dose of 100 mg/min/m3 produces casualties, a dose of 1,500 mg/min/m^3 is lethal. Residual lethality lasts up to 2–8 weeks.
> Distilled Mustard (DM)
> Nitrogen Mustard (HN)
> Lewisite (L)
> Phosgene Oxime (CX)
> Mustard Lewisite (HL)

Figure 10.3 (Continued)

Choking Agents: Agents that cause the blood vessels in the lungs to hemorrhage, and fluid to build-up, until the victim chokes or drowns in his or her own fluids (pulmonary edema). Provide quick warning though smell or lung irritation. Can be absorbed through inhalation. Immediate to delayed action The only treatment is inhalation of oxygen and rest. Symptoms emerge in periods after exposure of seconds up to three hours:

> Phosgene (CG)
> Diphosgene (DP)
> PS Chloropicrin
> Chlorine Gas

Blood Agents: Kill through inhalation. Provide little warning except for headache, nausea, and vertigo. Interferes with use of oxygen at the cellular level. CK also irritates the lungs and eyes. Rapid action and exposure either kills by inhibiting cell respiration or it does not—casualties will either die within seconds to minutes of exposure or recover in fresh air. Most gas masks have severe problems in providing effective protection against blood agents:

- Hydrogen Cyanide (AC) A dose of 2,000 mg/min/m3 produces casualties, a respiratory dose of 5,000 mg/min/m3 is lethal. Lethality lasts 1–4 hours.
- Cyanogen Chloride (CK) A dose of 7,000 mg/min/m3 produces casualties, a respiratory dose of 11,000 mg/min/m3 is lethal. Lethality lasts 15 minutes to one hour.

Toxins: Biological poisons causing neuromuscular paralysis after exposure of hours or days. Formed in food or cultures by the bacterium clostridium Botulinum. Produces highly fatal poisoning characterized by general weakness, headache, dizziness, double vision and dilation of the pupils, paralysis of muscles, and problems in speech. Death is usually by respiratory failure. Antitoxin therapy has limited value, but treatment is mainly supportive:

> Botulin toxin (A) Six distinct types, of which four are known to be fatal to man. An oral dose of 0.001 mg is lethal. A respiratory dose of 0.02 mg/min/m^3 is also lethal.

Developmental Weapons: A new generation of chemical weapons is under development. The only publicized agent is perfluoroisobutene (PFIB), which is an extremely toxic odorless and invisible substance produced when PFIB (Teflon) is subjected to extreme heat under special conditions. It causes pulmonary edema or dry-land drowning when the lungs fill with fluid. Short exposure disables and small concentrations cause delayed death. Activated charcoal and most existing protection equipment offers no defense. Some sources refer to "third" and "fourth" generation nerve gasses, but no technical literature seems to be available.

continued

Figure 10.3 (Continued)

Control Agents: Agents which produce temporary irritating or disabling effects which in contact with the eyes or inhaled. They cause flow of tears and irritation of upper respiratory tract and skin. They can cause nausea and vomiting: can cause serious illness or death when used in confined spaces. CN is the least toxic gas, followed by CS and DM. Symptoms can be treated by washing of the eyes and/or removal from the area. Exposure to CS, CN, and DM produces immediate symptoms. Staphylococcus produces symptoms in 30 minutes to four hours, and recovery takes 24–48 hours. Treatment of Staphylococcus is largely supportive:

> Tear
> Chlororacetophenone (CN)
> O-Chlorobenzyl-malononitrile (CS)
> Vomiting: Cause irritation, coughing, severe headache, tightness in chest, nausea, vomiting:
> Adamsite (DM)
> Staphylococcus

Incapacitating Agents: Agents, which normally cause short-term illness, psychoactive effects, (delirium and hallucinations). Can be absorbed through inhalation or skin contact. The psychoactive gases and drugs produce unpredictable effects, particularly in the sick, small children, elderly, and individuals who already are mentally ill. In rare cases they kill or produce a permanent psychotic condition. Many produce dry skin, irregular heart beat, urinary retention, constipation, drowsiness, and a rise in body temperature, plus occasional maniacal behavior. A single dose of 0.1 to 0.2 milligrams of LSD-25 will produce profound mental disturbance within a half-hour that lasts 10 hours. The lethal dose is 100 to 200 milligrams:

> BZ
> LSD
> LSD Based BZ
> Mescaline
> Psilocybin
> Benzilates

Source: Adapted from Matthew Meselson and Julian Perry Robinson, "Chemical Warfare and Chemical Disarmament," *Scientific American*, Vol. 242, No. 4, April, 1980, pp. 38–47; "Chemical Warfare: Extending the Range of Destruction," *Jane's Defense Weekly*, August 25, 1990, p. 267; Dick Palowski, *Changes in Threat Air Combat Doctrine and Force Structure*, 24th Edition, Fort Worth: General Dynamics DWIC-01, 1992, pp. II-335–II-339; U.S. Marine Corps, "Individual Guide For NBC Defense," Field Manual OH-11-1A, August, 1990; and unpublished testimony to the Special Investigations Subcommittee of the Government Operations Committee, U.S. Senate, by Mr. David Goldberg, Foreign Science and Technology Center, U.S. Army Intelligence Center on February 9, 1989.

Figure 10.4
Typical War-Fighting Uses of Chemical Weapons

Mission	Quantity
Attack an infantry position: Cover 1.3 square kilometers of territory with a "surprise dosage" attack of Sarin to kill 50% of exposed troops.	216 240mm rockets (e.g. delivered by 18, 12 tube Soviet BM-24 rocket launchers, each carrying 8 kilograms of agent and totaling 1,728 kilograms of agent.
Prevent launch of enemy mobile missiles: Contaminate a 25 square kilometer missile unit operating area with 0.3 tons of a persistent nerve gas like VX per square kilometer.	8 MiG-23 or 4 Su-24 fighters, each delivering 0.9 tons of VX (totaling 7.2 tons).
Immobilize an air base: Contaminate a 2 square kilometer air base with 0.3 tons of VX twice a day for 3 days.	1 MiG-23 with six sorties or any similar attack aircraft.
Defend a broad front against large-scale attack: Maintain a 300 meter deep strip of VX contamination in a front of a position defending a 60 kilometer wide area for 3 days.	65 metric tons of agent delivered by approximately 13,000 155-mm artillery rounds.
Canalize 1st and 2nd Echelon attacking forces: Force attacking Or retreating forces into fixed lines of movement. Guard flanks. Disrupt rear area operations.	8 MiG-23 or 4 Su-24 fighters, each delivering 0.9 tons of VX (totaling 7.2 tons).
Terrorize population: Kill approximately 125,000 unprotected civilians in a densely populated (10,000 square kilometer) city.	8 MiG-23 or 4 Su-24 fighters, each delivering 0.9 tons of VX (totaling 7.2 tons) under optimum conditions.

Source: Adapted by Anthony H. Cordesman from Victor A. Utgoff, *The Challenge of Chemical Weapons*, New York: St. Martin's, 1991, pp. 238–242; and Office of Technology Assessment, *Proliferation of Weapons of Mass Destruction: Assessing the Risks*, Washington, DC: U.S. Congress OTA-ISC-559, 1993, pp. 56–57.

Figure 10.5
Biological Weapons That May Be in the Middle East

Disease	Infectivity	Transmissibility	Incubation Period	Mortality	Therapy
Viral					
Chikungunya fever	high?	none	2–6 days	very low (–1%)	none
Dengue fever	high	none	5–2 days	very low (–1%)	none
Eastern equine encephalitis	high	none	5–10 days	high (+60%)	developmental
Tick borne encephalitis	high	none	1–2 weeks	up to 30%	developmental
Venezuelan equine encephalitis	high	none	2–5 days	Low (–1%)	developmental
Hepatitis A	–	–	15–40 days	–	–
Hepatitis B	–	–	40–150 days	–	–
Influenza	high	none	1–3 days	usually low	available
Yellow fever	high	none	3–6 days	up to 40%	available
Smallpox (Variola)	high	high	7–16 days	up to 30%	available
Rickettsial					
Coxiella Burneti (Q-fever)	high	negligible	10–21 day	Low (–1%)	antibiotic
Mooseri	–	–	6–14 days	–	–
Prowazeki	–	–	6–15 days	–	–
Psittacosis	high	moderate–high	4–15 days	moderate–high	antibiotic
Rickettsi (Rocky mountain spotted fever)	high	none	3–10 days	up to 80%	antibiotic
Tsutsugamushi	–	–	–	–	–
Epidemic typhus	high	none	6–15 days	up to 70%	antibiotic/vaccine

Bacterial

Anthrax (pulmonary)	moderate–high	negligible	1–5 days	usually fatal	antibiotic/vaccine
Brucellosis	high	none	1–3 days	~2-5%	antibiotic
Cholera	low	high	1–5 days	up to 80%	antibiotic/vaccine
Glanders	high	none	2–1 days	usually fatal	poor antibiotic
Meloidosis	high	none	1–5 days	usually fatal	moderate antibiotic
Plague (pneumonic)	high	high	2–5 days	usually fatal	antibiotic/vaccine
Tularemia	high	negligible	1–10 days	low to 60%	antibiotic/vaccine
Typhoid fever	moderate–high	moderate–high	7–21 days	up to 10%	antibiotic/vaccine
Dysentery	high	high	1–4 days	low to high	antibiotic/vaccine

Fungal

Coccidioidomycosis	high	none	1–3 days	low	none
Coccidiodes Immitis	high	none	10–21 days	low	none
Histoplasma					
Capsulatum	—	—	15–18 days	—	—
Norcardia Asteroides	—	—	—	—	—

Toxins[a]

Botulinum toxin	high	none	12–72 hours	high neromuscular paralysis	vaccine
Mycotoxin	high	none	hours or days	low to high	?
Staphylococcus	moderate	none	24–48 hours	incapacitating	?

[a]Many sources classify as chemical weapons because toxin are chemical poisons.

Source: Adapted by Anthony H. Cordesman from "Report of the Secretary General, Department of Political and Security Affairs, Chemical and Bacteriological (Biological) Weapons and the Effects of Their Possible Use," New York: United Nations, 1969, pp. 26, 29, 37–52, 116–117; *Jane's NBC Protection Equipment,* 1991–1992; James Smith, "Biological Warfare Developments," *Jane's Intelligence Review,* November, 1991, pp. 483–487.

Figure 10.6
The Comparative Effects of Biological, Chemical, and Nuclear Weapons Delivered against a Typical Urban Target in the Middle East

Using missile warheads: Assumes one Scud-sized warhead with a maximum payload of 1,000 kilograms. The study assumes that the biological agent would not make maximum use of this payload capability because this is inefficient. It is unclear this is realistic.

	Area Covered in Square Kilometers	Deaths Assuming 3,000–10,000 people Per Square Kilometer
Chemical		
300 kilograms of Sarin nerve gas with a density of 70 milligrams per cubic meter	0.22	60–200
Biological		
30 kilograms of Anthrax spores with a density of 0.1 milligram per cubic meter	10	30,000–100,000
Nuclear		
One 12.5 kiloton nuclear device achieving 5 pounds per cubic inch of over-pressure	7.8	23,000–80,000
One 1 megaton hydrogen bomb	190	570,000–1,900,000

Using one aircraft delivering 1,000 kilograms of Sarin nerve gas or 100 kilograms of anthrax spores
Assumes the aircraft flies in a straight line over the target at optimal altitude and dispensing the agent as an aerosol. The study assumes that the biological agent would not make maximum use of this payload capability because this is inefficient. It is unclear this is realistic.

	Area Covered in Square Kilometers	Deaths Assuming 3,000–10,000 people Per Square Kilometer
Clear sunny day, light breeze		
Sarin Nerve Gas	0.74	300–700
Anthrax Spores	46	130,000–460,000
Overcast day or night, moderate wind		
Sarin Nerve Gas	0.8	400–800
Anthrax Spores	140	420,000–1,400,000
Clear calm night		
Sarin Nerve Gas	7.8	3,000–8,000
Anthrax Spores	300	1,000,000–3,000,000

Source: Adapted by Anthony H. Cordesman from Office of Technology Assessment, *Proliferation of Weapons of Mass Destruction: Assessing the Risks*, Washington, DC: U.S. Congress OTA-ISC-559, 1993, pp. 53–54.

Figure 10.7
The Relative Killing Effect of Chemical versus Biological Weapons of Mass
Destruction for a 1,000-Kilogram Bomb or Warhead

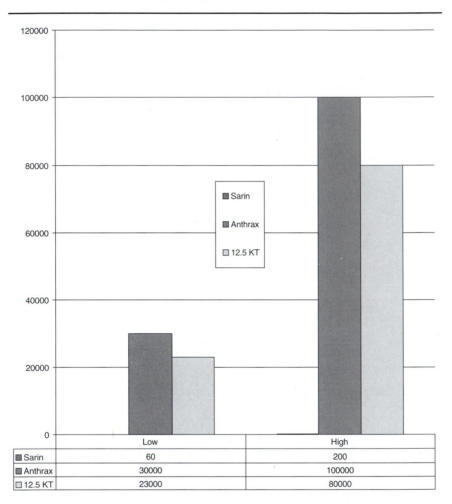

	Low	High
■ Sarin	60	200
■ Anthrax	30000	100000
□ 12.5 KT	23000	80000

The Thermal and Blast Effects of Nuclear Weapons—
Radius of Effect in Kilometers

Yield in Kilotons	Metals Vaporize	Metals Melt	Wood Burns	3rd Degree Burns	5 psi/ 160 mph Winds	3 psi/ 116 mph Winds
10	0.337	0.675	1.3	1.9	1.3	1.6
20	0.477	0.954	1.9	2.7	2.0	2.5
50	0.754	1.6	3.0	4.3	2.7	3.3
100	1.0	2.0	4.3	5.7	3.5	4.3
200	1.5	2.8	5.7	8.0	4.5	5.4

Source: Adapted by Anthony H. Cordesman from Royal United Services Institute, *Nuclear Attack: Civil Defense*, London: RUSI/Brassey's, 1982, pp. 30–36.

- Advanced warheads probably may require actual testing, but advances in the state-of-the-art in simulation and measurement increasingly mean that nuclear weapons can be designed with a high probability of effectiveness using implosion and gun testing without fissile material.

- Yields above 20 kilotons require advanced weapons designs known as "boosted" weapons, with some of the design characteristics of thermonuclear weapons. These may be beyond the state-of-the-art for any nation other than Israel. This does, however, present serious problems for some delivery systems like missiles, which may not be accurate enough to deliver a regular fissile weapon within the area where it has high effectiveness.

- Similarly, yields of about 200 kilotons require thermonuclear weapons—which are still extremely difficult technical challenges—and long-range missiles may be inaccurate or unreliable to the point that such yields are required.

- There are no simple ways to summarize radiation and fallout effects, but lowering the height of burst of a weapon can radically increase fallout and long-term radiation and contamination effects at the cost of reducing blast and thermal effects.

At the same time, the kind of lethality data presented in Figures 10.4 to Figure 10.7 can exaggerate the threat posed by such weapons. The models for making such calculations have dubious credibility, in terms of estimating both immediate and long-term effects. Chemical weapons have never achieved anything like the lethality in practice that they have in theory, and there have been no actual uses of modern biological weapons in warfare. The nuclear effects models assume flat open areas, and have limited credibility in estimating long-term effects against humans and the environment.

The actual process of weaponization is critical in determining effectiveness. Even the most lethal agent or weapon can be ineffective if a bomb or warhead design is not highly advanced and does not operate perfectly in actual use. The reliability and accuracy of the delivery system, the quality of targeting, and the choice of targets are also critical factors. Many developing countries lack the systems integration, command and control, and tactical capabilities to both develop and deploy effective forces using weapons of mass destruction, and most may lack the strategic and tactical skills to employ them effectively in sophisticated attacks.

It should also be noted that ballistic missiles often receive undue attention, as if they were the only major delivery systems for such weapons. Aircraft, helicopters, artillery, and covert delivery are all effective methods of delivering such weapons. Missiles are only one of many possible delivery systems and often not the most effective.

THE PROLIFERATORS, THEIR MOTIVES, AND WAR-FIGHTING ISSUES

Many Middle Eastern states have not proliferated, or have resisted the temptation to deploy, such weapons. At the same time, there are strong regional incentives to proliferate—at least to the point of developing the capability to rapidly manufacture and deploy some form of weapon of mass destruction. These incentives include:

- Prestige
- Deterrence
- War-fighting
- Lessons of the Iran-Iraq and Gulf Wars: missiles and weapons of mass destruction have been used against military and civilian targets
- Arms race with neighbors: Algeria-Libya-Morocco, Egypt-Israel-Syria, Iran-Iraq-Southern Gulf
- Inability to know the future enemy, characterize risk
- The "greater Middle East"—growing overlap of arms races listed above, plus impact of North Korea and India-Pakistan arms race
- Deterrence and safeguards: no way to know the scale of the efforts of key threats and other major regional actors
- Intimidation
- Alternative to expensive conventional investments
- Compensate for conventional weakness and cost of conventional weapons
- "Glitter factor"
- Limit or attack U.S. and others outside power projection options
- Create existential threat
- Force arms control, react to absence of meaningful arms control regimes
- Momentum of arms race/respond to proliferation elsewhere
- State, proxy, or private terrorism
- Exploit lack of effective civil and critical facility defense and antitactical ballistic missile defense capabilities

Proliferation already shapes the regional military balance in ways that affect the peacetime balance of power and influence, the structure of regional deterrence, and options for future war-fighting:

- Israel relies on nuclear weapons, deterrence, and "soft strike" preemption.
- Iran has chemical and probably biological weapons, nuclear effort continues.
- Iraq's massive pre–Gulf War efforts gave it a major "break out" effort the moment UN and U.S. containment efforts ceased and may give a successor some break out capability in spite of the Iraq War.
- Syria has significant chemical warfare capabilities and will soon acquire significant biological capabilities—if it does not have them.
- Libyan chemical effort continues.
- Algerian and Egyptian efforts uncertain.

- Saudi Arabia is studying options as a result of its CSS-2 replacement planning.
- Terrorists, extremists, and "proxies" are also making efforts to acquire such capabilities.

This, in turn, has already created the following unstable mix of possible combinations of adversaries and contingencies:

- Iran versus Iraq
- Iraq versus Southern Gulf, United States, and/or Israel
- Israel versus Syria
- Iran versus Southern Gulf, United States, and/or Israel
- Libyan and Algerian wild cards
- Vestigial Yemeni use of gas
- Saudi Arabia joins the club in reaction to Iranian and Iraqi proliferation, changing the nature of war-fighting involving the Southern Gulf
- The United States extends deterrence, compellance, and/or retaliation in reaction to an attack on an Arab ally or Israel
- Egypt joins the club after arms control efforts fail, and finds itself involved against Iraq or dragged into confrontation with Israel

There are a number of war-fighting options wherein proliferation could affect the balance:

- Covert-indirect, unconventional warfare, "terrorism"
- Surprise attack to support conventional war-fighting
- Avoid conventional defeat
- Pose political threat—intimidation
- Regional deterrence—threatened or illustrative use
- Attack power projection facilities
- Counterproliferation
- Extended deterrence
- Controlled escalation ladder
- Asymmetric escalation/escalation dominance
- "Firebreaks"
- Launch on warning/launch under attack
- Seek to force conflict termination
- Destroy enemy as state
- Martyrdom
- Alter strategic nature of ongoing conflict

These lists illustrate the fact that there is no way to know how each pro-liferating nation has developed or will develop its war-fighting doctrine, war plans, safety procedures, leadership control procedures, release doctrine and procedures, targeting doctrine and capabilities, civil defense capabilities, and damage estimation and assessment capabilities. It seems unlikely that most leadership elites will consider major existential risks or behave recklessly except under extreme crisis conditions. However, risk-taking and miscal-culation are long-standing historical realities, and war-fighting analysis that is based on scenarios and actions that seem prudent in peacetime can be terribly misleading.

The following factors need to be considered:

- The WMD arms race is multipolar and cuts across subregions, making it dif-ficult to contain the scope of conflicts.
- Technologies are new and there is little or no combat experience; operations research and exercises are difficult.
- Acquisition does not mean war planning, policy statements do not mean war planning, doctrine does not mean war planning.
- Lies, denial, and covert efforts make it extremely difficult to predict oppos-ing force and enemy actions.
- Impossible to predict ride out capability and survival of retaliatory forces in many cases, possible "use or lose" reaction.
- War-fighting concepts are likely to lack clear structure and be highly volatile in terms of enemy, targets, and crisis behavior:
  - Only a few leadership and military elites—such as Egypt and Israel—have shown a concern with highly structured strategic planning in the past.
  - The Iran-Iraq and Gulf Wars have demonstrated missiles and weapons of mass destruction will be used, and that escalation can be unpredictable.
  - Israeli actions in 1967 and attack on Osirak, and Egyptian and Syrian attack on Israel in 1973 demonstrate regional focus on surprise and preemption.
  - Iraq has already demonstrated regional concern with launch on warning, launch under attack options. Syria probably has some option of this kind.
- Concentration of population and leadership in single or a few urban areas makes existential attacks possible and attractive.
- Covert, terrorist, and proxy attacks are increasingly possible, particularly using biological weapons.
- Employment is unlikely to be irrational or reckless, but restraint in attacking civilian targets or mass employment against armed forces may be limited. Regimes also take existential risks in escalating if they feel they are likely to lose power. The use of proxies and unconventional delivery means may well be improvised without warning.

The region has at least some leaders who believe in personal rule, are impatient with technical details, and may be poorly prepared for crises when they do occur. The region's military experts also tend to be far more interested in acquiring new weapons than the details of employing them, and it may be difficult for many countries to estimate weapons reliability and effects—particularly when weapons development is covert. Restraint and rational deterrence in peacetime could quickly turn into uncontrolled escalation in a major crisis—particularly if leaders were confronted with the perceived need to preempt or a "use or lose" contingency. It is important to note that while some states may be proliferating, they may not yet have decided exactly how these weapons that they are producing are to be used.

Many countries do not articulate detailed war plans and employment doctrine beyond the prestige of acquiring such weapons, broad threats, and efforts to intimidate their neighbors and the West. Even where nations appear to articulate a strategy of deterrence or employment, this may often consist more of words than detailed war-fighting capabilities. Most proliferating nations will engage in concealment, denial, and compartmentation—focusing more on the acquisition and development effort than employment. Targeting plans, test and evaluation, and understanding of lethality will be limited. Joint warfare concepts will rarely be articulated, and doctrine will not be practiced.

CBRN forces will often be covert or compartmentalized from other forces, and under the direct control of ruling elites with little real military experience. Separate lines of C^4I/BM reporting directly to the leadership will be common. Actual weapons may be held separately from delivery systems and by special units chosen more for loyalty than capability. Any actual employment will be crisis-driven, and utilization and escalation will be more a product of the attitudes and decisions of a narrow ruling political elite than any part of the military command chain. Risk-taking will often be leader-specific and based on perceptions of a crisis shaped more by internal political attitudes than an objective understanding of the military situation.

The covert nature of proliferation also makes it almost impossible for any nation to be sure its opponent has actually reduced its weapons to zero, and the very nature of biotechnology means that no presently conceivable arms control regime can deny states in the region a steadily growing "breakout" capability to build and use bioweapons capable of decimating an opponent's capital city, potentially disrupting its government and threatening its existence as a state. This makes it essential to consider the threat of terrorist use of weapons of mass destruction.

All of these factors could, in the worst case, lead to the use of chemical and biological weapons in areas of dense population. The easily accessible agents as well as the multitude of dense population centers in the Middle East make these scenarios increasingly probable. While many of the examples provided here include scenarios regarding states, it is important to note the many possibilities of a terrorist attack using these weapons:

- Unconventional and terrorist delivery of weapons of mass destruction can offer major advantages.
- Powers like Iran and Syria have used terrorists and extremists as proxies in attacking neighbors.
- Biological warfare—the easiest way to achieve extremely high lethalities—is best conducted in this manner.
- Past terrorist attacks have shown it can take months to years to firmly characterize the enemy, and this is particularly true when terrorism has indirect or direct support from a state like Libya, Syria, or Iran. "Plausible deniability" may exist indefinitely and a state subject to an existential attack has no meaningful way to retaliate.

CHANGES IN TECHNOLOGY

As Figure 10.8 shows, advances in technology present growing problems for both achieving regional military stability and for arms control at every level. While there have been no breakthroughs in the production of fissile material, there is a vast amount of fissile material in the former Soviet Union, and more and more countries could produce an aircraft-deliverable nuclear device in a matter of a few months or years if they could buy weapons grade material. The very nature of biotechnology means all of the countries in the Middle East are steadily acquiring the capability to make extremely lethal dry-storable biological weapons, and can do so with fewer and fewer indicators in terms of imports of specialized technology, with more use of dual-use or civilian production facilities, and in smaller spaces. In most cases, their civil infrastructure will provide the capability to create such weapons without dedicated major military imports.

As Figure 10.9 shows, these changes in technology affect both defense and offense. Long-range ballistic missile systems are being deployed in Iran and Syria, as well as Israel; better strike fighters with performance capabilities superior to yesterday's bombers are becoming commonplace. The kind of cruise missile technology suited to long-range delivery of both nuclear and biological weapons against area targets like cities is becoming available to nations like Egypt, Iran, Iraq, Israel, and Syria. While improved air defenses and theater ballistic missile defenses—such as Patriot, Arrow, and THAAD—offer a potential countermeasure to such delivery systems, the peace process also will create more open borders and more civilian commercial traffic of a kind that makes it easier to use unconventional delivery means.

These technical developments create new uncertainties for war-fighting and arms control. Nations that are just beginning to acquire a few nuclear weapons or serious biological weapons tend to see wars involving such weapons in terms of threats to enemy population centers and have little option other than to strike or concede if intimidation fails. They also tend

Figure 10.8
Technological Developments and Imperatives: 2010–2020

Missiles and Other Delivery Systems

- Satellite targeting and weather models, GPS launch location data.

- Cheap cruise missiles, drones, aircraft conversions.

- Indigenous production of medium to long-range solid fuel designs and high payload, multi-stage liquid-fueled designs. "Add a stage" range extensions.

- Widespread deployment of systems with high range-payloads and very high terminal velocities. Some "smart" warhead technology for penetration and terminal guidance.

- Hardened or mobile launch facilities, large numbers of dispersed systems.

- Rapid launch with minimal warning indicators.

- Mobile, rapidly replaceable separate warheads. Easy conversion and concealment.

- Advanced computer modeling and simulation, test range facilities. Reduced testing requirements.

- Strike Aircraft with some stealth features.

- Advanced warhead and munitions designs with sophisticated fusing and dissemination systems.

- Highly sophisticated covert delivery systems and "terrorist" devices.

Chemical Weapons

- Rapid, often covert, precursor production. Complex precursor assembly combinations.

- Stable binary nerve agents for persistent and non-persistent agents.

- Rapid production of mustard and other incapacitating agents.

- Weapons with mixed agents or "cocktails" to help defeat antidotes and protection systems.

- "Breakout" facilities for rapid conversion to production.

- Effective cluster warheads and bombs, with reliable fusing and dissemination systems.

- Widespread deployment of systems with high range-payloads and very high terminal velocities. Some "smart" warhead technology for penetration and terminal guidance.

- Advanced weather and targeting data. Computer modeling of attack contours.

- Highly sophisticated covert delivery systems and "terrorist" devices.

Biological Weapons

- Genetic engineering—generational change capability to weaponize new weapons, defeat vaccines, detection, and protection systems.

- Widespread deployment of dry, storable agents.

continued

Figure 10.8 (Continued)

- Ability to rapidly convert civilian pharmaceutical, fermentation, and other facilities.
- Possible ability to weaponize infectious agents like Ebola.
- Ability to use complex cocktails of different biological weapons to defeat warning, detection, treatment, and protection.
- Lethality of small nuclear weapons.
- Advanced warhead and munitions designs with sophisticated fusing and dissemination systems. Line source dissemination systems.
- Rapidly convertible warheads and bombs.
- Advanced weather and targeting data. Computer modeling of attack contours.
- Highly sophisticated covert delivery systems and "terrorist" devices. Ability to delay effect of weapon.

Nuclear Weapons
- Widespread understanding of complex weapons designs and access to key computer modeling data.
- Reduced need for fissile material and sharply reduced weapon weight.
- Can reduce or eliminate need for testing.
- High speed, high capacity centrifuge capability.
- Power reactors can be rapidly converted or cannibalized?
- Indigenous design and production of explosive lenses, initiators, and boosting technology.
- Advanced computer modeling and simulation. Ability to use non-fissile material for most testing purposes.
- Advanced warhead designs with sophisticated fusing. Controlled height of burst and enhanced radiation weapons. Safe use of weapons near own and friendly territory.
- Advanced weather and targeting data. Computer modeling of fall out contours.
- Highly sophisticated covert delivery systems and "terrorist" devices.

---

to try to keep their capabilities covert, and remove them from their normal political decision-making process. This can lead to rapid massive escalation or surprise attacks—particularly if a given side fears preemption, structures its forces to launch under attack, and/or seeks to strike before its opponent can bring its retaliatory forces and air and missile defenses to full readiness. Fewer weapons do not mean greater stability and security, and they almost inevitably mean countervalue targeting.

Figure 10.9

Technological Developments and Imperatives: 2010–2020—Counterproliferation and Defensive Options

"Defensive" systems can protect:

- Missile and greatly improved air defenses.
- Major improvements in chemical and biological detection and warning.
- Some improvement in treatment and protection systems.
- Civil defense options.

"Defensive" systems can also threaten:

- Greatly improved access to satellite surveillance systems, ability to piggyback on any arms inspection efforts to ease targeting burden.
- Widespread access to long-range precision-guided strike systems and some ability to hit hardened targets.
- Possible access to small covert sensors and detection systems.
- Long-range UAVs, RPVs.
- Possible improvement in Sigint/Comint systems.

As the East-West arms race has shown, there is no easily definable stopping point in terms of either technology or weapons numbers. Broadening the number and type of weapons to allow strikes against military targets creates an incentive to be able to strike as many targets as possible. Obtaining the option to strike at tactical military targets lowers the threshold of escalation and may lead a given side to be more willing to attack. Reducing the vulnerability of steadily larger inventories of weapons and delivery systems may lead to a loss of control, or more lethal plans to preempt or launch under attack. Larger forces potentially increase the risk that weapons directed against military targets will hit population centers, and while the Middle East may not be filled with "one bomb" states, it is definitely filled with "few bomb" states. Further, a state under existential attack by one neighbor may lash out against other states—a pattern Iraq has already exhibited by launching missile attacks against Israel during the Gulf War.

COVERT AND TERRORIST ATTACKS AND THE RISK OF "SUPERTERRORISM"

As Figure 10.10 shows, however, it is also dangerous to view proliferation, and the technologies involved, in terms of advanced weapons and regular military forces. The advances in proliferation also aid terrorists,

Figure 10.10
Unconventional Attacks Using Weapons of Mass Destruction: Scenario Examples

- A radiological powder is introduced into the air conditioning systems of Saudi high-rise buildings or tourist hotels. Symptoms are only detected over days or weeks and public warning is given several weeks later. The authorities detect the presence of such a power, but cannot estimate its long-term lethality and have no precedents for decontamination. Tourism collapses, and the hotels eventually have to be torn down and rebuilt.

- A Country X-backed terrorist group smuggles parts for a crude gun-type nuclear device into Israel or bought in the market place. The device is built in a medium sized commercial truck. A physics student reading the U.S. Department of Defense weapons effects manual maps Tel Aviv to maximize fall out effects in an area filled with buildings with heavy metals and waits for a wind maximizing the fall out impact. The bomb explodes with a yield of only 8 kilotons, but with an extremely high level of radiation. Immediate casualties are limited but the long-term death rate mounts steadily with time. Peace becomes impossible and security measures become Draconian. Immigration halts and emigration reaches crisis proportions. Israel as such ceases to exist.

- Several workers move drums labeled as cleaning agents into a large shopping mall, large public facility, subway, train station, or airport. They dress as cleaners and are wearing what appear to be commercial dust filters or have taken the antidote for the agent they will use. They mix the feedstocks for a persistent chemical agent at the site during a peak traffic period. Large-scale casualties result, and Draconian security measures become necessary on a national level. A series of small attacks using similar "binary" agents virtually paralyze the economy, and detection is impossible except to identify all canisters of liquid.

- Immunized terrorists visit a U.S. carrier or major Marine assault ship during the first hours of visitor's day during a port call in the Middle East. They are carrying Anthrax powder in bags designed to make them appear slightly overweight. They slowly scatter the powder as they walk through the ship visit. The immediate result is 50% casualties among the ship's crew, its Marine complement, and the visitors that follow. The U.S. finds it has no experience with decontaminating a large ship where Anthrax has entered the air system and is scattered throughout closed areas. After long debates over methods and safety levels, the ship is abandoned.

- A Country X-backed terrorist group seeking to "cleanse" a nation of its secular regime and corruption introduces a modified type culture of Ebola or a similar virus into an urban area. It scatters infectious cultures in urban areas for which there is no effective treatment. By the time the attack is detected, it has reached epidemic proportions. Medical authorities rush into the infected area without proper protection, causing the collapse of medical facilities and emergency response capabilities. Other nations and regions have no alternative other than to isolate the nation or center under attack, letting the disease take its course.

- A Country X-backed terrorist group modifies the valves on a Japanese remote-controlled crop-spraying helicopter which has been imported legally for agricultural purposes. It uses this system at night or near dawn to spray a chemical or biological agent at altitudes below radar coverage in a line-source configuration. Alternatively, it uses a large home-built RPV with simple GPS guidance. The

Figure 10.10 (Continued)

device eventually crashes undetected into the sea or in the desert. Delivery of a chemical agent achieves far higher casualties than any conventional military warhead. A biological agent is equally effective and the first symptoms appear days after the actual attack—by which time treatment is difficult or impossible.

- A truck filled with what appears to be light gravel is driven through the streets of Riyadh, Kuwait City, Tehran, or Tel Aviv during rush hour or another maximum traffic period. A visible powder does come out through the tarpaulin covering the truck, but the spread of the powder is so light that no attention is paid to it. The driver and his assistant are immunized against the modified form of Anthrax carried in the truck which is being released from behind the gravel or sand in the truck. The truck slowly quarters key areas of the city. Unsuspected passersby and commuters not only are infected, but also carry dry spores home and into other areas. By the time the first major symptoms of the attack occur some 3–5 days later, Anthrax pneumonia is epidemic and some septicemic Anthrax has appeared. Some 40–65% of the exposed population dies and medical facilities collapse causing serious, lingering secondary effects.

- A Country X-backed terrorist group scatters high concentrations of a radiological, chemical, or biological agent in various areas in a city, and trace elements into the processing intakes to the local water supply. When the symptoms appear, the terrorist group makes its attack known, but claims that it has contaminated the local water supply. The authorities are forced to confirm that water is contaminated and mass panic ensues.

- Immunized terrorists carry small amounts of Anthrax or a similar biological agent onto a passenger aircraft like a B-747, quietly scatter the powder, and deplane at the regular scheduled stop. No airport detection system or search detects the agent. Some 70–80% of those on the aircraft die as a result of symptoms that only appear days later.

- Several identical nuclear devices are smuggled out of the FSU through Afghanistan or Central Asia. They do not pass directly through governments. One of the devices is disassembled to determine the precise technology and coding system used in the weapon's PAL. This allows users to activate the remaining weapons. The weapon is then disassembled to minimize detection with the fissile core shipped covered in lead. The weapon is successfully smuggled into the periphery of an urban area outside any formal security perimeter. A 100 kiloton ground burst destroys a critical area and blankets the region in fall out.

- The same device is shipped to Israel or a Gulf area in a modified standard shipping container equipped with detection and triggering devices that set it off as a result of local security checks or with a GPS system that sets it off automatically when it reaches the proper coordinates in the port of destination. The direct explosive effect is significant, but "rain out" contaminates a massive local area.

- Country X equips a freighter or dhow to spread Anthrax along a coastal area in the Gulf. It uses a proxy terrorist group, and launches an attack on Kuwait City and Saudi oil facilities and ports. It is several days before the attack is detected, and the attacking group is never fully identified. The form of Anthrax involved is dry and time encapsulated to lead to both massive prompt casualties and force

continued

Figure 10.10 (Continued)

time-consuming decontamination. Country X not only is revenged, but also benefits from the resulting massive surge in oil prices.

- A Country X-backed terrorist group scatters small amounts of a biological or radiological agent in a Jewish area during critical stages of the final settlement talks. Near panic ensures, and a massive anti-Palestinian reaction follows. Israeli security then learns that the terrorist group has scattered small amounts of the same agent in cells in every sensitive Palestinian town and area, and the terrorist group announces that it has also stored some in politically sensitive mosques and shrines. Israeli security is forced to shut down all Palestinian movement and carry out intrusive searches in every politically sensitive area. Palestinian riots and exchanges of gunfire follow. The peace talks break down permanently.

- Country X equips dhows to spread Anthrax. The dhows enter the ports of Kuwait as commercial vessels—possibly with local or other Southern Gulf registrations and flags. It is several days before the attack is detected, and the resulting casualties include much of the population of Abu Dhabi and government of the UAE. The UAE breaks up as a result, no effective retaliation is possible, and Iran achieves near hegemony over Gulf oil policy.

- A Country X-backed terrorist group attempting to drive Western influence out of Saudi Arabia smuggles a large nuclear device into Al Hufuf on the edge of the Ghawar oil field. It develops a crude fall out model using local weather data which it confirms by sending out scouts with cellular phones. It waits for the ideal wind, detonates the devices, shuts down the world's largest exporting oil field, and causes the near collapse of Saudi Arabia.

- Alternatively, the same group takes advantage of the security measures the U.S. has adopted in Saudi Arabia, and the comparative isolation of U.S. military personnel. It waits for the proper wind pattern and allows the wind to carry a biological agent over a Saudi airfield with a large U.S. presence from an area outside the security perimeter. The U.S. takes massive casualties and has no ability to predict the next attack. It largely withdraws from Saudi Arabia.

- A freighter carrying fertilizer enters a Middle Eastern port and docks. In fact, the freighter has mixed the fertilizer with a catalyst to create a massive explosion and also carries a large amount of a chemical, radiological, and/or biological agent. The resulting explosion destroys both the immediate target area and scatters the chemical or biological weapon over the area.

- A large terrorist device goes off in a populated, critical economic, or military assembly area—scattering mustard or nerve gas. Emergency teams rush in to deal with the chemical threat and the residents are evacuated. Only later does it become clear that the device also included a biological agent and that the response to this "cocktail" killed most emergency response personnel and the evacuation rushed the biological agent to a much wider area.

states in conducting covert attacks, and the potential use of extremist or terrorist movements as proxies for regional powers. Moreover, the kind of scenarios outlined in Figure 10.10 illustrate how difficult it could be to identify the attacker in some scenarios, and the risk deception and false flags will be used to try to direct any response toward other movements or states.

The Central Intelligence Agency (CIA) has issued unclassified reports that make it clear that such threats are not theoretical. The CIA reported in June 2003 that

> [a]l-Qaeda and associated extremist groups have a wide variety of potential agents and delivery means to choose from for chemical, biological, radiological, or nuclear (CBRN) attacks. Al-Qaeda's end goal is the use of CBRN to cause mass casualties; however, most attacks by the group—and especially by associated extremists—probably will be small scale, incorporating relatively crude delivery means and easily produced or obtained chemicals, toxins, or radiological substances. The success of any al-Qaeda attack and the number of ensuing casualties would depend on many factors, including the technical expertise of those involved, but most scenarios could cause panic and disruption.
>
> - Several groups of mujahadeen associated with al-Qaeda have attempted to carry out "poison plot" attacks in Europe with easily produced chemicals and toxins best suited to assassination and small-scale scenarios. These agents could cause hundreds of casualties and widespread panic if used in multiple simultaneous attacks.
>
> - Al-Qaeda is interested in radiological dispersal devices (RDDs) or "dirty bombs." Construction of an RDD is well within its capabilities as radiological materials are relatively easy to acquire from industrial or medical sources. Osama Bin Laden's operatives may try to launch conventional attacks against the nuclear industrial infrastructure of the United States in a bid to cause contamination, disruption, and terror.
>
> - A document recovered from an al-Qaeda facility in Afghanistan contained a sketch of a crude nuclear device.
>
> - Spray devices disseminating biological warfare (BW) agents have the highest potential impact. Both 11 September attack leader Mohammad Atta and Zacharias Moussaoui expressed interest in crop dusters, raising our concern that al-Qaeda has considered using aircraft to disseminate BW agents.
>
> - Analysis of an al-Qaeda document recovered in Afghanistan in summer 2002 indicates the group has crude procedures for making mustard agent, sarin, and VX.[1]

The CIA reported in November 2003 that

> [t]he threat of terrorists using chemical, biological, radiological, and nuclear (CBRN) materials remain[s] high. Many of the 33 designated foreign terrorist organizations and other nonstate actors worldwide have expressed interest in

CBRN. Although terrorist groups probably will continue to favor long-proven conventional tactics such as bombings and shootings, the arrest of ricin plotters in London in January 2003 indicated that international mujahadeen terrorists were actively plotting to conduct chemical and biological attacks.

Increased publicity surrounding the anthrax incidents since the September 11 attacks has highlighted the vulnerability of civilian and government targets to CBRN attacks.

One of our highest concerns is al-Qaeda's stated readiness to attempt unconventional attacks against us. As early as 1998, Osama Bin Laden publicly declared that acquiring unconventional weapons was "a religious duty."

Individuals from terrorist groups worldwide undertook poison training at al-Qaeda-sponsored camps in Afghanistan and have ready access to information on chemical, biological, radiological, and to some extent, even nuclear weapons, via the Internet, publicly available scientific literature, and scientific conferences, and we know that al-Qaeda was working to acquire some of the most dangerous chemical agents and toxins. A senior Bin Laden associate on trial in Egypt in 1999 claimed his group had chemical and biological weapons. Documents and equipment recovered from al-Qaeda facilities in Afghanistan show that Bin Laden had a more sophisticated unconventional weapons research program than was previously known.

We also know that al-Qaeda has ambitions to acquire or develop nuclear weapons and was receptive to any outside nuclear assistance that might become available. In February 2001, during the trial on the al-Qaeda bombings of the American Embassies in Tanzania and Kenya, a government witness—Jamal Ahmad Fadl—testified that al-Qaeda pursued the sale of a quantity of purported enriched uranium (which in fact probably was scam material) in Sudan in the early 1990s.

We assess that terrorist groups are capable of conducting attacks using crude radiological dispersal devices—i.e., ones that would not cause large-scale casualties, even though they could cause tremendous psychological effects, and possibly create considerable economic disruption as well. This type of threat first appeared in November 1995 when Chechen rebels placed a package containing radioactive cesium on a bench in Moscow's Izmailovo Park. In addition, we are alert to the very real possibility that al-Qaeda or other terrorist groups might also try to launch conventional attacks against the chemical or nuclear industrial infrastructure of the United States to cause panic and economic disruption.[2]

This raises the following issues regarding "superterrorism" and the effect it may have on the military future of the region:

- The role of covert warfare, proxy warfare, independent nonstate actors.
- The dangers posed by the fact that the conventional military strength of the United States and its allies creates a growing incentive for both proliferation and covert/indirect attack.
- The ability of both states and nonstate actors to use CBRN weapons in a variety of new methods of attack.

- The risk that terrorist and extremist movements may develop or gain access to weapons of mass destruction.

- While many analysts focus on the nuclear worst case, chemical and biological weapons are easier to manufacture and obtain.

- Commercial technologies like cell phones, GPS navigation systems, advanced timers, and local weather models can greatly increase the effectiveness and lethality of covert and terrorist attacks.

- What forms of superterrorism are possible that do not involve weapons of mass destruction?

- Information warfare attacks on critical systems?

- Manportable and light precision weapons attacks on critical facilities like power plants, water/desalination plants/grids, high-rise closed buildings, and mall complexes?

- What form of arms control is relevant in dealing with covert, proxy, and terrorist attacks?

- Can a regime be established to monitor the possible use of CBRN and superterrorist weapons and attacks, limit the ability to conduct covert attacks, and identify the state or nonstate attacker?

- What level of control on technology transfer is possible and relevant? To what extent can the flow of relevant technologies be controlled to either state or nonstate actors?

ARMS CONTROL ISSUES

While many countries in the Middle East seek arms control as a method of defense, others see it as hindering their potential power and influence in the region. Further difficulties exist in the political arena, where signing a treaty might be seen as "giving in" to other nations or as a weakness in the leader signing it. The following factors affect the pursuit of arms control and counterproliferation:

- Egyptian-Israeli dispute has paralyzed ACRS and all near-term progress.

- NPT aids in early to midphases of proliferation. Transfer of technology for fuel cycle.

- IAEA inspection and "visits" to declared facilities help, but can also be manipulated to disguise proliferation.

- Dual-use technology now allows states to carry out virtually all aspects of weapons design and manufacture—including simulated tests.

- In spite of Iraq's grandiose effort, the ability to carry out all aspects of nuclear proliferation except acquiring fissile materials is becoming steadily cheaper, smaller in scale, and easier to conceal.

- The CWC only affects signer countries and large efforts or those disclosed through SIGINT; it cannot prevent development and assembly of up to several hundred weapons and warheads.

- The steady expansion of petrochemical, industrial process plants, and insecticide plants will make it progressively easier to produce chemical weapons without extensive imports of telltale feedstocks.

- The technology to purify and stabilize mustard and nerve agents is now well known, as is the need for more lethal warhead technology. All major proliferators have nerve gas technology.

- The BWC has no enforcement provisions and no near- to midterm prospects of acquiring them.

- Advances in biotechnology, food processing systems, and pharmaceuticals mean all regional states will soon be able to covertly mass produce dry storage biological weapons in optimal aerosol form.

- The MTCR slows things down and is very valuable, but it has not prevented any determined regional actor from getting missiles.

- All credible regional proliferators already have long-range strike aircraft and a wide range of unconventional delivery options.

- Only a broadly based UNSCOM/IAEA effort of the kind going on in Iraq—supported by even more intrusive inspection and higher levels of technology—can really enforce arms control, and it might not work for biological weapons.

Figure 10.11 shows that many Middle Eastern states are parties to arms control agreements designed to prevent or limit proliferation. In practice, however, the preceding risks pose critical problems for global arms control regimes like the Nuclear Non-Proliferation Treaty and Biological Weapons Convention, and are a serious problem with the Chemical Weapons Convention.

Figure 10.12 summarizes the continuing technological duel between the detection and concealment of weapons of mass destruction. It illustrates the fact that arms control is often an extension of war, or at least the struggle to acquire military power, by other means.

Figure 10.13 lists the major risks in regional arms control, and shows the broader limits to the ability of such agreements in providing verifiable military security. It shows that effective arms control, must rely on intrusive technical means and unimpeded, sudden challenge inspection. Even then, it is far from clear that any regional arms control agreement can offer absolute assurance, no matter how many countries may be included or how demanding the proposed inspection system may be.

BROADER APPROACHES TO COUNTERPROLIFERATION

Yet it is again important not to exaggerate the impact of "worst case" risks or their probability. Such possibilities do not alter the basic rules of rational behavior. Arms control can also be mixed with broader-based counterproliferation efforts of the kind described in Figure 10.13.

Figure 10.11
The Status of Major Arms Control Agreements

Country	Geneva Protocol	NNPT	BWC	CWC	Treaty of Pelindaba*	CTBT
North Africa						
Algeria	R	R	—	R	R	SRR
Libya	R	R	A	—	S	—
Morocco	R	R	S	R	R	S
Tunisia	R	R	R	R	S	S
Near/Middle East						
Egypt	R	R	S	—	S	SRR
Israel	R	—	—	S	NA	SRR
Jordan	R	R	R	A	NA	R
Lebanon	R	R	R	—	NA	—
Syria	R	R	S	—	NA	—
Gulf						
Bahrain	R	R	A	R	NA	S
Iran	R	R	R	R	NA	SRR
Iraq	R	R	R	—	NA	—
Kuwait	R	R	R	R	NA	S
Oman	—	R	R	R	NA	—
Qatar	R	R	R	R	NA	R
UAE	—	R	S	S	NA	S
Yemen	R	R	R	S	NA	S
Periphery						
Ethiopia	R	R	R	R	S	S
Eritrea	—	R	—	—	S	—
Sudan	R	R	—	—	S	—
India	R	—	R	R	NA	NSRR
Pakistan	R	—	R	R	NA	NSRR

R = Ratified, S = Signed, A = Acceded, NA = Not Applicable, SRR = Signed—Ratification Required, and NSRR = Not signed—Ratification Required.
*African Nuclear Weapons Free Zone Treaty.
Source: State Department.

Figure 10.12
The Changing Technology of Detection and Concealment

Changes in Concealment
- Counter-Satellite: Covered buildings, monitor overhead coverage, deception (including media/commercial satellites), conversion of existing facilities, dual use facilities.
- Counter EW/ELINT/ESSM: Secure encryption, line of sight, pulse code modulation.
- Breakout versus openly deploy or stockpile.
- Cell-like structures.
- Parallel programs.
- Computer simulation backed by limited tests.
- C^{4}I/BM/sensor advances, rather than hardware.

Changes in Detection
- Near advanced satellite imaging.
- Use of UAVs. Micro UAVs.
- New unattended sensors: soil and water.
- Non-encryption agreements.
- Challenge inspection.
- Sensors that can see through shelters, inspect underground facilities.

The following factors affect such counterproliferation efforts:

- No one area of focus can be effective.
- There is no present prospect that any combination of arms control and active/passive counter proliferation can fully secure the region, any state in the region, or Western power projection forces.
- However, a synergistic effort blending arms control, containment, preemptive options, deterrence, retaliation, and civil defense should offer significant stability.
- There is no present prospect that such stability can be offered without at least tacit U.S. threats to retaliate with nuclear weapons.
- Such policies cannot work by enforcing restraint on friends without enforcing them on enemies. There is no near- to midterm prospect that Israel can give up nuclear weapons.
- Creeping proliferation will follow the line of least resistance.
- There is no present prospect that any combination of measures can defend against biological warfare, and many proposed forms of counterproliferation act as incentive to develop biological weapons and use unconventional means of delivery.
- Theater missile defense will be meaningless without radical improvements in defense against air attacks, cruise missiles, and unconventional means of delivery.

Figure 10.13
Major Risks in Regional Arms Control

- Does not affect non-state or terrorist groups except to degree reduces ability of states to transfer such weapons. However, also acts as an incentive to states to carry out covert development or attacks on their own or use terrorist or extremist groups as proxies.
- "Breakout": Technology allows sudden or covert break out of weapons production and delivery capability—particularly in terms of biological weapons.
- "Squeezing the balloon": Limiting one area of proliferation simply increases activity in another.
- "Liar's contest": Accept agreements that do not intend to honor. Carry out covert efforts and deny them. Obtain access to technology and equipment.
- "Only the honest suffer:" Limit moderate states, but fail to contain and deter rogue or high-risk states. License technology transfer to nations that claim to comply, but do not.
- "War fighting risk": Create a covert climate of proliferation involving sudden activation of forces with limited planning and/or control, higher risk of misunderstandings, accidents, unnecessary preemption, launch under and through attack, and escalation.
- "Existential minimalism": Reducing weapons to minimal levels creates an added use or lose risk, leads to countervalue (civilian casualties and damage)/existential threats and targeting.
- "Destabilizing truth": Added transparency, inspection, declarations either stimulate arms race or lead to constantly increasing pressure to reveal or reduce more.
- "Climate of illusions": Inspection, verification, declarations give the impression of added transparency and stability without being trustworthy.
- "Conventional paradox": Reducing or constraining weapons of mass destruction increases risk of conventional war.
- "Nth Weapon" problem in trying to eliminate all weapons when a few concealed nuclear or biological weapons can produce existential damage.
- "Valid Paranoia": Can encourage covert delivery and strikes, use of third parties and terrorists.
- "Arms control is an extension of war by other means": Well, yes!

Figure 10.14 gives some examples of possible counterproliferation policies that states in the Middle East would need in order to achieve some form of arms control in the region. In addition, there will need to be force improvements to regulate any possible agreements and weapons development. These could result in major budgetary problems for each of the countries participating in such efforts.

Figure 10.14
Key Force Improvements Affecting Counterproliferation Policy

- Detection and characterization of biological and chemical agents. This initiative is intended to accelerate the fielding of stand-off and point detection and characterization systems by up to six years. It also addresses the integration of sensors into existing and planned carrier platforms, emphasizing man-portability and compatibility with UAVs.

- Detection, characterization, and defeat of hard, underground targets. The U.S. is seeking new sensors, enhanced lethality, and penetrating weapons to increase the probability of defeating the target while minimizing the risk of collateral damage.

- Detection, localization and neutralization of weapons of mass destruction inside and outside the U.S. The U.S. is seeking to identify and evaluate systems, force structures, and operational plans to protect key military facilities and logistic nodes, and conduct joint exercises to improve the capability to respond to potential biological and chemical threats.

- Development and deployment of additional passive defense capabilities for U.S forces, including development and production of biological agent vaccines. This program will develop and field improved protective suits, shelters, filter systems, and equipment two to five years faster than previously planned. It also restores funding to the development of improved decontamination methods.

- Support for weapons of mass destruction related armed control measures include strengthening the NNPT, CTB, and BWC. They include establishing a COCOM successor regime, and improving controls on exports and technology by strengthening the MTCR, Nuclear Suppliers Group and Australia Group.

- Missile defense capabilities, with primary emphasis on theater ballistic missile defenses. This activity involves improvements in active and passive defenses, attack operations, and improvements in BM/C^{4}I as well as the deployment of theater missile defenses. The primary focus, however, is on anti-ballistic missile defenses, and in the near-term, this involves the development of the Patriot Advanced Capability Level-3 (PAC-3/ERINT), Navy area theater missile defense (Aegis), and theater high altitude area defense (THAAD).

- Publicized counterstrike options. Options ranging from a convincing declared capability to conduct precision mass air and missile strikes with conventional weapons that can devastate user states to use of nuclear weapons escalating to the destruction of population centers.

- New force tailored to dealing with terrorist and unconventional threats. New intelligence and tracking systems dedicated to the prevention of mass terrorism, and tailored special forces to detect and attack terrorist groups and deal with unconventional uses of weapons of mass destruction.

COUNTRY-BY-COUNTRY THREAT ANALYSIS

Figures 10.15 through 10.22 attempt to summarize the state of proliferation by country. The reader should understand, however, that any unclassified assessment at this level of detail is extremely uncertain.

Figures 10.23 through 10.24 show that the failure to find stockpiles of weapons of mass destruction in Iraq, and the uncertainties surrounding proliferation in Iran and North Korea, have shown that there are major problems in current intelligence and collection capabilities to deal with this aspect of the military balance. The uncertainties in intelligence collection capability are summarized in Figure 10.23, and the uncertainties in analysis capability are summarized in Figure 10.24.

Figure 10.15
Possible Counterproliferation Policies

- Dissuasion to convince non-weapons of mass destruction states that their security interests are best served through not acquiring weapons of mass destruction.

- Denial to curtail access to technology and materials for weapons of mass destruction through export controls and other tools.

- Arms co Missile Treaty clarification efforts to allow U.S. deployment of advanced theater ballistic missile defenses.

- Region-wide arms control agreements backed by intelligence sharing and ruthless, intrusive challenge inspection without regard for the niceties of sovereignty.

- International pressure to punish violators with trade sanctions to publicize and expose companies and countries that assist proliferators, and to share intelligence to heighten awareness of the proliferation problem.

- Defusing potentially dangerous situations by undertaking actions to reduce the threat from weapons of mass destruction already in the hands of selected countries—such as agreements to destroy, inspect, convert, monitor, or even reverse their capabilities.

- Military capabilities to be prepared to seize, disable, or destroy weapons of mass destruction in time of conflict.

- Improve tracking and detection of sales, technology transfer, research efforts, extremist groups.

- Defensive capabilities, both active (theater missile defenses) and passive (protective gear and vaccines) that will mitigate or neutralize the effects of weapons of mass destruction and enable U.S. forces to fight effectively even on a contaminated battlefield.

- Declared and convincing counterstrike options ranging from conventional strikes devastating a user nation's economy, political structure, and military forces to the use of nuclear weapons against the population centers of user nations and groups.

Figure 10.16
Algeria's Search for Weapons of Mass Destruction

Delivery Systems

• 28 Su-24 long-range strike aircraft.

• 28 MiG-23BN fighter ground attack aircraft.

• Tube artillery and multiple rocket launchers.

• Possible modification of Soviet SS-N-2B Styx.

Chemical Weapons

• Possible development. No evidence of deployed systems.

Biological Weapons

• Some low-level research activity.

• No evidence of production capability.

Nuclear Weapons

• Deliberately sought to create a covert nuclear research program under military control with Chinese support.

• Secretly built a research reactor (Es Salam) at the Ain Oussera nuclear research facility. This was announced to be a 10–15 megawatt reactor using heavy water and low enriched uranium. The size of its cooling towers, however, indicated it might be as large as 60 megawatts. It was also located far from population centers, had no visible electric generating facilities and was defended by SA-5s. There were also indications Algeria might be constructing a facility to separate out weapons grade plutonium.

• In May 1991, following the exposure of the reactor by U.S. intelligence, Algeria agreed to place the reactor under IAEA safeguards. As early as December 1993, Algerian officials pledged adherence to the NPT, and on January 12, 1995, Algeria formally acceded to the Treaty. On March 30, 1996, Algeria signed a comprehensive IAEA safeguards agreement providing for IAEA inspections of all of Algeria's nuclear facilities and IAEA technical assistance to Algeria. The agreement went into effect on January 7, 1997.

• Algeria signed a "second stage" agreement of nuclear cooperation with China on June 1, 1996. According to an October 1996 "letter of intent," China was to assist Algeria with the construction of facilities for the research and production of radioactive isotopes for use in the medical, industrial, and agricultural sectors. China and Algeria intend to move into a third phase of cooperation under which China will share the know-how to enable Algeria to operate hot cells in the facility (mentioned previously) at the Es Salam compound. These hot cells would give Algeria the capability to separate plutonium from spent fuel. Algeria claims that the hot cells are intended for the purpose of producing medical isotopes, and the U.S. is reportedly "satisfied" that the hot cells will be operated under IAEA safeguards.

• While it appears that the government is cautiously expanding Algeria's civil nuclear research program in compliance with the NPT, uncertainties about the long-term goals of the nuclear research program and Algeria's political future make the program a potential threat. The possibility remains that Algeria could

Figure 10.16 (Continued)

continue its civil program and then suddenly announce its intention to withdraw from the NPT 90 days hence and "go nuclear" quickly. This would be pursuant to Article Ten of the NPT.

- Algeria has uranium deposits west of Tamanrasset in southeast Algeria, has a 1 megawatt reactor (Nur) at Draria on the coast east of Algiers, and has hot cells for the production of radioactive isotopes at Draria.

- A Spanish paper, *El Pais*, made an unconfirmed claim on August 23, 1998 that Spain's military secret service, the CESID, had issued a report that said that Algeria will be able in two years to produce military-grade plutonium, a key ingredient for making atomic weapons. The report is said to have concluded that Algeria, had forged ahead with a nuclear program with Chinese and Argentine technical support that far exceeded its civilian needs, despite having signed the international nuclear non-proliferation treaty. The report is said to have been submitted to the Spanish government in July and to have sounded a warning of the danger involved if Algeria decided to divert its nuclear program to military purposes. The report indicated that the nuclear complex at Birine, 250 km (155 miles) south of Algiers, already had a heavy-water reactor in operation capable of producing weapons-grade plutonium. The CESID report stated that Algeria "has all the installations needed to carry out activities linked to the complete cycle for the creation of military plutonium" by the end of the century, the newspaper said. CESID concluded that if the Algerian government decided to change its current policy of not acquiring atomic weapons, "the knowledge gathered by a significant team of technicians and scientists, in addition to the availability of facilities . . . will place this country in the position of initiating a program of military purposes."

Figure 10.17
Libya's Search for Weapons of Mass Destruction

- By mid-March 2004, Libya seemed to have transferred all technical data, material, and weapons production equipment for its nuclear weapons program to the U.S. and allowed full IAEA inspection. It also seemed to have transferred most or all of its chemical weapons program and missiles with a range over 150 kilometers.

- Libya claimed to have ended its efforts to acquire weapons of mass destruction and long range missiles in November 2003, and agreed to International Atomic Energy Agency inspection of its nuclear facilities in December 2003, as well as inspection of it's other WMD sites by the international community. On December 19, 2003, President Bush and Prime Minister Blair announced that Libyan leader Moammar Qadaffi had agreed to surrender all CBRN programs and activities and give up Libya's efforts to develop nuclear weapons. This followed some nine months of secret negotiations and two secret visits by U.S. and British experts to Libya.

continued

Figure 10.17 (Continued)

- In response to Libya's actions and Qadaffi's statement that Libya would seek to take part in "building a new world free from WMD and from all forms of terrorism," the U.S. rescinded the ban on travel and business activities to and in the country.[1] Business activity has been temporarily limited to companies who had holdings in Libya prior to the implementation of sanctions. The U.S. invited Libya to establish an Interests Section in Washington, D.C., to coordinate humanitarian efforts, efforts to eliminate WMD, and with an eye to greater diplomatic contacts in the future. On February 28, a contingent from the U.S. Agency for International Development and the department of Health and Human Services arrived in Libya. This group acted as consultants on a variety of health care related issues.

Delivery Systems

- FROG-7 rocket launchers with 40-kilometer range.
- Deployed 80 Scud B launchers with 190 mile range in 1976, but could not successfully operate system. Many of the launchers and missiles sold to Iran.
- According to press reports Libya has confirmed that it has Scud-C missiles in its inventory, and that these missiles have a range of 750 km to 800 km. This would confirm Israeli assertions in 1999–2000 that Libya had received the same Scud-C variants that were shipped to Syria.[2]
- Fired Scud missiles against the Italian island of Lampadusa in 1987.
- Purchased SS-N-2C and SSC-3 cruise missiles. Little operational capability.
- Pursued other missile development programs with little success.
- There are unconfirmed reports of some Libyan interest in the Iranian Shahab 3 program.
- Reports has developed a liquid-fueled missile with a range of 200 kilometers. No evidence of deployment.
- Other reports indicate development of Al-Fatih solid-fueled missile with 300–450 mile range reported to have been under development with aid of German technical experts, but no signs of successful development.
  - Other indigenous programs include the Al-Jadid, which is thought to be based on or related to the Scud C (Hwasong 6).
  - The Al-Fajr program to produce solid-fueled rockets of about 300 km range is thought to have ended.
- Libya has a number of combat aircraft that could be used to deliver CBRN weapons. They include:
  - 6 Tu-22 bombers with minimal operational capability.
  - 6 Su-24MK long-range strike fighters. These are operational and have with limited refueling capability using C-130s.
  - 30 Mirage 5D/DE and 14 Mirage 5DD fighter ground attack aircraft.
  - 14 Mirage F-1AD fighter ground attack aircraft.
  - 40 MiG-23BN Flogger F and 15 MiG-23U fighter ground attack.
  - A total of 53 Su-20 and Su-22 Fitter E, J. F fighter ground attack aircraft.

Figure 10.17 (Continued)

- Possible short range and tactical delivery systems include tube artillery and multiple rocket launchers.

- Numerous allegations have been made regarding foreign assistance to Libya's missile program. Organizations from a number of nations have been implicated, including Serbia, Ukraine, China, India, Iran, Argentina, Brazil, Germany, Taiwan and most frequently, North Korea.

- The CIA estimated in January 1999 that, Libya continued to obtain ballistic missile-related equipment, materials, and technology during the first half of 1998. Outside assistance is critical to keeping its fledgling ballistic missile development programs from becoming moribund.

  - June 1999, unconfirmed reports that Libya attempted to import blueprints, manuals and 148 crates of production equipment for Scud B and Scud C missiles.[3]

  - Libya reported to be smuggling Scud components from Hontex in Southern China which were being shipped from Taiwan via BA to Malta in November 1999. The parts include elements for the rocket propulsion system. The shipment was said in 32 crates disguised as automobile parts.

- Reports of Libyan acquisition of production equipment for Scud C missiles and subsequent installation at Rabta and Tarhuna.[4]

- Conflicting reports regarding Libyan purchase, assembly and/or manufacture of North Korean No Dong missiles seem to have sharply exaggerated Libyan activity:

  - Reports in early 2000 cite the Spanish intelligence agency CESID as claiming Libya was in the process of procuring No Dong missiles from North Korea.

  - A senior analyst at the state-sponsored think-tank, the Korean Institute of Defense Analysis reported in 2001 that Libya had purchased and received 50 No Dong missiles. Analyst claims his report was based on data from the Korean Defense Ministry and the U.S. Defense Intelligence Agency.[5]

  - Israeli intelligence sources claim that Libya had received two shipments of No Dong missiles, launchers and North Korean technicians by 2002.

  - The Italian foreign intelligence agency indicates in 2002 that Libya lacked a strong ballistic missile capability and that it was extremely unlikely that Libya had managed to acquire complete No Dong missiles.

  - U.S. CIA and DoD reports indicate in 2002 that Libya has been seeking a medium-range capability, but was likely to remain heavily dependant on foreign assistance and had not yet been able to obtain complete No Dong missiles. Additionally, U.S. sources are cited as claiming that Libya and North Korea were still in negotiations for future shipments of technology, hardware and production equipment.

- *Jane's Intelligence Review* estimated in 2003 that Libya possessed a missile inventory of 210–405 missiles as follows:[6]

  - 0–5 Al Fatah prototypes with one or two launchers

  - 150–250 Scud B with 60–70 Transporter-Erector-Launcher (TEL) units

  - 50–100 Scud C (Hwasong 6) with 6–12 TELs

continued

Figure 10.17 (Continued)

- 10–0 No Dong missiles with 7 mobile launchers and an unknown number of rail and fixed launchers.
- The Center for Nonproliferation Studies at the Monterey Institute of International Studies has compiled a chronology of North Korean assistance to Libya through 2003[7]:

Date	Item(s)	Remarks
Early 1990s	Missile production technology	North Korea reportedly assists Libya in establishing a Scud production facility near Tripoli.
1990s	Unknown number of Scud-B and Scud-C missiles	
1999 June	Blueprints for the Scud-B and Scud-C; 148 crates of machinery for missile production, including: heavy duty steel presses, a plate bending machine, torroidal air bottles, and two sets of theodolites	Intercepted; North Korea ship is detained by India and returns to North Korea without delivering cargo.
1999 November	Scud and No Dong missile components	Intercepted by British customs at Gatwick Airport; shipment was bound for Tripoli
2000	50 No Dong missiles, seven TELs, and nine North Korean missile technicians	No Dong and launcher delivery begins in July—part of $600 million deal signed in October 1999.
2000	No Dong missiles and TELs	Unconfirmed; North Korean firm Ch'ongchon'gang reportedly delivers 50 No Dong missiles and seven TELs to Syria. Missiles possibly procured on behalf of Iraq, Egypt and Libya for $600 million.

- The CIA reported in November 2003 that "The suspension of UN sanctions in 1999 allowed Libya to expand its efforts to obtain ballistic missile–related equipment, materials, technology, and expertise from foreign sources. During the first half of 2003, Libya continued to depend on foreign assistance—particularly from Serbian, Indian, Iranian, North Korean, and Chinese entities—for its ballistic missile development programs. Libya's capability therefore may not still be limited to its Soviet-origin Scud-B missiles. With continued foreign assistance, Libya will likely achieve an MRBM capability—a long-desired goal—probably through direct purchase from North Korea or Iran."
- Although Libya is not a signatory to the Missile Technology Control Regime (MTCR), it has agreed to dispose of any missiles with more than 300 km range and 500 kg payload, and seems to have complied.
  - This agreement permits Libya to keep its Scud-B and FROG-7 missiles.
  - Libya would be required to dispose of the inventory of Scud-C missiles they have admitted to, and seems to have done so.
  - Libya has not directly confirmed, so far, that they possess any No-Dong missiles. If Libya has any of these, then they too will have to be dismantled.[8]
- Unconfirmed reports suggest that as late as September 23003, North Korea had been encouraging Iran to sell Libya it's 1,300–1,500 km Shahab-3 missile and

Figure 10.17 (Continued)

launchers. These reports indicate that Libya and Iran had been in negotiation over purchase of a less advanced model than the Shahab-3 missile. As of the date of the report no deal appeared imminent.[9]

- Unconfirmed reports tend to suggest that there was a great deal of cooperation between Iran, Egypt, Libya and North Korea on issues pertaining to ballistic missiles.[10]
- When nuclear material was shipped to the United States for cataloging and destruction, the materials inventoried also included missile guidance sets for longer-range missiles.[11]

Chemical Weapons

- Libya has acceded to the CWC on January 6, 2004 (entry into force on February 5, 2004). Libya had previously asserted that it would not sign the CWC as long as other states have nuclear weapons.
- Libya has until 2007 to comply with the CWC's deadline for destruction of the materials.[12]
- May have some stocks of nerve agents Sarin and Tabun, blister agents Mustard Gas and Lewisite, and the choking agent Phosgene.
- May have used mustard gas delivered in bombs by AN-26 aircraft in final phases of war against Chad in September 1987. Libya asserts that it has never used chemical weapons and the Organization for the Prohibition of Chemical Weapons has never found enough evidence to send an investigation team to Chad.[13]
- Pilot plant near Tripoli has been producing small amounts of chemical weapons since early 1980s.
  - Are probably two other small research/batch production facilities.
- Main nerve and mustard gas production facilities in an industrial park at chemical weapons plant at Rabta. This plant can produce both the poison gas and the bombs, shells, and warheads to contain it. Are probably two other research facilities.
- Rabta Plant seems to have started test runs in mid-1988. It is a 30 building facility defended by SAM batteries and special troops. Has sheltered underground areas.
  - Libya has acquired large stocks of feedstocks for mustard gas like thiodiglycol, and precursors for nerve gas, and extensive amounts have been sent to Rabta. Though Libyan scientists could produce mustard gas domestically, reports indicate that the production of nerve gas required the help of foreign governments or corporations.[14]
  - At least 100 metric tons of blister and nerve agents have been produced at Rabta since the late 1980s, but production rate has been very low and plant is either not successful or is not being utilized because of fear of attack.
  - The plant would have a capacity of 100 metric tons per year if operated at full capacity.
  - Fabricated fire at Rabta in 1990 to try to disguise the function of plant and fact was operating.

continued

Figure 10.17 (Continued)

- German courts have convicted a German national in October 1996, for selling Libya a computer designed for use in chemical weapons programs and helping Libya to import equipment to clean the waste emissions from poison gas production from India using an Irish dummy corporation.
- Additional major chemical weapons plant in construction in extensive underground site near Tarhunah, a mountainous area 65 kilometers southeast of Tripoli, but few recent signs of activity.
  - Tarhunah has been designed to minimize its vulnerability to air attack and has twin tunnels 200–450 feet long, protected by 100 feet of sandstone above the tunnels and a lining of reinforce concrete. This is far beyond the penetration capabilities of the U.S. GBU-27B and GBU-28 penetration bombs. The GBU-28 can penetrate a maximum of 25–30 meters of earth or 6 meters of concrete.
- Libya rejected the proposal of President Mubarak that it open the Tarhuna facility to third country inspection to prove it was not a chemical weapons facility in April 1996.
- South African chemical warfare experts thought to have sold their expertise to Libya during the mid–1990s.
- Reports of construction of another sheltered major facility near Sabha, 460 miles south of Tripoli.
- Reports of Chinese, North Korean, German, Swiss, and other European technical support and advisors.
- Reports of shipments of chemical weapons to Syria and Iran do not seem valid.
- Other confirmed preliminary reports indicate that Libya maintained stocks of precursors for other chemical agents.
  - The CIA estimated in January 1999 that Libya remains heavily dependent on foreign suppliers for precursor chemicals and other key CW–related equipment. UN sanctions continued to severely limit that support during the first half of 1998. Still, Tripoli has not given up its goal of establishing its own offensive CW capability and continues to pursue an independent production capability for the weapons.
  - The CIA reported in November 2003 that, "Libya…remained heavily dependent on foreign suppliers for CW precursor chemicals and other key related equipment. Following the suspension of UN sanctions, Tripoli reestablished contacts with sources of expertise, parts, and precursor chemicals abroad, primarily in Western Europe. Libya has indicated—as evidenced by its observer status at the April 2003 Chemical Weapons Convention Review Conference and previous Convention Conferences of States Parties—a willingness to accede to the CWC. Such efforts are consistent with steps that Tripoli is taking to improve its international standing. Tripoli still appeared to be working toward an offensive CW capability and eventual indigenous production."
- Approximately one month after Colonel Qadaffi's declaration that Libya would give up its CBRN programs, British and American teams representing agencies such as the Defense Threat and Reduction Agency arrived in Libya to prepare for operations.[15]

Figure 10.17 (Continued)

- Coincident with the formal accession of Libya to the CWC on February 5th, 2004, experts from the Organisation for the Prohibition of Chemical Weapons (the supervising body of the CWC) began operations in Libya. This group of approximately a dozen joined teams of British and American experts already in country to supervise the technical aspects of compliance with CWC requirements that all materials Libyan stocks be declared by March 5, 2004.[16]
- The experts from the OPCW will be responsible for technical supervision of the prohibited materials. The American and British personnel will be responsible for the verifiable destruction of forbidden material.[17]
  - Prohibited materials include not only stocks of chemical weapons, but chemical-capable weapons, equipment necessary to the manufacture of chemical weapons.
  - Preliminary reports indicate that Libya destroyed stocks that included 23 tons of mustard gas, some of it weaponized in the form of air-deliverable bombs.
  - Very low quality weapons designs with poor fusing and lethality.
- Additional holdings include a facility to produce more mustard gas, as well as equipment sufficient to build a second chemical weapons production facility.[18]
  - Destroyed 3,300 unfilled chemical weapon bomb assemblies.
- The Organization for the Prohibition of Chemical Weapons will build a facility within Libya to destroy the mustard gas.[19]

Biological Weapons
- Some early research activity.
- No evidence of serious development or production capability.
- The CIA reported in November 2003 that, "Evidence suggested that Libya also sought dual-use capabilities that could be used to develop and produce BW agents."
- Although a state party to the BTWC, Libya did not submit any materials per established Confidence Building Measures from 1997–2002.
- Investigations of Libya's biological weapons program were still ongoing in early 2004. Dual-use facilities are of particular interest.

Nuclear Weapons
- Has sought to create a development and production capability.
- Historical background:
  - Unsuccessfully attempted to buy nuclear weapons from China in the 1970s.
  - Qadaffi called for Libyan production of nuclear weapons on April 29, 1990.
  - Explored for uranium, but no active mines or uranium mills.
  - 10 megawatt, Soviet-supplied nuclear research reactor at Tajura acquired from the USSR in 1970s. Operates under IAEA safeguards.
  - Discussions with Russia over cooperation on nuclear power resulted in an agreement to upgrade the Tajura facility. Ongoing discussions about providing a power reactor.

continued

Figure 10.17 (Continued)

- Had plan to build a 440 megawatt, Soviet-supplied reactor near the Gulf of Sidra in the 1970s, but canceled project.
- Ratified NPT is 1975. Declares all facilities under IAEA safeguards.
- Continued to train nuclear scientists and technicians abroad.
- Shifted focus in 1980s and 1990s to acquiring nuclear weapons designs and centrifuge designs and equipment from Pakistan.
- This situation has changed strikingly since the fall of 2003:
- The U.S. and Britain intercepted a German freighter, the *BBC China*, bound for Libya at the Italian port of Taranto on October 4, 2003. The freighter was intercepted with help from the German government. The specific centrifuges intercepted were manufactured by a third party in Malaysia, based on Pakistani designs and then shipped to Libya. This was the first action under a new Proliferation Security Initiative, which was an 11-nation agreement to stop the shipment of materials carried banned material for CBRN programs and long-range missile programs.
  - A total of 5 containers to Libya was seized following allegations it contained certain components for "centrifuge." The containers were sent by BSA Tahir from Dubai. Several items inside the container that is said to be components of a "centrifuge" are as follows:

Description	Part Numbers	Total
Casing	4	2,208
Molecular Pump	5	2,208
Top spacer	6	608
Positioner	8	10,549
Top end	9	1,680
Crash Ring	12	2,208
Stationary Tube	59	1,056
Clamp holder	73	400
Flange	77	4,525

- All the above items, were made of "quality aluminum" and were in wooden boxes with the SCOPE logo. This was part of the "transshipment" delivered by SCOPE to Aryash Trading Company, Dubai. The shipment of the items or components by Bsa Tahir to Libya via the vessel *BBC China* was outside the knowledge of the management of SCOPE.
- The intercepted centrifuges were maraging steel designs based on a German design stolen and copied by Pakistan, and manufactured for Libya by a third party in Malaysia.[20]
- These discoveries, combined with Libya's desire to reshape its image as a rogue state, fully free itself of international sanctions, and obtain foreign investment and technology for its economy led it to state it would give up all of its long-range missile and CBRN programs.

Figure 10.17 (Continued)

- On December 19, 2003, President Bush and Prime Minister Blair announced that Libyan leader Muammar Qaddafi had agreed to surrender all CBRN programs and activities and give up Libya's efforts to develop nuclear weapons. This followed some nine months of secret negotiations and two secret visits by U.S. and British experts to Libya.

- On December 22, 2003, Libya agreed to allow IAEA inspectors to examine the country's nuclear program.

- Libya's past compliance with arms control treaties has been a major issue, but seems to be changing:

  - The CIA reported in November 2003 that, "An NPT party with full-scope IAEA safeguards, Libya continued to develop its nuclear infrastructure. The suspension of UN sanctions provided Libya the means to enhance its nuclear infrastructure through foreign cooperation and procurement efforts. Tripoli and Moscow continued talks on cooperation at the Tajura Nuclear Research Center and a potential power reactor deal. Such civil-sector work could have presented Libya with opportunities to pursue technologies also suitable for military purposes. In addition, Libya participated in various technical exchanges through which it could have tried to obtain dual-use equipment and technology that could have enhanced its overall technical capabilities in the nuclear area. Although Libya made political overtures to the West in an attempt to strengthen relations, Libya's assertion that Arabs have the right to nuclear weapons in light of Israel and its nuclear program—as Qadhafi stated in a televised speech in March 2002, for example—and Tripoli's continued interest in nuclear weapons and nuclear infrastructure upgrades raised concerns."

  - Libya signed the Comprehensive Test Ban Treaty in 2001, but did not ratify the treaty until January 6, 2004.

  - Under the auspices of the agreement the Comprehensive Test Ban Treaty Organization maintains a radionuclide monitoring station at Misratah to observe compliance with the provisions of the agreement.

  - Libya indicated in 2003 that it would sign the Additional Protocols to the Nuclear Non-Proliferation Treaty. Until the treaty is legally in force, they will voluntarily comply with its provisions.

  - British and American experts (from the U.S. Department of Energy, Los Alamos Laboratories, the Defense Threat Reduction Agency, among other places) are cooperating with IAEA inspectors. The 10 IAEA inspectors will have "a role, but only with the technical aspects" of confirming Libyan compliance.[21] So far inspection teams have visited from ten to dozens of nuclear sites.

  - The first flight shipping materials from Libya was a chartered 747 from Libya to Dulles and is thought to have carried back Libyan designs for a warhead. Reportedly, the designs were found wrapped in plastic bags from an Islamabad dry cleaner.[22] This is thought to be further confirmation of the links between Dr. A. Q. Kahn and the proliferation of nuclear weapons. The design found was based on a Chinese design from the 60's and is for a simple implosion device.[23] The warhead, as designed, weighs some 500 kg and is approximately 80 cm in diameter.

continued

Figure 10.17 (Continued)

- Libya does not posses a delivery system sufficient to carry such a device; however, missiles currently in service with Iran and North Korea could carry such a warhead.
- Other developments related to Libya's decision to give up its CBRN weapons include:
  - Unconfirmed reports indicate that on December 30, 2003, Libya sent some 150 Pakistanis back to Pakistan from Libya on a special charter flight.[24]
  - Reports that the U.S. has shipped some 55,000 pounds of material to the Oakridge National Laboratory on two C-17s in mid-late January 2004.
  - The first shipment contained, among other things the "most sensitive" documentation associated with Libya's nuclear program. The second flight, arriving on January 26th, included among other things, uranium hexafluoride and centrifuge parts.
  - The discovery that Libya began the purchase of components for the less-efficient aluminum centrifuges in the late 1990s. After acquiring the parts for about 100 centrifuges, they began to focus on a more sophisticated high-performance centrifuges made from maraging steel, based on a German design acquired by Pakistan. Libya had acquitted parts for thousands by the time of the December 19th, 2003 declaration.[25]
    - Some of this material was still in packing crates had had not been assembled.
    - During the 1980's a number of sources reported that Libya obtained more than 450 tons of yellowcake from Niger, and transferred 150 tons to Pakistan. The remaining 300 tons could produce 30 kg of HEU. The whereabouts of the yellowcake is not entirely certain at this point.[26]
    - Some unconfirmed reports suggest that some of the Niger yellowcake had been used jointly by Libya and Iraq. These reports continue on to suggest that Qadaffi opted to sacrifice his WMD program to prevent American investigations from revealing that the Iraqi and Libyan uranium had continued to reside in Libya for use by both countries.[27]
    - These reports then go on to assert that the December 29, 2003 visit of Libyan officials to Niamey, the Niger capital, while undertaken for ostensibly normal purposes, was in fact to ensure that there would be no leaks from Niger on the details of the uranium exports to Libya.[28]
- Weapons experts found large amounts of equipment used in making enriched uranium, the essential ingredient in nuclear weapons. That discovery helped expose a rogue nuclear trading network that officials say funneled technology and parts to Libya as well as Iran and North Korea. A central figure in the network, Pakistani metallurgist Abdul Qadeer Khan, acknowledged in a televised confession last month that he had passed nuclear secrets to others.
- On February 15, 2004, the *Washington Post* reported that the U.S. had discovered that the nuclear weapons designs Libya obtained through a Pakistan had come from a smuggling network that originated in China. The bomb designs and other papers turned over by Libya to the included text in Chinese, with detailed, step-by-step instructions for assembling a 1,000 pound implosion-type nuclear

Figure 10.17 (Continued)

bomb that could fit atop a large ballistic missile. The device was similar to a weapon known to have been tested by China in the 1960s. Although of an older design, the bomb design is a moderate-sized implosion device that uses use precision-timed conventional explosives to squeeze a sphere of fissile material and trigger a nuclear chain. Pakistan's first nuclear test in 1998 involved a more modern design than the one sold to Libya.

- The documents included technical instructions for manufacturing components for the device. The package of documents was turned over to U.S. officials in November following Libyan leader Moammar Qadaffi's decision to renounce weapons of mass destruction and open his country's weapons laboratories to international inspection.

- The documents were "copies of copies of copies." The primary documents were entirely in English, while a few ancillary papers contained Chinese text. The package also included open-literature articles on nuclear weapons from U.S. weapons laboratories, officials familiar with the documents stated.

- Although most essential design elements were included, some key parts were missing. The Post reported that investigators speculated that the missing papers could have been lost, or were being withheld pending additional payments. Libyan scientists claimed they had not seriously studied them and were unaware that anything was missing.

- The IAEA reported on February 20, 2004 that Libya produced small amounts of plutonium, and assembled a small set of gas centrifuges for producing enriched uranium, with the goal of producing 10,000 more. The IAEA inspectors had visited 18 sites in Libya, and found that plutonium was produced in "very small quantities" at the Tajura National Research Center.

- The IAEA also finds that Libya imported 2,263 tons of uranium ore concentrate between 1978 and 1981, and acquired Uranium Hexaflouride in 1985, 2000, and 2001—a material used in producing HEU.

- It conducted secret uranium conversion experiments on a small scale in the 1980s, and received a portable conversion facility in 1986, and stored the modules in locations around Tripoli. It did not conduct tests until 2002.

- Libya worked on domestic efforts to produce HEU during the 1980s and early 1990s, with foreign technical assistance. In 1997, it ordered 20 assembled centrifuges, and components for 200 more. In September 200, Libya ordered 10,000 centrifuges based on more advanced designs. The components began to arrive in December 2002, and further deliveries were on the ship intercepted in October 2003.

- On February 20, 2004 the Malaysian police issue a report on the smuggling of nuclear weapons components to Libya. The report confirms the details of Libyan proliferation found by the IAEA and notes that:

- In November 2003, representatives from the CIA and MI6 contacted their Malaysian counterparts to tell them about some of the activities of AQ Khan and Bsa Tahir, a close associate of the Pakistani nuclear scientist.

continued

Figure 10.17 (Continued)

- Alleged that a Pakistani nuclear arms expert was involved in the "onward proliferation of Pakistani nuclear technology to third countries, notably Libya."
- Tahir used a front company to "produce components for the centrifuge unit for the uranium enrichment programme."
- Bsa Tahir, a Sri Lankan businessman based in Dubai was a trusted and close confidante of the arms expert and was actively involved in supplying centrifuge components for Libya's uranium-enrichment program; and made use of SCOPE, a subsidiary of Scomi Group BHD, a company involved in the petroleum services industry. As a subsidiary, SCOPE is also involved in precision engineering services which involves the production of components for a variety of equipments including parts for cars, petroleum and gas.
- BSA Tahir alleged that his involvement with the nuclear expert started sometime in 1994/1995. That year, the latter had asked Bsa Tahir to send two containers of used centrifuge units from Pakistan to Iran. Bsa Tahir organized the transshipment of the two containers from Dubai to Iran using a merchant ship owned by a company in Iran. Bsa Tahir said the payment for the two containers of centrifuge units, amounting to about USD$3 million was paid in UAE Dirham currency by the Iranian. The cash was brought in two briefcases and kept in an apartment that was used as a guesthouse by the Pakistani nuclear arms expert each time he visited Dubai.
- Libya had contacted the nuclear arms expert in 1997 to obtain help and expertise in the field of uranium-enrichment centrifuge. Several meetings between the arms expert and representatives from Libya took place:
- Meeting in Istanbul sometime in 1997. During this meeting, the nuclear arms expert was accompanied by Bsa Tahir while Libya was represented by Mohamad Matuq Mohamad and another person known only as Karim. During this meeting, the Libyans asked the arms expert to supply centrifuge units for Libya's nuclear program; and
- Between 1998 and 2002. During this time, several meetings were held between the arms expert, accompanied by Bsa Tahir and the Libyans headed by Mohamad Matuq Mohamad. One discussion was held in Casablanca, Morocco and several discussions in Dubai.
- Around 2001, the nuclear arms expert informed Bsa Tahir that a certain amount of UF6 (enriched uranium) was sent by air from Pakistan to Libya. Bsa Tahir could not remember the name of the Pakistan Airlines which transported the uranium;
- Year 2001/2002. The nuclear arms expert informed Bsa Tahir that a certain number of centrifuge units were sent to Libya directly from Pakistan by air. There is a possibility that the design of the centrifuge units that were sent were of the P1 model, i.e. a Dutch designed model;
- Project Machine Shop 1001. This was a project to set up a workshop in Libya to make centrifuge components which could not be obtained from outside Libya. The machines for the workshop were obtained from Spain and Italy. Bsa Tahir

Figure 10.17 (Continued)

said the middleman involved in this project was Peter Griffin, a British citizen who is believed to have once owned Gulf Technical Industries (GTI) based in Dubai. Peter Griffin is said to be retired and living in France. The management of GTI has been taken over by his son Paul Griffin. Bsa Tahir also said that the plans for the Machine Shop 1001 was prepared by Peter Griffin.

- The full pattern of European support involved Late Heinz Mebus, an engineer. He is alleged to have been involved in discussions between the nuclear arms expert and Iran to supply centrifuge designs about 1984/85. Gotthard Lerch, a German citizen residing in Switzerland. Gotthard Lerch once worked for Leybold Heraeus, a German company that is alleged to have produced vacuum technology equipment. Gotthard Lerch is alleged to have tried to obtain supplies of pipes for the Machine Shop 1001 Project by sourcing from South Africa but failed to obtain it even though payment had been made by Libya earlier. Gunas Jireh, a citizen of Turkey who had once worked for the German company Siemens. Gunas Jireh is alleged to have supplied aluminum casting and dynamo to Libya at the request of the nuclear arms expert; Selim Alguadis, a citizen of Turkey. Also said to be an engineer. Alleged to have supplied electrical cabinets and power supplier-voltage regulator to Libya. Two weeks after action against the ship BBC China in Taranto, Italy on 4 Oct 2003.

- Bsa Tahir is alleged to have arranged the transshipment of electrical cabinets and power supplier-voltage regulator to Libya through Dubai on behalf of Selim Alguadis. Peter Griffin, a citizen of the United Kingdom, who has business interests in Dubai and currently residing in France. Alleged to have supplied the lay-out plan for the Machine Shop 1001 as a workshop to enable Libya to produce centrifuge; About 2001/2002, Peter Griffin is alleged to have supplied a lathe machine to Libya for the Machine Shop 1001 Project. After that Peter Griffin arranged to send 7 to 8 Libyan technicians to Spain, twice, to attend courses on how to operate the machine.

- At the same time, Peter Griffin is said to have supplied an Italian–made furnace to Libya for the workshop. Usually, lathe machines are used to make cylindrical objects, while the furnace is essential in the process of heating and refining during the manufacture of certain components; Friedrich Tinner, mechanical engineer, alleged to have had dealings with the nuclear arms expert since 1980s. Friedrich Tinner was reported to have prepared certain centrifuge components, including safety valves, and he sourced many of the materials that were made in several companies in Europe. Friedrich Tinner did not keep the stock himself but arranged for the supply to reach Dubai and then on to Libya. Friedrich Tinner is also the President of CETEC, a company in Switzerland; and Urs Friedrich Tinner is the son of Friedrich Tinner. Urs Tinner is a consultant arranged by Bsa Tahir to set up the SCOPE factory in Shah Alam. He was actively involved in the manufacturing operations in the SCOPE factory.

- Bsa Tahir claimed that together with the seized components on board *BBC China* on October 4, 2003, was a consignment sent by Gunas Jireh, a Turkish national who supplied "aluminum casting and dynamo" to Libya for its "machine shop 1001" project. These items were delivered through DUBAI using

continued

Figure 10.17 (Continued)

---

the services of TUT Shipping (TS) via vessel *BBC China*. It is surprising that the consignment from Gunas Jireh direct to Libya was allowed without any action; and two weeks after action taken against *BBC China*, Bsa Tahir claimed to have arranged a "transshipment of electrical cabinet and power supplier-voltage regulator" to Libya through Dubai on behalf of Selim Alguadis. These transshipment too arrived in Libya without any obstruction and this is unusual. Selim Alguadis is said to have known AQK since the 1980s.

---

[1]Quoted in the Statement by the Press Secretary, Office of the Press Secretary, February 26, 2004. Available at http://www.whitehouse.gov/news/releases/2004 /02/20040226-2.html#2.

[2]David C. Isby, "Libya can keep its 'SCUD' and 'FROG' missiles," *Jane's Missiles and Rockets*, February 1, 2004.

[3]Center for Nonproliferation Studies, Monterey Institute of International Studies, "North Korean Missile Exports and Technical Assistance to Libya," http://www.nti.org/db/profiles/dprk/msl/ie/NKM_EelibyGO.html, accessed March 2003.

[4]Joseph Bermudez, "Ballistic missile development in Libya," *Jane's Intelligence Review*, January 2003, pp. 26–31.

[5]AP Worldstream, April 6, 2001; "Report: North Korea exported over 540 missiles to Middle East countries."

[6]Joseph Bermudez, "Ballistic missile development in Libya," *Jane's Intelligence Review*, January 2003, pp. 26–31.

[7]Center for Nonproliferation Studies, Monterey Institute of International Studies, "North Korean Missile Exports and Technical Assistance to Libya," http://www.nti.org/db/profiles/dprk/msl/ie/NKM_EelibyGO.html, accessed March 2003.

[8]David C. Isby, "Libya can keep its 'SCUD' and 'FROG' missiles," *Jane's Missiles and Rockets*, February 1, 2004.

[9]Jason Fuchs, "Libya, Iran, DPRK Discuss New Strategic Missile Procurement," *Defense & Foreign Affairs Daily*, September 4, 2003.

[10]Jason Fuchs, "Libya, Iran, DPRK Discuss New Strategic Missile Procurement," *Defense & Foreign Affairs Daily*, September 4, 2003.

[11]Robin Huges, "Libya ships nuclear weapon material to U.S.," *Jane's Defense Weekly*, February 4, 2004.

[12]Stephen Fidler, "Libya had sizeable chemical weapons programme," The Financial Times of London, February 7, 2004, p. 8.

[13]Judith Miller, "Libya Discloses Production of 23 Tons of Mustard Gas," *New York Times*, March 6, 2004, p. 5.

[14]Judith Miller, "Libya Discloses Production of 23 Tons of Mustard Gas," *New York Times*, March 6, 2004, p. 5.

[15]Patrick Tyler, "British and U.S. experts return to dismantle Libya arms program," *The International Herald Tribune*, January 20, 2004, p. 3.

[16]Stephen Fidler, "Libya had sizable chemical weapons programme," *The Financial Times of London*, February 7, 2004, p. 8.

[17]*Jane's Intelligence Digest*, "Libya: In from the cold?" January 9, 2004.

[18]*Jane's Intelligence Digest*, "Libya: In from the cold?" January 9, 2004.

[19]Judith Miller, "Libya Discloses Production of 23 Tons of Mustard Gas," *New York Times*, March 6, 2004, p. 5.

[20]Stephen Fidler, Mark Huband, and Roula Khalaf, "Success of Libya's nuclear procurement effort revealed—Inspection findings," *The Financial Times of London*, January 22, 2004.

[21]Jane's Intelligence Digest, "Libya: In from the cold?" January 9, 2004.

[22] William J. Broad, "Libya's A-Bomb Blueprints Reveal New Tie To Pakistani," *New York Times*, February 9, 2004.

Figure 10.17 (Continued)

[23]George Jahn, "Libya Nuke Drawings Likely From Pakistan," *Associated Press*, February 15, 2004.
[24]*Defense & Foreign Affairs Daily*, "Qadhafi 'Rear Guard' Action Attempts to Halt U.S. Discovery of WMD Link With Iraq," January 22, 2004.
[25]Stephen Fidler, Mark Huband, and Roula Khalaf, "Success of Libya's nuclear procurement effort revealed—Inspection findings," *The Financial Times of London*, January 22, 2004.
[26]Jack Boureston, Yana Feldman, Charles Mahaffey, "Putting together Libya's nuclear puzzle," *Jane's Intelligence Review*, February 1, 2004.
[27]*Defense & Foreign Affairs Daily*, "Qadhafi 'Rear Guard' Action Attempts to Halt U.S. Discovery of WMD Link With Iraq," January 22, 2004.
[28]*Defense & Foreign Affairs Daily*, "Qadhafi 'Rear Guard' Action Attempts to Halt U.S. Discovery of WMD Link With Iraq," January 22, 2004.

Figure 10.18
Egypt's Search for Weapons of Mass Destruction

Delivery Systems

- Began three major design programs based on the V-2 missile in the 1950s, with help from German scientists. Tested two missiles by 1965: A 350 kilometer range al-Zafir and a 600 kilometer range Al Kahir. A 1,500-kilometer range Ar-Ra'id was designed but never tested. These missiles were liquid-fueled aging designs and development ceased around 1967.

- Cooperated with Iraq in paying for development and production of "Badr 2000" missile with a 750–1,000 kilometer range. This missile is reported to be a version of the Argentine Condor II or Vector missile. Ranges were reported from 820–980 kilometers, with the possible use of an FAE warhead.

  - Egyptian officers were arrested for trying to smuggle carbon materials for a missile out of the U.S. in June 1988.

  - Covert U.S. efforts seem to have blocked this development effort.

  - The Condor program seems to have been terminated in 1989–1990.

- Has Scud B TELs and missiles with approximately 100 missiles with 300 kilometers range.

- Reports have developed plant to produce an improved version of the Scud B, and possibly Scud C, with North Korean cooperation.

  - North Korean transfers include equipment for building Scud body, special gyroscope measuring equipment and pulse-code modulation equipment for missile assembly and testing.

  - Unconfirmed reports in June 1996 that has made major missile purchase from North Korea, and will soon be able to assemble such missiles in Egypt. Seven shipments from North Korea reported in March and April.

  - Other unconfirmed reports that Egypt had another liquid-fueled missile under development known as 'Project T' with an estimated range of 450 kilometers.

continued

Figure 10.18 (Continued)

It is believe to be an extended-range Scuds designed with North Korean assistance. These unconfirmed reports indicate Egypt may have as many as 90 Project T missiles.

- Media reports that U.S. satellites detected shipments of Scud C missile parts to Egypt in February–May, 1996—including rocket motors and guidance devices—do not seem correct. The Scud C has a range of roughly 480 kilometers.
- The CIA reported in June 1997, that Egypt had acquired Scud B parts from Russia and North Korea during 1996.

- The CIA reported in January 1999 that Egypt continues its effort to develop and produce the Scud B and Scud C and to develop the two–stage Vector short-range ballistic missiles (SRBMs). Cairo also is interested in developing a medium-range ballistic missile (MRBM). During the first half of 1998, Egypt continued to obtain ballistic missile components and associated equipment from North Korea. This activity is part of a long-running program of ballistic missile cooperation between these two countries.
- U.S. suspects Egypt is developing a liquid-fueled missile called the Vector with an estimated range of 600–1,200 kilometers.
- FROG 7 rocket launch units with 40 kilometers range.
- Cooperation with Iraq and North Korea in developing the Saqr 80 missile. This rocket is 6.5 meters long and 210-mm in diameter, and weighs 660 kilograms. It has a maximum range of 50 miles (80 kilometers) and a 440 pound (200 kilogram) warhead. Longer range versions may be available.
- AS-15, SS-N-2, and CSS-N-1 cruise missiles.
- 28 F-4E fighter ground attack aircraft.
- 20 Mirage 5E2 fighter ground attack.
- 53 Mirage 2000EM fighters.
- 33 F-16A/B and 174 F-16C/D fighters.
- Multiple rocket launcher weapons.
- Tube artillery.
- The Center for Nonproliferation Studies at the Monterey Institute of International Studies has compiled a chronology of North Korean assistance to Egypt through 2003[1]:

Date	Item(s)	Remarks
1987	Technical assistance for Scud-B production plant	
1989	Scud-B parts, improved missile components, such as guidance systems	Information from retired Israeli Brigadier General Aharon Levran.
Early 1990s	Scud-C missile production technology	North Korea reportedly helps Egypt set-up Scud-C production facility outside of Cairo.

466

Figure 10.18 (Continued)

1996 March-April	Seven shiploads of equipment and materials for producing Scud-C missiles	Could have included steel sheets for Scuds and support equipment, rocket engines and guidance systems. Possible assistance for producing Scud-C TELs.
1997	Several shipments of equipment for Scud-C production	
1999 July	Specialty steel	Probably maraging steel; shipped by Chinese firm in Hong Kong.
1999-2001	50 to 300 missile experts	
2000	No Dong missiles and TELs	Unconfirmed; North Korean firm Ch'ongchon'gang reportedly delivers 50 No Dong missiles and seven TELs to Syria. Missiles possibly procured on behalf of Iraq, Egypt and Libya for $600 million.
2001	24 to 50 No Dong engines	Unconfirmed; some reports claim that delivery occurred in the first half of 2001, but others claim engines have yet to be delivered. Egypt insists that missile cooperation with North Korea ended in 1996.

Chemical Weapons

- Produced and used mustard gas in Yemeni civil war in 1960s, but agents may have been stocks British abandoned in Egypt after World War II. Effort was tightly controlled by Nasser and was unknown to many Egyptian military serving in Yemen.

- Completed research and designs for production of nerve and cyanide gas before 1973.

- Former Egyptian Minister of War, General Abdel Ranny Gamassay stated in 1975, that, "if Israel should decide to use a nuclear weapon in the battlefield, we shall use the weapons of mass destruction that are at our disposal."

- Seems to have several production facilities for mustard and nerve gas. May have limited stocks of bombs, rockets, and shells. Unconfirmed reports suggest that Egypt had developed VX nerve gas.

- Unconfirmed reports of recent efforts to acquire feedstocks for nerve gas. Some efforts to obtain feedstocks from Canada. May now be building feed stock plants in Egypt.

- Industrial infrastructure present for rapid production of cyanide gas.

- Egypt is thought to have an offensive chemical warfare capability, but the extent of this capability is unknown.

Biological Weapons

- Research and technical base.

- Unconfirmed Israeli sources allege that Egypt has pursued research into anthrax, plague, botulinum toxin, and Rift Valley fever virus for military purposes, but no other open-source data confirms these allegations.

continued

Figure 10.18 (Continued)

- Egypt is thought to have a significant microbiological capability, but no substantiated, open-source evidence exists that suggests Egypt has pursued biological weapons.
- No evidence of major organized research activity.

Nuclear Weapons

- Research and technical base.
- Egypt currently operates two research reactors, both of which are under IAEA safeguards.
  - A 2 MW Soviet built reactor 40 km from Cairo which started operation in 1961
  - A 22 MW Argentine reactor at the Ishas facility, 60 km from Cairo, started operation in 1997. The Argentine reactor is thought to be capable of producing as enough plutonium for one weapon each year.[2]
- Numerous discussions over the years with the U.S., China and other nations for large-scale power generation facilities. No current agreements for construction of power reactors.
- No evidence of major organized research activity for development of a usable weapon.
- President Mubarak did say in October 1998, that Egypt could acquire nuclear weapons to match Israel's capability if this proves necessary,[3] "If the time comes when we need nuclear weapons, we will not hesitate. I say 'if' we have to because this is the last thing we think about. We do not think of joining the nuclear club." This speech was more an effort to push Israel towards disarmament talks, however, than any kind of threat.
- Mubarak also said that Israel "enhances its military expenditure and develops its missile systems that are used for military purposes. It knows very well that this will not benefit it or spare it from harm. Its efforts to use the help of foreign countries will plunge the region into a new arms race which serves nobody's interests." Egypt has supported the indefinite extension of the NNPT, has long been officially committed to creating a nuclear weapons-free zone in the Middle East, and had advocated an agreement that would ban all weapons of mass destruction from the region

[1]Center for Nonproliferation Studies, Monterey Institute of International Studies, "North Korean Missile Exports and Technical Assistance to Egypt," http://www.nti.org/db/profiles/dprk/msl/ie/NKM_EeegptGO.html, accessed March 2003.

[2]*The Risk Report*, "Egypt's Budding Nuclear Program," September–October 1996, http://www.wisconsinproject.org countries/egypt/nuke.html.

[3]*Jane's Defense Weekly*, October 14, 1998.

Figure 10.19
Israel's Search for Weapons of Mass Destruction

Delivery Systems

- There are convincing indications that Israel has deployed nuclear-armed missiles on mobile launchers. Most outside sources call the first of these missiles the "Jericho I," but Israel has never publicly named its long-range missile systems.

  - These missiles were near-copies of the two-stage, solid-fueled, French MD-620 missile. Some reports claim the first 14 were built in France.

  - A number of sources indicate that Israel deployed up to 50 "Jericho I" (YA-1) missiles on mobile launchers in shelters in the hills southwest of Jerusalem, with up to 400 miles range with a 2,200 pound payload, and with possible nuclear warhead storage nearby. (Some reports give the range as 500 kilometers.)

  - Israel is thought to have conventional, chemical and nuclear warheads for the Jericho I.

  - The current deployment of the "Jericho I" force is unclear. Some sources say it has been phased out for the Jericho II missile.[1]

- Israel has since gone far beyond the Jericho I in developing long-range missile systems. It has developed and deployed the "Jericho II" (YA-2).

  - The "Jericho II" began development in the mid-1970s, and had its first tests in 1986.[2] Israeli carried out a launch in mid-1986 over the Mediterranean that reached a range of 288 miles (460 kilometers). It seems to have been tested in May 1987. A flight across the Mediterranean reached a range of some 510 miles (820 kilometers), landing south of Crete.[3] Another test occurred on September 14, 1989.

  - Israel launched a missile across the Mediterranean that landed about 250 miles north of Benghazi, Libya. The missile flew over 800 miles, and U.S. experts felt it had a maximum range of up to 900–940 miles (1,450 kilometers)—which would allow the Jericho II to cover virtually all of the Arab world and even the Southern USSR.[4]

  - The most recent version of the missile seems to be a two-stage, solid-fueled missile with a range of up to 900 miles (1,500 kilometers) with a 2,200 pound payload.

  - Commercial satellite imaging indicates the Jericho II missile may be 14 meters long and 1.5 meters wide. Its deployment configuration hints that it may have radar area guidance similar to the terminal guidance in the Pershing II and probably has deployed these systems.

  - Some Jericho IIs may have been brought to readiness for firing during the Gulf War.

  - Israel began work on an updated version of the Jericho II no later than 1995 in an effort to stretch its range to 2,000 km. At least part of this work may have begun earlier in cooperation with South Africa.

- Israel has done technical work on a TERCOM type smart warhead. It has examined cruise missile guidance developments using GPS navigation systems. This system may be linked to a submarine launch option.

continued

469

Figure 10.19 (Continued)

- Israel is also seeking technology to improve its accuracy, particularly with gyroscopes for the inertial guidance system and associated systems software.

- Israel is actively examining ways to lower the vulnerability of its ballistic missiles and nuclear weapons. These include improved hardening, dispersal, use of air-launched weapons, and possible sea-basing. Israel seems especially interested in basing ballistic missiles in Israel's Dolphin-class submarines.

- There are also reports that Israel is developing a Jericho III missile, based on a booster it developed with South Africa in the 1980s.

  - The tests of a longer-range missile seem to have begun in the mid-1980s.[5] A major test of such a booster seems to have taken place on September 14, 1989, and resulted in extensive reporting on such cooperation in the press during October 25 and 26, 1989.

  - It is possible that that both the booster and any Israeli-South African cooperation may have focused on satellite launches.[6] Since 1994, however, there have been are numerous reports among experts that Israel is seeking a missile with a range of at least 4,800 kilometers, and which could fully cover Iran and any other probable threat.

  - *Jane's* estimates that the missile has a range of up to 5,000 kilometers and a 1,000 kilogram warhead. This estimate is based largely on a declassified DIA estimate of the launch capability of the Shavit booster that Israel tested on September 19, 1988.[7]

- Reports of how Israel deploys its missiles differ.

  - Initial reports indicated that 30–50 Jericho I missiles were deployed on mobile launchers in shelters in the cases southwest of Tel Aviv. A source claimed in 1985, that Israel had 50 missiles deployed on mobile erector launchers in the Golan, on launchers on flat cars that could be wheeled out of sheltered cases in the Negev. (This latter report may confuse the rail transporter used to move missiles from a production facility near Be'er Yaakov to a base at Kefar Zeharya, about 15 kilometers south of Be'er Yaakov.)

  - More recent reports indicate that Jericho II missiles are located in 50 underground bunkers carved into the limestone hills near a base near Kefar Zeharya. The number that are on alert, command and control and targeting arrangements, and the method of giving them nuclear warheads has never been convincingly reported.[8]

  - *Jane's Intelligence Review* published satellite photos of what it said as a Jericho II missile base at Zachariah (God remembers with a vengeance) several miles southeast of Tel Aviv in September 1997.[9] According to this report, the transport-erector-launcher (TEL) for the Jericho II measures about 16 meters long by 4 meters wide and 3 meters high. The actual missile is about 14 meters long and 1.5 meters wide. The TEL is supported by three support vehicles, including a guidance and power vehicle. The other two vehicles include communications vehicle and a firing control vehicle. This configuration is somewhat similar to that used in the U.S. Pershing II IRBM system, although there are few physical similarities.

470

Figure 10.19 (Continued)

- The photos in the article show numerous bunkers near the TEL and launch pad, and the article estimates a force of 50 missiles on the site. It also concludes that the lightly armored TEL would be vulnerable to a first strike, but that the missiles are held in limestone caves behind heavy blast-resistant doors. It estimates that a nuclear-armed M-9 or Scud C could destroy the launch capability of the site. [10]

- The same article refers to nuclear weapons bunkers at the Tel Nof airbase, a few kilometers to the northwest. The author concludes that the large number of bunkers indicates that Israel may have substantially more nuclear bombs than is normally estimated—perhaps up to 400 weapons with a total yield of 50 megatons. [11]

- 76 F-15, 232 F-16, 20 F-4E, and 50 Phantom 2000 fighter-bombers capable of long-range refueling and of carrying nuclear and chemical bombs.

- Israel bought some Lance missile launchers and 160 Lance missiles, with 130 kilometers range, from the U.S. in the 1970s. The U.S. removed them from active duty during 1991–1994. The status of the Israeli missiles is unknown.

  - IISS reports that Israel currently has some 20 Lance launchers in storage.

  - The Lance has a range of 130 km with a 450 kg payload.

  - Reports indicate that Israel has developed conventional cluster munitions for use with the Lance rocket.

- Reports of a May 2000 test launch seem to indicate that Israel is developing a cruise missile with 1,500 km that can be launched from its new Dolphin-class, German-built submarines.[12]

  - It is believed that such a cruise missile, an extended-range, turbofan powered variant of the Popeye cruise missile, called the Popeye Turbo, can carry a nuclear warhead.

- There are reports of the development of a long-range, nuclear-armed version of Popeye with GPS guidance and of studies of possible cruise missile designs that could be both surface-ship and submarine based.

  - Variant of the Popeye air-to-surface missile believed to have nuclear warhead.

  - The MAR-290 rocket with 30 kilometers range is believed to be deployed.

  - MAR-350 surface-to-surface missile with range of 56 miles and 735 lb. payload believed to have completed development or to be in early deployment.

  - Israel seeking super computers for Technion Institute (designing ballistic missile RVs), Hebrew University (may be engaged in hydrogen bomb research), and Israeli Military Industries (maker of "Jericho II" and Shavit booster).

  - Israel current review of its military doctrine seems to include a review of its missile basing options, and the study of possible hardening and dispersal systems. There are also reports that Israel will solve its survivability problems by deploying some form of nuclear-armed missile on its new submarines.

Chemical Weapons

- Reports of mustard and nerve gas production facility established in 1982 in the restricted area in the Sinai near Dimona seem incorrect. May have additional

continued

Figure 10.19 (Continued)

facilities. May have capacity to produce other gases. Probable stocks of bombs, rockets, and artillery.

- According to some reports, Israel revitalized its chemical warfare facilities south of Dimona in the mid-1980s, after Syria deployed chemical weapons and Iraq began to use these weapons in the Iran-Iraq War.

- Extensive laboratory research into gas warfare and defense.

- An El Al 747–200 cargo plane crashed in southern Amsterdam on October 4, 1992, killing 43 people in the apartment complex it hit. This led to extensive examination of the crash and the plane was found to be carrying 50 gallons of dimethyl methylphosphonate, a chemical used to make Sarin nerve gas. The chemical had been purchased from Solkatronic Chemicals in the U.S. and was being shipped to the Israel Institute for Biological Research. It was part of an order of 480 pounds worth of the chemical. Two of the three other chemicals used in making Sarin were shipped on the same flight. Israel at first denied this and then claimed it was only being imported to test gas masks.[13]

- Israel may have the contingency capability to produce at least two types of chemical weapons and has certainly studied biological weapons as well as chemical ones. According to one interview with an Israeli source of unknown reliability, Israel has mustard gas, persistent and non-persistent nerve gas, and may have at least one additional agent.

- Development of defensive systems includes Shalon Chemical Industries protection gear, Elbit Computer gas detectors, and Bezal R&D aircrew protection system.

- Extensive field exercises in chemical defense.

- Gas masks stockpiled, and distributed to population with other civil defense instructions during first Gulf War and the Iraq War.

- Warhead delivery capability for bombs, rockets, and missiles, but none now believed to be equipped with chemical agents.

- An unconfirmed October 4, 1998 report in the *Sunday Times* of London quotes military sources as stating that Israeli F-16s can carry out attacks using chemical and biological weapons produced at the Nes Ziona facility.[14]

Biological Weapons

- Extensive research into weapons and defense.

- Ready to quickly produce biological weapons, but no reports of active production effort.

- Israel has at least one major research facility with sufficient security and capacity to produce both chemical and biological weapons.[15] There are extensive reports that Israel has a biological weapons research facility at the Israel Institute for Biological Research at Nes Tona, about 12 miles south of Tel Aviv, and that this same facility also has worked on the development and testing of nerve gas. This facility has created enough public concern in Israel so that the mayor of Nes Tona has asked that it be moved away from populated areas. The facility is reported to have stockpiled Anthrax and to have provided toxins to Israeli intelli-

Figure 10.19 (Continued)

gence for use in covert operations and assassinations like the attempt on a Hamas leader in Jordan in 1997.[16]

- The Israel Institute for Biological Research is located in a 14-acre compound. It has high walls and exceptional security, and is believed to have a staff of around 300, including 120 scientists. A former deputy head, Marcus Kingberg, served 16 years in prison for spying for the FSU.
- U.S. experts privately state that Israel is one of the nations included in U.S. lists of nations with biological and chemical weapons. They believe that Israel has at least some stocks of weaponized nerve gas, although they may be stored in forms that require binary agents to be loaded into binary weapons.
  - They believe that Israel has fully developed bombs and warheads capable of effectively disseminating dry, storable biological agents in micropowder form and has agents considerably more advanced than anthrax. Opinion differs over whether such weapons are actively loaded and deployed. Unconfirmed reports by the British *Sunday Times* claimed that IAF F-16s are equipped for strikes using both these weapons and chemical weapons.[17]

Nuclear Weapons

- Director of CIA indicated in May 1989, that Israel may be seeking to construct a thermonuclear weapon.
- Has two significant reactor projects: the 5 megawatt HEU light-water IRR I reactor at Nahal Soreq; and the 40–150 megawatt heavy water, IRR-2 natural uranium reactor used for the production of fissile material at Dimona. Only the IRR-1 is under IAEA safeguards.
- Dimona has conducted experiments in pilot scale laser and centrifuge enrichment, purifies UO_2, converts UF_6 and fabricates fuel for weapons purpose.
- Uranium phosphate mining in Negev, near Beersheba, and yellowcake is produced at two plants in the Haifa area and one in southern Israel.
- Pilot-scale heavy water plant operating at Rehovot.
  - *Jane's Intelligence Review* published an article in September 1997 which refers to nuclear weapons bunkers at the Jericho 2 missile base at Zachariah (God remembers with a vengeance) several miles southeast of Tel Aviv and at Tel Nof airbase, a few kilometers to the northwest. The author concludes that the large number of bunkers indicates that Israel may have substantially more nuclear bombs than is normally estimated—perhaps up to 400 weapons with a total yield of 50 megatons. [18]
- Estimates of numbers and types of weapons differ sharply.
  - Stockpile of at least 60–80 plutonium weapons.
  - May have well over 100 nuclear weapons assemblies, with some weapons with yields over 100 kilotons.
  - U.S. experts believe Israel has highly advanced implosion weapons. Known to have produced Lithium-6, allowing production of both tritium and lithium deuteride at Dimona. Facility no longer believed to be operating.

continued

Figure 10.19 (Continued)

- Some weapons may be ER variants or have variable yields.
- Total stockpile of up to 200–300 weapons is possible.
- There exists a possibility that Israel may have developed thermonuclear warheads.
- Major weapons facilities include production of weapons grade Plutonium at Dimona, nuclear weapons design facility at Nahal Soreq (south of Tel Aviv), missile test facility at Palmikim, nuclear armed missile storage facility at Kefar Zekharya, nuclear weapons assembly facility at Yodefat, and tactical nuclear weapons storage facility at Eilabun in eastern Galilee.

Missile Defenses

- Patriot missiles with future PAC-3 upgrade to reflect lessons of the Gulf War.
- Arrow 2 two-stage ATBM with slant intercept ranges at altitudes of 8–10 and 50 kilometers speeds of up to Mach 9, plus possible development of the Rafal AB-10 close in defense missile with ranges of 10–20 kilometers and speeds of up to Mach 4.5. Taas rocket motor, Rafael warhead, and Tadiran BM/C^{4}I system and "Music" phased array radar.
  - The Arrow 2 has been tested six times and the most recent test successfully intercepted a Sparrow missile. IAF sources claim that the Arrow 2 can intercept the Iranian Shahab missile series.[19]
  - Israel plans to deploy three batteries of the Arrow to cover Israel, each with four launchers, to protect up to 85% of its population. The first battery was deployed in early 2000 at the Palmuchim Air Force Base, south of Tel Aviv, with an official announcement declaring the system operational on March 12, 2000.
  - The second Arrow battery components are being assembled at Eim Shemer near Hadera.
  - The Arrow program has three phases:
    - Phase I: Validate Defense Concept and Demonstrate Pre-prototype Missile.
      - Fixed price contract: $158 million.
      - The U.S. pays 80%, Israel pays 20%.
      - Completed in December 1982.
    - Phase II: Demonstrate Lethality, develop and demonstrate tactical interceptor and launcher.
      - Fixed price contract: $330 million.
      - The U.S. pays 72%, Israel pays 28%.
      - Began in July 1991.
      - Successfully completed.
    - Phase III: Develop and integrate tactical system, conduct weapon system tests, and develop and implement interoperability.
      - Program cost estimated at: $616 million.
      - The U.S. pays 48%, Israel pays 52%.

Figure 10.19 (Continued)

- Began in March 1996.
- System integration in progress.
- The Arrow will be deployed in batteries as a wide area defense system with intercepts normally at reentry or exoatmospheric altitudes. Capable of multi-target tracking and multiple intercepts.
- Israel has designed the Nautilus laser system for rocket defense in a joint project with the USA. It has developed into the Theater High Energy Laser (THEL). The project has recently been expanded to include interception of not only short-range rockets and artillery, but also medium-range Scuds and longer-range missiles such as Iran's Shahab series.
- Israel is also examining the possibility of boost-phase defenses. The Rafael Moab UAV forms part of the Israeli Boost-phase Intercept System. This is intended to engage TBMs soon after launch, using weapons fired from a UAV. Moab would launch an improved Rafael Python 4 air-to-air missile. Range is stated as 80–100km depending on altitude of release.

Advanced Intelligence Systems

- Israeli space program to date:

Satellite	Launch Date	Status	Function
Ofeq 1	9/19/1988	Decayed 1/14/1989	Experimental
Ofeq 2	4/3/1990	Decayed 7/9/1990	Communications experiments.
Ofeq 3	4/5/1995	Decayed 10/24/2000	Reconnaissance/experimental?
Ofeq 4 (Eros A)	1/22/1998	Launch failed during second-stage burn	Reconnaissance/commercial imaging?
Eros A1	12/5/2000	In orbit	Reconnaissance/commercial imaging?
Ofeq 5	5/28/2002	In orbit	Reconnaissance

Note: This chart does not include Israel's commercial communications satellite ventures.

- The Shavit launched Israel's satellite payload on September 19, 1989. It used a three stage booster system capable of launching a 4,000 pound payload over 1,200 miles or a 2,000 pound payload over 1,800 miles. It is doubtful that it had a payload capable of intelligence missions and seems to have been launched, in part, to offset the psychological impact of Iraq's missile launches.
  - It is believed that the vehicle was launched for experimentation in generation of solar power and transmission reception from space; verification of system's ability to withstand vacuum and weightless conditions; data collection on space environment conditions and Earth's magnetic field.
- Ofeq 2 launched in April 3, 1990—one day after Saddam Hussein threatens to destroy Israel with chemical weapons if it should attack Baghdad.
  - This vehicle used the Ofeq 1 test-bed. Little open-source information exists on this vehicle although it is believed to be a test-bed for communications experiments.

continued

Figure 10.19 (Continued)

- Israel launched first intelligence satellite on April 5, 1995, covering Syria, Iran, and Iraq in orbit every 90 minutes. The Ofeq 3 satellite is a 495-pound system launched using the Shavit 1 launch rocket, and is believed to carry an imagery system. Its orbit passes over or near Damascus, Tehran, and Baghdad.

    - The Shavit 1 differs from the Shavit only in the use of a somewhat different first stage. This change has not significantly affected vehicle performance. The Ofeq 3 and all subsequent launches have used the Shavit 1.

    - Reports conflict regarding whether this was an experimental platform or Israel's first surveillance satellite. Although it is thought to carry visible and ultraviolet wavelength imaging technology, the resolution is thought to be on the order of feet. The relatively low resolution, combined with its orbit, suggest to some observers that the satellite was capable of producing imagery of limited military usefulness.

- On January 22, 1998, the Ofeq 4/Eros A satellite was launched. Due to a failure in the second-stage the satellite never made orbit. Reports conflict about whether this was a launch of a military reconnaissance satellite or was intended for producing commercial satellite imagery.

- The Eros A1 satellite was launched on December 5, 2000 on a Russian Start-1 rocket from Svobodny launch site. This satellite produces commercially available satellite images. At a basic level, multi-spectral images with resolutions of 1.8 meters can be obtained. Currently, image processing techniques can yield resolutions of 1 meter. This is expected to improve to 0.6~0.7 meter resolutions in the next year or two. Some reports indicate that the Israeli government is a primary consumer of EROS imagery.

    - The successor craft, the Eros B, will have a baseline ability to produce images with a panchromatic resolution of 0.87 meters and 3.5 meters for multi-spectral images. Launch on board a Russian vehicle is expected in early 2004.

- On May 28, 2002, the Ofeq 5 reconnaissance satellite was launched successfully.

- Development of the Ofeq 6 reconnaissance satellite has started for a 2007 launch.

- Agreement signed with the U.S. in April 1996 to provide Israel with missile early warning, launch point, vector, and point of impact data.

- Israeli Aircraft Industries, the manufacturer of the Shavit series SLV, is developing the additional launchers to place satellites in polar orbits:

    - LK-A—For 350kg-class satellites in 240×600km elliptical polar orbits.

    - LK-1—For 350kg-class satellites in 700km circular polar orbits.

    - LK-2—For 800kg-class satellites in 700km circular polar orbits.

    - It is likely that these SLVs designed to place satellites in polar orbits could not be launched from Israel and would require an overseas launching site, such as the American site at Wallops Island.

---

[1]Some reports give the range as 500 kilometers; *Jane's Defense Weekly*, March 10, 1999, pp. 50–64.

[2]*Baltimore Sun, November 23, 1988; Washington Post,* September 16, 1989.

[3]*Tass International*, 1216 GMT, September 15, 1989; *Washington Post*, September 16, 1989; *Jane's Defense Weekly,* November 19, 1988, September 23, 1989, p. 549; *Washington*

Figure 10.19 (Continued)

Times, July 22, 1987, p. D-4; *International Defense Review*, 7/1987, p. 857, and *New York Times*, July 22, 1987, p. A-6, July 29, 1987; Mideast Markets, November 23, 1987, p. 11; in Harold Hough, "Israel's Nuclear Infrastructure, *Jane's Intelligence Weekly*, November, 1994, pp. 505–511.

[4]BBC and ITV reporting efforts seem to give more credibility to the idea that Israel has some form of relatively short-range nuclear armed missile. Ranges of anywhere from 750–930 NM have been reported, with accuracy's of anywhere from 0.1 Km to radar correlator guidance packages capable of CEPs of 10 meters. Bulletin of Atomic Scientists, Vol. 46, Jan/Feb. 19980, p. 48; *Washington Post*, September 16, 1989, p. A-17, November 15, 1989, p. A-14; Economist, August 1, 1987, p. 41; *Washington Times*, July 22, 1987, p. D-4; July 24, 1987, p. A-9 and April 4, 1988, p. 17; *International Defense Review*, 7/1987, p. 857, and *New York Times*, July 29, 1987, p. A-10.

[5]*Tass International*, 1216 GMT, September 15, 1989; *Washington Post*, September 16, 1989; *Jane's Defense Weekly*, November 19, 1988, September 23, 1989, p. 549; *Washington Times*, July 22, 1987, p. D-4; *International Defense Review*, 7/1987, p. 857, and *New York Times*, July 22, 1987, p. A-6, July 29, 1987; Mideast Markets, November 23, 1987, p. 11; in Harold Hough, "Israel's Nuclear Infrastructure, *Jane's Intelligence Weekly*, November, 1994, pp. 505–511.

[6]*Washington Post*, October 26, 1989, p. A-36; *Boston Globe*, October 30, 1989, p. 2; *Newsweek*, November 6, 1989, p. 52.

[7]*Jane's Intelligence Review*, September, 1997, pp. 407–410; *Jane's Defense Weekly*, March 10, 1999, pp. 50–64; *International Defence Review*, Extra, 2/1997, p. 2.

[8]It is also possible that Israel may have deployed nuclear warheads for its MGM-55C Lance missiles. Israel has 12 Lance transporter-erector-launchers, and at least 36 missiles. The Lance is a stored liquid fueled missile with inertial guidance and a range of 5–125 kilometers. It has a warhead weight of 251 kilograms, and a CEP of 375 meters. It was deployed in U.S. forces with the W-70 nuclear warhead. *International Defense Review*, 7/1987, p. 857; Economis t, May 4, 1968, pp. 67–68; *New York Times*, July 22, 1987, p. A-6; *Washington Times*, July 22, 1987, p. D-4; *Defense and Foreign Affairs*, June, 1985, p. 1; *Aerospace Daily*, May 1, 1985, p. 5 and May 17, 1985, p. 100; *Aerospace Daily*, May 1, 1985, May 7, 1985; Shuey, et al., Missile Proliferation: Survey of Emerging Missile Forces, p. 56; CIA, "Prospects for Further Proliferation of Nuclear Weapons, "DCI NIO 1945/74, September 4, 1974; NBC Nightly News, July 30, 1985; *New York Times*, April 1, 1986; U.S. Arms Control and Disarmament Agency, World Military Expenditures and Arms Transfers, Washington, GPO, 1989, p. 18; Michael A. Ottenberg, "Israel and the Atom," *American Sentinel*, August 16, 1992, p. 1.

[9]Harold Hough, "Could Israel's Nuclear Assets Survive a First Strike?," *Jane's Intelligence Review*, September, 1997, pp. 407–410.

[10]Harold Hough, "Could Israel's Nuclear Assets Survive a First Strike?," *Jane's Intelligence Review*, September, 1997, pp. 407–410.

[11]Harold Hough, "Could Israel's Nuclear Assets Survive a First Strike?," *Jane's Intelligence Review*, September, 1997, pp. 407–410.

[12]Uzi Mahnaimi and Matthew Campbell, "Israel Makes Nuclear Waves With Submarine Missile Test," *Sunday Times* (London), June 18, 2000; Walter Pincus, "Israel Has Sub-Based Atomic Arms Capability," *Washington Post*, June 15, 2002, p. A-1.

[13]*Associated Press*, October 5, 1998, 0316, October 8, 1998, 1350; *Philadelphia Inquirer*, November 1, 1998, p. A-7.

[14]Uzi Mahnaimi, "Israeli Jets Equipped for Chemical Warfare," *Sunday Times* (London), October 4, 1998.

[15] This information is unconfirmed, and based on only one source. Israel does, however, have excellent research facilities, laboratory production of poison gas is essential to test protection devices as is the production of biological weapons to test countermeasures and antidotes.

continued

Figure 10.19 (Continued)

[16]*Philadelphia Inquirer*, November 1, 1998, p. A-7; Associated Press, October 8, 1998, 1350.

[17]*Washington Times*, October 7, 1998, pp. A-14.

[18]Harold Hough, "Could Israel's Nuclear Assets Survive a First Strike?," *Jane's Intelligence Review*, September, 1997, pp. 407–410.

[19]Robin Hughes and Alon Ben-David, "Arrow 2 Test Exceeds Israeli Expectations," *Jane's Defense Weekly.* http:jdw.janes.com, Accessed March 12, 2004.

Figure 10.20
Syria's Search for Weapons of Mass Destruction

Delivery Systems

- Possible short range and tactical delivery systems include:
  - 18 FROG-7 launchers and rockets.
  - Multiple rocket launchers and tube artillery.
- Syria has numerous aircraft that could be used to deliver a nuclear weapon or modified for use as a UAV. They include:
  - 20 Su-24 long range strike fighters.
  - 44–60 operational MiG-23BN Flogger F fighter ground attack aircraft.
  - 50 Su-22 fighter ground attack aircraft.[1]
- Four SSM brigades: 1 with FROG, 1 with Scud Bs, 1 with Scud Cs, and 1 with SS-21s.
  - Has 18 SS-21 launchers and at least 36 SS-21 missiles with 80–100 kilometers range. May be developing chemical warheads.
  - According to the May 1998 estimate of the Center for Nonproliferation Studies at the Monterey Institute of International Studies, Syria possessed 200 SS-21 Scarab missiles.[2]
  - Some experts believe some Syrian surface-to-surface missiles armed with chemical weapons began to be stored in concrete shelters in the mountains near Damascus and in the Palmyra region no later than 1986, and that plans have long existed to deploy them forward in an emergency since that date.
  - Up to 12 Scud B launchers and 200 Scud B missiles with 310 kilometers range. Believed to have chemical warheads. Scud B warhead weighs 985 kilograms. The inventory of Scud B missiles is believed to be approximately 200.
  - The Monterey Institute of International Studies' Center for Nonproliferation Studies reports that the Chinese provided technical assistance to upgrade Scud B missiles in 1993.[3]
  - New long-range North Korean Scud Cs deployed
- *Jane's* cites an American Department of Defense document published in 1992 that is said to report that Syria had purchased 150 Scud C missiles.

Figure 10.20 (Continued)

- Two brigades of 18 launchers each are said to be deployed in a horseshoe shaped valley. This estimate of 36 launchers is based on the fact there are 36 tunnels into the hillside. The launchers must be for the Scud C since the older Scud Bs would not be within range of most of Israel. Up to 50 missiles are stored in bunkers to north as possible reloads. There is a maintenance building and barracks.

- Underground bunkers are thought to have sufficient storage for some 1,000 Scud-C missiles according to a fall 2002 article in the Middle East Quarterly.[4]

- Estimates indicate that Syria has 24–36 Scud launchers for a total of 260–300 missiles of all types. The normal ratio of launchers to missiles is 10:1, but Syria is focusing on both survivability and the capability to launch a large preemptive strike.

- The Scud Cs have ranges of up to 550–600 kilometers. They have a CEP of 1,000–2,600 meters. Nerve gas warheads using VX with cluster bomblets seem to have begun production in early 1997. Syria is believed to have 50–80 Scud C missiles.

- A training site exists about 6 kilometers south of Hama, with an underground facility where TELs and missiles are stored.

- *Jane's* reports that "It was reported in early 1998 that Israeli intelligence experts had estimated that there were between 24 and 36 'Scud' launchers at most Syrian missile sites—far more launchers than previously estimated." Traditionally, armies deploying Scuds stock about 10 missiles per launcher. The higher number of Syrian launchers suggests a ratio closer to 2 missiles per launcher—this would enable Syria to launch a large first-wave strike before launchers were destroyed.

- Syria may be able to build the entire Scud B and Scud C. Some Israeli sources claim it has sheltered and/or underground missile production/assembly facilities at Aleppo, Hama, and near Damascus, which have been built with aid from Chinese, Iranian, and North Korean technicians. Possibly some Russian technical aid.

  - Israeli defense officials have been reported as stating that Syria has been producing about 30 Scud C missiles per year at an underground facility.[5]

  - A missile test site exists 15 kilometers south of Homs where Syria has tested missile modifications and new chemical warheads. It has heavy perimeter defenses, a storage area and bunkers, heavily sheltered bunkers, and a missile storage area just west of the site.

  - According to some reports, Syria has built two missile plants near Hama, about 110 miles north of Damascus, one is for solid fueled rockets and the other is for liquid fueled systems. North Korea may have provided the equipment for the liquid fuel plant, and Syria may now be able to produce the missile.

- Reports of Chinese deliveries of missiles but little hard evidence:

  - Reports of PRC deliveries of missile components by China Precision Machinery Company, maker of the M-11, in July 1996. The M-11 has a 186-mile (280 kilometer) range with a warhead of 1,100 pounds. Missile components may have included "contained sensitive guidance equipment."[6]

continued

Figure 10.20 (Continued)

- Reports of Syrian purchases and production of Chinese M-9 missile are unconfirmed and of uncertain value:
    - Some sources believe M-9 missile components, or M-9-like components deliv-
    ered to Syria. Missile is reported to have a CEP as low as 300 meters.
    - Some intelligence reports indicate that 24 M-9 launchers were sighted in late
    1991.[7] Other reports suggest that the 1991 missile deliveries were subsequently
    cancelled due to U.S. pressure.
    - "Since 1989 there have been persistent rumors that Syria was trying to import
    the M-9 from China. Up to the mid-1990s, Israeli sources believed that these
    attempts ended in failure—Beijing reportedly backed out of the deal due to
    U.S. pressure. The reports surfaced again in the late 1990s, with suggestions
    that the M-9 had been delivered from China—possibly in kit form, or partly
    assembled."
    - *Jane's* reported in March 1999 that Syria had created a production facility to
    build both the M-11 (CSS-7/DF-11) and M-9 missiles with ranges of 280 and
    600–800 kilometers respectively. It reports that production of the booster stage
    of the M-11 began in 1996, and that missile production is expected to start
    "soon."
    - An April 1993 report in Jane's Intelligence Review report indicated that North
    Korea and Iran (with Chinese assistance) helped in the construction of under-
    ground production facilities for the Scud C and M-9 missiles. At the time of
    the article (April 1993), production of the Scud C was believed to be 12–18
    months off, while M-9 production was believed to be 2–3 years away.[8]
- Senior administration officials were quoted as stating that China had sold missile technology to Syria. 30–90 tons of chemicals for solid propellant were sold
to Syria by mid 1992.[9]
- Some Israeli sources report that Syria has also developed, with North Korean assistance, a Syrian version of the Korean No Dong (sometimes referred to as the
Scud-D).
    - A number of sources reported the September 23, 2000 test flight of the Syrian
    No Dong.
    - Four tunnels for shelters for No Dong launchers have been excavated, as of
    late 2002.[10]
    - Syria expected to produce or have already started production at the rate of
    about 30 missiles per year.[11]
    - Israeli officials claimed that Syria was developing "multiple warhead clusters"
    in a bid to defeat Israel's Arrow missile defense system.[12]
    - Syria has shorter range systems:
        - Short-range M-1B missiles (up to 60 miles range) seem to be in delivery from
        PRC.
        - SS-N-3, and SSC-1b cruise missiles.
- The Center for Nonproliferation Studies at the Monterey Institute of International
Studies has compiled the following chronology of North Korean assistance to
Syria through 2000[13]:

Figure 10.20 (Continued)

Date	Item(s)	Remarks
1991 March	24 Scud-Cs and 20 TELs	Syria pays approximately $250 million, and Libya reportedly helps finance transaction.
1991 April	60 Scud-Cs and 12 TELs	First delivery after agreement for Syria to acquire 150 Scud-Cs for an estimated $500 million.
1991 May	36 Scud-Cs	Missiles transported by Yugoslavian freighter.
1991 summer	Unknown number of Scud-Cs	Missiles delivered by North Korean ship *Mupo* and transferred to Syria via Cyprus.
1992	24 Scud-C missiles; missile-production and assembly equipment	Delivered by North Korean freighter *Tae Hung Ho* in March. Part of the shipment was airlifted to Syria via the Iranian port of Bandar Abbas, and the remaining cargo was transported directly to the Tartus. The manufacturing equipment reportedly destined for suspected missile factories in Hama and Aleppo.
1992	Approximately 50 Scud-Cs	A North Korean ship carrying 100 Scud-Cs depart for the Iranian port Bandar Abbas in October. Half of the delivery transported overland to Syria.
1993	seven MAZ 543 chassis and unknown number of Scud-Cs	In August, two Russian Condor aircraft transport the missiles and chassis from Sunan International Airport to Damascus. According to Israeli Foreign Minister Shimon Peres, North Korea offered to stop the delivery if Israel paid $500 million.
1994	Unknown number of Scud-C missiles and TELs	
1994	Unknown number of Scud-C cluster warheads	
1996	Missile expertise	Syrian missile technicians spend two weeks training in North Korea.
1999	10 tons of powdered aluminum	Originally from China, shipment delivered to the Centre des Etudes de Recherche Scientifique, the institute in charge of Syria's missile program.
2000	Scud-D missile	Unconfirmed; Syria conducted Scud-D flight test on 23 September 2000.
2000	No Dong missiles and TELs	Unconfirmed; North Korean firm Ch'ongchon'gang reportedly delivers 50 No Dong missiles and seven TELs to Syria. Missiles possibly procured on behalf of Iraq, Egypt and Libya for $600 million.

- Sheltered or underground missile production/assembly facilities at Aleppo and Hamas have been built with aid from Chinese, Iranian, and North Korean technicians. Possibly some Russian technical aid.
- May be converting some long range surface-to-air and naval cruise missiles to use chemical warheads.
- Syria has improved its targeting capability in recent years by making extensive direct and indirect use of commercial satellite imagery, much of which now offers

continued

481

Figure 10.20 (Continued)

3 meter levels of resolution and comes with coordinate data with near GPS-like levels of accuracy. One-meter levels of resolution will become commercially available.

- Unconfirmed reports indicate Syria is interested in purchasing Russia's Iskander-E (SS-X-26) ballistic missile when once it has finished development.[14]
- The CIA estimated in January 1999 that Syria continued work on establishing a solid-propellant rocket motor development and production capability. Foreign equipment and assistance have been and will continue to be essential for this effort.
- The CIA reported in November 2003 that, "During the first half of 2003, Damascus continued to seek help from abroad to establish a solid-propellant rocket motor development and production capability. Syria's liquid-propellant missile program continued to depend on essential foreign equipment and assistance—primarily from North Korean entities. Damascus also continued to manufacture liquid-propellant Scud missiles. In addition, Syria was developing longer-range missile programs such as a Scud D and possibly other variants with assistance from North Korea and Iran."

Chemical Weapons

- First acquired small amounts of chemical weapons from Egypt in 1973.
- Began production of non-persistent nerve gas in 1984. May have had chemical warheads for missiles as early as 1985.
- Experts believe has stockpiled 500 to 1,000 metric tons of chemical agents. Holdings thought to include persistent (VX) and non-persistent nerve agents (Sarin) as well as blister agents.
- Believed to have begun deploying VX in late 1996, early 1997.
  - CIA reported in June 1997 that Syria had acquired new chemical weapons technology from Russia and Eastern Europe in 1996.
  - Unconfirmed reports of sheltered Scud missiles with unitary Sarin or Tabun nerve gas warheads, now being replaced by cluster warheads with VX bomblets, deployed in caves and shelters near Damascus.
  - Tested Scuds in manner indicating possible chemical warheads in 1996.
  - Seems to have cluster warheads and bombs.
  - May have VX and Sarin in modified Soviet ZAB-incendiary bombs and PTAB-500 cluster bombs. Reports stated that U.S. intelligence source had obtained information indicating a late October 1999 test of a live chemical bomb dropped by a Syrian MiG-23.[15]
- Acquired design for Soviet Scud warhead using VX in 1970s.
- Major nerve gas, and possible other chemical agent production facilities north of Damascus. Two to three plants.
  - One facility is located near Homs and is located next to a major petrochemical plant. It reportedly produces several hundred tons of nerve gas a year.
  - Reports is building new major plant at Safira, near Aleppo.

Figure 10.20 (Continued)

- Reports that a facility co-located with the Center d'Etdues et de Recherche Scientifique (CERS) is developing a warhead with chemical bomblets for the Scud C.
- Many parts of the program are dispersed and compartmented. Missiles, rockets, bombs, and artillery shells are produced/modified and loaded in other facilities. Many may be modified to use VX bomblets.
- Wide range of potential delivery systems:
  - Extensive testing of chemical warheads for Scud Bs. May have tested chemical warheads for Scud Cs. Recent tests include a July 2001 test of a Scud B near Aleppo and a May 1998 test of a Scud C with a VX warhead near Damascus.
  - Shells, bombs, and nerve gas warheads for multiple rocket launchers.
  - FROG warheads may be under development.
  - Reports of SS-21 capability to deliver chemical weapons are not believed by U.S. or Israeli experts.
  - Israeli sources believe Syria has binary weapons and cluster bomb technology suitable for delivering chemical weapons.
  - The CIA estimated in January 1999 that Chinese entities sought to supply Iran and Syria with CW-related chemicals during this reporting period.
- The CIA reported in November 2003 that, "Syria continued to seek CW-related expertise from foreign sources during the reporting period. Damascus already held a stockpile of the nerve agent sarin, but apparently tried to develop more toxic and persistent nerve agents. Syria remained dependent on foreign sources for key elements of its CW program, including precursor chemicals and key production equipment."

Biological Weapons

- Signed, but not ratified the 1972 Biological and Toxin Weapons Convention. Extensive research effort.
- U.S. State Department, Bureau of Arms Control report in August 1996 indicated that, "it is highly probably that Syria is developing an offensive biological capability."
- Extensive research effort. Reports of one underground facility and one near the coast.
- Probable production capability for anthrax and botulism, and possibly other agents.
- Israeli sources claim Syria weaponized botulinum and ricin toxins in early 1990s, and probably anthrax as well.
- Limited indications may be developing or testing biological variations on ZAB-incendiary bombs and PTAB-500 cluster bombs and Scud warheads.
  - Major questions exist regarding Syria's strike capabilities. Older types of biological weapons using wet agents, and placed in older bomb and warhead

continued

Figure 10.20 (Continued)

designs with limited dissemination capability, can achieve only a small fraction of the potential effectiveness of biological weapons. Dry micropowders using advanced agents—such as the most lethal forms of Anthrax—can have the effectiveness of small theater nuclear weapons. It is difficult to design adequate missile warheads to disseminate such agents, but this is not beyond Syrian capabilities—particularly since much of the technology needed to make effective cluster munitions and bomblets for VX gas can be adapted to the delivery of biological weapons.[16]

- The design of biological bombs and missile warheads with the lethality of small nuclear weapons may now be within Syrian capabilities, as is the design of UAV, helicopter, cruise missile, or aircraft-borne systems to deliver the agent slowly over a long line of flight and taking maximum advantage of wind and weather conditions. U.S. and Soviet texts proved that this kind of "line source" delivery could achieve lethalities as high as 50–100 kiloton weapons by the late 1950s, and the technology is well within Syria's grasp. So is the use of proxy or covert delivery.
  - The CIA reported in November 2003 that "It is highly probable that Syria also continued to develop an offensive BW capability."

Nuclear Weapons

- Ongoing low-level research effort seems likely.
- No evidence of major progress in development effort.
- Announced nuclear reactor purchase plans including 10 megawatt research reactor from Argentina. Discussions with Argentina were resumed in the mid-1990s, but plans to build a Syrian reactor were scrapped under U.S. pressure.
- Syria tried to obtain six power reactors (for a total of 6,000 megawatts of generating capacity) in 1980s from a number of countries, including the Soviet Union, Belgium, and Switzerland, but plans were never implemented.
- The Center for Nonproliferation Studies at the Monterey Institute of International Studies quotes a *Jane's Intelligence Review* article from 1993 claiming Syria attempted to purchase "large (thousand ton) quantities" of yellowcake from Namibia.[17]
- In December 1991 Syria purchased a 30 kilowatt neutron-source research reactor from China, reactor is not suitable for weapons production. The Atomic Energy Commission of Syria received 980.4 g of 90.2% enriched Uranium 235 as part of the deal.
- Russia and Syria have approved a draft of a plan for cooperation on civil nuclear power, which is expected to provide opportunities for Syria to expand its indigenous nuclear capabilities.[18] Reports surfaced in January of 2003 indicating that Syria and Russia had reached an agreement on the construction of a $2 billion facility that would include a nuclear reactor. Although within several days, Russian Foreign Ministry officials had indicated that no reactor would be sold.[19]

Missile Defenses

- Seeking Russian S-300 or S-400 surface-to-air missile system with limited anti-tactical ballistic missile capability.

Figure 10.20 (Continued)

[1]Numbers of aircraft are from various editions of IISS, "The Military Balance."
[2]Center for Nonproliferation Studies, Monterey Institute of International Studies, "Syria Weapons of Mass Destruction Profile," May 1998, http://www.cns.miis.edu/research/wmdme/syria.html, accessed March 2003.
[3]Michael Eisenstadt, "Syria's Strategic Weapons," *Jane's Intelligence Review*, April 1993, pp. 168–173.
[4]Dani Shoham, "Poisoned Missiles: Syria's Doomsday Deterrent," *Middle East Quarterly*, Fall 2002.
[5]*Jane's Defense Weekly*, June 19, 2002. p. 40.
[6]Sid Balman Jr., UPI, 23 July 1996; in Executive News Service, July 24, 1996.
[7]*Far Eastern Economic Review*, August 22, 1991, p. 6.
[8]Michael Eisenstadt, "Syria's Strategic Weapons," *Jane's Intelligence Review*, April 1993, pp. 168–173
[9]Elaine Sciolino with Eric Schmitt, "China Said to Sell Parts for Missiles," *New York Times*, January 31, 1992, pp. A-1, A-2.
[10]Dani Shoham, "Poisoned Missiles: Syria's Doomsday Deterrent," *Middle East Quarterly*, Fall 2002.
[11]Steven Rodan and Andrew Koch, "Syria Preparing to Build Extended-Range 'Scud,'" *Jane's Defense Weekly*, June 19, 2002, p. 40.
[12]*Jane's Sentinel Security Assessment*, posted June 28, 2001.
[13]Center for Nonproliferation Studies, Monterey Institute of International Studies, "North Korean Missile Exports and Technical Assistance to Syria," http://www.nti.org/db/profiles/dprk/msl/ie/NKM_EesyriGO.html, accessed March 2003.
[14]*Jane's Sentinel Security Assessment*, posted June 28, 2001.
[15]Bill Gertz and Rowan Scarborough, "Syrian Gas Practice," *Washington Times*, November 26, 1999, p. A-10.
[16]*Jane's Defense Weekly*, September 3, 1997. p. 3.
[17]Michael Eisenstadt, "Syria's Strategic Weapons," *Jane's Intelligence Review*, April 1993, pp. 168–173, in Center for Nonproliferation Studies, Monterey Institute of International Studies, "Country Overviews: Syria (Nuclear)," http://www.nti.org, accessed March 2003.
[18]Central Intelligence Agency, "Unclassified Report to Congress on the Acquisition of Technology Relating to Weapons of Mass Destruction and Advanced Conventional Munitions, 1 July Through 31 December 2001."
[19]"Russian Nuclear Assistance to Syria: Scam or Scandal?," *Middle East Intelligence Bulletin*, Vol. 5 No. 1, January 2003.

Figure 10.21
Iran's Search for Weapons of Mass Destruction

Delivery Systems

- The Soviet-designed Scud B (17E) guided missile currently forms the core of Iran's ballistic missile forces—largely as a result of the Iran-Iraq War.

  - Iran only acquired its Scuds in response to Iraq's invasion. It obtained a limited number from Libya and then obtained larger numbers from North Korea. It deployed these units with a special Khatam ol-Anbya force attached to the air element of the Pasdaran. Iran fired its first Scuds in March 1985. It fired as many as 14 Scuds in 1985, 8 in 1986, 18 in 1987, and 77 in 1988. Iran fired

continued

Figure 10.21 (Continued)

77 Scud missiles during a 52 day period in 1988, during what came to be known as the "war of the cities." Sixty-one were fired at Baghdad, nine at Mosul, five at Kirkuk, one at Tikrit, and one at Kuwait. Iran fired as many as five missiles on a single day, and once fired three missiles within 30 minutes. This still, however, worked out to an average of only about one missile a day, and Iran was down to only 10–20 Scuds when the war of the cities ended.

- Iran's missile attacks were initially more effective than Iraq's attacks. This was largely a matter of geography. Many of Iraq's major cities were comparatively close to its border with Iran, but Tehran and most of Iran's major cities that had not already been targets in the war were outside the range of Iraqi Scud attacks. Iran's missiles, in contrast, could hit key Iraqi cities like Baghdad. This advantage ended when Iraq deployed extended range Scuds.

- The Scud B is a relatively old Soviet design which first became operational in 1967, designated as the R-17E or R-300E. The Scud B has a range of 290–300 kilometers with its normal conventional payload. The export version of the missile is about 11 meters long, 85–90 centimeters in diameter and weighs 6,300 kilograms. It has a nominal CEP of 1,000 meters. The Russian versions can be equipped with conventional high explosive, fuel air explosive, runway penetrator, submunition, chemical, and nuclear warheads.

- The export version of the Scud B comes with a conventional high explosive warhead weighing about 1,000 kilograms, of which 800 kilograms are the high explosive payload and 200 are the warhead structure and fusing system. It has a single stage storable liquid rocket engine and is usually deployed on the MAZ-543 eight-wheel transporter-erector-launcher (TEL). It has a strap-down inertial guidance, using three gyros to correct its ballistic trajectory, and uses internal graphite jet vane steering. The warhead hits at a velocity above Mach 1.5.

- Most estimates indicate that Iran now has 6–12 Scud launchers and up to 200 Scud B (R-17E) missiles with 230–310 KM range.

- Some estimates give higher figures. They estimate Iran bought 200–300 Scud Bs from North Korea between 1987 and 1992, and may have continued to buy such missiles after that time. Israeli experts estimate that Iran had at least 250–300 Scud B missiles, and at least 8–15 launchers on hand in 1997.

- U.S. experts also believe that Iran can now manufacture virtually all of the Scud B, with the possible exception of the most sophisticated components of its guidance system and rocket motors. This makes it difficult to estimate how many missiles Iran has in inventory and can acquire over time, as well as to estimate the precise performance characteristics of Iran's missiles, since it can alter the weight of the warhead and adjust the burn time and improve the efficiency of the rocket motors.

- Iran has new long range North Korean Scuds—with ranges near 500 kilometers.
  - The North Korean missile system is often referred to as a "Scud C." Typically, Iran formally denied the fact it had such systems long after the transfer of these missiles became a fact. Hassan Taherian, an Iranian foreign ministry official, stated in February 1995, "There is no missile cooperation between Iran and North Korea whatsoever. We deny this."

Figure 10.21 (Continued)

- In fact, a senior North Korean delegation traveled to Tehran to close the deal on November 29, 1990, and met with Mohsen Rezaei, the former commander of the IRGC. Iran either bought the missile then, or placed its order shortly thereafter. North Korea then exported the missile through its Lyongaksan Import Corporation. Iran imported some of these North Korean missile assemblies using its B-747s, and seems to have used ships to import others.
- Iran probably had more than 60 of the longer range North Korean missiles by 1998, although other sources report 100, and one source reports 170.
    - Iran has begun to test its new North Korean missiles. There are reports it has fired them from mobile launchers at a test site near Qom about 310 miles (500 kilometers) to a target area south of Shahroud. There are also reports that units equipped with such missiles have been deployed as part of Iranian exercises like the Saeqer-3 (Thunderbolt 3) exercise in late October 1993.
    - The missile is more advanced than the Scud B, although many aspects of its performance are unclear. North Korea seems to have completed development of the missile in 1987, after obtaining technical support from the People's Republic of China. While it is often called a "Scud C," it seems to differ substantially in detail from the original Soviet Scud B. It seems to be based more on the Chinese-made DF-61 than on a direct copy of the Soviet weapon.
    - Experts estimate that the North Korean missiles have a range of around 310 miles (500 kilometers), a warhead with a high explosive payload of 700 kilograms, and relatively good accuracy and reliability. While this payload·is a bit limited for the effective delivery of chemical agents, Iran might modify the warhead to increase payload at the expense of range and restrict the using of chemical munitions to the most lethal agents such as persistent nerve gas. It might also concentrate its development efforts on arming its Scud C forces with more lethal biological agents. In any case, such missiles are likely to have enough range-payload to give Iran the ability to strike all targets on the southern coast of the Gulf and all of the populated areas in Iraq, although not the West. Iran could also reach targets in part of eastern Syria, the eastern third of Turkey, and cover targets in the border area of the former Soviet Union, western Afghanistan, and western Pakistan.
    - Accuracy and reliability remain major uncertainties, as does operational CEP. Much would also depend on the precise level of technology Iran deployed in the warhead. Neither Russia nor the People's Republic of China seem to have transferred the warhead technology for biological and chemical weapons to Iran or Iraq when they sold them the Scud B missile and CSS-8. However, North Korea may have sold Iran such technology as part of the Scud C sale. If it did so, such a technology transfer would save Iran years of development and testing in obtaining highly lethal biological and chemical warheads. In fact, Iran would probably be able to deploy far more effective biological and chemical warheads than Iraq had at the time of the Gulf War.
    - Iran may be working with Syria in such development efforts, although Middle Eastern nations rarely cooperate in such sensitive areas. Iran served as a transshipment point for North Korean missile deliveries during 1992 and 1993.

continued

Figure 10.21 (Continued)

Some of this transshipment took place using the same Iranian B-747s that brought missile parts to Iran. Others moved by sea. For example, a North Korean vessel called the *Des Hung Ho*, bringing missile parts for Syria, docked at Bandar Abbas in May, 1992. Iran then flew these parts to Syria. An Iranian ship coming from North Korea and a second North Korean ship followed, carrying missiles and machine tools for both Syria and Iran. At least 20 of the North Korean missiles have gone to Syria from Iran, and production equipment seems to have been transferred to Iran and to Syrian plants near Hama and Aleppo.

- Iran may have 5–10 Scud C launchers, each with several missiles. This total seems likely to include four new North Korean TELs received in 1995.
- Iran can now assemble Scud B and Scud C missiles using foreign-made components. It may soon be able to make entire missile systems and warhead packages in Iran.
- Iran seems to want enough missiles and launchers to make its missile force highly dispersible.
- Iran has created shelters and tunnels in its coastal areas which it could use to store Scud and other missiles in hardened sites and reduce their vulnerability to air attack.
- Iran is developing an indigenous missile production capability with both solid and liquid fueled missiles. Seems to be seeking capability to produce MRBMs.
  - The present scale of Iran's production and assembly efforts is unclear. Iran seems to have a design center, at least two rocket and missile assembly plants, a missile test range and monitoring complex, and a wide range of smaller design and refit facilities.
  - The design center is said to be located at the Defense Technology and Science Research Center, which is a branch of Iran's Defense Industry Organization, and located outside Karaj—near Tehran. This center directs a number of other research efforts. Some experts believe it has support from Russian and Chinese scientists.
  - Iran's largest missile assembly and production plant is said to be a North Korean-built facility near Isfahan, although this plant may use Chinese equipment and technology. There are no confirmations of these reports, but this region is the center of much of Iran's advanced defense industry, including plants for munitions, tank overhaul, and helicopter and fixed-wing aircraft maintenance. Some reports say the local industrial complex can produce liquid fuels and missile parts from a local steel mill.
- A second missile plant is said to be located 175 kilometers east of Tehran, near Semnan. Some sources indicate this plant is Chinese-built and began rocket production as early as 1987. It is supposed to be able to build 600–1,000 Oghab rockets per year, if Iran can import key ingredients for solid fuel motors like ammonium perchlorate. The plant is also supposed to produce the Iran-130.
- Another facility may exist near Bandar Abbas for the assembly of the Seersucker. China is said to have built this facility in 1987, and is believed to be helping the naval branch of the Guards to modify the Seersucker to extend its

Figure 10.21 (Continued)

range to 400 kilometers. It is possible that China is also helping Iran develop solid fuel rocket motors and produce or assemble missiles like the CS-801 and CS-802. There have, however, been reports that Iran is developing extended range Scuds with the support of Russian experts, and of a missile called the Tondar 68, with a range of 700 kilometers.

- Still other reports claim that Iran has split its manufacturing facilities into plants near Pairzan, Seman, Shiraz, Maghdad, and Islaker. These reports indicate that the companies involved in building the Scuds are also involved in Iran's production of poison gas and include Defense Industries, Shahid, Bagheri Industrial Group, and Shahid Hemat Industrial Group.

- Iran's main missile test range is said to be further east, near Shahroud, along the Tehran-Mashhad railway. A telemetry station is supposed to be 350 kilometers to the south at Taba, along the Mashhad-Isfahan road. All of these facilities are reportedly under the control of the Islamic Revolutionary Guards Corps.

- There were many reports during the late 1980s and early 1990s that Iran had ordered the North Korean No Dong missile, which was planned to have the capability to carry nuclear and biological missile ranges of up to 900 kilometers. This range would allow the missile could reach virtually any target in Gulf, Turkey, and Israel. The status of the No Dong program has since become increasingly uncertain, although North Korea deployed some developmental types at test facilities in 1997.

  - The No Dong underwent flight tests at ranges of 310 miles (500 kilometers) on May 29, 1993. Some sources indicate that Iranians were present at these tests. Extensive further propulsion tests began in August 1994, and some reports indicate operational training began for test crews in May 1995. Missile storage facilities began to be built in July 1995, and four launch sites were completed in October 1995.

  - The progress of the program has been slow since that time, and may reflect development problems. However, mobile launchers were seen deployed in northeast North Korea on March 24, 1997. According to some reports, a further seven launcher units were seen at a facility about 100 kilometers from Pyongyang.

  - The No Dong 1 is a single-stage liquid-fueled missile, with a range of up to 1,000 to 1,300 kilometers (810 miles), although longer ranges may be possible with a reduced warhead and maximum burn. There are also indications that there may be a No Dong 2, using the same rocket motor, but with an improved fuel supply system that allows the fuel to burn for a longer period.

  - The missile is about 15.2 meters long—four meters longer than the Scud B— and 1.2 meters in diameter. The warhead is estimated to weigh 770 kilograms (1,200–1,750 pounds) and a warhead manufacturing facility exists near Pyongyang. The No Dong has an estimated theoretical CEP of 700 meters at maximum range, versus 900 meters for the Scud B, although its practical accuracy could be as wide as 3,000–4,000 meters. It has an estimated terminal velocity of Mach 3.5, versus 2.5 for the Scud B, which presents added problems

continued

Figure 10.21 (Continued)

for tactical missile defense. The missile is transportable on a modified copy of the MAZ-543P TEL that has been lengthened with a fifth axle and which is roughly 40 meters long. The added support stand for the vertical launch modes brings the overall length to 60 meters, and some experts questioned whether a unit this big is practical.

- Other reports during the later 1980s and early 1990s indicated that Iran was also interested in two developmental North Korean IRBMs called the Tapeo Dong 1 and Tapeo Dong 2.

  - The Tapeo Dong 1 missile has an estimated maximum range of 2,000 kilometers, and the Tapeo Dong 2 may have a range up to 3,500 kilometers.

  - Both Tapeo Dongs are liquid fueled missiles which seem to have two stages.

  - Unlike the No Dong, the Tapeo Dongs must be carried to a site in stages and then assembled at a fixed site. The No Dong transporter may be able to carry both stages of the Tapeo Dong 1, but some experts believe that a special transporter is needed for the first stage of the Tapeo Dong 1, and for both stages of the Tapeo Dong 2.

- Since the early 1990s, the focus of reports on Iran's missile efforts have shifted, and it has since become clear that Iran is developing its own longer-range variants of the No Dong for indigenous production with substantial Russian and some Chinese aid:

  - As early as 1992, one such missile was reported to have a range of 800–930 miles and a 1,650 pound warhead. Reports differ sharply on its size. *Jane's* estimates a launch weight up to 16,000 kilograms, provided the system is derived from the No Dong. It could have a launch weight of 15,000 kilograms, a payload of 600 kilograms, and a range of 1,700–1,800 kilometers if it is based on a system similar to the Chinese CSS-5 (DF-21) and CSS-N3 (JL-1). These systems entered service in 1983 and 1987.

  - A longer-range missile was said to have improved guidance components, a range of up to 1,240 miles and a warhead of up to 2,200 pounds.

  - IOC dates were then estimated to be 1999–2001.

  - Russia agreed in 1994 that it would adhere to the terms of the Missile Technology Control Regime and would place suitable limits on the sale or transfer of rocket engines and technology. Nevertheless, the CIA has identified Russia as a leading source of Iranian missile technology, and the State Department has indicated that President Clinton expressed U.S. concerns over this cooperation to President Yeltsin. This transfer is one reason the President appointed former Ambassador Frank Wisner, and then Robert Gallucci, as his special representatives to try to persuade Russia to put a firm halt to the transfer of missile technology to Iran.

  - These programs are reported to have continuing support from North Korea, and from Russian and Chinese firms and technicians. One such Chinese firm is Great Wall Industries. The Russian firms include the Russian Central Aerohydrodynamic Institute, which has provided Iran's Shahid Hemat Industrial Group (SHIG) with wind tunnels for missile design, equipment for manufacturing missile models, and the software for testing launch and reentry performance. They may also include Rosvoorouzhenie, a major Russian arms-export agency; NPO Trud, a rocket motor manufacturer; a leading research

Figure 10.21 (Continued)

center called the Bauman Institute; and Polyus (Northstar), a major laser test and manufacturing equipment firm.

- The CIA reported in June 1997 that Iran obtained major new transfers of new long-range missile technology from Russian and Chinese firms during 1996. Since that time, there have been many additional reports of technology transfer from Russia.

- The reports on Chinese technology transfers involve the least detail:
  - There have been past reports that Iran placed orders for PRC-made M-9 (CSS-6/DF-15) missile (280–620 kilometers range, launch weight of 6,000 kilograms).
  - It is more likely, however, that PRC firms are giving assistance in developing indigenous missile R&D and production facilities for the production of an Iranian solid fueled missile.
  - The U.S. offered to provide China with added missile technology if it would agree to fully implement an end of technology transfer to Iran and Pakistan during meetings in Beijing on March 25–26, 1998.

- Recent reports and tests have provided more detail on the Shahab system:
  - Some U.S. experts believe that Iran tested booster engines in 1997 capable of driving a missile to ranges of 1,500 kilometers. Virtually all U.S. experts believe that Iran is rapidly approaching the point where it will be able to manufacture missiles with much longer ranges than the Scud B.
  - It is less clear when Iran will be able to bring such programs to the final development stage, carry out a full range of suitable test firings, develop highly lethal warheads, and deploy actual units. Much may still depend on the level of foreign assistance.
  - Eitan Ben Eliyahu—the commander of the Israeli Air Force—reported on April 14, 1997 that Iran had tested a missile capable of reaching Israel. The background briefings to his statement implied that Russia was assisting Iran in developing two missiles—with ranges of 620 and 780 miles. Follow-on intelligence briefings that Israel provided in September 1997 indicated that Russia was helping Iran develop four missiles. U.S. intelligence reports indicate that China has also been helping Iran with some aspects of these missile efforts.
  - These missiles included the Shahab ("meteor") missiles, with performance similar to those previously identified with Iranian missiles adapted from North Korean designs.
  - The Israeli reports indicated that the Shahab 3 was a liquid-fueled missile with a range of 810 miles (1,200–1,500 kilometers) and a payload of 1,550 pounds (700 kilometers).
  - Israel claimed the Shahab might be ready for deployment as early as 1999.

- Iran tested the Shahab 3 on July 21, 1998, claiming that it was a defensive action to deal with potential threats from Israel.
  - The missile flew for a distance of up to 620 miles, before it exploded about 100 seconds after launch. U.S. intelligence sources could not confirm whether

continued

491

Figure 10.21 (Continued)

the explosion was deliberate, but indicated that the final system might have a range of 800–940 miles (a maximum of 1,240 kilometers), depending on its payload. The test confirmed the fact the missile was a liquid fueled system.

- Gen. Mohammad Bagher Qalibaf, head of the Islamic Revolutionary Guards Corps' air wing publicly reported on August 2, 1998 that the Shahab-3 is 53-foot-long ballistic missile that can travel at 4,300 mph and carry a one-ton warhead at an altitude of nearly 82,000 feet. He claimed that the weapon was guided by an Iranian-made system that gives it great accuracy: "The final test of every weapon is in a real war situation but, given its warhead and size, the Shahab-3 is a very accurate weapon."

- Other Iranian sources reported that the missile had a range of 800 miles. President Mohammad Khatami on August 1, 1998 stated that Iran was determined to continue to strengthen its armed forces, regardless of international concerns: "Iran will not seek permission from anyone for strengthening its defense capability."

- Martin Indyck, the U.S. Assistant Secretary for Near East Affairs testified on July 28, that the U.S. estimated that the system needed further refinement but might be deployed in its initial operational form between September 1998 and March 1999.

- Iran publicly displayed the Shahab 3 on its launcher during a parade on September 25, 1998. The missile carrier bore signs saying, "The U.S. can do nothing" and "Israel would be wiped from the map."

- There are some reports of a Shahab-3B missile with extended range and a larger booster.

- The resulting system seems to be close to both the No Dong and Pakistani Ghauri or Haff-5 missile, first tested in April 1998, raising questions about Iranian-North Korean-Pakistani cooperation.

- North Korean parades exhibiting the Tapeo Dong in September 1999 exhibited a missile with rocket motor and nozzle characteristics similar to those of the Shahab 3.

- Iran conducted further tests of the Shahab 3.
  - Tests on July 15, 2000 and May 23, 2003 were successful.
  - An additional test on September 21, 2000 was claimed to be successful test launch by Iran, although U.S. officials claim that the missile exploded shortly after launch.
  - A July 2002 test was also determined to be unsuccessful. On whole, test firings of the Shahab 3 series have met with success in approximately half of all launches.

- Sources quote unconfirmed reports by Turkish intelligence that the Shahab 3 is now in production. Additionally, Israeli intelligence is quoted as saying that Iran may have as many as 20 missiles.[1]

- On July 4, 2000, Iran's Islamic Revolutionary Guards Corps claimed to have formed five new missile units, apparently to be equipped with Shahab 3 missiles.[2]

Figure 10.21 (Continued)

- In September 1999, the Revolutionary Guard exhibited another missile called the Zelzal, which it stated was "now in mass production." The missile was said to have taken four and one-half years to develop and to be derived from the Zelzal 2, which the IRGC had exhibited earlier. Some estimates indicate that it can carry a warhead of 500 kilograms for up to 900 kilometers. However, the missile exhibited in Tehran was a rocket on a truck-mounted launch rail that seemed more likely to have a range of 150–200 kilometers.
  - There have been growing reports that Iran might be using Russian technology to develop long-range missiles with ranges from 2,000 to 6,250 kilometers.
- Israeli and U.S. intelligence sources have reported that that Iran is developing the Shahab 4, with a range of 2,000 kilometers (1,250 miles), a payload of around 2,000 pounds, and a CEP of around 2,400 meters. Some estimates indicate that this system could be operational in 2–5 years. The U.S. Assistant Secretary for Near East Affairs testified on July 28, 1998, that the U.S. estimated that the system still needed added foreign assistance to improve its motors and guidance system.
  - Some reports indicate that the Shahab 4 is based on the Soviet SS-4 missile. Others that there is a longer range Shahab 5, based on the SS-4 or Tapeo Dong missile. Reports saying the Shahab is based on the SS-4 say it has a range of up to 4,000 kilometers and a payload in excess of one ton.
  - Iran may have two other missile programs include longer-range systems, variously reported as having maximum ranges of 3,650, 4,500–5,000, 6,250, or 10,000 kilometers.
  - It seems clear that Iran has obtained some of the technology and design details of the Russian SS-4. The SS-4 (also known as the R-12 or "Sandal") is an aging Russian liquid fuel design that first went into service in 1959, and which was supposedly destroyed as part of the IRBM Treaty. It is a very large missile, with technology dating back to the early 1950s, although it was evidently updated at least twice during the period between 1959 and 1980. It has a CEP of 2–4 kilometers and a maximum range 2,000 kilometers, which means it can only be lethal with a nuclear warhead or a biological weapon with near-nuclear lethality.
  - At the same time, the SS-4's overall technology is relatively simple and it has a throwweight of nearly 1,400 kilograms (3,000 pounds). It is one of the few missile designs that a nation with a limited technology base could hope to manufacture or adapt, and its throw weight and range would allow Iran to use a relatively unsophisticated nuclear device or biological warhead. As a result, an updated version of the SS-4 might be a suitable design for a developing country.
- Iran is reported to have carried out the test of a sea-launched ballistic missile in 1998.
- Russia has been a key supplier of missile technology.
  - Some sources have indicated that Russian military industries have signed contracts with Iran to help produce liquid fueled missiles and provide specialized

continued

Figure 10.21 (Continued)

wind tunnels, manufacture model missiles, and develop specialized computer software. For example, these reports indicate that the Russian Central Aero-hydrodynamic Institute is cooperating with Iran's Defense Industries Organization (DIO) and the DIO's Shahid Hemmat Industrial Group (SHIG). The Russian State Corporation for Export and Import or Armament and Military Equipment (Rosvoorouzhenie) and Infor are also reported to be involved in deals with the SHIG. These deals are also said to include specialized laser equipment, mirrors, tungsten-coated graphite material, and maraging steel for missile development and production. They could play a major role in help Iran develop long range versions of the Scud B and C, and more accurate variations of a missile similar to the No Dong.

- The Israeli press reported in August 1997 that Israeli had evidence that Iran was receiving Russian support. In September 1997, Israel urged the U.S. to step up its pressure on Iran, and leaked reported indicating that private and state-owned Russian firms had provided gyroscopes, electronic components, wind tunnels, guidance and propulsion systems, and the components needed to build such systems to Iran.

- President Yeltsin and the Russian Foreign Ministry initially categorically denied that such charges were true. Following a meeting with Vice President Gore, President Yeltsin stated on September 26, 1997 that, "We are being accused of supplying Iran with nuclear or ballistic missile technologies. There is nothing further from the truth. I again and again categorically deny such rumors."

- Russia agreed, however, that Ambassador Wisner and Yuri Koptyev, the head of the Russian space program, should jointly examine the U.S. intelligence and draft a report on Russian transfers to Iran. This report reached a very different conclusion from President Yeltsin and concluded that Russia had provided such aid to Iran. Further, on October 1, 1997—roughly a week after Yeltsin issued his denial—the Russian security service issued a statement that it had "thwarted" an Iranian attempt to have parts for liquid fuel rocket motors manufactured in Russia, disguised as gas compressors and pumps.

- Russian firms said to be helping Iran included the Russian Central Aero-hydrodynamic Institute which developed a special wind tunnel; Rosvoorouzhenie, a major Russian arms-export agency; Kutznetzov (formerly NPO Trud) a rocket motor manufacturer in Samara; a leading research center called the Bauman National Technical University in Moscow, involved in developing rocket propulsion systems; the Tsagi Research Institute for rocket propulsion development; and the Polyus (Northstar) Research Institute in Moscow, a major laser test and manufacturing equipment firm. Iranians were also found to be studying rocket engineering at the Baltic State University in St. Petersburg and the Bauman State University.

- Russia was also found to have sold Iran high strength steel and special foil for its long-range missile program. The Russian Scientific and Production Center Inor concluded an agreement as late as September 1997 to sell Iran a factory to produce four special metal alloys used in long-range missiles. Inor's director, L. P. Chromova worked out a deal with A. Asgharzadeh, the director of an Iranian factory, to sell 620 kilograms of special alloy called 21HKMT, and provide Iran with the capability to thermally treat the alloy for missile

Figure 10.21 (Continued)

bodies. Iran had previously bought 240 kilograms of the alloy. Inor was also selling alloy foils called 49K2F, CUBE2, and 50N in sheets 0.2–0.4 millimeters thick for the outer body of missiles. The alloy 21HKMT was particularly interesting because North Korea also uses it in missile designs. Inor had previously brokered deals with the Shahid Hemat Industrial Group in Iran to supply maraging steel for missile cases, composite graphite-tungsten material, laser equipment, and special mirrors used in missile tests.

- The result was a new and often tense set of conversations between the U.S. and Russia in January 1998. The U.S. again sent Ambassador Frank Wisner to Moscow, Vice President Gore called Prime Minster Viktor Chernomyrdin and Secretary of State Madeline Albright made an indirect threat that the Congress might apply sanctions. Sergi Yastrzhembsky, a Kremlin spokesman, initially responded by denying that any transfer of technology had taken place.

- This Russian denial was too categorical to have much credibility. Russia had previously announced the arrest of an Iranian diplomat on November 14, 1997, that it caught attempting to buy missile technology. The Iranian was seeking to buy blueprints and recruit Russian scientists to go to Iran. Yuri Koptev, the head of the Russian Space Agency, explained this, however, by stating that that, "There have been several cases where some Russian organizations, desperately struggling to make ends meet and lacking responsibility, have embarked on some ambiguous projects . . . they were stopped long before they got to the point where any technology got out."

- The end result of these talks was an agreement by Gore and Chernomyrdin to strengthen controls over transfer technology, but it was scarcely clear that it put an end to the problem.

- Prime Minister Chernomyrdin again promised to strengthen his efforts to restrict technology transfer to Iran in a meeting with Gore on March 12, 1998. The U.S. informed Russia of 13 cases of possible Russian aid to Iran at the meeting and offered to increase the number of Russian commercial satellite launches it would license for U.S. firms as an incentive.

- New arrests of smugglers took place on April 9, 1998. The smugglers had attempted to ship 22 tons of specialized steel to Iran via Azerbaijan, using several Russia shell corporations as a cover.

- On April 16, 1998, the State Department declared 20 Russian agencies and research facilities were ineligible to receive U.S. aid because of their role in transferring missile technology to Iran.

- A U.S. examination of Iran's dispersal, sheltering, and hardening programs for its antiship missiles and other missile systems indicate that Iran has developed effective programs to ensure that they would survive a limited number of air strikes and that Iran had reason to believe that the limited number of preemptive strikes Israel could conduct against targets in the lower Gulf could not be effective in denying Iran the capability to deploy its missiles.

- Iran has shorter missile range systems:
  - In 1990, Iran bought CSS-8 surface-to-surface missiles (converted SA-2s) from China with ranges of 130–150 kilometers.

continued

Figure 10.21 (Continued)

- Has Chinese sea- and land-based antiship cruise missiles. Iran fired 10 such missiles at Kuwait during Iran-Iraq War, hitting one U.S.-flagged tanker.

- Iran has acquired much of the technology necessary build long-range cruise missile systems from China:

- Such missiles would cost only 10% to 25% as much as ballistic missiles of similar range, and both the HY-2 Seersucker and CS-802 could be modified relatively quickly for land attacks against area targets.

- Iran reported in December, 1995 that it had already fired a domestically built antiship missile called the Saeqe-4 (Thunderbolt) during exercises in the Strait of Hormuz and Gulf of Oman Other reports indicate that China is helping Iran build copies of the Chinese CS-801/CS-802 and the Chinese FL-2 or F-7 antiship cruise missiles. These missiles have relatively limited range. The range of the CS-801 is 8–40 kilometers, the range of the CS-802 is 15–120 kilometers, the maximum range of the F-7 is 30 kilometers, and the maximum range of the FL-10 is 50 kilometers. Even a range of 120 kilometers would barely cover targets in the Southern Gulf from launch points on Iran's Gulf coast. These missiles also have relatively small high explosive warheads. As a result, Iran may well be seeking antiship capabilities, rather than platforms for delivering weapons of mass destruction.

- A platform like the CS-802 might, however, provide enough design data to develop a scaled-up, longer-range cruise missile for other purposes, and the Gulf is a relatively small area where most urban areas and critical facilities are near the coast. Aircraft or ships could launch cruise missiles with chemical or biological warheads from outside the normal defense perimeter of the Southern Gulf states, and it is at least possible that Iran might modify antiship missiles with chemical weapons to attack tankers—ships which are too large for most regular antiship missiles to be highly lethal.

- Building an entire cruise missile would be more difficult. The technology for fusing CBW and cluster warheads would be within Iran's grasp. Navigation systems and jet engines, however, would still be a major potential problem. Current inertial navigation systems (INS) would introduce errors of at least several kilometers at ranges of 1,000 kilometers and would carry a severe risk of total guidance failure—probably exceeding two-thirds of the missiles fired. A differential global positioning system (GPS) integrated with the inertial navigation system (INS) and a radar altimeter, however, might produce an accuracy of 15 meters. Some existing remotely piloted vehicles (RPVs), such as the South African Skua claim such performance. Commercial technology is becoming available for differential global positioning system (GPS) guidance with accuracies of 2 to 5 meters.

- There are commercially available reciprocating and gas turbine engines that Iran could adapt for use in a cruise missile, although finding a reliable and efficient turbofan engine for a specific design application might be difficult. An extremely efficient engine would have to be matched to a specific airframe. It is doubtful that Iran could design and build such an engine, but there are over 20 other countries with the necessary design and manufacturing skills.

Figure 10.21 (Continued)

- While airframe-engine-warhead integration and testing would present a challenge and might be beyond Iran's manufacturing skills, it is inherently easier to integrate and test a cruise missile than a long-range ballistic missile. Further, such developments would be far less detectable than developing a ballistic system if the program used coded or low altitude directional telemetry.

- Iran could bypass much of the problems inherent in developing its own cruise missile by modifying the HY-2 Seersucker for use as a land attack weapon and extending its range beyond 80 kilometers, or by modifying and improving the CS-801 (Ying Jai-1) antiship missile. There are reports that the Revolutionary Guards are working on such developments at a facility near Bandar Abbas.

- China has delivered approximately 150 of 400 C-802 missiles ordered by Iran.[3]

- A number of reports claim that Chinese companies have provided extensive technical assistance to Iranian cruise missile efforts, in engineering, production assistance, critical materials and equipment upgrades.

- Su-24 long-range strike fighters with range-payloads roughly equivalent to U.S. F-111 and superior to older Soviet medium bombers.

- F-4D/E fighter-bombers with capability to carry extensive payloads to ranges of 450 miles.

- Can modify HY-2 Silkworm missiles and SA-2 surface-to-air missiles to deliver weapons of mass destruction.

- Iran has made several indigenous long-range rockets.

  - The Iran-130, or Nazeat, since the end of the Iran-Iraq War. The full details of this system remain unclear, but it seems to use commercially available components, a solid fuel rocket, and a simple inertial guidance system to reach ranges of about 90–120 kilometers. It is 355 mm in diameter, 5.9 meters long, weighs 950 kilograms, and has a 150 kilogram warhead. It seems to have poor reliability and accuracy, and its payload only seems to be several hundred kilograms.

  - The Shahin 2. It too has a 355-mm diameter, but is only 3.87 meters long, and weighs only 580 kilograms. It evidently can be equipped with three types of warheads: A 180 kilogram high explosive warhead, another warhead using high explosive submunitions, and a warhead that uses chemical weapons.

  - Iranian Oghab (Eagle) rocket with 40+ kilometers range.

  - New SSM with 125 mile range may be in production, but could be modified FROG.

- Large numbers of multiple rocket launchers and tube artillery for short range delivery of chemical weapons.

- The CIA reported in January 1999 that entities in Russia and China continue to supply missile-related goods and technology to Iran. Tehran is using these goods and technologies to achieve its goal of becoming self-sufficient in the production of MRBMs. The July flight test of the Shahab-3 MRBM demonstrates the success Iran has achieved in realizing that goal. Iran already is producing Scud

continued

Figure 10.21 (Continued)

SRBMs with North Korean help and has begun production of the Shahab-3. In addition, Iran's Defense Minister has publicly acknowledged the development of the Shahab-4 ballistic missile, with a "longer range and heavier payload than the 1,300-km Shahab-3."

- Iran's earlier success in gaining technology and materials from Russian companies accelerated Iranian development of the Shahab-3 MRBM, which was first flight tested in July 1998.

- The CIA report on missile proliferation in September 1999 estimated that Iran is the next hostile country most capable of testing an ICBM capable of delivering a weapon to the United States during the next 15 years.

  - Iran *could test* an ICBM that could deliver a several-hundred kilogram payload to many parts of the United States in the between 2005 and 2010, using Russian technology and assistance.

  - Iran *could pursue* a Taepo Dong-type ICBM. Most analysts believe it could test a three-stage ICBM patterned after the Taepo Dong-1 SLV or a three-stage Taepo Dong-2-type ICBM, possibly with North Korean assistance, in the next few years.

  - Iran is *likely to test* an SLV by 2010 that—once developed—could be converted into an ICBM capable of delivering a several-hundred kilogram payload to the United States.

- Analysts differ on the likely timing of Iran's first flight test of an ICBM that could threaten the United States. Assessments include:

  - *likely* before 2010 and *very likely* before 2015 (noting that an SLV with ICBM capabilities will *probably be tested within the next few years)*;

  - no more than an *even chance* by 2010 and a *better than even chance* by 2015;

  - and less than an even chance by 2015.

- The CIA reported in November 20003 that, "Ballistic missile-related cooperation from entities in the former Soviet Union, North Korea, and China over the years has helped Iran move toward its goal of becoming self-sufficient in the production of ballistic missiles. Such assistance during the first half of 2003 continued to include equipment, technology, and expertise. Iran's ballistic missile inventory is among the largest in the Middle East and includes some 1,300-km-range Shahab-3 medium-range ballistic missiles (MRBMs) and a few hundred short-range ballistic missiles (SRBMs)—including the Shahab-1 (Scud-B), Shahab-2 (Scud C), and Tondar-69 (CSS-8)—as well as a variety of large unguided rockets. Already producing Scud SRBMs, Iran announced that it had begun production of the Shahab-3 MRBM and a new solid-propellant SRBM, the Fateh-110. In addition, Iran publicly acknowledged the development of follow-on versions of the Shahab-3. It originally said that another version, the Shahab-4, was a more capable ballistic missile than its predecessor but later characterized it as solely a space launch vehicle with no military applications. Iran is also pursuing longer-range ballistic missiles."

- The Center for Nonproliferation Studies at the Monterey Institute of International Studies has compiled a chronology of North Korean assistance to Iran through 2003[4]:

Figure 10.21 (Continued)

Date	Item(s)	Remarks
1980s	About 100 Scud missile launchers	
Late 1984-Early 1985	Technical assistance for Scud-B production facility	In October 1983 Iran and North Korea reach agreement for assistance in setting up missile production capability.
1987-88	100 modified Scud-B missiles and 12 TELs	
1987	Technical assistance for modified Scud-B production	
1987-88	Unknown number of HY-2 Silkworm anti-ship missiles	Agreement signed in 1986; some believe that the missiles were supplied by China, but Beijing insists Pyongyang was supplier.
1987-92	200-300 Scud-B missiles	
1988 Early	40 Scud-B missiles	Probably part of the 100 Scuds reportedly shipped in 1987-1988.
1988 January	four Styx anti-ship missiles and at least one HY-2 Silkworm anti-ship missile	
1988 February	80 HY-2 Silkworm anti ship missiles and 40 Scud-B missiles	Report says missiles came from both China and North Korea.
1990 Early	20 Scud-B missiles	
1990 December	Missile technicians	North Korean technicians arrive in eastern Iran to convert a missile maintenance facility into a missile production plant.
1991	170 Scud-C missiles	Uncertain; Iran probably had not received all 170 missiles by 1991 because, according to estimates, North Korea would not have been able to produce 170 Scud-C missiles by this time.
1992 March	Unknown; suspected Scud-B missiles	US officials suspect Iranian ship with Scud missiles travels from Singapore to the Iranian port of Char Bahar.
1992 Second Half	A few No Dong-1 prototypes	
1992 October	100 Scud-C missiles	Half of the Scud-C shipment possibly transferred to Syria.
1993	Unknown number of Scud-C missiles	Possibly the same shipment of 100 Scud-Cs reported in late October 1992.
1994 Mid to Late	No Dong-1 components or a small number of complete missiles	In April 1993 North Korea reportedly agreed to sell 150 No Dongs to Iran in exchange for access to test facilities and financial support.
Late 1994-Early 1995	At least four Scud-C TELs and possibly a No Dong MEL	
1995 Early	At least 12 No Dong missiles	Based on an Israeli intelligence report; in April 1996, *Jane's Defense Weekly* reports that North Korea may have exported as many as 20 No Dongs.
1997	Unknown missile components	
1997 Early	Computer software for No Dong production	
1999 November	12-20 No Dong engines	
2001 March	Engines and airframes; unspecified number of missile components	US reconnaissance satellite detects missile components being loaded onto an Iranian Il-76 transport plane at Sunan International Airport near Pyongyang.

continued

Figure 10.21 (Continued)

Chemical Weapons

- Iran purchased large amounts of chemical defense gear from the mid-1980s onwards. Iran also obtained stocks of non-lethal CS gas, although it quickly found such agents had very limited military impact since they could only be used effectively in closed areas or very small open areas.

- Acquiring poisonous chemical agents was more difficult. Iran did not have any internal capacity to manufacture poisonous chemical agents when Iraq first launched its attacks with such weapons. While Iran seems to have made limited use of chemical mortar and artillery rounds as early as 1985—and possibly as early as 1984—these rounds were almost certainly captured from Iraq.

- Iran had to covertly import the necessary equipment and supplies, and it took several years to get substantial amounts of production equipment, and the necessary feedstocks. Iran sought aid from European firms like Lurgi to produce large "pesticide" plants, and began to try to obtain the needed feedstock from a wide range of sources, relying heavily on its Embassy in Bonn to manage the necessary deals. While Lurgi did not provide the pesticide plant Iran sought, Iran did obtain substantial support from other European firms and feedstocks from many other Western sources.

- By 1986–1987, Iran developed the capability to produce enough lethal agents to load its own weapons. The Director of the CIA, and informed observers in the Gulf, made it clear that Iran could produce blood agents like hydrogen cyanide, phosgene gas, and/or chlorine gas. Iran was also able to weaponize limited quantities of blister (sulfur mustard) and blood (cyanide) agents beginning in 1987, and had some capability to weaponize phosgene gas, and/or chlorine gas. These chemical agents were produced in small batches, and evidently under laboratory scale conditions, which enabled Iran to load small numbers of weapons before any of its new major production plants went into full operation.

- These gas agents were loaded into bombs and artillery shells, and were used sporadically against Iraq in 1987 and 1988.

- Reports regarding Iran's production and research facilities are highly uncertain:
  - Iran seems to have completed completion of a major poison gas plant at Qazvin, about 150 kilometers west of Tehran. This plant is reported to have been completed between November 1987 and January 1988. While supposedly a pesticide plant, the facility's true purpose seems to have been poison gas production using organophosphorous compounds
  - It is impossible to trace all the sources of the major components and technology Iran used in its chemical weapons program during this period. Mujahideen sources claim Iran also set up a chemical bomb and warhead plant operated by the Zakaria Al-Razi chemical company near Mahshar in southern Iran, but it is unclear whether these reports are true.
  - Reports that Iran had chemical weapons plants at Damghan and Parchin that began operation as early as March, 1988, and may have begun to test fire Scuds with chemical warheads as early as 1988–1989, are equally uncertain.
  - Iran established at least one large research and development center under the control of the Engineering Research Centre of the Construction Crusade (Jahad

Figure 10.21 (Continued)

e-Sazandegi), had established a significant chemical weapons production capability by mid-1989.

- Debates took place in the Iranian parliament or Majlis in late 1988 over the safety of Pasdaran gas plants located near Iranian towns, and that Rafsanjani described chemical weapons as follows: "Chemical and biological weapons are poor man's atomic bombs and can easily be produced. We should at least consider them for our defense. Although the use of such weapons is inhuman, the war taught us that international laws are only scraps of paper."

- Post Iran-Iraq War estimates of Iran chemical weapons production are extremely uncertain:

  - U.S. experts believe Iran was beginning to produce significant mustard gas and nerve gas by the time of the August, 1988 cease-fire in the Iran-Iraq War, although its use of chemical weapons remained limited and had little impact on the fighting.

  - Iran's efforts to equip plants to produce V-agent nerve gases seem to have been delayed by U.S., British, and German efforts to limit technology transfers to Iran, but Iran may have acquired the capability to produce persistent nerve gas during the mid 1990s.

  - Production of nerve gas weapons started no later than 1994.

  - Began to stockpile of cyanide (cyanogen chloride), phosgene, and mustard gas weapons after 1985. Recent CIA testimony indicates that production capacity may approach 1,000 tons annually.

- On August 2, 2002, the NSC's Director for the Near East indicated that Iran is producing and stockpiling blister, blood and choking agents.

- The Defense Department's 2001 Report "Proliferation: Threat and Response" suggests that Iran, in addition to producing and stockpiling blister, blood and choking agents, has weaponized these agents for use with artillery shells, mortars, rockets and bombs. The report also states that Iran is continuing its research into nerve agents.

- Weapons include bombs and artillery. Shells include 155-mm artillery and mortar rounds. Iran also has chemical bombs and mines. It may have developmental chemical warheads for its Scuds, and may have a chemical package for its 22006 RPV (doubtful).

- There are reports that Iran has deployed chemical weapons on some of its ships. Training for Iranian naval forces suggests that they are preparing for the possibility of operating in a contaminated environment.

- Iran has increased chemical defensive and offensive warfare training since 1993.

- Iran is seeking to buy more advanced chemical defense equipment, and has sought to buy specialized equipment on world market to develop indigenous capability to produce advanced feedstocks for nerve weapons.

  - CIA sources indicated in late 1996, that China might have supplied Iran with up to 400 tons of chemicals for the production of nerve gas.

continued

Figure 10.21 (Continued)

- One report indicated in 1996, that Iran obtained 400 metric tons of chemicals for use in nerve gas weapons from China—including carbon sulfide.

- Another report indicated that China supplied Iran with roughly two tons of calcium-hypochlorate in 1996, and loaded another 40,000 barrels in January or February of 1997. Calcium-hypochlorate is used for decontamination in chemical warfare.

- Iran placed several significant orders from China that were not delivered. Razak Industries in Tehran, and Chemical and Pharmaceutical Industries in Tabriz ordered 49 metric tons of alkyl dimethylamine, a chemical used in making detergents, and 17 tons of sodium sulfide, a chemical used in making mustard gas. The orders were never delivered, but they were brokered by Iran's International Movalled Industries Corporation (Imaco) and China's North Chemical Industries Co. (Nocinco). Both brokers have been linked to other transactions affecting Iran's chemical weapons program since early 1995, and Nocinco has supplied Iran with several hundred tons of carbon disulfide, a chemical uses in nerve gas.

- Another Chinese firm, only publicly identified as Q. Chen, seems to have supplied glass vessels for chemical weapons.

- The U.S. imposed sanctions on seven Chinese firms in May 1997 for selling precursors for nerve gas and equipment for making nerve gas, although the U.S. made it clear that it had "no evidence that the Chinese government was involved." The Chinese firms were the Nanjing Chemical Industries Group and Jiangsu Yongli Chemical Engineering and Import/Export Corporation. Cheong Yee Ltd., a Hong Kong firm, was also involved. The precursors included thionyl chloride, dimethylamine, and ethylene chlorohydril. The equipment included special glass lined vessels, and Nanjing Chemical and Industrial Group completed construction of a production plant to manufacture such vessels in Iran in June 1997.

- Iran sought to obtain impregnated alumina, which is used to make phosphorous oxychloride—a major component of VX and GB—from the U.S.

- It has obtained some equipment from Israelis. Nahum Manbar, an Israeli national living in France, was convicted in an Israeli court in May 1997 for providing Iran with $16 million worth of production equipment for mustard and nerve gas during the period from 1990 to 1995.

- CIA reported in June 1997 that Iran had obtained new chemical weapons equipment technology from China and India in 1996.

- India is assisting in the construction of a major new plant at Qazvim, near Tehran, to manufacture phosphorous pentasulfide, a major precursor for nerve gas. The plant is fronted by Meli Agrochemicals, and the program was negotiated by Dr. Mejid Tehrani Abbaspour, a chief security advisor to Rafsanjani.

- A recent report by German intelligence indicates that Iran has made major efforts to acquire the equipment necessary to produce Sarin and Tabun, using the same cover of purchasing equipment for pesticide plants that Iraq used for its Sa'ad 16 plant in the 1980s. German sources note that three Indian companies—Tata Consulting Engineering, Transpek, and Rallis India—have approached German pharmaceutical and engineering concerns for such equipment

Figure 10.21 (Continued)

and technology under conditions where German intelligence was able to trace the end user to Iran.

- Iran ratified the Chemical Weapons Convention in June 1997.
  - It submitted a statement in Farsi to the CWC secretariat in 1998, but this consisted only of questions in Farsi as to the nature of the required compliance.
  - It has not provided the CWC with any data on its chemical weapons program.
- The CIA estimated in January 1999 that Iran obtained material related to chemical warfare (CW) from various sources during the first half of 1998. It already has manufactured and stockpiled chemical weapons, including blister, blood, and choking agents and the bombs and artillery shells for delivering them. However, Tehran is seeking foreign equipment and expertise to create a more advanced and self-sufficient CW infrastructure.
- The CIA stated that Chinese entities sought to supply Iran with CW-related chemicals during 1997–1998 period. The U.S. sanctions imposed in May 1997 on seven Chinese entities for knowingly and materially contributing to Iran's CW program remain in effect.
- There exists a large number of sites in Iran that are alleged to be related to Iran's chemical warfare effort[5]:
  - Abu Musa Island: Suspected site of a large number of chemical weapons, principally 155mm artillery shells, in addition to some weaponized biological agents.
  - Bandar Khomeni: Allegedly the location of a chemical weapons facility, run by the Razi chemical corporation, established during the Iran-Iraq war to manufacture chemical weapons.
  - Damghan: Either a chemical weapons plant or warhead assembly facility. Primarily involved in 155mm artillery shells and Scud warheads.
  - Isfahan: Suspected location of a chemical weapons facility, possibly operated by the Poly-Acryl Corporation.
  - Karaj: Located about 14 km from Tehran, this is the site of an alleged storage and manufacturing facility for chemical weapons. Reports suggest that this facility was built with Chinese assistance.
  - Marvdasht: The Chemical Fertilizers Company is suspected to have been a manufacturing facility for mustard agents during the Iran-Iraq War.
  - Parchin: The location of at least one munitions factory and is suspected of being a major chemical weapons production facility. Reports of uncertain reliability indicate that the plant was in operation no later than March 1988. In April 1997, a German newspaper reported that, according to the German Federal Intelligence Service, the factories at Parchin were producing primary products for chemical warfare agents.
  - Qazvin: A large pesticide plant at this location is widely believed to produce nerve gas.
  - Mashar: Iranian opposition groups have made allegations, of uncertain reliability, that a warhead filling facility is operated at this location.

continued

Figure 10.21 (Continued)

- A number of reports indicate that China has provided Iran with the ability to manufacture chemical weapons indigenously as well as providing precursors since at least 1996.[6]
- The CIA reported in November 2003 that, "Iran is a party to the Chemical Weapons Convention (CWC). Nevertheless, during the reporting period it continued to seek production technology, training, and expertise from Chinese entities that could further Tehran's efforts to achieve an indigenous capability to produce nerve agents. Iran likely has already stockpiled blister, blood, choking, and probably nerve agents—and the bombs and artillery shells to deliver them—which it previously had manufactured."

Biological Weapons

- Extensive laboratory and research capability.
- Weapons effort documented as early as 1982. Reports surfaced that Iran had imported suitable type cultures from Europe and was working on the production of mycotoxins—a relatively simple family of biological agents that require only limited laboratory facilities for small-scale production.
- U.S. intelligence sources reported in August 1989, that Iran was trying to buy two new strains of fungus from Canada and the Netherlands that can be used to produce Mycotoxins. German sources indicated that Iran had successfully purchased such cultures several years earlier.
- The Imam Reza Medical Center at Mashhad Medical Sciences University and the Iranian Research Organization for Science and Technology were identified as the end users for this purchasing effort, but it is likely that the true end user was an Iranian government agency specializing in biological warfare.
- Many experts believe that the Iranian biological weapons effort was placed under the control of the Islamic Revolutionary Guards Corps, which is known to have tried to purchase suitable production equipment for such weapons.
- Since the Iran-Iraq War, Iran has conducted research on more lethal active agents like Anthrax, hoof and mouth disease, and biotoxins. In addition, Iranian groups have repeatedly approached various European firms for the equipment and technology necessary to work with these diseases and toxins.
  - Unclassified sources of uncertain reliability have identified a facility at Damghan as working on both biological and chemical weapons research and production, and believe that Iran may be producing biological weapons at a pesticide facility near Tehran.
  - Some universities and research centers may be linked to biological weapons program.
  - Reports surfaced in the spring of 1993 that Iran had succeeded in obtaining advanced biological weapons technology in Switzerland and containment equipment and technology from Germany. According to these reports, this led to serious damage to computer facilities in a Swiss biological research facility by unidentified agents. Similar reports indicated that agents had destroyed German bio-containment equipment destined for Iran.
  - More credible reports by U.S. experts indicate that Iran has begun to stockpile anthrax and Botulinum in a facility near Tabriz, can now mass manufac-

Figure 10.21 (Continued)

ture such agents, and has them in an aerosol form. None of these reports, however, can be verified.

- The CIA has reported that Iran has, "sought dual-use biotech equipment from Europe and Asia, ostensibly for civilian use." It also reported in 1996 that Iran might be ready to deploy biological weapons. Beyond this point, little unclassified information exists regarding the details of Iran's effort to "weaponize" and produce biological weapons.

- Iran may have the production technology to make dry storable and aerosol weapons. This would allow it to develop suitable missile warheads and bombs and covert devices.

- Iran may have begun active weapons production in 1996, but probably only at limited scale suitable for advanced testing and development.

- CIA testimony indicates that Iran is believed to have weaponized both live agents and toxins for artillery and bombs and may be pursuing biological warheads for its missiles. The CIA reported in 1996 that, "We believe that Iran holds some stocks of biological agents and weapons. Tehran probably has investigated both toxins and live organisms as biological warfare agents. Iran has the technical infrastructure to support a significant biological weapons program with little foreign assistance."

- CIA reported in June 1997 that Iran had obtained new dual use technology from China and India during 1996.

- Iran announced in June 1997 that it would not produce or employ chemical weapons including toxins.

- The CIA estimated in January 1999 that Iran continued to pursue purchasing dual-use biotechnical equipment from Russia and other countries, ostensibly for civilian uses. Its biological warfare (BW) program began during the Iran-Iraq war, and Iran may have some limited capability for BW deployment. Outside assistance is both important and difficult to prevent, given the dual-use nature of the materials and equipment being sought and the many legitimate end uses for these items.

- The CIA reported in November 2003 that, "Even though Iran is part of the Biological Weapons Convention (BWC), Tehran probably maintained an offensive BW program. Iran continued to seek dual-use biotechnical materials, equipment, and expertise. While such materials had legitimate uses, Iran's biological warfare (BW) program also could have benefited from them. It is likely that Iran has capabilities to produce small quantities of BW agents, but has a limited ability to weaponize them."

- Russia remains a key source of biotechnology for Iran. Russia's world-leading expertise in biological weapons makes it an attractive target for Iranians seeking technical information and training on BW agent production processes.

Nuclear Weapons

- The Shah established the Atomic Energy Organization of Iran in 1974, and rapidly began to negotiate for nuclear power plants.

continued

Figure 10.21 (Continued)

- He concluded an extendible ten-year nuclear fuel contract with the U.S. in 1974, with Germany in 1976, and France in 1977.

- In 1975, he purchased a 10% share in a Eurodif uranium enrichment plant being built at Tricastin in France that was part of a French, Belgian, Spanish, and Italian consortium. Under the agreement the Shah signed, Iran was to have full access to the enrichment technology Eurodif developed, and agreed to buy a quota of enriched uranium from the new plant.

- He created an ambitious plan calling for a network of 23 power reactors throughout Iran that was to be operating by the mid-1990s, and sought to buy nuclear power plants from Germany and France.

- By the time the Shah fell in January 1979, he had six reactors under contract, and was attempting to purchase a total of 12 nuclear power plants from Germany, France, and the U.S. Two 1,300 megawatt German nuclear power plants at Bushehr were already 60% and 75% completed, and site preparation work had begun on the first of two 935 megawatt French plants at Darkhouin that were to be supplied by Framatome.

- The Shah also started a nuclear weapons program in the early to mid-1970s, building upon his major reactor projects, investment in URENCO, and smuggling of nuclear enrichment and weapons related technology from U.S. and Europe.

  - 5 megawatt light-water research reactor operating in Tehran.

  - 27 kilowatt neutron-source reactor operating in Isfahan.

  - Started two massive 1,300 megawatt reactor complexes.

  - The Shah attempted to covertly import controlled technology from the U.S.

- U.S. experts believe that Shah began a low-level nuclear weapons research program, centered at the Amirabad Nuclear Research Center. This research effort included studies of weapons designs and plutonium recovery from spent reactor fuel.

- It also involved a laser enrichment program which began in 1975, and led to a complex and highly illegal effort to obtain laser separation technology from the U.S. This latter effort, which does not seems to have had any success, continued from 1976 until the Shah's fall, and four lasers operating in the critical 16 micron band were shipped to Iran in October 1978.

- At the same time, Iran worked on other ways to obtain plutonium, created a secret reprocessing research effort to use enriched uranium, and set up a small nuclear weapons design team.

- In 1976, Iran signed a secret contract to buy $700 million worth of yellowcake from South Africa, and appears to have reached an agreement to buy up to 1,000 metric tons a year. It is unclear how much of this ore South Africa shipped before it agreed to adopt IAEA export restrictions in 1984, and whether South Africa really honored such export restrictions. Some sources indicate that South Africa still made major deliveries as late as 1988–1989.

- Iran also tried to purchase 26.2 kilograms of highly enriched uranium; the application to the U.S. for this purchase was pending when the Shah fell.

Figure 10.21 (Continued)

- The Shah did eventually accept full IAEA safeguards but their value is uncertain.
- In 1984, Khomeini revived nuclear weapons program begun under Shah.
  - Received significant West German and Argentine corporate support in some aspects of nuclear technology during the Iran-Iraq War.
  - Limited transfers of centrifuge and other weapons-related technology from PRC, possibly Pakistan.
  - It has a Chinese-supplied heavy-water, zero-power research reactor at Isfahan Nuclear Research Center, and two-Chinese supplied sub-critical assemblies—a light water and graphite design.
  - It has stockpiles of uranium and mines in the Yazd area. It may have had a uranium-ore concentration facility at University of Tehran, but status unclear.
  - Some experts suspect that the IRGC moved experts and equipment from the Amirabad Nuclear Research CenterAmirabad Nuclear Research Center to a new nuclear weapons research facility near IsfahanIsfahan in the mid-1980s, and formed a new nuclear research center at the University of Isfahan in 1984—with French assistance. Unlike many Iranian facilities, the center at Isfahan was not declared to the IAEA until February 1992, when the IAEA was allowed to make a cursory inspection of six sites that various reports had claimed were the location of Iran's nuclear weapons efforts.
  - Bushehr I & II, on the Gulf Coast just southwest of Isfahan, were partially completed at the time of the Shah's fall. Iran attempted to revive the program and sought German and Argentine support, but the reactors were damaged by Iraqi air strikes in 1987 and 1988.
  - Iran may also have opened a new uranium ore processing plant close to its Shagand uranium mine in March 1990, and it seems to have extended its search for uranium ore into three additional areas. Iran may have also begun to exploit stocks of yellowcake that the Shah had obtained from South Africa in the late 1970s while obtaining uranium dioxide from Argentina by purchasing it through Algeria.
  - Iran began to show a renewed interest in laser isotope separation (LIS) in the mid-1980s, and held a conference on LIS in September 1987.
  - Iran opened a new nuclear research center in Isfahan in 1984, located about four kilometers outside the city and between the villages of Shahrida and Fulashans. This facility was built at a scale far beyond the needs of peaceful research, and Iran sought French and Pakistani help for a new research reactor for this center.
  - The Khomeini government may also have obtained several thousand pounds of uranium dioxide from Argentina by purchasing it through Algeria. Uranium dioxide is considerably more refined than yellowcake, and is easier to use in irradiating material in a reactor to produce plutonium.
- The status of Iran's nuclear program since the Iran-Iraq War is highly controversial, and Iran has denied the existence of such a program.

continued

Figure 10.21 (Continued)

- On February 7, 1990, the speaker of the Majlis publicly toured the Atomic Energy Organization of Iran and opened the new Jabir Ibn al Hayyan laboratory to train Iranian nuclear technicians. Reports then surfaced that Iran had at least 200 scientists and a work force of about 2,000 devoted to nuclear research.

- Iran's Deputy President Ayatollah Mohajerani stated in October 1991, that Iran should work with other Islamic states to create an "Islamic bomb."

- The Iranian government has repeatedly made proposals to create a nuclear-free zone in the Middle East. For example, President Rafsanjani was asked if Iran had a nuclear weapons program in an interview in the CBS program *60 Minutes* in February 1997. He replied, "Definitely not. I hate this weapon."

- Other senior Iranian leaders, including President Khatami have made similar categorical denials. Iran's Foreign Minister, Kamal Kharrazi, stated on October 5, 1997, that, "We are certainly not developing an atomic bomb, because we do not believe in nuclear weapons. . . . We believe in and promote the idea of the Middle East as a region free of nuclear weapons and other weapons of mass destruction. But why are we interested to develop nuclear technology? We need to diversify our energy sources. In a matter of a few decades, our oil and gas reserves would be finished and therefore, we need access to other sources of energy. . . . Furthermore, nuclear technology has many other utilities in medicine and agriculture. The case of the United States in terms of oil reserve is not different from Iran's. The United States also has large oil resources, but at the same time they have nuclear power plants. So there is nothing wrong with having access to nuclear technology if it is for peaceful purposes . . ."

- The IAEA reports that Iran has fully complied with its present requirements, and that it has found no indications of nuclear weapons effort, but IAEA only inspects Iran's small research reactors.

  - The IAEA visits to other Iranian sites are not inspections, and do not use instruments, cameras, seals, etc. These are informal walk-throughs.

  - The IAEA visited five suspect Iranian facilities in 1992 and 1993 in this manner, but did not conduct full inspections.

  - Iran has not had any 93+2 inspections and its position on improved inspections is that it will not be either the first or the last to have them.

  - Iranian officials have repeatedly complained that the West tolerated Iraqi use of chemical weapons and its nuclear and biological build-up during the Iran-Iraq War, and has a dual standard where it does not demand inspections of Israel or that Israel sign the NPT.

  - The IAEA has inspected the uranium enrichment facility at Natanz, although it is unclear what kind of future inspection regime will be put in place.

  - Despite agreeing to discuss concluding an Additional Protocol for inspections with the IAEA, during a March 13, 2003 interview with *Le Monde*, the Iranian Vice President Gholamreza Aghazadeh indicated that Iran would not sign such a protocol unless the United States lifted economic sanctions.

- These are reasons to assume that Iran still has a nuclear program:

  - Iran attempted to buy highly enriched fissile material from Kazakhstan. The U.S. paid between $20 million and $30 million to buy 1,300 pounds of highly

Figure 10.21 (Continued)

enriched uranium from the Ust-Kamenogorsk facility in Kazakhstan that Iran may have sought to acquire in 1992. A total of 120 pounds of the material—enough for two bombs—cannot be fully accounted for.

- Iran has imported maraging steel, sometimes used for centrifuges, by smuggling it in through dummy fronts. Britain intercepted a 110-pound (50 kilogram) shipment in August 1996. Seems to have centrifuge research program at Sharif University of Technology in Tehran. IAEA "visit" did not confirm.

- Those aspects of Iran's program that are visible indicate that Iran has had only uncertain success. Argentina agreed to train Iranian technicians at its Jose Balaseiro Nuclear Institute, and sold Iran $5.5 million worth of uranium for its small Amirabad Nuclear Research Center reactor in May 1987. A CENA team visited Iran in late 1987 and early 1988, and seems to have discussed selling sell Iran the technology necessary to operate its reactor with 20% enriched uranium as a substitute for the highly enriched core provided by the U.S., and possibly uranium enrichment and plutonium reprocessing technology as well. Changes in Argentina's government, however, made it much less willing to support proliferation. The Argentine government announced in February 1992, that it was canceling an $18 million nuclear technology sale to Iran because it had not signed a nuclear safeguards arrangement. Argentine press sources suggested, however, that Argentina was reacting to U.S. pressure.

- In February 1990 a Spanish paper reported that Associated Enterprises of Spain was negotiating the completion of the two nuclear power plants at Bushehr. Another Spanish firm called ENUSA (National Uranium Enterprises) was to provide the fuel, and Kraftwerke Union (KWU) would be involved. Later reports indicated that a 10 man delegation from Iran's Ministry of Industry was in Madrid negotiating with the Director of Associated Enterprises, Adolofo Garcia Rodriguez.

- Iran negotiated with Kraftwerke Union and CENA of Germany in the late 1980s and early 1990s. Iran attempted to import reactor parts from Siemens in Germany and Skoda in Czechoslovakia. None of these efforts solved Iran's problems in rebuilding its reactor program, but all demonstrate the depth of its interest.

- Iran took other measures to strengthen its nuclear program during the early 1990s. It installed a cyclotron from Ion Beam Applications in Belgium at a facility in Karzaj in 1991.

- Iran conducted experiments in uranium enrichment and centrifuge technology at its Sharif University of Technology in Tehran. Sharif University was also linked to efforts to import cylinders of fluorine suitable for processing enriched material, and attempts to import specialized magnets that can be used for centrifuges, from Thyssen in Germany in 1991.

- In 1992, Iran attempted to buy beryllium from a storage site in Kazakhstan that also was storing 600 kilograms of highly enriched uranium. These contacts then seem to have expanded to an attempt to try the material. In 1994, they helped lead the U.S. to buy the enriched material and fly it out of the country.

continued

Figure 10.21 (Continued)

- It is clear from Iran's imports that it has sought centrifuge technology ever since. Although many of Iran's efforts have never been made public, British customs officials seized 110 pounds of maraging steel being shipped to Iran in July 1996.

- Iran seems to have conducted research into plutonium separation and the Iranians published research on uses of tritium that had applications to nuclear weapons boosting. Iran also obtained a wide range of U.S. and other nuclear literature with applications for weapons designs. Italian inspectors seized eight steam condensers bound for Iran that could be used in a covert reactor program in 1993, and high technology ultrasound equipment suitable for reactor testing at the port of Bari in January 1994.

- Other aspects of Iran's nuclear research effort had potential weapons applications. Iran continued to operate an Argentine-fueled five megawatt light water highly enriched uranium reactor at the University of Tehran. It is operated by a Chinese-supplied neutron source research reactor, and subcritical assemblies with 900 grams of highly enriched uranium, at its Isfahan Nuclear Research Center. This Center has experimented with a heavy water zero-power reactor, a light water sub-critical reactor, and a graphite sub-critical reactor. In addition, it may have experimented with some aspects of nuclear weapons design.

- The German Ministry of Economics has circulated a wide list of such Iranian fronts which are known to have imported or attempted to import controlled items. These fronts include the:
  - Bonyad e-Mostazafan;
  - Defense Industries Organization (Sazemane Sanaye Defa);
  - Pars Garma Company, the Sadadja Industrial Group (Sadadja Sanaye Daryaee);
  - Iran Telecommunications Industry (Sanaye Mokhaberet Iran);
  - Shahid Hemat Industrial Group, the State Purchasing Organization, Education Research Institute (ERI);
  - Iran Aircraft Manufacturing Industries (IAI);
  - Iran Fair Deal Company, Iran Group of Surveyors;
  - Iran Helicopter Support and Renewal Industries (IHI);
  - Iran Navy Technical Supply Center;
  - Iran Tehran Kohakd Daftar Nezarat, Industrial Development Group;
  - Ministry of Defense (Vezerate Defa).

- Iran claims it eventually needs to build enough nuclear reactors to provide 20% of its electric power. This Iranian nuclear power program presents serious problems in terms of proliferation. Although the reactors are scarcely ideal for irradiating material to produce Plutonium or cannibalizing the core, they do provide Iran with the technology base to make its own reactors, have involved other technology transfer helpful to Iran in proliferating and can be used to produce weapons if Iran rejects IAEA safeguards.

- Russian has agreed to build up to four reactors, beginning with a complex at Bushehr—with two 1,000–1,200 megawatt reactors and two 465 megawatt reactors, and provide significant nuclear technology.

Figure 10.21 (Continued)

- Russia has consistently claimed the light water reactor designs for Bushehr cannot be used to produce weapons-grade plutonium and are similar to the reactors the U.S. is providing to North Korea.

- The U.S. has claimed, however, that Victor Mikhaliov, the head of Russia's Atomic Energy Ministry, proposed the sale of a centrifuge plant in April 1995. The U.S. also indicated that it had persuaded Russia not to sell Iran centrifuge technology as part of the reactor deal during the summit meeting between President's Clinton and Yeltsin in May 1995.

- It was only after U.S. pressure that Russia publicly stated that it never planned to sell centrifuge and advanced enrichment technology to Iran, and Iran denied that it had ever been interested in such technology. For example, the statement of Mohammed Sadegh Ayatollahi, Iran's representative to the IAEA, stated that, "We've had contracts before for the Bushehr plant in which we agreed that the spent fuel would go back to the supplier. For our contract with the Russians and Chinese, it is the same." According to some reports, Russia was to reprocess the fuel at its Mayak plant near Chelyabinsk in the Urals, and could store it at an existing facility, at Krasnoyarsk-26 in southern Siberia.

- The CIA reported in June 1997 that Iran had obtained new nuclear technology from Russia during 1996.

- A nuclear accident at plant at Rasht, six miles north of Gilan, exposed about 50 people to radiation in July 1996.

- Russian Nuclear Energy Minister Yevgeny Adamov and Russian Deputy Prime Minister Vladimir Bulgak visited in March 1998 and Iran and dismissed U.S. complaints about the risk the reactors would be used to proliferate.

  - Russia indicated that it would go ahead with selling two more reactors for construction at Bushehr within the next five years.

- The first 1,000-megawatt reactor at Bushehr has experienced serious construction delays. In March 1998, Russia and Iran agreed to turn the construction project into a turn key plant because the Iranian firms working on infrastructure had fallen well behind schedule. In February, Iran had agreed to fund improved safety systems. The reactor is reported to be on a 30- month completion cycle.

- The U.S. persuaded the Ukraine not to sell Iran $45 million worth of turbines for its nuclear plant in early March 1998, and to strengthen its controls on Ukrainian missile technology under the MTCR.

- The CIA reported in January 1999 that Russia remained a key supplier for civilian nuclear programs in Iran and, to a lesser extent, India. With respect to Iran's nuclear infrastructure, Russian assistance would enhance Iran's ability to support a nuclear weapons development effort. Such assistance is less likely to significantly advance India's effort, given that India's nuclear weapons program is more mature. By its very nature, however, even the transfer of civilian technology may be of use in the nuclear weapons programs of these countries.

- Following intense and continuing engagement with the United States, Russian officials have taken some positive steps. Russia has committed to observe

continued

Figure 10.21 (Continued)

certain limits on its nuclear cooperation with Iran, such as not providing militarily useful nuclear technology.

- In January 1998, the Russian Government issued a broad decree prohibiting Russian companies from exporting items known or believed to be used for developing WMD or related delivery systems, whether or not these items are on Russia's export control list. In May 1998, Russia announced a decree intended to strengthen compliance of Russian businesses with existing export controls on proliferation-related items. These actions, if enforced, could help to counter the proliferation of WMD and their delivery systems.

- However, there are signs that Russian entities have continued to engage in behavior inconsistent with these steps. Monitoring Russian proliferation behavior, therefore, will have to remain a very high priority for some time to come.

- On January 14, 2000, Russia's Minister of Defense Igor Ivanavov met with Hassan Rowhani, the secretary of Iran's Supreme National Security Council, and promised that Russia would maintain defense cooperation, and that Russia, "intends to fulfill its obligations under the agreements made in 1989–1990."

- The same day, Vice Minister Ilya Klebanov met with Hassan Rowhani, and announced that Iran might order three additional Russian reactors.

- The CIA warned in January 2000 that Russia might have sold Iran heavy water and graphite technology.

- China is reported to have agreed to provide significant nuclear technology transfer and possible sale of two 300 megawatt pressurized water reactors in the early 1990s, but then agreed to halt nuclear assistance to Iran after pressure from the U.S.

  - Iran signed an agreement with China's Commission on Science, Technology, and Industry for National Defense on January 21, 1991, to build a small 27-kilowatt research reactor at Iran's nuclear weapons research facility at Isfahan. On November 4, 1991, China stated that it had signed commercial cooperation agreements with Iran in 1989 and 1991, and that it would transfer an electromagnetic isotope separator (Calutron) and a smaller nuclear reactor, for "peaceful and commercial" purposes.

  - The Chinese reactor and Calutron were small research-scale systems and had no direct value in producing fissile material. They did, however, give Iran more knowledge of reactor and enrichment technology, and U.S. experts believe that China provided Iran with additional data on chemical separation, other enrichment technology, the design for facilities to convert uranium to uranium hexaflouride to make reactor fuel, and help in processing yellowcake.

  - The U.S. put intense pressure on China to halt such transfers. President Clinton and Chinese President Jiang Zemin reached an agreement at an October 1997 summit. China strengthened this pledge in negotiations with the U.S. in February 1998.

  - In March 1998, the U.S. found that the China Nuclear Energy Corporation was negotiating to sell Iran several hundred tons of anhydrous hydrogen fluo-

Figure 10.21 (Continued)

ride (AHF) to Isfahan Nuclear Research Corporation in central Iran, a site where some experts believe Iran is working on the development of nuclear weapons. AHF can be used to separate plutonium, help refine yellowcake into uranium hexaflouride to produce U-235, and as a feedstock for Sarin. It is on two nuclear control lists. China agreed to halt the sale.

- Iran denied that China had halted nuclear cooperation on March 15, 1998.

- Even so, the U.S. acting Under Secretary of State for Arms Control and International Security Affairs stated that China was keeping its pledge not to aid Iran on March 26, 1998.

- The CIA reported in January 1999 that during the first half of 1998, China continued to take steps to strengthen its control over nuclear exports. China promulgated new export control regulations in June 1998 that cover the sale of dual-use nuclear equipment. This follows on the heels of the September 1997 promulgation of controls covering the export of equipment and materials associated exclusively with nuclear applications. These export controls should give the Chinese Government greater accounting and control of the transfer of equipment, materials, and technology to nuclear programs in countries of concern.

- China pledged in late 1997 not to engage in any new nuclear cooperation with Iran and to complete work on two remaining nuclear projects—a small research reactor and a zirconium production facility—in a relatively short period of time. During the first half of 1998, Beijing appears to have implemented this pledge. The intelligence community will continue to monitor carefully Chinese nuclear cooperation with Iran.

- During the reporting period, Chinese entities provided a variety of missile-related items and assistance to several countries of proliferation concern. China also was an important supplier of ACW to Iran through the first half of 1998.

- The control of fissile material in the FSU remains a major problem:

  - U.S. estimates indicate the FSU left a legacy of some 1,485 tons of nuclear material. This includes 770 tons in some 27,000 weapons, including 816 strategic bombs, 5,434 missile warheads, and about 20,000 theater and tactical weapons. In addition, there were 715 tons of fissile or near-fissile material in eight countries of the FSU in over 50 sites: enough to make 35,000–40,000 bombs.

  - There are large numbers of experienced FSU technicians, including those at the Russian weapons design center at Arzamas, and at nuclear production complexes at Chelyabinsk, Krasnoyarsk, and Tomsk.

  - These factors led the U.S. to conduct Operation Sapphire in 1994, where the U.S. removed 600 kilograms of highly enriched uranium from the Ulba Metallurgy Plant in Kazakhstan at a time Iran was negotiating for the material.

  - They also led to Britain and the U.S. cooperating in Auburn Endeavor, and airlifting fissile material out of a nuclear research facility in Tiblisi, Georgia. There were 10 pounds of material at the institute, and 8.8 pounds were HEU. (It takes about 35 pounds to make a bomb.) This operation was reported in

continued

Figure 10.21 (Continued)

the *New York Times* on April 21, 1998. The British government confirmed it took place, but would not give the date.

- The *Jerusalem Post* reported on April 9, 1998 that Iran had purchased four tactical nuclear weapons from Russian smugglers for $25 million in the early 1990s, that the weapons had been obtained from Kazakhstan in 1991, and that Argentine technicians were helping to activate the weapon.
  - It quoted what it claimed was an Iranian report, dated December 26, 1991, of a meeting between Brigadier General Rahim Safavi, the Deputy Commander of the Revolutionary Guards and Reza Amrohalli, then head of the Iranian atomic energy organization.
  - It also quoted a second document—dated January 2, 1992—saying the Iranians were awaiting the arrival of Russian technicians to show them how to disarm the protection systems that would otherwise inactivate the weapons if anyone attempted to use them.
  - The documents implied the weapons were flawed by did not indicate whether Iran had succeeded in activating them.
  - The U.S. intelligence community could not find any evidence that such a transfer had taken place.
- The most detailed reports of Iran's nuclear weapons program are the least reliable, and come from the People's Mujahideen, a violent, anti-regime, terrorist group. Such claims are very doubtful, but the People's Mujahideen has reported that:
  - Iran's facilities include a weapons site called Ma'allem Kelayah, near Qazvin on the Caspian. This is said to be an IRGC-run facility established in 1987, which has involved an Iranian investment of $300 million. Supposedly, the site was to house the 10 megawatt reactor Iran tried to buy from India.
  - Two Soviet reactors were to be installed at a large site at Gorgan on the Caspian, under the direction of Russian physicists.
  - The People's Republic of China provided uranium enrichment equipment and technicians for the site at Darkhouin, where Iran once planned to build a French reactor.
  - A nuclear reactor was being constructed at Karaj; and that another nuclear weapons facility exists in the south central part of Iran, near the Iraqi border.
  - The ammonia and urea plant that the British firm M. W. Kellog was building at Borujerd in Khorassan province, near the border with Turkestan, might be adapted to produce heavy water.
  - The Amir Kabar Technical University, the Atomic Energy Organization of Iran (AEOI) (also known as the Organization for Atomic Energy of Iran), Dor Argham Ltd., the Education and Research Institute, GAM Iranian Communications, Ghoods Research Center, Iran Argham Co., Iran Electronic Industries, Iranian Research Organization, Ministry of Sepah, Research and Development Group, Sezemane Sanaye Defa, the Sharif University of Technology, Taradis Iran Computer Company, and Zakaria Al-Razi Chemical Company are all participants in the Iranian nuclear weapons effort.

Figure 10.21 (Continued)

- Other sources based on opposition data have listed the Atomic Energy Organization of Iran, the Laser Research Center and Ibn-e Heysam Research and Laboratory Complex, the Bonab Atomic Energy Research Center (East Azerbaijan), the Imam Hussein University of the Revolutionary Guards, the Jabit bin al-Hayyan Laboratory, the Khoshomi uranium mine (Yazd), a possible site at Moallem Kalayeh, the Nuclear Research Center at Tehran University, the Nuclear Research Center for Agriculture and Medicine (Karaj), the Nuclear Research Center of Technology (Isfahan), the Saghand Uranium mine (Yazd), the Sharif University (Tehran) and its Physics Research Center.

- The CIA estimated in January 1999 that Iran remains one of the most active countries seeking to acquire WMD technology and ACW. During the reporting period, Iran focused its efforts to acquire WMD-related equipment, materials, and technology primarily on two countries: Russia and China. Iran is seeking to develop an indigenous capability to produce various types of nuclear, chemical, and biological weapons and their delivery systems.

- Iran actively sought relevant production technology to lessen its dependence on foreign sources.

- Russian entities continued to market and support a variety of nuclear-related projects in Iran during the first half of 1998, ranging from the sale of laboratory equipment for nuclear research institutes to the construction of a 1,000-megawatt nuclear power reactor in Bushehr, Iran, that will be subject to International Atomic Energy Agency (IAEA) safeguards. These projects, along with other nuclear-related purchases, will help Iran augment its nuclear technology infrastructure, which in turn would be useful in supporting nuclear weapons research and development.

  - The completion date of the light-water reactor at Bushehr has been moved forward from 2005 to the end of 2003.

  - Russia has indicated that it would provide fuel for the reactor, in a bid to decouple the construction of the reactor from the Iranian fuel production program.

  - Russia has agreed to provide fuel only if Iran returns the spent fuel to Russia. This is intended to deny Iran the fuel rods needed for plutonium production.

- Russia has committed to observe certain limits on its nuclear cooperation with Iran. For example, President Yeltsin has stated publicly that Russia will not provide militarily useful nuclear technology to Iran. Beginning in January this year, the Russian Government has taken a number of steps. For example, in May 1998, Russia announced a decree intended to strengthen compliance of Russian businesses with existing export controls on proliferation-related items.

- China continued to work on one of its two remaining projects—to supply Iran's civil nuclear program with a zirconium production facility. This facility will be used by Iran to produce cladding for reactor fuel. As a party to the Nuclear Nonproliferation Treaty, Iran is required to apply IAEA safeguards to nuclear fuel, but safeguards are not required for the zirconium plant or its products. During the U.S.-China October 1997 Summit, China pledged not to engage in

continued

Figure 10.21 (Continued)

any new nuclear cooperation with Iran and to complete cooperation on two ongoing nuclear projects in a relatively short time. This pledge appears to be holding. In addition, China promulgated new export regulations in June 1998 that cover the sale of dual-use nuclear equipment. The regulations took effect immediately and were intended to strengthen control over equipment and material that would contribute to proliferation. Institution of these regulations fulfills Jiang Zemin's commitment to the United States last fall to implement such controls by the middle of 1998.

- Iran claims to desire the establishment of a complete nuclear fuel cycle for its civilian energy program. In that guise, it seeks to obtain whole facilities, such as a uranium conversion facility, that, in fact, could be used in any number of ways in support of efforts to produce fissile material needed for a nuclear weapon. Despite outside efforts to curtail the flow of critical technologies and equipment, Tehran continues to seek fissile material and technology for weapons development and has set up an elaborate system of military and civilian organizations to support its effort.

- U.S. estimates of Iran's progress in acquiring nuclear weapons have changed over time.

  - In 1992, the CIA estimated that Iran would have the bomb by the year 2000. In 1995, John Holum testified that Iran could have the bomb by 2003.

  - In 1997, after two years in which Iran might have made progress, he testified that Iran could have the bomb by 2005–2007.

  - In 1999, the NIE on proliferation estimated that Iran could test a missile that could reach the U.S. by 2010, but did not change the 1997 estimate or when Iran might acquire a bomb.

  - In early 2000, the *New York Times* reported that the CIA had warned that Iran might now be able to make a nuclear weapon. The assessment stated that the CIA could not monitor Iran closely enough to be certain whether Iran had acquired fissile material from an outside source.

  - U.S. experts increasingly refer to Iran's efforts as "creeping proliferation" and there is no way to tell when or if Iranian current efforts will produce a weapon, and unclassified lists of potential facilities have little credibility.

  - Timing of weapons acquisition depends heavily on whether Iran can buy fissile material—if so it has the design capability and can produce weapons in 1–2 years—or must develop the capability to process plutonium or enrich uranium—in which case, it is likely to be 5–10 years.

- On August 14, 2002, the representative office of the National Council of Resistance of Iran (NCRI), an Iranian opposition group which includes the People's Mujahideen, held a press briefing in which they released information about Iran's nuclear program.

  - The construction of a large site in Natanz which, according to the allegations, is to have been completed by March 2003.

  - The construction of a heavy water production facility at Arak.

  - Additional nuclear projects at a number of facilities:

Figure 10.21 (Continued)

- The Bushehr power reactor complex.
- The Nuclear Fuel Center in Isfahan.
- The Nuclear Research Center at Karaj.
- Research Center of Bonab.
- Saghand Research Center of Yazd.
- Amirabad Research and Reactor Center in Tehran.
- The Natanz site was previously unknown. By late 2002, the facility had been identified as a uranium enrichment facility.
  - In September 2002, Iran informed the IAEA of the existence of the facility. In a March 17, 2003 report the IAEA had confirmed their February 21, 2002 inspection of the facility.
  - At the time of the inspection, the IAEA Director General Mohamed El Baradei observed approximately 164 gas centrifuges operating at a pilot plant, with parts for perhaps an additional 1,000 centrifuges. When the IAEA delegation visited the facility, no uranium was in any of the centrifuges.
    - The Iranian government has stated that uranium hexaflouride will be produced at Isfahan and then shipped to Natanz for separation and processing. A March 14, 2003 Iranian state television broadcast indicated that on March 3, 2003, the Secretary of the Supreme National Security Council stated that the Isfahan facility for converting yellowcake into uranium hexaflouride was complete.
  - News stories quoting government sources, independent analysis of commercially-available satellite imagery and reports from the NCRI all note that the two main halls are quite large (between 25,000 m² and 32,000 m²), are several meters underground and have walls in excess of two meters thick.
    - The size of the halls tends to suggest that the total number of centrifuges may total roughly 50,000 or more—contradicting recent media reports which claim that Natanz is intended only to house 5,000 centrifuges.[7] This number may merely reflect an interim goal for the site.
    - Previously the Iranian government had announced that it intended to achieve complete self-sufficiency throughout the entire fuel cycle for a projected generation capacity of 6,000 megawatts over the next 20 years.
    - The total capacity of the Natanz facility depends on the efficiency of the centrifuges. At the low end, a complex housing 50,000 centrifuges would produce a quarter of the fuel need for the Bushehr reactor—which is only about 4 percent of the total stated goal of the Iranian nuclear program. At the high end, 50,000 centrifuges could produce 25% more than the amount called for in publicly stated nuclear program objectives.
      - The throughput of the centrifuges depends on the quality of the materials used in manufacturing the centrifuges, as well as their design.
      - Unconfirmed reports quoting western governmental sources suggest that the Iranian centrifuges may tend towards the upper bounds of the range of production capabilities.

continued

517

Figure 10.21 (Continued)

- The amount of separation capacity needed to meet the stated goals of providing sufficient fuel for 6,000 MW is sufficient to produce enough highly-enriched uranium for 180 weapons annually.

- It is uncertain what portion, if any, of the separation capacity at Natanz will be dedicated to producing highly-enriched, weapons-grade uranium versus low-enriched uranium for use in power reactors.

- More significantly, the ability to construct a plant of this scale suggests that there may exist ample capacity to produce separation equipment for use in a weapons program. Such equipment could be located at other, unknown, sites.

- National Council of Resistance of Iran (NCRI) also released information about a heavy water production facility at Arak during it's August 14, 2002, press briefing.

  - The construction of a heavy-water production facility is puzzling to many observers, as Iran has no reactor that utilizes heavy water.

    - Heavy water can be used in a reactor that uses natural uranium fuel.

    - Analysts note that heavy water is a key material used in plutonium production.

- On February 9, 2003, Iranian President Khatami made a televised speech on Iran's nuclear program in which a number of pronouncements were made indicating the scope and scale of the Iranian nuclear program.

  - Iran has started mining uranium near the city of Yazd.

  - A facility for converting ore into yellowcake has been built in the same province as the mines.

  - Iran is building or operating uranium mines, uranium concentration and conversion facilities and fuel fabrication plants.

  - A statement made the next day by the head of Iran's Atomic Energy Organization, stated that the Isfahan facility would convert yellowcake into uranium oxide, uranium hexaflouride and uranium metal.

  - Uranium metal has very few civil uses, but is a key to the construction of nuclear weapons.

  - On March 3, 2003, the state-run Islamic Republic News Agency reported that the Isfahan facility was completed and would begin operation.

- Statements made over the last few months by the Iranian government regarding fuel-cycle self-sufficiency had troubled some observers, including the U.S. State Department, as these statements could be interpreted to mean that Iran is pursuing the ability to reprocess spent fuel.

  - Reprocessing of spent fuel produces plutonium.

  - Russia's earlier agreements regarding the construction of the reactor at Bushehr included an agreement for Russia to provide reactor fuel. This agreement was contingent on Iran returning spent fuel rods to Russia.

- On December 13, 2002, IAEA Director General Mohammed El-Baradei indicated that the reports by Iranian opposition groups and Western governments on Iranian nuclear facilities at Natanz and Arak was not a surprise, citing discussions with Iranian authorities over the last 6 months.

  - On February 22, 2003, Iran permitted three IAEA personnel to visit the Natanz enrichment facility. More detailed inspections began on March 10, 2003.

Figure 10.21 (Continued)

- During the visit, personnel observed between 160–200 active centrifuges at the Natanz pilot plant. However, none of these centrifuges appeared to have contained uranium hexaflouride. It is possible that some UF_6 has been processed somewhere in Iran, at least on a trial basis.

- Inspectors also observed parts for about an additional 1,000 centrifuges.

- Iranian authorities promised to provide information on centrifuge design no later than 60 days before the start of processing of uranium hexaflouride. Under existing agreements, Iran would also be required to provide IAEA with data covering the number of centrifuges installed as well as the total facility throughput.

- The United States and other western governments have pressured the IAEA to more aggressively monitor the Iranian nuclear program and have encouraged the IAEA to seek additional, more comprehensive, inspection agreements. Iran originally indicated some willingness to make such an agreement, although recently they appear to be more inclined to extract concessions in exchange for further inspections.

- The CIA reported in November 2003 that, "The United States remains convinced that Tehran has been pursuing a clandestine nuclear weapons program, in violation of its obligations as a party to the Nuclear Nonproliferation Treaty (NPT). To bolster its efforts to establish domestic nuclear fuel-cycle capabilities, Iran sought technology that can support fissile material production for a nuclear weapons program.

  - Iran tried to use its civilian nuclear energy program to justify its efforts to establish domestically or otherwise acquire assorted nuclear fuel-cycle capabilities. In August 2002, an Iranian opposition group disclosed that Iran was secretly building a heavy water production plant and a "nuclear fuel" plant. Press reports later in the year confirmed these two facilities using commercial imagery and clarified that the "fuel" plant was most likely a large uranium centrifuge enrichment facility located at Natanz. Commercial imagery showed that Iran was burying the enrichment facility presumably to hide it and harden it against military attack. Following the press disclosures, Iran announced at the International Atomic Energy Agency (IAEA) September 2002 General Conference that it had "ambitious" nuclear fuel cycle plans and intended to develop all aspects of the entire fuel cycle.

  - By the end of 2002, the IAEA had requested access to the enrichment facility at Natanz, and the IAEA Director General (DG) for the first time visited the facility in February 2003. The IAEA is investigating the newly disclosed facilities, and previously undisclosed nuclear material imports to determine whether Iran has violated its NPT-required IAEA safeguards agreement in developing these facilities and their related technologies. At the June 2003 Board of Governors meeting, the IAEA DG presented a report on the Iranian program noting Tehran had failed to meet its safeguards obligations in a number of areas. The DG's report described a pattern of Iranian safeguards failures related to the undeclared import and processing of uranium compounds in the early 1990s, expressed concern over the lack of cooperation from Iran with IAEA inspections, and identified a number of unresolved concerns in Iran's program that the IAEA will continue to investigate. The IAEA Board on 19

continued

519

Figure 10.21 (Continued)

June welcomed the report and called on Iran to answer all IAEA questions, cooperate fully with IAEA inspectors, and sign and implement an Additional Protocol immediately and unconditionally.

- Although Iran claims that its nascent enrichment plant is to produce fuel for the Russian-assisted construction projects at Bushehr and other possible future power reactors, we remain concerned that Iran is developing enrichment technology to produce fissile material for nuclear weapons under the cover of legitimate fuel cycle activities. Iran appears to be embarking on acquiring nuclear weapons material via both acquisition paths—highly enriched uranium and low burn-up plutonium. Even with intrusive IAEA safeguards inspections at Natanz, there is a serious risk that Iran could use its enrichment technology in covert activities. Of specific proliferation concern are the uranium centrifuges discovered at Natanz, which are capable of enriching uranium for use in nuclear weapons. Iran claims its heavy water plant is for peaceful purposes. In June, Iran informed the IAEA that it is pursuing a heavy water research reactor that we believe could produce plutonium for nuclear weapons. We also suspect that Tehran is interested in acquiring fissile material and technology from foreign suppliers to support its overall nuclear weapons program."

- Iran agreed to sign the NNPT protocol allowing full IAEA challenge inspections, and to IAEA inspections of suspect nuclear facilities in late 2003, after the discovery of undeclared centrifuge and heavy water facilities, and the IAEA discovered it was conducting a variety of activities illegal under the NNPT. It did so in the face of UN condemnation and possible sanctions.

- The IAEA, in early 2004, found traces of highly enriched uranium at an Iranian nuclear facility. The uranium, the uncommon 235 isotope, had been refined to 90 percent, making it of a quality usually used in a nuclear bomb.

  - Iran claimed that its equipment must have been contaminated by uranium while being shipped to its facilities. Iran stated that the exact time and location of the contamination was impossible to determine due to the fact that the parts had been shipped through five different countries.

  - The IAEA suggested that the contamination may have occurred in Pakistan as a result of the alleged collusion between Iranian officials and the Pakistani scientist, Abdul Qadeer Kahn. The IAEA requested that Pakistan allow the organization to take samples from its enrichment sites to determine whether or not the contamination occurred in Pakistan.

  - The Iranian Defense Minister, Ali Shamkhani, admitted that centrifuge production had taken place under military supervision and were designed to enrich uranium. These centrifuges, he maintained, were solely for use in civilian power plants. Kamal Kharrazi, the Foreign Minister, accused the U.S. of using every opportunity to pressure Iran and indicated that the actions of the U.S. could "complicate" Iran's cooperation with the IAEA. Kharrazi insisted that Iran would resume enriching uranium for "peaceful purposes" after the IAEA was satisfied with Iran's compliance.[8]

  - The U.S. has threatened to refer Iran to the UN Security Council if the country refused to reveal or tried to conceal developments in its nuclear research. The European nations have been reluctant to support such a measure, be-

Figure 10.21 (Continued)

lieving that it would rule out further Iranian cooperation with the IAEA. The revelation of highly enriched uranium and the Iranians' decision to suspend further IAEA inspections until April on March 11, 2004, however, has caused them to reevaluate their positions with regard to Iran.

- On March 13, 2004, the IAEA passed a resolution that criticized Iran for failing to reveal all aspects of its nascent nuclear weapons program. In response, Iran suspended IAEA inspections indefinitely. The IAEA's main concerns were[9]:

  - Iran had failed to reveal the full extent of its past and current nuclear program as requested by the IAEA in November.

  - Iran had signed the Additional Protocol but had failed to ratify it as the IAEA called for in November.

  - The IAEA found additional equipment and designs not disclosed by Iran. They included a more advanced centrifuge design, centrifuge research, centrifuge testing, and centrifuge manufacture. The IAEA found the designs for two hot cells at the Arak heavy water research reactor and two mass spectrometers for the laser enrichment process. Iran has not provided the IAEA with the reason for the planned construction of a second heavy-water reactor. These issues require greater investigation but are consistent with an active nuclear weapons research program.

  - Iran failed to show the extent of its research and development in uranium enrichment. Iran failed to provide the IAEA with the source of the uranium contamination.

  - No sufficient explanation has been given for Iran's experiments with polonium-210.

Missile Defenses
  - Seeking Russian S-300 or S-400 surface-to-air missile system with limited anti tactical ballistic missile capability.

---

[1]www.globalsecurity.org

[2]Ed Blanche, "Iran Forms Five Units for Shahab Ballistic Missiles," *Jane's Defense Weekly*, July 12, 2000, p. 16.

[3]John Mintz, "Tracking Arms: a Study in Smoke; Ambiguity Clouds French Role in China-Iran Deal," *Washington Post*, April 3, 1999, p. A-03.

[4]Center for Nonproliferation Studies, Monterey Institute of International Studies, "North Korean Missile Exports and Technical Assistance to Iran," http://www.nti.org/db/profiles/dprk/msl/ie/NKM_EeiranGO.html, accessed April 2003.

[5]Merav Zafary, "Iranian Biological and Chemical Weapons Profile Study," *Center for Nonproliferation Studies, Moneterey Institute of International Studies*, February 2001.

[6]Shirly Kan, "China's Proliferation of Weapons of Mass Destruction," Congressional Research Service, March 1, 2002, CRS IB 9256.

[7]David Albright and Corey Hinderstein, "The Iranian Gas Centrifuge Uranium Enrichment Plant at Natanz: Drawing From Commercial Satellite Images," *The Institute for Science and International Security*, March 14, 2003.

[8]Craig S. Smith, "Alarm Raised Over Quality of Uranium Found in Iran," *New York Times*, March 11, 2004 p. A-11.

[9]International Atomic Energy Agency, Board of Governors, "Implementation of the NPT Safeguards Agreement in the Islamic Republic of Iran," March 13, 2004 http://www.iaea.org/Publications/Documents/Board/2004/gov2004-21.pdf.

Figure 10.22
Saudi Arabia's Search for Weapons of Mass Destruction

Delivery Systems

- Between 30 and 60 modified CSS-2 missiles purchased from China in 1988. The CSS-2 is based on the Russian SS-4 and has an estimated range of 2,650 km, a payload of 2,150 kg, with a CEP of 2.5 km.
  - Saudi Arabia is thought to possess 9 launchers.
  - The missiles are deployed in two installations al-Sulayil and al-Joffer 500 and 100 km south of Riyadh, respectively.
  - XX Tornado fighter ground attack aircraft.
  - XX F-15s of various models.
  - Tube artillery and multiple rocket launchers.

Chemical Weapons

- Possible development. No evidence of deployed systems.

Biological Weapons

- Possible development. No evidence of deployed systems.

Nuclear Weapons

- There has been a great deal of ongoing speculation regarding Saudi nuclear intentions. None of these suspicions have been confirmed although the allegations are persistent.
- The Saudis are alleged to have first open a nuclear research center at Al-Kharj in 1975.
- Later, there have been many reports of nuclear cooperation between Saudi Arabia and Iraq, prior to the 1990 invasion of Kuwait. Reportedly, Saudi Arabia offered to pay for the rebuilding of the Osirak reactor, following its destruction in 1981.
- In 1994 a Saudi diplomat, the second-in-command of the Saudi mission to the United Nations sought political asylum.[1]
  - He brought more than 10,000 documents with him, including letters written in 1989 from the China Nuclear Energy Industry Corporation to a Saudi prince discussing the purchase of miniature neutron source reactors.
  - The veracity of these letters and the validity of these allegations have never been established.
- On October 22, 2003, an article citing an unnamed Pakistani source indicated that Saudi Arabia and Pakistan had reached a secret agreement on the exchange of nuclear weapons technology for cheap oil.[2]
  - Both Pakistan and Saudi Arabia have vehemently denied this and no evidence has been produced to support this allegation.
- Other unverified reports speculate that Pakistan will be seeking a joint control and command of Pakistani nuclear weapons in Saudi Arabia. The article argues

Figure 10.22 (Continued)

that this would increase Saudi prestige and safety, while giving Pakistan a complex second strike capability against India.[3]

• Saudi Arabia is a signatory to the nuclear non-proliferation treaty.

[1]Paul Lewis, "Defector Says Saudis Sought Nuclear Arms," *New York Times*, August 7, 1994, p. 20.

[2]Arnaud de Borchgrave, "Pakistan, Saudi Arabia in secret nuke pact; Islamabad trades weapons technology for oil," *The Washington Times*, October 22, 2003, p. A-01.

[3]*Defense & Foreign Affairs Daily*, "Saudi Arabia Takes Steps to Acquire Nuclear Weapons," October 29, 2002.

Figure 10.23
**Problems in Collecting Data on WMD Capabilities and Delivery Systems:
Iraq as a Case Study**

Even a cursory review of this list of U.S. and British charges about Iraq's WMD capabilities shows that point after point that was made was not confirmed during war or after the first two months of effort following the conflict. Despite all of the advances in their IS&R capabilities, the United States and Britain went to war with Iraq without the level of evidence needed to provide a clear strategic rationale for the war, and without the ability to fully understand the threat that Iraqi weapons of mass destruction posed to U.S., British, and Australian forces. This uncertainty is not a definitive argument against carrying out a war that responded to grave potential threats. It *is* a definitive warning that this intelligence and targeting are not yet adequate to support grand strategy, strategy, and tactical operations against proliferating powers or to make accurate assessments of the need to preempt.

It is difficult to put these problems into perspective without access to classified material. Past declassified U.S. intelligence reporting on proliferation has made it clear, however, that proliferation presents very serious problems for intelligence collection and analysis. UNSCOM and UNMOVIC reports show that Iraq was well aware of these problems and how to exploit them:

• Iraq and other powers sophisticated enough to proliferate are also sophisticated enough to have a good understanding of many of the strengths and limitations of modern intelligence sensors, the timing and duration of satellite coverage, and the methods use to track imports and technology transfer. They have learned to cover and conceal, to deceive, and to create smaller and better disseminated activities.

• Intelligence collection relies heavily on finding key imports and technology transfers. Such reports, however, only usually cover a small fraction of the actual effort on the part of the proliferating country, and the information collected is often vague and uncertain, in part because importers and smugglers have every incentive to lie and are also familiar with many the ways to defeat intelligence collection and import controls. When information does become available, it is often impossible to put in context, and a given import or technology transfer can often be used in many difficult ways, often was other than proliferation. Such import data can hint at the character of a proliferation effort, but give no picture of the overall character of the activity.

continued

Figure 10.23 (Continued)

- Even when data are available on given imports or technology transfers, they generally present three serious problems. One is that there is no way to know the end destination and use of the import and how it is integrated into the overall effort. The second is there is no way to know if it is integrated into an ongoing research and development effort, a weapons production effort, being procured or stockpiled for later use, or simply an experiment or mistake that is never further exploited. The third is that many imports have civilian or other military uses. These so-called "dual-use" imports may have legitimate use.

- The very nature of arms control agreements like the Nuclear Non-Proliferation Treaty (NNPT), Biological Weapons Convention (BWC), and Chemical Weapons convention (CWC) encourages proliferating nations to lie and conceal as effectively as possible. The same is true of supplier agreements like the Missile Technology Control Regime (MTCR) and Australia List, and any form of sanctions. Arms control only encourages compliance among non-proliferators and non-sellers, and current enforcement efforts are too weak to be effective while their provisions effective license technology transfer to those nations who succeed in lying or concealing.

- The technology of proliferation generally permits the research and development effort to be divided up into a wide range of small facilities and projects. Some can be carried out as legitimate civil research. Others can be hidden in civil and commercial facilities. As proliferators become more sophisticated, they learn to create dispersed, redundant and parallel programs, and mix high secret covert programs with open civil or dual-use programs. Chemical, biological, and cruise missile programs are particularly easy to divide up into small cells or operations. However, this is increasingly true of nuclear weapons centrifuge programs, plutonium processing and fuel cycles, and the testing and simulation of nuclear weapons that does not involve weapons grade materials. Many key aspects of ballistic missile R&D, including warhead and launch system design fit into this category.

- Iraq and most other proliferators have, in the past, focused on creating stockpiles of weapons for fighting theater conflicts against military forces. These stockpiles require large inventories, large-scale deployments, and generally mixes of training and warfighting preparations that create significant intelligence indicators. There are, however, other strategies and many proliferators may now be pursuing them. One is to bring weapons to full development, and to wait until a threat becomes imminent to actually produce the weapon. A second is to follow the same course, but create large dual-use civil facilities that can be rapidly converted to the production of weapons of mass destruction. These can include pharmaceutical plants, food-processing plants, breweries, petrochemical plants, and pesticide plants, but key assembly lines can be concealed in a wide range of other commercial activities.[1] Weapons production facilities can be stockpiled for a later and sometimes sudden breakout. A third is to focus on creating as few highly lethal biological or nuclear weapons to attack key political or civilian facilities in a foreign country, rather than its military forces. Highly lethal non-infectious or infectious biological agents are one means of such an attack, biological weapons directed at crops or livestock are another.

- Countries can pursue very different strategies in dealing with their past inventories of weapons. They can disclose and destroy them, knowing they do not face

Figure 10.23 (Continued)

an urgent war-fighting need, better weapons are coming, and this suits current political objectives. They can claim to destroy and hide the remaining weapons in covert areas known only to a few. They can claim to destroy, or lie, and disperse weapons where they can be used for warfighting purposes. In many cases, intelligence collection may not be able to distinguish between such strategies, and a given proliferator like Iraq can pursue a mix of such strategies—depending on the value of the weapon.

- In many cases, there is no clear way to know whether a program is R&D, production and weapons deployment, or production capable/breakout oriented. The problem is further complicated by the fact that Iraq and other countries have learned to play a "shell game" by developing multiple surface and underground military facilities and dual-use facilities and to create relatively mobile mixes of trailer/vehicle mounted and "palletized" equipment for rapid movement. Large special-purpose facilities with hard to move equipment often still exist, but they are by no means the rule. Intelligence collection takes time and may often lag behind country activities.

- Unless a country keeps extremely accurate records of its programs, it is often far easier to estimate that maximum scale of what it might do than provide an accurate picture of what it has actually done.

- In most cases, it is impossible to know how far a given project or effort has gotten and how well it has succeeded. The history of proliferation is not the history of proliferators overcoming major technical and manufacturing problems. It is the history of massive management and systems integration problems, political failures, lying technical advocates and entrepreneurs, project managers who do not tell their political masters the truth, and occasional sudden success. Short of an intelligence breakthrough, it is rarely possible to assess the success of a given effort and even on the scene inspection can produce vary wrong results unless a given project can be subjected to detailed technical testing. For example, UNSCOM and the IAEA found that virtually all of their preliminary reporting on Iraq's nuclear effort in 1992–1993 tended to exaggerate Iraqi capabilities once they had had the time to fully assess the efficiency of key efforts like the Calutron and centrifuge programs.

- The only definitive way to counter most of these collection problems is to have a reliable mix of redundant human intelligence (HUMINT) sources within the system or as defectors. The United States, however, has never claimed or implied it had such capabilities in any proliferating country, and the history of U.S., British, UNSCOM, and UNMOVIC efforts to deal with Iraq makes it painfully clear both that such transparency was totally lacking in Iraq and that most Iraqi defectors and intelligence sources outside Iraq made up information, circulated unsubstantiated information, or simply lied. Breakthroughs do occur, but HUMIMT is normally inadequate, untrustworthy, or a failure, and these shortcomings cannot generally be corrected with data based on other intelligence means. Either inside information is available or it is not. When it is, imagery and signals intelligence generally do far more to indicate that HUMINT is wrong or suspect than to reveal the truth.[2]

continued

Figure 10.23 (Continued)

- In many cases, even the leaders of a proliferating country may not have an accurate picture of the success of their efforts, and most probably do not have a clear picture of the accuracy, lethality and effects, and reliability of their weapons. U.S. and British research efforts have long shown that even highly sophisticated technical models of the performance and lethality of chemical, biological, and nuclear weapons and delivery systems can be grossly wrong, or require massive levels of human testing that simply are not practical even for closed authoritarian societies. No declassified intelligence report on any proliferation effort in any developing country has yet indicated that Iraq or any other proliferator has sophisticated technical and testing models in these areas. Intelligence cannot collect data that do not exist.

---

[1] For an interesting discussion of the problems in assessing dual-use facilities in Iraq, see Walter Pincus, "Weapons Linked to Dual Use Facilities in Iraq," *Washington Post*, June 2, 2003.
[2] For some additional data on this aspect of these assessments made of Iraq, see Bill Gertz, "Iraqi Group Aid CIA Intelligence," *Washington Times*, June 12, 2003; John Diamond, "Broad Purges Wiped Out Most Iraqis Helping CIA," *USA Today*, June 17, 2003; John Diamond, "Weak Spy Network Hurt Hunt for Arms," *USA Today*, June 17, 2003.

Figure 10.24
Problems in Analyzing WMD Capabilities and Delivery Systems:
Iraq as a Case Study

Many of the resulting problems in the analysis of the WMD capabilities of Iraq and other countries are the result of the previous problems in collection. The details of U.S., British, and allied intelligence analyses remain classified. At the same time, background discussions with intelligence analysts and users reveal the following additional problems in analyzing the WMD threat:

- The uncertainties surrounding collection on virtually all proliferation and weapons of mass destruction programs are so great that it is impossible to produce meaningful point estimates. As the CIA has shown in some of its past public estimates of missile proliferation, the intelligence community must first develop a matrix of what is and is not known about a given aspect of proliferation in a given country, with careful footnoting or qualification of the problems in each key source. It must then deal with uncertainty by creating estimates that show a range of possible current and projected capabilities—carefully qualifying each case. In general, at least three scenarios or cases need to be analyzed for each major aspect of proliferation in each country—something approaching a "best," "most likely," and "worst case."[1]
- Even under these conditions, the resulting analytic effort faces serious problems. Security compartmentation within each major aspect of collection and analysis severely limits the flow of data to working analysts. The expansion of analytic staffs has sharply increased the barriers to the flow of data, and has brought large number of junior analysts into the process that can do little more than update past analyses and judgments. Far too little analysis is subjected to technical re-

Figure 10.24 (Continued)

view by those who have actually worked on weapons development, and the analysis of delivery programs, warheads and weapons, and chemical, biological, and nuclear proliferation tends to be compartmented. Instead of the free flow of data and exchange of analytic conclusions, or "fusion" of intelligence, analysis is "stovepiped" into separate areas of activity. Moreover, the larger staffs get, the more stovepiping tends to occur.

- Analysis tends to focus on technical capability and not on the problems in management and systems integration that often are the real world limiting factors in proliferation. This tends to push analysis towards exaggerating the probable level of proliferation, particularly because technical capability is often assumed if collection cannot provide all the necessary information.

- Where data are available on past holdings of weapons and the capability to produce such weapons—such as data on chemical weapons feedstocks and biological growth material—the intelligence effort tends to produce estimates of the maximum size of the possible current holding of weapons and WMD materials. While ranges are often shown, and estimates are usually qualified with uncertainty, this tends to focus users on the worst case in terms of actual current capability. In the case of the Iraq, this was compounded by some 12 years of constant lies and a disbelief that a dictatorship obsessed with record keeping could not have records if it had destroyed weapons and materials. The end result, however, was to assume that little or no destruction had occurred whenever UNSCOM, UNMOVIC, and the IAEA reported that major issues still affected Iraqi claims.

- Intelligence analysis has long been oriented more towards arms control and counterproliferation rather than war fighting, although DIA and the military services have attempted to shift the focus of analysis. Dealing with broad national trends and assuming capability is not generally a major problem in seeking to push nations towards obeying arms control agreements, or in pressuring possible suppliers. It also is not a major problem in analyzing broad military counterproliferation risks and programs. The situation is very different in dealing with war fighting choices, particularly issues like preemption and targeting. Assumptions of capability can lead to preemption that is not necessary, overtargeting, inability to prioritize, and a failure to create the detailed collection and analysis necessary to support warfighters down to the battalion level. This, in turn, often forces field commanders to rely on field teams with limit capability and expertise, and to overreact to any potential threat or warning indicator.

- The intelligence community does bring outside experts into the process, but often simply to provide advice in general terms rather than cleared review of the intelligence product. The result is often less than helpful. The use of other cleared personnel in U.S. laboratories and other areas of expertise is inadequate and often presents major problems because those consulted are not brought fully into the intelligence analysis process and given all of the necessary data.

- The intelligence community does tend to try to avoiding explicit statements of the short comings in collection and methods in much of its analysis and to repeat past agreed judgments on a lowest common denominator level—particularly

continued

527

Figure 10.24 (Continued)

---

in the form of the intelligence products that get broad circulation to consumers. Attempts at independent outside analysis or "B-Teams," however, are not subject to the review and controls enforced on intelligence analysis, and the teams, collection data, and methods used are generally selection to prove given points rather than provide an objective counterpoint to finished analysis.[2]

More broadly, the users of intelligence are at best intolerant of analysis that consists of a wide range of qualifications and uncertainties even at the best of times, and the best of times do not exist when urgent policy and warfighting decisions need to be made. Users inevitably either force the intelligence process to reach something approaching a definitive set of conclusions, or else they make such estimates themselves.

Intelligence analysts and managers are all too aware of this fact. Experience has taught them that complex intelligence analysis—filled with alternative cases, probability estimates, and qualifications about uncertainty—generally go unused or make policy makers and commanders impatient with the entire intelligence process. In the real world, hard choices have to be made to provide an estimate that *can* actually be used and acted upon, and these choices must either by the intelligence community or the user.[3]

---

[1]Earlier unclassified CIA reports on problems like the ballistic missile threat often projected alternative levels of current and future capability. The qualifications and possible futures are far less well defined in more recent reports. For example, see CIA, Unclassified Summary of a National Intelligence Estimate, Foreign Missile Developments and the Ballistic Missile Threat Through 2015," National Intelligence Council, December 2001, http://www.cia.gov/nic/pubs/other_products/Unclassifiedballisticmissilefinal.htm.

[2]There is no way to determine just how much the Special Plans Office team set up within the office of the Secretary of Defense to analyze the threat in Iraq was designed to produce a given conclusion or politicized intelligence. The Department has denied this, and stated that the team created within its policy office was not working Iraqi per se, but on global terrorist interconnections. It also stated that the Special Plans Office was never tied to the Intelligence Collection Program—a program to debrief Iraqi defectors—and relied on CIA inputs for its analysis. It states that simply conducted a review, presented its findings in August 2002, and its members returned to other duties. See Jim Garamone, "Policy Chief Seeks to Clear Intelligence Record," American Forces Information Service, June 3, 2003; and Briefing on policy and intelligence matters, Douglas J. Feith, undersecretary of defense for policy, and William J. Luti, deputy under secretary of defense for special plans and Near East and South Asian affairs, June 4, 2003, http://www.defenselink.mil/transcripts/2003/tr20030604-0248.html.

Some intelligence experts dispute this view, however, and claim the team's effort was used to put press on the intelligence community. Such "B-teams" also have a mixed history. They did help identify an intelligence community tendency to underestimate Soviet strategic nuclear efforts during the Cold War. The threat analysis of missile threats posed to the United States by the "Rumsfeld Commission," however, was a heavily one-sided assessment designed to justify national missile defense. Also see Greg Miller, "Pentagon Defends Role of Intelligence Unit on Iraq," *Los Angeles Times*, June 5, 2003; and David S. Cloud, "The Case for War Relied on Selective Intelligence," *Wall Street Journal*, June 5, 2003.

Figure 10.24 (Continued)

---

[3]Some press sources cite what they claim is a deliberate effort to ignore a September 2002 DIA report on Iraqi chemical weapons capabilities called "Iraq-Key WMD Facilities-An Operational Support Study." See James Risen, "Word that U.S. Doubted Iraq Would Use Gas," *New York Times*, June 18, 2003 and Tony Capaccio, "Pentagon 2002 Study Reported No Reliable Data on Iraq Weapons," *USA Today*, June 6, 2003.

In fact, the unclassified excerpts from the DIA report, show that DIA was not stating that Iraqi did not have chemical weapons, but rather that it had, No reliable information on whether Iraq is producing and stockpiling chemical weapons, or where Iraq has—or will—establish its chemical weapons facilities." The report went on to say that, "although we lack any direct information, Iraq probably possess CW agent in chemical munitions, possibly include artillery rockets, artillery shells, aerial bombs, and ballistic missile warheads. Baghdad also probably possess bulk chemical stockpiles, primarily containing precursors, but that also could consist of some mustard agent of stabilized VX."

If anything, the report is a classic example of what happens when intelligence reports do state uncertainty and of how the user misreads or misuses the result.

Notes

CHAPTER 1

1. For a modern and well-structured Israeli assessment of the balance, see *The Middle East Military Balance*, Tel Aviv University, Jaffe Center for Strategic Studies.

CHAPTER 4

1. For further details, see U.S. State Department, Bureau of Arms Control, *World Military Expenditures and Arms Transfers*.

2. This discussion draws heavily on interviews and the details provided in *Jane's Fighting Ships, 2003–2004*, and the country section in IISS, *The Military Balance, 2003–2004*.

3. IISS, *The Military Balance, 2003–2004*.

4. This discussion draws heavily on interviews and the details provided in *Jane's Fighting Ships, 2003–2004*, plus other data from London, Jane's Information Group, and the country section in IISS, *The Military Balance, 2003–2004*.

5. *Jane's Defense Weekly*, October 25, 2000, p. 15.

6. "Algeria to Get Night-Upgraded Mi-171 Helicopters," *Jane's Defense Weekly*, January 15, 2003, http://jdw.janes.com, accessed January 8, 2004. Labeled Baetjer 1.

7. This discussion draws heavily on interviews and the details provided in *Jane's Fighting Ships, 2003–2004*, p. 1, and the country section in IISS, *The Military Balance, 2003–2004*.

8. This is a report from one source. The creation of a coast watch seems erratic even for Libya.

9. Reports that Libya acquired 12 Soviet SS-12M (SS-22) missiles between mid-1980 and mid-1981 do not seem accurate. Yoseff Bodansky and Vaughn Forrest,

Chemical Weapons in the Third World, p. 4; *Libya's Chemical-Biological Warfare Capabilities,* Task Force on Terrorism and Unconventional Warfare, House Republican Research Committee, U.S. House of Representatives, Washington, DC, June 12, 1990, p. 3; M. Sicker, *The Making of a Pariah State* (New York: Praeger, 1987), pp. 104–105; John K. Colley, *Libyan Sandstorm* (New York: Holt, Rinehart, and Winston, 1982), pp. 248–251.

10. *Aviation Week and Space Technology,* April 10, 1989, pp. 19–20; *New York Times,* April 5, 1989, September 7, 1989; *Washington Times,* January 16, 1989; FBIS/NES, April 10, 1989.

11. Foreign technicians could provide effective support in the use of radar reconnaissance data. The basic problems with daylight reconnaissance photography are that it is not as discriminating as radar or electro-optics, cannot be processed until the aircraft lands, takes several hours to process, and requires expert interpretation. This is adequate against static targets, but even infantry units often move too quickly to use such data for targeting purposes.

12. "Libya's Armed Forces," *IISS Strategic Comments* 6, no. 10, December 2000.

CHAPTER 5

1. Gal Luft, "All Quite on the Eastern Front?: Israel's National Security Doctrine After the Fall of Saddam," Saban Center for Middle East Policy Analysis Paper Number 2, Brookings Institution, March 2004, pp. 14–15. Data is adapted from Jaffee Center for Strategic Studies.

2. Gal Luft, "All Quite on the Eastern Front?: Israel's National Security Doctrine After the Fall of Saddam," Saban Center for Middle East Policy Analysis Paper Number 2, Brookings Institution, March 2004, p. 14.

3. Gal Luft, "All Quite on the Eastern Front?: Israel's National Security Doctrine After the Fall of Saddam," Saban Center for Middle East Policy Analysis Paper Number 2, Brookings Institution, March 2004, p. 15. Data is adapted from Jaffee Center for Strategic Studies.

4. "Israel, Turkey Sign Security Accord," *Jane's Defense Weekly,* January 21, 2004, http://jdw.janes.com, accessed January 27, 2004; and "Russia Halts Plans to Sell Igla to Syria," *Jane's Defense Weekly,* November 6, 2002, http://jdw.janes.com, accessed January 9, 2004.

5. Barbara Opall-Rome, "Tactical Successes, Strategic Failures," *Defense News,* December 22, 2003, p. 32.

6. Barbara Opall-Rome, "Israel Security Experts Seek Strategy," *Defense News,* December 22, 2003, p. 6.

7. Barbara Opall-Rome, "Tactical Successes, Strategic Failures," p. 34.

8. Barbara Opall-Rome and Riad Kawahji, "Rendering Assad Unviable," *Defense News,* October 20, 2003, p. 1.

9. Alon Ben-David, "Extensive Cuts to Hit Israeli Ground Forces the Most," *Jane's Defense Weekly,* July 16, 2003, p. 16.

10. Opall-Rome, "Israel Security Experts Seek Strategy," p. 6.

11. Alon Ben-David, "IDF Branches Sparring for Share of U.S. Funding," *Jane's Defense Weekly,* January 28, 2004, http://jdw.janes.com, accessed January 27, 2004.

12. "Israel Decides Not to Develop Merkava Mk5," *Jane's Defense Weekly,* October 2, 2003, http://jdw.janes.com, accessed January 8, 2004. Labeled as 2.

13. Barbara Opall-Rome, "Israel Eyes Merkava MBT Replacement," *Defense News,* November 10, 2003, p. 34.

14. Barbara Opall-Rome, "IMI Proposes Buy of Merkava Production Line," *Defense News,* January 12, 2004, p. 6.

15. Arieh O'Sullivan, "IDF Plans to Buy Stryker APC," *Jerusalem Post,* February 3, 2004, accessed via http://ebird.afis.osd.mil/ebfiles/e20040203254221.html.

16. "Israel Eyes Stryker Vehicle to Update Infantry Units," *Jane's Defense Weekly,* August 27, 2003, http://jdw.janes.com, accessed January 8, 2004. Labeled as 3.

17. *Jane's Sentinel Security Assessment,* Eastern Mediterranean, Israel, Procurement, November 6, 2002, http://jdw.janes.com, accessed January 28, 2003. Labeled 4.

18. Clifford Beal, "Israel's Spike Weapon Goes Network-Centric," *Jane's Defense Weekly,* October 1, 2003, http://jdw.janes.com, accessed January 8, 2004. Labeled 7.

19. *Jane's Sentinel Security Assessment,* Eastern Mediterranean, Israel, Procurement, November 6, 2002, http://jdw.janes.com, accessed January 28, 2003. Labeled 5.

20. Barbara Opall-Rome, "LORA Missile Called No Threat," *Defense News,* November 24, 2003, p. 6. Labeled 6. There is some concern that the LORA could be altered in such a way as to be in violation of arms control limits. The Israeli Missile Defense Organization vehemently denies this.

21. Alon Ben-David, "All Quiet on the Eastern Front, so Israel will Revise IDF Organization and Doctrine," *Jane's Defense Weekly*, March 1, 2004, http://jdw.janes.com. Accessed March 12, 2004.

22. Robin Hughes, "Israel Orders Surveillance Coverage," *Jane's Defense Weekly,* September 3, 2003, http://jdw.janes.com, accessed January 8, 2004. Labeled 8.

23. Barbara Opall-Rome, "Israel Army Taps Elbit UAV for Over-the-Hill Missions," *Defense News,* February 4, 2004, www.defensenews.com, accessed February 5, 2004.

24. Barbara Opall-Rome, "Israel Plans $550M JSTARS-Like Fllet," *Defense News,* November 3, 2003, p. 14. Labeled 15.

25. Ibid., p. 14. Labeled 16.

26. Clifford Beal, "New Radio Units Primed for Israeli Forces," *Jane's Defense Weekly,* September 19, 2003, http://jdw.janes.com, accessed January 8, 2004. Labeled Baetjer 9.

27. Alon Ben-David, "All Quiet on the Eastern Front, so Israel will Revise IDF Organization and Doctrine," *Jane's Defense Weekly*, March 1, 2004, http://jdw.janes.com. Accessed March 12, 2004.

28. Barbara Opall-Rome, "From Foot Soldier to Network Node," *Defense News,* October 20, 2003, p. 30.

29. Robin Hughes, "Israel Extols 'Solid Mirror,'" *Jane's Defense Weekly,* October 3, 2003, http://jdw.janes.com, accessed January 8, 2004. Labeled 17.

30. Alon Ben-David, "Israeli Navy Opts for Fewer, but Flexible Vessels," *Jane's Defense Weekly,* September 17, 2003, http://jdw.janes.com, accessed January 8, 2004. Labeled 18.

31. Barbara Opall-Rome, "Israel Reaches for New Combat Ships," *Defense News*, December 22, 2003, p. 15.

32. Alon Ben-David, "Israel Seeks More Dolphins," *Jane's Defense Weekly*, January 21, 2004, http://jdw.janes.com, accessed January 27, 2004.

33. *Jane's International Defense Review*, April 1998, p. 29.

34. Opall-Rome, "Israel Reaches for New Combat Ships." Labeled 19.

35. *Jane's Fighting Ships*, various editions; IISS, *The Military Balance*, various editions.

36. IISS, *The Military Balance*, "Israel," various editions; *Jane's Fighting Ships*, "Israel," various editions; *Jane's Sentinel, Eastern Mediterranean*, "Israel," various editions.

37. Barbara Opall-Rome, "Israel Air Force Protects Gunships from IR Threats," *Defense News*, March 22, 2004, p. 38.

38. Barbara Opall-Rome, "Israel's Air Force Looks Beyond FLIRS to Multi-spectral Sensors," *Defense News*, January 19, 2004, www.defensenews.com, accessed February 5, 2004.

39. Barbara Opall-Rome, "Israel Air Force to Buy More Apache Longbows," *Defense News*, October 6, 2003, p. 44. Labeled 11. One retired general insisted that the helicopter had mostly failed its missions in Iraq.

40. "Boeing Wins Israeli JDAM Contract," *Jane's Defense Weekly*, October 8, 2003, http://jdw.janes.com, accessed January 8, 2004. Labeled 10.

41. Robin Hughes, "Israel Orders Gulfstream to Fulfill Early-Warning Need," *Jane's Defense Weekly*, September 10, 2003, http://jdw.janes.com, accessed January 8, 2004. Labeled 12.

42. The defecting pilot was on maneuver near the Golan, and suddenly turned toward Israel and flew very low and fast low over the Golan and the central Galilee. He landed in a remote civil strip near Megido. This led to a great deal of media comment in Israel, but such incidents are almost unavoidable. Although he flew for seven minutes without being intercepted, he flew at a time when IAF E-2Cs were not in the air and now nearby aircraft were scrambled, when the IAF was in a state of low alert, and flew without using any radar or communications emissions. He also stated later that he did receive warning he was being tracked by Israeli radar. Israel later used the MiG-23ML (G) for training and test and evaluation purposes. *Washington Post*, October 13, 1989, p. A-35, October 14, 1989, p. A-18; *New York Times*, October 12, 1989, p. A-10, October 14, 1989, p. A-2; *Philadelphia Inquirer*, October 12, 1989, p. 18A, October 13, 1989, p. 17A; *Washington Times*, October 12, 1989, p. A-8; *Jane's Defense Weekly*, February 10, 1990, p. 221.

43. The Arrow is a joint project between the United States and Israel. It has successfully intercepted target missiles during several tests. Concerns over Israel's ability to mass produce Arrow parts have been alleviated by the construction of a parallel plant in the United States. See Barbara Opall-Rome, "Israel Boosts Arrow Arsenal as War Looms," *Defense News*, November 25–December 1, 2002, p. 14, for additional information. Labeled 13.

44. Israel Defense Forces Official Website, "The IDF has Conducted an Test Launch 'Patriot' and 'Hawk' Missiles," IDF Homepage News, posted May 19, 2004, http://wwwl.idf.il. Accessd May 20, 2004.

45. Alon Ben-David, "Rafael, IAI Unveil Surface-to-Air Missile Combo," *Jane's Defense Weekly*, January 21, 2004, http://jdw.janes.com, accessed January 27, 2004.

46. "Israel, U.S. to Pursue Mobile Laser Concept," *Jane's Defense Weekly*, September 3, 2003, http://jdw.janes.com, accessed January 8, 2004. Labeled 14.

47. "Egypt to Augment M1A1 Fleet," *Jane's Defense Weekly*, January 7, 2004, http://jdw.janes.com, accessed January 8, 2004. Labeled 21.

48. "Egypt Seeks M88A2 Sale," *Jane's Defense Weekly*, October 8, 2003, http://jdw.janes.com, accessed January 8, 2004. Labeled 20.

49. Nikolai Novichkov, "Belarus to Upgrade Egyptian BTR-50PKs," *Jane's Defense Weekly*, September 18, 2002, http://jdw.janes.com, accessed January 9, 2004. Labeled 22.

50. Robin Hughes, "Egypt Seeks All-Terrain Vehicles," *Jane's Defense Weekly*, September 17, 2003, http://jdw.janes.com, accessed January 8, 2004. Labeled 23.

51. IISS, *The Military Balance,* "Egypt," various editions; *Jane's Fighting Ships*, "Egypt," various editions; *Jane's Sentinel, Eastern Mediterranean,* "Egypt," various editions.

52. *Jane's Defense Weekly*, November 20, 2003, http://jdw.janes.com, accessed January 8, 2004. Labeled 29.

53. *Jane's Defense Weekly*, August 6, 2003, http://jdw.janes.com, accessed January 8, 2004. Labeled 28.

54. Robin Hughes, "Egypt Receives First Upgraded Hawkeye," *Jane's Defense Weekly*, March 12, 2003, http://jdw.janes.com, accessed January 8, 2004. Labeled 25.

55. Robin Hughes, "Egypt Seeks Foreign Military Sales," *Jane's Defense Weekly*, July 30, 2003, http://jdw.janes.com, accessed January 8, 2004. Labeled 26. Robin Hughes, "Egypt's Apaches to Receive Mission-Planning Systems," July 2, 2003, *Jane's Defense Weekly*, p. 19.

56. Robin Hughes, "Egypt's Apaches to Receive Mission-Planning Systems," *Jane's Defense Weekly*, July 2, 2003, p. 19.

57. "BAE Systems Wins Egyptian F-16 Contract," *Jane's Defense Weekly*, January 15, 2003, http://jdw.janes.com, accessed January 8, 2004. Labeled 24.

58. Christopher Foss, "UK Design to Make Jordan's Tanks More Lethal," *Jane's Defense Weekly*, September 19, 2003, http://jdw.janes.com, accessed January 8, 2004. Labeled 33.

59. Rupert Pengelley, "Jordan Studies Interim 'Hybrid Turret' Upgrade for Challenger 1 Fleet," *Jane's Defense Weekly*, August 20, 2003, http://jdw.janes.com, accessed January 8, 2004. Labeled 34.

60. Robin Hughes, "Jordan Awards Contract for M60 Tank Upgrade," *Jane's Defense Weekly*, December 17, 2003, http://jdw.janes.com, accessed January 8, 2004. Labeled 32.

61. Lale Sariibrahimoglu, "Jordan Signs for Turkish Armoured Combat Vehicles," *Jane's Defense Weekly*, July 16, 2003, http://jdw.janes.com, accessed January 8, 2004. Labeled 31.

62. Robin Hughes, "Jordan Orders Al-Jawad Armoured Troop Carrier," *Jane's Defense Weekly*, October 18, 2002, http://jdw.janes.com, accessed January 9, 2004. Labeled 30.

63. Robin Hughes, "Jordan First with Dutch Gun," *Jane's Defense Weekly*, February 5, 2003, http://jdw.janes.com, accessed January 8, 2004. Labeled 35.

64. Christopher Foss, "BAE Pointing System Wins Orders in the Middle East," *Jane's Defense* Weekly, August 27, 2003, http://jdw.janes.com, accessed January 8, 2004. Labeled 36.

65. *Jane's Fighting Ships*, various editions; IISS, *The Military Balance*, various editions.

66. IISS, *The Military Balance*, "Jordan," various editions; *Jane's Fighting Ships*, "Jordan," various editions; *Jane's Sentinel*, "Jordan," various editions.

67. Robin Hughes, "Amman Increases Air Force Assets," *Jane's Defense Weekly*, September 24, 2003, http://jdw.janes.com, accessed January 8, 2004. Labeled 37.

68. "Jordan Receives Patriot Batteries," *Jane's Defense Weekly*, February 12, 2003, http://jdw.janes.com, accessed January 8, 2004. Labeled 38.

69. IISS, *The Military Balance*, "Lebanon," various editions; *Jane's Fighting Ships*, "Lebanon," various editions; *Jane's Sentinel, Eastern Mediterranean*, "Lebanon," various editions.

70. *Jane's Fighting Ships*, various editions; IISS, *The Military Balance*, various editions.

71. Riad Kahwaji, "Analysts: Syria May Broaden Proxy Wars into Golan Heights," *Defense News*, December 1, 2003, p. 14.

72. Alon Ben-David, "Syria Upgrades T-72 Tanks," *Jane's Defense Weekly*, August 6, 2003, http://jdw.janes.com, accessed January 8, 2004. Labeled 39.

73. Elizabeth Konstantinova, "Bulgarian Arms Exports Investigated," *Jane's Intelligence Review*, February 1, 2003, http://jir.janes.com, accessed January 8, 2004. Labeled 40.

74. *Jane's Defense Weekly*, November 2, 1999, p. 20.

75. United Press International, "Syria Plans Russian Arms Purchase," February 17, 1999.

76. Ed Blanche, "Syria Discusses Buying Advanced Russian Systems," *Jane's Defense Weekly*, May 19, 1999, p. 17.

77. Simon Saradzhyan, "Bombing Spurs Interest in Russian Craft, Defenses," *Defense News*, July 19, 1999, p. 11.

78. Sharon LaFraniere, "Russia, Syria Hint at Weapons Deal," *Washington Post*, July 7, 1999, p. A6.

79. Damian Kemp, "Russia Pushes Defense Sales as Exports Hit Highest for Years," *Jane's Defense Weekly*, July 14, 1999, p. 17.

80. *Jane's Defense Weekly*, November 2, 1999, p. 20.

81. "Russia Halts Plans to Sell Igla to Syria," *Jane's Defense Weekly*, November 6, 2002, http://jdw.janes.com, accessed January 9, 2004. Labeled 41.

82. Interviews; IISS, *The Military Balance, 1998–1999* and *1999–2000*.

83. The strength estimates here are based on interviews, various editions of IISS, *The Military Balance*, and *Jane's World Armies* no. 2, "Syria."

84. Based on data in the relevant country section of IISS, *The Military Balance, 1998–1999* and *1999–2000*. Estimates in other sources differ.

85. IISS, *The Military Balance*, "Syria," various editions; *Jane's Fighting Ships*, "Syria," various editions; *Jane's Sentinel, Eastern Mediterranean*, "Syria," various editions.

86. *Jane's Fighting Ships, 1998–1999* and *1999–2000*; IISS, *The Military Balance, 1998–1999* and *1999–2000*.

87. Interviews; *Jane's Sentinel*, "Syria."

88. Ibid.

89. *Jane's Fighting Ships, 1998–1999* and *1999–2000;* IISS, *The Military Balance, 1998–1999* and *1999–2000.*

90. *Defense News,* June 30, 1997, p. 4.

91. *Flight International,* August 24, 1993, p. 12.

92. Based on interviews with British, U.S., and Israeli experts. *Washington Times,* January 16, 1992, p. G-4; *Washington Post,* February 1, 1992, p. A1, February 2, 1992, pp. A1, A25, February 5, 1992, p. A-19; *Financial Times,* February 6, 1992, p. 4; *Christian Science Monitor,* February 6, 1992, p. 19; *Defense News,* February 17, 1992, p. 1.

CHAPTER 6

1. IISS, *The Military Balance, 1997–1998; Jane's Sentinel: The Gulf States, 1997,* p. 24.

2. There are reports that the lighter and smaller formations in the regular army include an Airmobile Forces group created since the Iran-Iraq War, which includes the 29th Special Forces Division, which was formed in 1993–1994, and the 55th Paratroop Division. There are also reports that the regular army and IRGC commando forces are loosely integrated into a corps of up to 30,000 men with integrated helicopter lift and air assault capabilities. The airborne and special forces are trained at a facility in Shiraz. These reports are not correct. Note that detailed unit identifications for Iranian forces differ sharply from source to source. It is unclear that such identifications are accurate, and now dated wartime titles and numbers are often published, sometimes confusing brigade numbers with division numbers.

3. No reliable data exist on the size and number of Iran's smaller independent formations.

4. The estimates of Iran's AFV and APC strength are based on interviews with Israeli, British, and U.S. civilian experts, and on IISS, *The Military Balance,* "Iran," and *Jane's Sentinel: The Gulf States,* "Iran."

5. Christopher Foss, "Iran Reveals Up-Armoured Boraq Carrier," *Jane's Defense Weekly,* April 9, 2003, http://jdw.janes.com, accessed January 8, 2004. Labeled 42.

6. Lyubov Pronina, "U.S. Sanctions Russian Firm for Alleged Iran Sales," *Defense News,* September 22, 2003, p. 12. Labeled 43.

7. *Jane's Defense Weekly,* January 15, 2003, http://jdw.janes.com, accessed January 8, 2004. Labeled 45.

8. Dough Richardson, "Iran's Raad Cruise Missile Enters Production," *Jane's Missiles and Rockets.*

9. *International Defense Review,* July 1996, pp. 23–26; Anthony H. Cordesman, *Iran's Weapons of Mass Destruction,* CSIS, April 1997.

10. "Iran Enhances Existing Weaponry by Optimising Shahab-3 Ballistic Missile" *Jane's Missiles and Rockets,* January 20, 2004.

11. Ibid.

12. See *Time,* March 21, 1994, pp. 50–54, November 11, 1996, pp. 78–82. Also see *Washington Post,* November 21, 1993, p. A-1, August 22, 1994, p. A-17, October 28, 1994, p. A-17, November 27, 1994, p. A-30, April 11, 1997, p. A-1, April 14, 1997, p. A-1; *Los Angeles Times,* November 3, 1994, pp. A-1, A-12; Deutsche

Presse-Agentur, April 17, 1997, 11:02; Reuters, April 16, 1997, BC cycle, April 17, 1997, BC cycle; *The European,* April 17, 1997, p. 13; *The Guardian,* October 30, 1993, p. 13, August 24, 1996, p. 16, April 16, 1997, p. 10; *New York Times,* April 11, 1997, p. A1; Associated Press, April 14, 1997, 18:37; *Jane's Defense Weekly,* June 5, 1996, p. 15; Agence France Press, April 15, 1997, 15:13; BBC, April 14, 1997, ME/D2892/MED; Deustcher Depeschen via ADN, April 12, 1997, 07:43; *Washington Times,* April 11, 1997, p. A22.

13. For typical reporting by officers of the IRGC on this issue, see the comments of its acting commander in chief, Brigadier General Seyyed Rahim Safavi, speaking to reporters during IRGC week (December 20–26, 1995). FBIS-NES-95-250, December 25, 1995, IRNA 14:06 GMT.

14. Interviews and *Washington Times,* May 12, 1997, p. A-13, October 11, 1997, p. A-6; *Jane's Defense Weekly,* June 25, 1997, p. 14, October 1, 1997, p. 19; Reuters, July 3, 1997, 04:52, July 9, 1997, 1655, September 28, 1997, 0417, October 6, 1997, 16:00.

15. The reader should be aware that much of the information relating to the Quds is highly uncertain and is drawn from Israeli sources. Also, however, see the article from the Jordanian publication *Al-Hadath* in FBIS-NES-96-108, May 27, 1996, p. 9, and in *Al-Sharq Al-Awsat,* FBIS-NES-96-110, June 5, 1996, pp. 1, 4; A. J. Venter, "Iran Still Exporting Terrorism," *Jane's Intelligence Review,* November 1997, pp. 511–516.

16. *New York Times,* May 17, 1998, p. A-15; *Washington Times,* May 17, 1998, p. A-13; *Washington Post,* May 21, 1998, p. A-29.

17. Venter, "Iran Still Exporting Terrorism," pp. 511–516.

18. "Iran," *Jane's,* October 29, 2001.

19. *World Missiles Briefing,* Teal Group Corporation.

20. *Jane's Defense Weekly,* June 25, 1997, p. 3; Associated Press, June 17, 1997, 17:51; United Press, June 17, 1997, 04:28; *International Defense Review,* June 1996, p. 17.

21. *Washington Times,* March 27, 1996, p. A-1.

22. *Defense News,* January 17, 1994, pp. 1, 29.

23. Only two torpedo tubes can fire wire-guided torpedoes. *Defense News,* January 17, 1994, pp. 1, 29.

24. See David Miller, "Submarines in the Gulf," *Military Technology,* June 1993, pp. 42–45; David Markov, "More Details Surface of Rubin's 'Kilo' Plans," *Jane's Intelligence Review,* May 1997, pp. 209–215.

25. In addition to the sources listed at the start of this section, these assessments are based on various interviews, prior editions of IISS, *The Military Balance; Jaffee Center Middle East Military Balance; Jane's Sentinel: The Gulf States,* "Iran"; *Jane's Defense Weekly,* July 11, 1987, p. 15.

26. A. Kozhikhov and D. Kaliyeva, "The Military Political Situation in the Caspian Region," *Central Asia's Affairs,* no. 3.

27. Ibid.

28. The range of aircraft numbers shown reflects the broad uncertainties affecting the number of Iran's aircraft which are operational in any realistic sense. Many aircraft counted, however, cannot engage in sustained combat sorties in an extended air campaign. The numbers are drawn largely from interviews; *Jane's Intelligence Review,* Special Report no. 6, May 1995; *Jane's Sentinel: The Gulf*

Staffs, 1997, "Iran"; IISS, *The Military Balance, 1997–1998,* "Iran"; Andrew Rathmell, *The Changing Balance in the Gulf,* Whitehall Paper no. 38 (London: Royal United Services Institute, 1996); Andrew Rathmell, "Iran's Rearmament: How Great a Threat?" *Jane's Intelligence Review,* July 1994, pp. 317–322; *Jane's World Air Forces* (CD-ROM).

29. *Wall Street Journal,* February 10, 1995, p. 19; *Washington Times,* February 10, 1995, p. A-19.

30. Robert Hewson, "Iran's New Combat Aircraft Waits in the Wings," *Jane's Defense Weekly,* November 20, 2002, p. 15. Labeled 43.

31. Periscope, "Nations/Alliances/Geographic Regions/Middle East/North Africa: Plans and Programs." Labeled 69.

32. Reports that the IRGC is operating F-7 fighters do not seem to be correct.

33. Reuters, June 12, 1996, 17:33.

34. "Iran Reveals Shahab Thaqeb SAM Details," *Jane's Defense Weekly,* September 4, 2002, http://jdw.janes.com, accessed January 9, 2004. Labeled 44.

35. Based on interviews with British, Israeli, and U.S. experts; Anthony H. Cordesman, *Iran and Iraq: The Threat from the Northern Gulf* (Boulder, CO: Westview, 1994); Anthony H. Cordesman and Ahmed S. Hashim, *Iran: the Dilemmas of Dual Containment* (Boulder, CO: Westview, 1997); IISS, *The Military Balance, 1997–1998,* "Iran"; *Jane's Sentinel: The Gulf States, 1997,* "Iran"; USNI Database; Anoushiravan Ehteshami, "Iran's National Strategy," *International Defense Review,* April 1994, pp. 29–37; "Military Technology," *World Defense Almanac: The Balance of Military Power* 17, no. 1 (1993), pp. 139–142; working data from the Jaffee Center for Strategic Studies; Rathmell, "Iran's Rearmament," pp. 317–322; Ahmed Hashim, *The Crisis of the Iranian State,* Adelphi Paper no. 296 (London: IISS, 1995), pp. 7–30, 50–70; Andrew Rathmell, *The Changing Military Balance in the Gulf,* Whitehall Series (London: RUSI, 1996), pp. 9–23; Michael Eisenstadt, *Iranian Military Power, Capabilities, and Intentions* (Washington, DC: Washington Institute, 1996), pp. 9–65; Anoushiravan Enreshami, "Iran Strives to Regain Military Might," *International Defense Review,* July 1996, pp. 22–26.

36. *Jane's Defense Weekly,* September 4, 1996, p. 4.

37. Michael Gordon, "U.S. Attacked Iraqi Air Defenses Starting in 2002," *New York Times,* July 20, 2003; Bradley Graham, "U.S. Moved Early for Air Supremacy," *Washington Post,* July 20, 2003.

38. As the previous chapter showed, these conclusions track well with the other data available on this aspect of the war. See Terry McCarthy, "Whatever Happened to the Republican Guard," *Time,* May 12, 2003, p. 38; Molly Moore, "A Foe That Collapsed from Within," *Washington Post,* July 20, 2003, p. A-1.

39. Elliot Blair Smith, "Marine Tanks May Fire First Shots," *USA Today,* March 18, 2003, p. 5.

40. Moore, "Foe That Collapsed from Within," p. A-1.

CHAPTER 7

1. Pierre Tran, "Thales, Saudi Arabia Close in on Border Security Deal," *Defense News,* January 30, 2004, http://www.defensenews.com, accessed February 5, 2004.

2. "Middle East Defence Spending to Rise," *Jane's Defense Weekly*, December 3, 2003, http://jdw.janes.com, accessed January 8, 2004. Labeled 47.

3. The IISS reports 90 GCT-1s, but Giat only reports the sale of 51.

4. David Long, *The Kingdom of Saudi Arabia* (Gainesville: University of Florida Press, 1997).

5. Robin Hughes, "Modernisation Drive for Saudi National Guard," *Jane's Defense Weekly*, December 3, 2003, http://jdw.janes.com, accessed January 8, 2004. Labeled 48.

6. Richard Scott, "New Saudi Frigates to Receive Oto Melara Guns," *Jane's Defense Weekly*, November 27, 2002, http://jdw.janes.com, accessed January 9, 2004. Labeled 50.

7. Periscope, "Nations/Alliances/Geographic Regions Middle/East/North Africa: Saudi Arabia." Labeled as Baetjer 1.

8. J.A.C. Lewis, "Saudis Move Closer to NH 90 Purchase for Navy," *Jane's Defense Weekly*, December 24, 2003, http://jdw.janes.com, accessed January 8, 2004. Labeled 51.

9. Based on *Jane's Fighting Ships, 1996–1997, 1999–2000,* and *2000–2001*; IISS, *The Military Balance, 1996–1997, 1999–2000,* and *2001–2002*.

10. USCENTCOM, *Atlas, 1996*; MacDill Air Force Base, USCENTCOM, 1997; IISS, *The Military Balance, 1996–1997, 1999–2000, 2000–2001,* and *2001–2002*.

11. USCENTCOM, *Atlas, 1996*; MacDill Air Force Base, USCENTCOM, 1997; IISS, *The Military Balance, 1996–1997, 1999–2000, 2000–2001,* and *2001–2002*.

12. *Defense News*, September 9, 1996, p. 26.

13. Riad Kahwaji, "Bahrain to Scrutinize Future Defense Buys," *Defense News*, February 2, 2004, p. 3.

14. "Iran and Kuwait Agree on Military Cooperation," *Jane's Defense Weekly*, October 16, 2002, http://jdw.janes.com, accessed January 9, 2004. Labeled 52.

15. Riad Kahwaji, "Parliament-MoD Row Delays C⁴I Deal in Kuwait," *Defense News*, December 1, 2003, p. 34.

16. Ibid.

17. Jiri Kominek, "Two Gulf States Weigh up Heavy Transporter Bids," *Jane's Defense Weekly*, July 2, 2003, p. 18.

18. "Kuwait Selects SINCGARS," *Jane's Defense Weekly*, November 13, 2002, http://jdw.janes.com, accessed January 9, 2004. Labeled 54.

19. "Kuwait Buys Aerostat," *Jane's Defense Weekly*, December 10, 2003, http://jdw.janes.com, accessed January 8, 2004. Labeled 55.

20. "Kuwait's Apache Deal Moves On," *Jane's Defense Weekly*, October 22, 2003, http://jdw.janes.com, accessed January 8, 2004. Labeled 53.

21. Christopher Foss, "Oman Gets Chinese Armoured Personnel Carriers," *Jane's Defense Weekly*, September 24, 2003, http://jdw.janes.com, accessed January 8, 2004. Labeled 56.

22. Robin Hughes, "Oman and UAE Bolster Coastal Protection," *Jane's Defense Weekly*, February 11, 2004, http://jdw.janes.com, accessed February 18, 2004.

23. "Lockheed Wins Omani F-16 Contract," *Jane's Defense Weekly*, June 25, 2003, http://jdw.janes.com, accessed January 8, 2004. Labeled 57.

24. Robin Hughes, "Omani F-16s to Get Reconnaissance Pods," *Jane's Defense Weekly*, February 11, 2004, http://jdw.janes.com, accessed February 18, 2004.

25. "PANTERA Pods for Oman and Poland," *Jane's Defense Weekly*, January 7, 2004, http://jdw.janes.com, accessed January 8, 2004. Labeled 58.

26. Richard Scott, "Qatar Orders Fast Interceptor Craft," *Jane's Defense Weekly*, February 12, 2003, http://jdw.janes.com, accessed January 8, 2004. Labeled 59.

27. Kominek, "Two Gulf States," p. 18.

28. Christopher Foss, "Gulf States Near to Chem-Bio Vehicle Choice," *Jane's Defense Weekly*, October 22, 2003, http://jdw.janes.com, accessed January 8, 2004. Labeled 60.

29. Riad Kahwaji, "Abu Dhabi Shipyard Raises Export Profile," *Defense News*, March 3, 2003, p. 25. Labeled 65.

30. Hughes, "Oman and UAE."

31. Riad Kahwaji, "UAE Doubles Mirage Orders, Halts Swiss Hawks Purchase," *Defense News*, June 23, 2003, p. 1. Labeled 61.

32. Andrew Chuter, "Trainer Aircraft Makers Court UAE Air Force," DefenseNews.com, December 15, 2003, http://www.defensenews.com, accessed January 8, 2004. Labeled 62.

33. Riad Kahwaji, "UAE Seeks E-2C Deal, Upgrade of Ex-Libyan CH-47s," *Defense News*, December 1, 2003, p. 32.

34. Ibid.

35. Riad Kahwaji, "Iraq War Stalls GCC Missile Defense Plans," *Defense News*, December 1, 2003, p. 1.

36. "EADS to Upgrade UAE Radar Systems," *Jane's Defense Weekly*, December 17, 2003, http://jdw.janes.com, accessed January 8, 2004. Labeled 66.

37. Sam Dagher, "UAE Military Air Flight Center Could Become Regional Force," DefenseNews.com, December 9, 2003, http://www.defensenews.com, accessed January 8, 2004. Labeled 64.

38. Joseph Bermudez, "Yemen Continues Ballistic Missile Procurement Programme," *Jane's Intelligence Review*, April 1, 2003, http://jir.janes.com, accessed January 8, 2004. Labeled 68.

39. Ian Bostock, "Yemen Orders Patrol Boats," *Jane's Defense Weekly*, June 18, 2003, http://jdw.janes.com, accessed January 8, 2004. Labeled 67.

CHAPTER 9

1. There have also been cases of state-sponsored attacks. These include the Libyan bombings of Pan Am flight 103 over Scotland in 1988 and the bombing of UTA flight 772 over Chad in 1989. The bombing of Pan Am flight 103 killed 259 people on board and 11 people on the ground, and the bombing of UTA flight 772 killed 171 people on board.

2. For historical background on bin Laden, see Kenneth Katzman, "Persian Gulf: Radical Islamic Movements," Washington, DC: Congressional Research Service, 96–731-F, August 30, 1996.

CHAPTER 10

1. CIA, "Terrorist CBRN: Materials and Effects," Washington, DC, Director of Central Intelligence, June 2003, http://www.cia.gov/cia/reports/terrorist_cbrn/terrorist_cbrn.htm.

2. CIA, "Unclassified Report to Congress on the Acquisition of Technology Relating to Weapons of Mass Destruction and Advanced Conventional Munitions, 1 January Through 30 June 2003," Washington, DC, November 2003, http://www.cia.gov/cia/reports/721_reports/jan_jun2003.htm.

Index

Note: Page numbers in *italic* type refer to figures.

State Department. *See* U.S. State
  Department
Stockholm International Peace
  Research Institute (SIPRI), 10
Submarines: Gulf conditions for, 272;
  Iran, 270–73
Sudan, 388, 390, 412
Sunni extremism, 399, 408
Superterrorism, 17, 442–43
Surveillance. *See* IS&R (intelligence,
  surveillance, and reconnaissance)
Sustainability: assessment of, 28; and
  changing nature of warfare, 16, 28;
  new tempo of, 18–19; weakness of
  less advanced powers in, 22
Switzerland, 456
Syria, 205–18; air defense in, 169,
  215–18, 225; air force in, 215–18,
  223–24; Arab-Israeli conflict and,
  4–5; Argentina and, 484; armored
  operations in, 160, 213, 220; arms
  agreements and deliveries by, *221*;
  arms imports by, 147; artillery in,
  213–14, 221; assessment of military
  in, 211–12; and asymmetric warfare,
  205; and biological weapons, 483–
  84; and chemical weapons, 137,
  482–83; China and, 210, 479–80,
  483, 484; conscript force funding
  by, 8; as crucial state in Arab-Israeli
  military balance, 136; delivery
  systems for WMD, 478–82; economic situation in, 31; force
  strength versus Israel, *220*; force
  structure imbalance in, 137; force
  trends in, *206–8*; helicopters in, 216;
  and Hezbollah, 201; Iran and, 479,
  487–88; Israeli-Palestinian War and,
  137; Israeli versus, 218; Israel
  versus, 153; land forces in, 212–14;
  Lebanon and, 195, 200; manpower
  quality in, 9; military expenditures
  by, 35, *40*, 138, 143; military
  situation in, 205, 209–12; missile
  defenses in, 484; modernization in,
  209–10, 218; naval forces in, 214–
  15, *227*; North Korea and, 210,

479–82; and nuclear weapons, 484;
  and proxy warfare, 205; recapitalization crisis in, *209*; reserve system
  in, 213; Russia and, 35, 147, 210–
  11, 217–18, 482, 484; terrorism
  sponsored by, 393; and weapons of
  mass destruction, 478–84

Taha, Musa, Rifa'i, 400
Taherian, Hassan, 486
Tahir, Bsa, 458, 461–64
Taiwan, 453
Taliban, 408
Al-Tamimi, Assad Bayud, 203
Tanker war, 5, 244
Tanks. *See* Armored operations
Tanzania, embassy bombing in, 389,
  407
Taradis Iran Computer Company, 514
Targeting, near–real time integration in,
  18
Tata Consulting Engineering, 502
Technology: and changing nature of
  warfare, 19; Israel and integration
  of, 153–54, 167; vulnerabilities of
  advanced powers, *25–26*; vulnerabilities of less advanced powers,
  21–24
Tempo, revolution in military affairs
  and operations, 18
Terrain, weakness of less advanced
  powers regarding, 23
Terrorism: advanced powers' vulnerability to, 25; causes and targets of,
  390; and CBRN weapons, 437–43;
  and changing nature of warfare, 16;
  impact of, 389–91; as major military
  force, xxiii; military expenditures
  affected by, 35; state supported,
  392–93; U.S. State Department lists
  concerning, 397–413; and weapons
  of mass destruction, 393, 433–34,
  437–43. *See also* Counterterrorism;
  Extremist movements; Islamic
  extremism; Superterrorism; War on
  terrorism
Thyssen, 509

About the Author

ANTHONY H. CORDESMAN is a Senior Fellow and holds the Arleigh A. Burke Chair in Strategy at the Center for Strategic and International Studies. He is an analyst for ABC News and a frequent commentator on National Public Radio. He is the author of numerous books on security issues and has served in a number of senior positions in the U.S. government.